Framing Law and Crime

The Fairleigh Dickinson University Press
Series in Law, Culture, and the Humanities

The Fairleigh Dickinson University Press Series in Law, Culture, and the Humanities publishes scholarly works in which the field of Law intersects with, among others, Film, Criminology, Sociology, Communication, Critical/Cultural Studies, Literature, History, Philosophy, and the Humanities.

General Editor: Caroline Joan "Kay" S. Picart, M.Phil.
(Cantab), Ph.D., J.D., Esquire
Attorney at Law/Of Counsel, Tim Bower Rodriguez, P.A.

Publications

Caroline Joan "Kay" S. Picart, Michael Hviid Jacobson, and Cecil Greek, eds., *Framing Law and Crime: An Interdisciplinary Anthology* (2016)
Caroline Joan "Kay" S. Picart, *Law In and As Culture: Intellectual Property, Minority Rights, and the Rights of Indigenous Peoples* (2016)

On the Web at http://www.fdu.edu/fdupress

Framing Law and Crime

An Interdisciplinary Anthology

Edited by
Caroline Joan "Kay" S. Picart,
Michael Hviid Jacobsen, and Cecil Greek

Fairleigh Dickinson

FAIRLEIGH DICKINSON UNIVERSITY PRESS
Madison • Teaneck

Published by Fairleigh Dickinson University Press
Copublished by The Rowman & Littlefield Publishing Group, Inc.
4501 Forbes Boulevard, Suite 200, Lanham, Maryland 20706
www.rowman.com

Unit A, Whitacre Mews, 26-34 Stannary Street, London SE11 4AB

British Library Cataloguing in Publication Information Available

Library of Congress Cataloging-in-Publication Data

Names: Picart, Caroline Joan, 1966- editor. | Jacobsen, Michael Hviid, 1971- editor. | Greek, Cecil E., editor.
Title: Framing law and crime : an interdisciplinary anthology / edited by Caroline Joan "Kay" S. Picart, Michael Hviid Jacobsen and Cecil Greek.
Description: Madison : Fairleigh Dickinson University Press ; Lanham, Maryland : Copublished by The Rowman & Littlefield Publishing Group, Inc., 2016. | Series: Fairleigh Dickinson University Press Law, Culture, and the Humanities Series | Includes bibliographical references and index.
Identifiers: LCCN 2015044314 (print) | LCCN 2015048399 (ebook) | ISBN 9781611477054 (cloth : alk. paper) | ISBN 9781611477061 (Electronic)
Subjects: LCSH: Justice, Administration of, in motion pictures. | Justice, Administration of, on television. | Law in motion pictures. | Law on television. | Crime films--History and criticism. | Crime on television.
Classification: LCC PN1995.9.J8 F83 2016 (print) | LCC PN1995.9.J8 (ebook) | DDC 791.43/6554—dc23
LC record available at http://lccn.loc.gov/2015044314

∞™ The paper used in this publication meets the minimum requirements of American National Standard for Information Sciences—Permanence of Paper for Printed Library Materials, ANSI/NISO Z39.48-1992.

Printed in the United States of America

Contents

Acknowledgments

The editors thank the following for licenses and permissions to reprint or adapt some of the chapters: (1) the *International Journal of Drug Policy* (Elsevier) for permission to reprint Susan Boyd's chapter, which originally appeared as: Susan Boyd, 2013, "A Canadian Perspective on Documentary Film: *Drug Addict*," *International Journal of Drug Policy* 24: 589–96; (2) Naomi Mezey and Mark C. Niles for permission to adapt an article, of which they own copyright, into a chapter for this edited collection; that article originally appeared as Naomi Mezey and Mark C. Niles, 2005, "Screening the Law: Ideology and Law in American Popular Culture," adapted from *Columbia Journal of Law and the Arts* 28: 91–185; (3) Palgrave Macmillan for granting a license to reprint a chapter that originally appeared as: Caroline Joan "Kay" S. Picart, 2012, "Race and Serial Killing in the Media: The Case of Wayne Williams," In *Speaking of Monsters: A Teratological Anthology*, edited by Caroline Joan "Kay" S. Picart and John Edgar Browning, 173–91, New York: Palgrave Macmillan; and (4) the Institute for Holocaust Research, University of Haifa, and Taylor & Francis Ltd., for granting a license to reprint an article that originally appeared as: Caroline Joan "Kay" S. Picart, 2015, "Nationalities, Histories, Rhetorics: Real / Reel Representations of the Holocaust and Holocaust Trials and a Poethics of Film and Law," *Dapim: Studies on the Holocaust* 29(2): 114–33, copyright © Institute for Holocaust Research, University of Haifa, reprinted by permission of Taylor & Francis Ltd, www.tandfonline.com, on behalf of Institute for Holocaust Research, University of Haifa. The editors also thank IFC and Sundance Selects for camera-ready prints and copyright permission to use the photos of Werner Herzog and the screen shot from *Into the Abyss*. The majority of the images were found in the public domain, but the editors owe a debt of gratitude to Susan Gilbert for her digital magic and tirelessness in converting images that would have been unsuitable for printing into print-quality images. Additionally, the editors thank the University of South Florida Department of Sociology and University of South Florida Publications Council for a generous grant financing the production of the index for this book and Lynn Weber for her excellent indexing. Finally, the editors thank all contributors for their professionalism and patience with the process of putting together an edited collection, as well as the director and editorial and production staff of the Fairleigh Dickinson University Press and Rowman & Littlefield, most notably Harry Keyishian, Brooke Bures, Zachary Nycum, and Hannah Fisher for their helpfulness and support.

Caroline (Kay) is greatly indebted to John Edgar Browning and Margaret Petty for their tireless and conscientious assistance with finding suitable and relevant images in the public domain. She thanks Katheryn Russell Brown and John Stinneford for prior comments on earlier drafts of her two chapters, and is grateful for the collaboration with Michael Hviid Jacobsen and Cecil Greek. She dedicates this book to the Picart, Terrell, and Rivera families, and most especially her beloved husband, Jerry Rivera.

Introduction

Attempting To Frame Law and Crime: An Experiment in Interdisciplinary Commensurability

Caroline Joan "Kay" S. Picart,
Michael Hviid Jacobsen, and Cecil Greek

The inspiration for this anthology, for Caroline Joan "Kay" S. Picart, began as a Kuhnian thought-experiment. Phrased probably in an oversimplified way for the purposes of this introduction, Thomas S. Kuhn's notion of "incommensurability" posited that given the paradigm-specific nature of knowledge, members of different disciplines, even when they used the same terms, would "inevitably talk through each other" rather than to each other because of an "incompleteness of logical contact" between the different disciplinary matrices (Kuhn 1970, 110).[1] What would therefore result, assuming Kuhn were correct, if one were to place scholars of law, sociology, criminology, and film criticism all together in one room to discuss screen depictions of law and crime, would be that a complex Babel of discourses would erupt, with no one truly communicating with another because of the problem of incommensurability.

Picart, having formed successful interdisciplinary collaborations in the past, was curious to enact the thought experiment, and was delighted when Michael Hviid Jacobsen and Cecil Greek agreed to join her in spearheading the project, and when a cadre of eminent scholars of law, sociology, criminology, and film criticism agreed to join the project. The result, as described below, is less a tumult of incommensurabilities than a complex tapestry of different connections and divergences. Of course, there are discipline-specific terms and points of entry, but there are also a remarkable number of convergences, in terms of issues, themes, and aspirations, to name a few such confluences. The exercise was certainly "fruitful," in Kuhn's sense: inspiring questions and answers in an intricate spiral.

The first set of chapters, titled "Cinematic Histories and Real/Reel Dystopias of Law and Crime," brings together accounts of the history of the law and cinema movement (Stefan Machura); the birth of a new genre ripe for analysis for criminologists, "post-apocalyptic fiction" (Majid Yar); and a sociohistorical analysis of the genesis of a policy-shaping Canadian documentary, *Drug Addict*, which generated Canadian policy regarding drugs, drug addiction, and law enforcement for illegal drugs and addiction (Susan Boyd). All three chapters implicate a central thematic to be explored, in detail, in the third section of the book: the complex interplay between the "real" and the "reel." Yar, in particular, heralds the dystopic landscape characteristic of many, but not necessarily all, cinematic narratives about crime and law.

Machura's "Law and Cinema Movement" is a general sketch of the history of the law and cinema movement. Machura argues that beginning roughly in the 1980s, a new type of sociolegal scholarship emerged—one focused on depictions of legal phenomena in popular films. Machura's chapter hinges on deploying Harold Lasswell's (1949, 37) formula: "Who says what to whom in which channel with which effect?" in relation to specific films that depict lawyers and legal proceedings. Thus, Machura's chapter uses Lasswell's questions to crystallize findings on law in film and to map out the "law and cinema movement" itself. The chapter concludes by outlining areas for future development of the sociolegal study of film and reflecting on lessons learned for how academic subjects develop.

Part of Machura's argument is that the law and cinema movement flows from both the practical and political concerns of legal scholars. For Machura, although some distortion occurs in these fictional cinematic depictions of law, nevertheless resulting in real-world consequences, he finds that the typical fictional portrayal of law and the legal professions tends on balance to be positive, therefore contributing to public trust. Furthermore, Machura points to two positive and concrete legacies the law and cinema movement has forged: (1) the blossoming of classes, in law schools, which use film as an educational tool to supplement the traditional teaching of law; and (2) an increasing number of scholarly publications on film and law.

Yar's "The Crisis of Law and the Imaginary of Disaster: Reading Post-Apocalyptic Fictions" begins with the observation, which intersects with Machura's reflections regarding the ubiquity of scholarship regarding law and film, that criminology has of late extended its gaze to include fictional discourses (such as films, television series, and novels), exploring their constructions of crime and law. Yar argues that although the clearly identifiable genre of crime fiction (including the likes of police procedurals, courtroom dramas, prison movies, and serial killer thrillers) has been the subject of burgeoning analysis, criminology has yet to look beyond this to explore how issues of crime, victimization, law-and-order, justice, and vengeance are configured in the genre of post-apocalyptic fictions, despite the fact that such texts are replete with crime-related themes, plots and references.

It is this deficiency that Yar intends to address, opening the way to new themes in a yet-unexplored genre. Yar's chapter attempts a first step toward this endeavor, focusing in particular upon how the "crisis of law" is dramatized using post-apocalyptic scenarios in which the social order has collapsed and crime runs rampant. Yar paints a graphic picture of how this sense of crisis is articulated through a dualistic discourse in which law is both missing, and reappears as an authoritarian perversion of itself—two sides of a response to a scenario in which law and order appears to be failing. Thus, Yar argues that what this duality gestures toward are existing social and cultural cleavages and tensions around the efficacy of law in creating and sustaining a stable society. In some ways, Yar's thesis parallels Robin Wood's (1986, 78)[2] well-documented thesis regarding how horror films, as a genre, depict the repressed fears of a particular historical era and a particular culture, visualized as monstrous.[3] In a parallel fashion, Yar argues, the monstrous scenarios that these post-apocalyptic narratives depict reveal long-standing fears about the failure of law to protect citizens or adequately punish offenders with the explosion of predatory and violent behavior once the institutional apparatus of law enforcement disappears. Additionally, Yar argues that such apocalyptic cinematic narratives turn a skeptical gaze on the growing tendency to suspend rights and liberties in light of a supposed "state of emergency" (such as the "war on terror"), by visualizing law as a tool of tyrannical authority.

Boyd's "A Canadian Perspective on Documentary Film: *Drug Addict*" brings to this collection on law, crime, and film, a thought-provoking analysis of a policy-shaping Canadian documentary, *Drug Addict* (National Film Board 1948). *Drug Addict* was the first National Film Board (NFB) documentary, in Canada, about illegal drugs, trafficking, and addiction. Boyd's chapter aims to provide a sociohistorical context for the documentary in order to ground the claims and representations in the film about law enforcement, people who use illegal drugs, and treatment, within the context that produced that film. Boyd deploys a qualitative methodological framework that is consistent with its critical theoretical perspective, drawing from Stuart Hall's perspectives on visual and textual representation and cultural criminology.

Boyd argues that *Drug Addict* is significant because the documentary provides insight into early foundational law enforcement discourses and practices about illegal drugs, addiction, and treatment, including obstacles to drug substitution and maintenance programs. Furthermore, reminiscent of Michel Foucault's argumentative strategies in *The Birth of the Clinic* (1994) and *Discipline and Punish* (1995), Boyd argues that the film also highlights the emergence of psychiatry as a new knowledge producer in the area of drug treatment and transmits ideas about the criminal nature of addicts and the need for punitive criminal justice control. Ultimately, Boyd concludes that *Drug Addict* captures some past and contemporary tensions related to Canadian drug policy. Hence, the documentary provides another lens to understand some of the foundational frameworks of Canadian drug policy such as the dominance of criminal justice, and its practices of knowledge production, the resistance espoused by institutions to diverse models of treatment such as drug maintenance programs, and the power of visual representation.

The second section of the book, titled "Jurisprudence in International Films" turns to the examination of a range of international or global films, with an eye to assessing the strengths, frailties, and possible functions of law, as depicted in fictional cinema. All three chapters implicitly problematize the foundations of a natural-law based jurisprudence (that law is accessible through reason and that whatever force humanly created law has stems from natural law) in favor of exploring other alternatives, whether they be of legal positivism (that the force of law stems from social facts, not some inherent connection between law and morality); legal realism (the real-world practice of law is what determines what "law" is); or critical legal studies (that law principally reflects the policy goals of the dominant social group and is contradictory), among others. All three problematize the adequacy of a principally punitive-based model of justice in different ways: Carrie Menkel-Meadow by exploring the conditions of possibility of a transitional, reconciliation-based justice; Orit Kamir by pushing the limits of a purely punitive model; and Peter Robson by noting how the theme of vigilantism in popular film has progressive potential.

Menkel-Meadow's chapter focuses on *In the Land of Blood and Honey* (Jolie 2011), to analyze how the film explores and raises questions about crimes against humanity and transitional or restorative (and not simply punitive) justice in Angelina Jolie's fictional narrative of hapless lovers caught in the violent history of Bosnia-Herzegovina's ethnic conflicts. Kamir's chapter juxtaposes an Iranian film, *A Separation* (Farhadi 2001), with an iconic Japanese film, *Rashomon* (Jingo 1950), to show how both films train their viewers to use multiple perspectives (a technique she calls "multifocal judgment") to critique how effectively legal proceedings can bring justice to complex situations; Kamir argues that despite the radical critique of Iranian patriarchy embedded in *A Separation*, the film ironically pulls back from that critical perspective to justify and strengthen the patriarchal foundations of Iranian society. Robson's chapter, like Machura's chapter in the first section, is a sprawling and ambitious history of depictions of law in cinema, but this time, ranging from westerns to rape-revenge films, among others, which are characterized by a narrative focus on themes of vigilantism and a politics of resistance that erupt, when, as in Yar's chapter, a regime of law seems ineffectual. Toward the end of his chapter, Robson gestures toward how recent trends have begun to depict real vigilante groups, such as the pink clad Gulabi Gang on the screen in *Gulaab Gang* (Sen 2014) with their focus on such issues as domestic violence, the dowry system, rape, and education, indicating that perhaps, following Theodor W. Adorno and Max Horkheimer's (1979) view, there is an ongoing shift from an "individual, conservative" perspective to a "communitarian" view, and that the boundary between the "real" and the "reel" is convoluted and porous.

Menkel-Meadow's "*In the Land of Blood and Honey*: What's Fair or Just in Love and War Crimes? Lessons for Transitional Justice" examines a contemporary representation of crimes against humanity in film, focusing specifically on Angelina Jolie's *In the Land of Blood and Honey* as an illustration of the depiction of war crimes, now including crimes against woman, and the complexities of learning from such films for modern legal developments in transitional justice institutions and processes. Menkel-Meadow follows the trajectory set by scholars of the Holocaust in relation to the questions of how effectively cinematic depictions of the Holocaust can represent the "negative sublime" of mass atrocities, humanely portray individual narratives of suffering and trauma, against the larger backdrop of systematized violence, or even educate its viewers. The connection to Holocaust film scholarship is resonant with Menkel-Meadow's autoethnographic nod to her personal history as the child of Holocaust survivors. Menkel-Meadow envisages her chapter as oriented by theory on whether or not horrific acts against groups and masses of people, as well as individuals, can be "represented" in different media, doing adequate "justice" to the reality of the harm and what we should "learn" from such representations. To initiate her reflections on Jolie's film, Menkel-Meadow, in an abstract that is not included in this book, poses a variety of questions:

> Can popular cultural representations of inhumanity, in film, TV, music, pictures, and such aid in the development of empathy and reactions to such harms and spur more border-crossing action of legal and humane intervention? How do the variety of popular cultural treatments of human-caused harms deepen our understanding of historical events, motivations and

> actions? Do they help us see the human, for possible reconciliation, or the inhumanity, for need of retribution, punishment or revenge? Do popular culture media overly simplify or distort "what really happened," or help us to see the layers of history, collective and individual experiences, that produce mass atrocities, genocides, civil wars, and conflicts? What might be the relationship of more complex popular cultural representations of criminal acts and human rights violations to the increasing diversity of formal and informal justice and truth seeking institutions and processes?

Menkel-Meadow interprets *In the Land of Blood and Honey* as one female filmmaker's "intervention" into spaces long dominated by more conventional (male?) representations in film, as well as more conventional juridical forms of punishment and retribution. Menkel-Meadow reads the film as a modern retelling of the familiar cross-group Romeo and Juliet prohibited love story, set against a backdrop of rape, abuse, genocide, and mass atrocities, in which the audience is compelled to witness complicated relationships of desire, love, rape, capture, and degradation. Menkel-Meadow's ultimate aim is to study the potential impact of such films for configuring more culturally and legally diverse forms of transitional or restorative, not only punitive, justice.

Also using a feminist lens, Kamir's "Multifocal Judgment, Intersecting Legal Proceedings, and Conservativism: *A Separation* and *Rashomon*" similarly offers a close reading of *Separation* in comparison with *Rashomon*, demonstrating that these two acclaimed law-films establish a unique, non-Anglo-American sophisticated and effective cinematic critique of law and judgment, while subtly and discretely taking a conservative sociopolitical stand. Kamir aims to render visible the ways in which *Separation* (much like *Rashomon*) trains its audience in judgment through the complex conjunction of multiple perspectives. Kamir notes that *A Separation* bluntly places the viewer on the judge's bench, instructing him or her to perform complex, multifocal judgment, relying on characters' mutual accusations and their comparison with characters cast as their doubles. However, this apparently neutral judicial stance is undercut by the centrality of a noncritical character, who, instead of judging the other characters, merely loves them.

For Kamir, *A Separation* voices some of its jurisprudential insights through its multiple views of the main characters, enabling other characters to weigh and challenge them. For Kamir, perhaps the most radical jurisprudential insight is revealed by the film's intersection of two onscreen legal proceedings whose juxtaposition reveal that a criminal proceeding cannot resolve a complex emotional situation, such as a family dispute. Finally, for Kamir, *A Separation* mirrors the social action of the legal system that it portrays ("film acts like [an] onscreen legal system"). In a manner similar to the events of the cinematic family court, the movie too allows its leading female character to express her critical view of Iran—only to ignore her criticism altogether. Kamir's interpretation of *A Separation* notes both progressive and conservative elements; for Kamir, the film offers a radical criticism of law, but does not challenge its conservative, patriarchal society. In so doing, Kamir argues that the film mirrors the frailties and inequities of that society, without offering sufficient challenge, and eventually, ironically strengthens and supports that society.

Robson's "Beyond the Courtroom: Vigilantism, Revenge, and Rape-Revenge Films in the Cinema of Justice" begins with a nod to the history of scholarship on the representations of law in film (Bergman and Asimow 1996; Denvir 1996; Black 1999; Greenfield, Osborn, and Robson 2001; 2010; Machura and Robson 2001; Lucia 2005; Kamir 2006), television (Jarvis and Joseph 1998; Rapping 2003; Villez 2005; 2010; Asimow 2009; Robson and Silbey 2012 , popular fiction (Meyer 1993; 2001; Robson 1996; 2001; 2014) and graphic novels (Dailly and Davidson 2011). Robson, in an abstract that is not included in this book, locates the development of his own scholarship on vigilante films against this backdrop, stating:

> My interest in this area and focus derive from a concern during the early years of the twenty-first-century that taking the law into one's own hands and meting out justice on an *ad hoc* basis was a theme which seemed to be becoming a constant theme in mainstream film (see appendix 1 [of chapter 6]). These works, presented in a realist style, offered a simple solution to the time-consuming and variable quality of state justice. The films seemed to laud the primitive urge to revenge and seemed to have limited negative consequences for the actor and harked back to the crude stereotypes of the Death Wish series (see appendix 2 [of chapter 6]).

Like Menkel-Meadow, Robson keeps a strong autoethnographic element to his analysis. Thus, in the abstract, he writes: "While being no blind adherent to a belief that the state is always right or that miscarriages of justice never occur, it did represent a worrying development to me. On further investigation, there seemed to be something more than the classical revenge motif involved and on the assumption that film has some kind of impact I started to explore whether my casual observations amounted to something more significant." To guide his analysis, Robson draws inspiration from Adorno and Horkheimer: "The whole world is made to pass through the filter of the culture industry. The old experience of the movie-goer, who sees the world outside as an extension of the film he has just left (because the latter is intent upon reproducing the world of everyday perceptions), is now the producer's guideline" (Adorno and Horkheimer 1979). Following Adorno and Horkheimer's lead, which again gestures to the complex relationships binding the "real" and the "reel," Robson remarks: "How exactly film is read by viewers in the media-saturated twenty-first-century and precisely how it affects us is a distinct topic but this chapter assumes that a steady supply of films with successful vigilante actions has at least the potential to influence action along with other aspects of popular culture." Robson reads the trajectory of vigilante films to reveal "more than just a challenge to the rule of law if the focus shifts to the victim in rape-revenge films." Eventually, Robson shifts his attention to "the link between the politics of resistance and language of vigilantism in relation to recent films, linking these two earlier themes and dealing with various resistance groups operating at the time of writing."

After the international focus of the second section, the third section focuses on "Law and Crime in American Film and Television." This section's expansion beyond film narratives to include television series attempts to broaden the scope of the collection, in terms of media discussed; it is also a nod to how the big screen, although still a dominant force in American popular culture, now has to compete, to some extent, with the small screen, for influence over the collective American popular cultural imaginary. Mathieu Deflem's chapter focuses on an iconic British auteur, Alfred Hitchcock, whose cinematic works came to signify both a mastery of, and subversion of, Hollywood cinematic formulae, of in particular the thriller genre. Drawing from the theories of Émile Durkheim (1912; 1914) and Victor W. Turner (1967; 1969; 1974), Deflem draws out two central characteristics of Hitchcock's films: the liminality of its characters, and the porousness and universality of guilt. In a converging conclusion, though very differently executed, John Denvir's chapter, on the all-too-human protagonists of the television series, *The Wire*, finds that it is precisely the characters' struggles with frailties and imperfections that make them contemporary heroes worthy of emulation and identification. Matthew Sorrento's chapter performs a genealogy of the emergence of the director-as-"avenger," who ensures the narrative return to law and order in recent American crime documentaries, such as Errol Morris's *Thin Blue Line* (Lipson and Morris 1988), whose narrative techniques aim to simulate or reproduce authenticity or verisimilitude and whose directorial narrative choices bring a certain form of justice to the accused. Naomi Mezey and Mark C. Niles's comprehensive chapter compares and contrasts how law is ideologically represented in American popular film and television; for them, although film possesses a greater potential for profound critical commentary, compared with television, such potential is seldom realized.

Summarized in greater detail, in Deflem's chapter, "Alfred Hitchcock: Visions of Guilt and Innocence," Deflem explores dimensions and modalities of guilt and innocence in the movies of a director whose films are well-known for both their mastery and subversion of formulaic Hollywood film narratives: Alfred Hitchcock. Miming the Hitchcock whom he describes as a skilled practitioner of liminality, Deflem situates the approach he takes at the intersection of the sociology of law and cultural sociology and conceives of Hitchcock's films as manifestations of liminality that are essentially marked by a process of transition from one state to another. Through what Deflem describes as a ritualistic experience of transformation, which, to Deflem, includes both diegetic and nondiegetic interactions, the ritual subjects are not only transformed but also subjected to, and actively experiencing, a transitional existential process that escapes from, and often even contradicts, the usual structures and demands of the social order. Deflem concludes, in a manner reminiscent of Hitchcock's subversion of the voyeuristic gaze in *Psycho* (Hitchcock 1960), that the accompanying visions of guilt and innocence in Hitchcock's movies involve a demarcation between private guilt and public guilt, the transference of guilt across subjects, and a generalized universality of guilt.

In the next chapter, "Heroes for Hard Times: *The Wire*'s 'Good Police,'" Denvir turns a pragmatic and grounded eye to a popular American television series, *The Wire* (Simon 2002–2006)—a series that has been aptly described as "social science-fiction" (Penfold-Mounce, Beer, and Burrows 2011). For Denvir, unlike most television shows and movies that feature fantasy heroes who win incredible victories by unbelievable means, *The Wire* refuses to provide its audience easy solutions to contrived problems. Denvir arrives at a similar conclusion as Yar does, regarding post-apocalyptic films, but phrases his conclusion regarding the less than happy endings of the series episodes in a quintessentially American manner: "As in life, the 'good guys' often lose." Denvir disagrees with the popular view that the series, because of its bleak narrative landscape, is a "downer," and concludes that whether we judge their efforts by what they accomplish for the community, or by the satisfaction they feel as professionals giving their all for a cause they believe in, the "good police" on *The Wire* are not only heroes, but also heroes with whom we can identify and emulate.

Matthew Sorrento's "Documenting Crime: Genre, Verity, and Filmmaker as Avenger" focuses on American traditions of documentary filmmaking in relation to the evolution of narratives of crime and law. Sorrento analyzes how recent crime documentaries (a largely ignored genre) since Errol Morris's *The Thin Blue Line* (1988) feature a filmmaker taking the role of "avenger." Sorrento argues that the avenger, a principal crime film figure, along with the "criminal" and the "victim," ensures resolution to ordeals or the triumph of law and order. Sorrento notes that in the nondiegetic (or "true") stories featured in crime documentaries, an actual avenger is not available (or ineffective) to fill that cathartic gap. Sorrento argues that the filmmaker takes the role to bring some form of justice for the accused or convicted. Sorrento observes that in the history of American film, crime films, as a genre, have generally striven for authenticity, if not realism. Hence, Sorrento notes that early narrative crime films (in the 1930s and 1940s) featured place and soon thereafter, actual location to depict verity. Sorrento further argues for cross-genre pollination and emphasizes that this relevance on place would lead to adaptations of true crime in the *noir* tradition, the celebrated example being Truman Capote's *In Cold Blood* as a book (Capote 1966) and film (Brooks 1967). Sorrento tracks this realistic crime trend to culminate in Morris's cornerstone film (*The Thin Blue Line*), the first work of documentary in which the filmmaker becomes avenger for the case being filmed which in turn inspired a series of recent filmmaker-as-avenger documentaries. As examples, Sorrento argues that Joe Berlinger and Bruce Sinofsky work as avengers assisting the accused in *Brother's Keeper* (1992) and the *Paradise Lost* series (1996; 2000; 2011), with both projects featuring the "deliberation" process of the law. Additionally, Sorrento points to the work of Nick Broomfield (1992 and 2003), in his films on Aileen Wuornos, and Werner Herzog (2011), in his death row film *Into the Abyss*. For Sorrento, Broomfield and Herzog account for the humanity of the condemned in films featuring the "disposition" stage of the law.

Rounding off the section, "Screening the Law: Ideology and Law in American Popular Culture," by Mezey and Niles, explores the role that ideology plays in the representation of law within the two dominant popular media, film and television by deploying cultural theory to assess the various ways that legal ideology is developed, communicated, and recreated in mass-mediated popular culture. In a manner similar to Robson's Adorno and Horkheimer-inspired theoretical turn to exploring how the "real" and the "reel" interact in complex ways, Mezey and Niles survey the abundant images of and arguments about the law in film and television in order to assess what those images and arguments can tell us about the legal ideology and popular understandings of legal institutions and the role of law in society. In comparing how American popular film and television visualize narratives regarding law and crime, Mezey and Niles distinguish between a potential for radical critique in film versus a more domesticated narrative, characteristic of television. Nevertheless, in a manner reminiscent of Kamir's appraisal of *A Separation*'s nonfulfilment of its potential for radical critique, they conclude that despite that difference, both media generally tend to reinforce dominant and pro-status quo perspectives on law. In an abstract that is not included in this book, they note:

> [W]hile all mass-mediated popular culture serves a pervasive ideology-reinforcing role in our society, the models of ideological production endemic

> to television and film are decidedly different. Television more consistently produces quite crude versions of legal ideology while film is more likely to portray more complex images of law and legal institutions. Notwithstanding these differences, a strong ideological message about law's ability to achieve justice in our society is consistently communicated by both media, and neither offers many subversive or counterhegemonic perspectives on law, although film has the greater potential, tantalizingly if rarely realized, to offer truly oppositional messages.

The fourth section, titled "Film, Crime, and the Social World," brings together several chapters that attempt to instantiate how a "Gothic Criminology" could be useful, as an interpretative framework in analyzing depictions of law and crime in film and television. The concept of what a Gothic Criminology is was preliminarily explored by Caroline Joan "Kay" S. Picart and Cecil Greek in an earlier edited collection, *Monsters In and Among Us: Toward a Gothic Criminology* (Picart and Greek 2008). Briefly summarized, noting the ubiquity of Gothic modes of narration and visualization in American popular culture, academia and even public policy, Picart and Greek proposed a framework, which they described as a Gothic Criminology to attempt to map the complex interactions between the "real" and the "reel" in the flow of Gothic metaphors and narratives regarding criminological phenomena that populate not only popular culture but also academic and public policy discourses. Although there are intersections in the way Picart and Greek deploy the tools of Gothic Criminology, which is adapted from Stanford M. Lyman's "Gothic sociology" (Lyman 1990), there are also differences. Picart uses Gothic Criminology to mean the mapping of the "social construction of crime and the nature of criminality, focusing specifically on the proliferation of Gothic tropes and *mise-en-scene* in the media's accounts, often fluctuating between fact and fiction and teratological rhetorics (i.e., 'monster talk')" (Picart, 2014). Picart's work thus far has remained focused principally on tracking evolving representations of a particular type of "monster"—serial killers—along the registers of race, class, gender, and sexuality. What the general body of Picart's work has striven to show is that these registers (of race, class, gender, and sexuality) of "real"/"reel" serial killers, result in different narratives. For example, Hannibal Lecter, a fictional character with affinities to Jeffrey Dahmer and Ted Bundy, is cinematically depicted as a hyper-intelligent, classy, heterosexual, white, male cannibal associated with the image of the glamorous vampire (with his hypnotic gaze; dark, swirling cape; and rakish Borsalino hat). In contrast, a lesbian serial killer, Aileen Wuornos, is cinematically depicted as metaphorically similar to the Frankensteinian Creature—white trash eternally in search of love and companionship.

Picart's first chapter in this book, "Race and Serial Killing in the Media: The Case of Wayne Williams" flows from the trajectory of that analysis; she now uses the tools of Gothic Criminology to analyze how these factors (race, class, gender, sexuality) interact in the media coverage of Wayne Williams, a fair-skinned black man convicted as the serial killer responsible for the Atlanta Child Murders. Picart notes that the media coverage of Wayne Williams differed from those of other typical black male serial killers in its scope, and in the grandiosity and refractoriness of the monstrous metaphors that proliferated the media discourse during the trial, divided generally (but not solely) along racial lines: for the prosecution and the generally white community, Wayne Williams was comparable to Attila the Hun, Adolf Hitler, and Idi Amin. In contrast, for the predominantly black civil rights community, the monsters were the racist criminal justice and legal systems that produced the lies of the one-drop rule; the "half-breeds" who hoped to be treated as white; and the mentality of complicity in these institutions and myths. Picart, deploying critical tools derived from legal scholarship, film criticism, and the sociological analysis of crime, principally uses the tools of Gothic Criminology to unveil the social construction of Otherness in relation to crime, through the use of "monster talk"; the target of her scholarly focus is how the perpetuation of teratological rhetorics (Picart and Browning 2012),[4] using Gothic modes of story-telling and visualization reinforces stereotypes, reifying them as self-perpetuating narratives.

In comparison, Greek's interpretation of Gothic Criminology is broader than Picart's. While not necessarily excluding Picart's focus on teratological rhetorics, Greek's scholarly interest appears to be an "ongoing fascination with evil, as simultaneously repellent, both in the Hollywood film, criminological case studies, popular culture, and even public policy" (Picart and Greek 2008, 17). Thus, Greek's work focuses on Gothic-inspired themes such as "blood lust, compulsion, fear, godlike vengeance, power, and domination" (Picart and Greek 2008, 31), and has a stronger affinity with theological themes than Picart, though he also draws from sociological and criminological frameworks. The latest evolution of his writings using a Gothic Criminological approach turns to a more comprehensive model. Greek calls this model a "Behemoth Model," which focuses on Hollywood films whose narratives hinge on themes related to how modern militarized societies attempt to maintain order, often by using overwhelming force and domination. Greek mines these films to offer a unique sociological interpretation of understanding postmodern international relations. In his first and solo-authored chapter in this section, "Globalization and the Rise of the Behemoth: A Study in Gothic Criminology," Greek notes the emergence of a predominant interpretation of the impact of globalization that has emerged from Hollywood.

Akin to Yar's observations regarding dystopic narratives that emerge in post-apocalyptic fictional films, Greek observes that within contemporary films globalization is depicted as a force unleashing terrible consequences, which now appear to be beyond human amelioration. Greek argues that a coherent theoretical framework, derived from an analysis of the Gothic images that predominate cinematic depictions of our post–Cold War problems such as terrorism, continuing instability in the Middle East, and illegal arms and drug shipments; and ongoing exploitation of the developing nations by the superpowers can be articulated—one described as a "Behemoth perspective rooted in chaos theory." Greek explains, in an abstract that is not included in this book, the theoretical foundations of his Gothic Criminological model in the following way:

> Drawing upon the concept of the Behemoth as it appears in Jewish apocryphal literature and the work of social scientist Franz Neumann (1963), the United States in particular and the developed Western world are depicted as a Behemoth, creating additional chaos in the world while claiming to be bringing order to what are existing sources of instability on the planet. The Western-led capitalist countries justify their continuing domination of the planet, including economic, medical, and legal concerns, by depicting the rest of the world needing governing leadership, including military intervention at times, to stave off forces which might otherwise thrust the planet into an irreversible chaotic state. To avoid the coming apocalypse, ultimately predicted by science fiction films set in the near future, a Behemoth has emerged which itself may bring that future to fruition rather than prevent it.

To exemplify how this model works, Greek focuses his analysis on four films: *The Constant Gardener* (Abberley and Mierelles 2005), *Battle in Seattle* (Aloe and Townsend 2007), *Lord of War* (Cage and Niccol 2005), and *Syriana* (Clooney and Gaghan 2005)—all of which were "made at the height of President George W. Bush's global campaigns against terrorism, 2002–2008." Greek selects these films because "each film deals with a different aspect of chaos (international medical policies, global economic policy, terrorism and the Middle East, and illicit weapons sales and their impact on ongoing civil strife), and how the West perpetuates chaos to justify its Behemoth strategies."

In the last chapter of the section, "A Depiction of Evil, Order, and Chaos: The Symbiotic Relationship of Law and the Supernatural in Film and Television," Farah Britto and Cecil Greek focus on the horror genre in film and television to analyze depictions of law and the supernatural. They argue that law and the supernatural are portrayed repeatedly and at odds in film and television programming, creating a dichotomy between the "real" realm of law and order and the "perceived" world of religious and supernatural forces, which provides the narrative *frisson* for supernatural thrillers in both film and television media. Britto and Greek show how tools of narrative and discourse analysis of six horror films and eight episodes from two horror television series reveal this strained symbiotic relationship, while also exposing the ways in which these different media formats portray evil while incorporating themes regarding law and the supernatural. Britto and Greek's theoretical framework is informed by Gothic Criminology, monster theory, and dystopia theory, which they use to reflect upon how evil is depicted differently in their selected samples of television versus film narratives. Eventually, they argue that in film, the evil resides in supernatural monsters, rendering the law powerless to defend victims of supernatural forces; on television, the evil resides in people, making the law a tangible way to vindicate victims and exact punishment. For Britto and Greek, it is important to note that in the horror genre, the law is rarely capable of fulfilling hopes for restoring order, and the dichotomy of an ordered universe rooted in law versus a world dominated by chaos and unchecked evil becomes an important component in this genre. This limits their depictions of horror to contemporary or modern horror, as opposed to classic Hollywood narratives of horror, for example, which is unsurprising, given the samples they choose to analyse. For Britto and Greek, the horror genre depiction of law and supernatural themes is well suited for Gothic criminological representation, as it includes Gothic visual elements, representations of evil and monsters, and features criminology and criminal justice. Like Picart, though in a more expansive manner, as Picart has a more pronounced rhetorical focus, Britto and Greek draw from "Monster" theory, and like Yar, from theories of dystopia, in the attempt to understand how law and supernatural discourse interact in both television and film formats.

The fifth and final section of this book is titled "Pedagogy, Epistemology, and Ethics in Films of Law and Crime." Michael Hviid Jacobsen and Anders Petersen's chapter proposes four methodological strategies (distillation, dramatization, distortion, and anecdotal data) for both pedagogical and scholarly criminological purposes. Jon Frauley argues against a hard and fast fact versus fiction dichotomy as an obstacle that must be overcome for a more effective epistemological model in studying criminological sources. Steve Greenfield argues against the reductive use of film as a source for examples that illustrate ethics as compliance to a professional code of responsibility, and argues for a more interdisciplinary use of film in relation to ethics and law. Caroline Joan "Kay" S. Picart maps the trajectory of American and Russian Holocaust documentaries and docudramas in relation to their functions as "witnesses" to the atrocities of the Holocaust in Holocaust-related trials in order to explore an emergent "poethics" of the production and reception of such representations of collective trauma and suffering.

Jacobsen and Petersen's chapter, "Contours of a Cinematic Criminology: Distillation, Dramatization, Distortion, and Anecdotal Data," begins with the observation that until relatively recently, the discipline of criminology did not pay particular attention to the treasure trove of knowledge provided by popular film. During the last decade, however, still more research literature on the fertile relationship between criminology and film has been published. Drawing from this ample trove of scholarly sources on intersections connecting film, law, and crime, Jacobsen and Andersen aim to highlight some of the methodological potentials for research in what is defined as "Cinematic Criminology." In this chapter, Jacobsen and Petersen—inspired by the work of Penney C. Hills and L. Rust Hills in a much-forgotten book, *How We Live* (1968), as well as the notion of "liquid criminology" (Jacobsen and Walklate 2016)—suggest four specific methodological strategies or approaches—distillation, dramatization, distortion, and anecdotal data—for thinking and researching with film which may, in each their way, assist the criminologist in comprehending and analyzing specific research topics more creatively as well as, at times, perhaps even more fully. After defining, instantiating, exemplifying, and analyzing each of these strategies, Jacobsen and Petersen conclude with an illustration of how crime-themed film may not only aid and abet criminological research but also be used creatively and imaginatively in teaching sessions for criminology students.

The next chapter, Frauley's "Fact, Fantasy, Fallacy: Division Between Fanciful Musings and Factual Mutterings," adopts a reflexive realist approach to the study of literature and film, arguing that novels and fiction films contain within them traces of empirical reality and that they also reflect upon that reality. Frauley's scholarly focus is again on the complex and porous nature of the relationships binding the "real" and the "reel"—a theme that has preoccupied a number of scholars in this collection, but this time recast into the familiar "fact" versus "fiction" dichotomy, which Frauley problematizes. Frauley argues that because fictional realities are empirical entities, and contain within them traces of the actual material and discursive conditions under which they were created, they are amenable to criminological analysis and are just as valuable as data sources as "factual" works such as diaries and letters. As Frauley convincingly argues, the setting up of this dichotomy casts the familiar fact-fiction division as an obstacle to criminological knowledge production and as a challenge to be overcome. Frauley's ultimate concern has epistemological consequences; his chapter discusses the fact-fiction dichotomy and the fallacy of the correspondence view of truth that supports this dichotomy (and its empiricist underpinning) and then enlists a brief discussion of texts and films that may be familiar to the reader to illustrate the faulty premise on which much sociology and criminology rests.

Greenfield's chapter is titled "Tobias Beecher: Law as a Refuge from Uncertainty?" Greenfield begins by noting that in legal scholarly and pedagogical circles, the analysis of depictions of screen lawyers has generally been limited to a discussion of whether or how a portrayal relates to actual law practice, particularly in relation to issues of professional responsibility. Without denigrating this approach, Greenfield nevertheless finds that this way of using film is unduly restrictive and limits the field of enquiry by placing actual legal practice at the core and confines the film or television show to its specific legal jurisdiction. Drawing from his own collaborative work (Greenfield, Osborn, and Robson 2001; 2010), Greenfield argues for the need for interdisciplinary theoretical frameworks that could potentially enrich a perspective informed purely by legal practice; for him, the question of ethics in relation to law is not reducible to mere compliance to a code of professional responsibility. He notes that one of the major challenges for the subject is to move beyond a narrow framework of analysis. Eclectic approaches with different aims also permit engagement with a wider range of portrayals further expanding and diversifying the subject base.

Like Denvir's chapter on the mortal and flawed heroes of the television series, *The Wire*, Greenfield's chapter focuses on Tobias Beecher, a middle-class lawyer who features heavily in the prison drama, *Oz* (Fontana 1997–2003), who has been convicted of vehicular manslaughter, incarcerated, and disbarred. Greenfield draws his theoretical framework from identity theory within social psychology which posits that individuals in a period of uncertainty will change their behavior and relationship to groups. Uncertainty theory has been used to explain the attraction of fundamental religious groups during uncertainty (Hogg, Kruglanski, and van den Bos 2013) because those facing uncertainty are attracted to groups and ideas that provide a solid bedrock. Greenfield observes that Beecher does not, because of his background, have access to such groups, which are the gangs operating within the prison system. As a lone individual, he must struggle with the question of what role the law plays in his search for meaning and identity. Thus, the guiding compass of Greenfield's chapter is: How does Beecher's relationship with the law, a previous fixture in his life, evolve and what security does it offer?

Picart's second chapter, "Nationalities, Histories, Rhetorics: Real/Reel Representations of the Holocaust and Holocaust Trials and a Poethics of Film and Law," converges with Menkel-Meadow's concern with the adequacy and ethics of representing trauma, suffering and violence using, in Picart's case, principally documentary or docudramatic film, in relation to the Holocaust and Holocaust-related trials. Picart's chapter examines the general trajectory of the role film has played in relation to evolving historical and legal narratives of the Holocaust, a complex historical arc relative to other forms of representation of the Holocaust. Thus, Picart's second chapter begins by analyzing an American documentary film, *Nazi Concentration Camps* (Nuremberg Trial Proceedings 1945), which functioned as a "self-evident" witness during the Nuremberg International Military Tribunal (IMT). From there, Picart then reflects upon and analyzes the cinematic techniques used in American docudramatic depiction, which embedded documentary footage into fictional rendition, as in Stanley Kramer's *Judgment at Nuremberg* (1961). Next, Picart turns to methodically examining *Film Documents of Atrocities Committed by the German-Fascist Invaders* (*Kinodukumenty o zver-stvack nemetsko-fashistskikh zakhvatchikov*) (1945), the Russian equivalent of *Nazi Concentration Camps*, and its contemporaries. Finally, Picart comparatively examines *Sud Naradov* (*The Judgment of the Nations*) (Karmen and Svilova 1947), the Russian feature film about the Nuremberg Trial.

Picart argues that the historical evolution of representations of the Holocaust and Holocaust trials is important because these form part of the rhetoric of the "spectacular" and "educational," especially within the context of World War II. While Picart's methodology is initially genealogical and deconstructive, analyzing the mechanics of film (as "language" and rhetoric) as it depicts the "real"/"reel" within differing national contexts (American and Russian), Picart's concern, like Greenfield's attempts to explore a broader, interdisciplinary examination of what "ethics" could mean, in the face of these horrific representations of crime and law. Picart ultimately raises the possibility of a "poethics" (to borrow and adapt Richard Weisberg's [1992] term) of production and reception in relation to the evolution of representations of the Holocaust and Holocaust trials. Eventually, Picart, drawing from Weisberg, affirms the educational value of such representations, provided their audiences engage in a critical ethics of reception.

With this collection of cross-disciplinary studies we hope to show how alternative ways of framing the themes of law and crime—such as through film or television—may enhance our appreciation and understanding of these phenomena. We hope to show how drawing on the bountiful experiences embedded within each researcher's creative insights, playful experiments, lucky hunches, or sudden associations can demonstrate that rethinking what it is we are doing within our own compartmentalized scientific disciplines, or thinking across disciplinary boundaries and circumventing the status quo of Kuhnian "normal science," holds the promise of novelty, surprise, and ingenuity—something succinctly summarized by Mary Catherine Bateson's spot-on observation that "the most creative thinking occurs at the meeting places of disciplines. At the center of any tradition, it is easy to become blind to alternatives. At the edges, where the lines are blurred, it is easier to imagine that the world might be different. Vision sometimes arises from confusion" (1991).

NOTES

1. Admittedly, Kuhn, at that point in time was talking about hard sciences, but his use of the term "paradigm," which he later revised to "disciplinary matrix," has long been adopted by other disciplines.

2. Wood writes: "Popular films, then, respond to interpretation as at once the personal dreams of their makers and the collective dreams of their audiences—the fusion made possible by the shared structures of a common ideology. It becomes easy, if this is granted, to offer a simple definition of horror films: they are our collective nightmares. The conditions under which a dream becomes a nightmare are that the repressed wish is, from the point of view of consciousness, so terrible that it must be repudiated as loathsome, and that is so strong and powerful as to constitute a serious threat."

3. The notion that horror and science fiction films allow for the expression of otherwise tabooed Jungian "shadow" figures has also been developed by Janice Hocker Rushing and Thomas S. Frentz, among others. See, for example, Janice Hocker Rushing and Thomas S. Frentz, *Projecting the Shadow* (Chicago: University of Chicago Press, 1995) and Caroline Joan S. Picart, *Remaking the Frankenstein Myth on Film: Between Laughter and Horror* (Albany, NY: State University of New York Press, 2003).

4. See also Caroline Joan "Kay" S. Picart, "'Jihad Cool/Jihad Chic': The Roles of the Internet and Imagined Relations in the Self-Radicalization of Colleen LaRose (Jihad Jane)," *Societies* 5 (April 2015): 354–83; doi: 10.3390/soc5020354.

REFERENCES

Abberley, Jeff (producer) and Fernando Mierelles (director). 2005. *The Constant Gardener* [Motion Picture]. United States: Focus Features.

Adorno, Theodor and Max Horkheimer. 1979. *Dialectic of Enlightenment.* London: Verso. (First published 1944 in German as *Dialektik der Aufklarung.*)

Aloe, Mary (producer) and Stuart Townsend (director). 2007. *Battle in Seattle* [Motion Picture]. United States: Metropolitan Films.

Asimow, Michael (ed.). 2009. *The Lawyer in Your Living Room: TV Lawyers.* Washington, American Bar Association.

Bateson, Mary Catherine. 1991. *Composing a Life.* London: Grove Press.

Bergman, Paul and Michael Asimow. 1996. *Reel Justice—The Courtroom Goes to the Movies.* Kansas City: Andrews and McMeel.

Berlinger, Joe and Bruce Sinofsky (producers and directors). 1992. *Brother's Keeper* [Motion Picture]. United States: New Video Group.

———. 1996. *Paradise Lost.* [Motion Picture]. United States: Home Box Office.

———. 2000. *Paradise Lost 2: Revelations.* [Motion Picture]. United States: Home Box Office.
———. 2011. *Paradise Lost 3: Purgatory.* [Motion Picture]. United States: Home Box Office.
Black David. 1999. *Law in Film: Resonance and Representation.* Urbana, IL: University of Illinois Press.
Brooks, Richard (producer and director). 1967. *In Cold Blood* [Motion Picture]. United States: Columbia Pictures.
Broomfield, Nick (producer and director). 1992. *Aileen Wuornos: The Selling of a Serial Killer* [Motion Picture]. United States: Strand Releasing.
———. 2003. *Aileen: Life and Death of a Serial Killer* [Motion Picture]. United States: Columbia TriStar Home Entertainment.
Cage, Nicholas (producer) and Andrew Niccol (director). 2005. *Lord of War* [Motion Picture]. United States: Lions Gate Films.
Capote, Truman. 1966. *In Cold Blood.* New York: Random House.
Clooney, George (producer) and Stephen Gaghan (director). 2005. *Syriana* [Motion Picture]. United States: Warner Brothers.
Dailly, James and Ryan Davidson. 2011. *The Law of Superheroes.* New York: Gotham.
Denvir, John (ed.). 1996. *Legal Reelism: Movies as Legal Texts.* Urbana, IL: University of Illinois Press.
Durkheim, Emile. (1912) 1965. *The Elementary Forms of the Religious Life.* New York: The Free Press.
———. (1914) 1973. "The Dualism of Human Nature and Its Social Conditions." In *Emile Durkheim on Morality and Society,* edited by Robert N. Bellah, 149–63. Chicago: University of Chicago Press.
Farhadi, Asghar (producer and director). 2001. *A Separation.* [Motion Picture]. Iran: Asghar Farhadi.
Fontana, Tom (producer). 1997–2003. *Oz* [Television Program]. New York: HBO.
Foucault, Michel. 1994. *The Birth of the Clinic: An Archeology of Medical Perception.* New York: Vintage Books.
———. 1995. *Discipline and Punish: The Birth of the Prison.* New York: Vintage Books.
Greenfield Steve, Guy Osborn, and Peter Robson. 2001. *Film and the Law: The Cinema of Justice.* London: Cavendish.
———. 2010. *Film and the Law: The Cinema of Justice,* second edition. Oxford: Hart.
Herzog, Werner (producer and director). 2011. *Into the Abyss* [Motion Picture]. United States: IFC Films.
Hills, Penney C. and L. Rust Hills (eds.) (1968): *How We Live—Contemporary Life in Contemporary Fiction.* New York: Macmillan.
Hitchcock, Alfred (producer/director). 1960. *Psycho* [Motion Picture]. United States: Paramount.
Hogg, Michael, A., Arie Kruglanski, and Kees van den Bos. 2013. "Uncertainty and the Roots of Extremism." *Journal of Social Issues* 69(3): 407.
Jacobsen, Michael Hviid and Sandra Walklate (eds.). 2016. *Liquid Criminology.* Farnham, U.K.: Ashgate.
Jarvis, Robert and Paul Joseph. 1998. *Prime Time Law: Fictional Television as Legal Narrative.* Durham, NC: Carolina Academic Press.

Jingo, Minoru (producer) and Akira Kurosawa (director) 1950. *Rashomon* [Motion Picture]. Japan: Daiei Motion Picture Company.
Jolie, Angelina (director, writer, and producer). 2011. *In the Land of Blood and Honey* [Motion Picture]. GK Films.
Kamir, Orit. 2006. *Framed: Women in Law and Film*. Durham, NC: Duke University Press.
Karmen, Roman and Yelizaveta Svilova (directors). 1947. *The Judgment of the Nations* (*Sud Naradov*) [Motion Picture]. United States: Artkino Pictures.
Kramer, Stanley (director). 1961. *Judgment at Nuremberg* [Motion Picture]. United States: United Artists.
Kuhn, Thomas S. 1970. *The Structure of Scientific Revolutions*. Chicago: University of Chicago Press.
Lasswell, Harold. 1949. *The Analysis of Political Behaviour: An Empirical Approach*. New York: Oxford University Press.
Lipson, Mark (producer) and Errol Morris (director). 1988. *The Thin Blue Line* [Motion Picture]. United States: Criterion Collection.
Lucia, Cynthia. 2005. *Framing Female Lawyers: Women on Trial in Film*. Austin, TX: University of Texas Press.
Lyman, Stanford. 1990. "Rereading Robert E. Park: Toward a Gothic Perspective on Capitalism and Imperialism." In *Explorations: The Age of Enlightenment* (Volume IV), edited by M. W. duQuesnay, 29–108. Lafayette, LA: University of Southwestern Louisiana Foundation.
Machura, Stefan and Peter Robson (eds.). 2001. *Law and Film*. Oxford: Blackwell.
Meyer Phil. 1993. "Visual Literacy and the Legal Culture: Reading Film as Text in the Law School Setting." *Legal Studies Forum* 17(1): 73–93.
———. 2001. "Why a Jury Trial is More Like a Movie Than a Novel." In *Law and Film*, edited by Machura Stefan and Peter Robson, 133–46. Oxford: Blackwell.
National Film Board. 1948. Royal Canadian Mounted Police (Producers) and Robert Anderson (Director), *Drug Addict*. [Motion Picture]. Canada: NFB.
Neumann, Franz. 1963. *Behemoth: The Structure and Practice of National Socialism, 1933–1944*. New York: Octagon Books, Inc.
Nuremberg Trial Proceedings. 1945. *Charter of the International Military Tribunal*, Volume 1. Accessed July 7, 2013 at: avalon.law.yale.edu/imt/imtconst.asp#art19.
Penfold-Mounce, Ruth, David Beer, and Roger Rurrows. 2011. "*The Wire* as Social Science-Fiction?" *Sociology* 45(1): 152–67.
Picart, Caroline Joan "Kay" S. 2003. *Remaking the Frankenstein Myth on Film: Between Laughter and Horror*. Albany, NY: State University of New York Press.
———. 2014. "Media Myths Regarding Serial Killers: A Gothic Criminology." In *The Poetics of Crime*, edited by Michael Hviid Jacobsen, 173–91. Farnham, U.K.: Ashgate.
———. 2015. "'Jihad Cool/Jihad Chic': The Roles of the Internet and Imagined Relations in the Self-Radicalization of Colleen LaRose (Jihad Jane)." *Societies* 5(April): 354–83.
Picart, Caroline Joan "Kay" S. and John Edgar Browning (eds.). 2012. *Speaking of Monsters: A Teratological Anthology*. New York: Palgrave Macmillan.

Picart, Caroline Joan "Kay" S. and Cecil Greek. 2008. "Introduction: Toward a Gothic Criminology." In *Monsters In and Among Us: Toward a Gothic Criminology*, edited by Caroline Joan "Kay" S. Picart and Cecil Greek, 11–43. Madison, NJ: Fairleigh Dickinson University Press.

Rapping, Elayne. 2003. *Law and Justice As Seen in TV*. New York: New York University Press.

Robson, Peter. 1996. "Images of Law in the Fiction of John Grisham." In *Tall Stories? Reading Law and Literature*, edited by John Morison and Christine Bell, 201–22. Aldershot: Dartmouth Publishing.

———. 2001. "Adapting the Modern Law Novel: Filming John Grisham." In *Law and Film*, edited by Machura Stefan and Peter Robson, 147–63. Oxford: Blackwell.

———. 2014. "The Law through the Eye of the Courtroom Comedy: The Light Legal Procedural in Context." In *Law and Popular Culture: International Perspectives*, edited by Michael Asimov, Kathryn Brown and David Papke, 233–52. Cambridge: Cambridge University Press.

Robson, Peter and Jessica Silbey (eds.). 2012. *Law and Justice on the Small Screen*. Oxford, UK: Hart.

Rushing, Janice Hocker and Thomas S. Frentz. 1995. *Projecting the Shadow*. Chicago: University of Chicago Press.

Sen, Soumik (director). 2014. *Gulaab Gang* [Motion Picture]. India: Benaras Mediaworks.

Simon, David (producer). 2002–2006. *The Wire*. [Television Program]. New York: HBO.

Turner, Victor W. 1967. *The Forest of Symbols*. Ithaca, NY: Cornell University Press.

———. 1969. *The Ritual Process: Structure and Anti-Structure*. Ithaca, NY: Cornell University Press.

———. 1974. *Dramas, Fields, and Metaphors: Symbolic Action in Human Society*. Ithaca, NY: Cornell University Press.

Villez, Barbara. 2005. *Séries Télé: visions de la justice*. Paris: Presses Universitaires de France.

———. 2010. *Television and the Legal System*. London: Routledge.

Weisberg, Richard. 1992. *Poethics and Other Strategies of Law and Literature*. New York: Columbia University Press.

Wood, Robin. 1986. *Hollywood from Vietnam to Reagan*. New York: Columbia University Press.

I

CINEMATIC HISTORIES AND REAL/REEL DYSTOPIAS OF LAW AND CRIME

1

Law and Cinema Movement

Stefan Machura

Scholars engaged in sociolegal studies often want to inform jurisprudence and legal practice. In outlining the importance of law for society, sociolegal studies also contribute to social sciences. It is in this context that a new variety of scholarship developed, which is dedicated to the depiction of legal phenomena in the popular medium of film. For more than a hundred years, audiences consumed films related to law, to legal institutions and to lawyers. In all likelihood this has formed many people's views and may then have influenced their actions. Consequently, sociolegal scholars have reason to study law in film. Harold Lasswell's (1949, 37) formula "Who says what to whom in which channel with which effect?" has served as an agenda for communication analysis. This chapter uses Lasswell's questions to crystallize findings on law in film and to map out the "law and cinema movement"[1] itself.

LAW AND CINEMA MOVEMENT

Social and intellectual movements usually have a lot of predecessors. The decision to single out which of the pioneers possible to mention remains a question of preference. It is not so long ago that the academic field of law and cinema has developed. In fact, its presence is so new that there has been little attempt to (re-)construct its history up to now. From the view of sociolegal studies, the law and cinema movement originated roughly from 1986 to 1987. Journal articles of, to name but a few, Anthony Chase (1986), Stewart Macaulay (1987), and Lawrence M. Friedman (1989) opened a path for following authors. Macaulay's (1987) was based on his presidential address at the annual meeting of the Law and Society Association in Chicago in 1986. He took the opportunity to draw attention to a promising new field of sociolegal scholarship. "I'm not suggesting that we waste time on trivial matters. The familiar images shown again and again on film and television and both the formal and hidden curricula of our schools reflect, teach, and reinforce what most people know about things legal. And these ideas and attitudes matter" (214).

The topic of law in the movies fit into the older concept of "popular legal culture." According to Friedman (1985, 191), legal culture is about

> ideas, opinions, values, and attitudes about law, that people carry about with them in their heads. If you ask, which people? the answer is: whichever people you like, whatever group, and at whatever level of generality. It is possible to talk about the legal culture of Germans in general, or of Berliners, or of elderly people in Berlin, (. . .) or any class, group or community whatever.

"Popular legal culture" refers to what "the people" think of and do with law and not to lawyers' law. It consists of depictions of law and legal personnel in entertainment media rather than of the self-description of the legal system and its professionals. This distinction, however, should not mislead us to deny the influence of the legal system on popular legal culture. Klaus F. Röhl (2002a, 317) expresses skepticism about the role of genuine folk-customs today. He stresses the importance of modern institutions and of professionals. Popular legal culture exists "in narratives which reproduce parts of the official legal system in a more or less distorted fashion" (317). In modern Western societies, state law has increasingly seized the positions and importance formerly held by folk legal custom in everyday life. Nevertheless, with global streams of migration, traditional and religiously based customs make themselves felt more, again (Röhl and Machura 2013). The media industry has utilized and appropriated, to a large extent, folk music, plays, and other forms of popular culture. Media professionals have a key role today in the communication of cultural products, and lawyers largely contribute to media portrayals of the law. Lawyers influence people's legal expectations and behavior. They are writing film plots, giving advice to film directors and producers, and sometimes they even fill in these core positions. However, their impact on the portrayal of law, legal institutions, and personnel is never complete since films, as well as TV series, are a team product.

Popular legal culture was but one root of law and cinema. Arguably, the study of law and cinema would have hardly become as widespread if there had not been a second factor in academic life. The "law and literature movement" and an approach to analyze "law as text" (e.g., Porsdam 1999) contributed to a rise of sociolegal studies in the United States and in Britain. Almost certainly, the view also diffused to movies and TV productions (e.g., Lüderssen 2002). "Much of legal writing about film has identified itself, in one way or another, with legal writing on literature," stated David A. Black (1999, 117; similar Silbey 2002, 141–42; see Denvir 1996a). However, Greenfield, Osborn, and Robson (2001, 196) rightly argue that few law and film authors are also known from law and literature work. Nevertheless, because law and literature was earlier accepted by some legal scholars, it has prepared ground for law and film.

The availability of VCR technology—and later DVD—in classrooms facilitated the use of films in academic teaching. Surprised professors detected the "visual literacy" of their students (Meyer 1993). Growing up with television, today's students are able to read a movie in multiple ways that often offer intellectual surprises for their teachers. Also, legal scholars have developed methods to scrutinize films and to relate them to their historical surrounding. These methods offer rich insights into their functioning as pieces of art and into their sociopolitical environment.

In the process of writing the present chapter, it sometimes appeared as if the categories of author and audience, and even more, the categories of message and effect began to partially lose their contours. Films, as complex entities, are the product not only of a work team but also of a society (or, at least certain segments of society). Broader social communications, myths, stories, and stereotypes are filling in the spaces of films, as if the audience has a say in the production. Similarly, law and film scholars do not only talk to their audience but they are sharing the audience's thoughts in many respects. They adapt to their modes of thinking and they are even somehow writing for them, or instead of them. Directors of movies receive suggestions from the audience on future film products (e.g., Smoodin 2005). Furthermore, it is at times hard to describe the messages of law and film scholars without talking about intended and "real" effects. Often, we are reading the intentions of film-people and scholarly writers into their works. In discussions about intents of films, the absence of a clear method for the falsification of interpretations makes itself painfully felt. Society today—defined as the totality of "communications" which are reachable for each other—tends to be a world-society with national states as crucial entities of its political organization (Luhmann 2000, 220–27). Legal films as cultural products refer almost exclusively to national legal institutions and culture. But they are watched worldwide. At the same time, American cinema is dominating the film market, transporting American legal themes to places in which audiences live with different experiences and knowledge.[2] Certainly, people in the

Western (including East European) countries are likely to share certain basic values regarding fairness and the rule of law.[3] What they lack, however, is the special cultural background to read all the signs in American movies. Similarly, American law and film scholarship addressing flaws and shortcomings in the American legal system often encounter barriers for an understanding by scholars from other countries. The cultural factor can also be stressed, quoting Chase (2002, 81) who mentions a "deep and pervasive, if unconscious, familiarity with both legal and cinematic conventions shared by audience and filmmakers alike" in American cinema.

A terminological question has to be raised at this point. What constitutes a legal film? For the purpose of the present chapter, it may be helpful to engage with an early attempt at a definition by Steve Greenfield, Guy Osborn, and Peter Robson (2001, 24): "In order to qualify as a law film the following characteristic(s) must be present in some shape or form: the geography of law, the language and dress of law, legal personnel and the authority of law." This definition extends the focus on a field much larger than the traditional courtroom genre: films with a significant part happening inside a courtroom and in a running trial. Legal films may find their story outside of the courtroom, for instance in the lawyers' offices or in other legal forums, for example, an unofficial "quasi-court," like the gathering of the criminals in the film *M* (Nebenzal and Lang 1931; see figure 1.1) or the barn in *The Devil and Daniel Webster* (Glett and Dieterle 1941). But there may be no resemblance to legal locations (Greenfield, Osborn, and Robson 2010, 33), as in *The Ox-Bow Incident* (Trotti and Wellman 1943) or in *Spur der Steine* (Dormeier and Beyer 1966). The language of law evokes connections between morality and law, power (dominance, politics) and law, and sometimes religion and law. At times, it is reduced to a "legalese," which documents a gap between the "real" and the legal sphere. The dress of law is more obvious in films showing front-stage behavior of legal personnel. "Dress . . . has a crucial purpose in identifying the main players in the courtroom" (Greenfield, Osborn, and Robson 2010, 39), here: which are the central legal figures? Jurors and other lay judges may count as legal personnel. Films on law have to deal with binding rules and with their authority over people. Although there is not necessarily a restriction to state law, mere conventions would not count. To summarize, at times Greenfield, Osborn, and Robson's (2001) definition may be too narrow, depending on the actual research interest. It has to be admitted that most of the following still deals with examples from the traditional courtroom genre. Courtroom dramas form the core of the legal films and they are widely consumed.

Figure 1.1. *M*—The Quasi-Court. Image in the public domain, optimized by Susan Gilbert.

LAW IN THE MOVIES

It is not very rewarding to draw a sharp distinction between the depiction of law and lawyers in movies made for cinema and movies made for TV. These categories have merged more and more in the media industry. Nevertheless, this text concentrates on law on the broad screen primarily. The majority of academics have turned their attention to films made for cinema. The big movies often provide the ideas or the elements that are used in TV productions. Self-reference is a main characteristic of the system of art (Luhmann 1997), to which movies and made for TV films mainly belong. They are primarily responding to previous films, using their plots, sequences, role constellations, and such. Only very recently, the success and complexity of TV series like *The Wire* (Thorson and Simon 2001–2008) and *The Good Wife* (King and King 2009–present) set in motion a significant shift of influence.

Hart's War (Hoblit 2002) offers an example for the self-reference of film. The German commander of a World War II prison camp asks the American POWs whether they are going to conduct a trial just like in their American movies. *Hart's War* plays with the twenty-first-century audience's memory of prior films. Only a member of the film team with an excellent grasp of film history might have known that American courtroom scenes appeared on German screens during Nazi rule. In 1939, for example, a Nazi propaganda film *Sensationsprozess Casilla* (Holder and Borsody 1939) attacked the American legal system. The film used conventions of American courtroom dramas to denounce the American legal system and society (Drexler 2001, 75–76). Previous representations like "the real world of law" provide bricks for the constructions of movies and TV shows (Machura and Ulbrich 2001).

The Communicator(s)

It certainly is a complicated question to clarify the authorship of films. Some European and American (among them, e.g., John Ford, perhaps Sidney Lumet) directors had at some point of their career reached such a status, that they were more or less able to decisively determine a film. However, their dominance can never be complete since film is a team product to which workers of very different crafts contribute. Sometimes actors can have a lasting impact on a film. Producers in Hollywood reserved the right of the "final cut." Certainly, the laws of the market rule the film industry. Market influences were even the driving force behind the famous Production Code of Hollywood (Maltby 1983), which dictated: "Law, natural or human, shall not be ridiculed, nor shall sympathy be created for its violation" (General Principles 1930, No. 3). But what can be said about the film market? It is influenced not exclusively by a capitalist economy. Certainly, the film industry is a very speculative business. But it is also influenced by social values, by ideologies, and by grand stories, which are told again and again in various cultural products—including films.

The Message(s) of the Movies

Almost everywhere nowadays, narratives are stressed as important constitutive elements of real trials and courtroom films. This follows the narration model (story model) of court trials. The narration model has become widespread in sociolegal studies and underlies lawyers' strategies in cases (overviews: Ewick and Silbey 1995; Jackson 1996; Löschper 1999). "In the courtroom, whoever tells the best story wins," states attorney John Quincy Adams in *Amistad* (Spielberg 1997). Narratives are not only formulated by the competing parties at a trial, but are also incorporated—albeit in a condensed form—in legal precedence and in the paragraphs of law. They do not exist independently from cultural narratives in a broader sense, quite to the contrary. It is often the craft of the lawyer to link a story to a shared pattern of cultural understanding. Some authors distinguish between a "story in the trial," an event in the past which is judged now, and a "story of the trial," which is formed by the events of the trial itself (Jackson 1996, 27). The latter can also be formed after broader cultural narratives: for example, the corrupt police forge evidence. Edith Hall (1995, 49), a student of ancient Greek legal dramas related narratives to another factor: "The outcome of a case must often have depended not on discovery of the factual truth or falsity of the two versions of events rendered, but on their competitive plausibility; this in turn was dependent on the credibility of those rendering them."

All of that forms a powerful constellation for law films and they often combine both elements: the credibility of competing stories and of the protagonists. Even the apparent absence of a final solution can make a successful film, as in *Rashomon* (Minoura and Kurosawa 1950) with its different stories told about the same crime. But usually one of the competing versions of events triumphs over the other. *Inherit the Wind* (Kramer 1960) provides a particularly interesting example of dealing with narratives. Based on the famous Scope's trial (Kuzina 2000, 290–96), the film contrasts a Creationist's outlook and a Darwinist's perspective on the origins of life. A young teacher is prosecuted for telling his class about Darwin's theory. This constituted an offense according to local state law of the time. In a final scene, we see Spencer Tracy as a victorious defense lawyer. He weighs both books, which were introduced during the trial, in his hands: the Bible and Darwin's. The grey-haired Tracy plays a believable figure in this film as a righteous man of the law in numerous others; as a star, he stands generally for liberal American values. So he is the man qualified to argue and to judge. In a sudden move, he decides to pick up both volumes, reconciling both culturally dominant narratives: the religious and the scientific.

It could be said that not only are the messages of law movies very diverse and open to viewer interpretation, but also that there is a message behind certain national movies at a given period of time. Movies are complex entities emphasizing aspects of the story told. Even the same plot filmed twice may slightly shift the meaning of the film. This can be tested by viewing *Twelve Angry Men*, the famous movie of 1957 (Fonda and Lumet) and its 1997 TV version *12 Angry Men* (Donnelly and Friedkin). The later version casts the role of the racist juror with a militant African-American man and the hand camera produces an atmosphere which appears more fluid. Over time, the initial social meaning of a film can get lost. A young viewer nowadays might not even imagine the provocation lying in *Sergeant Rutledge* (Goldbeck and Ford 1960). This movie depicts a black cavalry soldier with all the attributes of a John Wayne hero. Some films win the audience's respect for discriminated groups, for example, *Philadelphia* (Saxon and Demme 1993). Others simply exploit social stereotypes held against certain groups, for example, women (like a series of movies in the 1980s about female lawyers). Legal doctrines and legal political conceptions may find their way into law films. In the United States, for example, older law movies shared the impetus of the liberal reforms in the Warren Era. Plots in the 1980s often supported a backlash (Berets 1996). In older movies, Chief Justice Earl Warren of the U.S. Supreme Court stands as a symbol for the defense of citizens' rights. Later—after the interlude of the 1970s—American society became more concerned with crime control. Films on crime and criminal law, according to Chase (2002, 68), "not surprisingly simply mirror the central dichotomy between crime control and due-process values within an adversary system of criminal justice." After a review of films, he further clarifies: "Traditional due-process films . . . dealt with efforts to vindicate the innocent. But later due-process films go further and brand government officials as frame-up artists" (76).

Chase (2002, 108–13) presents a thorough analysis of films on tort litigation. He argues that the American popular legal culture lacks a narrative that does not depict large firms as villains. "Could a motion picture manage to tell the story of a victimized corporation wrongly accused of negligence in the popular press and in civil court, only to be exonerated by a no-nonsense jury in the film's upbeat ending?" (Chase 2002, 112). This, despite the fact that American politicians often buy the industry's "deep pockets hypotheses." The "master discourse" (119) is different: David wins against Goliath, as in *Erin Brockovich* (DeVito and Soderbergh 2000).

The portrayal of lawyers in movies has been systematically analyzed by Asimow (2000a). It changed from dominantly positive in the 1950s and 1960s to the depiction of what Asimow calls "bad lawyers" especially in fictional movies. (However, positive characters are prevailing in films based on "real" events.) The change in the characterization of lawyers took place in the 1970s, a period in which comparably few American pictures on courts were made. In American films, the reputation of law firms and their lawyers is especially bad. Asimow (2001) writes they are depicted as greedy and as serving the interests of big money at the expense of justice. Sometimes they even take part in organized crime. In TV series with lawyers as main protagonists, their characters appear much more positively depicted. Asimow (2000a, 557–58) explains this with the need of TV stations to constantly attract viewers in order to receive high amounts of advertisement money. Positive characters are more likeable and people switch on to watch the series more often. Also, according to standard plot lines, bad characters often have to be punished and disappear from the screen. Greenfield, Osborn, and Robson (2001) objected to Asimow's criteria distinguishing between "good" and "bad" lawyers. The dispute is interesting here for at least two reasons. The three British authors argued that characterizations as "good" and "bad" depend on subjective evaluation and that several of the older lawyer heroes also show behavior that is, for example, rude and ethically questionable. Recent research conducted in laboratory situations with brain and eye-movement scanners also suggests that viewers are mainly attracted by the figures shown in TV series. Situations, history, and scenery would just serve as framing (Schulz 2013). However, even if they would be the side dish, they are consumed nevertheless.

Contents transported by movies may vary, as clearly evidenced by national cinemas. Italian, French, or German films often have their special atmosphere and they depict law and its personnel in special ways. There are differences from typical American plots. German law films deal with an inquisitorial system, but take up patterns of the adversarial system as depicted by American movies. In this way they are often confusing both legal worlds.[4] In French and Italian films, a typical figure is the investigating judge or the police officer as loner. He is fighting against criminals as well as against the bureaucracy in which he is working. Finally he—it is usually a male figure—may find out that the two (the criminal world and the "legal" authorities) have merged and the lesson learned is a bitter one (e.g., *The Octopus*, Damiani 1984). Similarly, American detective films, as Macaulay (1987, 203–4) mentioned, are sending messages about hierarchies, but here the fittest protagonists are able to bend the rules in order to achieve "justice." The same would apply to the German TV commissioner Schimanski (*Tatort* 1981–1991), or his Italian colleague Montalbano (Degli Esposti and Sironi 1999–2013).

There are categories of law films that can be identified, among them:

- the traditional courtroom drama,
- the lawyer-film without a focus on the courtroom,
- films about court martials.[5]

A typical court-martial film, like *A Few Good Men* (Brown and Reiner 1992), is both a film about military justice and contains significant courtroom scenes. The latter aspect also makes it a courtroom drama.[6] Films belonging to this category have pivotal parts of the story happening in the courtroom, like *To Kill a Mockingbird* (Pakula and Mulligan 1962). The contents of the three categories of films vary considerably. Court-martial films commonly have political intentions, depicting a clash between the systems of the military or the formalized law on the one hand and individual needs, individual justice on the other. *A Few Good Men* (Brown and Reiner 1992) is a rather harmless example of the genre with a questionable ending for the two men who tortured their comrade. *Paths of Glory* (Harris and Kubrick 1957) formulates a powerful critique of a military under the command of generals who only follow personal career objectives (Strübel 2002, 210–11). Racism and ethnic hostility are targeted by films like *Sergeant Rutledge* (Goldbeck and Ford 1960) and *Breaker Morant* (Carroll and Beresford 1980).

Movies and TV court shows are fascinating because they are not only about law, but also about morality. Television shows, especially, usually "offer more explicit lessons about moral boundaries than news broadcasts" (Macaulay 1987, 208). Movie lawyers like the protagonist in *Young Mr. Lincoln* (MacGowan and Ford 1939) and Atticus Finch in *To Kill a Mockingbird* (Pakula and Mulligan 1962) have clear moral orientations. Films and court shows pit good and bad characters against each other. The viewer thus gets emotionally involved. Which moral rules have to be observed? In an American society becoming increasingly diverse, TV court shows like *The People's Court* (Levin 1981–1993) and *Judge Judy* (Douthit 1996–present) or the German *Richterin Barbara Salesch* (Marx 1999–2012) are places where positions are qualified by a judge having superior legal consciousness and common sense (Porsdam 1999; Machura 2012). The good film judge—or lawyer—preserves the mores of the people even when the people have started losing their faith in them.

Films on law depict institutions of law. This portrayal does not mirror legal reality exactly but emphasizes certain aspects. Movies deal more often with criminal law and procedures than with civil law and procedures although the latter are much more frequent in the real world (Robson 1996, 2–3). Many movies show jury trials. The audience may easily get the impression that jury trials are much more used than they actually are. Bench trials, plea bargaining in criminal cases, settlements in civil matters, mixed tribunals of professional and lay assessors, and all the other forms of courts and modes of case resolution appear less often on the screen. In the real world, the costly trial by jury is a last resort. For dramaturgical reasons it is the preferred choice in movies (Machura and Ulbrich 2001, 118).

The Audience of the Movies

The audience of movies has changed a lot since the times of the *Prisoner of Shark Island* (D. F. Zanuck and Ford 1936) and *The Winslow Boy* (Grunwald, and Asquith 1948). Nowadays families rarely go out for the movies together. Since the 1960s, younger audiences have predominantly filled the cinemas. They want to see more action (and sometimes more sex) in the films. And the law movies also followed this trend. As did many films and TV series in the meantime. In the long run however, the age distribution of moviegoers in the aging Western countries changed again (for Germany already; Neckermann 2000, 409). The family audience before the TV screen now receives a cocktail of films produced at different times following different trends.

Nicole Hahn Rafter (2000) convincingly argued that with minorities soon outnumbering the white U.S. audience and American society (like the European) aging significantly, the film industry will change its products. A number of American movies made for TV with black or Hispanic protagonists have already appeared. Rafter (2000, 167) wrote, including courtroom films into her topic "crime films": "In the years ahead, crime film heroes will become more diverse in terms of age, race and ethnicity, gender, and sexual preferences. The youngish, heterosexual white males who have long dominated the imagery of heroism will be joined by new hero types that will ultimately make crime movies a more democratic form of entertainment." Following Rafter, an older audience would also prefer to watch classical detective work and not so much action. Generally speaking, film as a commodity has to adapt to the audience. Unless, of course, it is subsidized massively by public money, as sometimes is the case in Germany.

The Means of Communication

Greenfield and Osborn (1995, 120) once talked about "lego-films." And indeed, many scenes or plot ideas recur again and again. Hardly any courtroom film comes without cross-examinations. Frequently, cross-examination as a turning point brings out a surprise confession in open court, for example, in *Sergeant Rutledge* (Goldbeck and Ford 1960), or *Witness for the Prosecution* (Hornblow and Wilder 1957). A powerful dramaturgical device, surprise confessions reached by cross-examination are nevertheless rare in real courtrooms. Moreover, confessions are, in practice, often unreliable and need further corroborative evidence. *The Lady from Shanghai* (Wilson and Welles 1948) does not raise this legal critique but apparently mocks the ritual of cross-examination when the defending barrister calls himself to the witness stand, then cross-examines himself in place of the prosecutor and re-examines himself in his capacity as defender. There are other films, in which last-minute evidence in the court saves the day (e.g., *Libel* [Grunwald and Asquith 1959]). In *Young Mr. Lincoln* (MacGowan and Ford 1939), the final confession of the culprit (and false witness) follows after Lincoln has produced a farmers' calendar.

Lincoln goes on to argue that at the day of the murder there has not been enough moonlight to see what happened.

Symbolism is a recurring element of storytelling, especially in American films. Many courtroom films make use of establishing shots showing the court-building, courtrooms, and busy people in them, ongoing trials and so on. Famous examples are the movies . . . *And Justice for All* (Wizan and Jewison 1979) with its camera moving through the courtrooms and corridors (e.g., Silbey 2001, 101–2), and *Witness for the Prosecution* (Hornblow and Wilder 1957), where a worker is cleaning the sculptured figure of justice on the dome of the courthouse. Law is part of the American civil religion, as Helle Porsdam (1999) wrote. American culture has developed an arsenal of commonly understood symbols of law and justice. It even encompasses an icon of justice and law like Abraham Lincoln. He reappears in a number of courtroom dramas and Westerns (Böhnke 2001, 51–52; 2002, 97; 2007). The jury symbolizes the people and also stands for the film audience (Machura and Ulbrich 2001, 126–27). In other countries, like Germany and Russia, law has fewer, and arguably weaker, symbols. In the two countries mentioned, this is probably an effect of discontinuous political developments. At times, the legal system was perverted in both countries, resulting in a de-legitimation. As a surrogate to domestic symbols, German films try to borrow from Hollywood portrayals of law, lawyers, and courts.

The modern state rests on the expectation that the "rule of law" and not "the rule of man" shall reign. Legal films are often constructed around this concept, as illustrated for instance when a mean and corrupt judge or prosecutor threatens the correct application of the procedural or substantive law (Machura and Ulbrich 1999, 176; Chase 2002, 67–68). However, it appears as if this constellation is not the message itself, for that would be indeed trivial. Some commercial productions may simply use this powerful dramaturgical device to earn money (is there a message behind, for example, *A Few Good Men* [Brown and Reiner 1992]?). But in a number of films, among them . . . *And Justice for All* (Wizan and Jewison 1979), *The Verdict* (Zanuck and Lumet 1982), or *The Star Chamber* (Yablans and Hyams 1983), the warning of an abuse of power becomes a political message and a vehicle for raising sincere questions. The corrupt and mean individual represents the realization that something has gone wrong with the legal system (Machura 2004).

Law films have at their disposal the whole array of general cinematic styles and patterns regarding plot structure, light and sound, effects, and more. But they nevertheless have their own recurring elements copied from previous law films, which often causes a feeling that this has already been seen before.

The Effects of Law-Related Movies

A first, system-immanent effect of law films is that the success of former films in terms of money and appraisals sparked ideas to produce so many more of them. As a late response to the growing number of media portrayals, the law and cinema movement, with its classes, publications, and conferences forms another effect. Many scholars believe in films having an impact on the legal thinking and behavior of the audience, as expressed by Macaulay (1987). Systematic studies on media effects on the public are difficult to conduct and often have complicated results that do not fulfil a desire for simple facts.[7]

Sometimes films made about real events change the lives of the people depicted. In one case a man convicted wrongfully was finally released from prison after the film *The Thin Blue Line* (Lipson and Morris 1988) attracted new attention to his case (Bergman and Asimow 1996, 50–51; Kuzina 2000, 287). *The Onion Field* (Coblenz and Becker 1979) evoked such a public outcry that the parole board decided against one of the convicted perpetrators (Bergman and Asimow 1996, 40; Kuzina 2000, 315). Anecdotal evidence is quickly at hand. Part of an explanation as to why it is hard to determine the effects of such films is that each viewer can construct her own meaning out of the material of a film. "Just as a Rorschach ink blot," Macaulay (1987, 201) says. Moreover, it might be even one of the joys of film consumption that the recipient actually has to construct their own opinion.

Richard Sherwin (2000) wrote that the American legal system is about to adapt to pop culture as the result of deliberate, although backfiring, policies of conservative high court justices. They opened the courts to cameras. What was intended to strengthen public support ended in a public relations disaster, when the media covered trials selectively following media-specific criteria. The media focuses on extreme cases and disputable outcomes.

Sherwin's argument may serve as a warning. One should not attribute too much of the public's opinion on law, lawyers, and legal institutions to films. Media exposure also means the influence of not only court TV but also, for example, of infotainment in news shows, of reality-TV, or of advertisement for legal services (forbidden for lawyers in Germany, but even televised in the United States and the United Kingdom).

Michael Asimow (2000a, 556) employs psychological cultivation theory to explain the cumulative effects of film viewing. Frequent and recent exposure to films with negative portrayals of lawyers, he argues, amounts to a negative opinion of this professional group. However, frequent dealings with lawyers can also contribute to negative stereotypes (Macaulay 1987, 187; Asimow 2000a, 542).

According to an American study by Michael Pfau, Lawrence J. Mullen, Tracy Dietrich, and Kirsten Garrow (1995, 321) the public, despite its viewing of television, does not hold a better opinion on the character of lawyers as lawyers themselves have about their group. Pfau, Mullen, Dietrich, and Garrow summarize their findings:

> In short, prime-time network television appears to influence public perceptions of attorneys, particularly in terms of front region behaviors, such as composure, physical attractiveness, and presence, all of which may contribute to attorneys' public roles, especially their prowess in arguing cases in court. . . . The public perceives attorneys as upper class and powerful, images that are conveyed through prime-time television programming. Perhaps as a consequence, they also view attorneys as low in character, an image albeit contrary to that projected in network prime-time programming. (Pfau, Mullen, Dietrich, and Garrow 1995, 326)

While this relates to evaluation, what about knowledge? American films with appearances of law and lawyers are often broadcasted in Germany. The German public seems to be influenced by this in its knowledge of legal institutions (Wolf 1997). German children are convinced that judges bang gavels (film cliché of American judges) and wear wigs (England). This has been noted by psychologists in an attempt to develop a book for the preparation of child witnesses (Hille 1997). German judges do not have gavels or wigs.

In a study with law students, more than half of the respondents stated that they were influenced by the popular media of film and fictional books in their views of lawyers. Respondents were students in law schools and countries as diverse as the University of California at Los Angeles (United States), University of Westminster (London), Strathclyde University (Glasgow, Scotland), Ruhr University Bochum (Germany), Buenos Aires University Law School (Argentine), and University of Wollongong (Australia). Only news media were more important to them in forming their opinion on lawyers (Asimow 2005). In a subsequent study, Bochum students of law, geography, and political science were interviewed about their views on courts and about sources of information. It turns out that the consumption of TV court shows and court series, as well as the consumption of legal movies had no detrimental effect on trust in German courts. There were even slightly positive correlations between law-related media consumption on the one hand, estimated prestige of courts, and a belief in the fair treatment of citizens at court on the other hand (Machura 2006).

Kimberlianne Podlas (2001) tried to discern the influence of TV court show judges like *Judge Judy* (Douthit, 1996–present) on juror's perception of court rules. There are several of such shows on U.S. television. The behavior of the judges there is much more emotional and investigative than in real U.S. courts. Podlas expressed concern about the expectations that jurors might develop from watching such shows. They might misunderstand the actual behavior patterns at court. Respondents were individuals called for jury duty in three courthouses. Frequent viewers of TV court shows stated more often than nonfrequent viewers that judges should have an opinion regarding the verdict, should make that opinion "clear and obvious" to the jurors and that they as jurors would affirmatively "look for clues" supporting the judge's opinion or "try to figure out" the judge's opinion (Podlas 2001, 12). Also, frequent viewers attributed the silence of a judge to that judge's favoring of either the plaintiff or the defendant (13). The vast majority of the frequent viewers believed that judges should ask questions during the trial and thought that a judge should be "aggressive with the litigants or express his or her displeasure with their testimony or behavior" (14). Nonfrequent viewers were much closer with their expectations to the traits of the U.S. legal system. According to Thym (2003), university students viewing similar German TV court shows were more likely to believe in a rude style of behavior in court, which includes attacking the opposite party. They also expected, for example, frequent last minute confessions from the witness stand. In a study with high school and college students, assumptions of aggressive behavior at court were not related to viewing TV judge shows, but rather to influences from novels and movies, and also by TV and radio reports (Machura and Kammertöns 2010).

But what about the general population? From April to June 2005, a telephone survey was conducted in the area of Bochum in Germany involving 1,015 residents above the age of fourteen (Machura 2012). The survey suggested that TV judge shows "cultivate" stereotypes that trials involve aggression, contingency, and emotion. The results led to the main points:

- These stereotypes may encourage viewers to mobilize the law in case of conflict. They are more likely to go to a lawyer or to court if they suffer damage. Viewers feel the need to avail themselves of legal remedies to solve problems.
- Consequently, those who share these stereotypes also expect to be exposed to aggressive behavior (be ridiculed, subjected to awkward attacks, etc.) once they find themselves in court.
- The more respondents believed they would suffer as a party in court, the less they actually trusted courts. Accordingly, TV judge shows may actually have a detrimental long term effect (Machura 2015, 408).

Watching U.S. courtroom and lawyer movies correlated with slightly less favorable views of lawyer prestige and lawyer character and respondents feeling influenced by novels, TV and films tended to doubt that lawyers deserve their income.

A quote by Vladimir Lenin used to be installed above cinema screens in the Soviet Union: "The most important art for us is cinema." In 1917, about 90 percent of the Russian population was illiterate (Steiner 2001, 14). Films about law are often used as instruments to sell political concepts to a broader public. The Nazi film *Jud Süß* (Lehmann and Harlan 1940) stands as an example for inhuman, terrible propaganda (Ecke 2002). In the eighteenth-century Duchy of Württemberg, the finance politician Süß Oppenheimer was sentenced to death under violation of existing law. He was a scapegoat for local political problems. The historical events were distorted in the film *Jud Süß* (Lehmann and Harlan 1940) for an anti-Jewish agitation. The film formed a special project of Nazi propaganda minister Joseph Goebbels. In post-war Germany, the director Veit Harlan was tried for contributing to a public atmosphere that lead to the Holocaust. An initial conviction was not upheld at the appellate court. More recently, a courtroom documentary *Jud Süß—Ein Film als Verbrechen?* (Milker and Königstein 2002) addressed Harlan's guilt and whether a film constitutes a crime. *Jud Süß* is still forbidden in Germany. The government argues it would evoke vicious feelings among right-wing youth.

Today, social science methodology is available to investigate the impression of a film on the audience. However, there seems to be no study that nails down propaganda effects for law films. The movie *Philadelphia* (Saxon and Demme 1993) is said to have contributed to breaking the taboo that surrounded homosexual orientation and AIDS in the 1980s. But there is no systematic evidence.

According to anecdotal evidence from countries as diverse as the United States, Argentina, and Germany, law films (Greenfield, Osborn, and Robson (2001, 10–11), TV series and TV court shows have attracted many students to the study of law. Barbara Salesch, with her court show (Marx, 1999–2012) the German equivalent to *Judge Judy* (Douthit 1996–present) in the United States, claimed that judicial office would have become the number one career objective of German girls thanks to her onscreen appearance (Broder 2002, 180). A survey of German high school students showed no influence of TV lawyer series and judge series on the attractiveness of becoming a lawyer or judge, but a significant influence on selecting paralegal as "dream job" (Machura and Kammertöns 2009, 251–52). Asimow (2000a, 583) suspects that lawyer figures he understands as "negative" ironically serve as role models for American law students: "Lawyers on the big screen are teaching lawyers and law students that uncivil and unethical behavior is rewarded in law practice. Law students are taught that they must be Rambo with a briefcase to be successful; perhaps young people who find that model attractive are disproportionately choosing legal careers."

But the audience's response to American movie lawyers is not necessarily negative, especially where they violently engage in noble causes. Moreover, in countries previously under dictatorships, where the judges and lawyers were subjugated under political authorities, the adversarial qualities of the American legal system appear as attractive. In Russia, people sometimes learned about a Western legal system and the role of lawyers from American films. It is this picture that later formed the ideal (Lempert 1996, 365; Korolkov 2002, 1).

Indeed, although there are many critical portrayals, the overall effect of law films is most likely propaganda in favor of the law (not necessarily any particular law) and its professional figures: lawyers, judges, and even public prosecutors. That legal process and lawyers are legitimized by lawyer films has been concluded by Greenfield and Osborn (1995, 120). "[G]ood people working within a fair system or, at least, a system that delivers justice in some shape or form" (Greenfield, Osborn, and Robson 2001, 27). There are films on miscarriages of justice, but "[t]he beauty of these films is that they do not disturb our faith in the law; the failings are those of individuals, normally police officers, who are shown as corrupt. The ideal of law is shown as subverted by individual or even communal dishonesty" (ibid.).

People's opinions may also be related to self-selection of their personal media diet. According to Cynthia Cohen (2006, 12; 2009, 30), people who watch TV representations of lawyers tend to trust them. Those who think negatively about lawyers avoid them on TV and stick to their negative stereotypes. In countries where the legal sector is on the whole working quietly and reasonably, the majority of citizens would hold a favorite view, reflecting, and at the same time constituting, a positive climate (Machura 2011). Media messages may then further strengthen this level of trust (ibid.). The legal institutions themselves can add to this through appearance. Analyzing public support for national high courts James L. Gibson, Gregory A. Caldeira, and Vanessa Baird (1997, 33) suggested a "positivity bias": "to be aware of a court is to be supportive of it." Courts display and manipulate legitimizing symbols. Immediately, the decorum of robes and court architecture, the formalities of procedure, the use of arguments, the role play, and other aspects spring to mind, which are exploited to the full in popular legal culture.

But something else is also happening with the viewers. Film as a unit of moving pictures, cut, and sound draws attention from abstract legal rules to single cases. Personalization of public topics is a major trait of picture media. The needs of individuals often stand against abstract rules (Chase 2002). Pain and suffering are effectively depicted in films.

In *To Kill a Mockingbird* (Pakula and Mulligan 1962), the wrongly accused defendant breaks out in tears at the witness stand. He feels hopelessly entangled in a net of racist prejudice. The forum of the southern U.S. court room does not allow him an effective defense. In order to explain what happened, he must talk about "the unspeakable in our society." He does and is punished for having broken the taboo—admitting to feeling sorry for a white girl (Maier 2002, 116). Films like this can move the audience and win their sympathy for the cause of the depicted. But not only the characters of the parties are becoming important in the picture media: the personae of the decision makers also receive more attention (Röhl and Ulbrich 2000, 381–82). The morality of the parties and of the persons holding legal authority gets questioned in legal films. Where are the moral limits of behavior? What is just? How well are the institutions working? Who has been entrusted with power? These topics appear over and again. In rare moments the society looks at its own shortcomings and injustices. Nevertheless, at least in those Western societies, which are at peace with their legal authorities, the pop cultural portrayal of law constitutes a predominantly conservative force (Machura 2011) thanks to patterns of story-telling, audience preferences, and the predispositions of most of the producers.

LAW AND FILM SCHOLARSHIP

A lot of literature has been written on the topic of law and film. The previous sections of this chapter have already introduced some of its contents. Especially productive have been American scholars, but there are some British contributions, too. The number of Continental European publications remains smaller in this sector. One of the first German publications seems to have been an article by Oliver Castendyk (1992), who was very much influenced by the rise of popular American legal culture literature and American films. In his article, little is said about Germany itself. The first German book by Matthias Kuzina in 2000 was dedicated to the American courtroom drama. Only slowly, the European films came into the sight of German authors, who were mainly fascinated by Hollywood films (e.g., Neuhaus 1994/1995). In several other European countries, the movement seems to have started later (France and Italy), or may be lacking entirely (e.g., Russia).

The ever-growing body of literature speaks in favor of an analysis of the law and cinema movement. The Lasswell question can be applied to the literature and scholarship on legal films. As mentioned earlier, Laswell asks: "Who says what to whom in which channel with what effect?"

The Scholars

The scholars engaged in the field of legal films are quite diverse. As mentioned, Continental European lawyers are only infrequently—if ever—addressing the field of law and cinema. To their camp, law still is almost exclusively black-letter law and the use of pictures of any kind beyond a narrow use in legal history or criminology appears highly unprofessional. In his critique of the picture-phobia shown by German lawyers, Röhl (2002b, 3, 35) argues that the effect of pictures on an audience is less predictable than the effect of a legal text. Pictures are more complex than language and more open to interpretations. This makes them vulnerable to the suspicion of a number of lawyers. Although the American legal historian Anthony Chase (2002, 13) raises a point similar to Röhl, American lawyers first used films in their teaching and first dealt with law films in their publications.

As Black (1999, 133) points out, film is for legal scholars "a tool for gaining access to important legal issues." Most of them are working with the objective to contribute to a better legal practice. "Law borrows from literature and film in the service of reaching its own telos. Film studies borrows, too, but its borrowings virtually amount to its substance," wrote Black (1999, 125). He wants to express the differences between the relation of the two academic disciplines to studying film. However, there also are authors who reach beyond a use in legal education and practice to a broader understanding of the functions of both law and film in society. Among them are lawyers with a strong law and society agenda.

Their Message(s)

The messages of law and film scholars vary considerably. A lot of them are writing politically critical articles. They are partly affiliated to the critical legal studies camp within jurisprudence. (Critical legal studies can be characterized as an attempt by legal scholars to use law as an instrument for social reforms to the benefit of disadvantaged groups.) Some are fighting for a more general reorientation of the public, for example, by attacking sex-role clichés in media or addressing stereotypes of homosexuals in movies (Moran 1996). Strictly theoretical papers are rare, since most authors are lawyers rooted in the black-letter tradition. This tradition coins two responses to a new problem, according to Greenfield, Osborn, and Robson (2001, 192): Answers are searched for within the system of law in force, and interest focuses on legality, not on the social functions of law. Theoretical offers from other disciplines and from the margins of jurisprudence are therefore often unimportant.

Some scholars admire the art of films (or filming) in a way in which law and literature exponents salute masterpieces of classical literature.

These authors have a lot to say about the contexts of films, the staging, the interplay of scenes, of sound, light, montage, and so on. They may relate movies based on literature to their original source or sketch out the history of legal movies.

Others, mainly lawyers, are concerned with the public image of the profession. They often tend to overemphasize negative portrayals. Film characterizations are not always positive. Film figures do gain significance when they have some edges, like personal problems or conflicts with their surroundings.

According to Black (1999, 142), film culture is obsessed with plausibility, as evidenced by what moviegoers tell each other about a film and also by film critique. Legal scholars are especially able to contribute to discussions on the legal plausibility of film plots and actions of film figures. A book like *Reel Justice: The Courtroom Goes to the Movies* by Paul Bergman and Michael Asimow (1996) may serve as an example. Scholars from outside of the United States are grateful for such assessments.

There is, however, a danger in several lawyer-authors' articles, as Cynthia Lucia (1999, 15) puts it, of "hitting something of an analytic dead-end once the question of accuracy or plausibility has been answered." Klaus Lüderssen reflects on the use of films as data for criminological research. An empirical check of depictions often becomes impossible. Even if the films contain a "real" core story, all that goes beyond that as an artistic compression or abstraction is hard to prove (Lüderssen 2002, 336–37).

A lot of critique focuses on legal faults in films that are not detectable from the knowledge of a layperson. Such comments of legal scholars are therefore out of touch with the films' impact (Chase 2002, 173). "What matters for the audience is the contrast between the screen portrayal and the mythical qualities and idealism of law and lawyers *as reflected in films*," Greenfield, Osborn, and Robson (2001, 115, emphasis in the original). This position argued against a trend in parts of the law and film scholar camp, which contrasted film portrayals and the "real."

There are more broadly shared ideals involved that are present not only in films, but also in other sources of popular culture, such as education, religious, and ethical beliefs. In addition, a conflict between the legal plausibility of law films and artistic aspirations makes itself felt throughout law and film scholarship. Some authors tend to favor one side, some the other, and the balance of both aspects is hard to find.

Still other scholars are interested in popular legal culture as a part of sociology of law. They tend to see both law and film in a more detached manner. But these are few. In Germany, scholars of American culture inevitably came to study law and cinema, and their works are closer to traditional film scholars' studies or focus on individual films or problems of genre, or they follow the lines of the critical legal studies (e.g., Baer 2011).

Greenfield, Osborn, and Robson (2001, and again 2010, 27–31), Francis M. Nevins (2003), as well as other authors also stress the service law and film classes can do for the education of lawyers.[8] American author Anthony Chase (2002, 134) emphasizes films of foreign countries as a device for classes on comparative law. Since clients are likely to know the law from popular cultural portrayals, Jessica Silbey (2002, 142) argues, law students should be confronted with legal films in order to prepare for their future work. Greenfield, Osborn, and Robson (2001, 6) formulated that it would be a "tragic waste" to confine legal films to the narrow role of another sort of traditional legal teaching material. Because of often dealing with moral issues, legal films may contribute to a general education of students (Greenfield, Osborn, and Robson 2001, 8). Skills that may be furthered are "viewing and listening, teamwork, presentation and research." Also, "films were used to replace texts that are often inaccessible to students at this point in their academic career." Theoretical problems of law can be addressed at an early time of the studies, and need not be delayed to the almost final courses, when everything revolves around legal craftsmanship (Greenfield, Osborn, and Robson 2001, 8).

Law and film classes can have an "empowering function" (Greenfield, Osborn, and Robson 2001, 9) to students who are exhausted by the traditional dogmatic content. In addition, students are learning to work with competing versions of reality (party narratives) and to familiarize themselves with the concept of discourse (Greenfield, Osborn, and Robson 2001, 10). In our own teaching experience with law in film classes in Bochum and Speyer (Germany) and Bangor (Wales), some students are often more motivated and they deliver better papers than otherwise as a result of exposure to these themes.

Chase welcomes the focus on individual needs versus abstract legal rules inherent in films and writes about the emergence of a "[c]inematic jurisprudence—a way of looking at law through the lens of the camera that projects an alternative view of legality, one every bit as likely to undermine ruling ideas about fairness and formal legal equality as it is to reinforce them" (Chase 2002, xiii). "The popular art of motion pictures may be one of the most effective instruments ever invented for providing just that sensibility for particularity in law (Chase 2002, 30).

For the time being, this appears rather visionary, bearing in mind the "fear of pictures" (Chase 2002, 13) in jurisprudence, which has already been discussed as a reason why German law scholars are reluctant to use films as instruments of legal education. Chase knows that picture-phobia also exists in the United States.

Their Audiences

The role of the audience for law and film scholars should not be underestimated. The target audience, according to Black (1999, 134), makes the difference as to whether a work belongs to film scholarship or legal scholarship. It is not difficult to determine who the main audiences for law and film publications are. Two groups can be identified mainly: lawyers and legal scholars (in their majority situated in the United States) and students of law and film studies (again most often United States). The success story of Bergman and Asimow's *Reel Justice* (1996) tells us much about the audience of law and film scholarship. The book was initially planned as a kind of video guide with academic comments. Bergman and Asimow have sold some twenty thousand copies of its first edition alone. The authors made presentations in book stores. Thousands of books have been bought after the authors gave talks to Bar Associations. There also were TV appearances. The buyers have been lawyers mainly (Asimow, personal communication, April 2002 and December 2013). The analysis of the channels of communication for law and cinema scholarship also reveals that lawyers are most interested in the field. Students of law may be motivated by their personal affection for film portrayals of law people and legal institutions. Students of film science want to know more about the recipes of the successful genre and they want to present their pre-knowledge when they enter law and film classes. Also, such classes provide a welcome alternative to overly theoretical film courses.

Channels of Communication

Most frequently, law journals are the places of publication for work on law in film. Increasingly, separate publications have come out: books, some of which are already mentioned, and special issues of (printed) journals[9] as well as an online journal (*Picturing Justice* 1997–2006) and internet Web pages. The trend is another sign of the development of law and cinema into an academic field.

From the beginning, the verbal paraphrase of film plots has been the preferred means for law and film literature (Black 1999, 131–32). A significant number of essays were constructed around reports of plotlines, or of other analyses of one or a limited number of films. Text may occasionally be accompanied with pictures. In the meantime, more articles and books appeared that used film stills to illustrate verbal descriptions. Sometimes, historic film advertisement material was also utilized to give readers an idea about the film distribution policy and even a cartoon was drafted to point at the historical function of an actor (e.g., Isensee and Drexler 2002).

Increasingly, different means have become employed to communicate findings of law and film scholars.

Not the least important channel of communication is classes of students. Nevins (report in Nevins 2003) taught intellectual property law in St. Louis. Works of literature and films served as objects of study. A bridge between classic dogmatic teaching of law and film was built. Further examples may illustrate the scope of classes focusing exclusively on law and film. At London's University of Westminster, Greenfield and Osborn (Osborn 2001) taught law in film to first year law students. In Bochum, from 1995 to 2003, a course on "law in film" was taught regularly (Machura and Ulbrich 1999). Students of law and of film studies filled the audience. After a film was presented and a break was taken, two hours were reserved for presentations by students and a general discussion. Students were mainly in their third or fourth academic year. Another format was employed by Asimow in California: Students had to apply, showing practical experience in the film industry to enter the class. With his colleague Shannon Mader, Asimow authored a course book *Law and Popular Culture* (2004). A decade ago, Asimow (personal communication, April 2002) already estimated that there were no less than between forty and fifty classes on law and film at U.S. universities alone. Today, their number would have at least doubled (personal communication, December 2013).

Another channel of communication are talks before lawyers, like the presentations of Bergman and Asimow before Bar Associations, but also at scholarly events like the Annual Meeting of the Law and Society Association, or the Meetings of the Research Committee on Sociology of Law and at other conferences, both regional and national.

THE EFFECT OF THE LAW AND CINEMA MOVEMENT

More and more scholars are interested in the field of law and film and an ever wider readership and audience is reached by publications, classes, and presentations. This proves the main effect of the movement. While in Black's (1999, 139) analysis legal scholarship does not contribute to discussions of film scholars, this might already be changing since the number and quality of publications is rising. Direct effects of law and film scholarship on film production are unknown. A number of film people are lawyers themselves and they provide feedback from the realm of law to the production sphere of films. Because of this, they can draw on their own knowledge rather than law and film scholarship.

In a way, do law and film scholars amplify the messages and effects of law films? The answer seems to be a resounding "Yes." Even critical authors often come to appreciate certain aspects of films and the legal world. What they attack in detail—for example, rigid views and prejudice, discrimination, harsh penalties, distorted representations—is often rejected by the educated audience, too. So authors are often endorsing pre-existing views. Fierce critique of legal actions, myths, and institutions implies, to many, that there should be more "just" laws and better lawyers. The critique becomes a call for reform.

THE FUTURE

While there will still be publications in the future that will draw on a description of just one or only a few films, the time is ripe for more comprehensive and more systematic studies. A number of approaches can be suggested. A few of them are discussed below.

Systematic content analyses have been started. As mentioned, Asimow (2000a) classified portrayals of lawyers, reviewing a great number of films.[10] A group of European scholars, headed by Antoine Garapon, reviewed their national cinema productions in order to assess the portrayal of the legal system and its representatives.

- Focused interviews (Merton and Kendall 1979, 171–72) can be conducted after a film has been watched by the audience. For that purpose, researchers would prepare with a content analysis of the film and they would formulate questions about the impression the film has. Such a controlled experimental approach would provide insights on how certain aspects of law films are experienced and what the immediate effects on the audience are.
- Opinion surveys can be employed to find out which films are consumed and remembered by the audience (or certain segments of it, e.g., law students). Also, potential effects of that media experience can be isolated when effects of personal encounters with the law, legal institutions, and legal personnel are controlled for (e.g., Machura 2011; Machura, Ramos, Rooney, and Warmald 2013; Machura and Kammertöns 2009; 2010).
- Among other topics, further research may address the politics behind law films. From time to time, political aspirations of U.S. filmmakers are discussed (e.g., Böhnke 2002, 92–93; Machura and Davies 2013).

Also, the portrayal of law, legal agencies, lawyers, and police under the influence of the Hollywood Production Code has been analysed (e.g., Asimow 2000b). There are articles on law-related films as propaganda instruments in Nazi Germany (Drexler 1999, 2001; Ecke 2002; Isensee and

Drexler 2002). But Western scholars know little about political influences on law films in a number of countries (among them China and Russia). As the law and cinema movement broadens, researchers from countries like Poland, Italy, or Spain will certainly raise their voices. A strange example of political influences on the depiction of courts is reported from the United States in the aftermath of September 11, 2001. Military trials against members of al-Qaeda were planned to exclude the public. An episode of the military court TV series *JAG* (Bellisario 2002), called *The Tribunal*, served as an instrument for the U.S. defense ministry, because these pictures would be the only ones the Americans would ever see, according to both the producer and the Pentagon (Hupertz 2002).

Most efforts of law and film scholarship concentrated on "big" movies made for cinema. The cinematic qualities of films often clearly served as a selection criteria. Against this, it can be argued that the minor films may not be less important for the audience. And important are, of course, the numbers of TV movies and TV series on law and law people that are broadcast. Arguably, their effect on popular legal culture can be decisive.

The topic of law and cinema already has its special publications in books and journals. It remains to be seen, whether further steps for an establishment as a fully recognized academic subject will be taken, such as the founding of scientific associations and of university chairs or research institutes. In any case, we have witnessed the birth of a new, challenging academic field over the last two decades, one of truly transdisciplinary character.

BROADER LESSONS LEARNED

To analyze not only social communication in the "field" as social scientists usually describe it but also to include the meta-communication of scholarly authors might be a promising idea for further communication studies. While the present chapter tried this for law movies and TV products as well as for law and film scholars, other research might relate, for example, works on war movies, on fashion magazines, or on governmental public relations to the scientific community dedicated to it. If there is some similarity, we would expect that personal fascination, professional engagement, and critical aspirations, partly of political origin, come into play. The law and cinema movement is very much motivated by a wish to enhance methods and results of academic teaching. Other academic fields may be more infuriated by political endeavors or by economic calculus.

In the case of the law and cinema movement, it has to be noted that scholarly authors are mainly lawyers. They are bringing forward a field of study that has been almost overlooked before. As a coalition of scholars coming from different academic backgrounds, it gained momentum. It is one example more for the argument that transdisciplinary studies are very promising. Perhaps, future prospects for law and the social sciences lie here in the working together of scholars from different disciplines, employing different methods and representing different cultural origins. Products from the Americas, India, Europe, or Japan reach out across the globe. There, on foreign soil, they are consumed by people who interpret them against their specific backgrounds. This text has mentioned American courtroom dramas reflecting Common Law tradition, which are seen by a Continental European audience. But it would be a tragic waste to focus on local or national specifics only and to overlook the manifold ways in which people from different cultures share common expectations and patterns of consumption. These are partly a result of a cultural globalization which in its extent is not second to economic globalization.

NOTES

1. The author has first detected the phrase "law and cinema movement" in Rosenberg (1991, 215).

2. In German cinemas, for example, American films held an average market share of 81 percent in the years between 1991 and 1999 (Neckermann 2000, 407).

3. As a case study for Russia: consider Machura (2003) and Machura, Donskow, and Litvinova (2003). In some patriarchal and Islamic cultures, however, discrimination along the lines of status and gender by an authority is seen as just legitimate (Bierbrauer 1994, 258).

4. German court procedures have adversarial aspects but the films often distort them. For example in criminal trials, the presiding professional judge questions witnesses first. Later prosecution and defense may continue. In films it often appears that they start the interrogation, which is very rare in reality. There isn't something like a witness for the defense or for the prosecution. Even the thought is alien to the inquisitorial German system.

5. Black (1999, 59) and Greenfield and Osborn (2002, 6) argue to include prison films. Prison films often contrast the punishment allotted to the prisoners by law and courts with private regimes of abusive punishments and with cruelties by corrupt or hateful prison officers (e.g., *The Prisoner of Shark Island*, D. F. Zanuck and Ford 1936) or sadistic fellow inmates. The films sometimes provide flashbacks to the trial and the events leading to it, sometimes state law is contrasted with the rules of social subgroups (Black 1999, 162–68).

6. On subgenres of courtroom drama Kuzina 2000; on court-martial films Kuzina 2002; 2005.

7. For instance, Dowler's (2002) study about media influences on citizen attitudes toward police effectiveness showed little effects. But the author has been unaware of what crime dramas viewers have seen. The search for effects of law-related films needs to be much more focused.

8. A few other examples from a variety of teaching tasks: Sarah Gatson (1997) suggested the use of films in a law and society class, Lee Stuesser (1999, 100–1) to show *The Star Chamber* (Yablans and Hyams 1983) in order to introduce the topic of reasonable expectation of privacy to law students, and a group of social psychologists favored films as a means for the undergraduate education in legal psychology (Fulero, Hans, Nietzel, Small, and Wrightsman 1999, 144).

9. See Denvir 1996b; Symposium 1997; Machura and Robson (eds.) 2001; Asimow (ed.) 2001; Marder (ed.) 2007.

10. The leading questions for a classification of lawyers as "positive" or "negative" by Asimow and his research assistants were whether they would like to have a film character as a friend or as their lawyer (Asimow 2000a, 562). Further attempts may employ a more complex scheme, probably to the expense of the number of movies watched by the researchers.

REFERENCES

Asimow, Michael. 2000a. "Bad Lawyers in the Movies." *Nova Law Review* 24: 533–91.

———. 2000b. "Divorce in the Movies: From the Hays Code to Cramer v Kramer." *Legal Studies Forum* 24: 221–67.

———. 2001. *Embodiment of Evil: Law Firms in the Movies* (Research Paper Series No. 01-8). University of California, Los Angeles, School of Law.

——— (ed.). 2001. Law and Popular Culture [Special issue]. *UCLA Law Review* 48 (6).

Asimow, Michael, Steve Greenfield, Guillermo Jorge, Stefan Machura, Guy Osborn, Peter Robson, Cassandra Sharp and Robert Sockloskie. 2005. "Perceptions of Lawyers—A Transnational Study of Student Views on the Image of Law and Lawyers." *International Journal of the Legal Profession* 15: 407–36.

Asimow, Michael and Shannon Mader. 2004. *Law and Popular Culture. A Course Book*. New York: Peter Lang.

A Symposium on Film and the Law [Special issue]. 1997. *Oklahoma City University Law Review* 22 (1).

Baer, Susanne. 2011. *Rechtssoziologie* [Sociology of Law]. Baden-Baden: Nomos.

Bellisario, Donald P. (producer). 2002. "The Tribunal" [Television series episode]. In *JAG*, United States: CBS-TV.

Berets, Ralph. 1996. "Changing Images of Justice in American Films." *The Legal Studies Forum* 20: 473–80.

Bergman, Paul and Michael Asimow. 1996. *Reel Justice: The Courtroom Goes to the Movies*. Kansas City, KS: Andrews and McMeel.

Bierbrauer, Günter. 1994. "Toward an Understanding of Legal Culture: Variations in Individualism and Collectivism Between Kurds, Lebanese, and Germans." *Law and Society Review* 28: 243–64.

Black, David A. 1999. *Law in Film. Resonance and Representation*. Urbana, IL: University of Illinois Press.

Böhnke, Michael. 2001. "Myth and Law in the Films of John Ford." In *Law and Film*, edited by Stefan Machura and Peter Robson, 47–63. Oxford: Blackwell Publishers.

———. 2002. "Der Mythos des Rechts in Filmen von John Ford" [The Myth of Law in the Films of John Ford]. In *Recht im Film*, edited by Stefan Machura and Stefan Ulbrich, 89–110. Baden-Baden, Germany: Nomos Verlag.

———. 2007. Abraham Lincoln—Politische Ikonographie im amerikanischen Film [Abraham Lincoln—Political Iconography in the American Film]. Unpublished Master thesis, Faculty for Philology, Ruhr-Universität Bochum, Germany.

Broder, Henryk M. 2002. March 30. "Die vierte Instanz" [The Fourth Instance]. *Der Spiegel*: 176–81.

Brown, David (producer) and Rob Reiner (producer/director). 1992. *A Few Good Men* [Motion Picture]. United States: Columbia Tri Star.

Carroll, Matthew (producer) and Bruce Beresford (director). 1980. *Breaker Morant* [Motion Picture]. Australia: Panavision.

Castendyk, Oliver. 1992. "Recht und Rechtskultur. Das Recht im Fernsehen als 'Popular Legal Culture'—ein vielversprechender Ansatz aus den USA?" [Law and Legal Culture. Law in Television as "Popular Legal Culture"—a promising approach from the USA?]. *Zeitschrift für Rechtspolitik* 25: 63–67.

Chase, Anthony. 1986. "Towards a Legal Theory of Popular Culture." *Wisconsin Law Review*: 527–69.

———. 2002. *Movies on Trial. The Legal System on the Silver Screen*. New York: New Press.

Coblenz, Walter (producer) and Harold Becker (director). 1979. *The Onion Field* [Motion Picture]. United States: Black Marble.

Cohen, Cynthia R. 2006. Media Influences on Public Perceptions of Lawyers. Paper presented at the Task Force on Image of the Profession, American Bar Foundation Section of Litigation Annual Conference, Los Angeles, 20 April 2006, www.verdictsuccess.com/pdf/Media_Influences_on_Public_Perceptions_of_Lawyers.pdf.

———. 2009. "Media Effects from Television Shows—Reality or Myth?" In *Lawyers in Your Living Room! Law on Television*, edited by Michael Asimow, 27–35. Chicago: American Bar Association Press.

Damiani, Damiano (director). 1984. *The Octopus* [Television Broadcast]. Italy: Rai Uno Televisione.

Degli Esposti, Carlo and Alberto Sironi. 1999–2013. *Il commissario Montalbano* [Television Broadcast]. Italy: Palomar and RAI Fiction.

Denvir, John (ed.). 1996a. *Legal Reelism: Movies as Legal Texts*. Urbana, IL: University of Illinois Press.

——— (ed.). 1996b. Symposium: Picturing Justice: Images of Law and Lawyers in the Visual Media [Special Issue]. *University of San Francisco Law Review* 30(4).

DeVito, Danny (producer) and Steven Soderbergh (director). 2000. *Erin Brockovich* [Motion Picture]. United States: Columbia Tri Star.

Donnelly, Terance A. (producer) and William Friedkin (director). 1997. *12 Angry Men*, TV production [Teleplay]. United States: MGM Home Entertainment.

Dormeier, Dieter (producer) and Frank Beyer (director). 1966. *Spur der Steine* [Traces of Stone, Motion Picture]. Germany: DEFA.

Douthit, Randy (executive producer/director). 1996–present. *Judge Judy* [Television Broadcast]. United States, Paramount.

Dowler, Kenneth. 2002. "Media Influences on Citizen Attitudes toward Police Effectiveness." *Policing and Society* 12: 227–38.

Drexler, Peter. 1999. "Der deutsche Gerichtsfilm 1930–1960. Annäherungen an eine problematische Tradition" [The German Courtroom Movie 1930–1960: On a Problematic Tradition]. In *Verbrechen—Justiz—Medien. Konstellationen in Deutschland von 1900 bis zur Gegenwart*, edited by Joachim Linder and Claus-Michael Ort, 387–402. Tübingen, Germany: Max Niemeyer Verlag.

———. 2001. "The German Courtroom Film During the Nazi Period: Ideology, Aesthetics, Historical Context." In *Law and Film*, edited by Stefan Machura and Paul Robson, 64–78. Oxford: Blackwell Publishers.

Ecke, Felix. 2002. "Braune Leinwand. Antisemitische Rechtspropaganda im Film des Dritten Reiches" [Brown Screen: Anti-Semitic Law Propaganda in the Film of the Third Reich]. In *Recht im Film*, edited by Stefan Machura and Stefan Ulbrich, 54–69. Baden-Baden, Germany: Nomos Verlag.

Ewick, Patricia and Susan S. Silbey. 1995. "Subversive Stories and Hegemonic Tales: Toward a Sociology of Narrative." *Law and Society Review* 29: 197–226.

Fonda, Henry (producer/actor) and Sidney Lumet (director). 1957. *Twelve Angry Men* [Motion Picture]. United States: United Artists.

Friedman, Lawrence M. 1985. "Transformations in American Legal Culture 1800–1985." *Zeitschrift für Rechtssoziologie* 6: 191–205.

———. 1989. "Law, Lawyers and Popular Culture." *Yale Law Journal* 98: 1579–1606.

Fulero, Solomon F., Edith Greene, Valerie Hans, Michael T. Nietzel, Mark A. Small, and Lawrence S. Wrightsman. 1999. "Undergraduate Education in Legal Psychology." *Law and Human Behavior* 23: 137–53.

Gatson, Sarah N. 1997, June. *"It's About Law" Accessible Teaching Sources for Law and Society*. Paper presented at the annual meeting of the Law and Society Association, Toronto, Canada.

General Principles. 1930. *The Motion Picture Code of 1930 (Hays Code)*. www.artsreformation.com/a001/hays-code.html.

Gibson, James L., Gregory A. Caldeira, and Vanessa Baird. 1997, June. *On the Legitimacy of National High Courts*. Paper presented at the annual meeting of the Law and Society Association, St. Louis, MO.

Glett, Charles L. (producer) and William Dieterle (director). 1941. *The Devil and Daniel Webster* [Motion Picture]. United States: RKO.

Goldbeck, Willis (producer) and John Ford (director). 1960. *Sergeant Rutledge* [Motion Picture]. United States: Warner.

Greenfield, Steve and Guy Osborn. 1995. "Where Cultures Collide: The Characterisation of Law and Lawyers in Film." *International Journal of the Sociology of Law* 23: 107–30.

———. 2002, April. *Prison Movies and Court Martials; Thoughts on the Issue of Genre*. Paper presented at the international workshop on law and film of the International Institute for the Sociology of Law, Oñati, Spain.

Greenfield, Steve, Guy Osborn, and Peter Robson. 2001. *Film and the Law*. London: Cavendish.

———. 2010. *Film and the Law. The Cinema of Justice*. Oxford: Hart.

Grunwald, Anatole de (producer) and Anthony Asquith (director). 1948. *The Winslow Boy* [Motion Picture]. Great Britain: British Lion.
———. 1959. *Libel* [Motion Picture]. Great Britain: MGM.
Hall, Edith. 1995. "Lawcourt Dramas: The Power of Performance in Greek Forensic Oratory." *Bulletin of the Institute of Classical Studies* 40: 39–58.
Harris, James B. (producer) and Stanley Kubrick (director). 1957. *Paths of Glory* [Motion Picture]. United States: United Artists.
Hille, Petra. 1997. *Verbesserung der Situation kindlicher Zeugen vor Gericht—Entwicklung und Evaluation von Informationsmaterial für Kinder* [Enhancing the Situation of Children Witnesses at Court: Development and Evaluation of Information Material for Children]. Unpublished diploma thesis, Institut für Psychologie, Christian-Albrechts-Universität, Kiel, Germany.
Hoblit, Gregory (producer/director). 2002. *Hart's War* [Motion Picture]. United States: Metro-Goldwyn-Mayer.
Holder, Erich (producer) and Eduard von Borsody (director). 1939. *Sensationsprozess Casilla* [Motion Picture]. Germany: UFA.
Hornblow, Arthur Jnr. (producer) and Billy Wilder (director). 1957. *Witness for the Prosecution* [Motion Picture]. United States: United Artists.
Hupertz, Heike. 2002, May 2. "Nur das Wahrheitsserum bleibt im Giftschrank" [Only the Truth Serum Stays in the Poison-Chest]. *Frankfurter Allgemeine Zeitung*.
Isensee, Eike (under collaboration of Peter Drexler). 2002. "Das Bild der Justiz im NS-Film am Beispiel der Filme Der Verteidiger hat das Wort und Der Gasmann" [The Picture of Legal Institutions in Nazi Films using the Example of Der Verteidiger hat das Wort and Der Gasmann]. In *Recht im Film*, edited by Stefan Machura and Stefan Ulbrich, 70–88. Baden-Baden, Germany: Nomos Verlag.
Jackson, Bernard S. 1996. "'Anchored Narratives' and the Interface of Law, Psychology and Semiotics." *Legal and Criminological Psychology* 1: 17–45.
King, Michelle and Robert King (writers). 2009–present. *The Good Wife*. USA, TV series.
Korolkov, Igor. 2002. "New Basis for Legal Proceedings—New Criminal Procedure Code Takes Effect in Russia." *The Current Digest of the Post-Soviet Press* 54 (27): 1–3 (Original published in Russian in *Moskovskiye novosti*, No. 25, 2002, 21).
Kramer, Stanley (producer/director). 1960. *Inherit the Wind* [Motion Picture]. United States: United Artists.
Kuzina, Michael. 2000. *Der amerikanische Gerichtsfilm. Justiz, Ideologie, Dramatik* [The American Courtroom Movie: Justice, Ideology, Dramatics]. Göttingen, Germany: Vandenhoeck and Ruprecht.
———. 2002. "Die amerikanische Militärjustiz im Film: The Caine Mutiny Court-Martial (1988)" [The American Military Justice in Film: The Caine Mutiny Court-Martial (1988)]. In *Recht im Film*, edited by Stefan Machura and Stefan Ulbrich, 126–54. Baden-Baden, Germany: Nomos Verlag.
———. 2005. "Das Kriegsgerichtsverfahren als Filmsujet: US-amerikanische Erzählmuster" [The Court-Martial as Film Sujet: U.S.-American Patterns of Telling]. In *Krieg im Film*, edited by Stefan Machura and Rüdiger Voigt, 185–236. Munster, Germany: Lit.

Lasswell, Harold. 1949. *The Analysis of Political Behaviour. An Empirical Approach.* New York: Oxford University Press.
Lehmann, Otto (producer) and Veit Harlan (director). 1940. *Jud Süß* [Motion Picture]. Germany: Terra.
Lempert, David. 1996. "Pepsi-Stroika: American Cultural Influence on the Russian Political and Legal System." *The Legal Studies Forum* 20: 345–65.
Levin, Harvey. 1981–1993. *The People's Court.* USA, TV court show.
Lipson, Mark (producer) and Errol Morris (director). 1988. *A Thin Blue Line* [Motion Picture]. United States: Third Floor.
Löschper, Gabriele. 1999. *Bausteine für eine psychologische Theorie richterlichen Urteilens* [Contributions to a Psychological Theory of Judging]. Baden-Baden, Germany: Nomos Verlag.
Lucia, Cynthia. 1999. "'Has the Jury Reached Its Verdict?': Deliberating the Case of Cinema and the Law." *Cineaste* 25: 14–18.
Lüderssen, Klaus. 2002. *Produktive Spiegelungen* [Productive Reflections]. 2nd ed. Baden-Baden, Germany: Nomos Verlag.
Luhmann, Niklas. 1997. *Die Kunst der Gesellschaft* [The Art of Society]. Frankfurt am Main, Germany: Suhrkamp Verlag.
———. 2000. *Die Politik der Gesellschaft* [The Politics of Society]. Frankfurt am Main, Germany: Suhrkamp Verlag.
Macaulay, Stewart. 1987. "Images of Law in Everyday Life: The Lessons of School, Entertainment and Spectator Sports." *Law and Society Review* 21: 185–218.
MacGowan, Kenneth (producer) and John Ford (director). 1939. *Young Mr. Lincoln* [Motion Picture]. United States: Twentieth Century-Fox.
Machura, Stefan. 2003. "Fairness, Justice and Legitimacy: Experiences of People's Judges in South Russia." *Law and Policy* 25: 123–50.
———. 2004. "Procedural Unfairness in Real and Film Trials. Why Do Audiences Understand Stories Placed in Foreign Legal Systems?" In *Law and Popular Culture,* edited by Michael Freeman, 148–59. Oxford: Oxford University Press.
———. 2006. "Fernsehgerichtshows: Spektakel des Rechts" [TV-Court Shows: Spectacles of Law]. *Paragrana* 15 (1): 174–88.
———. 2011. "Media Influence on the Perception of the Legal System." In *Understanding Law in Society,* edited by Knut Papendorf, Stefan Machura, and Kristian Andenæs, 239–83. Zurich, Switzerland: Lit Verlag.
———. 2012. "Television Judges in Germany." In *Law and Justice on the Small Screen,* edited by Peter Robson and Jessica Silbey, 251–69. Oxford: Hart.
———. 2015. "Empirische Beobachtungen zum Prestige der deutschen Anwälte" [Empirical Observations on the Prestige of German Lawyers]. In *Menschenrechte und Solidarität im internationalen Diskurs. Festschrift für Armin Höland,* edited by Wolfhard Kohte and Nadine Absenger, 390–405. Baden-Baden: Nomos.
Machura, Stefan, and Llewellyn Davies. 2013. "'Law is an Odd Thing': Liberalism and Law in the TV-series 'The Good Wife'." *Kriminologisches Journal* 45: 279–94.
Machura, Stefan, Dmitry Donskow, and Olga Litvinova. 2003. *Ehrenamtliche Richter in Südrussland* [People's Judges in South Russia]. Munster, Germany: Lit.
Machura, Stefan and Annette Kammertöns. 2009. "Recht im Schulunterricht, Medieneinflüsse und die Attraktivität von Rechtsberufen." [Legal Education

at School, Media Influences and the Attraction of Legal Careers]. *Zeitschrift für Rechtssoziologie* 30: 235–59.

———. (2010). "Deterred From Going to Court? A Survey at German Schools on Media Influences." *Entertainment and Sports Law Journal* 8 (2).

Machura, Stefan, Nelson M. Correia Ramos, Torie Rooney and Shanna Warmald. 2013. "How Studying Law, Media and Experience Influence Trust in the Courts and the Police. A Comparison of Law and Language Students at Bangor University." In *Der Kampf ums Recht. Akteure und Interessen im Blick der interdisziplinären Rechtsforschung*, edited by Josef Estermann, 150–67. Vienna, Austria and Beckenried, Switzerland: Lit Verlag and Orlux Verlag.

Machura, Stefan and Peter Robson (eds.). 2001. *Law and Film*. Oxford: Blackwell Publishers [also released as special issue of *Journal of Law and Society* 28(1), 2001].

Machura, Stefan and Stefan Ulbrich. 1999. "Recht im Film: Abbild juristischer Wirklichkeit oder filmische Selbstreferenz?" [Law in Film: Depiction of Legal Reality or Self-Reference of Film?]. *Zeitschrift für Rechtssoziologie* 20: 168–82.

———. 2001. "Law in Film: Globalizing the Hollywood Courtroom Drama." In *Law and Film*, edited by Stefan Machura and Peter Robson, 117–32. Oxford: Blackwell Publishers.

Maier, Susanne M. 2002. "Recht und Gerechtigkeit in der amerikanischen Literaturverfilmung: *To Kill a Mockingbird* und *Snow Falling on Cedars*" [Law and Justice in the American Literature Film: *To Kill a Mockingbird* and *Snow Falling on Cedars*]. In *Recht im Film*, edited by Stefan Machura and Stefan Ulbrich, 111–25. Baden-Baden, Germany: Nomos Verlag.

Maltby, Richard. 1983. *Harmless Entertainment. Hollywood and the Ideology of Consensus*. Metuchen, NJ: Scarecrow.

Marder, Nancy (ed.). 2007. Symposium: The 50th Anniversary of 12 Angry Men [Special issue]. *Chicago-Kent Law Review* 82(2).

Marx, Gisela (producer). 1999–2012. *Richterin Barbara Salesch* [Judgess Barbara Salesch. Television Broadcast]. Berlin, Germany: Sat 1.

Merton, Robert K. and Patricia L. Kendall. 1979. "Das fokussierte Interview" [The Focused Interview]. In *Qualitative Sozialforschung*, edited by Christel Hopf and Elmar Weingarten, 171–204. Stuttgart, Germany: Klett-Cotta.

Meyer, Philip N. 1993. "Visual Literacy and the Legal Culture: Reading Film as Text in the Law School Setting." *The Legal Studies Forum* 17: 73–93.

Milker, Reiner (producer) and Horst Königstein (director). 2002, November 24. *Jud Süß—Ein Film als Verbrechen?* [Jew Süss—A Film as Crime? Television Broadcast]. Hamburg, Germany: Norddeutscher Rundfunk.

Minoura, Jingo (producer) and Akira Kurosawa (director). 1950. *Rashomon* [Motion Picture]. Japan: Daiei.

Moran, Leslie 1996. "Heroes and Brothers in Love: The Male Homosexual as Lawyer in Popular Culture." *Studies in Law, Politics and Society* 18: 3–27.

Nebenzal, Seymore (producer) and Fritz Lang (director). 1931. *M* [Motion Picture]. Germany: Nero Film.

Neckermann, Gerhard. 2000. "Kinobranche im Umbruch" [Cinema Industry Under Transition]. *Media Perspektiven*, No. 9: 406–13.

Neuhaus, Kai Jochen. 1994/1995. "Jura Goes Hollywood." *JUSTUF*. Part 1: 1994, no. 2: 36–42, and Part 2: 1995, no. 1: 34–40.

Nevins, Francis M. 2003. "Using Fiction and Film as Law School Tools." In *Recht—Gesellschaft—Kommunikation*, edited by Stefan Machura and Stefan Ulbrich, 175–81. Baden-Baden, Germany: Nomos Verlag.

Osborn, Guy. 2001. "Borders and Boundaries: Locating the Law in Film." In *Law and Film*, edited by Stefan Machura and Peter Robson, 164–76. Oxford: Blackwell Publishers.

Pakula, Alan J. (producer) and Robert Mulligan (director). 1962. *To Kill a Mockingbird* [Motion Picture]. United States: Universal Pictures.

Pfau, Michael, Lawrence J. Mullen, Tracy Diedrich and Kirsten Garrow. 1995. "Television Viewing and Public Perceptions of Attorneys." *Human Communications Research* 21: 307–30.

Picturing Justice. The On-Line Journal of Law and Popular Culture. 1997–2006. www.usfca.edu/pj/.

Podlas, Kimberlianne. 2001. "Please Adjust Your Signal: How Television's Syndicated Courtrooms Bias Our Juror Citizenry." *American Business Law Journal* 39: 1–24.

Porsdam, Helle. 1999. *Legally Speaking. Contemporary American Culture and the Law.* Amherst, MA: University of Massachusetts Press.

Rafter, Nicole. 2000. *Shots in the Mirror. Crime Films and Society*. Oxford University Press.

Robson, Peter. 1996, July. *Law and Lawyers in Film—Globalising Atticus Finch*. Paper presented at the joint meetings of the Law and Society Association and the Research Committee on Sociology of Law, Glasgow, Scotland.

Röhl, Klaus. F. 2002a. "Law and Popular Culture: Popular Legal Culture as Media Legal Culture." In *Empirische Rechtssoziologie*, edited by Dieter Strempel and Theo Rasehorn, 315–23. Baden-Baden, Germany: Nomos Verlag.

———. 2002b. *"Recht anschaulich": Visualisierung in der Juristenausbildung* [Illustrative Law: Visualization in Legal Education]. Ruhr-Universität Bochum, Lehrstuhl für Rechtssoziologie und Rechtsphilosophie.

Röhl, Klaus F. and Stefan Machura. 2013. "100 Jahre Rechtssoziologie: Eugen Ehrlichs Rechtspluralismus heute." [100 Years Sociology of Law: Eugen Ehrlich's Legal Pluralism Today]. *Juristenzeitung* 68: 1117–28.

Röhl, Klaus F. and Stefan Ulbrich. 2000. "Visuelle Rechtskommunikation" [Visual Legal Communication]. *Zeitschrift für Rechtssoziologie* 21: 315–23.

Rosenberg, Norman. 1991. "Young Mr. Lincoln: The Lawyer as Super-Hero." *The Legal Studies Forum* 15: 215–31.

Saxon, Edward (producer) and Jonathan Demme (producer/director). 1993. *Philadelphia* [Motion Picture]. United States: Tri Star.

Schulz, Stefan. 2013, December 7. "Ich schau Dir in die Augen, Kleiner" [I Am Looking into Your Eyes, Little One]. *Frankfurter Allgemeine Zeitung*.

Sherwin, Richard K. 2000. *When the Law Goes Pop. The Vanishing Line between Law and Popular Culture*. Chicago: University of Chicago Press.

Silbey, Jessica. 2001. "Patterns of Courtroom Justice." In *Law and Film*, edited by Stefan Machura and Peter Robson, 97–116. Oxford: Blackwell Publishers.

———. 2002. "What We Do When We Do Law and Popular Culture." *Law and Social Culture* 27: 139–68.

Smoodin, Eric. 2005. "'Everyone Went Wild Over It': Film Audiences, Political Cinema, and Mr. Smith Goes to Washington." In *Law on the Screen*, edited by Austin Sarat, Laurence Douglas and Martha Merrill Umphrey, 231–52. Stanford, CA: Stanford University Press.

Spielberg, Stephen (producer/director). 1997. *Amistad* [Motion Picture]. United States: Dream Works.

Steiner, Helmut. 2001. "Die Herausbildung von Sozialstrukturen im gegenwärtigen Rußland" [The Emergence of Social Structures in Contemporary Russia]. In *Sitzungsberichte der Leibniz-Sozietät*, Vol. 41/2000, no. 6. Berlin, Germany: Trafo Verlag.

Strübel, Michael. 2002. "Krieg als Produkt der Filmindustrie" [War as Product of the Film Industry]. In *Medien zwischen Krieg und Frieden*, edited by Ulrich Albrecht and Jörg Becker, 205–22. Baden-Baden, Germany: Nomos Verlag.

Stuesser, Lee. 1999. In *Techniques for Teaching Law*, edited by Gerald F. Hess and Steven. Friedland. Durham, NC: Carolina Academic Press.

Tatort [TV broadcast]. 1981–1991. Germany: Westdeutscher Rundfunk.

Thorson, Karen L. (producer) and David Simon (creator). 2002–2008. *The Wire*. US, TV series.

Thym, Barbara. 2003. *Kultivierung durch Gerichtsshows. Eine Studie unter Berücksichtigung von wahrgenommener Realitätsnähe, Nutzungsmotiven und persönlichen Erfahrungen* [Cultivation Through Court Shows: A Study Under Consideration of Perceived Proximity to Reality, Motivation for Use and Personal Experiences]. Unpublished master's thesis, Ludwig-Maximilians-Universität München, Munich, Germany.

Trotti, Lamar (producer) and William Wellman (director). 1943. *The Ox-Bow Incident* [Motion Picture]. United States: Twentieth Century-Fox.

Wilson, Richard (producer) and Orson Welles (director). 1948. *The Lady from Shanghai* [Motion Picture]. United States: Columbia Pictures.

Wizan, Joe (producer) and Norman Jewison (director). 1979. *. . . And Justice for All* [Motion Picture]. United States: Columbia Pictures.

Wolf, Petra. 1997. *Was wissen Kinder und Jugendliche über Gerichtsverhandlungen?* [What do Children and Youth Know about Court Proceedings?]. Regensburg, Germany: Roderer.

Yablans, Frank (producer) and Peter Hyams (director). 1983. *The Star Chamber* [Motion Picture]. United States: Twentieth Century-Fox.

Zanuck, Darryl F. (producer) and John Ford (director). 1936. *The Prisoner of Shark Island* [Motion Picture]. United States: Twentieth Century-Fox.

Zanuck, Richard D. (producer) and Sidney Lumet (director). 1982. *The Verdict* [Motion Picture]. United States: Twentieth Century-Fox.

2

The Crisis of Law and the Imaginary of Disaster

Reading Post-Apocalyptic Fictions

Majid Yar

In the realm of modern popular culture, one doesn't have to look very far to find the apocalypse. Setting aside the complex historical, theological, and religious meanings of the term, we can suggest that in modern parlance the apocalypse refers to an event, act, or occurrence (accidental or otherwise) that brings about the end of the world. Cultural discourses (such as films, novels, and comics) that deal with such matters can be termed apocalyptic in tone, tenor, and content. These representations may deal with events leading up to "the end," and depict heroic attempts (successful or doomed) to prevent catastrophe. Alternatively, post-apocalyptic culture imagines what comes after disaster has been visited upon us (Renner 2012: 204). The end of the world may be interpreted in a most literal manner. For example, in the Hollywood movie *End of Days* (1999), Satan attempts to usher in the end of the world on the eve of the new millennium. In *The Core* (2003), the molten iron core of the Earth stops spinning; without the magnetic field that its rotation generates, the planet will become a lifeless rock, irradiated by the sun's emissions to such an extent that no life will be able to survive. In *Sunshine* (2007) the sun again threatens to eradicate all life on Earth, this time because it is dying. However, more commonplace are tales in which the Earth, humanity, and life persist, but in a world where the familiar coordinates of social, cultural, political, economic, and moral organization are gone—in other words, what has ended is the world as we know it. As Yuen (2012: xiii) puts it: "The end of the world rarely is the end, at least in popular culture. Instead, it's the beginning of a new world, a world that is devoid of strong central government and traditional social institutions." It is such post-apocalyptic scenarios, centered upon human existence in the wake of a radical break with life-as-we-know-it, that provide the focus for analysis in this chapter.

SITUATING POST-APOCALYPTIC FICTIONS

There is a rich abundance of research and analysis that reflects upon apocalyptic and post-apocalyptic popular culture. For example, scholars from film studies have explored such fictions as manifestations of twentieth-century fears about imminent nuclear war (Newman 1999; Shapiro 2002). Others have related our preoccupation with these tales to a broader *fin de siècle* anxiety, or a postmodern nihilism that brings with it a loss of belief in "grand narratives" (Lyotard 1984) of progress, peace, emancipation, or liberation. More specific crises, such as the legacy of the terrorist attacks of September 11, 2001, have also been adopted as a lens through which to understand the conspicuous popularity of apocalyptic fictions (Walliss and Aston 2011). Yet others have read such texts as indicators of a persistent (or perhaps resurgent) interest in religiosity (especially of an evangelical, ecstatic, and rapturous kind) in an otherwise supposedly secular era (Bendle 2005). However, despite this rich and diverse array of interventions, criminologists have been conspicuous by their absence when it comes to examining post-apocalyptic cultural discourses. Over the past few decades, there has of course emerged a vibrant strand within criminology (often identified with "cultural criminology") that focuses in significant part upon popular cultural forms such as film and television. Critical analysis of these products has aimed to uncover their contribution to reflecting, reinforcing, and sometimes reshaping commonplace understandings of crime and deviance (Rafter 2006; Young 2009; Yar 2010). Yet such interventions, as insightful as they are, have restricted their ambit to a clearly identifiable crime genre, examining films, TV shows, and novels centered upon policing, organized crime, drugs, prisons, homicide, serial killers, and the like (see, for example, Eschholz, Mallard, and Flynn 2004; Wilson and O'Sullivan 2005; Fleming 2007; Rafter and Brown 2011). In this chapter I seek to extend the gaze of critical cultural criminology beyond its most obvious textual materials to examine the post-apocalyptic genre. The relevance of such cultural outputs for criminology becomes clearer once we identify and acknowledge the extent to which they consistently deal with issues of crime, law and lawlessness, disorder, risk, and violence. There are in fact very few popular representations of the post-apocalyptic world that do not address in some way, shape or fashion, crime, law, and related issues.

The core contention in the analysis that follows can be stated fairly unambiguously, namely that post-apocalyptic fictions (like other popular genres) refract contemporary social concerns into the domain of storytelling, thereby dramatizing the tensions, conflicts, fears, and contradictions with which a society is wrestling. In other words, they:

> transcode the discourses (the forms, figures, and representations) of social life into . . . narratives. Rather than reflect a reality external to the . . . medium, [they] execute a transfer from one discursive field to another. As a result [they] become part of that broader system of cultural representations that construct social reality. (Ryan and Kellner 1990: 12)

Important here is an appreciation that cultural discourses cannot and should not be read as straightforward expression of a "dominant ideology" that seeks to "dupe" and thereby pacify the audience in the interests of maintaining the status quo. Such a reading of the political imperatives that configure popular culture has a long and influential history, most notably the theory and practice of "ideology critique" in the Marxist tradition (Althusser 1994; Murdock and Golding 2000; Barthes 2000). In lieu of such a reductive or deterministic approach, and following that of Ryan and Kellner (1990), I suggest that in fact cultural texts give voice to multiple and competing standpoints on the social and political issues of the day. Focusing on Hollywood films, they argue that:

> Much of what happens in Hollywood cinema is indeed ideological . . . but not all Hollywood . . . products are inherently ideological. The conception of cinematic ideology flattens out necessary distinctions between different films at different moments in history, and it overlooks the distinctive and multiple rhetorical and representational strategies and effects of films in varying social situations. (Ryan and Keller 1990, 1)

We can legitimately extend this standpoint in considering other popular cultural products (for example, novels, television shows, and comics) as well as films emanating from centers of production other than Hollywood. Consequently, one does not find in post-apocalyptic representations (nor in popular culture more broadly) a single, unified, or unambiguous perspective on matters related to crime, law, justice, and punishment. Instead we find a complex assembly of meanings and symbols, often contradictory in character. Again, this "incoherence" should not be taken as indication of artistic incompetence or confusion on the part of writers, directors, and producers, but as the inevitable reflection of a multiplicity of viewpoints, beliefs and judgements about crime, which we daily attempt to hold and reconcile in a precarious balance. One example of such ambivalence can be found in our simultaneous attachment both to a vision of law and order based in an objective system of justice, and a yearning for vengeance and retribution that sets-aside cool, calculated penal decision-making (Green 2011; Yar 2014). Such tensions and contradictions become readily apparent in post-apocalyptic visions of law and crime.

CRIME, MODERNITY, AND THE CRISIS OF LAW

The first significant trend in the depiction of post-apocalyptic disorder centers upon concerns about the erosion of law, particularly its power to constrain human behavior and contain violent and acquisitive appetites. The longstanding discussion of a supposed "crisis of law and order," manifest in alienated urban environments beset with incivility and predation, is extended to its logical endpoint in post-apocalyptic fictions—law and order implode under the weight of a catastrophic event (be it a zombie plague, nuclear war, ecosystemic, or economic collapse) leaving a vacuum in which evil runs loose, and the innocent and vulnerable are bereft of protection. Such narratives are underpinned by a "disenchanted" understanding of human nature, of the kind that can be traced to Hobbes's discourse on the "state of nature." In *Leviathan* (1968 [1651]), Hobbes witheringly rejects classical philosophy's presumptions about a teleological ordering of human existence, one that roots in human nature an imperative toward ethical behavior and social coexistence (a prime example being Aristotle's insistence that humans are *zoa politikon,* by their nature "political animals" oriented toward a collective and co-operative life) (Yar 2002). On the contrary, for Hobbes human beings are essentially animalistic and individualistic, governed by their appetites and self-interest, and driven by fear and distrust to pursue violence in the struggle for survival. It is this "war of all against all" that legitimates Hobbes vision of political power—the necessity for an absolute sovereign power whose word is law, and who can mobilize force so as to command and constrain humans into a condition of peaceable coexistence, suppressing their natural inclinations toward conflict. Hobbes's account of the problem of human nature, and its resolution through the exercise of sovereign power, provides the template for the modern state—an entity that abrogates unto itself a monopoly on the legitimate use of violence (Weber 1965), enforcing the limits and rules upon behavior, which are codified in law, and enacted by its nominated agents (such as armies, police forces, prison warders, and executioners). A parallel view of human nature is given an explicit criminological twist in Lombroso's concepts of degeneration and atavism—the ever-present risk of a return to an ancestral primitivism in which moral sensibilities are overridden by animal instincts. It is worth noting that the concept of degeneration, as developed in nineteenth-century quasi-evolutionary discourses on crime, was seen to affect not only individuals but also whole societies (Beccalossi 2010). Contemporary fears about the collapse of law and order and the reversion to violence recode such notions and play out their consequences upon the fantastic stage of the post-apocalyptic scene.

The anticipation of a fatal erosion of law-and-order, and the concomitant liberation of destructive appetites, is explored in a number of popular fictions that may be termed proto-apocalyptic—while these do not explicitly rehearse end-of-the-world scenarios, they nevertheless provide an influential discursive template that is recuperated into post-apocalyptic imaginaries. A particularly significant example is William Golding's novel *The Lord of the Flies* (published in 1955, and subsequently adapted as a feature film in 1963, and again in 1976, 1990, and 2010). Golding's tale unfolds against the background of an unspecified wartime emergency, in which groups of schoolchildren are being evacuated from the conflict area (echoing the wartime evacuations of British children from cities to the countryside, which was a common practice during World War II). A plane carrying evacuated children crashes on an isolated and uninhabited Pacific island, and the only survivors are pre-adolescent and adolescent boys. An important feature of this scenario is the absence of any adult authority figures, the accompanying teachers having perished in the crash. The boys are therefore left to their own devices, without direction from those who would normally impose rules upon proper behavior—in Hobbes's terms, they are subjects without a sovereign. As the narrative unfolds, civilization and self-restraint slowly give way to conflict, cruelty, and superstition, culminating in theft, torture, and murder. *The Lord of the Flies* can thus be read as a pointed allegory about the ugly substrate of human nature, which comes to the surface when lawful authority is no longer present. As Golding himself elaborated:

> Before the Second World War I believed in the perfectibility of social man; that a correct structure of society would produce goodwill; and that therefore you could remove all social ills by a reorganization of society . . . but after the war I was unable to. I had discovered what one man could do to another . . . understanding that man produces evil as a bee produces honey . . . I believed that the condition of man was to be a morally diseased creation. (Golding, in Spitz 1970, 22–23)

If mankind is in fact "morally diseased," and disposed by nature toward evil acts, then lawful authority is the best and only defense of the social order—without this, we quickly revert to savagery.

Golding's pessimistic conclusions about human nature are echoed in subsequent popular fictions. Depictions of crime-as-evil are conditioned by particular social contexts. Golding's was explicitly shaped by the atrocities of World War II, but we see other, less dramatic but equally telling, cultural responses to social dislocation and crisis. For example, the 1970s stands as a landmark decade in the post-war development of Western societies. It marked the end of a sustained period of prosperity, with economic recession, mass unemployment, and deindustrialisation replacing growth, rising living standards and upward socioeconomic mobility. The urban landscape of "advanced" industrial economies bore the imprints of these developments; for example, in the United States the flight of the white upper-middle classes to suburbs accelerated a process of urban decline, leaving the former heartlands of industrial production to fall into dereliction and neglect (Frey 1979; Wacquant 1993; Cullen and Levitt 1999). This period also saw a concomitant cultural reaction to social change manifested in a new climate of fear about street crime and the threat posed by a range of "dangerous others," including drug dealers and users, sexual predators, serial killers, gangs, and ethnic minorities. We can note how Hollywood film of this era paints an increasingly frantic and anxious picture of the breakdown of law and order in the post-industrial city. Two such proto-apocalyptic representations of the crisis of law can be found in John Carpenter's *Assault on Precinct 13* (1976) and Walter Hill's *The Warriors* (1979). In Carpenter's film, Hollywood's traditional scenario of criminals pursued (and ultimately cornered) by the forces of law-and-order is inverted. Set in a depopulated Los Angeles ghetto, *Assault* depicts a small force of police officers besieged inside a rundown station house by a heavily armed gang on a murderous rampage ("an army of street killers," as they are described in the film's original tagline). In the streets of Anderson, the agents of the law no longer exercise meaningful control over its residents—the law has in effect given up and is in the retreat, attested in the fact that Precinct 13 is in fact being decommissioned at the start of the movie. Throughout the siege, no one comes to investigate the hail of automated gunfire that the gang ("Street Thunder") unleash upon the precinct's occupants, and they are left to defend this last local bastion of the law against overwhelming odds. The evacuation of lawful authority from the spaces of the city is similarly highlighted in *The Warriors*, which takes as its protagonists a number of rival New York street gangs who use the city as a staging ground for their vendettas, a war of attack and retaliation as they maraud the streets, parks, and subways, armed with chains, knives, and guns. The police are notable largely by their absence, and their inability to restore any sense of order or bring about a cessation to the violence. These films exemplify the sense that the city has become a lawless zone, one where crime is rampant and no one is safe.

Themes of lawlessness and its consequences are equally a common feature in post-apocalyptic films, often serving as one of the genre's main concerns. Luc *Besson's Le Dernier Combat* (*The Last Battle*) (1983) features a world laid waste by some unspecified disaster. Survivors scavenge among the depopulated vestiges of civilization, routinely resorting to theft and violence so as to secure food and other materials. The film's main characters (identified only by monikers such as "The Man," "The Doctor," and "The Brute") live as isolated individuals, apparently having lost the impetus toward sociality. The absence of collective life and association is highlighted by the fact that, as a consequence of the unnamed catastrophe, humans appear to have lost the ability to speak (there is no dialogue in the film, with the exception of the word "*bonjour*"—"hello"—which is uttered twice). Without language humans are reduced to an atavistic state, bereft of the means to generate and sustain a normative order that could mediate and limit conflicts over resources. Such motifs are likewise examined in Michael Haneke's post-apocalyptic drama *Le Temps du Loup* (*The Time of the Wolf*) (2003). The film is set in France in the aftermath of a catastrophe which has contaminated the food and water supply. It follows a family (the Laurents) who flee the city, seeking refuge in the village where they have a country house. However, upon arrival they find their property already occupied by strangers, and the father of the family (Georges) is killed in the ensuing argument with the present occupiers; his wife (Anne) and their two children are repeatedly turned-away by their former friends and neighbors, as they grow increasingly desperate. They eventually find a rudimentary community of survivors, under the control of a brutal authoritarian named Koslowski, where life is organized through a system of barter and brutal violence. Significantly, when Georges's killer later arrives and joins the group, Anne (Isabel Huppert) is helpless to exact any kind of justice for the murder, as the structures and systems of law enforcement no longer exist (Johnston 2007). As critic Peter Bradshaw puts it, they are "cast adrift in a rural landscape where law and order have broken down, an unending nightmare of fear and horror in which neighbour turns on neighbour . . . well-to-do comfortable folk have become terrified animals" (Bradshaw 2003). The dualism of human and animal is adduced in the film's title—the wolf has, of course, long served as a cultural metaphor for the destructive urges that lurk inside seemingly civilized individuals, consolidated for example in the horror genre's fascination with the werewolf (du Coudray 2006).

The crisis of law is most clearly and directly explored in those post-apocalyptic fictions that feature police officers as their protagonists. The policeman is, after all, the heroic embodiment of law-in-action, enforcing its prohibitions and apprehending offenders. In the post-apocalyptic world, the lawman (and it is almost always a man) struggles in vain to uphold a system of rules and sanctions whose institutional underpinnings are simply no longer present (there are no organized police forces, courts, lawyers, judges, or prisons). One of the most famous popular incarnations of the post-apocalyptic lawman is Max Rockatansky, the eponymous anti-hero of George Miller's 1979 cult film *Mad Max* (and of its sequels—*The Road Warrior* [1981] and *Mad Max: Beyond Thunderdome* [1985]). The film deserves detailed consideration in light of both its dramatization of law, crime, and justice in the context of social breakdown, and its significant influence upon the post-apocalyptic genre as a whole. It furnished the template for many subsequent post-apocalyptic road movies, spawning numerous imitations. The social setting for the Mad Max trilogy appears to be one of progressive breakdown. In *Mad Max*, the material and institutional base of society is still intact, though starting to unravel—it is afflicted with growing lawlessness and material scarcity. In *The Road Warrior*, the decline has accelerated, with people roaming across a desolate wasteland in search of fuel, which has become the scarcest and most precious of commodities. By the time we reach the third, concluding film in the sequence, society as we know it appears to have dissolved altogether, and there are intimations that the world has been unmade through a nuclear war.

The collapse of the social order, especially the system of law enforcement, is visually encoded in the opening minutes of Mad Max, through a triptych of signs. The opening shot of the film shows a large metal gate adorned with the words "HALLS OF JUSTICE"—the symbolization of law rendered tangible in wrought iron. However, the letters in "JUSTICE" are hanging precariously from their mounting, with the "U" about to fall off entirely—a simple, sly but effective allusion to the parlous state of the system. After a "fade," accompanied with the words "A FEW YEARS FROM NOW," we see another sign, this time on an empty and dusty highway—it reads simply "Anarchie Road 3km." Shortly thereafter, we are presented with a second roadside sign—this one states that the highway is "MONITORED BY MAIN FORCE PATROL" (MFP—the law enforcement agency of which, we soon learn, Max is an officer). However, someone has vandalized the sign, painting a letter "A" in place of the "O" in "FORCE"—it now reads "MONITORED BY MAIN FARCE PATROL." Hence, without the benefit of any additional commentary or voice-over, we are informed that justice is falling apart, anarchy is close at hand, and the police are perceived as a joke. These three images, presented in quick succession, provide the interpretive frame within which the movie's plot unfolds.

The narrative of *Mad Max* recuperates fairly well-trodden themes of good-versus-evil and revenge. It begins with a member of a motorcycle gang (Nightrider) escaping custody by killing a cop and stealing a police vehicle. The MFP engage in a high-speed pursuit that results in carnage before Max (Mel Gibson) finally catches up to the fleeing prisoner; Nightrider crashes the car and is killed in the ensuing explosion. Max is later told by his boss that the gang is now seeking revenge against him for the death of their fallen friend. Our first encounter with the gang itself (led by the psychopathic Toecutter) features their arrival in a small outback town whose residents they terrorize. They administer beatings to the locals; chain one man to a motorbike and drag him at speed along the road; and gang rape a young woman whom they subsequently chain-up like a dog. Max and his partner (Goose) speed to respond to the incident, freeing the woman and capturing one of the gang members (Johnny the Boy). However, back at the Halls of Justice, they are forced by lawyers to release Johnny, as the residents are too terrified to file a complaint against the bikers, for fear of reprisals. The gang later tracks down Goose, and burn him alive in a car, reproducing Nightrider's death. Disillusioned and distraught, Max resigns his position in the MFP and takes a road-trip with his wife (Jessie) and their young son (Sprog). Inevitably, the gang catches up with the family, killing Sprog and leaving Jessie near death. Max, hell-bent on revenge, steals the MFP's fastest pursuit vehicle and then sets about extracting information about the gang's whereabouts through torture. He subsequently kills the bikers one by one. In the final scene, he handcuffs Johnny the Boy to a wrecked car, and gives him a hacksaw—Johnny can attempt escape by sawing through either the handcuffs or his own ankle, provided he can do so before the car catches fire. The closing shot is a close-up of Max's expressionless face as he drives away, and we see the car explode in the background.

The film recasts into a post-apocalyptic frame themes already familiar in 1970s crime films, especially the failure of law and order, the cop disgusted by a "broken system," and the recourse to extra-judicial torture and killing in the service of retributive justice (popularized, for example, by the character of Harry Callaghan (Clint Eastwood) in *Dirty Harry* (1971) and its sequels *Magnum Force* (1973) and *The Enforcer* (1976) (Ryan and Kellner 1990: 42). However grim and pessimistic the tone of conventional cop films, there is at least in their contemporary settings the possibility of a collective social and political response to "the crime problem"—be it achieved through a program of humane reform and rehabilitation, or through (much more commonly) a "tough on crime" strategy that promotes the likes of "zero tolerance," tougher sentencing or use of the death penalty. In contrast, the disordered world of the post-apocalyptic marks the passage beyond a point where the law is efficacious (or even continues to exist at all in any meaningful sense). The visceral horror of a world without law is amplified by the very personal consequences of crime—Max, after all, loses to the gang the three people most dear to him—his best friend, his beloved wife, and infant son. However, the fantastic projection of crime and lawlessness into a disastrous future incites a deeply ambivalent moral and affective reaction. On the one hand, it is meant to express the feelings of fear and anxiety that accompany contemporary public discourse on crime, violence and "terror." One the other, it enjoins its audience in a pleasurable anticipation of vengeance and retribution. Alongside popular tales of everyday vigilantism (such as *Death Wish* [1974]) and the violent, sometimes sadistic, punishment meted out by superheroes (such as *The Punisher* [2004]), *Mad Max* speaks to an ever-present yearning to answer evil in the most uncompromising and merciless terms. It gives a full-throated voice to the raw and visceral emotions of outrage, and the desire for symbolic restoration of a damaged world through exemplary, immediate, and sometimes extravagant punishment for wrong-doing (Yar 2014).

Let us continue with the exploration of crime and disorder as embodied in the figure of the post-apocalyptic law-keeper. Insightful in this regard is the hit television series *The Walking Dead* (2010–present), adapted by Frank Darabont from an ongoing comic book series authored by Robert Kirkman. Both the television show and comic books (despite significant narrative divergence) start from the same premise, namely the struggle for survival in the wake of a "zombie apocalypse" that turns most humans into cannibalistic monsters. *The Walking Dead* is at the forefront of a recent popular cultural resurgence of interest in the post-apocalyptic zombie genre, including not only films (such as *28 Days Later*, *28 Weeks Later*, *Resident Evil: Apocalypse*, *World War Z*, and *The Zombie Diaries*) and TV shows (such as *Z Nation*, *Helix*, and *In the Flesh*), but also a burgeoning attendant culture industry:

> There are popular "Zombie 5k Runs," "Zombie, Run" fitness apps for iPhones and Android . . . "zombie student clubs" that sponsor human vs. zombie Nerf tag and other activities, and a very lucrative zombie/apocalypse industry that sells self-defense gear and manuals to those who want to survive the looming end of days. (Weiss and Taylor 2014, i)

This abundance of cultural production and popular interest makes the zombie genre a particularly useful avenue for exploring the post-apocalyptic imaginary, including its configurations around issues of "race," gender, sexuality, and class, as well as crime, law, violence, and political power. The figure of the zombie itself has been read as a metaphor for everything from the racialized "other" and the "queer," to the subject of consumer culture and neoliberalism (Linnemann, Wall, and Green 2014; McAlister 2012; Reyes 2014; Harper 2002; Lanci 2014). At present, however, we shall focus upon significance of the lawman in *The Walking Dead*.

The first episode of the series starts with a familiar depiction of the agents of law and order. Two southern cops are sitting in a patrol car, eating fast food, while one (Shane—played by John Bernthal) regales his partner (Rick—played by Andrew Lincoln) with sexist anecdotes (referring to women as "chicks" and "pairs of boobs"). Rick, meanwhile, laments the parlous state of his marriage, citing his wife's claims that he's unwilling to communicate or share his feelings. Shane and Rick appear as stereotypes of the American police officer, complete with antiquated views of women, a hyper-masculine disdain for emotional self-expression, all wrapped-up in a certain blue-collar patriarchal swagger in keeping not only with popular cultural representations, but also classic studies of "cop culture" (Crank 2004, 229–33; Reiner 2010; Chan, Doran, and Marel 2010). Echoing the plot of *Mad Max*, they are dispatched, along with their colleagues, to apprehend a group of armed fugitives who have already shot and injured a police officer. In the ensuing gun battle, all three fugitives are killed, but not before Rick is shot and seriously injured.

When Rick regains consciousness, he is in a hospital bed, an unknown amount of time having passed. The hospital is eerily silent and his calls for help go unanswered. Stumbling into the corridors, he finds disarray—walls riddles with bullet holes and smeared with blood, and a mutilated corpse. Horrible groaning sounds come from behind a padlocked door, upon which someone has painted the words "DON'T OPEN DEAD INSIDE." Outside the building there are piles of fly-ridden corpses, abandoned military vehicles, and deserted streets. He encounters his first zombie—an emaciated creature, the bottom half of its body missing, dragging itself along the ground, hissing and gurgling sounds the only thing issuing from its mouth. He makes his way home to find his wife (Lori) and son (Carl) gone. Disoriented and injured, he is rescued by a father and son (Morgan and Duane); as they nurse him back to health, they update him on the events of the past month, since the beginning of the plague. Anyone who is infected dies, but then "comes back" as a "walker"—mindless and driven only by an appetite to feed on living flesh, further spreading the infection through bites. Sufficiently recovered, Rick takes Morgan and Duane to his police station. Rick showers, shaves, and then dons his police uniform—thereby reclaiming his role, his "master status," as a police officer. He decides to head for Atlanta, where there are supposedly refugee camps set up by the army, and where the Center for Disease Control (CDC) is said to be working on a cure for the plague. Running out of gas, he abandons his police car, and finds a horse on an uninhabited farm; he rides into the city, uniformed and armed, like the lawmen of old (Leisner 2009). The image is redolent of the opening scene of numerous Westerns:

> A lone rider, sitting easily in the saddle of his dusty horse, travels across the plains towards a small, new town. . . . He wears a tattered, wide-brimmed hat . . . and one gun rests naturally at his side in a smooth, well-worn holster. (Wright 1992, 4)

Rick's arrival in Atlanta thus recuperates a set of sedimented meanings, most particularly those of the heroic law-keeper who represents order and justice in an otherwise wild and unruly land (Andrew Lincoln reportedly modelled his portrayal of Rick upon Gary Cooper's roles in classic Westerns such as *High Noon* [1952] [Roberts 2010]). In a world thrown into chaos, Rick—uniform, hat, badge, guns, horse, and all—represents the last remaining embodiment of law in the post-apocalyptic wasteland. As the show's narrative unfolds, Rick attempts to sustain his role and responsibility as the agent of law enforcement. He finally finds his wife and son, who have joined with a small band of survivors, led by his erstwhile partner Shane. Rick and Shane soon take joint control as the group's leaders (with Rick ultimately supplanting his friend), their status as police officers according them a special authority in the eyes of the others. Rick's authority stems, in effect, from the others' investment in what he symbolizes—the promise of some vestige of rule-bound order, a restoration of the kinds of predictability that have disappeared along with the collapse of society. As Slavoj Zizek (1991, 33) writes of the king or sovereign:

> The subjects think they treat a certain person as a king because he is already in himself a king, while in reality this person is king only insofar as the subjects treat him as one . . . the king's charisma [is] a performative effect of their symbolic ritual.

Rick struggles to sustain the law as a symbolic order, and his place as its embodiment, by insisting that the demands of survival must nevertheless be constrained with the "old" system of norms and prohibitions. Over time, however, this proves increasingly untenable—encounters with other bands of survivors are as likely to end in violent confrontation and death as they are in cooperation. Rick's symbolic efficacy (materialized in his uniform, badge, and hat) is undermined because he is a lawman in a world where law no longer exists, and his articulation of authority is at best an empty gesture, and at worst a cruel reminder of a way of life that has been destroyed. His efforts to maintain the precepts of lawful behavior are a desperate, last-ditch attempt to pretend that, in the end, "nothing has changed" when in fact nothing remains the same. In the face of cumulative failures (including killing an increasingly unstable Shane, and the death of Lori) Rick ultimately hangs up his uniform and holster, and turns his back on the role of leader.

LAW AS TYRANNY IN THE POST-APOCALYPTIC STATE OF EMERGENCY

Thus far, we have considered post-apocalyptic culture's reflections on the crisis of law imagined as a deficit—the trepidation we experience in the face of the law's disappearance, leaving in its wake a society (if it can any longer be described as such) in which actions are no longer subject to limitation and constraint. In this section we shall turn to consider a diametrically opposed scenario that equally haunts the post-apocalyptic landscape—a fear not of the law's lack, but of its reappearance in a monstrous and distorted form, taking shape as an excess that partakes of the logic of brutal subjection. Law, in this rendition, becomes an instrument of the tyrannical sovereign, its edicts directed solely by a desire to reestablish some semblance of order, irrespective of the violence that is exercised in its name.

A fruitful theoretical framework for considering the violent excess of post-apocalyptic law is provided by the political philosopher Georgio Agamben, most especially his influential book *Homo Sacer: Sovereign Power and Bare Life* (1998). Agamben's starting point lies with Michel Foucault's conceptualization of modern forms of power as configured around the bios—the essential biological existence of human beings. Across his many works, Foucault explored the emergence of regimes of what he calls "biopower," which serve to produce, govern, and discipline subjects by "taking hold" of the body. Biopower thus refers to "the set of mechanisms through which the basic biological features of the human species became the object of a political strategy" (Foucault 2007, 116). Extending this to the analysis of sovereignty, Agamben argues that its ultimate basis lies in gathering unto itself the power over the basic biological existence of its subjects, "bare life," including the sole right to decide who lives and who dies. The institution of law, as dictated by sovereign power (be this the ancient emperor, the medieval monarch, or the modern state) is thus bound up with violence (the right to determine life or death), even as it forbids its subjects this same capacity (Agamben 1998, 42). Paradoxically, then, just as the law sets limits on the behavior of its subjects and holds them accountable, it is itself unconstrained by limits and accountable to nothing other than itself; sovereign power exists in a "state of exception" from its own laws. This state of exception is exemplified for Agamben by the figure of the concentration camp, a space in which human beings are stripped of all rights and reduced to a "bare life" that is subject to total domination, the exercise of power without limit, restraint, or refusal (Agamben 1998, 71). The camp, however, is not just a singular instance of the state of exception, but a logic that increasingly comes to characterize the exercise of sovereign power in modern societies:

> the camp was originally an "exceptional" space . . . in which the life of the "citizen" was reduced to "bare life," stripped of form and value. . . . However . . . the production of bare life is today extended well beyond the walls of the concentration camp. That is, today, the logic of the camp is generalized; the exception is normalized. (Diken and Lausten 2005, 5)

We see the proliferation of what Diken and Lausten (2002) call "zones of indistinction" in which sovereign power suspends its own laws in the name of a "state of emergency." Over the past decade, on the grounds of an existential risk to society posed by "terror," such exception to lawful limits has become normalized and permanent, distributed across society as such; hence the paradoxically "lawful lawlessness" of states that license themselves to engage in "extraordinary rendition," detention without trial in secret facilities, the systematic use of torture against "terror suspects," assassinations using unmanned drone strikes, limitations on freedom of speech and assembly, and mass covert surveillance of citizens, all in the name of safety and security (Neal 2006; Aradau and van Munster 2009; Hudson 2009).

The aforementioned exceptions to the "normal" exercise of sovereign power, resorting routinely to a suspension of law on grounds of national and international "emergency," have been met with sustained concern and criticism on the part of lawyers and human rights activists (Lustick 2006; Blum and Heymann 2013). They have also found articulation in popular cultural discourses that depict the crisis of law in terms of the exercise of state power without constraint and accountability. In the post-9/11 context, films such as *The Bourne Ultimatum* (2007), *Rendition* (2007), *Redacted* (2007), and *Green Zone* (2010), take critical aim variously at war crimes, extra-lawful imprisonment, torture, state-sponsored assassination programs, and mass surveillance. Beyond films that explicitly address the issues raised by the "war on terror," we can also suggest that these developments have found a resonance in a broader sphere of cultural production, one in which the specter of tyrannical law reappears in metaphorical explorations of the post-9/11 world. While bearing in mind Wallis and Aston's (2011, 53–54) caution that we must take care in "stressing an overarching link between the events of 9/11 and its influence on cultural production," it is nevertheless possible to discern its impact upon popular culture. They go on to suggest that there has "been a significant increase in apocalyptic imagery and themes post-9/11 across a variety of popular media," and that there "have been a large number of apocalyptic films that have directly or indirectly sustained [a] connection" between the apocalyptic and 9/11 (Wallis and Aston 2011, 54). While many such potential affinities may be considered, in keeping with our focus upon crime and disorder, the following discussion will confine itself to the representation of tyrannical law in post-apocalyptic scenarios.

We can resume here the previous section's analysis of *The Walking Dead*. I suggested that, with its representation of the policeman, the text offers a sustained reflection on the "crisis of law and order," through the projection of a disordered world in which the lawful restraint and regulation of behavior is no longer possible. The first two seasons of the show can be read as a "lament for the law," exemplified by Rick Grimes's heroic but doomed attempts to uphold a system of rules whose societal anchors (the state, government, police, courts) have been destroyed. It is not coincidental that, in season 2, Rick and his fellow survivors find refuge in a prison. What was once a space (like Agamben's camp) in which occupants were confined in a "state of exception," their rights and liberties suspended, is now inverted as a fragile oasis of civilization and order, facing an outside world where the logic of the camp (the reduction of human existence to "bare life") is now the norm. Inevitably, the survivors' attempt to reinstate something resembling a functioning social order (akin to the *polis*) ends in failure, and they are cast out once again into the zombie-infested wilderness. In contrast to this discourse on the crisis of law as deficit, season 3 confronts us with its counterpart—the law turned monstrous and excessive in a permanent "state of emergency."

In the third episode of season 3, we are introduced to the town of Woodbury. An erstwhile member of Rick's group, Andrea, is found by armed men and taken away in a vehicle, passing out from the illness she has been suffering. She awakens indoors, being administered to by a doctor. She learns that she is in Woodbury, a town with seventy-three residents. Compared to the life she has known since the onset of the plague (one of endless fear, flight, hunger, hardship, and danger) the town seems like a paradise: it has heavily fortified wooden walls protected from the "walkers" by patrols of armed guards; children play in the streets; there is no apparent shortage of clean clothes, food, water, and other essential amenities; and the town has suffered no losses to the zombies since the previous winter. She is introduced to the town's leader, known simply as The Governor (David Morrissey). The Governor appears to have built a properly functioning and well-ordered community, one that is safe and secure from the dangers outside its walls, and which can provide for the needs, well-being, and security of its residents. The townspeople are organized, cooperative, and grateful to have found a way not only to survive, but to thrive under The Governor's benign but decisive and determined stewardship. However, we soon learn that things are not entirely as congenial as they may seem. The townspeople hear of a group of National Guard soldiers who are seemingly stranded nearby. The Governor leads a rescue mission, vowing to bring the soldiers back to the safety of Woodbury. However, when he and his men find the group, they simply open fire, killing them all, and then take their supplies of food, medicines, and weapons back to town. The Governor tells the residents that he regrettably arrived too late, and that the soldiers had already been bitten and "turned" by the zombies, so he could nothing other than collect their abandoned supplies and return with them. As the subsequent episodes unfold, we are allowed to the see terrifying reality of The Governor's regime, as he routinely (and in secret from all but a handful of his most trusted subordinates) resorts to kidnapping, torture, imprisonment, and execution as and when he deems it necessary in order to secure the town and his own unquestioned authority over it. When he learns about the group of survivors at the prison, he captures and tortures two of them (Glenn and Maggie), seeking information about their strength and numbers; he keeps this hidden from the residents. Rick's group stages a rescue attempt to retrieve their friends from Woodbury. In the wake of this incursion, The Governor addresses the town:

> I should tell you that we'll be okay, that we're safe, that tomorrow we'll bury our dead and endure. But I won't, cos I can't, cos I'm afraid . . . I'm afraid of these terrorists, who want what we have, who want to destroy us!

He whips up the residents into a frenzy, as they chant in unison "Kill them! Kill them!" The Governor then leads his people in an assault on the prison, with the intention of killing anyone who is not under his absolute control (and in the course of which he also summarily guns-down a number of his own men who express reservations about going to war against the prison-dwellers).

The representation of Woodbury, its governor and their war with Rick's group offers a clear allegory of America in the post-9/11 era. Like George W. Bush (a real-life former southern Governor) Woodbury's fictional leader declares a war of annihilation against "terrorists" who are deemed to seek the destruction of his people and their "way of life." In service to this war, all rights to question or criticize The Governor's leadership are tantamount to "treason," and punishable by death. The enemy cannot be bargained with, and their very existence cannot be tolerated—only their complete destruction can ensure safety, order, and freedom from fear. In this state of emergency, the only law that can be allowed is the absolute authority of a tyrannical sovereign.

The Walking Dead's transcoding of contemporary anxieties about the law's excess in the state of emergency is likewise echoed in other recent apocalyptic cultural productions. *Under the Dome* (2013–present), a television series adapted from Stephen King's novel of the same name, is similarly preoccupied with the figure of the tyrannical sovereign. It is set in the small town of Chester's Mill, Maine. Suddenly and inexplicably, the town is enveloped in a mysterious, invisible "dome," a force-field that allows nothing other than air to pass its wall. The residents find themselves trapped inside, cut off from the outside world. The authorities are unable to either understand the nature of the dome, or find a way to remove, bypass or destroy it. Under the dome, we see unfolding a familiar post-apocalyptic scenario, where the shortage of food, water, and medicines incrementally leads to conflict and violence as the residents struggle for survival. By an unfortunate happenstance, most of the town's elected officials were outside the dome when it "came down," so there is a vacuum of legitimate political authority in Chester's Mill. The exception is "Big Jim" Rennie (Dean Norris), an ambitious (and rather shady) local entrepreneur and town councilman. As the only remaining councilman, he grasps for himself the role of leader, a move that the frightened and confused townsfolk readily accept. He soon begins to assert absolute control over the residents, using the town's small police force as a means to coerce the reluctant into obedience. He organizes a program of firearms confiscation, taking all weapons in the town into his personal control, thereby monopolizing the means of violence. If others seek to oppose his one-man rule, he resorts to murder. When possibilities emerge to escape the dome's confinement, Big Jim covertly moves to sabotage such attempts; without the dome, he is just a small-town used car salesman, but within its walls he is sovereign and all-powerful. A challenge to his authority emerges in the character of Dale "Barbie" Barbara (Mike Vogel). A former soldier-turned-debt collector for organized crime, Barbie is an outsider who gets trapped in Chester's Mill while visiting on business. When an increasing number of people start to look to Barbie as an alternative leader, Big Jim frames his rival for murders he himself commits, then organizes a manhunt to capture the "criminal." Once Barbie is apprehended, Big Jim orders the construction of a gallows in front of the courthouse. Acting as both judge and jury, he unilaterally declares Barbie guilty, and sentences him to hang. Like The Governor, Big Jim serves as an exemplification of the horrors unleashed when law is granted unlimited power in the name of safety and survival—the price of security and the restoration of order is the suspension of rights and liberties, including the citizen's right to a fair trial, due process and to life itself.

CONCLUSION

Over the course of this chapter we have explored how post-apocalyptic popular culture dramatizes anxieties about a crisis of social order, through a corresponding crisis of law. This is articulated through a dualistic discourse in which law is both missing, and reappears as an authoritarian perversion of itself—two sides of a response to a scenario in which law-and-order appears to be failing. This duality represents, I argue, existing social and cultural cleavages and tensions around the efficacy of law in creating and sustaining a stable society. Long-standing fears about the failure of law to both protect citizens or adequately punish offenders, finds voice in those post-apocalyptic narratives that stress the explosion of predatory and violent behavior once the institutional apparatus of law enforcement disappears. Conversely, concerns about the growing tendency to suspend rights and liberties in light of a supposed "state of emergency" (such as the "war on terror"), find expression through an imagery of law as a tool of tyrannical authority.

REFERENCES

Agamben, Giorgio. 1998. *Homo Sacer: Sovereign Power and Bare Life.* Stanford, CA: Stanford University Press.

Althusser, Louis. 1994. "Ideology and Ideological State Apparatuses (Notes Towards an Investigation)." In *Mapping Ideology*, edited by Slavoj Zizek, 100–40. London: Verso.

Aradau, Claudia and Rens van Munster. 2009. "Exceptionalism and the 'War on Terror': Criminology Meets International Relations." *British Journal of Criminology*, 49(5): 686–701.

Barthes, Roland. 2000. *Mythologies.* London: Vintage.

Beccalossi, Chiara. 2010. "Lombroso, Cesare: The Criminal Man." In *Encyclopedia of Criminological Theory*, edited by Francis T. Cullen and Pamela Wilcox, 560–65. Thousand Oaks, CA: Sage.

Bendle, Mervyn F. 2005. "The Apocalyptic Imagination and Popular Culture." *Journal of Religion and Popular Culture*, 11(1): 1–7.

Blum, Gabrialla and Philip B. Heymann. 2013. *Laws, Outlaws and Terrorists: Lessons from the War on Terrorism.* Cambridge, MA: MIT Press.

Bradshaw, Peter. 2003. "Time of the Wolf." In *The Guardian*, 17 October, online at: www.theguardian.com/film/2003/oct/17/michael-haneke-isabelle-huppert.

Broderick, Mick. 1993. "Heroic Apocalypse: Mad Max, Mythology and the Millennium." In *Crisis Cinema: The Apocalyptic Idea in Postmodern Narrative Fiction*, edited by Christopher Sharrett, 251–72.Washington, DC: Maisonneuve Press.

Chan, Janet, Sally Doran, and Christina Marel. 2010. "Doing and Undoing Gender in Policing." *Theoretical Criminology*, 14(4): 425–46.

Crank, John P. 2004. *Understanding Police Culture*, 2nd edition. London: Routledge.

Cullen, Julie Berry and Steven D. Levitt. 1999. "Crime, Urban Flight, and the Consequences for Cities." *Review of Economics and Statistics*, 81(2): 159–69.

Darabont, Frank (creator). 2010. *The Walking Dead* [television series]. United States: AMC

Diken, Bulent and Carsten Bagge Lausten. 2002. "Zones of Indistinction: Security, Terror, and Bare Life." *Space and Culture*, 5(3): 290–307.

———. 2005. *The Culture of Exception: Sociology Facing the Camp*. Abingdon: Routledge.

Du Coudray, Chantal Bourgault. 2006. *The Curse of the Werewolf: Fantasy, Horror and the Beast Within*. London: I. B. Taurus.

Eschholz, Sarah, Matthew Mallard, and Stacey Flynn. 2004. "Images of Prime Time Justice: A Content Analysis of *NYPD Blue* and *Law & Order*." *Journal of Criminal Justice and Popular Culture*, 10(3): 161–80.

Fleming, Thomas. 2007. "The History of Violence: Mega Cases of Serial Murder, Self-Propelling Narratives, and Reader Engagement." *Journal of Criminal Justice and Popular Culture*, 14(3): 277–91.

Foucault, Michel. 2007. *The Birth of Biopolitics: Lectures at the Collège de France, 1978–1979*. Basingstoke: Palgrave Macmillan.

Frey, William H. 1979. "Central City White Flight: Racial and Nonracial Causes." *American Sociological Review*, 44(3): 425–48.

Golding, William. 1954. *Lord of the Flies*. London: Faber & Faber

Golding, Peter and Graham Murdock, G. 2000. "Culture, Communications and Political Economy." *Mass Media and Society*, 3: 70–92.

Gordon, Lawrence (producer) and Walter Hill (director). 1979. *The Warriors* [motion picture]. United States: Paramount Pictures

Green, Simon T. 2011. "Vengeance and Furies: Existential Dilemmas in Penal Decision-Making." In *Crime, Governance and Existential Predicaments*, edited by James Hardie-Bick and Ronnie Lippens, 61–84. Houndmills: Palgrave Macmillan.

Harper, Stephen. 2002. "Zombies, Malls, and the Consumerism Debate: George Romero's *Dawn of the Dead*." *Americana: The Journal of American Popular Culture*, 1(2), online at: www.americanpopularculture.com/journal/articles/fall_2002/harper.htm.

Heiduschka, Veit (producer) and Michael Haneke (director). 2003. *Les temps du Loup* [motion picture]. France: Canal +

Hobbes, Thomas. (1968 [1651]). *Leviathan*, edited by C. B. Macpherson. Harmondsworth: Penguin.

Hudson, Barbara. 2009. "Justice in a Time of Terror." *British Journal of Criminology*, 49(5): 702–17.

Johnston, Ian. 2007. "Lost World: Michael Haneke's *Time of the Wolf* Reconsidered." *Bright Lights Film Journal*, 1 May, online at: brightlightsfilm.com/lost-world-michael-hanekes-time-wolf-reconsidered/#.VKvVsHt7YtE.

Jolivet, Pierre (producer) and Luc Besson (director). 1983. *Le Dernier Combat* [motion picture]. France: Les Films du Loup.

Kaplan, J. Stein (producer) and John Carpenter (director). 1976. *Assault on Precinct 13* [motion picture]. United States: CKK Corporation.

Kennedy, Byron (producer) and George Miller (director). 1979. *Mad Max* [motion picture]. Australia: Kennedy Miller Productions

Lanci, Yari. 2014. "Zombie 2.0: Subjectivation in Times of Apocalypse." *Journal for Cultural and Religious Theory*, 13(2): 25–37.

Leisner, Andreas. 2009. "Law and (Dis) Order: The Janus-Faced Myth of the Lawman in US History and Popular Culture." In *Legal Narratives: European Perspectives on U.S. Law in Cultural Context*, edited by Gudron Grabher and Anna Gamper, 101–21. New York: Springer.

Linnemann, Travis, Tyler Wall, and Edward Green. 2014. "The Walking Dead and Killing State: Zombification and the Normalization of Police Violence." *Theoretical Criminology*, 18(4): 506–27.

Lustick, Ian. 2006. *Trapped in the War on Terror*. Philadelphia: University of Pennsylvania Press.

Lyotard, Jean-Francois. 1984. *The Postmodern Condition: A Report on Knowledge*. Manchester: Manchester University Press.

McAlister, Elizabeth. 2012. "Slaves, Cannibals, and Infected Hyper-Whites: The Race and Religion of Zombies." *Anthropological Quarterly*, 85(2): 457–86.

Neal, Andrew W. 2006. "Foucault in Guantánamo: Towards an Archaeology of the Exception." *Security Dialogue*, 37(1): 31–46.

Newman, Kim. 1999. *Millennium Movies: End of the World Cinema*. London: Titan Books.

Rafter, Nicole. 2006. *Shots in the Mirror: Crime Films and Society*, 2nd Edition. New York: Oxford University Press.

Rafter, Nicole and Michelle Brown. 2011. *Criminology Goes to the Movies: Crime, Theory and Popular Culture*. New York: New York University Press.

Reiner, Robert. 2010. *The Politics of the Police*, 4th edition. Oxford: Oxford University Press.

Renner, Karen J. 2012. "The Appeal of the Apocalypse." *Lit: Literature Interpretation Theory*, 23: 203–11.

Reyes, Xavier A. 2014. "Beyond the Metaphor: Gay Zombies and the Challenge to Heteronormativity." *Journal for Cultural and Religious Theory*, 13(2): 1–12.

Ryan, Michael and Douglas Kellner. 1990. *Camera Politica: The Politics and Ideology of Contemporary Hollywood Film*. Bloomington, IN: Indiana University Press.

Shapiro, Jerome F. 2002. *Atomic Bomb Cinema: The Apocalyptic Imagination on Film*. London: Routledge.

Spitz, David. 1970. "Power and Authority: An Interpretation of Golding's *Lord of the Flies*." *The Antioch Review*, 30(1): 21–33.

Vaughan, Brian K. (creator). 2013. *Under the Dome* [television series]. United States: Amblin Entertainment

Wacquant, Louis. J. 1993. "Urban Outcasts: Stigma and Division in the Black American Ghetto and the French Urban Periphery." *International Journal of Urban and Regional Research*, 17(3): 366–83.

Walliss, John and James Aston. 2011. "Doomsday America: The Pessimistic Turn of Post-9/11 Apocalyptic Cinema." *The Journal of Religion and Popular Culture*, 23(1): 53–64.

Weber, Max. (1965). "Politics as a Vocation." In *From Max Weber: Essays in Sociology*, edited by H. H. Gerth and C. Wright Mills, 77–128. New York: Oxford University Press.

Weiss, Dennis M. and Victor E. Taylor. 2014. "The Cultural Un/Life of Zombies." *Journal for Cultural and Religious Theory*, 13(2): i–vi.
Wilson, David and Sean O'Sullivan. 2005. "Re-theorizing the Penal Reform Functions of the Prison Film: Revelation, Humanization, Empathy and Benchmarking." *Theoretical Criminology*, 9(4): 471–91.
Wright, Will. 1992. *Sixguns and Society: A Structural Study of the Western*. Los Angeles, CA: University of California Press.
Yar, Majid. 2002. "From Nature to History and Back Again: Blumenberg, Strauss and the Hobbesian Community." *History of the Human Sciences*, 15(3): 53–73.
———. 2010. "Screening Crime: Cultural Criminology Goes to the Movies." In *Framing Crime: Cultural Criminology and the Image*, edited by Keith J. Hayward and Mike Presdee, 68–82. London: Routledge.
———. 2014. "Imaginaries of Crime, Fantasies of Justice: Popular Criminology and the Figure of the Superhero." In *The Poetics of Crime: Understanding and Researching Crime and Deviance through Creative Sources*, edited by Michael Hviid-Jacobson, 193–207. Farnham: Ashgate.
Young, Alison. 2009. *The Scene of Violence: Cinema, Crime, Affect*. Abingdon: Routledge.
Yuen, Wayne. 2012. "Philosophy for the Dead." In *The Walking Dead and Philosophy: Zombie Apocalypse Now*, edited by Wayne Yuen, xiii–xv. Chicago, IL: Open Court Publishing.
Zizek, Slavoj. 1991. *Looking Awry*. Cambridge, MA: MIT Press.

3

A Canadian Perspective on Documentary Film

Drug Addict

Susan Boyd

While conducting research for a study on fictional drug films, I became aware of the first National Film Board (NFB) documentary produced in Canada about illegal drugs, trafficking, and addiction.[1] The documentary is titled *Drug Addict* and was directed by Robert Anderson. The National Film Board of Canada with the Royal Canadian Mounted Police (RCMP) produced *Drug Addict* in 1948 for the Division of Narcotic Control and the Department of National Health and Welfare. This thirty-four-minute black and white, "realist" voice-over documentary was created as an educational tool for law agents and medical professionals. *Drug Addict* was praised in Canada and won a Genie Award in 1949.

Drug Addict was not publicly viewed in the United States following its release. U.S. researchers John Galliher, David Keys, and Michael Elsner (1998) claim that *Drug Addict* is a significant film because of its opposition to the U.S. Federal Bureau of Narcotic's (FBN) policy at that time to demonize illegal drug users. To this end, FBN censored oppositional ideas, including films such as *Drug Addict*. The work by Galliher, Keys, and Elsner, however, does not examine the role of documentary or drug policy in Canada in order to contextualize the film *Drug Addict*.

I agree with Galliher, Keys, and Elsner that *Drug Addict* is a significant film; however, in this chapter my focus is quite different. I argue that *Drug Addict* is a significant documentary and worthy of further investigation because it provides insight into some early foundational discourses about illegal drugs, law enforcement, addiction, and treatment, including drug maintenance, that still resonate in Canada today. The documentary *Drug Addict* reveals how the RCMP and law agents in Canada in 1948 thought about people who used or sold illegal drugs and the associated ideas about managing and regulating these people. This chapter provides a sociohistorical context for the documentary *Drug Addict*. Viewing the film through the lens of Canadian history gives readers a better context to understand the claims and representations in the film. I also argue that law enforcement discourses have been constituted in part through documentary representation. To this end, this chapter explores the medium of documentary to educate individuals about social issues such as drug crime, addiction, and treatment options. By taking into account Canadian history and the cultural, political, legal, and social environment, we can better understand the narrative and visual representations in the documentary *Drug Addict*.

SOCIOHISTORICAL CONTEXT

The origins of drug regulation in Canada have been explored by a number of researchers (see Boyd 1984; Carstairs 2006; Giffen, Endicott, and Lambert 1991). Against the backdrop of the international anti-opium movement and the professionalization of physicians and pharmacists and their support of the regulation of patent medicines, Canada enacted the Opium Act (the first federal drug legislation outside of alcohol prohibition for those labelled Status Indians under the Indian Act) in 1908 with little parliamentary debate or pharmacological evidence to support the regulation of this drug. The Opium Act was shaped by moralism, and race, class, and gender fears (Boyd 1984; Boyd 2015). The legislation was aimed at regulating opium in smoking form, an activity linked to Chinese men, and not the elixirs and patent medicines that contained opiates or other drugs such as cocaine and marijuana commonly used by white settlers. Early legislation was enacted with the understanding that it would not be used against Anglo-Saxon Canadians (Solomon and Green 1988). However, each subsequent drug law increased penalties, the list of criminalized drugs, police profiling, budgets, and powers.

Smoking and liquid forms of opium became less available following prohibition, and as an illegal market emerged, these substances were replaced by refined morphine and heroin and the use of the hypodermic needle. Whereas early law enforcement focused on Chinese Canadians, later regulation centered on white poor and working-class heroin, morphine, and cocaine users (Giffen, Endicott, and Lambert 1991, 594, 596). Nevertheless, illegal drug use was confined to a very small portion of the Canadian population.

Another significant aspect of drug prohibition in Canada was the restriction on prescribing narcotics for drug maintenance purposes to anyone identified as an "addict." This was unlike Britain, where doctors retained the right to prescribe narcotics for drug maintenance purposes, or the United States, where narcotic clinics were initially established (see Acker 2002; Brecher et al. 1972; Campbell 2007; Musto 1987). In Canada, following prohibition, no public drug treatment provisions were set up for individuals who used or were addicted to newly criminalized drugs. In 1920 the Division of Narcotic Control was established and the RCMP became the enforcers of Canada's new federal drug laws. The RCMP are a federal paramilitary policing force and following prohibition they pushed for harsher legislation to control Chinese Canadians and regulate newly criminalized drugs (Hewitt 2006, 59–60). Special narcotic prosecutors were set up to investigate and prosecute drug users, sellers, and errant doctors who were thought to be prescribing narcotics to criminals.

Scholars in Canada argue that law enforcement played a significant role in shaping drug treatment regime and drug policy more generally (Carstairs 2006; Debeck, Montaner, and Kerr 2006; Giffen, Endicott, and Lambert 1991; Nolin and Kenny 2003). Early on the Division Chief of Narcotic Control and the RCMP became the dominant players in perpetuating criminal addict discourse in Canada (Giffen, Endicott and Lamber 1991). In 1929, Canadian Chief, Division of Narcotic Control, Colonel Sharman (formerly of the Mounted Police and Canadian Army), advanced three categories of "addicts": medical patients, respectable citizens such as doctors and nurses, and, those who were deemed criminals (Giffen, Endicott, and Lambert 1991, 158–59). For those people labeled criminals, "addiction" was believed to be less important than their criminal tendencies. It was claimed by the Division that these individuals were criminals prior to using illegal drugs and would, therefore, remain a menace to society even if their addiction were "cured" through abstinence. Thus, harsh criminal sanctions were necessary and treatment was ineffective for criminal addicts. The RCMP and the Division insisted that criminal addicts were different and deserving of harsher punishment than other moral Canadians such as doctors or medical patients who found themselves addicted to criminalized drugs.

The Division created case files for "Addicts" and "Traffickers" (from 1928 to the early 1970s). The Addict files were also categorized into two separate files: "Criminal users" and "Doctors" (see Carstairs 2006). The individual Addict files contained mug shots, police reports, and extensive correspondence with doctors, prosecutors, and parole boards (Carstairs 2006). The individuals involved were subject to intense surveillance by law enforcement and the RCMP/police could search without a warrant.

Legal and social discrimination, long prison sentences, whipping, and deportation (of those who were foreign born) was the fate of most visible drug users in Canada, especially those who were poor or working class.

Although the medical profession contributed to knowledge about narcotic addiction in Canada following prohibition, law enforcement became the primary knowledge producers about newly criminalized drugs and the individuals who used, sold, or produced them. Until 1947, the RCMP was responsible for 80 percent of drug convictions under the Opium and Narcotic Drug Act in Canada (Josie 1947, 62). The Division of Narcotic Control and the RCMP also shaped professional practice (i.e., medicine and social work). In the 1940s and early 1950s, psychiatry produced new knowledge about people addicted to criminalized drugs. However, rather than contest the dominance of law enforcement, historian Carolyn Acker notes that the criminal justice and psychiatry professions solidified new knowledge about criminalized drugs and people addicted to them, working hand-in-hand with one another to broaden the social control of those labeled criminal addicts (2002, 212). Although no unitary explanation emerged, following World War II, psychiatric experts in Canada claimed addiction to narcotics stemmed from a psychopathic personality type, and abstinence was required in order to "cure" the "addict" (see the Canadian study by Stevenson, Lingley, Trasov, and Stansfield 1956). Thus, in Canada, people addicted to illegal drugs, at least those outside the category of "Doctor addicts," were represented by psychiatry as doubly deviant: criminal and pathological. These perspectives were highlighted in the documentary *Drug Addict*.

In the year that *Drug Addict* was produced, 1948, there were only 286 drug convictions in Canada (Giffen, Endicott, and Lambert 1991, 599). Although drug arrests do not tell us how many people in Canada used criminalized drugs, as noted above, illegal drug use was not widespread at this time, although a small group of drug law offenders were well-known to law enforcement. These were poor and working-class white people, mostly heroin and morphine users living in Montreal, Quebec, and Vancouver, British Columbia. Heroin users in British Columbia were referred to as an "Addict colony" residing in the East End of Vancouver (Stevenson et al. 1956). The RCMP also depicted poor people who used or sold illegal drugs as a threat to the security and morality of the nation (Giffen, Endicott, and Lambert 1991; Grayson 2008).

Under the direction of Colonel Sharman, the Chief of the Division of Narcotic Control from 1927 to 1946, and K. C. Hossick from 1946 to 1959, Canada's punitive drug policy solidified. In fact, legendary drug-war advocate Harry J. Anslinger, the U.S. Commissioner of Narcotics from 1930 to 1962, publicly praised Colonel Sharman for his law-and-order stance, abstinence ideology, and opposition to narcotic clinics and maintenance therapy for addicts (Anslinger and Tompkins 1953, 206). Internationally, Canada was also an active participant in global efforts to initiate punitive domestic and global drug control systems (Giffen, Endicott, and Lambert 1991, 598).

Yet, the primacy of law-and-order and criminal addict discourse in Canada was challenged by other institutional players. From 1927 to the early 1930s, Canada's Department of Health's annual reports called for the setting up of treatment services. Although it was against the law, individual doctors continued to prescribe to people addicted to criminalized drugs (Giffen, Endicott, and Lambert 1991, 361, 363). From the 1930s until his death in 1957, Ernest Winch, Co-operative Commonwealth Federation (CCF) member of British Columbia's provincial legislature, tirelessly argued that Canada should adopt what was referred to in North America as the "British System" (referring to doctors' legal right in Britain to prescribe drugs such as heroin and morphine to people addicted to narcotics) (Giffen, Endicott, and Lambert 1991, 363; Steeves 1977, 142–45). In 1955, Winch argued before the Senate Special Committee on Narcotic Drug Traffic in Vancouver, British Columbia, for the establishment of "legalized medical clinics for the treatment of certified chronic drug addicts for the purpose of administering the minimum amount which will enable them to carry on their means of livelihood and refrain from having to resort to underworld sources of drug supply" (Senate of Canada 1955, 211). Winch also argued that publicly funded treatment and legal narcotic clinics should be made available because many people addicted to drugs are not criminals: "they have no criminal record prior to their addiction . . . imprisonment does not prevent, nor does it cure, drug addiction" (Senate of Canada 1955, 215). Other witnesses communicated similar messages to the Senate Committee (Senate of Canada 1955). Winch also claimed that professional addicts had the resources to pay for private sanitariums, had easier access to drugs, and could pay others to obtain them if needed. Thus, he argued that the effects of Canadian drug laws were visited primarily on poor and working-class people who were profiled by the police.

Additionally, a comprehensive study, *A Report on Drug Addiction in Canada*, by the Ministry of National Health and Welfare in 1947, challenged official RCMP discourse about criminal addicts and drug policy (Josie 1947, 39). The report highlights research that demonstrated that "law-breaking by addicts consists mainly of infractions of the narcotic laws" and the majority of convictions at that time were for possession (Josie 1947, 69).

Outside of Canada, other challenges to law enforcement perspectives on addiction were emerging including Alfred Lindesmith's study, *Opiate Addiction and the Law*, which was published in the United States in 1947.

Lindesmith forcefully critiqued Anslinger's drug policies and argued that people addicted to narcotics were neither psychopathic nor criminal, and most narcotic users used these drugs in order to feel normal and to ward off withdrawal symptoms. Lindesmith also criticized the medical profession for aligning itself with federal drug policy (Lindesmith 1947).

Yet the Senate, the Division of Narcotic Control, and the RCMP were not persuaded by facts, advocates of drug reform, or drug policy regimes that did not reflect the primacy of law enforcement. Rather, deeply entrenched ideas about criminal addicts and the efficiency of punishment shaped early Canadian drug policy and approaches to drug treatment. The RCMP further formalized their stance on the criminal addict in their annual report in 1946 (Boyd 2008; Carstairs 2006; Giffen, Endicott, and Lambert 1991; Stevenson et al. 1956). Compulsory abstinence based treatment, preferably in a prison cell, was their only concession. As I will discuss below, in the documentary *Drug Addict*, some of these contradictory notions about the nature of addiction and the addict were represented.

THEORIZING DOCUMENTARY FILM

Since the advent of film in the late 1800s, knowledge has often been transmitted through this medium rather than the written word or radio. From the early 1920s, British and later U.S. governments and businesses recognized the "powers of propaganda and persuasion" of documentary film, and invested in film production (Druick 2007, 33). Early on, Canadian "cinema was conceived as a documentary medium" rather than a "fictional" film industry for entertainment (Hogarth 2002, 23). Thus, in 1939, Canada established the state-sponsored National Film Board (NFB) to promote the production of documentaries. Other researchers have examined the emergence of the NFB and cinema in Canada and analyzed specific topics (although, not criminalized drugs or drug policy) featured in documentary films (Druick 2007; Gittings 2002; Hogarth 2002; Melnyk 2004; Morris 1978).

At its inception, one of the primary goals of the NFB was to educate Canadians about themselves, and citizen training and national unity were key themes of early documentary/educational films (Druick 2007). In Canada, documentary films produced by the NFB and other filmmakers provided a "realist visual" medium to communicate about emerging social problems. New knowledge and practice were relayed through film to professionals and the general public, including knowledge communicated by law enforcement about newly criminalized drugs and the people who used or sold them.

Documentary films differ significantly from fictive film and print media. Druick (2007, 8) argues that NFB documentaries have a "complex relationship between cultural policy" and social science. Documentary films reflect "ways of knowing" by professional groups and help to "predict," "manage," and regulate specific populations (Druick 2007, 5), such as people who use criminalized drugs and drug traffickers. The realist and visual format of documentaries captures observations, ideological assumptions, ways of knowing, practices, and new directions by law enforcement and criminal justice. Documentary films were and continue to be a significant medium communicating new knowledges about drug policy and practice in Canada.

Although documentary studies inform this chapter, this case study of *Drug Addict* draws from critical sociology, cultural criminology, feminist studies, and cultural studies. Stuart Hall has long been interested in the politics of representation and crime, racialized discourse, the ideological significance of visual images, and the interdependency of narrative and image in popular culture (Hall 1981; 2009). Hall argues that there are historical moments where certain discourses are produced that alter our understanding of topics (Hall 2009). Thus, what we think we know about illegal drugs, crime, and addiction in a specific era has a bearing on how we regulate and manage these issues and the people involved.

In this chapter, Hall's insights are supplemented by the work of cultural criminologists. Cultural criminology is a critical theoretical framework whose central focus is the domain of law, justice, and crime. It is "a mode of analysis that embodies sensitivities to image, meaning, and representation" and the proliferation of media depictions of crime and deviance (Ferrell and Websdale 1999, 3; Hayword and Young 2004, 259). Cultural criminology questions the dominance and expansion of criminal justice policies and practices. These perspectives provide a lens to understand the historical, social, cultural, and political factors that shape documentary film representations of illegal drugs, trafficking, addiction, and crime in *Drug Addict*.

Although a small number of researchers have also begun to examine fictional films about illegal drugs, trafficking, addiction, and/or criminality/crime (Boyd 2008; Shapiro 2003; Starks 1982; Stevenson 2000), documentary films are not analyzed in depth in these studies. Thus examining *Drug Addict* more closely will contribute to a new field of inquiry.

In order to examine the narrative and visual images in *Drug Addict*, an analysis of the documentary was conducted (Bacchi 2009; Hall 2009; Hesse-Biber and Leavy 2011). This project's qualitative methodological framework is consistent with its critical theoretical perspective. A case study was conducted drawing from Hall's perspectives on visual and textual representation and cultural criminology and Druick's observation that there is a "close connection between social policy and documentary narrative" (Druick, 2007, 26). Bacchi notes that implicit representations of problems lead to specific courses of action. In relation to analyzing documentary, questions introduced by Bacchi (2009, 2) were applied: (1) What is the problem represented to be? (2) "What assumptions underlie this representation of the 'problem'?" (3) "How has this representation of the 'problem' come about?" (4) "What is left unproblematic in this problem representation? What are the silences? Can the problem be thought of differently?" In keeping with an analysis of visual media, my analysis attended to image, meaning, and representations of deviance, crime, and control. Thus, discourses related to criminal justice, illegal drug users, drug trafficking, addiction, and treatment were coded and analyzed with attention to representations of race, class, and gender.

DRUG ADDICT: TRAFFICKING

Drug Addict is largely a voice-over dramatization, using "real" people who used illegal drugs to enact scenes set in Montreal, Quebec. Similar to early U.S. fictive drug films like *Reefer Madness* (1936), *Drug Addict* begins with a postscript, a popular film format at that time to lend authority to both fictive and documentary film. *Drug Addict*'s postscript states that "this is a film about drug addiction in Canada. . . . Many actual addicts who appear in the film gave valuable assistance." An authoritative male narrator then explains that the "conditions it portrays are typical of most of the larger cities" in Canada. All of the scenes in *Drug Addict* are scripted reenactments of events.

The film opens with dramatic music. The narrator explains that the Commission of Narcotic Drugs of the United Nations regulates which nations can grow opium legally. The opening scene depicts poppy fields and Asian-looking farmers splitting opium pods, reminding viewers that these are foreign lands upon which illegal drugs produced by foreign others are then smuggled into Canada. The next scene depicts men in a rowboat in the night picking up a bag from a larger vessel. The rowboat comes to shore and an Asian man carrying the bag hops out on land. The narrator states that the profits are immense for drug smuggling. The narrator claims that a "pound of opium can be bought in Bombay" and by the time it reaches the streets of Canada it is worth "$15,000" and drugs are a "commodity of organized crime." The hierarchy of the trade is discussed and shown visually by depicting farmers, smugglers, high-level traffickers, chemists, and street peddlers. The illegal drug trade is depicted as the domain of criminal men. Although the narrator states that all peoples participate in the drug trade, visually this is not so in the first section of the film. After the film opens in foreign lands, Asian men are depicted smuggling opium into Canada and then the next scene shows an Asian man giving both refined and crude opium to another Asian man. The second man is shown lying down smoking opium from a long pipe with his drug paraphernalia in front of him. This scene reactivates old tropes about racialized men running the illegal opium drug trade and opium dens, and enslaving innocent people to a life of addiction and crime (Boyd 2008).

Following the opening scenes, the film centers on white, male traffickers and street peddlers, and white working-class and poor users in Montreal. The narrator explains that most opium dens are closed in Canada now and most addicts now inject narcotics. He notes that addicts on the street (in contrast to "Doctor addicts") steal and are involved in a life of crime and that most of their life is spent in prison. Numerous scenes of street dealing, passing cash for drugs, and petty crime such as stealing from a store are depicted. The film also reinforces criminal justice dominance in the field of drug policy and control. The film includes numerous scenes of law enforcement, undercover police, and training squads of the RCMP going about their work by rounding up traffickers and street peddlers, as well as people who use criminalized drugs. The narrator emphasizes the importance of law enforcement work in Canada and "enforcement bodies throughout the world" to stem the trade in illegal drugs and to control the people who use these drugs.

The misuse of drugs and the illegal drug trade is described by the narrator of *Drug Addict* as a "stain on the body politic," and the need for global and national criminal justice control is stressed. Nowhere does the narration acknowledge that the illegal drug trade is a consequence of criminalization and drug prohibition. The narrator does slightly acknowledge the failures of prohibition by noting that "complete control of illicit drugs is impossible" as there are "thousands of hiding places." The narrator then refers to illegal drug use and states, "this is the practice that society has condemned as a contagious and evil thing." Near the end of the film, we see "unscrupulous drug chemists" and a drug lab that produces illegal synthetic drugs; the narrator expresses that this is "a new challenge to RCMP" as one factory could "flood the whole world with these toxic substances." At the end of the film the key role of law enforcement is reinforced as we see agents conducting a drug raid and the narrator concludes: "Law enforcement and control always [have a] dominant role in drug regulation."

DRUG USERS AND ADDICTION

The documentary moves from depictions of drug smuggling and trafficking to addiction and people who use criminalized drugs. In the film, the narrator notes that drugs have medicinal benefits and all people are vulnerable to addiction to drugs. Examples include doctors who have easy access to drugs and "criminal addicts," such as an older white male heroin user who is shown preparing heroin that he then injects. The narrator states that the heroin user has been using drugs for twenty-nine years. The narrator claims that the "solution to addiction to drugs is found only in curing the addict." However, he notes that there are "no proper facilities in Canada for the cure of addiction" and jail does not necessarily solve the problem for first-time offenders. The street and domestic scenes of criminalized drug users in the documentary now focus on white users and peddlers. These people are depicted as looking healthy and conventionally attired; almost all the men wear suits and overcoats and all the women wear dresses. Yet, the film reaffirms discourse about the criminal nature of these "addicts." Although the narrator says that it is "very seldom that" a narcotic "addict [would] commit a crime of violence," he nevertheless notes, "they steal to get the money" to feed their addiction and they have "long records" of criminal offences and spend half their life in prison. Several scenes of people buying drugs from street peddlers are shown.

Unlike the men, women in the film who use illegal drugs are portrayed as immoral street workers who support their own and their boyfriends' drug habits. However, women represented in the film are quite secondary to the male characters; we only see women in relation to men (with their boyfriends and street peddlers) and the documentary does not focus on them. Reflecting the era, there are no women experts in the film or RCMP or among the police officers. However, the small scenes of women portrayed as illegal narcotic users are revealing because of their moral tone. At the time that the film was produced, women who used heroin or cocaine were perceived as especially "sexually immoral" and deviant (see Boyd 2008; Campbell 2000; Stevenson et al. 1956, 96).

An explicit scene (for the times) is shown of a white male heroin user preparing and then injecting the drug into a vein in his arm. The narrator states that the "addict must have it several times a day, it is a habit he must satisfy, he has no choice." In one scene, the door to the Mental Health Division is shown. Inside sits a doctor who speaks directly to the camera telling the viewer that "some addicts want treatment" and others want to go on using narcotics. The scene than shifts to an older white man, who also speaks directly to the camera. He says, "If I could procure them [drugs] at a clinic at cost price for a dollar and a half a week instead of paying $150 to $200 a week, I could get a job and avoid dodging the police and spending half my life in jail." The camera cuts back to the doctor who quickly discounts the elderly man's opinion by stating [maintenance] "clinics spread addiction which is dangerously contagious." The doctor then notes that instead of feeding their "appetite for drugs," new psychiatric knowledge offers more promise because this body of knowledge can address the fact that "addicts" suffer from a "weakness in personality that can be corrected" and the "solution to addiction to drugs is curing the addict." The narrator of the film states that "curing the addict" is almost impossible without professional help and that help could be easily provided through the introduction of compulsory treatment in prisons. The narrator then notes that there are no such facilities in Canada and he suggests that new prison wards for compulsory treatment be set up to cure the addict in the future. Thus, the film's narrative firmly rejects narcotic clinics or drug maintenance programs in Canada and the narrator underscores this point by explaining that it is an "offence to supply habitual users drugs." The film also promotes emerging discourses about the role that contagion plays in promoting addiction. The narrator states that it is an "accepted fact that much of addiction begins with contact and associating with addicts." Not surprisingly for the times, rather than examining the social and cultural roots of addiction, addiction is represented in the film as "contagious," and addicts as criminal and pathological.[2]

In another scene, young and old men are depicted in prison. One young white man is shown hearing about heroin from older prisoners while incarcerated. The narrator explains that once he is released from prison he is labeled a convict and he will thus eventually turn to the friendships he made in prison. The narrator explains that it is an "accepted fact that much of addiction begins with contact and association with addicts." Thus, for young people, the "seeds are sown" in prison. Later the young man (all the characters are nameless) is depicted trying heroin with a group of older users. We then see a series of scenes depicting his quick spiral into addiction and crime, such as stealing, to support his habit. He is shown lying in bed; his new girlfriend, who is also an "addict," is in a separate bed next to his. The young man looks contemplative. The narrator makes clear that he is debating whether to use or not, to stop or continue the downward spiral of addiction and crime. The narrator explains that the young man knows all too well what his fate will be if he does not stop, and the camera captures the young man looking over at the sleeping woman in the other bed and the camera rests on her sleeping body. In the film, she embodies both his temptation and his downfall.

The film's sympathy toward young white men newly introduced to a life of crime and addiction is noteworthy. Although a 1947 Department of National Health and Welfare Report on Drug Addiction in Canada challenges RCMP assertions about a wave of youth narcotic use, it does appear that, from 1949 on, more people in their twenties were convicted than before. However, claims about the number of young users seem to be greatly exaggerated (Josie 1947, 19–20, 68). The narrative in *Drug*

Addict can show understanding and even sympathy about the fate of young white male bodies. In contrast, previous media products (such as newspapers and fictive film) that featured the racialized body carried no such concern. In fact it was racialized residents and citizens of Canada who were the impetus for, and suffered the brunt of, early drug legislation in Canada (Boyd, 2008). Any sympathy for the fate of female bodies is similarly absent. The film uses young white male bodies to generate sympathy but to focus this sympathy in such a way that it can be used to advance law-and-order initiatives.

Throughout *Drug Addict* the problem of addiction is repeatedly represented, as are solutions and actions based on the film's diagnosis of the problem (see Bacchi 2009). Near the end of the film, the narrator introduces psychiatry as a profession that can work with criminal justice to provide treatment for some young white men—those new to the world of heroin—in secure psychiatric units in prisons. The narrator argues that in secure psychiatric units, young "addicts" would be separate from long-term criminal addicts in the general prison population. The film's narrator again strongly opposes all forms of drug maintenance treatment for people addicted to narcotics and reasserts the claim that drug maintenance "clinics spread addiction."

FOLLOWING *DRUG ADDICT*

As we know today, law enforcement and control remain the dominant instruments of drug prohibition in Canada. Law enforcement, especially the RCMP, has prevailed as a dominant knowledge producer and enforcer of drug policy in Canada, especially prior to the 1960s. Yet, *Drug Addict* does represent a slight crack in the dominance of law enforcement with the introduction of psychiatry for people addicted to narcotics and the acknowledgment that treatment might benefit some people, especially young white men new to heroin use. However, following the immediate release of the documentary *Drug Addict*, Canadian federal drug policy became harsher. Nevertheless, opposition to the dominance of criminal justice approaches grew in Canada, especially on the west coast.

Although there were already some individuals opposed to Canada's drug policy, the first drug treatment movement emerged in Vancouver, British Columbia, in the late 1940s and early 1950s. The Community Chest and Council of Greater Vancouver's Special Committee on Narcotics was established. Committee chair Dr. Ranta released the Ranta Report of 1952 stating that narcotic addiction was a health rather than a criminal justice matter (Stevenson et al. 1956, appendix A). The committee recommended that provincial narcotic clinics (providing legal drug maintenance) be set up in Canada (Stevenson et al. 1956, appendix A). At that time the recommendations were ignored by both the RCMP and the federal government (Boyd et al. 2009). The Ranta Report also argued that narcotic addition is a "medical problem with definite psychiatric implications" (Stevenson et al. 1956, appendix A), and this belief is expressed in the documentary *Drug Addict.* This approach was echoed in both Canada and the United States, as psychiatrists claimed that addiction to criminalized drugs was a psychiatric disorder as well as a criminal activity (Acker 2002; Stevenson et al. 1956).

In 1954, following the release of *Drug Addict,* law enforcement successfully called for more punitive drug laws and amendments to the Canadian Opium and Narcotic Drug Act. A new offence of "possession for the purpose of trafficking" was introduced and the act further pushed the "burden of proof" of innocence to the accused (however, I am not claiming that these events stemmed from the film). In addition, the Senate Special Committee on Narcotic Drug Traffic was established in 1955. The proceedings of the federal Senate committee commented on drug trafficking around Vancouver, British Columbia, and suggested it was a problem of both "alarming and increasing proportions affecting the youth of our country" (Senate of Canada 1955, 8). The Senate proceedings mostly focused on heroin and cocaine trafficking and made repeated references to criminals and addicts. The committee noted that of the prisoners they consulted at Oakalla Prison Farm in British Columbia, "without exception they all advocated the legalized provision of drugs" (Senate of Canada 1955, 344). In fact, in a more in-depth study at Oakalla from 1953 to 1956, the majority of "addicts" interviewed stated that they would "like to continue to use narcotics, if legally available" (Stevenson et al. 1965, 154). Some of the prisoners who met with the Senate committee were quite "bitter" about the way they were treated in comparison to "medical and professional" addicts in Canada. The prisoners told the Senate committee that the medical and professional addicts were treated differently because they had "sufficient money with which to support their habits" (Senate of Canada 1955, 344).

The Senate committee did not act on the recommendations and grievances expressed by witnesses calling for drug maintenance programs, including prisoners at Oakalla. Similar to the response given to the elderly drug user depicted in *Drug Addict,* the prisoners' insights and recommendations for drug maintenance and narcotic clinic programs were ignored. Instead the Senate proceedings solidified Canada's federal response to criminalized drugs in the 1950s by advocating, once again, heavy penalties and increased enforcement. Although the Senate rejected setting up narcotic clinics, it did recommend that the provinces provide some treatment, but only in the form of abstinence-based programs.

Meanwhile the British Columbia Oakalla Research Project was completed in 1956. The final report of this project is now known as the Stevenson Report. Stevenson, a professor of psychiatry, had already testified to the earlier Senate committee prior to the release of the final report. Stevenson strongly recommended to the Senate that drug maintenance programs not be established in Canada and he provided misleading information about the "British System" in the United Kingdom and the early clinics in the United States (see Stevenson et al. 1956, appendix I). Stevenson was to become a very vocal and influential opponent of the drug treatment movement in British Columbia as well as the recommendations outlined in the Ranta Report for the establishment of narcotic clinics. Stevenson argued that drug addiction is part of a "general personality disorder" and "anti-social tendencies"; thus, he argued that providing narcotic clinics and drug maintenance would not change addicts into mature law-abiding citizens (Stevenson, in Stevenson et al. 1956, appendix H). Rather, Stevenson recommended psychiatric treatment and abstinence from drugs (ibid.). Still, efforts for change were brewing in Canada, especially in the province of British Columbia. The Narcotic Addiction Foundation of British Columbia (TNAFBC) was established in 1955 and by 1958 had set up a small four-bed residential facility for men addicted to narcotics. By 1959, despite opposition to the use of methadone by the Senate committee, TNAFBC began to prescribe methadone to ease withdrawal for some patients (TNAFBC 1967, 2). This was made possible because some of the restrictions on physicians were finally lifted in the Narcotic Control Act of 1957 and 1961, allowing physicians to begin to provide some alternative care and treatments (TNAFBC 1967).

Law enforcement officials had continued to push for new and harsher legislation, resulting in the Narcotic Control Act of 1961. These legislative changes gave Canada the distinction of enacting some of the harshest drug laws of any Western nation (Narcotic Control Act, S.C. 1961, c.35). Drug substitution programs were again firmly rejected by law enforcement officials (Giffen, Endicott, and Lambert 1991, 389). In fact, under the new law anyone convicted of a drug offence could be sentenced to an "indefinite period" in prison to undergo treatment, including up to ten years for first-time offenders (Carstairs 2006, 156), and the first compulsory prison drug treatment ward was set up at Matsqui Institution in British Columbia in 1966, with an emphasis on psychiatric treatment (Williams 1966, 5).

In the same year that Canada enacted the Narcotic Control Act of 1961, it also signed the International Single Convention on Narcotic Drugs. The goal of the international treaty was to eliminate illegal production and nonmedical use of cannabis, cocaine, opioids, and later synthetic pharmaceutical drugs (Room and Reuter 2012). Yet, these goals have still not been realized in Canada or globally. In fact, contemporary researchers argue that international drug conventions have not decreased the drug trade, which is now global. Nor have they reduced addiction or drug use rates (see Room and Reuter 2012). Robin Room and Peter Reuter note that drug prohibition and international conventions have "worsened the human health and wellbeing of drug users by increasing the number of imprisoned drug users, discouraging effective counter measures to the spread of HIV and HCV by injecting drug users, and creating an environment characterized by discrimination and punishment conducive to the violation of drug users' human rights" (2012, 84).

In the late 1960s, Canada and many other Western nations saw a dramatic increase in drug use, especially marijuana use by white middle-class youth, and debates about the role of drugs and their control expanded to include new claims-makers (Martel 2006). Though these debates and their accompanying legislative and policy shifts are outside the domain of this chapter, it should be noted that they affected the course of Canadian drug policy. One of Canada's responses to public debates about increased use of marijuana and other criminalized drugs was the creation of the Canadian Commission of Inquiry into the Non-Medical Use of Drugs (also known as the Le Dain Commission) in 1969 (Commission of Inquiry into the Non-Medical Use of Drugs 1973). The Commission's role was to examine the phenomenon of illegal drugs and make recommendations for domestic and international policy and legislative changes. The commission was critical of law enforcement and recommended that the federal government should help support provincial treatment programs and methadone maintenance programs. Some of these recommendations have been realized in Canada. Examples are the expansion of drug treatment services and the establishment of methadone maintenance programs, now publicly funded, although not universally available throughout Canada (Carter and MacPherson 2013; Luce and Strike 2011).

REPRESENTATION

Drug Addict exemplifies the unchecked ways in which professionals in Canada could make assumptions about the nature of addiction and "addicts" with little public challenge. Even today discussions about the appropriate ways to spend public monies to address substance use issues take place mostly behind closed doors without the input of the people most affected by these policies. Stuart Hall argues that stereotyping occurs when there are extreme "inequalities of power" (2009, 258). He makes clear how power is represented in not only economic or coercive restraint, but by representational practices and stereotyping that are key elements in the "exercise of symbolic violence" commonly expressed in cultural products such as film and other media products (Hall 2009, 258). These practices and stereotyping reduce illegal drug use to a limited set of representational tropes, and thus shape how governments and other institutions regulate and control the lives of their citizens. If we understand that the problem of drug use can be found in the personalities and criminal nature of people who use criminalized drugs, these understandings are then reflected in policy. As the NFB's first documentary on illegal drugs, *Drug Addict* can be understood to contribute to symbolic violence by reiterating old law-and-order discourse, rejecting drug maintenance, and introducing new discourses about criminal and pathological people addicted to, or selling, criminalized drugs. Although we are told that "actual addicts" are acting in scenes in *Drug Addict*, their voices are absent. The lone "addict" depicted in the film who speaks directly into the camera about his experience and the necessity of narcotic clinics is part of a scripted dialogue inserted in the film by the director so that the "expert doctor" can swiftly dismiss such allusions.

Examining reports and research produced in the few years before and after the film's production, we can see that people who used criminalized drugs and were incarcerated in Canada at this time had strong opinions and made recommendations to researchers and government officials when they could. They stated that they were discriminated against and that legal narcotic clinics should be set up. Yet these recommendations were rejected. This dismissal gives us some insight into the incredible marginalization and legal and social discrimination that poor and working-class people who used criminalized drugs in Canada experienced. From a contemporary vantage point, the dissenting voices of people who used criminalized drugs stand out in reports and research produced in the same era. Of course, it is difficult to know with certainty what viewers thought about *Drug Addict* when it was released and whether they sympathized with the lone man recommending narcotic clinics. However, given the fact that the film won a Genie Award in 1949, its sympathy and recommendations toward young white people addicted to illegal drugs must have resonated with some audiences. In addition, the drug treatment movement that emerged in British Columbia in the late 1940s and early 1950s was precipitated by the questioning of official drug policy.

DOCUMENTARY FILM AND DRUG POLICY

By more closely examining the social, legal, and cultural factors that shaped drug policy in Canada from the advent of drug prohibition to the early 1960s, we can better understand the narrative and visual discourses present in *Drug Addict*. The way in which this film identified the problem of drugs and then offered solutions that drew on a hybrid of law enforcement and medical approaches reflects some of the ways that illegal drug use is still viewed in Canada. These discourses also present significant barriers to drug law and policy reform. Acker notes that in order for drug substitution or maintenance programs to take hold, "the idea that addicts' character flaws would prevent them from improving under a maintenance regimen had to be overturned" (2002, 215). This claim holds true in Canada in relation to those people labelled criminal addicts. In Canada, slight shifts in discourse and practice led to the expansion of publicly funded drug treatment programs outside of prison in the late 1960s and early 1970s as new discourses about addiction and treatment emerged. However, negative discourses about the criminal and pathological nature of people who use criminalized drugs (especially heroin and cocaine), producers, and sellers continue today. Their difference and otherness from moral citizens has been marked (Hall 2009, 230). Many of these ideas about the nature of the so-called criminal and pathological "addict" that were apparent in *Drug Addict* still underscore contemporary opposition to drug maintenance and harm reduction programs.

Today, the state along with a wide range of professions including medicine, psychiatry, and social work, together with nonprofessionals like Narcotics Anonymous and drug users themselves, all create discourses about illegal drugs, drug users, drug trafficking, addiction, and crime. They also provide a wide range of services, including harm reduction services throughout Canada. However, since 2006 and the election of the Conservative Prime Minister Stephen Harper, federal drug policy has been reconfigured to a law-and-order mandate that more strongly adheres to the notion of the "criminal addict." Harm reduction initiatives have been rejected and in 2007 responsibility for the management of the National Drug Strategy was moved from Health Canada to the Justice Department and renamed the National Anti-Drug Strategy. In March 2012, the Conservative government also reinforced Canada's long-standing punitive approach to drugs by enacting the Safe Streets and Communities Act, which amends the Canadian Controlled Drugs and Substances Act by introducing mandatory minimum sentences for a number of drug offences. The Federal National Anti-Drug Strategy budget for 2012–2017 also reflects the government's priorities. Health Canada's budget for community initiatives and drug treatment has decreased. In contrast, the budget for the RCMP Drug Enforcement Program and criminal prosecution services increased substantially (Department of Justice Canada 2012). The government also chooses to ignore the positive findings of the NAOMI clinical trial in Canada and other international studies that demonstrate the efficacy of heroin-assisted therapy and safe injection sites. In fact, Canada is the only country that did not continue to provide heroin-assisted therapy (HAT) to its patients following its first clinical trial even though the study demonstrated that HAT improved physical and psychological health (Boyd and NAOMI Patients Association 2013; NAOMI Study 2008). These attitudes and policies ensure that the establishment of permanent narcotic clinics, so keenly supported (even if scripted) by the lone man speaking directly to the camera in *Drug Addict*, remains unrealized in Canada. Despite the present federal government's antipathy toward harm reduction and people who use criminalized drugs, drug reform efforts remain strong in Canada and these efforts are part of a larger global drug reform movement (e.g., Boyd and NAOMI Patients Association 2013; Boyd, MacPherson, and Osborn 2009; Carter and MacPherson 2013; Oscapella and CDPC 2012; Vienna Declaration 2013; Global Commission on Drug Policy, 2011).

Not all documentary films such as *Drug Addict* are state sponsored or institutionally based. Documentary films also provide a social space to resist stereotypical references and to provide alternative discourse and practice. In other words, I argue that documentary film representations are potentially unstable in the meanings they convey about illegal drugs and the people who use them (Boyd 2011, 60). Thus, they have the potential to introduce new discourse, interrogating and contesting dominant representations, or to reiterate old tropes, such as the primacy of criminal justice control.

In this chapter, I conclude that since its inception, Canada's drug policy and practice has been accompanied by symbolic violence; this is commonly expressed in cultural products such as documentary films (and other mediums such as fictive film and print media) (Boyd 2008; Boyd and Carter 2010; 2011). Films can reproduce stereotypical references that work to reiterate social hierarchies and drug prohibition, contributing to a "regime of representation" through which "'difference' is represented at any one historical moment" (Hall 2009, 232). State sponsored films such as *Drug Addict* provide a way to understand the problem of illegal drugs and by extension those groups of people deemed to threaten the security and morality of the nation. The documentary also introduces its audience to a "way of knowing" by professional groups, primarily law agents and, to a lesser degree, psychiatry (see Druick 2007). The film then offers solutions to the problem by these same professionals (see Bacchi 2009). One of the key messages in *Drug Addict* is to ensure that the audience understands that the central "problem" is the drug user, not the laws and policies that prohibit drugs.

The scenes in *Drug Addict* help to cement ideas and images about the nature of people who use, produce, and sell drugs, and the nature of crime and addiction. Viewers are introduced to law enforcement and psychiatric discourses about the criminal and pathological nature of people addicted to criminalized drugs, and the film advocates prison and mandatory psychiatric treatment as solutions to these problems. *Drug Addict* brings to light entrenched institutional discourses and practices about people who use criminalized drugs, along with stereotypes and myths—symbolic violence—that can be easily reactivated. We see this with the current Conservative federal party of Canada and their penchant for punishment and prison as a solution and their vilification of illegal drug users and harm reduction services. The film also provides another lens to understand some of the foundational frameworks of Canadian drug policy such as the dominance of criminal justice, knowledge production and practice, resistance to diverse models of treatment, and the power of representation.

NOTES

1. This chapter is reprinted with permission from *International Journal of Drug Policy* (Elsevier): Boyd, S. 2013. A Canadian Perspective on Documentary Film: *Drug Addict*. *International Journal of Drug Policy* 24: 589–96. The author thanks Elsevier Global Rights Division for a license to reproduce this article.

2. The film also reaffirms discourse about the violent and delusionary nature of cocaine users. The narrator states that cocaine is associated with crime and "violent courage" that is drug induced.

REFERENCES

Acker, Caroline. 2002. *Creating the American Junkie: Addiction Research in the Classic Era of Narcotic Control*. Baltimore: The John Hopkins University Press.

Anslinger, Harry and William Tompkins. 1953. *The Traffic in Narcotics*. New York: Funk and Wagnalls.

Bacchi, Carol. 2009. *Analyzing Policy: What's the Problem Represented to Be?* Melbourne: Pearson Australia.

Boyd, Neil. 1984. "The Origins of Canadian Narcotics Legislation: The Process of Criminalization in Historical Context." *Dalhousie Law Journal* 8: 102–36.

Boyd, Susan. 2008. *Hooked: Drug War Films in Britain, Canada, and the United States*. New York: Routledge.

———. 2011. "Pleasure and Pain: Representations of Illegal Drug Consumption, Addiction and Trafficking in Music, Film and Video." In *The Drug Effect: Health, Crime and Society*, edited by Suzanne Fraser and David Moore, 57–72. New York: Cambridge University Press.

———. 2015. *From Witches to Crack Moms: Women, Drug Law, and Policy*, 2nd ed. Durham, NC: Carolina Academic Press.

Boyd, Susan and Connie Carter. 2010. "Methamphetamine Discourse: Media, Law, and Policy." *Canadian Journal of Communication* 35: 219–37.
———. 2001. "Using Children: Marijuana Grow-ops, Media, and Policy," *Critical Studies in Media Communication* 29: 238–57.
Boyd, Susan, Donald MacPherson, and Bud Osborn. 2009. *Raise Shit! Social Action Saving Lives*. Black Point, NS: Fernwood.
Boyd, Susan and NAOMI Patients Association. 2013. "Yet They Failed to Do So: Recommendations Based on the Experiences of NAOMI Research Survivors and a Call for Action," *Harm Reduction Journal* 10. Accessed June 18, 2013 at www.harmreductionjournal.com/content/10/1/6.
Brecher, Edward and the Editors of *Consumer Reports*. 1972. *Licit & Illicit Drugs*. Boston: Little, Brown & Company.
Campbell, Nancy. 2000. *Using Women: Gender, Drug Policy, and Social Justice*. New York: Routledge.
———. 2007. *Discovering Addiction: The Science and Politics of Substance Abuse Research*. Ann Arbor: University of Michigan Press.
Carstairs, Catherine. 2006. *Jailed for Possession: Illegal Drug Use, Regulation, and Power in Canada, 1920–1961*. Toronto: University of Toronto Press.
Carter, Connie and Donald MacPherson. 2013. *Getting to Tomorrow: A Report on Canadian Drug Policy*. Vancouver, BC: Canadian Drug Policy Coalition. Accessed June 11, 2013 at www.drugpolicy.ca/progress/getting-to-tomorrow.
Commission of Inquiry into the Non-Medical Use of Drugs. 1973. *Final Report*. Ottawa: Information Canada.
Debeck, Kora, Julio Montaner and Thomas Kerr. 2009. "Canada's New Federal 'National Anti-Drug Strategy': An Informal Audit of Reported Funding Allocation." *International Journal of Drug Policy* 20: 188–91.
Department of Justice Canada. 2012. *Supplementary Tables—Horizontal Initiatives—National Anti-Drug Strategy*. Ottawa: Author. Accessed December 24, 2012 at www.tbs-sct.gc.ca/rpp/2012-2013/inst/jus/st-ts03-eng.asp. This data can be compared to the supplementary tables for the 2007–2012 period. Accessed at www.tbs-sct.gc.ca/hidb-bdih/plan-eng.aspx?Org=37&Hi=28&Pl=164.
Druick, Zoe. 2007. *Projecting Canada: Government Policy and Documentary Film at the National Film Board*. Montreal: McGill-Queen's University Press, 2007.
Ferrell, Jeff and Neil Websdale. 1999. "Materials for Making Trouble." In *Making Trouble: Cultural Constructions of Crime, Deviance, and Control*, edited by Jeff Ferrell and Neil Websdale, 3–21. New York: Aldine de Gruyter.
Galliher, John, David Keys, and Michael Elsner. 1998. "Lindesmith v. Anslinger: An Early Government Victory in the Failed War on Drugs." *The Journal of Criminal Law & Criminology* 88: 661–82.
Giffen, P. J., Shirley Endicott, and Sylvia Lambert. 1991. *Panic and Indifference: The Politics of Canada's Drug Laws*. Ottawa: Canadian Centre on Substance Abuse.
Gittings, Chris. 2002. *Canadian National Cinema*. New York: Routledge.
Global Commission on Drug Policy. 2011. *War on Drugs: Report of the Global Commission on Drug Policy*. Accessed December 10, 2013 at www.globalcommissionondrugs.org/reports.
Grayson, Kyle. 2008. *Chasing Dragons: Security, Identity, and Illicit Drugs in Canada*. Toronto: University of Toronto Press.

Hall, Stuart. 1981. "The Determination of News Photographs." In *The Manufacture of News: Social Problems, Deviance and the Mass Media*, Revised ed., edited by Stuart Cohen and Jock Young, 226–43. London: Constable.

———. 2009. *Representations: Cultural Representations and Signifying Practices*. London: Sage, 2009 edition.

Hayword, Keith and Jock Young. 2004. "Cultural Criminology: Some Notes on the Script." *Theoretical Criminology* 8: 259–73.

Hesse-Biber, Sharlene and Patricia Leavy. 2011. *The Practice of Qualitative Research*. London, UK: Sage.

Hewitt, Steve. 2006. *Riding to the Rescue: The Transformation of the RCMP in Alberta and Saskatchewan, 1914–1939*. Toronto: University of Toronto Press.

Hogarth, David. 2002. *Documentary Television in Canada: From National Public Service to Global Marketplace*. Montreal: McGill-Queen's University Press.

Josie, Gordon. 1947. *A Report on Drug Addiction in Canada*. Ottawa, Canada: Department of National Health and Welfare.

Lindesmith, Alfred. 1947. *Opiate Addiction*. Bloomington, IN: Principia Press, 1947.

Luce, Janine and Carol Strike. 2011. *A Cross-Canada Scan of Methadone Maintenance Treatment Policy Developments*. Ottawa: Canadian Executive Council on Addictions. Accessed March 1, 2013 at www.ccsa.ca/ceca/activities.asp.

Martel, Marcel. 2006. *Not this Time: Canadians, Public Policy, and the Marijuana Question 1961–1975*. Toronto: University of Toronto Press.

Melnyk, George. 2004. *One Hundred Years of Canadian Cinema*. Toronto: University of Toronto Press.

Morris, Peter. 1978. *Embattled Shadows: A History of Canadian Cinema, 1895–1939*. Montreal: McGill-Queen's University Press.

Musto, David. 1987. *The American Disease: Origins of Narcotic Control*, expanded edition. New York: Oxford University Press.

NAOMI Study Team. 2008. *Reaching the Hardest to Reach—Treating the Hardest-to-Treat: Summary of the Primary Outcomes of the North American Opiate Medication Initiative (NAOMI)*, 18. Accessed October 17, 2008 at www.naomistudy.ca/documents.html

Narcotic Addiction Foundation of British Columbia. 1967. *A Short History of Narcotic Dependence and Treatment in British Columbia*. Vancouver, BC: Author.

National Film Board. 1948. Royal Canadian Mounted Police (Producers) and Robert Anderson (Director), *Drug Addict*. [Motion picture]. Canada: NFB.

Nolin, Pierre and Colin Kenny. 2003. *Cannabis: Report of the Senate Special Committee of Illegal Drugs*. Toronto: University of Toronto Press.

Oscapella, Eugene and Canadian Drug Policy Coalition Policy (CDCP) Working Group. 2012. *Changing the Frame: A New Approach to Drug Policy in Canada*. Accessed December 10, 2013 at drugpolicy.ca/solutions/publications/.

Room, Robin and Peter Reuter. 2012. "How Well do International Drug Conventions Protect Public Health?" *The Lancet* 379: 84–91.

Senate of Canada. 1955. Senate of Canada Proceedings of the Special Committee on the Traffic in Narcotic Drugs in Canada. Ottawa: Queen's Printer.

Shapiro, Harry. 2003. *Shooting Stars: Drugs, Hollywood, and the Movies*. London: Serpent's Tail.

Solomon, Robert and Melvin Green. 1988. "The First Century: The History of Nonmedical Opiate Use and Control Policies in Canada, 1870–1970," In *Illicit Drugs in Canada* (pre-publication ed.), edited by Judith Blackwell and Patricia Erickson, 88–116. Toronto: Methuen Publications.

Starks, Michael. 1982. *Cocaine Fiends and Reefer Madness: An Illustrated History of Drugs in the Movies*. New York: Cornwall Books.

Steeves, Dorothy. 1977. *The Compassionate Rebel: Ernest Winch and the Growth of Socialism in Western Canada*. Vancouver, BC: The Boag Foundation.

Stevenson, George, Lewis Lingley, George Trasov and Hugh Stansfield. 1956. *Drug Addiction in British Columbia: A Research Survey*. Unpublished manuscript. Vancouver: University of British Columbia.

Stevenson, Jack. 2000. *Addicted: The Myth and Menace of Drugs in Film*. New York: Creation Books.

The Vienna Declaration. Accessed December 10, 2013 at www.viennadeclaration.com/.

Williams, H. R. 1966. *Treatment and Rehabilitation of Drug Users*. Vancouver: BC: The Narcotic Addiction Foundation of British Columbia.

II

JURISPRUDENCE IN INTERNATIONAL FILMS

4

In The Land of Blood and Honey

*What's Fair or Just in Love and War Crimes? Lessons for Transitional Justice**

Carrie Menkel-Meadow

In 1990, the University of California at Los Angeles (UCLA) held a conference on "Probing the Limits of Representation: Nazism and the Final Solution" during which leading international scholars of history, literature, cultural studies, philosophy, critical theory, arts, language, sociology, and psychology explored the question of whether the mass atrocities of Nazism and the Final Solution to exterminate all European Jewry could be represented in anything other than "factual" historical documentation and narrative (Friedlander 1992; White 1992; LaCapra 1996). This was some years after the first documentaries and "fictionalized" films on the Holocaust had appeared, after *Judgment at Nuremberg* (Kramer 1961), but before *Schindler's List* (Spielberg 1993) and after various cultural critics had said such things as "there can be no poetry after Auschwitz" (attributed to Theodor Adorno), and no morally acceptable artistic representation could be made of the Shoah (Friedlander 1992). The conference explored what were then called "limits to representation" of certain "truths," so reprehensible, so mass and, at the same time, so specific or so exceptional (the "German" problem; Maier 1988), that no genre could fully, morally, or "accurately" depict either the systematic evil or the mass pain, death, and injury that is the Holocaust.

As the child of Holocaust survivors, I attended that conference as both scholar and one generation removed "victim," having spent a lifetime listening to my family's stories and seeing many visual images of both their own stories and the larger international one that was World War II.

I could watch some Holocaust movies (*Schindler's List* and *Sophie's Choice*, Pakula 1982) and had to turn away from others (*Life is Beautiful*, Benigni 1998), as I experienced the tension of what representations, in what genres, were "true" to the horror of the experience and what was said or depicted about humanity, in all its horrors, resistances, adaptations, and bravery. I began a lifelong interest in what artistic, documentary, and now digital and other media, can depict about man's inhumanity to man (and woman and child) and for what purposes—redemptive, retributive, documentary, educative, punitive, reconciliative, restorative, or offensive and propagandist.

REPRESENTATIONS OF WAR CRIMES AND DOING JUSTICE

Whatever scholars may think and analyze about the visual depiction of human atrocities and crimes, filmmakers and filmgoers now have created a vast portfolio of documentaries, "true-story" films, fictionalized accounts, short subjects, and even cartoons[1] and graphic novels (*Maus*, Spiegelman 1986), showing the worst of acts that human beings commit against each other—mass murder, rape, torture, beatings, beheadings, assault, injury, burnings, property theft and destruction, and other horrible crimes. Some films depict the acts themselves; others the pain and consequences in their aftermath or after death and destruction; still others depict the now familiar genre form of trials, confrontations, truth telling, and legal sanctions, or the depiction of less lawful acts of revenge and counter-atrocity, now also shown in the dystopias so common in the violence of our modern media world.

As the artistic genres have expanded and proliferated, subject to creative morphing of familiar themes and formats, the law and legal processes, designed to deal with the many ways (new and old) human beings have developed to be cruel to each other, have also expanded, developed, and diversified, to include not only more substantive efforts at policing the boundaries of international crimes (The *Rome Treaty* creating the International Criminal Court) (1998, 2002 in force), but also creating new legal tribunals and different processes which attempt to deal with crimes against humanity, both with more punishment and sanction, but also with more "alternative" genres of processes which hope to reconcile and "restore" nations comprised of perpetrators, victims, and bystanders.

In this chapter I explore what one film, *In the Land of Blood and Honey* (Jolie 2011), has accomplished in demonstrating what popular culture can do to deepen our understanding of international crimes against humanity (by, among other things, depicting specific crimes against women) in their most human and real forms, and what this film suggests we think about when we consider what forms of retributive, reparative, restorative, or transitional justice we should pursue. As popular culture appeals both to the masses and to the individual (telling individual and specific stories), justice and law must also speak to the general polity (the citizens of the world and particular nation-states), as well as to the needs of the specific people, groups, cities and nations affected by criminal acts of inhumanity, whether or not contained by a knowable boundary. Can or should films and other popular cultural forms encourage us to be citizens of the world, responsive to and responsible for the criminal acts that we (both far-away strangers, and closer to home kinsmen) commit against each other? What is the relationship of cultural production to legal or social justice and individual and collective responsibilities?

IN THE LAND OF BLOOD AND HONEY

In the Land of Blood and Honey (a film written, produced, and directed by actress and UN Advisor, Angelina Jolie) is a powerful, painful, sad, brave, and strangely beautiful, filmed representation of so many of the issues raised above. There are and were controversies about the "shooting" of the film, the story it told, the representativeness of the film to the actual events of the Bosnian War, the uses to which it might and could be put, and whether or not it properly educated about and represented reactions to war; ethnic cleansing; rape; war atrocities; Serbs; Bosniaks (Bosnian Muslims); the international (inactive) community; the role of national, subnational, and international law; and myths or stereotypes about all of the above. Heralded and applauded by many (including victims of the rapes and other atrocities depicted) and criticized by others (some victims groups, many Serbs, some women's groups, and many film critics), this film well-illustrates virtually all of the issues in filmic representation of modern atrocities.

This compelling and moving film, using a *Romeo and Juliet* (Shakespeare 1597) forbidden love story in the midst of the Bosnian ethnic cleansing war of 1992–1995, raises the harrowing question of how could these horrific events (rapes, murders, concentration camps, burnings, property destruction, firing squads, and genocides) possibly be happening in 1992–1995 (a modern, post-war, international, anti-genocide legal treaty, and "United Nations" world), after so many legal, cultural, and human claims of "Never Again!"[2] Jolie was reported to have been motivated to make this film by similar incredulity that this horrible war could occur in the modern (and European) post–World War II reality and thought that her film would bring greater attention, both to the horrific events, and to the inaction of the world community, obligated by modern treaty imperatives (*Convention on the Prevention and Punishment of the Crime of Genocide*, 1948) to take action against genocides. The making of the film produced individual and group enmity, opposition by at least one women's victims group, and a halt to filming in Bosnia, as contesting groups argued about its significance and portrayal of perpetrators and victims before, during, and after the film's "shooting" (how ironic a process in a war film!) (Hopkins 2011).

The film tells the (improbable?) story of a relationship between a Bosniak (Muslim) woman, Ajla (Zana Marjanovic), who is a gentle painter, and Danijel (Goran Kostic), a Serbian male police officer, son of the harsh Serbian general, Nebojŝa (Rade Serbedzija), who becomes her captor and protector as the Bosnian war (conducted 1992–1995) leads to mass murders, firing squads, rapes, ethnic cleansing, detention and concentration camps, and massive property destruction. Estimates of the actual harm of this war include over 100,000 dead, a single massacre of eight thousand mostly male Muslims, and displacement of thousands of women and children (Srebrenica 1995), and anywhere from twelve thousand to fifty thousand rapes (Pégorier 2013). The film is located in and around Sarajevo and was filmed on location until the protests of one victims group led to the Bosnian government withdrawing permission for filming and the film moved to Hungary for completion. All of the actors were local, and, remarkably, Jolie (as both writer and director) had the film shot in both English and in local (Serbo-Croatian and Bosnian) languages (by the same local actors) so it could be seen locally and internationally. (This effort at parallel language versions for local and international viewership and "participation" is an exemplar of how parallel international, local, and hybrid tribunals could, but so far, have not, operated. See, e.g., Stromseth, Wippman, and Brooks 2006.)

Ajla and Danijel open the film in a pre-credits prologue with a romantic dance at a seemingly peaceful multicultural bar/café in what we are told is a culturally diverse and peaceful community, before a bomb explodes. Like many scenes in the film, there are clear references to that iconic romance across conflict zones, Shakespeare's *Romeo and Juliet* (1597) (the opening ball where the young lovers meet, act I, scenes 4 and 5, and the dance at the gym in the twentieth-century *West Side Story*, film version, Wise and Robbins 1961). Like the tragic-comedy of *Romeo and Juliet*, scenes of enmity, rivalry, and death in *In the Land of Blood and Honey* alternate with tender scenes of love (and sex) and artful elegance. The bomb shatters the peace of the town and the budding romance of Ajla and Danijel (who is seen dancing with his police epaulets to signal his "official" position), as the lovers are represented as painter and policeman/soldier (art/humanity; softness and femininity; and life vs. order, war, duty, and probable death). Ajla has been seen babysitting for her baby nephew Adi, who will later be killed by Serbian soldiers who toss the baby out of a many-storied modern apartment building (corresponding to the death of Mercutio in *Romeo and Juliet*?). The juxtaposition of the modern (apartment living quarters, color on the walls, in Ajla's paintings, in the women's clothes and jewelry, cars, modern European café life) to the scenes of destruction and war that follow is Jolie's directorial *cri de coeur*—how can this be happening in a post–World War II, modern world?

For those who remember the real scenes of exodus of refugees from the many Balkan wars covered contemporaneously on television news, here are people of the late twentieth-century being killed and tortured and removed from their homes in track and running suits, sneakers, colorful scarves, high heels, holding on to electronics, toys, and what little they can carry from their otherwise normal lives. (I was a tourist in Yugoslavia in 1975 and saw many of the historical and modern buildings later seen damaged or destroyed on the evening news in the 1990s. My Serbian friend at UCLA in the early 1990s complained that the U.S. media were covering only Serbian destruction and not what "the others had done and were doing.") Jolie was criticized for taking a partisan side against the "brutish Serbs" (Hopkins 2011).

In a remarkable set of short sequences, the "history" of conflict in Bosnia-Herzegovina is narrated by one character to another. Danijel's father, the great and merciless general, Nebojŝa Vujovich, recounts the five hundred years of Serbian war with the Turks, the 1914 war, the "one million Serbs who died fighting against Hitler and the Bosniak and Croat enemies,"[3] and the need to "cleanse" the Muslims who "hid their faces" under Tito. There is much talk of oppressive Turk/Muslim rule and later "regaining" 80 percent of some vague territory the Serbs claim as theirs. Though not part of this movie, Nebojŝa also refers to the Battle of Kosovo (1448), to remind us how far back all of this enmity goes. Later Nebojŝa personalizes this history by telling Ajla "her" people (Turks/Muslims) murdered his mother who had worn and dirty hands from working in the fields so that Ajla's women relatives could wear "fine silks." Danijel's grandmother and three uncles were mercilessly killed in a field, while the implication is that the "higher class" Muslim women of their village (Ajla, who has "lady's hands" and is a painter, whose work is on display in the Sarajevo Museum of Art) enjoyed an easy life, at the expense of the lower class and oppressed Serbs. Before the bomb blast which opens the film, Ajla's relatives and friends are seen enjoying a modest middle-class life with beautiful things. Ajla later spends a secretive "night in the (partially destroyed) museum" educating Danijel about art and the beauty of quiet and "empty spaces," reminiscent of the few secret meetings of Romeo and Juliet or Tony and Maria before their respective tragedies (foretelling, for those who know those stories, what is likely to happen to Danijel and Ajla).

The trashed museum and devastated buildings shown in the film (and commonly reported and shown on the nightly news during the Balkan conflicts) vividly portray the complexity of the uses, abuses, and manipulations of the various "pasts" as each group attempts to destroy the artistic, architectural, and religious achievements of its enemies. Using the artistic signs and references of *Romeo and Juliet*, Jolie positions Danijel and Ajla at forbidden windows, escaping and communicating across enemy and prison lines and "borders." Will these lovers be able to transcend the borders of enmity between their people and escape the familiar plot lines of those older stories of forbidden love, while those around them seek to destroy each other's (ethnic) families?

These constant juxtapositions of long-suffering resentments and tribal hostilities in the often narrated cultural/ethnic/national histories, interspersed with interpersonal connections and love scenes, as well as fellow-feeling, are referred to often in many film sequences. In one scene, a brutish Serb soldier interrogating a captured Bosniak (who has just rescued Ajla from her own captivity) recognizes the Bosniak, a baker, as one who "made the best pastries in the town." In another scene, captured Bosniaks cry "we are all Bosnians," hoping to appeal to a higher humanity, rather than to a to-be-slaughtered ethnic and "different" form of being. Ajla tells General Nebojŝa that her father was a Partisan (in World War II fighting against Hitler) and taught her "there were no differences among Serbs, Croats and Muslims." When asked if she is Danijel's enemy she says no—though we see this as both her love and desire for him, and the coerced loyalty he can silently enforce as her lover/captor.

The vast sweep of conflict and history is deftly (in my view) displayed in both battles in the woods, and destroyed cities, and in the interpersonal pain seen in the eyes and cries of the protagonists. Who cannot cry with Ajla's sister, Lejla (Vanessa Glodjo), when her baby is found on the cold snowy ground on which he seems to have been thrown? Who cannot wince when snipers expertly cut down single people walking on a road to escape? The horror of war, and, worse, genocide, when people kill their neighbors and steal their children, wives, and lovers, as well as housing and property, is conveyed in scenes alternating with the ardent love-making of Danijel and Ajla and the all too human honey-colored flesh, surrounded by the red and black blood of wounds inflicted by guns, whips, and grenades.

In the Land of Blood and Honey is a specific tale of the Bosnian war, but it is also one of the first films about such ethnic conflicts and war to put women's particular suffering at its center. Though firing squads, snipers, bomb blasts, and formal modern battles punctuate the film, the horror of rape, beating, and humiliation of women is at the core of this film. At a Christmas celebration of the soldiers, the oldest Muslim women are humiliatingly asked to strip in front of laughing soldiers and their tarted up prostitute escorts—women enjoying the humiliation of other women. In the opening sequences of the film Serbian soldiers select the youngest and prettiest women to be sent to a detention camp to be their servants, cooks, and rape victims. The lines of choice and prisoner selection echo the horrors of the Holocaust's concentration camps and its now vivid depictions in other films, *Sophie's Choice* (Pakula 1982) and *Schindler's List* (Spielberg 1993), to name a few, a now familiar trope of cinematic mimesis for the horrors of ethnic sorting and family separation—lines of (temporarily) spared lives, or torture, beatings, death, forced labor, rape, exploitation, and inhumanity. In an early scene, one woman who volunteers to sew and help the men in order to save her life is asked "do you fuck?" and then is publicly raped in front of the rest of the women, dramatizing what human rights lawyers have fought for for decades—recognition of this specific inhumanity against women. Rape is now a war crime and this war has led to the first formal legal convictions (Franke 2006; Pégorier 2013). Perhaps another "border" has been crossed—formal legal recognition of women's suffered harms in war, but only after we can really *see* it, as in such films.

Like many drawn to the senselessness of group conflict, Jolie uses the device of a "cross-border" love story (Montagues-Capulets, Jets and Sharks, Israeli and Palestinian, Northern Irish Catholic and Protestants [Andrew Lloyd Weber's The *Beautiful Game* (2000), a musical which never made it to the screen]) to show how the human connection of love can sometimes transcend such profound group hatred. But here, too, Jolie has modernized the story. Ajla certainly feels something for Danijel—a powerful sexual attraction, and tenderness, but we never really know if she truly loves him—she is his captive, servant, and portrait painter, he is her (sometimes) protector, though he eventually kills her when he thinks it was her sister who betrayed him (see figure 4.1). (Once again borrowing the tropes of *Romeo and Juliet* and the denouement of *West Side Story* where Anita, Maria's sister, does betray the Jets when a few of them rough her up [a "softer" rape for the 1960s theater and film public?]). Ajla and Danijel have passionate sex, he feeds her, she paints him, she teaches him about art, but all the same she is protected from further abuse only because he has told his men "she is my property!" Like women for thousands of years of human history, Ajla is "protected" as chattel and when Danijel doesn't "get rid of her" as his father orders, she is raped and defiled by one of Nebojŝa's men. At first Danijel can't decide if he has been betrayed by Ajla—who can be trusted in these times of war and conflict?—but eventually he uses his own form of justice—he kills her

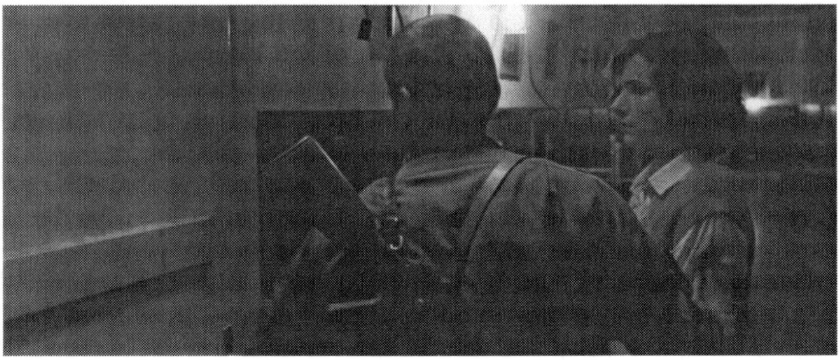

Figure 4.1. Captive, Prisoner, or Lover? *In the Land of Blood and Honey*. Image in the public domain, optimized by Susan Gilbert.

rapist, while the rest of his men continue to abuse Ajla's friends, family, and other women.

Ajla wears the colors of female passivity and beauty, yellow, while in the detention center serving as cook and private servant and later (amazingly, still delicate and clean), she wears white shifts and floating nightdresses, all while being kept in a white room, conjuring up the unreality of the story as a captive princess, a painting (talented) beautiful "ethnic" Rapunzel. Ajla is a captive prisoner of war, and does what she can to survive (who wouldn't?, we seem to be asked) as women have done for thousands of years.

Though some film critics accused Jolie of painting too harsh a picture of the Serbs, Danijel emerges as a complex figure, seen to save a few individuals by refusing to shoot, a reluctant warrior unless he has to fight or is seen by his soldiers, almost, but not quite helpless, before his commanding father, challenging his overly harsh ways, but still seemingly loved by his men, and brutal when he needs to be. Jolie uses these characters to explore the tensions between groupthink and obedience to orders (Danijel is a soldier) and individual choice. Though Ajla spends some time reunited with her "people" in hiding, she does nothing to sabotage her captors when she is recaptured, and is seen lollygagging in relative luxury in her confinement. If the fairytale has a slightly Hollywood shine to it, I prefer to see the fairytale stories of the Brothers Grimm—Ajla occasionally seems a protected princess but she dies a brutal and bloody death at the hand and gun of her lover. The film craftily uses color and beautifully framed scenes to communicate the paradoxical relations of love (honey) and death (blood).

To conclude the film with its anticipated Shakespearean end, Jolie importantly reminds us it is 1995, not 1595, and the law of war and intergroup conflict has changed. Danijel, having killed his lover (having himself been mortally wounded by a bomb sent into a Christian church in which he was hiding), staggers across a bridge or no-man's land to a U.N. peace officer and declares, as he falls to his operatic death, "I am Daniel Vukojovich, I am a war criminal!" Jolie had consulted with Richard Holbrooke, chief negotiator of the Dayton Accords which brought an end to the violence of the Bosnian War, as well as with others who monitored or covered the war for the United Nations, United States, and various media outlets, and so was legally and diplomatically advised in her scriptwriting to conclude the film with a reference to an acknowledged international criminal law declaration of confession and guilt. Is this a filmic version of a "truth" commission that has not occurred in real life?

Some film critics also accused Jolie, who has served as a U.N. Human Rights Advisor for some years, of making a U.N. "anti-war propaganda" film, or worse, a "war-porn" film. Other critics, and some victims, have criticized the film for its improbability or lack of reality or "truth," or cultural exaggeration or stereotyping. Yet, when the film was shown to survivors and victims of the war, many cried or vomited with recognition and the re-living of their experiences; including a group of Bosnian rape victims who thanked her for telling their story (Hopkins 2011).

The film, its pre- and post-production, and as shown by reactions to it, painfully demonstrates just how contested the terrain (both literally and figuratively) is in the "representation" of war crimes and human rights violations. The conflicts about the film parallel many disputes in the fields of international criminal law, transitional justice, and human rights activism—how much should the stories and experiences of individuals be told, shown, acknowledged, and remediated? Do individual stories (testimonies) tell the larger collective "truth"? How do individual stories emerge from group harms and atrocities and collective guilt in trial testimonies, truth commissions, documentaries—should there be room for defenses—individual or collective? Can individual stories depart from the collective truth that emerges in prosecutions, trials, truth and reconciliation commissions, and the many layered international, national, and local justice processes? Must all individual stories conform to a single narrative of guilt and wrongdoing or are more complicated stories of complicity, collaboration, and ethically comprised survival actions permitted to be told? When individual and collective stories about who began the aggression and who is engaging in "self-defense" differ, whose story is allowed to dominate the narrative? (Luban 2015). Does telling the story of individual or group harm encourage human empathy and motivation for reconciliation, or judicially authorized punishment, or does it empower and justify those seeking revenge, or those who glorify or simplify "victimhood" (Fletcher and Weinstein 2016)? Can one victim's story ever tell the whole truth? How much punishment is required to prevent further crimes? What is the role or possibility of "honey" or forgiveness, apology, reconciliation or simple, difficult, but nonviolent, co-existence in the aftermath of such mass atrocity?

As international law practitioners and scholars debate and practice with an ever-increasing set of new processes and institutions, films like *In the Land of Blood and Honey* can help us see the dilemmas and multiple layers of truth and meaning, and emotions that complicatedly inhabit the multiple realities of such complex stories.

CONFLICT IN THE FORMER YUGOSLAVIA: BOSNIA HERZEGOVINA AND THE LAND OF "BLOOD AND BELONGING"

The events depicted in *In the Land of Blood and Honey* are a smaller, but brutal, part of the larger conflict of the post-1989 fall of the Soviet Bloc and disintegration of the former Yugoslavia. The indicted, but dead-before-finally-convicted at the International Criminal Court, dictator Serbian Slobodan Milošević, had planned a successor state to the former Yugoslavia, in which he hoped to be the new Tito, a new nation, dominated by ethnic Serbs, in a land comprising much of what is now Serbia, Bosnia-Herzegovina, Kosovo, and portions of Croatia. Milošević was known to have masterminded many of the Serbian-committed atrocities in the Balkan wars of the 1990s, including the first conflict between Serbs and Croatians (1991–1992) (Ignatieff 1993), the Bosnia conflict partially depicted in this film (1992–1995), and the later conflicts in Kosovo (1998–1999) (Hagan 2003). In the communist days of Tito's rule it was illegal to call oneself a "Serb," "Croat," "Slovenian," or "Bosnian"—a punishable crime of "nationalism" and "chauvinism"—all citizens were communist Yugoslavs. With the fall of the Berlin Wall and the demise of the Soviet bloc (and Tito's earlier death in 1980), the forced "unity" of Yugoslavia returned to ancient and enduring nationalisms of the Orthodox Serbs, identifying with the Byzantine, sometimes Turkish and also Slav, identifying often with the Ottoman Empire; the Croatians calling themselves Catholic and European (and identifying with the Austro-Hungarian empire); and the Bosniaks, a smaller Muslim community in its loyalty. The Balkans were the fissure points for the older rivalry of the Ottoman and Austro-Hungarian empires, supposedly put down by the post–World War I, new boundaries drawn by victors of that war, but undermined two decades later in complex loyalties to different sides of the Allied-Axis powers of

World War II (calling each other genocidal Croat "Ustashe assassins" and Serbian "Chetnik [pro-Hitler] beasts").

As Michael Ignatieff recounts in his field-defining book and TV series, *Blood and Belonging* (book 1993; BBC TV Series 1993), the Freudian "narcissism of small differences" helped define identity politics of the region, so that one was a Croat by "not being a Serb" and vice versa: "Without hatred of the other, there would be no clearly defined national self to worship and adore" (Ignatieff 1993, 22). In fact, over fifty years of ethnic peace had reigned in the post–World War II country of Yugoslavia. Many historians insist that the civil wars of the 1980s and 1990s are fabricated or "refabricated" versions of Western European–bred ethnic and nationalist myths, borrowing from more ancient and contested battles, symbols, and religious differences, many which lay fallow and irrelevant to other problems and issues under Tito's enforced unity regime. Milošević was successful in stirring up a latent Serbian nationalism to counteract the Tito dictatorship which had attempted to accommodate, unify, and dominate the different ethnicities scattered within different areas of the nation's boundaries. The Balkans may be said to be "Balkanized" in part because the relevant land areas had more diverse, rather than totally homogenous populations, living together in complex geopolitical space. Civil wars developed in part because in each area "minority" groups have cohabited with whatever self-styled "majority" group controlled different areas.[4] Economic resentment fueled ethnic animosity as the richer Slovenian and Croatian regions believed themselves to be paying for the more "backward" Serbs and Bosnians (note here that similar economic resentment fuels a so-far more peaceful set of conflicts between Flemish and Walloon ethnic groups in Belgium) (Mnookin and Verbeke 2009).

For some commentators, the second modern Balkan war, the Bosnia-Herzegovina conflict, began as a continuing proxy of the Serbian-Croatian civil war (1991–1992) which led to the division of those two regions into two separate countries, "at the expense of the Bosnian Muslims" (Ignatieff 1993, 28), the war which is featured in *In the Land of Blood and Honey*. The territories comprising Croatia, Serbia, and Bosnia-Herzegovina saw some of the worst partisan and World War II fighting. Conflicts over numbers killed in concentration camps which imprisoned and murdered Jews, Roma (Gypsies), Serbs, and Communists continue to this day. From 1992 to 1995 the region saw the worst violence since World War II as "minority" Serbs fought both Croats and Bosniak (Muslims) for territory, possible unification with Serbia, and committed heinous crimes, including mass murders, rapes, assassinations, genocides, dislocations and removals, kidnapping, separation of families, detention in concentration camps, and massive property destruction (accounting for more than 90 percent of the war crimes charged and prosecuted at the International Criminal

Tribunal for the Former Yugoslavia, though a smaller group of Croatians and Bosniaks were also prosecuted) (Waller 2002). Proxies and outside fighters, including some German and Austrian neo-Nazis on the Croatian side, Greeks and Russians on the Serb side, and Muslims on the Bosniak side, fueled local devastation as an arms embargo supported by Europe and the UN tended to favor the Serbs, still armed by the former Yugoslav army resources.

The war finally ended after NATO and U.S. intervention (unilateral cessation of arms embargo to those fighting the Serbs) in 1995 with the conclusion of the Dayton Accords, negotiated by Assistant Secretary of State for the United States, Richard Holbrooke, with land partition, U.N. peacekeeping forces, and an uneasy peace, still reflected in complex political and on-going conflicts. Prosecutions for war crimes (of genocide, crimes against humanity, and for the first time, "mass or genocidal" rape) in the newly created International Criminal Tribunal for the former Yugoslavia (located in the Hague) began even before the hostilities were concluded. International lawyers and scholars still debate whether the conflict should be classified as a civil war or international war (depending on how the roles of sovereign Serbia and Croatia and their respective leaders are analyzed). For those who died, were brutally harmed, became refugees, or lost their physical and mental health, these international law categories may matter little. Many claim impunity continues and others claim disparate, discriminatory, and targeted prosecutions, and are used in the continuing politics of the new nations created by the conflicts.

Thus, film may more accurately depict the reality of human harms and pain, which law may not be able to fully remedy with its legal rules, evidentiary and categorical demands, and limited human and material resources. *In the Land of Blood and Honey* is only one of many films made about this war, including other American-made films, *The Peacemaker* (Leder 1997), and *The Hunting Party* (Shepard 2007); British productions, including *Welcome to Sarajevo* (1997), part of the BBC's popular *Prime Suspect* series, part 6 (Hooper 2003); and the Bosnian directed and Oscar-winning *No-Man's Land* (2001), a tragic-comedic look at the absurdities of war, man-made boundaries, and humanitarian law. Documentaries have been made, both about the events of the war, and some of the activity of the International Criminal Tribunal for the Former Yugoslavia in The Hague, and memoirs and books continue to be written about the war and its ongoing human tolls, see, for example *Zlata's Diary* (Filipović 2006) and Frederick Forsyth's *The Avenger* (2003).

The land depicted in the film is surely a land soaked with blood for decades at a time. It is also a land soaked with stories, both true and false, of different versions of the partisan versus fascist and now communist versus nationalist pasts. Lands soaked in conflicts will continue to tell different stories of the past to motivate present conflicts and violence, with the hope of literally "cementing" the future. (Consider the conflicting origin stories of Palestine-Israel and the "facts on the ground" of illegal settlements in the West Bank.)

The devastating violence of the Balkan Wars has many geopolitical explanations. There is the failure of Tito to build a successful succession; a weak single-party communist succession failed here as elsewhere in the former Soviet bloc. A potential democracy never took hold as the failed, multi-ethnic state imploded (despite the fact, that here, as in the similarly, but more quickly devastated, Rwanda, there was plenty of intermarriage, as suggested by the opening scene of *In the Land of Blood and Honey*—Ajla's sister helps her get ready for her date with a Serb, so dating and the promise of marriage in the future seem possible). The failure to attend to economic inequalities allowed demagogues like Miloŝević to substitute identity politics for a more differentiated problem-solving politics. Western euphoria over the fall of communism failed to take sufficient account of the consequences of the very "self-determination" and nationalist principles written into the founding documents of the post–World War II period, including the U.N. Charter (thus accounting for delay in interventions to prevent the genocides also prohibited by the treaties of the new world government). Political critics suggest that the United States and other Western powers were too obsessed with their own economic success in the early 1990s, and the continued memory of the losses of Vietnam to make good on antigenocide promises in modern treaties. The documentary *Ghosts of Rwanda* (Barker 2004) and the only slightly fictionalized *Hotel Rwanda* (George 2004), collect, in one PBS-produced documentary and a Hollywood film, the repeated and shameful attempts of Secretary of State Madeline Albright, President Clinton, and the various U.N. representatives to avoid using the "g" word ("genocide"), which might require them to take action as promised in the Genocide and Geneva Convention treaty-based obligations. American and European politicians, international law and foreign policy leaders, and academics struggled over the meanings and obligations of newer doctrines of "humanitarian intervention" (Gibbs 2009) and the "responsibility to protect," all as nightly news coverage, documentaries, and "fictionalized" films like *In the Land of Blood and Honey* (made later, after the carnage was more or less completed, but not yet fully accounted for) made all too real the human costs of wars and conflicts in the era after war was thought to be a thing of the past (Fukuyama 2006).

Whatever the causes of the many recent post–Cold War conflicts (I have always been a multicausal scholar and citizen), the advent of modern film, TV, cell phone, and digital photography, such as YouTube postings, has captured the horrors of wars, crimes against humanity, and human rights violations with an immediacy and vividness beyond even the newsreels of World War II[5] and Vietnam,[6] in my view, playing an integral role in the modern human rights movement's successful campaign for international legal and extralegal actions and reforms. Although the modern "transitional justice" movement was initially born out of the end of the South American dictatorships in Chile, Argentina, Brazil, Uruguay, Bolivia, and Paraguay (Teitel 2000; 2014), the terrible conflicts of Eastern Europe and Africa (particularly, but not exclusively the Rwandan genocide), and the more peaceful end to apartheid in South Africa (Gibson 2004), led to the development of new institutions for retributive justice and criminal prosecutions (the International Criminal Tribunal for the former Yugoslavia 1993; the International Criminal Tribunal for Rwanda 1994; and, eventually, the International Criminal Court 2002 (as yet unratified by United States), as well as more varied transitional justice processes in truth and reconciliation commissions (Hayner, 2011) and indigenous, local, as well as hybridized, courts (combined international and local courts, e.g., in Timor Leste, Cambodia, and Sierra Leone), and indigenous community processes (Stromseth 2003). These new institutions and processes have now produced a rich practical and scholarly literature for assessing their claims and controversies, which has begun to be documented in both reality-based and fictionalized films.

Some of the material presented in *In the Land of Blood and Honey* can help us understand the aspirations (in individual connections) and dangers (in collective grudge holding and uses of past histories) of both these formal prosecutorial justice institutions and the more informal and differently motivated truth and reconciliation commissions and other restorative processes. In fact, as the power of film and differently told stories demonstrates, to know the past is not to prevent its repetition (cf. Santayana 1905 "those who cannot remember the past are condemned to repeat it")—the uses of the past can be harnessed for punishment and deterrence, but also for revenge and retribution (Subotić 2009). The challenge is to determine what can be accomplished for both individuals and collectivities in not forgetting, but knowing and memorializing the past (Buckley-Zistel and Schäfer 2014), while victims, survivors, and successor polities have to decide what can be forgiven, what must be punished, and what must be done to heal, reconcile, or at least move forward with some hope for peaceful cohabitation.

LESSONS FOR AND FROM TRANSITIONAL JUSTICE IN POST CONFLICT SETTINGS

The tensions presented in *In the Land of Blood and Honey* between individual cross-ethnic love stories and collective atrocities reflect many of the controversies in the field of transitional justice today. The war crimes committed during the Balkan wars led to the establishment of the first international criminal tribunal, following the military tribunals of World War II in Nuremberg and Tokyo. Though many human rights advocates had argued for a permanent International Criminal Court earlier, the politics of the Cold War made the development of such an institution impossible (Goldstone and Smith 2008). The Rome Treaty of 1998 has now established an International Criminal Court with jurisdiction over defined war crimes, crimes of genocide, and crimes against humanity and aggression (now including rape and violence against women, thanks to the efforts of advocates following the Balkan wars, Bassiouni 1996; Nikolić-Ristanović 1999; Bell and O'Rourke 2007; Koenig 1994; Stiglmayer 1994; Yarwood 2013), but the United States is not a party, having not ratified the treaty.

When the atrocities of the actions in the former Yugoslavia came to light, even Russia and China joined the Security Council resolutions that led to the establishment, first of the International Criminal Tribunal for the Former Yugoslavia (1993) and then one year later after the Rwandan genocide (1994), the establishment of the International Criminal Tribunal for Rwanda (located in Arusha, Tanzania). The motivations behind these courts (which share a common appeals tribunal) were to use formal trial procedures (a hybrid of common law and civil law procedures and rules) to make public evidence of war crimes and crimes against humanity (genocide, ethnic cleansing, rape, targeted killings, kidnappings, forced deportation, serious bodily harm, imprisonment, torture, and other defined crimes) for international publicity, knowledge, and punishment, with the purposes of both retributive justice and deterrence. Today as these courts begin to transfer their activities, after twenty years of multinational and international legal prosecutions, to local courts, they are often criticized for their complexity, their enormous costs, and their inability to totally eliminate the impunity of crimes against humanity, as civil wars continue, especially in many African nations. (The ICC is now often criticized for indicting only African war criminals.) Appeals have been won, releasing some defendants, and reducing sentences for other Yugoslav war criminals. Milošević, denouncing the "victor's justice" of the tribunal in an unruly act of self-representation, managed to die before he was convicted, thus leaving no formal public adjudication of his responsibilities for many of the atrocities in the Balkan wars. Many of the worst perpetrators of war crimes remain at large, both in the former Yugoslavia, and in various African states. Furthermore, the effects of a court located in another country (the Netherlands or Tanzania), rather than near the scenes of the crimes, have permitted political exploitation of a critique of claimed "international elite victor's justice" with ongoing political conflicts at home (fueling continued Serbian nationalism and appeals to victimhood and discrimination in several of the new countries with Serbian populations). Most importantly, the international criminal tribunals, while recognizing crimes against, and committed by, groups of people, have continued the individualization of wrongdoing, through the cult of personality (both in defendants and legal leadership). In many cases, denial of culpability by individuals for their actions belies what many in the international human rights community feel are collective wrongs. At least modern international criminal law now allows actions against groups and organizations, as well as the now precedented indictment of sovereign leaders (a modern departure from sovereign immunity doctrine).

The end of the Balkan wars (more or less) coincided with at least four other major developments in global (dis)ordering—the end and increasing democratization of countries with former military dictatorships (1970s–1980s) in much of Southern and Central America (Argentina, Bolivia, Brazil, Chile, Paraguay, Peru, Uruguay, Guatemala, El Salvador, and Honduras, among others), the more or less peaceful end to apartheid in South Africa, the end of the political genocide of the Pol Pot regime in Cambodia, and a repetitive cycle of violent civil wars and struggles in Africa. A fifth global political earthquake in the "Arab Spring" now also raises significant issues of transitional justice (see *The Square*, Noujaim 2013). These varied historical developments, all with their own documentary and filmic portrayals (see appendix A: Filmography for a sample) spawned the new legal field of "transitional justice" (Teitel 2000; U.N. Rule of Law and Transitional Justice in Conflict and Post-Conflict Societies, Secretary-General Report 2004), with different processes and institutions to deal with movements away from violence into a new (if not clearly defined) "transitional" political order, including truth and reconciliation commissions (Hayner 2011; Gibson 2004; Minow 1998); hybrid international and local courts (Stromseth 2003) and use of indigenous "justice" and restorative healing processes, such as *gacaca* in Rwanda and *ubuntu* in Southern Africa (Menkel-Meadow 2007).

These new institutions and processes have often pitted conflict resolution and peace-seeking practitioners and scholars against, or in some conflict with, human rights and international criminal law advocates. Several new nongovernmental organizations (NGOs), such as Alliance for Peacebuilding and the Public International Law and Policy Group in Washington, DC, work in both fields and seek to "mediate" some of the issues in the controversies between formal prosecutorial accountability (seeking justice), and less formal and varied peace seeking reconciliation processes (seeking peace, cessation of violence or gentler reparative processes). The Balkan conflicts have actually spawned very little in the way of informal reconciliation processes. *In the Land of Blood and Honey* suggests that peace and reconciliation will not come easy to these lands (now comprising many different countries with continued heterogeneous populations). It would be interesting to compare intermarriage rates from the former Yugoslavia to the new countries of Serbia, Croatia, Bosnia-Herzegovina, and Kosovo (and Montenegro). How many Ajla and Danijel couplings have been successful, outside of the magic world of film?

This important new field of international criminal law and transitional justice now has its own set of competing goals, purposes and controversies (Leebaw 2008; Olsen, Payne, and Reiter 2010; Menkel-Meadow 2015), as one tries to imagine which of these might be useful or appropriate in the killing fields of Bosnia, including:

- *Prosecutions (international as in ICTFY, national—Bosnian courts or hybrids, as in special courts in Cambodia)*: Establishing "truth" and documenting mass harms and atrocities, whether by formal trial and evidentiary rules or
- *Truth and Reconciliation processes and commissions:* Acknowledgement of pain and suffering through victim testimonies in more informal "truth" commissions, in order to establish
- *Accountability* (individualized or collective): Identification of and naming of perpetrators, those responsible for actions, with either
- *Apology:* Formal verbal or written statements of perpetrators to victims and larger public acknowledging guilt and often narrating detailed information about crimes committed not known or acknowledged before and expressing regret, or
- *Amnesty:* Formal agreement not to prosecute (either through formal legal enactments, as in Chile and Argentina, now withdrawn in many cases, (Lessa, Olsen, Payne, Pereira, and Reiter 2014), or through process of TRC, following apology, as in South Africa) or with
- *Punishment*: Formal sanction, including detention (no more than thirty years and no death penalty in modern international tribunals) or
- *Lustration, purging, or "vetting":* Removal of perpetrators and guilty from ongoing governmental functions, with hopes of
- *Deterrence and prevention* of similar acts in the future ("never again"), and
- *Individual healing* (through cathartic/psychological/therapeutic and emotional processes, whether confrontational or narrative, either in formal tribunals or through individual psychiatric or social work, paid by the state) and
- *Reconciliation and collective healing* with varying degrees of

- *Forgiveness:* Actions by victims to understand and provide a moral "pardon" to the perpetrator. Forgiveness does not require "forgetting" the acts but allows victims and perpetrators to reconcile and co-inhabit the same society without ongoing and potentially explosive animosity; whether nonvictims or witnesses or other members of the harmed society, can or should "forgive" is a continuing issue (Margolit 2004); and
- *"Resolution":* of ongoing conflicts (or at least peaceful "management" and prevention of ongoing conflicts), with varying degrees of
- *Restoration and "remediation"* of physical, economic and emotional well-being, including both *"restorative justice"* and *"reparative justice,"* with varying degrees of economic, property or other compensation and
- *Memorialization* of past harms and education for prevention of future harms, through museums, memorials, artistic expressions, commemoration events, celebrations, holidays, street, and property naming and
- *Peacebuilding* efforts, through formal UN and international forces or civil society, NGO and local peace groups, with
- *Reformulation and reframing* of national/group narratives and histories, through both formal historical and narrative projects or NGO and civil society activities; and more controversially,
- Development of *"rule of law"* (rather than rule *by* law) in new constitutional commitments, new governmental structures, with more formal accountability and judicial independence (too often modeled on western "path dependence"), and
- *Democratization* and increased participation of all groups within the political order, in hopes of
- *Prevention of future mass atrocity and systemic violence* through both individual and collective learning and *"re-integration."* (assuming there was prior "integration").

These varied and many goals of transitional justice contain obvious tension points and potentially conflicting purposes: Can there be punishment and reconciliation, remembrance and forgiveness, compensation and remediation, and reintegration, all at the same time? Will all victims of the same atrocity or harm want the same processes (trials and punishment, truth and reconciliation commissions, healing circles) or outcomes (compensation, apology and forgiveness, or retribution)?[7] How can any restorative process fully compensate for destroyed lives, seized land and property, and changed boundaries? Can transitional justice offer a more complex menu of choices for new nations and for diverse victims, often with very different religions, social, political, and psychological value systems and needs?

Transitional justice has been unable to avoid the challenges of "distributive" scarce sum conflicts with limited resources (land, money, water, jobs, and positions), with continued allegiance to zero-sum identity conflicts, rather than focusing on future, multicultural, and regenerative or integrative new narratives and collaborative conditions on the ground. The claimed goals of some forms of transitional justice are, in fact, potentially in opposition to each other: Can there be a single "truth" in any contested conflict, without shared adjudicators or witnesses? Might accountability, lustration, and punishment lead to more waves of revenge seeking, rather than to reconciliation and healing? Will collective accountability prevent or encourage individual responsibility taking? Will efforts at "memorialization" lead to more, not fewer, conflicts as the past is revisited and partisanly retold, rather than transcended?

In the Land of Blood and Honey raises these issues, without resolving them, for the educated student of transitional justice theory and practice:

- Does knowing the past (Battle of Kosovo, Partisan vs. Fascist fighting in World War II, as told by those in conflict) explain, exacerbate, or pacify the differences among peoples? Knowing the past seems to perpetuate conflict here.
- Does group suffering build walls of hurt, wound, and insularity of group victimhood to prevent the connections of individuals from different groups? (Why does the *Romeo and Juliet/Tony and Maria/Ajla and Danijel* story get told in so many group conflict stories for so many centuries?)[8] When does reconciliation beyond the individual levels of love and even intermarriage between groups really happen? Was the Yugoslavian period under Tito really an "integrated" society? Could it ever be again after what we have witnessed and seen here?
- Will the particular suffering of women in war zones and crimes against all of humanity, including women and children (now finally recognized in international law [Franke 2006; Fineman and Zinsstag 2013]) be fully accounted for and redressed in formal justice institutions or not (Andrews 2012; Brown and Ni Aoláin 2014)? Is a female filmmaker's intervention in filmmaking enough to make up for the continued gendered structure of both formal and informal transitional justice (in theory and practice), as many have argued? (Charlesworth and Chinkin 2000; Copelon 1994). Does seeing these transgressions against women in the film encourage outrage and activism in response or depressed passivity and hopelessness?

- Does the tragedy of massive devastation and individual pain (and the "star-crossed lovers'" deaths) inspire us to prevent, repair, restore, and reconcile in conflict zones or to despair that human beings will ever learn to simply live and let live?
- Can individuals ever escape their chosen or imposed group identity?
- What is the relationship of individual to group agency in the commission of acts of grievous wrongs or kind and generous acts of humanity and empathetic fellow-feeling? (Menkel-Meadow 1992).

In the Land of Blood and Honey does not answer these questions; indeed, its sad conclusion with the death of the lovers and mass destruction and murder, with continued conflict, seems only to lead to a sense of helplessness and despair that human beings will ever really be able to get over their differences. Yet, I think Angelina Jolie made this film to contribute to the struggles for international human justice. Her hope (and mine), I believe, is that if we use film to depict human depravity and injustice (Blum 2004), we will work for its end—whether through formal legal accountability in international tribunals or through the less formal and "softer" versions of human contact, connection, and even forbidden love. We continue to tell and film these stories of conflict-ridden, ill-fated love affairs, and human relationships for their emotional power and hope they will spur action and response; at the same time as those of us who are lawyers continue to search for and design new legal and social processes for accountability, and hopes for reconciliation and new legal orders. If we can learn from seeing the human costs of violent conflict through film and other media representations, as I believe we can, from many different "truths" and points of view, then I think that popular representations of human rights violations and war atrocities are, in fact, another way to represent the continuing quest for legal, as well as human, justice. Jolie's film helps to represent the particular harms suffered by women in conflict zones, in a manner that is compelling and cathartic for some of its victims, as well as inspirational for those human rights advocates who seek to make real, as well as dramatize, the pain and loss that real people feel, across the globe, to many of us who may not read law books, watch the news, or who, fortunately, will never endure these crimes. It is possible, indeed, it is necessary, to "represent," in popular culture, great harms and pictures of man's inhumanity to man, so we can see them with our own eyes, and hopefully take action to end them forever. Each filmic and popular cultural representation of these criminal acts is another effort to make "Nunca mas! or "Nie wieder Krieg!" a more likely reality for future generations.

APPENDIX A: FILMOGRAPHY

Some Transitional Justice/Human Rights Films

Africa

Attenborough, Richard (director). 1987. *Cry Freedom* [Motion Picture]. United Kingdom: Marble Arch Productions.
August, Bille (director). 2007. *The Color of Freedom* [Motion Picture]. United States: Banana Films.
Barker, Greg (director and producer). 2004. *Frontline: Ghosts of Rwanda* [Documentary]. United States: Frontline PBS.
Boll, Uwe (director). 2009. *Attack on Darfur* [Motion Picture]. United States: Event Films; Pitchblack Pictures.
Caton-Jones, Michael (director). 2005. *Beyond the Gates* [Motion Picture]. United Kingdom, Germany: BBC Films; CrossDay Productions Ltd.
Chadwick, Justin (director). 2010. *The First Grader* [Motion Picture]. United Kingdom: BBC Films; UK Film Council.
——— (director). 2013. *Mandela: Long Walk to Freedom* [Motion Picture]. United Kingdom and South Africa: Videovision Entertainment; Distant Horizon; Film Afrika Worldwide.
Cohen, Rebecca Richman (director). 2010. *War Don Don* [Motion Picture]. Netherlands: Racing Horse Productions.
George, Terry (director). 2004. *Hotel Rwanda* [Motion Picture]. United States: Lions Gate Entertainment; United Artists.
Gibson, Angus and Menell, Jo (directors). 2014. *Mandela* [Motion Picture]. South Africa and United States: Clinica Estetico; Island Pictures.
Hoffmann, Deborah and Reid, Frances (directors). 2000. *Long Night's Journey into Day* [Motion Picture]. Australia: Reid-Hoffmann Productions.
Hormann, Sherry (director). 2009. *Desert Flower* [Motion Picture]. Germany: Desert Flower Filmproductions.
Laufer, Erez and Laufer, Miri (directors). 2012. *One Day After Peace* [Motion Picture]. Israel: Erez Laufer Films.
Lipper, Joanna (director and producer). 2014. *The Supreme Price* [Motion Picture]. United States: Vertunmus Productions.
MacDonald, Kevin (director). 2006. *The Last King of Scotland* [Motion Picture]. United Kingdom and Germany: DNA Films; Film 4.
Noyce, Phillip (director). 2006. *Catch a Fire* [Motion Picture]. France: StudioCanal.
Zwick, Edward (director). 2006. *Blood Diamond* [Motion Picture]. United States and Germany: The Bedford Falls; Virtual Studios; Initial Entertainment Group.

Anti-War (General)

Ashby, Hal (director). 1978. *Coming Home* [Motion Picture]. United States: Jerome Hellman Productions.
Coppola, Francis Ford (director). 1979. *Apocalypse Now* [Motion Picture]. United States: Zoetrope Studios.

Ignatieff, Michael (director). 1993. *Blood and Belonging* [Motion Picture]. United Kingdom: BBC Television.

Weir, Peter (director). 1981. *Gallipoli* [Motion Picture]. Australia: Associated R&R Films.

Asia

Annaud, Jean-Jacques (director). 1997. *Seven Years in Tibet* [Motion Picture]. United States and United Kingdom: Mandalay Pictures.

Attenborough, Richard (director). 1982. *Gandhi* [Motion Picture]. United Kingdom, India, United States: Goldcrest Films.

Besson, Luc (director). 2011. *The Lady* [Motion Picture]. France: EuropaCorp.

Briski, Rana and Kauffman, Ross (directors). 2004. *Born into Brothels: Calcutta's Red Lights Kids* [Documentary]. United States and India: Red Light Films.

Forster, Marc (director). 2007. *The Kite Runner* [Motion Picture]. United States: Sidney Kimmel Entertainment; Participant Productions; Paramount Classics.

Hansen, Renè Bo (director). 2009. *Eagle Hunter's Son* [Motion Picture]. Germany, Sweden, Denmark: Stomberg Productions; Eden Film.

Joffé, Roland (director). 1984. *The Killing Fields* [Motion Picture]. United Kingdom: Goldcrest.

Lemkin, Rob and Sambath, Thet (directors). 2009. *Enemies of the People* [Motion Picture]. Cambodia and United Kingdom: Old Street Films.

Nosheen, Habiba and Schellmann, Hilke (directors). 2013. *Outlawed in Pakistan* [Motion Picture]. Pakistan and United States: H2h Films.

Oppenheimer, Joshua and Cynn, Christine (directors). 2012. *The Act of Killing* [Motion Picture]. Norway, Denmark, United Kingdom: Final Cut for Real.

Europe

Gavras, Costa (director). 1969. *Z* [Motion Picture]. Algeria and France: Office National pour le Commerce et l'Industrie Cinématographique.

Goldberg, Andrew (director and producer). 2006. *The Armenian Genocide* [Documentary]. United States: Oregon Public Broadcasting.

Jolie, Angelina (director, writer, and producer). 2011. *The Land of Blood and Honey* [Motion Picture]. United States: GK Films.

Kondracki, Larysa (director). 2010. *The Whistleblower* [Motion Picture]. Canada, Germany, United States: Samuel Goldwyn Films.

Sakler, Madeleine (director). 2013. *Dangerous Acts Starring the Unstable Elements of Belarus* [Motion Picture]. United Kingdom: Great Curve Films.

Sheridan, Jim (director) 1993. *In the Name of the Father* [Motion Picture]. Ireland, United Kingdom, United States: Hell's Kitchen Films.

Tanović, Danis (director). 2001. *No Man's Land* [Motion Picture]. France: Noé Productions.

Winterbottom, Michael (director). 1997. *Welcome to Sarajevo* [Motion Picture]. United Kingdom: Damian Jones; Channel Four Films; Miramax.

Latin America

Campanella, Juan José (director). 2009. *El Secreto De Sus Ojos* [Motion Picture]. Argentina: Tornasol Films; Haddock Films; 100 Bares.

Farnsworth, Elizabeth and Leverton, Patricio Lanfranco (directors). 2008. *The Judge and the General* [Motion Picture]. United States: West Wind Productions and Independent Television Service (ITVS).

Gavras, Costa (director). 1982. *Missing* [Motion Picture]. United States: PolyGram Filmed Entertainment.

Kreuzpaintner, Marco (director). 2007. *Trade* [Motion Picture]. United States: VIP Medienfonds 4; Centropolis Entertainment.

Larraín, Pablo (director). 2012. *No!* [Motion Picture]. Chile: Fabula; Participant Media; Canana

Polanski, Roman (director). 1994. *Death and the Maiden* [Motion Picture]. United States, United Kingdom, France: Capitol Films; Channel Four Films (based on a play by Ariel Dorfman).

Puenzo, Luis (director). 1985. *The Official Story* [Motion Picture]. Argentina: Historias Cinematograficas Cinemania.

Toledo, Sérgio (director). 1991. *One Man's War* [Motion Picture]. United Kingdom: Channel 4.

Zeka, Alessandra and Kahn, Holen Sabrina (directors). 2014. *A Quiet Inquisition* [Motion Picture]. United States: Adrenaline Films.

Middle East

Abu-Assad, Hany (director). 2005. *Paradise Now* [Motion Picture]. Palestine, France, Germany, Netherlands, Israel: Augustus Films.

Avni, Ronit and Bacha, Julia (directors). 2006. *Encounter Point* [Motion Picture]. United States: Just Vision Films.

Barbeau-Lavalette, Anaïs (director). 2012. *Inch'Allah* [Motion Picture]. Canada: micro_scope.

Bolado, Carlos, Goldberg, B. Z., and Shapiro, Justine (directors). 2001. *Promises* [Motion Picture]. United States: Promises Film Project.

Daccache, Zeina (director and producer). 2013. *Scheherazade's Diary* [Motion Picture]. Lebanon: Catharsis.

Doueiri, Ziad (director). 2012. *The Attack* [Motion Picture]. Lebanon, France, Qatar, Belgium: 3B Productions.

Fox, Eytan (director). 2004. *Walk on Water* [Motion Picture]. Israel: Israeli Film Fund.

Ghobadi, Bahman (director). 2004. *Turtles Can Fly* [Motion Picture]. Iran, France, Iraq: Mij Film Co.; Bac Film.

Hood, Gavin (director). 2007. *Rendition* [Motion Picture]. Unites States: Anonymous Content; New Line Cinema.

Labaki, Nadine (director). 2011. *Where Do We Go Now?* [Motion Picture]. Lebanon: Les Films Des Tournelles.

Mayer, Michael (director). 2012. *Out in the Dark* [Motion Picture]. Israel: M7200 Productions.

Noujaim, Jehame (director) Karim Amer (producer). 2013. *The Square* [Motion Picture]. Egypt and United States: Noujaim Films.
Nowrasteh, Cyrus (director). 2008. *The Stoning of Soraya M* [Motion Picture]. United States: Mpower Productions.
Riklis, Eran (director). 2008. *Lemon Tree* [Motion Picture]. Israel: Heimatfilm.
Villeneuve, Denis (director). 2010. *Incendies* [Motion Picture]. Canada: micro scope.

Legal Processes

Stevens, Barry (director). 2011. *The Prosecutor* [Motion Picture]. Canada: White Pine Pictures.

World War II—Holocaust

Gavras, Costa (director). 1989. *Music Box* [Motion Picture]. United States: Carolco Pictures.
Kramer, Stanley (director). 1961. *Judgment at Nuremberg* [Motion Picture]. United States: Roxlom Films, Inc.
Pakula, Adam J. (director). 1982. *Sophie's Choice* [Motion Picture]. United States: ITC Entertainment.
Spielberg, Steven (director and producer). 1993. *Schindler's List* [Motion Picture]. United States: Amblin Entertainment.

NOTES

*With thanks to Aleksander Danielyan for research assistance and Robert Meadow for comments and good counsel.

1. As I complete this chapter, twelve cartoonists at the Paris based *Charlie Hebdo* publication have been murdered for their satiric depictions of religious and political material, demonstrating that the "borders" of representation and reality have in fact dissolved in a cruel and inhumane act. Representations clearly have "real" in the world consequences and no art form, including cartoons, humor, satire, is safe from the consequences of its expression. Destruction of lives and representations and "speech" as well as bodies is a particularly modern form of man's inhumanity to man. The UN Council on Human Rights is currently exploring investigations of specific cases for further development of international standards for the human right of freedom of expression and opinion (www.ohchr.org/EN/Issues/FreedomOpinion/Pages/OpinionIndex.aspx).

2. "Never again" ("nunca mas") has been the mantra, post–World War II and following the end of the military dictatorships in South America of the 1970s and 1980s, to express the international cry that genocides, mass killing, and war atrocities should never happen again, after what we have learned from the atrocities

of the Holocaust and the international legal machinery established by the United Nations and now the International Criminal tribunals, as well as the many Truth and Reconciliation Commissions (Hayner 2011), following modern conflicts. Actually pacifist movements since before World War I have used the phrase. The German artist Käthe Kollwitz was famous for her harrowing anti-war drawings (she lost a son in war), "nie wieder Krieg"—never again war! (de.wikepedia.org/wiki/K%C3%A4the_Kollwitz).

3. This is likely an inaccurate statement. According to Michael Ignatieff, many Serbs fought on Hitler's side; see Michael Ignatieff, *Blood and Belonging: Journeys into the New Nationalism* (1993) at 19.

4. Recall that India, separated from Pakistan, for religious reasons, still has one of the largest Muslim populations in the world. In absolute numbers there are almost as many Muslims in India as Pakistan, though as a percentage of the population Muslims are less than 15 percent of the population in India and over 95 percent of the population in Pakistan. Many regions of the world share the issues of nonhomogenous majority-minority cohabitation. If we do not solve the problem of intergroup (multiple identity) peaceful co-existence, we are doomed. See Amartya Sen, *Identity and Violence* (2007).

5. The classic genre of the international criminal trial, *Judgment at Nuremberg* (1961) included film clips of the liberation of German concentration camps in 1961 for viewing by a whole new generation who had not seen newsreels contemporaneously with the end of World War II.

6. *Apocalypse Now* (Coppola 1979), *The Deer Hunter* (Cimino 1979), and *Coming Home* (Ashby 1978) were probably the first films to bring the Vietnam War cost home to Americans on both sides of the debate about the legitimacy of the war and likely contributed to the growing reluctance in the American polity to "intervene" in other regions of the world.

7. The Ariel Dorfman play and film, *Death and the Maiden* (Polanski 1994; Luban 1998) is a superb rendition of how individual desires for retribution and punishment may not align with a successor state's need to "move on," trying to account for the past, create a new just regime and reconcile the nation's past with its future. Though a "fictional" story, the text is clearly rooted in the issues faced by both the Chilean and Argentinean truth and reconciliation, and now much delayed prosecution stories (see Lessa, Olsen, Payne, Pereira, and Reiter 2014).

8. In a new twist to the different group love story, a recent Israeli film portrays the (fatal) love story of two gay male lovers from both sides of the Palestine/Israel divide, *Out in the Dark* (Mayer 2012).

REFERENCES

Andrews, Penelope. 2012. *From Capetown to Kabul: Rethinking Strategies for Pursuing Women's Human Rights.* UK: Ashgate.

Ashby, Hal (director) and Jerome Hellman (producer). 1978. *Coming Home* [Motion Picture]. United States: United Artists.

Asimow, Michael, Kathryn Brown, and David Ray Papke (eds.). 2014. *Law and Popular Culture: International Perspectives.* Newcastle-on-Tyne: Cambridge Scholars Publishing.

Barker, Greg. 2004. "Ghosts of Rwanda." *Frontline* [Television Documentary]. Washington, DC: Public Broadcasting Studios.

Bassiouni, Cherif. 1996. *Sexual Violence: An Invisible Weapon of War in the Former Yugoslavia.* Chicago: International Human Rights Institute.

Bell, Christine and C. O'Rourke. 2007. "Does Feminism Need a Theory of Transitional Justice?" *International Journal of Transitional Justice* 1: 23–44.

Benigni, Roberto (director). 1998. *Life is Beautiful* [Motion Picture]. Italy: Miramax.

Blum, Carolyn Patty. 2004. "Film, Culture and Accountability for Human Rights Abuses." In *Law and Popular Culture,* edited by M. Freeman. Oxford: Oxford University Press.

Brown, Kris and Fionnuala Ni Aoláin. 2014. "Through the Looking Glass: Transitional Justice Futures through the Lens of Nationalism, Feminism and Transformative Changes." *International Journal of Transitional Justice* (forthcoming). University of Minnesota Research Paper No. 14-48.

Buckley-Zistel, Susanne and Stefanie Schäfer (eds.). 2014. *Memorials in Times of Transition.* Cambridge: Intersentia.

Charlesworth, Hilary and Christine Chinkin. 2000. *The Boundaries of International Law: A Feminist Analysis.* UK: Manchester University Press.

Cimino, Michael (director and producer). 1978. *The Deer Hunter* [Motion Picture]. United States: EMI, Columbia Pictures and Universal Pictures.

Comisión Nacional sobre la Desparición de Personas (CONADEP). 2006. *Nunca Mas!* 8th ed. Buenos Aires: Argentina: Eudeba.

Convention on the Prevention and Punishment of the Crime of Genocide. 1948. U.N.T.S. 277, 28 I. L.M. 754, Dec. 9, 1948. (US ratified, with reservations, Nov. 25, 1988; entered into force on January 12, 1951.)

Copelon, Rhonda. 1994. "Surfacing Gender: Re-engraving Crimes Against Women in Humanitarian Law." *Hastings Women's Law Journal* 5: 243–266.

Coppola, Francis Ford (director and producer). 1979. *Apocalypse Now* [Motion Picture]. United States: United Artists.

Dargis, Manohla. 2011. "In a Fractured Society, Ethnic War Kindles Both Hatred and Desire." *New York Times.* December 22.

Delage, Christian and Peter Goodrich (eds.). 2013. *The Scene of the Mass Crime: History, Film and International Tribunals.* London: Routledge.

Filipović, Zlata. 2006. *Zlata's Diary: A Child's Life in Wartime Sarajevo.* New York: Penguin Press.

Fineman, Martha Albertson and Estelle Zinstagg (eds.). 2013. *Feminist Perspectives on Transitional Justice: From International and Criminal to Alternative Forms of Justice.* Cambridge, UK: Intersentia.

Fletcher, Laurel E. and Harvey M. Weinstein. 2016. "Transitional Justice and the "Plight" of Victimhood." In *Research Handbook on Transitional Justice,* edited by Dov Jacobs. Northampton, MA: Edward Elgar.

Forsyth, Frederick. 2003. *The Avenger.* New York: Macmillan.

Franke, Katherine. 2006. "Gendered Subjects of Transnational Justice." *Columbia Journal of Gender and Law* 15(3): 813–28.

Freeman, Michael (ed.). 2005. *Law and Popular Culture, Current Legal Issues, Vol. 7.* Oxford: Oxford University Press.

Friedlander, Saul (ed.). 1992. *Probing the Limits of Representation: Nazism and "the Final Solution."* Cambridge, MA: Harvard University Press.

Fukuyama, Francis. 2006. *The End of History and the Last Man.* New York: Free Press.

General Assembly Resolution A/50/329. 1995. *Human Rights Questions: Human Rights Situations and Reports of Special Rapporteurs and Representatives—Rape and Abuse of Women in the Areas of Armed Conflict in the Former Yugoslavia.* 4 August 1995. UN DOC A/50/329.

George, Terry (director and producer). 2004. *Hotel Rwanda* [Motion Picture]. United States: Lionsgate United Artists.

Gibbs, David. 2009. *First Do No Harm: Humanitarian Intervention and the Destruction of Yugoslavia.* Nashville: Vanderbilt University Press.

Gibson, James L. 2004. *Overcoming Apartheid: Can Truth Resolve a Divided Nation?* New York: Russell Sage Foundation.

Goldstone, Richard J. and Adam M. Smith. 2008. *International Judicial Institutions: The Architecture of International Justice at Home and Abroad.* London: Routledge.

Hagan, John. 2003. *Justice in the Balkans: Prosecuting War Crimes in the Hague Tribunal.* Chicago: University of Chicago Press.

Hayner, Priscilla. B. 2011. *Unspeakable Truths: Transitional Justice and the Challenge of Truth Commissions,* 2nd edition. New York: Routledge.

Hooper, Tom (director) and David Boulter (producer). 2003. *Prime Suspect 6* [Motion Picture]. United Kingdom: Granada Television (Linda LaPlante, writer and creator).

Hopkins, Valerie. 2011. "Angelina Jolie Touched Our Souls—Bosnia's Rape Victims Have Their Say." *The Guardian.* Dec. 15.

Ignatieff, Michael. 1993. *Blood and Belonging: Journeys into the New Nationalism.* New York: Farrar, Straus and Giroux.

Jolie, Angelina (director, writer and producer). 2011. *In the Land of Blood and Honey* [Motion Picture]. GK Films.

Koenig, K. 1994. "Women and Rape in Ethnic Conflict and War." *Hastings Women's Law Journal* 5: 129–42.

Kramer, Stanley (director and producer). 1961. *Judgment at Nuremberg* [Motion Picture]. United States: United Artists.

LaCapra, Dominick. 1996. *Representing the Holocaust: History, Theory, Trauma.* Ithaca: NY: Cornell University Press.

Leder, Mimi (director) and Walter Parkes (producer). 1997. *The Peacemaker* [Motion Picture]. United States: DreamWorks.

Leebaw, Bronwyn Anne. 2008. "The Irreconcilable Goals of Transitional Justice." *Human Rights Quarterly* 30: 95–118.

Lessa, Francesca, Tricia D. Olsen, Leigh A. Payne, Gabriel Pereira, and Andrew Reiter. 2014. "Overcoming Impunity: Pathways to Accountability in Latin America." *International Journal of Transitional Justice* 8: 75–98.

Luban, David. (1998). "On Dorfman's *Death and the Maiden*." *Yale Journal of Law & the Humanities,* Vol. 10(1): Article 3.

———. 2016. "When Not to Fight." In *Oxford Handbook of the Ethics of War*, edited by Helen Frowe and Seth Lazar, forthcoming. New York: Oxford University Press.

Maier, Charles S. 1988. *The Unmasterable Past: History, the Holocaust and German National Identity.* Cambridge, MA: Harvard University Press.

Margolit, Avishai. 2004. *The Ethics of Memory.* Cambridge, MA: Harvard University Press.

Mayer, Michael (director). 2012. *Out in the Dark* [Motion Picture]. Israel.

Menkel-Meadow, Carrie. 1992. "Is Altruism Possible in Lawyering?" *Georgia State Law Review* 8: 385–419.

———. 2007. "Restorative Justice: What Is It and Does It Work?" 3 *Annual Review of Law and Social Science* 10.1–10.27 (Annual Reviews, Palo Alto, California).

———. 2015. "Process Pluralism in Transitional/Restorative Justice: Lessons from Dispute Resolution for Cultural Variations in Goals beyond Rule of Law and Democracy Development (Argentina and Chile)." *International Journal of Conflict Engagement and Resolution* 3(1): 3–32.

Minow, Martha. 1998. *Between Vengeance and Forgiveness: Facing History after Genocide and Mass Violence.* Boston: Beacon Press.

Mnookin, Robert and Alain Verbeke. 2009. "Persistent Non-Violent Conflict with no Reconciliation: The Walloons and Flemish in Belgium." *Law & Contemporary Problems* 72: 151–86.

Nikolić-Ristanović, Vesna (ed.). 1999. *Women, Violence and War: Wartime Victimization of Refugees in the Balkans.* Budapest: Central European University Press.

Noujaim, Jehane (director) and Karim Amer (producer). 2013. *The Square* [Motion Picture]. Egypt: Noujaim Films.

Olsen, Tricia D., Leigh A. Payne and Andrew Reiter. 2010. *Transitional Justice in Balance: Comparing Processes, Weighing Efficacy.* Washington, DC: United States Institute of Peace.

Pakula, Alan (director and producer). 1982. *Sophie's Choice* [Motion Picture]. United States: ITC Productions. Universal Studios.

Papke, David Ray, Christine Alice Corcos, Peter Henry Huang, Lenora P. Ledwon, Diane Mazur, Carrie Menkel-Meadow, Philip N. Meyer, Binny Miller, and Sean O'Brien. 2012. *Law and Popular Culture: Text Notes and Questions,* 2nd edition. (Ch. 14 International Law) LexisNexis.

Pégorier, Clotilde. 2013. "Denial, Impunity and Transitional Justice: The fate of female Rape Victims in Bosnia and Herzegovina," In *Women and Transitional Justice,* edited by Lisa Yarwood, chapter 6. London: Routledge.

Polanski, Roman (director). 1994. *Death and the Maiden* [Motion Picture]. United States, United Kingdom, France: Capitol Film: Fine Line Features (based on a play by Ariel Dorfman).

Pulver, Andrew. 2012. "*In the Land of Blood and Honey*-Review." *The Guardian.* London: February 10.

Rome Statute of the International Criminal Court (ICC) adopted by the United Nations Diplomatic Conference of Plenipotentiaries on the Establishment of an International Criminal Court on 17 July 1998, UN Document A/CONF. 183/9 (1998) (in force, ratified 2002).

Santayana, George. 1905. *The Life of Reason. Vol. 1: Reason in Common Sense.* New York: Prometheus Press (1998, Great Books of Philosophy).

Sen, Amartya. 2007. *Identity and Violence: The Illusion of Destiny.* New York: W.W. Norton.
Shakespeare, William. 1597. *Romeo and Juliet.* London: Arden Shakespeare, 2nd edition (Gibbons, ed. 1980).
Shepard, Richard (director) and Mark Johnson (producer). 2007. *The Hunting Party* [Motion Picture]. United States: The Weinstein Company.
Spiegelman, Art. 1986. *Maus.* New York: Pantheon.
Spielberg, Stephen (director and producer). 1993. *Schindler's List* [Motion Picture]. United States: Amblin Entertainment.
Statute of the International Criminal Tribunal for the Former Yugoslavia, (ICTFY) adopted on 25 May 1993 by Resolution of the Security Council, UN Document S/RES/827 (1993).
Statute of the International Criminal Tribunal for Rwanda (ICTR) adopted on 8 November 1994 by Resolution 955 of the Security Council, UN Document S/ RES/ 955/1994.
Stiglmayer, Alexandra (ed.). 1994. *Mass Rape: The War Against Women in Bosnia-Herzegovina.* Lincoln, NB: University of Nebraska Press.
Stromseth, Jane (ed.). 2003. *Accountability for Atrocities: National and International Responses.* Boston, MA: Martinus Nijhoff Publications.
Stromseth, Jane, David Wippman, and Rosa Brooks. 2006. *Can Might Make Rights: Building the Rule of Law After Military Intervention.* Cambridge: Cambridge University Press.
Subotić, Jelena. 2009. *Hijacked Justice: Dealing with the Past in the Balkans.* Ithaca, NY: Cornell University Press.
Tanović, Daniel (director and producer). 2001. *No-Man's Land* [Motion Picture]. Bosnia-Herzegovina: Ocean (France) and United Artists (US) distribution.
Teitel, Ruti G. 2000. *Transitional Justice.* New York: Oxford University Press.
———. 2014. *Globalizing Transitional Justice: Contemporary Essays.* Oxford: Oxford University Press.
United Nations Security Council. 2004. *The Rule of Law and Transitional Justice in Conflict and Post-Conflict Societies. Report of the Secretary General.* New York: United Nations. S/2004/616.
United Nations Security Council. 1993. *Resolution 827.* 25 May 1993, UN DOC 8/ RES827 (expressing concerns about reports of mass rapes of women in Bosnia).
Waller, James E. 2002. *Becoming Evil: How Ordinary People Commit Genocide and Mass Killing.* New York: Oxford Univ. Press.
Weber, Andrew Lloyd and Ben Elton. 2000. *The Beautiful Game* [Musical Play]. London: The Really Useful Group.
White, Hayden. 1992. "Historical Emplotment and the Problem of Truth." In *Probing the Limits of Representation,* edited by Saul Friedlander, 37–53. Cambridge, MA: Harvard University Press.
Wise, Robert and Jerome Robbins (director and producer). 1961. *West Side Story* [Motion Picture]. United States: United Artists.
Winterbottom, Michael (director) and Damien Jones (producer). 1997. *Welcome to Sarajevo* [Motion Picture]. United Kingdom: Miramax
Yarwood, Lisa (ed.). 2013. *Women and Transitional Justice: The Experience of Women as Participants.* London: Routledge.

5

Multifocal Judgment, Intersecting Legal Proceedings, and Conservativism

A Separation and *Rashomon*[1]

Orit Kamir

Law movies typically feature champions of justice—archaically dignified, like Gregory Peck's 1962 Atticus Finch (*To Kill A Mockingbird*, Pakula 1962) or bitterly disillusioned, like George Clooney's 2007 Michael Clayton (*Michael Clayton*, Clooney 2007), these champions are often what I have labeled "hero-lawyers" (Kamir 2009; 2012). Cinematic hero-lawyers embody natural justice combined with the law of the land. Often reluctantly, they come to the rescue, serving the law by doing "the right thing" at any cost. Their crusades are heroic, lonely, against all odds; but inherent integrity, loyalty, superior professional legalism, and unconditional devotion to the cause secure their moral victory, personal growth, and sometimes social acknowledgment. The hero-lawyers' terrain is the adversarial world of the Anglo-American common law.

While hero-lawyer movies are by far the most familiar and popular law-films, this chapter explores a different, non-Anglo-American format. Its focus is *A Separation*, Asghar Farhadi's (2011) Iranian movie—a powerful, Oscar winning law-film that does not even feature a lawyer. While following and presenting legal proceedings—in fact, two court cases—it exhibits none of the familiar law-film motifs. It portrays no victims or villains, no reluctant, reclusive heroes, or dramatic, adversarial courtroom battles. No one comes to the rescue; no justice is procured. It is very hard to assess whether any personal growth may be detected.

A Separation was warmly acclaimed and achieved great success including winning the Academy Award for Best Foreign Language Film in 2012, and the Golden Globe for Best Foreign Language Film. And yet, when I asked law students about their impression, they admitted to have found it difficult to follow or decipher. While touching them, the movie had left them puzzled and frustrated. They seemed to lack a key to access it. In response to that lack of access, in this chapter, I suggest that *A Separation* follows a path unexplored by most American law-films, but famously paved by Akira Kurosawa's renowned 1950 Japanese law-film, *Rashomon* (Jingo 1950). I propose that reading *A Separation* against the backdrop of *Rashomon* highlights an underlying structure shared by both films, revealing their unique "multifocal judgment" and "intersecting legal proceedings."

The second part of this chapter considers what I suggest we call "multifocal judgment." Both *Separation* and *Rashomon* offer judgmental perspectives and engage their viewers in judgment in complex ways. In both, judgment focuses on the characters of "husband" and "wife." These characters judge each other, are both judged against another, parallel couple, and most importantly, viewers are explicitly invited to partake in judging them. Many law-films engage in what I have referred to in previous works as socializing audiences to judgment (Kamir 2005a, 268); *Separation* and *Rashomon* share uniquely sophisticated structures of judging marital partners. Yet both films also undercut their judgmental zeal with equal sophistication and success.

The third part of this chapter unravels the "intersecting legal proceedings" of both films. Each presents two legal or legal-like proceedings. The intersection of these proceedings reveals much of the film's jurisprudential insight. In *Rashomon*, the intersection of criminal and lay proceedings (one held in a courtyard and the other at the Rashomon gate) highlights the advantages of the latter, social, informal proceeding. The lay "tribunal" of citizens reviews the evidence that was earlier examined by the criminal court, but, in the process of making social sense, relies on additional evidence (that was not available in the official proceeding) and resorts to common sense. Besides passing judgment, this procedure leads to redemption and rectification. *Separation* intersects criminal and family law proceedings, demonstrating the limited capacity of the criminal proceeding to grapple with the messy realities of human psychology and relationships. Concomitantly, the clear-cut accusations formed by the criminal law define and clarify the muted, sometimes suppressed grudges and resentments that muddle the waters of the more loosely formed family law procedure.

The fourth part of this chapter reveals the disguised (conservative) gender politics that underlie both movies, their silent acceptance of traditional honor norms (at the expense of full embrace of equal dignity), and the universalistic (rather than concrete political) nature of their social critiques.

Finally, in the conclusion, I map this chapter in terms of the three focal themes of my larger law-and-film endeavor: the analysis of law-films as social devices that induce audiences to engage in judgment; the exposé of popular jurisprudence suggested by law-films to their audiences; the illustration of law-films' mirroring of some social functions carried out by legal systems (Kamir 2005a).

With worldwide success, both *Rashomon* and *Separation* have become part and parcel of an international culture. It is in this context that the chapter examines them as remarkably influential law-films.

PART I: FILM SYNOPSES

A Separation

A Separation opens in a courtroom, in which Simin (Leila Hatami), an eloquent young woman in a modern garment and a minimal head cover, is pleading for divorce. She generously admits that her husband Nader (Peyman Moaadi) is a good, decent husband and father to their daughter Termeh (Sarina Ferhadi). Her grounds for petitioning divorce are that Nader has retracted from his previous willingness to leave Iran and settle in a country in which Termeh would enjoy more freedom. Nader, a soft-spoken young man, claims that he cannot leave his elderly father behind, since his father suffers from dementia, and Nader is responsible for him. The judge, who is never shown onscreen, finds Simin's request for divorce unfounded.

Simin packs her belongings and leaves Nader's (father's) apartment, despite the heart-wrenching pleas of both her father-in-law and daughter. With Simin's help, Nader hires a very conservatively dressed woman who, accompanied by her young daughter Somayeh (Kimia Hosseini), begins to take care of his father. The woman, Razieh (Sareh Bayat), is in desperate need of the income, and accepts the job despite the dread that her husband would prohibit it were he to discover she undertook such employment. She is deeply disturbed upon discovering that Nader's father is incontinent, and that she must help him dress and undress. From a conversation that Razieh holds in the living room with Termeh's teacher, we learn that she is pregnant and in need of medical care.

One afternoon, as Nader and Termeh return home, they find Nader's father injured, having fallen from his bed while tied to it. Startled, they attempt to revive him, as Razieh and her daughter return to the apartment. Furious, Nader fires Razieh, who was not supposed to have left his father alone, and even less so tie him to the bed. When Razieh returns to ask for her day's wage and insists on her right to receive it, he demands that she leave, and pushes her out, slamming the apartment door in her face. Later that night Simin is notified that Razieh has been hospitalized, and when she and Nader arrive at the hospital to visit her, they learn that she has miscarried. At the same time, Razieh's hot-blooded husband, Hojjat (Shahab Hosseini), realizes that Nader had employed his wife without his consent, and assaults him.

Razieh and Hojjat file a complaint against Nader, accusing him of having caused Razieh's miscarriage by shoving her forcefully out of the apartment, which resulted in her tumbling down the stairs. Nader is arrested and only Simin's intervention releases him on bail. He claims not to have known that Razieh was pregnant, and to have pushed her so mildly that it could not have possibly caused her fall. In turn, he files a complaint against Razieh, accusing her of neglecting her duties toward his father and causing his injuries and mental regression. The investigation of both allegations is carried out by an examining magistrate in a setting that seems to be a busy, crowded police station. The magistrate repeatedly asks Nader whether he overheard the conversation in which Razieh told Termeh's teacher of her pregnancy. In a dramatic scene, the judge interrogates Termeh. Termeh, who earlier confronted Nader on this point, knows that he was indeed privy to the women's conversation. Yet she adheres to his version, apparently believing him that in the moment of heat, when he pushed Razieh, he was oblivious to her state. Visiting Nader's residence, the magistrate examines whether Nader could have pushed Razieh hard enough to cause her fall down the stairs. Nader seems to prove that his action could not have precipitated the plunge.

Throughout the period of investigation, Hojjat repeatedly stalks Termeh, acting violently and threatening the girl and her teacher. Simin, horrified, is willing to pay Hojjat off in order to protect Termeh from him, but Nader refuses, arguing that it would make him look culpable. He accuses Simin of cowardice, while she accuses him of dishonesty and of risking his daughter's well-being.

Finally Nader consents, and, together with Simin, comes to Hojjat and Razieh's apartment. In the presence of witnesses (Hojjat's debtors) Nader seems willing to pay damages, if Razieh swears that he is indeed responsible for her miscarriage. Razieh refuses to swear. She discreetly confesses to Hojjat and his sister (as she did earlier to Simin) that a day prior to the dramatic clash with Nader, his father had left the apartment unnoticed; crossing the street to fetch him, she was hit by a passing car, and felt that the fetus might have been injured. Razieh fears that if she swears, as Nader demands, that he had caused the miscarriage, her false invocation of God's name might cause harm to her daughter. Hojjat demands that she swear, assuming responsibility for her guilt. But Razieh remains adamant.

The last scene returns the viewer[2] to the family courtroom. We learn from the invisible judge that Nader has consented to Simin's petition for divorce, and that both parents have left the custody decision to Termeh. With tears in her eyes, Termeh answers the judge that she has reached a decision, but prefers to give it to the judge in private. Simin and Nader leave the courtroom, the camera joining them. Termeh's decision is presumably rendered to the judge but not to the viewer, who is left to agonize in the corridor with Simin and Nader, separated by a glass door.

Rashomon[3]

Rashomon presents three men—a woodcutter (Takashi Shumura), a priest (Minoru Chiaki), and a commoner (Kichijiro Ueda)—who run into each other seeking shelter from the rain at the decaying Rashomon gate. Together they review testimonies delivered earlier during a legal proceeding that took place at the police courtyard. The judicial, criminal proceeding investigated the death of a samurai (Masayuki Mori), which occurred in a forest clearing, following a sexual encounter between the samurai's wife (Machiko Kyo) and an outlaw, Tajōmaru (Toshiro Mifune). Both woodcutter and priest were present at the courtyard, testified at the criminal proceeding, and heard the testimonies delivered by the outlaw, the samurai's wife, and the samurai's ghost. Deeply affected by the case, the woodcutter and the priest beseech the commoner to help them unravel the meaning of the event. Trapped by the rain, the commoner consents.

The woodcutter narrates to the commoner (through flashback) the testimony given by the outlaw in the courtyard. The outlaw admits to having slain the samurai after "taking" his wife. Four extended flashback-within-flashback scenes, representing his story on-screen, conjure up his courtyard narration. The outlaw recounts how, having glimpsed the angelic woman, he tricked the samurai into following him to a clearing in the wood, where he attacked and tied him up. We see him drag the horrified woman to the clearing, where she grabs her dagger and attacks the outlaw fiercely and skillfully. After a struggle, the outlaw "takes her." Then, he reveals, the woman demanded that the men fight over her. Accepting her proposal, the outlaw releases the samurai and the two engage in a lengthy, professional, heroic duel that leads to the samurai's honorable death.

Through a flashback to the courtyard, the priest at the Rashomon gate relates to the commoner the woman's testimony. The woman testifies that after the outlaw's departure, she rushed to the bound samurai, sobbing and throwing her arms around him. Through flashback-within-flashback we see how, encountering nothing but cold hatred and spite, she releases the samurai, offers him her dagger and demands that he kill her. Then, the dagger still in her hands, she faints. The woman says that awaking, she saw the dagger stabbed in her dead husband's chest. She claims that she then tried to drown herself in a pond, but failed.

At the gate, the commoner remarks: "Women lead you on with their tears. . . . They even fool themselves. Now, if I believed what she said I'd be really confused." The priest resumes his flashback narration, now of the dead man's testimony as delivered in the courtyard through a female medium. The dead samurai's version is presented as flashback-within-flashback. After the sexual encounter, the outlaw persuades the woman to follow him and leave her husband. But she insists that the outlaw kill the samurai first. Horrified by her cruelty, the outlaw asks the samurai what to do with his traitorous wife, but the woman escapes; the outlaw chases her. The samurai remains immobile, weeping and heartbroken. Then we see him grab the dagger and stab himself.

At the gate, the woodcutter paces up and down, proclaiming there was no dagger, but a sword. The commoner talks him into admitting what he really saw as he arrived at the scene of the crime. In the woodcutter's flashback narration, the woman is lying on the ground, weeping, while the outlaw beseeches her to come with him, promising to do anything for her and threatening to kill her if she refuses. In response, the woman replies that the men should fight over her, and that she would follow the winner. But the samurai refuses, denouncing the woman, and so the outlaw too loses interest in her. Accusing both men of cowardice, the woman incites them to fight to prove their manhood, which they finally do, reluctantly and clumsily. We see how this unheroic battle results in the pathetic death of the samurai.

At the gate, alerted by a cry, the commoner finds a baby, strips it of its expensive looking coat and good luck charm, and leaves with this booty. When the woodcutter confronts him, the commoner accuses him of finding the dagger in the samurai's body, stealing it, withholding evidence and covering up by fabricating a false narrative. For a long time the rain continues to pour, as the shamed woodcutter and the grieving priest stand silent. When the rain stops, the woodcutter offers to adopt the baby. At first the priest, suspicious of the woodcutter's motivation, grips the baby. But as the woodcutter reassures him that he merely wishes to raise the baby and care for him, the priest consents and gently places the baby in the woodcutter's arms. The glowing woodcutter carries the baby in his arms and walks into the light of a clear day.

PART II: MULTIFOCAL JUDGMENT AND BEYOND

On The Judge's Bench

Law films resort to various cinematic techniques to prompt their viewers to take an active stance and pass judgment on characters and situations (Kamir 2005a, 268–71). *Rashomon*'s technique is explicit and forceful: in all its courtyard (that is, the courtroom) scenes, the camera is placed on the bench of the unseen judge. This choice is curious, because the courtyard scenes are presented as flashbacks of the woodcutter's and the priest's points of view and neither of them could have seen the courtyard from the judge's seat. The cinematographic choice calls attention to its cinematic meaning, cueing to the viewer that he is invited to occupy the bench and assume the judge's role.[4] Concomitantly, the viewer is also invited to identify with the commoner at the Rashomon gate. Like the commoner, the viewer is an uninvolved passerby, asked to make sense of the second-hand testimonies presented to him. Through this shared role, the viewer joins the commoner in deciphering the events and judging them as the film's community's "reasonable man." By associating the viewer both with the official judge and with the lay "reasonable person," *Rashomon* invites him to perform a double judgment, from both legal and social perspectives (Kamir 2000, 74–78).

Separation renders a telling variation on this theme. *Rashomon*'s "camera on the judge's bench" technique is adopted in *Separation*'s first and last family courtroom scenes. In the film's criminal proceeding the judge is an onscreen character and the camera does not assume his point of view. The viewer is, thus, asked to preside not over the film's criminal case, but over the less formal, less legalistic family focused proceeding. Whereas *Rashomon* asks its viewer to be both judge in the criminal case and jury (so to speak) in the social tribunal, *Separation* clearly suggests that its viewer consider everything presented on screen while passing judgment over the family dispute. This choice seems to signal the centrality and importance of exercising judgment, and, more specifically, of judgment regarding the represented divorce and custody dispute. It seems to indicate that it is the family controversy that poses the issues which *Separation* requests its viewer to consider and judge.

Judgmental Spouses

Rashomon presents to its viewer four takes on the fatal event in the forest. The first and last versions, the outlaw's and the woodcutter's, point to the sword as the deadly weapon, presenting a duel between the outlaw and the samurai that results in the latter's death. The two versions offered by the samurai and his wife point to the woman's dagger as the deadly weapon. They differ in that the samurai condemns the woman for his death, whereas the woman blames the samurai.

According to the woman, after her rape, her husband's response to her was disgust, hatred, and a self-centered focus on his own wounded honor. Her anguish at the samurai's mental abandonment tormented her to the point of offering him the dagger, begging him to kill her. At this point she fainted, and perhaps her falling on top of him with the dagger in her hand caused his death.

In contrast, the samurai testifies how the intercourse with the outlaw unleashed in his wife savage hatred for him. The traitorous woman turned to the outlaw and demanded that he slaughter her husband. Her cold, merciless betrayal wounded the samurai's soul to the point where he stabbed himself with her dagger.

In *Separation*, Nader and Simin are similarly judgmental of each other. Simin admits that Nader is a decent man, yet she repeatedly claims that he is not proactive enough regarding Termeh's well-being, preferring his own interest to hers. She accuses him of insincerity, and of relinquishing their relationship by letting her go without a proper fight. Simin's accusations of her husband are not very different from those voiced by *Rashomon*'s woman.

Nader, on his part, accuses Simin of not standing by him steadfastly enough, deserting him, doubting him and turning Termeh against him. Nader, like the samurai, is disappointed that his wife does not manifest complete, unconditional loyalty to his well-being, as he defines it.

Ultimately, in both movies, husband and wife's mutual recriminations of insufficient commitment and empathy are presented before the viewer, who is cast as the bench. The parallel mutual imputations give rise, in both films, to the apprehension that, perhaps, neither husband nor wife are able to look outside him or herself far enough to discern the empathy and compassion that the other offers and seeks.

Judgment by Comparison: Parallel Sets of Characters

In *Rashomon*, the interaction between the three characters sitting in "social judgment" at the gate mirrors that between the triad involved in the violent event in the forest (*mise-en-abyme*). A comparison of the two corresponding groups casts a judgmental light on the samurai and his wife.

The samurai and his wife are an upper-class couple: he is a member of the military nobility, and she complements him, representing that which is delicate, emotional, and modest. The outlaw is a ruthless outsider who threatens the couple's virtue, relationship, and survival. In his self-serving attack on the normative couple, the outlaw wedges between them, setting them against each other and destroying both. Challenging them, he exposes their selfishness and greed, as well as their mutual blindness, expressed in their reciprocal accusation of lack of empathy, commitment, and devotion.

The Rashomon gate community features a different pair: the woodcutter, a member of the working class, and a gentle, emotional, meek priest. The commoner is the outsider: a shrewd and cynical drifter. He claims that all men are selfish and self-serving, and that he is no worse than the rest. In the process, he exposes the woodcutter's dishonesty, revealing that the woodcutter stole the woman's dagger and refrained from attesting to it. The revelation shames the woodcutter and shocks the priest. In response to the remorseful woodcutter, the priest offers him the helpless child, in a gesture that conveys his empathy, forgiveness, and faith. The woodcutter accepts these generous gifts with a glowing face.

Confronted with a challenging situation, the "couple" at the gate manifests the mutual compassion, generosity, and respect that the first couple so poignantly lacked. They support and enable each other to regain faith in one another and in human decency. Their moving, mutual benevolence atones for the first couple's selfishness; it also invites judgment-by-comparison of the upper-class couple. Through an interaction that revolves around parenting, the unselfish act of giving and taking responsibility for a vulnerable other, the priest and the woodcutter convey absolution and faith in each other. This distinguishes this couple from the samurai and wife, while judging the heterosexual couple as incapable of parenting.

Separation focuses on a married, middle-class couple and their daughter. Simin's departure entangles their lives with those of a lower-class family: Razieh, Hojjat, and their young daughter, Somayeh. Nader's loyalty to ancestral ties upsets Simin's quest for liberation—for herself and Termeh—from the prison house of kinship and country. Simin's demand for a divorce amounts to placing her daughter's well-being above her husband's. Later she sets Termeh's safety above her husband's honor, his reputation, and vindication when she insists that Nader pay Razieh and Hojjat blood money, even upon learning from Razieh herself that Nader was probably not responsible for the miscarriage. Nader feels deserted and betrayed. His response is passive yet stubborn: he neither yields to Simin's demands nor tries to dissuade her from leaving. She is frustrated and hurt by his aggressive passivity.

On the other side of Tehran, Hojjat's loss of his job, coupled with his volatile temper and irascibility, drive his family to distress and poverty. Razieh's secretive undertaking of the caretaker job to provide for her family shows that she values her daughter's well-being above her husband's honor. Later, when Simin convinces Nader to pay blood money, Razieh once again chooses her daughter's safety above her husband's honor when she refuses to invoke God's name in vain and accept the much-needed money. Despite Hojjat's aggressive pressure, Razieh does not budge. Hojjat loses his temper on both occasions, resorting to violence. Discovering that his wife worked for a man without his consent he attacks Nader. When Razieh refuses to swear, he slaps himself wildly in frustration and despair.

Razieh is Simin's *doppelganger*. Her devotion to her daughter mirrors Simin's. Like Simin, Razieh takes an independent, strong stand, upholding her daughter's best interests, refusing to succumb to her husband's demands. Razieh's persistence is viewed by her husband as an offensive and disloyal attitude to him, as well as a religious sin. Yet Razieh does not yield. In this, Razieh's character offers Simin strong moral support. The pious woman, whose chief concern is to do good, who calls a religious hotline to check whether it is sinful to help Nader's father undress, is as strong-headed regarding her daughter's well-being as Simin.

And yet, Razieh's character differs from Simin's in a significant way: Razieh disobeys her husband, refutes and shames him, but does so in agony and lament. Her pained expression, constant pleading, and passionate tears leave no room for doubt that hurting her husband causes her much anguish, and that she would have done anything to avoid it, had she felt she could. In contrast, Simin's attitude seems cold, unfeeling, and uncaring. This is the judgment of Simin that becomes rendered by comparison to Razieh.

A comparison to Hojjat makes Nader fare the better man. Both are hard-working, well-intentioned, and devoted family men who try to do their best for their respective daughters' sake. Inadvertently, both put their children at risk—Nader by triggering Hojjat's violent stalking of Termeh, and Hojjat by failing to provide a secure environment for Somayeh. Both Nader and Hojjat struggle against dire straits and experience frustration and aguish. Each of them tries to assume responsibility for his daughter's wellbeing and attempts to regain control over his family life. But whereas Hojjat fails to control his temper, flaring up, time and again, to everyone's distress, Nader manages to keep a lid on his emotions and to act rationally and civilly. Even when Hojjat assaults him physically, and Simin blames him for all their trouble, Nader maintains his composure. Hojjat's explosive character highlights Nader's serenity and self-control.

The lower-class husband and wife exhibit more emotion than the middle-class couple. "Judgment by comparison" works in favor of the middle-class man, who seems composed *vis-à-vis* his lower-class counterpart. The comparison to the lower-class woman reveals the middle-class one to be cold and uncaring: "less feminine."

Interestingly, a cross-gender comparison between the two couples is no less enlightening. Nader and Razieh are both directly involved in the conflict; Simin and Hojjat actively intervene, feeling that their respective spouses cannot be trusted to grapple with the situation on their own. Hojjat brings the contention before the court, pressing charges against Nader. His violent conduct pressures Simin to try and resolve the conflict by paying blood money. From this point on, both Hojjat and Simin seem eager to settle the affair out of court, disregarding the truth, as well as Nader and Razieh's feelings and wishes. Hojjat claims that he stands by the principles of fairness and equality; the viewer, however, cannot but suspect that his self-righteous zeal is triggered, at least partly, by injured honor, as well as by greed. Simin claims that her sole motivation is to ensure Termeh's well-being; the spectator, nevertheless, cannot help but feel that perhaps she, too, is partially impelled by a less-noble drive—the vindictive urge to reproach Nader and prove that only she can fix what he has broken. In their eagerness to settle the case, Hojjat and Simin thus seem somewhat insincere.

Unlike Hojjat and Simin, Nader and Razieh convey an impression of earnestness in their respective protestations. Each of them insists that the other is fully culpable. Yet, by the end of the film, it transpires that neither one was as truthful as she or he would have liked us to believe. Nader perjured himself by repeatedly and falsely testifying that he was oblivious to Razieh's pregnancy. Razieh withheld critically relevant evidence, known only to her, regarding the car accident. Nader and Razieh both try to justify withholding the truth. Nevertheless, they both know that they are less than completely truthful while assuming wholly innocent poses.

Nader and Razieh each point to a deficiency in the criminal law, which, they argue, causes a discrepancy between law and justice. Nader claims that criminal concepts and categories (such as the criminal *mens rea*) are too rigid and unidimensional to take into consideration a common psychological state of simultaneously knowing and suppressing knowledge. Razieh claims that the legal requirement of causality is unjust. She feels that when two distinct factors could have each separately caused the harmful outcome, they should each be held accountable, disregarding the other. But both place themselves above the law, and struggle to manipulate it in order to achieve what they each consider justice.

The cross-gender judgment by comparison does not prove favorable for either Simin or Nader; it exposes both their weaknesses and insincerities. Through the judgmental comparison, they both fare imperfect; human, all too human.

Nonjudgmental Judgment by Priest and Daughter

Rashomon and *Separation* both resort to complex cinematic devices to situate the theme of judgment at center stage. Each movie invites the viewer to judge by mounting the camera on the bench, and each weaves intricate relationships between its dramatis personae, that facilitate judgment by comparison of the husband and wife characters. Concomitantly these movies both add a redeeming gesture or character which undercuts the judgmental spirit and endows the viewing experience with forgiveness and redemption.

As *Rashomon*'s primary judge, the viewer stands in lieu of the unseen judge of the criminal proceeding and is also associated with the commoner at the Rashomon gate. The commoner is a witty, sharp character, and the spectator is drawn to his common-sense interpretation of the testimonies. But, in the final episode, when the commoner robs the helpless baby of its garments, the viewer is left to realize that he is too cynical to provide a trustworthy ethical reference point. Disillusioned, the spectator now finds himself in the rain with the woodcutter, harboring disappointment and dismay toward his insincerity and greed. It is a long awkward moment.

When the woodcutter finally moves to take the baby and the priest finds it in his heart to forgive him, the viewer feels invited to join the priest in this humane gesture. This shift is surprising, as the priest is the least charismatic character on screen. Yet in the final episode it is his compassionate move that provides the viewer's only course of relief. After two agonizing hours of intense judgment, the viewer is allowed to forgive and let go, and is grateful for the opportunity.

Separation associates its viewer, as judge, with the film's most captivating character—Termeh. The gentle yet repetitive camera focus on Termeh places her at the center of the film, inviting intense viewer identification. Termeh is onscreen much of the time both when the camera follows Nader or Simin and when it trails the grandfather, Razieh or Somayeh. In her interactions with her parents—as well as with the other characters—Termeh is inquisitive yet sensitive; her penetrating gaze complimented by deeply emotional facial expression. It is practically impossible not to connect with her.

This sensitive, thoughtful teenager watches, examines, and considers every move made by her parents. Throughout the film she sees and hears each of them condemning and feeling hurt by the other. She is privy to their strengths and weaknesses. She is aware of her mother's devotion to her, yet also faults her for leaving Nader and deserting the feeble grandfather and the family. She appreciates her father's efforts to take care of his aged parent as well as herself, yet demands to know whether he had lied to the investigating judge regarding his cognizance of Razieh's pregnancy. Termeh tries to mediate between her parents by talking Simin into coming back home, and Nader—into asking Simin to do so. She observes Razieh and Hojjat, and sees her parents in comparison (Somayeh's character helps to establish the analogy between the couples). She is intelligent enough to notice nuance, and mature enough to assess what she sees. Yet she is compassionate to both her parents throughout the film, and her judgment is conditioned by this powerful sentiment.

In *Rashomon*, the viewer is invited to pass harsh judgment throughout the film, and then to experience compassion and redemption at the very end. In *Separation*, the viewer is never left alone to judge: the film is focalized through Termeh, and her point of view is, above all else, a loving one. Scrutinizing and sharp as she is, Termeh has the empathy and acceptance that her parents lack in their mutual accusation and condemnation. Judgment by Termeh is nonjudgmental, and it is with her that the viewer is invited to judge. Termeh's love for her parents undercuts the film's judgmental spirit.

PART III: INTERSECTING LEGAL PROCEEDINGS

The Questions Posed by Legal Proceedings

In *Rashomon*, the criminal proceeding in the courtyard reviews the very case discussed by the lay tribunal at the Rashomon gate; both tribunals address the event of the samurai's death. Yet each of the proceedings focuses on a slightly different question. The question asked at the criminal court is simply who killed the samurai and how. The court is interested in determining what was the deadly weapon used to slaughter the man, and who caused the death. The legal conundrum results from the fact that the three eye witnesses that testify before the court offer three different testimonies leading in three different directions. The lay, social proceeding tackles the question of meaning, pondering on the social and moral significance of the Samurai's killing. The lay tribunal resorts to all the evidence presented before the criminal court, as well as to additional sources—the woodcutter's full testimony and shared common sense.

The mystery that *Rashomon* seems to present, which most of its scenes ostensibly tackle, and for which the film is universally renowned is the factual, criminal one: the puzzle of who killed the samurai and how. Known now as the Rashoman Effect, the film struggles to reach legal culpability as the accounts of the witnesses, suspects, and victims of a rape and murder are all different (Alia 2004, 29). But *Rashomon* never arrives at a conclusion that is "beyond reasonable doubt." The woodcutter's testimony, given at the gate, supports the outlaw's; the commoner, however, casts doubt on the truthfulness of the woodcutter's story. Thus, the viewer never learns whether the samurai died by sword or dagger; neither does the viewer find out whether the hand that held the weapon was the outlaw's, the samurai's own, or the woman's.

And yet, the testimonies submitted at the criminal court, allied with the lay discussion at the gate, seem to point to the woman's responsibility for her husband's death (Kamir 2000, 74–78). No less significant, at the final scene, both woodcutter and priest offer a different resolution to an interpersonal crisis that mimics the familial one at the forest, thus implying that both the samurai and his wife had failed in their task of overcoming a crisis and preserving the family. This seems to indicate that in *Rashomon*, the strict legal question is of secondary importance. The mystery built around it is a smoke screen. It is the question of social meaning, explored by the lay tribunal, which really matters. The legal proceeding, even when inconclusive, can reinforce a social conclusion. The resolution of the crisis at the Rashomon gate redresses the normative couple's failure, enabling society—and the audience—to overcome the trauma caused by the tragic crisis in the forest by virtue of catharsis.

Separation seems to offer a variation on the *Rashomon* formula, focusing attention on a factual and psychological criminal inquiry regarding the miscarriage, which merely echoes the underlying social enigma of family, partnership, and parenting.

The onscreen criminal proceeding focuses on the question of whether Nader is legally responsible for the death of Razieh's fetus. This question is twofold: did Nader's shoving of Razieh cause her miscarriage (*actus reus* and causality: did he shove her hard enough, and did this shove actually cause the miscarriage), and was he aware of her pregnancy at the time (*mens rea*). Neither legal issue, nor both, can resolve the underlying social concerns.

Unlike *Rashomon*, *Separation* does not hinge on witnesses' flashback testimonies providing contrasting onscreen versions of the disputed event. In a seemingly conventional cinematic manner, *Separation* presents the events to the viewer in chronological order, from diverse points of view. Only in retrospect does the viewer realize that she or he was never offered the relevant shots of the scenes that could have shed light on the two key aspects of the legal question. When the film presents Razieh's revealing conversation with Termeh's teacher, the camera remains with Razieh and does not follow Nader; the viewer has no way of knowing whether or not he overhears the women's conversation. Similarly, when Nader pushes Razieh out of his apartment, the camera, rather than follow Razieh, stays indoors with him, and the viewer has no way of knowing whether he causes her fall (or if, indeed, she fell). Even more dramatically, in the presentation of the episode in which Nader's father leaves the house and Razieh follows to fetch him, the film stops short of the scene in which the car hits her. So all the material information for the legal proceeding is discreetly concealed through editing choices; each choice of a focal point entails an occlusion, an inconspicuous editorial favoring of an ellipsis.

In *Separation*, as in *Rashomon*, most of the suspense revolves around the legal inquiry, and the viewer is constantly invited to reevaluate whether Nader's conduct caused the miscarriage and whether he was aware of Razieh's condition. And as in *Rashomon*, here, too, the legal mystery is merely the surface structure of the deeper issues at stake.

The family law proceeding with which *Separation* opens and closes tackles poignant sociocultural issues: what makes a family? What holds it together? What is the essence of spousal commitment? What makes a good spouse? What makes a good parent? How does one choose between one's parent and one's child? Which is a child's best interest: to grow up where she enjoys more civil liberties, or where she is culturally rooted? And more specifically: is Simin's request for divorce "justified"? Should she be granted the divorce she seeks? And with which of the two parents should Termeh stay? These are the issues over which the audience of the film is invited to sit in judgment.

Unlike *Rashomon*, *Separation* does reveal to its characters and viewer the "right answer" to the legal question. The information previously omitted is eventually disclosed: we learn from Nader, together with Termeh, that he did overhear Razieh's conversation regarding her pregnancy; we realize, together with the investigating judge, that Nader's push probably could not have caused Razieh's fall down the stairs; and we hear Razieh's disclosure to Simin (and later to the others) that a car had hit her before Nader pushed her out the door.

Does the legal verdict that absolves Nader from criminal responsibility due to lack of proof beyond reasonable doubt resolve the social questions raised by the family law proceeding? Clearly not. In fact, it hardly makes a difference, because in *Separation*, as in *Rashomon*, the criminal legal proceeding pursues "the objective truth" and cannot diffuse the real tension and suspense regarding the social meanings raised by the informal family proceeding.

As in *Rashomon*, the criminal proceeding is instrumental for supplying the necessary data to evaluate social meanings. Nader's choice to commit perjury before the court, Simin's disbelief of her husband's testimony, Termeh's decision to lie for her father, Razieh's refusal to swear to Nader's responsibility—those fragments of human, psychological information, revealed under the pressure of the criminal litigation, are the components from which social meaning arises and answers are construed in response to the difficult questions posed by the family law proceeding.

Legal (Criminal) Evidence in Social (Family) Court

Rashomon's social inquiry is fashioned around its criminal litigation. The lay tribunal at the Rashomon gate reiterates the testimonies presented in the official proceeding, comments on them and questions them, granting them social meaning.

The criminal proceeding that *Separation* presents does not refer directly to Simin and Nader's familial dispute. Yet, framed by the two scenes at the family court, the criminal proceeding duplicates, or mirrors, fundamental elements of the family dispute. In this framework, the criminal proceeding supplies the viewer, situated as the family court judge, with evidence relevant to Simin and Nader's conflict. The audience is invited to review the criminal case presented on screen and rely on it in determining the justification of Simin's plea for divorce.

Both Razieh's and Nader's arguments before the criminal judge reiterate Simin's and Nader's claims in the divorce case, amplifying and elaborating on them. Razieh's accusation of Nader, symbolically echoes Simin's accusation that he all but pushed her out of his home and ruined the future of her child. In this translation of Nader's alleged culpability (toward his own family) into criminal terms, his alleged betrayal of daughter and wife by failing his promise to leave Iran becomes—through mirroring and reverberation—homicide of a child and physical assault of the mother.

In his defense at the family court Nader invokes his loyalty and obligation toward his aging father. At the criminal court, this stand entails his accusation of the woman, Razieh, whose devotion to her child comes at the expense of her duties to the now helpless patriarch. The sight of Nader's father lying on the floor tied to his bed and suffocating is a vivid depiction of Nader's nightmare that Simin's plan to leave Teheran would doom the helpless old man to neglect and abuse.

The onscreen social interactions surrounding the criminal proceeding expose Nader and Razieh's emotional "behind the scenes." Nader admits that his frustrated devotion to and fear for his father overwhelmed and enraged him to the degree of suppressing his awareness of Razieh's pregnancy and his concern for the unborn child.

Razieh, on her part, admits that her accusation of Nader was a projection of her tormenting feeling of guilt over neglecting the old man, for rushing into the road carelessly and putting her fetus in harm's way. Last but not least, Razieh feels guilty toward Hojjat, whom she had deceived by taking the job without his permission. The denial of her own guilt toward the father, husband, and unborn son (three generations of men) leads Razieh to shift the accusation from herself and project it onto Nader, whose frustration, fear, and rage lead him to suppress his basic responsibility toward her.

The analogy between the criminal and the family law proceedings suggests that perhaps a similar emotional "behind the scenes" is at play in the divorce case. Perhaps underneath her relentless accusations of Nader lies Simin's sense of guilt toward her dependent father in law. Perhaps she feels guilty toward Nader and Termeh, of whom she demands that they abandon a dependent, beloved father and grandfather. Perhaps she even feels that she is betraying Nader by turning her back on her marital duties and vows. Her bold conduct and accusations infuriate Nader, who, agonizing at the sight of his languishing father, now feels ever more powerless, frustrated, trapped. In turn, these racing emotions suppress his ability to acknowledge Termeh's well-being and accept responsibility for her future. He is paralyzed into self-defense and caught up in accusing Simin. Simin's denied guilt and Nader's resentment, rage, and suppressed acknowledgment of responsibility thus feed into each other, forming a vicious cycle.

The film's criminal procedure cannot convict either Nader or Razieh; hence, they both remain innocent in the eyes of the law. But what of the family dispute between Nader and Simin? It does not call for proof beyond reasonable doubt, yet does require a resolution. The parties must either divorce or stay married, and, if they divorce—a decision must be reached regarding Termeh. Can the criminal proceeding be reinterpreted to shed light on the outcome of the family dispute? I believe that it can.

As Nader rightly explains to Termeh, the law only understands yes or no, black or white emotional situations; it cannot accommodate a vicious cycle of mutual denial. The only ones who could grapple with such a complex emotional reality are Simin and Nader. Had each of them shown integrity, courage, and compassion, they could each and both confront their fears and weaknesses. They could admit these shortcomings, accept them, and undergo a process of maturation. They could communicate openly and resolve their predicament, like the woodcutter and priest in *Rashomon*'s final scene.

But despite the insights supplied by the criminal proceeding, neither Nader nor Simin is strong enough to break free of the loop in which they have entrapped themselves and Termeh. Stubborn, silent, and cowardly, they remain locked in and chained to their insecurities and fears. Having reached a dead end, they both admit to the failure of their marriage, and agree to divorce, leaving Termeh to choose between them; typically, burdening her with their parental task.

The movie keeps us in the dark regarding Termeh's choice. It does not supply a conclusive answer to the legal aspect of the custody question. But it leaves us knowing that, much as in the criminal proceeding, the legal answer is of secondary importance. The heart of the issue lies beyond the reach of the law, and its "either or" questions and solutions. Both Termeh's parents are good people and good parents. They both love their daughter and are greatly involved and invested in her upbringing. Yet neither one of them shows the integrity, courage, and compassion necessary to do what Termeh really needs; neither is generous enough to admit, communicate, forgive, accept, and let go. Neither of them knows how to follow in the footsteps of their predecessors—the woodcutter and priest—and thus redeem themselves and save the family.

Termeh needs two adult parents who can face their guilt, assume responsibility for her future, and support each other with all their weaknesses. Such parents she does not have; hence no decision of hers can grant a happy ending. The real denouement in the family proceeding is that, regardless of who is granted custody, everyone loses.

Separation suggests that a criminal proceeding, with its "either or" logic, cannot do justice to a complex emotional situation, such as Simin and Nader's family dispute. In a family dispute, the scope of possible success is determined by the maturity of the parties: by their integrity, courage, and compassion.

PART IV: GENDER POLITICS, HONOR VERSUS DIGNITY, AND SOCIAL CRITIQUE

Gender Politics

I have argued elsewhere, in great detail, that *Rashomon*'s apparent relativistic—even anarchistic—stance regarding truth, evidence, and legal fact finding, conceals a deeper layer of meaning, in which the woman is socially condemned (Kamir 2000, 56–61, 66–67). I have shown how, relying on audiences' intuitive familiarity with Hollywood's common-law legal conventions, as well as with those of mystery stories and honor codes, *Rashomon* leads its audience to find the woman culpable for her husband's death. The legal evidence may not substantiate her guilt, but implied underlying social conventions do. A similar strategy is at play in *Separation*.

I have mentioned earlier that Razieh is Simin's double, and her devotion to her daughter mirrors Simin's. Both women maintain this stance at the expense of their husbands' respective interests. This theme is presented in the opening scene, in which Simin demands that Nader either leave his father and emigrate with her, or be forced by the family court to divorce her and let her take their eleven-year-old daughter out of Iran. It culminates in the scene, toward the end of the movie, in which Razieh discloses to Simin, confidentially, that her miscarriage may have been caused by a car accident. In fear for Somayeh's well-being, Razieh begs Simin not to pay Hojjat, despite his eagerness to receive compensation and repay his heavy debts. Rather than confide in her husband, trust him, believing that together they could best ascertain Somayeh's well-being, Razieh turns to Simin, attempting to conspire with her behind Hojjat's back.

But Simin is worried for her own daughter, who might be hurt by Hojjat if he is not paid and appeased. She clarifies that complying with Razieh's request may save Somayeh but endanger Termeh. The daughters are pitted against each other, and each mother prefers her own.

The next scene reveals that Simin does not trust Nader enough to share with him the crucial information disclosed by Razieh. Like Razieh, Simin chooses her daughter's interests, as she defines them, over those of her husband, as he defines them. She does not trust him enough to believe that, were he to choose between his own interests and his daughter's well-being, he would opt for Termeh's.

The distraught Razieh blames herself for the messy consequences. It is hard to refute her self-accusation that she is the source of turmoil. After Hojjat storms out of the failed mediation meeting, Razieh exclaims, "How can I live in this house now?" Her desperate outcry implies that she has destroyed her marital relationship.

This is followed by Simin and Nader's arrival at the family courtroom, their now confirmed divorce echoing Razieh's admission that she has wrecked her family. This shift from one woman to the other brings to mind that just as Razieh's unauthorized exit of Hojjat's home has led to upheaval and misfortune, so Simin's desertion of Nader's home led to the fateful hiring of Razieh and the calamity that ensued. Inasmuch as Razieh could have at least spared Hojjat the last blow (his humiliation before the creditors) had she entrusted him with the truth regarding the car accident, so Simin could have shown consideration for Nader's feelings by sharing with him Razieh's confession. Had she felt compassion, love, and loyalty for Nader, they could have planned together how to best settle the situation. But Simin withheld Razieh's secret from Nader, planning to let him pay for a miscarriage he did not cause, and dooming him to wonder forever about his guilt.

Separation leaves little doubt that cold, reserved Simin is guilty not merely of abandoning her father-in-law and home, but also of deserting her husband and causing the breakup of her family. Her culpability derives from being too active, self-reliant, strong, and suspicious, and due to her failure to trust, love, or share with a husband who is, as she herself admits, a good and decent man. Even empathetic Termeh tells her mother in no uncertain terms that—but for her desertion, none of this would have happened.

Separation does not acknowledge or admit its reliance on patriarchal gender norms and stereotypes; but its uncritical, unquestioning adherence to them renders them neutral and invisible, inviting the audience to blindly accept them as the yardstick against which to measure the characters and their actions.

Razieh's actions brought about her family's breakup only if we take for granted and do not question her husband's one-sided patriarchal right to control her employment choices. Her fear that this volcanic man might discover her "unauthorized" employment causes her to conceal both her work and the related car accident, a concealment that bears a disastrous entanglement and suffering. Had the film invited us to question Hojjat's patriarchal privilege, we might have concluded that Hojjat partook in a discriminating, oppressive regime. Perhaps we would have realized more clearly that accusation of Razieh is a form of victim blaming.

The same holds true for Simin and Nader. Were Simin not expected to do the housework and caretaking for Nader's father, she would not have been held responsible for Razieh's fateful presence in the household. Were it not considered improper for a woman to be active, independent, self-reliant, strong-headed, and critical—Simin would not have been cast in a negative light.

Nader and Simin are presented as a Westernized, egalitarian couple. Nader is portrayed as an active parent, very much involved in the upbringing of his daughter. This conceals the reality that in the onscreen world, Simin, like Razieh, is judged according to traditional, conservative patriarchal standards and norms. Those seem to be taken for granted by the film, and are thus inadvertently accepted and implemented by its implied viewer and audience. In this respect, the film uncritically mirrors the legal system that it portrays, supporting its logic and reasoning. Taken with Simin and Nader's modern lifestyle, as well as with Nader's open-mindedness, we become oblivious to the embedded patriarchal culture, and are invited to judge Simin by its standards. In this constellation, her guilt is blatant.

The following section suggests that uncritical grappling with the theme of traditional, patriarchal honor in *Separation* is an additional way in which the film invites judgment and condemnation of its female characters.

Dignity, Honor, and Gender: Latent Narratives in *Rashomon* and *Separation*

In the analysis of other films, I have suggested that sometimes a movie presents a dignity-based value system, while (also) upholding an honor-based one (Kamir 2005b, 67). Whereas a dignity-based value system commands absolute preservation and protection of each and every individual's human value, and fundamental human rights, an honor-based one encourages fierce, unqualified competition for honor, which assumes and perpetuates the distinction between men as subjects and women as objects and includes stereotypically gendered means of shaming competitors and humiliating them. (For further explication of honor and dignity see below.) Regarding *Rashomon,* I have claimed that under the guise of its famous relativistic posture, the movie discreetly invites its viewer to accept honor-based norms and implement them to assess the woman's conduct. Honor-based judgment is one way in which *Rashomon* invites its viewer to blame and condemn the woman. Here I claim that *Separation* does the same.

Each one of the four main adult characters in *Separation* claims to be devoted to the well-being of a dependent family member—Nader to his demented father, Hojjat to his miscarried, unborn son, Simin to Termeh, Razieh to Somayeh. The men claim that they are devoted to upholding the memory and rights of a male family member that they once loved or hoped to love, whereas the women are devoted to the well-being of their daughters. These four attachments may be described as commitments to human dignity.

Very simply put, I use "human dignity" to mean the inherent value ascribed to the category "human," and, therefore, to humankind and every member of the human family (Kamir 2006a, 5–10; 2006b, 143). Dignity, as constituted by the 1948 United Nation's Universal Declaration of Human Rights, is said to be inherent in the human nature of every human being, that is, in the humanity of each and every member of our human category. We can think of it as a stamp of human quality that is imprinted in each of us.

Nader still sees the innate human virtue of the old man who no longer communicates and wets his pants. Hojjat values the potential humanity of his unborn son, insisting that his death be treated seriously and respectfully by the authorities and the middle-class men and women involved in his demise. He demands recognition and compensation for the loss of this human life. Simin wants to offer her daughter—through exile—the option to realize her autonomy and human potential to the utmost. Razieh seeks to ensure Somayeh's well-being and protect her from harm by pleasing and appeasing God as dutifully as she can.

But beyond the ostensible dignity-based motivations, Nader and Hojjat also abide by their respective sense of honor, while both Simin and Razieh seem to have no compunction about dishonoring and shaming their respective husbands.

Let me clarify the meaning that I attribute to honor (Kamir 2006a, 5–10: 2006b; Miller 1993); in honor-and-shame societies, honor is the relative value attributed to a member of society in comparison to his peers. It implies social status, prestige, rank, and standing in a given group's hierarchical structure. Shame is the lack/loss of honor; dishonor. In most honor-and-shame societies, honor is partially bequeathed and mostly gained through a careful and disciplined adherence to the coded norms.

A meticulous observance of the appropriate set of norms entitles a person to honor; failure bestows shame.

In most traditional honor-and-shame societies, honor is closely linked with the ideal of manhood. Typically, only men are players in any group's honor game. Many societies offer men two routes to earn honor and status: one is success in the competition against other men (one's peers) in "manly" activities (such as warfare, accumulation of wealth); the other is conquering and maintaining sexual and familial control over women. Women are a means by which men may gain or lose honor. A wife's duty is to uphold her husband's honor by obeying him, particularly in public, and by being sexually accessible exclusively to him. A woman who disobeys her husband, especially in the open, or is "taken" sexually by another man, shames her husband extremely (Peristiany and Pitt-Rivers 1966; Pitt-Rivers 1977).

Hojjat has lost his job, and is unable to support his family. He feels intensely humiliated and emasculated. Losing a potential male son—a source of tremendous honor—is an additional blow. He experiences Razieh's disobedience as further humiliation, attesting to his loss of manly status and control. Nader is the man who, in Hojjat's mind, caused this humiliation and witnessed it. One cannot help but sense that Hojjat wants not just to redress the dignity of his unborn son, but also to avenge himself on Nader and receive from him compensation for his dishonor. But just as he is about to be somewhat reinstituted as a man of honor, his wife prevents it, by once again disobeying him in public and refusing to play the submissive role that he assigns her. Razieh is fully aware of this: Hojjat's sister urges her to take the oath that Nader requests, reminding her that Hojjat's honor is at stake. If Razieh were a good, obedient, dutiful wife, she would cherish her husband's honor, especially as she is partially responsible for tarnishing it. But she refuses, realizing fully the meaning of her action in an honor-and-shame society.

This interaction between Hojjat and Razieh mirrors the one between Nader and Simin. At the opening scene, Simin publicly shames Nader before the court with her drastic demands. We cannot help but sense that Nader's commitment to his father's dignity excuses his abiding by his manly honor as son, husband, and father. Nader refuses to abandon his father, which would mean colossal disgrace for both men, and stands on his honor-right to lead his family rather than follow his wife. A modern, Western man, who considers himself egalitarian, Nader denies Simin's accusation that he is driven by considerations of honor; but it is hard to deny the suspicion that in fact he is.

As if Simin's conduct were not disgraceful enough, Nader is further shamed when proven incapable of running his household without her. Imprisoned, and later released only thanks to her intervention, he is desperately shamed. When she demands that he pay Hojjat off, his shaming is complete: what kind of a *man* (of honor) is he, if he accepts responsibility for a homicide he is wrongly accused of, and pays the man who is threatening his daughter, all merely out of fear? Nader emphatically refuses. When Simin has the opportunity to restore some of Nader's sense of honor upon learning that he was indeed falsely accused, she declines to do so. Her explicit reason is concern for Termeh's dignity (she seems to fear that Nader would refuse to pay Hojjat, thus risking Termeh). But it is hard not to suspect, as well, that perhaps she is not too eager to help Nader recover some of his lost honor.

None of these interactions is openly acknowledged by the film, yet we sense them. The film's onscreen society is traditional, patriarchal, and honor-based. It is not hard to sense both men's acute humiliation, and their wives' continuing failure to relieve them of it. Left to our own devices, eschewing the issue of honor and its inherent ties to patriarchy, *Separation* (passive-aggressively?) allows us to comply with the honor norms of its onscreen society. Even if we are taken aback by Hojjat's blunt patriarchal conduct, we feel for both men's painful sense of dishonor, wishing their wives were more compassionate (more "feminine" in a traditional sense). We find the men merely human; the wives—uncaring and even cruel. Razieh, at least, suffers as she lets Hojjat down; Simin seems indifferent.

Social Critique

Rashomon does not offer explicit social critique, but in leaving the viewer under the impression of the woodcutter's last testimony, it winds up with a very critical view of the samurai, the bandit, and the woman. Through the woodcutter's eyes, all three are caught up in a vain struggle for honor, in which they lose sight of their own as well as their fellow humans' dignity. In their competition for prestige and esteem they become selfish, arrogant, and cruel, dooming themselves to ruin. Since this film was made in Japan in 1950, it is difficult not to think that it may have expressed critique of the Japanese social order that led the country into World War II and its disastrous aftermath. But since nothing in the film alludes to this historical interpretation, it is more likely to read the text as presenting and perhaps criticizing human nature and human interactions at large.

The only explicit reference to Iranian sociopolitical reality is made in *Separation* in its opening scene. Explaining why she insists on taking Termeh out of the country, Simin says that as a mother, she prefers not to raise her daughter in Iran. Aware that this line of argument is not likely to win the judge's sympathy, she stops short of mentioning that civil rights and liberties in Iran are greatly restricted; that women are silenced, marginalized, and subjected to patriarchal religious oppression. Nader joins the judge is pretending not to understand why Termeh would be better off elsewhere, and Simin chooses not to step into the trap that he sets her, and does not criticize the country's political regime. But her plea, as well as her discretion, frames the whole movie, and the little she says suffices for a contemporary Western implied viewer and audience to fill in the blanks.

But to keep sight of Simin's implied critique, a viewer must hold on to it with great determination, because from the second scene onward, *Separation* portrays daily life in Teheran as very normal and ordinary. The film almost splits itself from its opening scene. Termeh goes to school, does her homework and plays with other girls, while her parents go to work and are burdened with issues concerning their personal lives: an aging father, marital problems, a legal dispute. Neighbors, teachers, family members, judges—they all seem to be reasonable people; human interactions are familiar and casual.

The viewer is never shown a situation in which Simin or Termeh are oppressed, restricted, or discriminated against. Their head covers seem to be a matter of fashion. Razihe's veiling in the chador seems to be her own choice, as she is a very devout Muslim. Simin drives her own car, and in a scene at a gas station, Nader asks Termeh to fill the tank and teaches her to demand the change assertively. Nader and Simin seem to stand on an equal footing and the family court judge talks of their need to agree on both divorce and custody issues. It is significant that the homework that Termeh is shown doing with her father is in Iranian language and history; we are never shown classes in which she may be subjected to religious indoctrination and gender stereotyping. In one scene, Simin stands on a balcony with her back to the camera, and when she turns to face Nader and the viewer, it appears that she has been smoking. But unless one knows that it is prohibited in Iran to show women smoking, it is impossible to guess that this is a meaningful second.[5]

This creates the impression that women enjoy coequality with men, or, at least, that their situation is not very different from that of couples in the Western world.

Simply put, *Separation* naturalizes and normalizes everyday life in Iran, rendering it inconspicuous to the point that the viewer doubts whether Simin's concern about raising Termeh there is warranted. The film thus seems to embrace Nader's point of view and question the legitimacy of Simin's sociopolitical critique.

Simin's clear repudiation of the Iranian regime at the opening scene is thus blurred and her outcry is silenced by the ensuing uncritical presentation of Iranian life. The documentary-like character, seemingly objective perspective of *Separation* misleads the audience into feeling that real life in

Teheran is no different than in the West, and that there is no justification for Simin's insistence on traumatic exile and abandonment of Nader's father. In this, again, the film mimics the family court legal proceeding it portrays, offering it unacknowledged support.

It is this obliteration of Simin's point of view that renders *Separation* a universalistic examination of human nature, of husbands and wives and upper and lower classes, rather than a sociopolitical critique.

SUMMARY AND CONCLUSION

Summary

This chapter offers a close reading of *Separation* in comparison with *Rashomon*, demonstrating that these two acclaimed law films establish a unique, non-Anglo-American sophisticated and effective cinematic critique of law and judgment, while subtly and discretely taking a conservative sociopolitical stand.

The chapter reveals how *Separation* (like *Rashomon*) places judgment at large and judgment of interpersonal, family related concerns in particular, in the limelight. The cinematic choice of placing the camera and the viewer—on the bench of the family court judge; the onscreen mutual accusations and judgment of husband and wife; the judgment of a middle-class couple by comparison with a lower-class one—make up the multifocal ways in which the film not merely presents its audience with issues of family law and judgment, but also invites it to actively participate in complex, many-faceted family law decision-making. The film undercuts this intensely judgmental mood by establishing the feuding couple's loving, compassionate daughter as its supreme judge and the viewer's onscreen guide.

A comparison of the *Separation–Rashomon* cinematic reference to judgment with the more familiar one of the Anglo-American hero-lawyer law-film suggests that in the absence of courtroom drama, the *Separation–Rashomon* multifocal tactic is more nuanced, granting more weight to the undercutting nonjudgmental force.

The chapter further demonstrates how *Separation* (like *Rashomon*) engages the audience in a complex legal enigma (in the context of a criminal *whodunit* proceeding), concomitantly indicating that the resolution of legal conundrums does not impact the underlying interpersonal questions (posed by the less-formal family court proceeding). Still, the harshness and formalism of the criminal proceeding tease out information and responses that less formal proceedings cannot, and which are instrumental in the more subtle context of the family law case. The chapter illuminates how fragments of human, psychological information, revealed under the pressure of the criminal legal proceeding (such as Nader's decision to lie, Simin's disbelief of her husband's testimony, Termeh's decision to back her father despite his insincerity, Razieh's refusal to swear to Nader's responsibility)—are the building blocks of social meaning, illuminating the difficult issues posed by the family law proceeding.

A comparison with more conventional law-films suggests that the cinematic technique of intersecting legal proceedings leaves (Western) audiences in awe—as well as frustrating confusion. Legal detective investigations are aimed at discovering who did what, and who knew what when. The expectation is that once these investigations unravel the mystery, justice will be done, and conflicts satisfactorily resolved. In *Separation*, following such investigations, audiences appreciate the mystery and sense of complexity, but are perhaps baffled and discouraged when no legal solution in the criminal case sheds significant light on the underlying interpersonal family themes of the less-formal proceeding, leading to questions such as: "Should Nader and Simin divorce?" and "Who should get custody of Termeh?" The discord between the detective-like pursuit of legal answers within the criminal context and the complete irrelevance of these answers to the deeper level of human concerns addressed by the family focused procedure is shocking and, perhaps, paralyzing. Even as we realize that Nader is not guilty in the criminal case, no decision in the family case may grant a happy ending. This is a very difficult outcome for audiences, trained in happy legal endings that promise optimistic personal solutions and futures.

The last part of this chapter exposes how by ignoring the onscreen society's underlying patriarchal honor norms and discriminatory gender stereotypes, *Separation* (like *Rashomon*) induces its viewer to accept these conservative conventions. Withholding criticism of a particular patriarchal, honor-based society, frames the film as a universalistic, archetypal portrayal of the human condition.

In summary, the discussion in this chapter reveals that a non-Anglo-American law film featuring multifocal judgment and intersecting legal proceedings may be more radically critical and less optimistic than a conventional Anglo-American hero-lawyer law-film regarding the power of a legal investigation to shed light on fundamental social concerns or to reach the right decision and do justice in complex human situations. But this nihilistic skepticism regarding the legal system may go hand in hand with uncritical conformism regarding traditional, conservative sociopolitical realities, upholding patriarchy and honor-based norms. In fact, perhaps total skepticism regarding the rule of law necessitates acceptance of sociopolitical order. Perhaps *Separation* and *Rashomon*'s deep disbelief in the rule of positive law is part and parcel of adherence to conservative "natural law" ("the way things are"). Concomitantly, perhaps the optimistic stance of more conventional Anglo-American hero-lawyer law-films toward the rule of law cohabits with at least the possibility of profound criticism of sociopolitical reality.

Conclusion

In conclusion, let me connect this discussion of *Separation* with my long-standing law-and-film enterprise. I have repeatedly marked three perspectives that strike me as particularly exciting in the discussion of law and film. One is the examination of ways in which law-films train audiences in judging, and in legal-like ways of relating to the social world. Another is revealing law-films' jurisprudential commentary and insights. Finally, comparing law-film's social action to that of the legal systems they depict onscreen (Kamir 2005a; 2006a, 1–5).

In the second part of this chapter I have unraveled the ways in which *Separation* (much like *Rashomon*) trains its audience in judgment. The movie bluntly places the viewer on the judge's bench, instructing him or her to perform complex, multifocal judgment, relying on characters' mutual accusations and their comparison with characters cast as their doubles. Interestingly, *Separation* undercuts judgment by casting a compassionate, loving character as its supreme judge.

The third part of this chapter shows that some of *Separation*'s jurisprudential insights are voiced by its characters. One, perhaps the film's main character (Nader) claims that the law fails to address common psychological realities, such as knowledge suppressed due to stress. He believes that this justifies perjury, in order to supply the law with simple answers that it is capable of processing. Termeh, who is the film's main focal point, seems to be convinced by this argument. Is this a signal to the viewer regarding this jurisprudential point? Another main character (Razieh) faults the criminal law for its requirement of actual causality; she claims that if Nader's actions had sufficed to cause harm, he should be found guilty even if a different, unrelated factor actually caused the harmful result. Interestingly, at the very end of the movie she seems to retract (when, pushed to swear to Nader's culpability—she refuses). Is this a signal to the viewer regarding this jurisprudential point?

No less interesting is the film's implied jurisprudential claim, revealed in the intersection of the film's two legal proceedings. *Separation* shows that a criminal proceeding cannot resolve a complex emotional situation, such as a family dispute. The legal solutions may resolve formal, procedural conundrums, but remain completely irrelevant to the underlying human issues. Regarding these, the scope of possible success is determined by the maturity and humanity of the parties: by their integrity, courage, and compassion. In the summary, I suggest that this jurisprudential stand may strike audiences, trained in more conventional law films, as overly radical, perplexing, and unsatisfactory.

Last but not least, the fourth section of this chapter demonstrates how *Separation* mirrors the social action of the legal system that it portrays. The family court allows Simin to express her view that Iran is no place to raise a girl. But while speaking in a liberal, egalitarian voice, the law silences and ignores Simin's attempt to point to Iran's patriarchal, fundamentalist, conservative political and legal regime. *Separation* follows in the footsteps of its fictional legal system, offering it cinematic reinforcement. The film's choice to ignore its society's patriarchal honor norms and discriminating gender conventions ultimately silences Simin's voice and undermines her insistence that Termeh's well-being requires migration from Iran.

Some law-films, such as Marleen Gorris's Dutch, 1982, film *A Question of Silence* (van Heijningen 1982), present legal systems critically, inviting viewers to examine their assumptions and find them wanting (Kamir, 2006a, 218–42). *Separation,* much like *Rashomon,* calls our attention to its complex, sophisticated perspectives on judgment, and to radically critical jurisprudential commentary, while silently supporting its conservative onscreen patriarchal legal system. This complex structure seemingly reassures us of the film's critical, even radical nature, while silently inviting us to accept its underlying conservative worldview; much like the acclaimed *Rashomon.*

NOTES

1. I am deeply grateful to the generous support of the Emile Zola Chair for Human Rights; to the warm hospitality of the European University Institute in Florance, Italy; to Talia Trainin for her excellent professional work.

2. Throughout the chapter, "viewer" and "audience," refer to the "implied viewer"—as well as to real-world Western audiences, assuming that audiences, on the whole, accept the film's invitation and take on the role of its implied viewer. For discussion of this choice see Orit Kamir, 2006a, *Framed: Women in Law and Film* (Durham, NC: Duke University Press), xvi–xviii.

3. For a very detailed synopsis see Kamir, Orit, 2000, "Judgment by Film: Socio-Legal Functions of *Rashomon,*" *Yale Journal of Law & Humanities.* 12(1): 39, 44–56.

4. I use the male pronoun because *Rashomon* seems to construct a male hypothetical viewer.

5. I learned the significance of this scene from an interview with Leila Hatami who plays Simin. The interview appears in the "Special Features" of a DVD of the film. From this interview I also learned that Hatami was explicitly instructed to portray the image of a "cold" and very assertive woman, and that Simin's character is very well aware that the family court is biased against her.

REFERENCES

Alia, Valerie. 2004. *Media Ethics and Social Change*. Edinburgh; New York: Edinburgh University Press.

Clooney, George (producer) and Tony Gilroy (director). 2007. *Michael Clayton*. [Motion Picture]. United States: Castlerock Entertainment.

Farhadi, Asghar (producer and director). 2001. *A Separation*. [Motion Picture]. Iran: Asghar Farhadi.

Jingo, Minoru (producer) and Akira Kurosawa (director). 1950. *Rashomon*. [Motion Picture]. Japan: Daiei Motion Picture Company.

Kamir, Orit. 2000. "Judgment by Film: Socio-Legal Functions of *Rashomon*." *Yale Journal of Law & Humanities* 12(1): 44–88.

———. 2005a. "Why Law-and-Film and What Does it Actually Mean?" *Continuum: Journal of Media & Cultural Studies* 19: 268–71.

———. 2005b. "Anatomy of Hollywood's Hero-Lawyer: A Law-and-Film Study of Western Motifs, Honor-Based Values and Gender Politics Underlying Anatomy of a Murder's Construction of the Lawyer Image." *Studies in Law, Politics & Society* 35: 67–106.

———. 2006a. *Framed: Women in Law and Film*. Durham, NC: Duke University Press.

———. 2006b. "Law, Society and Film: Unforgiven's Call to Substitute Honor with Dignity." *Law and Society Review* 40: 193–235.

———. 2009. "Michael Clayton, Hollywood's Contemporary Hero-Lawyer: Beyond Outsider Within and Insider Without." *Suffolk University Law Review* 42: 829–48.

———. 2012. "Hollywood's Hero-Lawyer: A Liminal Character and Champion of Equal-Liberty." In *Treatise of Legal Visual Semiotics*, edited by Anne Wagner and Richard Sherwin. New York: Springer.

Miller, William Ian. 1993, *Humiliation and Other Essays on Honor, Social Discomfort and Violence*. Ithaca, NY: Cornell University Press.

Pakula, Alan (producer) and Robert Mulligan (director). 1962. *To Kill a Mockingbird*. [Motion Picture].United States: Universal.

Pitt-Rivers, Juliam. 1977. *The Fate of Shechem or the Politics of Sex: Essays in the Anthropology of the Mediterranean*. Cambridge, UK: Cambridge University Press.

Peristiany, J. G. and Julian Pitt-Rivers. 1966. *Honor and Shame: the Values of Mediterranean Society*. Chicago: Chicago University Press.

van Heijningen, Matthijs (producer) and Maurleen Gorris (director). 1982. *A Question of Silence*. [Motion Picture]. Holland: Sigma Film Productions.

6

Beyond the Courtroom

Vigilantism, Revenge, and Rape-Revenge Films in the Cinema of Justice

Peter Robson

This chapter[1] starts by contrasting different approaches to a group of films that share many characteristics. It looks at films with a vigilante theme and seeks to clarify what is involved. It then notes how a shift of perspective to focus on the victim of rape alters the nature of these films. The theme of revenge and, in particular, the revenge tragedy, is one that is encountered throughout myth and literature as is noted below. The chapter deals principally with films featuring action stemming from an individual's concern to right the situation and seek justice for a single evil event where the law has failed to provide a proper remedy. The quintessential modern vigilante has been the normal citizen, who if left alone by criminal elements, would have no reason to act outside the law or challenge the *status quo*. This simple revenge theme has cropped up in a series of films where the original perpetrators of the evil event are usually shown as having no redeeming qualities. Here the vigilante subsequently seeks to deal directly with a perpetrator to whom the legal system then fails to mete out proportionate justice. There is a clear connection between some of the aims of the vigilante—such as securing justice by means outside the normal channels of the justice system—and those of a number of other actors. These are not, in my reading, usefully called vigilantes. These include the romantic outcast Robin Hood figure, the social bandit encountered in many cultures (Hobsbawm 1960; 1969). The centrality of the social to the lives of many of these bandits varies considerably. At the most modest level are figures whose confrontations with the law are undertaken for purely personal motives but whose actions are taken as symbolic by others in society. Versions of group action also crop up in a number of different genres that are akin to vigilantism. For example, the Western genre moves from the replacement of random lawlessness and an individual response to it, to the emergence of official local law enforcement officers representing the community rather their own perspective. The political implications of the acceptance of the vigilante as a desirable feature in modern, urban, liberal societies are major and provide one of the sources of my concerns about how these films may be read.

A different set of issues, though, emerges when we look at these films of extra-legal justice from a victim's perspective. In *The Scene of Violence*, Young (2010) shifts the focus to the role of women seeking revenge in films involving rape. She focuses specifically on the extra-legal action of victims of rape and this theme is also explored in the work of Jacinda Read (2000), Alexandra Heller-Nicholas (2011), Claire Henry (2014), and on the Internet (Hephaestus 2011). This chapter also notes what light these alternative perspectives shed on issues of methodology in the scholarship of law and film. It concludes that it is worth making a distinction between the mainstream world of vigilante film and the underground world of the sexploitation films which for the most part are what rape-revenge films are. The political stance of vigilante films appears to be, for the most part, relatively straightforward while that of rape-revenge films is more complex.

VIGILANTES AND REVENGE

The notion of revenge such as in the blood feud is a theme encountered within the classical literary tradition. Greek mythology is suffused with tales of revenge and Greek and later writing on tragedy thrives on the consequences when revenge is sought for an offence against honor. From Aeschylus's *Oresteia Trilogy* in 458 B.C. (1977) and Sophocles's *Elektra* (2008) half a century later, through Seneca's *Thyestes* (1993) in the first century A.D. to the late sixteenth century with Christopher Marlowe's *Tamburlaine* (2002) and Shakespeare's *Titus Andronicus* and *Hamlet* (2004), it is clear that the phenomenon of bloody revenge is no modern artistic creation. It has also made its way into popular culture in both film and television, most frequently in historical dramas such as *El Cid* (Samuel Bronston and Anthony Mann 1961) and Westerns like *The Searchers* (C. V. Whitney and John Ford 1956). Most recently the portrayal of the feud between the Hatfields and McCoys has reached our screens in the form of the television miniseries, *Hatfields and McCoys* (Kevin Costner and Kevin Reynolds 2012) and *Hatfields and McCoys: Bad Blood* (Fred Olen Ray 2012).

These are truly the stuff of tragedy, but their very essence is the kind of justice that encountered in honor societies (Kamir 2002). Kamir contrasts the honor society and its underlying credo centered on status and its maintenance with liberal societies and their notions of rights (Kamir 2002, 2). Insofar as the films and legal systems being portrayed in the films discussed here are firmly within the liberal rights-based society, perceived breaches of rights and inadequate justice are the focus of this examination. It is worth noting, however, that there are nods to the existence of honor revenge as a major motivation in both *The Fourth Angel* (Allan Scott and Peter R Simpson; John Irvin 2001) and *Taken* 2 (Luc Besson and Olivier Megaton 2014). These films involve crime gangs from the Balkans where honor revenge is a driving force. The essence of *Taken 2* is the family revenge against Bryan Mills (Liam Neeson) for his actions in defence of his family in *Taken* (Luc Besson and Pierre Morel 2008).

THE VIGILANTE IN CONTEXT

Apart from the slew of films on vigilante themes in themselves, there are good reasons for debating the vigilante and vigilantes. In the current century we have witnessed Mexican American border vigilantes like the Minutemen (Minutemanproject.com 2014) and the destruction of computers by so-called "consumer vigilantes" in recent years (Gohring 2007). The current context for the discussion of how vigilantes have been portrayed over the years is the emergence of both individual and group vigilante activities across a wide range of countries, along with the widespread and indiscriminate use of the term "vigilante" action to describe almost any political activity where the individual takes action outside the parameters of standard law enforcement. This may be by way of revenge or as a warning. Activities include taking action against people suspected of having been involved in a range of activities. Most recently the focus has been on pedophiles and drug dealers. The responses have included alternative extra-legal "punishment" (Havery 2015). The term has also been used to describe those using the Internet to entrap those who would use social media devices to groom young people for sex and then passing their information to the police (Booth 2014; Tunick 2012).

It is also important to disentangle the casual use of the term vigilante to make a distinction between the temporary outlaw status of the lone vigilante and the law enforcement officer or government agent who does not "play by the rules." This chapter takes as its focus the individual vigilante. There is less ambivalence in the corresponding Spanish term "justiciero" and the French "justicier."[2] By focusing on the justice-seeking lawbreaker we are able to observe some common threads present in a series of films over the past thirty-five years. The commitment to securing fairness and justice rather than acting on behalf of sectional interests is, of course, not automatically dependent on the individual. There are groups like the fictional *Magnificent Seven* (John Sturges 1960)—saving a Mexican village from bandits or the real-life *Gulabi Gang* (Torstein Grude and Nishtha Jain 2012)—taking action with sticks against men who use violence against women. They act on behalf of the oppressed, whether on an *ad hoc* or organized basis, rather than on behalf of the rich and powerful. By the same token, the concept of justice espoused by individual vigilantes is often highly contested. The New York subway vigilante Bernhardt Goetz[3] and Florida's George Zimmerman[4] acted according to their own conception of what society needs. Whether or not they can be termed justice figures is moot. Suffice it to say, before embarking on a survey of the portrayal of the pursuit of alternative justice on the screen, the individual is normally the conduit through which this drive for decency and fairness is conducted. The use of groups in the modern vigilante film is rare.

What is found in the relationship between the vigilante/justiciero/justicier and the law is a breakdown of the system as far as the protagonist is concerned. The vigilante's concern is to right the situation and seek justice for the single event where the law has failed to provide a proper remedy. There is a relation to the social bandit insofar as the effect of their actions may overlap, but these are on the periphery of the vigilante spectrum. Looking at these various responses to the justice system when the public sees the justice system to be failing or to lack any kind of adequate markers of legitimacy, highlights the problematic and contingent nature of legality (Smith 2010; Ministry of Justice Report 2013).

THE VIGILANTE AND VIGILANTES

Words have symbolic power. The phrase "single parent" conjures up for the British public, courtesy, in this case, of the right wing press, images of an unemployed teenager in a council flat rather than a widow or widower in waged work. "On welfare" has the same power in the United States to denote race and gender. "Vigilante" has a loaded but variable meaning. It summons, on the one hand, Woody Guthrie's (1935) hired thug, vigilante man, cracking down on the poor and oppressed on behalf of rich exploitative employers.

On the other hand, counterposed to the company "goon" or protection of powerful interests, is the notion of vigilantism as a means of seeking justice. This can occur on behalf of the community. The object of the actions are robbers and "ne'er-do-wells" against whom the forces of law and order are powerless. The armed groups of vigilantes who have operated from time to time are acting not in their own narrow self-interests but on behalf of the many. These groups are generally either short-lived or they transmogrify into a more formal political group. The 1850s San Francisco Vigilance Committee (Quinn 1997), the Montana Vigilantes in the 1860s (Dillon 2013), and the Bald Knobbers in Taney County in the 1880s (Hartman and Ingenthron 1988; Anderson 2013) are all examples of short-lived extra-legal groups mobilized against lawlessness. Their appearance at a time of rudimentary state apparatus is quite distinctive. They can be seen as operating in a legal justice vacuum. These actions have sometimes been linked to political and labor struggles as with the Molly Maguires (Kenny 1998). Such activities have occasionally made it to the screen as with *The Molly Maguires* (Walter Bernstein and Martin Ritt 1970), *Missouri Breaks* (Elliott Kastner and Walter M. Sherman; Arthur Penn 1976) and *Harlan County War* (Tony Bill 2000). What has, however, captured the imagination of filmmakers, since the relaxation at the end of the 1960s of the Hays Code prohibition on showing successful extra-legal action, mentioned below, has been, not so much the group but the lone individual. They are portrayed seeking to secure justice for a wrong suffered by their families where the justice system is shown as incapable of dealing with this injustice effectively.

THE VIGILANTE/*JUSTICIERO*/*JUSTICIER* IN FILM

As is noted below, the vigilante film can be seen as a modern version of one of the recurrent themes in Westerns. The seeker of justice for a single event has a role in modern times in focusing debates about the viability and social function of the whole justice system. More than the trial movie, they allow the audience to weigh the true purpose of following formal rules and the problems with law enforcement that make phrases like "the rule of law" often seem hollow. Does the system offer a mere pretense of fairness providing a cloak of respectability for the powerful and leaving the rest of society to the shoddy application of law in an under-resourced and random way? Behind the walls of their gated communities or fortified apartments the rich are insulated from this ugly reality. The dystopian visions of the future in *Blade Runner* (Michael Deeley and Ridley Scott 1982) and *Judge Dredd* (Charles Lippincott, Beau E. L. Marks, and Danny Cannon 1995) provide merely an exaggerated version of the vigilante film world-view. The naked power of the "legal" can be seen as no more than codified tyranny. This chapter seeks to explore whether the films with vigilante themes encapsulate this potentially radical perspective or, alternatively, express a naïve and romantic attachment to a superficially attractive rugged individualism associated with a strongly conservative political stance.

THE PROHIBITION OF THE VIGILANTE FILM

The Motion Pictures Producers and Distributors of America (MPPDA), which later became the Motion Picture Association of America (MPAA), adopted a code on 31 March 1930, began enforcing it in 1934, and abandoned it in 1968, in favor of the subsequent MPAA film rating system (ArtsReformation.com 1930). This voluntary self-regulation by the industry, known as the Hays Code, sought to protect the viewing public in the United States, and by extension, much of the rest of the world, from what were seen as various malign influences—sex, sacrilege, and vulgarity as well as miscegenation—Particular Applications—articles II (2) and (3) and (6) and III. These were the principal targets identified in the years between 1930 and the late 1960s, which were the years when the code and equivalents elsewhere were in full vigor (Sperling and Millner 1998; Robertson 1989). Among the issues which the code frowned on was the belittling of the legal process and any film where the perpetrator of illegal acts did not get their just desserts. The general principles included the statement that "Law shall not be ridiculed nor shall sympathy be created for its violation" (General Principle 3).

This was discussed in greater detail later in the original text in the section Particular Applications:

> I. Crimes Against the Law. These shall never be presented in such a way as to throw sympathy with the crime as against law and justice or to inspire others with a desire for imitation.

Specifically later in the document, under the heading "Reasons Underlying the Particular Applications" any film where revenge was the theme was forbidden. This was to be subject to some leeway covering "lands and ages of less developed civilization" as well as in "places where no law exists."

> Revenge in modern times shall not be justified. In lands and ages of less developed civilization and moral principles, revenge may sometimes be presented. This would be the case especially in places where no law exists to cover the crime because of which revenge is committed.

The result was that we find what one might term the vindication of the lone justice figure flourishing in the Western. The point though, about the

Western, as Wright (1975) and Nevins (1996) make clear, is that it is the rule of law is often highly contested. There may well be a formal structure of law and order but it is often blatantly no more than a facade for the rule of the rich and powerful or mine owner with compromised/corrupt sheriffs such as in *Johnny Guitar* (Herbert J. Yates and Nicholas Ray 1957) or are under pressure from such interests as in *Rio Bravo* (Howard Hawks 1959). In many such Westerns the forces of law and order are a mere front for the interests of cattle barons and the sheriffs, marshals, and judges are "placemen" as we can see in *Shane* (George Stevens 1953), *El Dorado* (Howard Hawks 1966), and *Pale Rider* (Clint Eastwood 1985).

THE EMERGENCE OF THE MODERN VIGILANTE

The Essence of the Vigilante

The quintessential modern vigilante has been the character of Paul Kersey, particularly in the guise of the actor Charles Bronson, whose name in Britain effectively signifies rejection of the justice system.[5] We are talking about the normal citizen, who if left alone by criminal elements would have no reason to strike back. The simple revenge theme has cropped up in a whole series of films where the original perpetrators are shown as having no redeeming qualities. Their crimes are done almost for sport as in *Sudden Impact* (Clint Eastwood 1983), *Eye for an Eye* (Michael I. Levy and John Schlesinger 1996) and *The Limey* (John Hardy and Scott Kramer; Steven Soderbergh 1999). Here the vigilante seeks to deal directly with a perpetrator whom the legal system has failed to bring to justice. The twenty-first century also has its variants on this theme in the first decade with *Death Sentence* (Ashok Amrita, Howard Baldwin, and Karen Baldwin; James Wan 2007), *The Brave One* (Susan Downey and Joel Silver; Neil Jordan 2007), *Gran Torino* (Clint Eastwood, Bill Gerber, and Robert Lorenz; Clint Eastwood 2008), *Law Abiding Citizen* (Robert Katz, Kurt Wimmer, Gerard Butler, Mark Gill, and Lucas Foster; J. Gary Gray 2009), and *Harry Brown* (Matthew Vaughn, Kris Thykier, Matthew Brown, and Keith Bell; Daniel Barber 2009). More recently, in the second decade of the century, we have standard lone vigilantes making their appearance in *Seeking Justice* (Tobey Maguire, Ram Bergman, and James D. Stern; Roger Donaldson 2011) and *Vendetta* (Jonathan Sothcott and Stephen Reynolds 2013) and, most recently, *John Doe: Vigilante* (James M. Vernon, Kristy Vernon, Keith Sweitzer, and David Lightfoot; Kelly Dolen 2014), *A Walk among the Tombstones* (Danny de Vito, Michael Shamberg, Stacey Sher, Brian Oliver, and Tobin Armbrust; Scott Frank 2014) and *The Equalizer* (Todd Black, Jason Blumenthal, Tony Eldridge, Mace Neufeld, Alex

Siskin, Michael Sloan, Steve Tisch, Denzel Washington, and R. Wenk; Antoine Fuqua 2014).

The term vigilante is also sometimes bestowed on government operative agents "on the edge." Those operating loosely as agents of the government like John Rambo (Sylvester Stallone) in *First Blood*; (Buzz Feitshans, Mario Kassar and Andrew G. Vajna; Ted Kotcheff 1985); *Rambo: First Blood Part II* (Buzz Feitshans and George Cosmatos 1985); and *Rambo III* (Buzz Feitshans, Mario Kassar, and Andrew G Vajna; Peter MacDonald 1988) but with a cavalier disregard for procedure are not really vigilantes any more than the government spy James Bond, or special operative John McClane (Bruce Willis) in the *Die Hard* franchise from 1988 onward (Joel Silver and Lawrence Gordon; John McTiernan 1988; Joel Silver, Charles Gordon, and Lawrence Gordon; Renny Harlin 1990; John McTiernan and Michael Tadross 1995; Michael Fottrell and Len Wiseman 2007; Alex Young and Wyck Godfrey; John Moore 2013). These are merely servants of society who are boldly going where others fear to tread in protecting the status quo and the lawfully constituted authorities rather than acting as vigilantes ignoring the law.

There is also the related theme of disaffected legal system personnel who operate in ways that do not meet the expectations of their superiors. One would include within this group "gung ho" police operatives like Axel Foley (Eddie Murphy) in *Beverly Hills Cop* (Don Simpson and Jerry Bruckheimer; Martin Brest 1984) and *Beverly Hills Cop 2* (Don Simpson and Jerry Bruckheimer; Tony Scott 1987); and Martin Riggs (Mel Gibson) in the *Lethal Weapon* series from 1987 to 1998 (Richard Donner and Joel Silver 1987; 1989; 1992; 1998). Again the term vigilante has been applied to Harry Callahan (Clint Eastwood) of the *Dirty Harry* series with his cavalier attitude to the rights of suspects. They still operate, however, within the framework of police powers. *Magnum Force* (Robert Daley and Ted Post 1973) illustrates that, while Callahan is casual about the use of violence, he is not a self-appointed righter of wrongs. He is distinct from the gang of cops who urge him to join them in dealing with those whom the law's technicalities have set free. He is just "doing his job." Cutting procedural corners is simply his way of enforcing the law for all. Although, like Kersey, often seen as a vigilante, Callahan in *The Enforcer* (Robert Daley and James Fargo 1976), *Sudden Impact* (Clint Eastwood 1983), and *The Dead Pool* (David Valdes and Buddy Van Horn 1988) metes out justice in a way which is violent but within the framework of his police role. He meets deadly force with deadly force rather than engage in personal revenge. Finally in *The Dead Pool* (1988) his victims are seeking to kill him and those he is protecting, and it may be significant that the series ends when Callahan appears to step over this line and actually takes revenge on a perpetrator.

The blandishments which Callahan rejected to become a vigilante were also offered in an indirect way to Judge Steven R. Hardin (Michael Douglas) in *The Star Chamber* (Frank Yablans and Peter Hyams 1985). His decision to join this self-appointed group of professional judges to "retry" those whom the legal system had not convicted provides an interesting potential for discussion of the relationship between legal procedures, the rule of law, and justice. This discussion within the film is, however, somewhat truncated and we get for a major part of the film instead a chase thriller when the wrong men are identified as the Star Chamber's next victims.

There is also a clear connection between some of the aims of the vigilante—securing of justice by means outwith the normal channels of the justice system—and those of the romantic outcast figure encountered in many cultures, the social bandit mentioned above. The most obvious examples would be the gangsters of the Depression: from Bonnie Parker and Clyde Barrow and the Barker Gang to John Dillinger, Baby Face Nelson, and Pretty Boy Floyd. Their bank robberies do not seem to have been undertaken with any other goal than personal enrichment, but were widely applauded. The exploits of Charles Floyd, for instance, were encapsulated in the Woody Guthrie (1940) song, *The Ballad of Pretty Boy Floyd,* with the lines suggesting that there was an underlying socially conscious aspect to Floyd in contrast to the relentless exploitation of finance capital "when he is described as paying off mortgages to save farmers' homes." As Guthrie concludes, the difference between the robbery of the bandit and that of those operating an exploitative financial and legal system has never been easy to distinguish "between theft with a gun and being robbed by a 'legal' contract."

The power of the social bandit theme lives on and is found in the Michael Mann film *Public Enemies* (Kevin Misher and Michael Mann 2009). Here we see that the supportive public reaction in banks to the exploits of the Dillinger gang were such that they were seen as modern heroic Robin Hood figures counterposed to the unfeeling world of finance capital. This had particular resonance following the latest crisis of capitalism in the post Lehman Brothers banking meltdown in 2008 (Blackburn 2008).

There are also elements of individuals operating in ways that are sometimes casually referred to as vigilantism but who are not, in reality, seekers after justice. These include the individual under stress. It is worth making a distinction between the vigilantism of personal justice, which has something to say about the nature of inadequate law and those individuals under stress, who tip over into mental unbalance and take on the world like Joe Curran (Peter Boyle) in *Joe* (David Gil and John G. Avildsen 1970), Travis Bickle (Robert de Niro) in *Taxi Driver* (Julia Phillips and Michael Phillips; Martin Scorsese 1976), or D-Fens (Michael Douglas) in

Falling Down (Tommy Harris, Arnold Kopelson, and Herschel Weingrod; Joel Schumacher 1992). Here rage is directed against the whole system rather than an individual act. Their actions may be triggered by a specific event but it is the social order they are kicking against in their fury. Avenging one single action will not be enough.

The Creation of "Legality" and the "Collectivist Vigilante"

One of the reasons why the Hays Code made a distinction between modern revenge and the historical versions has to do with the recent emergence of the link between law and democracy which we see in *The Man Who Shot Liberty Valance* (Willis Goldbeck and John Ford 1959). The shift from random lawlessness and individual responses and the emergence of official local law enforcement officers representing the community rather than protecting the interests of the rich is the very essence of the Western genre. Hence, versions of group action also crop up in a way which is akin to vigilantism. *The Revengers* (Martin Rackin and Daniel Mann 1972) is an example along with *The Magnificent Seven* (John Sturges 1960). Here we move into the replacement of random lawlessness and individual response to it, to a community perspective. In time, as *The Man Who Shot Liberty Valance* (1959) shows us, the lawyer turned politician, Ranse Stoddard (James Stewart), replaces the frontier gunslinger Tom Doniphon (John Wayne). The dystopian nightmare of *Mad Max* (Byron Kennedy and George Miller 1979) and *Mad Max: Beyond Thunderdome* (Terry Hayes, George Miller, and Doug Mitchell; George Miller and George Ogilvie 1985) is where, in a post-apocalyptic future, we return to this reliance on the individual in place of a consensus-based law enforcement.

The introduction of the formality of the law places the individual justice figure into an ambivalent position in relation to the procedures and processes of law enforcement. Hence we can see the moral protagonists in *Shane* (George Stevens 1953) and in *Hannie Caulder* (Patrick Curtis and Burt Kennedy 1971) not as vigilantes but as proto-law officers. In the modern world, the reverse could be said to be appearing. In the Western, in The *Man Who Shot Liberty Valance* (1959), the random gun-justice of Tom Doniphon (John Wayne) was replaced by the legislature and state-sanctioned enforcement of Ranse Stoddart (James Stewart). In the modern cinematic world, the challenge to the inadequacy of lawful policing comes from a series of individuals seeking solutions on an *ad hoc* basis in the person of vigilantes like Paul Kersey (Charles Bronson), Karen McCann (Sally Field), and Erica Bain (Jodie Foster). This has had a resonance which collectivist actions by the likes of the Gulabi Gang (Berthod 2012) in India and *Los Justiceros de la Tierra Caliente* (Calderon 2014) in Mexico have not enjoyed thus far in popular culture (see below).

The Modern Vigilante Film Assessed

The essence of the modern vigilante film is to pose questions about the nature of justice in a much clearer way than occurs in the traditional courtroom drama but in the context of a thriller. What we get is the revenge motif with a family context. The vigilante focus tends to have more time devoted to moral conundrums and ambiguities than we find in the run-of the-mill trial movie. The courtroom dramas may also contain thriller elements but are centered on the skill, inadequacy, or personal crisis of the main lawyer protagonist. The moral center is often not in dispute—is the accused actually innocent of the crime? How will the legal team for the "David" side manage to overcome the obstacles they face? How will they establish that there is evidence to exculpate their client or to prove that the other side has breached their duties, for instance, not to pollute as in, for instance, A *Civil Action* (Robert Redford, Scott Rudin, and Rachel Pfeffer; Steven Zaillian 1999), or *Erin Brockovich* (Danny De Vito, Michael Shamberg, and Stacey Sher; Steven Soderbergh 2000) (Greenfield, Osborn, and Robson 2010, 164–65). Vigilante films are about what ordinary citizens do when the justice system does not meet their expectations and fails them. The extent and level of debate about these complex moral dilemmas is variable. Some return to the theme while others simply use the notion of "justice denied" as the catalyst for a thriller. Given the constraints of length in this chapter I have focused on the films that have been most successful in terms of box office, which have major stars and where a recognized director is involved—see appendix 2. There are many other films with a vigilante element or where the same kinds of themes appear and a full overview of the area would permit these more coverage. In fairness, many of these are concerned with system challenges rather than simply individuals. Those films which the various film guides (VideoHound 2008; 2014) and my own interpretation suggest fall into this category are noted in appendix 1. The films discussed are representative of the other lesser films. In this chapter we look at the conventions that can be seen in the most important films in this sub-genre of thrillers that center around a question at the heart of the justice system. This is encapsulated in the question posed on the poster advertising the film *The Brave One* (2007)—"What do you do when 'justice' fails?"

Narrative Conventions

The vigilante narrative conventions involve the contrast between the normality of family life and the disruption that assails it and a series of events that befall the luckless family, resulting in there being a vigilante response. This vigilante response succeeds, allowing an orderly return to normal life.

1. Setting the scene. The opening scene of the modern vigilante film shows the protagonist in their natural environment. This is invariably an ordinary decent family. We get just enough clues about the lives of the family to infer that this is a happy setting with a bright future beckoning. The family are going about either doing ordinary day-to-day tasks of shopping for instance. In *Death Wish* (1974) Paul Kersey's daughter (Kathleen Tolan) and wife (Hope Lange) have returned from getting the groceries and in *Law Abiding Citizen* (2009) father (Gerard Butler) and daughter (Ksenia Hulayev) are both constructing gifts for the mother (Brook Mills). In *Eye for an Eye* (1995) we see the excited preparations for a birthday party. In the most elaborate set up we see the home movies of the family growing up from birth through birthdays to near adulthood in *Death Sentence* (2007). Home movies of a contented childhood also feature in the less generic vigilante themed film *Dead Man's Shoes* (Mark Herbert and Louise Meadows; Shane Meadows 2004). The vigilante movie introduces this notion of the family in both a traditional form as with a wife and children as in *Eye for an Eye* (1995), *Death Sentence* (2007), and *Law Abiding Citizen* (2009) as well as a proto-family of vulnerable workplace colleagues in *The Equalizer* (2014). Even when the vigilante is a senior citizen we see evidence of past happy memories with family photos in *Harry Brown* (2009)

2. The disruptive random event. Into this calm and ordered world there is a sudden and unexpected irruption of stranger violence. The violence is almost always irrational. It is usually unexplained. The perpetrators are evil personified. They have no obvious redeeming social features. They are killing for thrills. In the case of *Death Sentence* (2007) they are doing this as part of a gang initiation rite or in *Harry Brown* (2009) because society has no role for them. They may be laughing "crazies" as we find *Death Wish* (1974) and *Law Abiding Citizen* (2009) or quiet, seemingly normal "loners" as in *Eye for an Eye* (1995). At best they are flagrantly taking irresponsible risks with innocent lives which we see in *The Fourth Angel* (2002) and *The Equalizer* (2014). They are classic examples of "stranger danger," which statistics tell us are far less likely to visit violence upon us than members of our immediate family or people whom we know (Office for National Statistics 2013).

3. The law takes its course. The essence of the perpetrators is that they should be in some way incompetent at evading the police and be immediately apprehended. They are charged and subjected to the rigors of the law in the apprehension phase of the justice system. This is the essence of the vigilante film. The legal system is shown to have the potential to apprehend. This aspect of the law's operation appears in vigilante films to be in sound working order as shown in *Death Wish* (1974), *Eye for an Eye* (1985), *Death Sentence* (2007), and *Law Abiding Citizen* (2009). The problem is what has happened to the court system. There is a slight variation in British vigilante films where we find that the problem arises because the prosecution authorities decline to take action and the matter does not reach the courts either for lack of reliable evidence in *Dead Man's Shoes* (2004), *Harry Brown* (2009), and *Vendetta* (2013), or a jurisdictional technicality in *The Fourth Angel* (2002). The law, then is shown as operative but also frequently compromised in the adjudicative phase.

4. The system malfunctions. The ease with which the malefactor is apprehended is in sharp contrast to the effectiveness of the trial or adjudicative phase. The conviction fails to materialize and the malefactor goes free. Plea bargaining or restrictive rules on the admissibility of evidence conspire together so that the malefactors are subjected to either no penalty or a mockery of what might reasonably have been predicted. Perhaps this is why the perpetrators are so casual about evading capture since they know that the conviction rate is so low and the system a joke. This theme is found in almost all the films in one form or another. It can include the problem of the adequacy of evidence (*Death Sentence* 2007). Other problems range from human foul-ups such as failing to provide the defense with DNA records (*Eye for an Eye* 1995) or being unable to use DNA evidence to convict both murderers and having to accept a plea bargain from one of the accused (*Law Abiding Citizen* 2009).

5. Tentative revenge reaction suppressed. The initial reaction of the affected individual is to accept the situation and try and get on with life. The victim is not naturally vengeful. There is more to life than feuding and revenge. Paul Kersey goes back to designing buildings in *Death Wish* (1974). Karen McCann (Sally Field) attends a self-help group in *Eye for an Eye* (1995), dealing with the loss of loved ones and her first thoughts are not of revenge. Erica Bain (Jody Foster), the radio presenter in *The Brave One* (2007), indeed, gets on with her life and returns to work. Even distraught Harry tholes the pain of missing his wife's death through the danger from local thugs preventing him reaching the hospital in time in *Harry Brown* (2009)

6. Trigger to revenge. There is, however, an event that shakes the victim out of their torpor. There is a realization that something must be done. Unchecked evil raises its ugly head and the protagonist is forced to do something or is put in a situation where action becomes inevitable. Karen McCann seeks counselling for her grief and it is only when she sees the murderer planning and then successfully carrying out another similar crime that she determines to get a gun and avenge her own daughter in *Eye for an Eye* (1995). In *The Brave One* (2007) the victim Erika Bain finds herself in a convenience store that is being robbed and responds to the threat to herself and the storeowner. She does not seek out evil. It comes to her not just once but twice. Spurred by her unexpected confrontations with further evil she determines to put right the original wrongs she has until then borne. The eponymous Harry Brown (Michael Caine) (2009) does nothing about the people terrorizing the housing estate where he lives until the death of his friend leads to a confrontation with a mugger and his accidental rediscovery of his Marine training skills. Up until that moment, he looks like a frail and frightened pensioner with emphysema.

7. Successful elimination of the "evil." Normally the victim manages to outwit the perpetrator whether or not it is museum administrator, Karen McCann (*Eye for an Eye* 1995), civil servant Jack Elgin (*The Fourth Angel* 2002), or radio program maker Erika Bain (*The Brave One* 2007). They may turn out to have hidden abilities as a killer or be drawing on their hitherto hidden past. In *Law Abiding Citizen* (2009) Gerard Butler's Clyde Shelton turns out to have been a government operative while Michael Caine's pensioner *Harry Brown* (2009) has been a Marine and gets out his old knife and obtains a weapon. Denzel Washington's Robert McCall has been involved in dark ops for the government in *The Equalizer* (2014) as has been Danny Dyer's Special Ops interrogation specialist, Jimmy Vickers, in *Vendetta* (2013). This is the basis for the success of the vigilante film, which allows a true thriller film to be operated within the framework of a moral revenge drama. This spells nemesis for those who appear to have escaped the clutches of the law. The perpetrators are brought down to earth in bloody confrontation. There is no opportunity for them to reflect on their past actions and to repent. Vengeance is exacted in a range of bloody ways. Sometimes these are appropriate to the nature of the original crime as in the burning alive of the gang leader in *Vendetta* (2013), but this is more a feature of the rape-revenge roster discussed below.

8. Coda. There is a brief moment for reflection after the elimination of the "evil." This "final scene" is one which seems to valorize the actions of the vigilante. The vigilante escapes the wrath of the law. There is, in many instances, connivance by the representatives of the forces of law and order to ensure that the vigilante escapes any punishment for their actions—from Paul Kersey, through Karen McCann and Erika Bain to Jack Elgin and Harry Brown—so that we are left to cheer the moral actions of the vigilante. Not only have they had their revenge on the perpetrator, but they have been allowed to return to their normal proper law-abiding lives. This ranges from simply surviving to live another day (*Eye for an Eye* 1995, *Outlaw* 2007, and *Harry Brown* 2009), sunning oneself on a yacht (*The Fourth Angel* 2002), or taking up the role of vigilante in a new location (*Vendetta* 2013). Vigilantism by part-time amateurs works in these movies. The only vigilantes who pay for their actions, and die, are the ones for whom life is already ended—physically with terminal cancer

(*Gran Torino* 2009), or psychologically with suicide (*Dead Man Shoes* 2004), or the ending is ambivalent (*Death Sentence* 2007).

THE VIGILANTE MORAL DILEMMA ON SCREEN

The advantage the vigilante film has over the traditional courtroom drama is the ability for it to be set firmly and credibly within the action movie genre. There is extensive use of chases and action sequences. This is not the land of suits, legal strategies, and gavels. Here we have tension, heightening music and short bite-sized discussions of the morality of acting or not acting. It does not involve an extended reflection on the human condition, which we find in, for instance, *Judgment at Nuremberg* (Stanley Kramer 1961) or *A Man for All Seasons* (Fred Zinnemann 1966), but it does have recognizable bad characters against whom the reasonable citizen might want to act. The revenge reflex is to an extent intellectualized and the nature of justice and its source assessed. There is even in the final shot of *Seeking Justice* (2011) a suggestion that a form of vigilantism has subverted the whole legal process with widespread vigilante actions being operated through a shadowy matrix-like underground. The mild reluctant avenging victim, Will Gerard (Nicolas Cage) is given a codeword to know that he is among those who offer mutual aid and carry out revenge attacks in the style of Hitchcock's *Strangers on a Train* (Alfred Hitchcock 1951) where unconnected people "swap" victims. He is required to kill a sex offender, Alan Marsh (Jason Davis), which he only manages to do by accident. He is arrested for murder but released when he is invited to complete the code phrase of the organization "The Hungry Rabbit Jumps." Everyone, it seems, is involved. The victim whose death he caused turns out to have been a reporter investigating vigilantes. A complicated story of blackmail unfolds at the end of which it seems vigilantism pervades the whole of the justice system.

What drew me to these films in the first place was that they were not cult specialist underground or even art house productions. These were standard mainstream fare available in today's multiplexes. The directors of these vigilante films were also major figures like John Schlesinger, Steven Soderbergh, Shane Meadows, Michael Winner, and Neil Jordan. These are directors whose work has been recognised both at Film Festivals and at Award Ceremonies as well as achieving major box office success (Radio Times 2015, 1620–40). The films had in the past and continue to attract such "A list" stars as Clint Eastwood, Jodie Foster, Kevin Bacon, Sally Field, Samuel L. Jackson, Michael Caine, Gerard Butler, Jamie Foxx, Nicolas Cage, Guy Pearce, Liam Neeson, Denzel Washington as well as others with solid box office track records like Chuck Norris, Sean Bean, and Danny Dyer. There is a consistent roster of films over the past thirty-five years that focus on stories which show that the system cannot cope and that the only approach is to settle accounts outwith the formal justice system. These films start with *Death Wish* (1974)—the original vigilante—and can be seen in a range of individual revenge plots mentioned above. This roster covers *An Eye for an Eye* (1981); *Eye for an Eye* (1995); *The Limey* (1999); *The Fourth Angel* (2002); *Dead Man's Shoes* (2004); *Red* (2004); *Death Sentence* (2007); *The Brave One* (2007); *Outlaw* (2007); *Gran Torino* (2009); *Law Abiding Citizen* (2009); *Harry Brown* (2009); *Seeking Justice* (2011); *Vendetta* (2013); *John Doe: Vigilante* (2014); *A Walk among the Tombstones* (2014); and *The Equalizer* (2014) (appendix 2). Although the films of Arnold Schwarzenegger, Steven Seagal, and Jean-Claude Van Damme often have simple revenge themes, they strike me as belonging to a fantasy action category all of their own for separate consideration another time along with superhero films. There are also many other films that have a revenge theme or that have vigilante elements within their storyline which do not, however, meet the criteria I have sought to place on this limited examination. These films tend to lack big names either directing or starring. They are often made for, or immediately go, straight to video. They do not get an airing in the everyday cinema houses across the world. In a number of instances, they have achieved a certain cult status. As appendix 1 indicates there are many of these films alongside extremely low-cost "fan films" produced with modern technology enabling revenge themes to be played out to a special interest audience such as *Left for Dead* (Phil Hobden and Ross Boyask 2005), *Ten Dead Men* (Phil Hobden and Mike Leeder; Ross Boyask 2008), and *Vigilante* (Robert Diaz and Aash Aaron 2009). Given the even cruder themes of "revenge is good and simple," which these films incorporate, they do nothing to allay my concerns about vigilante films. It does not seem unreasonable, however, for the purposes of this collection, to limit discussion to the quite extensive mainstream roster identified.

This, then, is an identifiable genre leading to homages and the like. Some of the films with vigilante themes provide these with a twist. In *Hot Fuzz* (Tim Bevan, Eric Fellner, and Nira Park; Edgar Wright 2007), a quiet peaceful crime-free town turns out to be the result, not of a good mix of effective policing and good citizens but of unbridled vigilantism by the "blue rinse brigade." In *Hero Wanted* (Danny Lerner, Johnny Martin, and Les Weldon; Brian Smrz 2008) an apparent victim, Liam Case (Cuba Gooding Jr), vows revenge on the perpetrators of the bank robbery that left an innocent bank clerk dead. All is, however, not as it seems. Liam set up the robbery to have the chance to impress the young female bank clerk, Kayla McQueen, (Christa Campbell) who ended up dead. Finally, in *Gran Torino* (2009), a xenophobe, Walt Kowalski, (Clint Eastwood) stands up for a group of incomers with whom he appears to have no common ties or interests. Again a twist confounds our expectations when we expect a serious culmination of evil confronted in a shoot-out. In a similar situation, although seriously outnumbered Butch and Sundance gun down their opponents in *Butch Cassidy and the Sundance Kid* (John Foreman and George Roy Hill 1969). This is parodied in a scene from *Blazing Saddles* (Michael Hertzberg and Mel Brooks 1974) where the Ringo Kid (Gene Wilder) singlehandedly shoots the guns from the hands of all eight of his opponents. Still expecting something on these lines and drawn in by the poster advertising the film showing Eastwood with rifle in hand, we get instead the ending from *Butch Cassidy* minus the truth-denying freeze-frame.[6] Eastwood, the hero of Spaghetti Westerns such as *Pale Rider* (Clint Eastwood 1985), in *Gran Torino* (Clint Eastwood 2008) is cut down in a hail of bullets, reaching, not for a gun, but for his cigarette lighter. The police arrive and the gang goes down for his murder. He has shown that there is another way to achieve revenge. In the process he has sacrificed himself but we know that he had only a short time to live. It seems to be a wry undercutting of the simplistic appeal of vigilantism. This chimes in with an earlier film directed by Eastwood, *Mystic River* (Judie G. Hoyt, Robert Lorenz, and Clint Eastwood 2003). Here the issue of the perils of vigilante justice was also subtly raised with the successful avengers suffering in a variety of ways and calling into question the whole revenge approach.

So what might we conclude? The cinema is suffused with themes of random stranger violence not reflected in crime surveys and statistics. These stereotypical misconceptions are allied to media themes of the routine malfunctioning of the justice system. Files are lost. The rules obstruct the way of "true justice" with public prosecutors and judges being obsessed with elaborate rules on what amounts to illegal search and seizure. The narrative conventions of the films are simple. The state has failed an ordinary, identifiable, sympathetic character whose life we know something about. There is a family. Their happiness has been brought to a jarring halt. Justice is denied to them and if the ordinary citizen cannot get justice what is to be done? The answer from vigilante cinema is to take back the night. The clear implications of these films briefly surveyed is that revenge as an option "works." The common final scene in the range of vigilante films is that justice has been effected informally and the world continues. Our *justiciero* has done what had to be done and the world can return to an even keel. It is little wonder that the Second Amendment to the United States Constitution maintaining the right to keep and bear arms has so many adherents since not only is there ever-present "stranger danger" but a strong chance that in order for this danger to be dealt with the individual will have to "seize the time." Life will go on but the "evil" is no more.[7]

There is an interesting development to observe for those looking at the film vigilante in the second decade of the twenty-first century. We have a continuing preoccupation with the fictional urban vigilante. Most recently we have a novel approach in the marketing of the Australian film *John Doe: Vigilante* (2014). This film premiered in March 2014 and at one level is absolutely standard fare. To quote from the publicity from the producers of the film at that time:

> Some call him a hero. Some call him a villain. He's "John Doe: Vigilante"—an ordinary man who decides to take the law into his own hands. Frustrated with a failing legal system that continues to allow violent criminals to go free, John Doe begins exacting justice the only way he knows how—by killing one criminal at a time. Soon he becomes a media sensation and inspires a group of copycat vigilantes, but who is the real John Doe—a pillar of justice or a cold-blooded murderer? You decide. (IMDB 2014)

In what was described as an "innovative marketing ploy," the producers of the film launched a free interactive game *Vigilante: Speak for the Dead* (2015). This was part of a campaign to publicize the film. To do this the producers explained that it enabled users to take the role of a vigilante and disarm other players while also forming powerful vigilante "Crews." The game poses questions such as: *What's your idea of justice? Will you steer clear of killing and only target hardened criminals? Or are you a psychotic killer, waxing j-walkers and speeding drivers?* This marks a recognition by those producing this films that these films have an impact on audiences beyond the time spent watching the action.[8]

AN ALTERNATIVE PERSPECTIVE: THE RAPE-REVENGE FILM

Alison Young and others also look at the theme of revenge, though from a different perspective. She looks not at the affected family member's reaction to trauma, but at the surviving victim's response in her discussion of rape-revenge films (Young 2010, chapter 3). This discussion is located within what is a recognizable genre. What she is talking about and examining is a scenario where there is violent revenge by the victim of "a shocking scene of gang rape" (Young 2010, 44). This will be "followed by a succession of episodes of violent retribution . . . after the victim, perhaps having sought legal assistance or the intervention of the police or equally having decided that no effective institutional assistance will be forthcoming decides to undertake the task of revenge" (Young 2010, 44). Here, then, is an alternative genre to the vigilante film also involving revenge and operating outside the law. The starting point, however, is different. The focus is narrower. Here we have a situation where "the agency of the victim can bring about justice in some form or other" (Young 2010, 66). Young's principal concern is that the depiction of rape in these films is exploitative and unacceptable and it is possible that "the depiction of sexual violence be imagined differently" (Young 2010, 73). We should "refuse the invitation to look at the crime image of rape" (Young 2010, 73). This reflects Young's desire to move beyond the focus in some law and film scholarship on narrative tropes. Her preoccupations are with the aesthetics of film and the process of spectatorship. Her notion that the portrayal of rape has pandered to the prurient and should be rejected seems to be entirely well put. The scenes in the films she discusses are evidence that, given an opportunity, filmmakers will dwell on the rape in a way that needs to be addressed.

There is clearly extensive common ground between rape-revenge films and those films in which those indirectly affected by stranger violence to family members seek justice. My initial concern from reading Young out of context was whether or not the films selected by her actually amounted to a film genre. *Thelma and Louise* (Mimi Polk Gitlin and Ridley Scott 1991) was selected despite it being a film principally about flight from the perceived unsympathetic justice system. The second of the films, *Blackrock* (David Elfick and Steven Vidler 1997), while it featured a gang rape and subsequent murder, did not deal with rape-revenge but rather the psychological consequences for a young man that failed to intervene. The Dirty Harry film, *Sudden Impact* (1983) in which rape-revenge was a subplot in a film famous for the phrase "Go ahead punk. Make my day," was the third film examined. Finally *The Accused* (Stanley R. Jaffe and Sherry Lansing; Jonathan Kaplan 1988), with its graphic gang rape scene revealed in the courtroom reconstruction was discussed. Young talks of revenge with the statute book and law reports being used as "weapons" (Young 2010, 67). This, though, is precisely the difference between using the law and going outside it. What Young discusses are films, however, which might possibly be added to an established mainstream of a clearly extant genre rather than its core. Henry, too, is of the view that *The Accused* and *Thelma and Louise* are "weaker examples of the genre than the earlier classic examples" (Henry 2014 15).

It becomes clear, however, from the material in Read (2000), Heller-Nicholas (2011), and Henry (2014), that there is, indeed, a considerable body of films produced over the years that share the themes to which Young draws attention. The reason for my unfamiliarity with these works was the obscurity of many of them. From the very beginning, with what Young refers to as the first film in the genre in 1978, *I Spit on Your* Grave,[9] there is a succession of films that are highly violent "gorefests" with prominent coverage of the rape element of the narrative from *Lipstick* (Freddie Fields and Lamont Johnson 1976) to *I Spit on Your Grave* 2 (Lisa

M. Hansen and Paul Hertzberg; Steven R. Monroe 2013). Many are catalogued in *Rape and Revenge Films* (Hephaestus 2011). Over fifty such films are noted here and in the rape-revenge scholarship of Read (2000), Heller-Nicholas (2011), and Henry (2014). There are occasional exceptions with some mainstream offerings like *Sleepers* (Steve Golin and Barry Levinson 1996). Although the victims of abuse by prison guards are boys in the criminal justice system the nature of their abuse is hinted at rather than made explicit here. It has also been suggested that *The Girl with the Dragon Tattoo* (Søren Stærmose and Niels Arden Oplev 2009) comes within the genre (Heller-Nicholas 2011, 172). There are also art-house products like *Irréversible* (Vincent Cassel, Brahim Chioua, Richard Grandpierre, and Christophe Rossignon; Gaspar Noé 2002), but the majority are for the DVD market with low production values and lacking any noted actors or directors. For the most part, they focus on the revenge as revenge without any concern for the consequences and with minimal focus on the post-revenge period. Such is the construction of their plots, their characterization and their dénouements that their likelihood of contributing to the debate about film's influence on the portrayal of the justice system might seem improbable.

These rape-revenge films, then, are largely obscure and well away from the multiplex fare of the vigilante films discussed in this chapter. *I Spit on Your Grave* (1978) is described in one of the film guides as a film "worth zero as a film; lots of violent terror and gory death; totally irresponsibly portrayed" (VideoHound 2009, 467; VideoHound 2015, 666) as well as being described by Henry as a "B movie" (Henry 2014, 15). It did not receive a cinematic release in Britain and went straight to video/DVD. Its 2010 remake treads the same path and went straight to DVD. What happens to the victim Jennifer Hills once she has killed the gang of rapists, one by one, we do not know. The film closes on her final act of revenge in both versions. Her relationship to the justice system remains unresolved. Whether or not she will suffer the fate of Aileen Wournos (Charlize Theron) in *Monster* (Mark Damon, Donald Kushner, Clark Peterson, Charlize Theron, and Brad Wyman; Patty Jenkins 2003) or that of Karen McCann (Sally Field) in *Eye for an Eye* (1995) we can only wonder. This strikes me as the crucial difference in the focus between the vigilante films I started out examining and the rape-revenge films which share the revenge element. The first set of films involve an ambivalent and shifting stance in relation to the justice system while the latter proceed on the assumption that it is irrelevant.

Responding to Carol Clover's work on the alleged pleasures of horror films (Clover 1992), Read addresses the issue of agency within the rape-revenge genre (Read 2000). She sees such films as transforming the victim into a heroine (Read 2000, 8). Given the dominant nature of the sexploitation trope in such films, whether these films can be seen as a way of making sense of feminism, as Read suggests, (2000, 10) seems questionable. It is a debate, however, that is beyond the scope of a chapter with its focus on the contingent nature of legality. Heller-Nicholas documents the production of such films across different cultures and across different genres (Heller-Nicholas 2011, chapters 2 and 3). She demonstrates that the underlying themes of rape-revenge go well beyond Anglophone cinema and can also be encountered in Argentina, Australia, Canada, France, Germany, Hong Kong, India, Japan, Spain, and Turkey (Heller-Nicholas 2011, chapter 3). The existence of the rape-revenge theme is also shown to exist across genres appearing in comedy, Westerns and horror films (Heller-Nicholas 2011, chapter 2). Her focus, though, as she explains, is to explore a "broader cultural confusion about rape generally" reflected in the way in which rape has been screened and to examine "simplistic assumptions about the ethics of rape and its representation on screen" (Heller-Nicholas 2011, 4).

As indicated above, that is not the focus of this chapter, although I would certainly concur with Heller-Nicholas's assessment that "many of the female-centred rape-revenge films . . . addressed in this book are undeniably sensational attempts to profit from the ugly desire to watch sexual violence" (Heller-Nicholas 2011, 4). Henry, for her part, is concerned with highlighting "affective response and ethical engagement" in her study (Henry 2014, 22). Henry looks at the rape-revenge films with a focus on genre and suggests that more recently a revisionist version of the rape-revenge film has emerged. These have a more ambivalent relationship to violent revenge. She cites the role of Adam (Danny Dyer) in *Straightheads* (Damian Jones and Kevin Loader; Dan Read 2007) (Henry 2014, 17). She also contrasts the more recent work such as *Twilight Portrait* (Olga Dykhovichnaya and Angelina Nikonova, 2011) and *Katalin Vargas* (Oona Giurgiu and Tudor Giurgiu; Peter Strickland 2009) with *Lipstick* (1976) to make this point (Henry 2014, 181). Again, all the modern films are far from the mainstream and subject to the same concerns as "the classics."

CONCLUSION

Before indicating my conclusions as to the developments in vigilante films two issues in relation to methodology strike me on examining these films. First, it might be argued that by situating the issue of rape-revenge within the context of the broader vigilante theme, the films are located more effectively in their social and political context. A richer picture emerges of how the cinematic world portrays extra-judicial justice. This does not prevent the principal focus being on the subset of victim-response films but I would argue that this context provides a clearer understanding of the way cinema has engaged with this extremely sensitive area. As Young points out, there is an element of the process of viewing the rape scene in *The Accused* (1988) whereby "the audience member watches as a witness to a crime . . . (as well as) . . . a spectator able to find entertainment in what is depicted" (Young 2010, 54). What is, to me, most interesting is whether, when one isolates rape victim protagonist films from other vigilante films, whether there are differences—has there been a development over time? Can viewers identify with the protagonists in a way that occurs in vigilante films where justice is achieved and normal service is resumed?

Looking at rape-revenge films in isolation for my own focus on the justice system's portrayal would be a rather limiting approach given the number of films which I have considered within the broader concept of vigilantism where there is rape-revenge as a theme but where the victim is avenged by another. This occurs in *Death Wish* (1974), *Death Wish 2* (1977), and *Eye for an Eye* (1995). In other films which shed a light on activity beyond the constraints of the formal legal system, such as *The Fourth Angel* (2002), *Harry Brown* (2009), or *Vendetta* (2013) what is being avenged is murder. The seriousness of the events being avenged is seldom less serious than rape and murder. That said, there have been exceptions such as revenge for a dog killing in *Red* (Steve Blair and Norman Dreyfuss; Trygve Allister Diesen and Lucky McKee 2008) and the comedy pastiche *Hot Fuzz* (2007) with its revenge for minor public nuisances. Thus, it would seem to me, more light is likely to be shed on the legitimacy of the justice system by the core of *The Brave One* (2007). Here the driving element is revenge of the boyfriend's death and the protagonist's own suffering rape rather than the loss of her dog.

The second issue is rather more positive, albeit tangential to the theme of legality. It provides us with a clear way of showing in concrete terms what is really meant by "different films having different meanings." It provides a fascinating insight into the way in which the vigilante/rape-revenge dichotomy illustrates the idea of films being read differently. It is not simply the interpretation of the signs and messages within films that are different. Rather we are talking about different questions within a different context. Neither perspective is right or wrong. They are simply operating within different problematics. This does not mean, however, that they cannot benefit from looking at the other perspective. In terms of pedagogy, the lessons to be derived are considerable. Here we are talking not simply of different reactions to events and perceptions of characters as heroic or flawed. Rather we are talking about the questions we are posing about the films (see also May 2015 on "backlash" films).

The examination of a number of the twenty-first-century women lawyer films illustrates this issue of how one can start off with different goals in one's work. *Legally Blonde* (Ric Kidney, Christian McLaughlin, David Nicksay, and Marc Platt; Robert Luketic 2001) and *Two Weeks Notice* (Sandra Bullock and Marc Lawrence 2002) are cases in point. By asking questions about the way in which women are processed in the legal systems where they are "players" as opposed to being its victims we can see a possible shift from the crude portrayal of women as being caring and intuitive as opposed to rational and logical in *Jagged Edge* (1985) and *Suspect* (1987). Both Elle Woods (Reese Witherspoon) in *Legally Blonde* (2001) and Lucy Kelson (Sandra Bullock) in *Two Weeks Notice* (2002) succeed by their legal skills rather than feminine wiles. They are not duped by men. In their battles and development they win. Alternatively, we can see these as just romantic comedies in which they both end up with the men of their dreams. Looking at these films in terms of satisfying the romantic-comedy conventions of "happiness-loss-happiness nearly regained-relost-finally happiness achieved," they satisfy the narrative conventions of the genre. They just happen to be set in legal offices and involve people who work as lawyers. Just as we can see films around revenge as illustrations of vigilantism or a new kind of nonvictim feminism—whether or not they are revenge for rape—*Death Wish* (1974), *Lipstick* (1976), *I Spit on Your Grave* (1978), and *Seeking Justice* (2012)—or murder—*Death Sentence* (2007) and *Harry Brown* (2009)—or often both—*Last House on the Left* (1972), *Eye for an Eye* (1995), *Death Wish* (1974), *Death Wish 2* (1982), *The Brave One* (2007), and *Law Abiding Citizen* (2011). It all depends where the focus is placed.

During the past thirty-five years between mild-mannered architect Paul Kersey (Charles Bronson) in *Death Wish* (1974) and model hardware store worker Robert McCall (Denzel Washington) in *The Equalizer* (2014), the basic theme of vigilante films has been almost constant. Vigilantism works. What has altered, though, has been the insertion into the narratives of an element of credibility. The modern vigilante protagonist is less likely to be a simple amateur. He or she will probably now have a background that makes the ability to take revenge effectively and efficiently and escape the consequences of these actions rather more believable. This background is likely to be in the military or police forces. It is unlikely to be revealed immediately and this allows us still to identify with the vigilante as a normal citizen whom the justice system has failed. This would suggest that that a rational reading of films with vigilante themes has not traditionally encapsulated any strong radical perspective but rather continue to express in a variety of ways an attachment to a simple world of empowering individualism. This may be coming under pressure. One possible optimistic development has been in the portrayal of actual vigilante groups like the pink clad Gulabi Gang on the screen in *Gulaab Gang*

(Sen 2014) with their focus on such issues as domestic violence, the dowry system, rape, and education.[10] This communitarian approach might come into greater prominence in the future and change what has hitherto been the vigilante film's dominant conservative individualistic theme. It depends on whether Theodor Adorno and Max Horkheimer's perspective holds true (Adorno and Horkheimer 1944/1979) and the line between the world of cinema and the world outside remains as it has been.

APPENDIX 1: VIGILANTE THEMED FILMS[11]—A MINI-GUIDE

American Commandos (1985): rape revenge theme minor aspect prior to Vietnam "mission."

Avenging Angel (1985): revenge of murder of policeman by person he helped.

Bad Ass (2012): Vietnam War hero becomes famous when he beats up two skinheads and becomes involved in solving a murder by a major drug dealer.

Best of the Best 3: No Turning Back (1995): fight against racist vigilantes.

Black Fox: Blood Horse (1994): vigilante attack on Native Americans part of action in a Western.

Boondock Saints (1995): brothers turn vigilante against Russian gangsters.

The Boondock Saints II: All Saints Day (2009): the brothers return to deal with a plot to frame a priest by the remnants of the gangsters in *Boondock Saints* (1995) and engage in various vigilante activities in a hugely complex plot.

Boy Wonder (2010): a young man who witnessed his mother's murder sets out to find the street scum responsible for this and other crimes.

The Brave One (2007): classic accidental vigilante by victim—see appendix 2.

Brutal Fury (1992): teenage vigilantes (the Fury) targeting drug dealers and rapists.

Bunny Whipped (2006): a sportswriter avenges the death of a rapper.

Combat Shock (1984): Vietnam veteran against lowlife street types trying to kill him.

Contract on Cherry Street (1977): vigilante hit on a gang member is part of rogue police officer's strategy to get evidence on the gang.

Cross (2011): a band of vigilantes roam the streets of Los Angeles looking for victims of kidnapping.

Dark Angel: The Ascent (1994): she-devil fired from hell takes on a vigilante role.

Dark Justice (2000): judge by day and avenger by night of those escaping through legal loopholes.

Death Sentence (2007): son killed and father takes revenge on the gang—see appendix 2.

The Death Squad (1973): police vigilantes tracked down by an ex-cop in TV movie.

Death Wish (1974): revenge of murder and rape of wife and daughter by liberal architect, Paul Kersey—see appendix 2.

Death Wish 2 (1982): revenge for trauma to daughter—see appendix 2.

Death Wish 3 (1985): further revenge on those dear to Kersey—see appendix 2.

Death Wish 4: The Crackdown (1987): Kersey attacks crack dealers after a friend's daughter dies of a drug overdose—see appendix 2.

Death Wish 5: The Face of Death (1994): revenge for treatment of business of Kersey's fiancée—see appendix 2.

Defiance (1979): stand against local street gang taken by ex-merchant seaman.

The Devil's Rejects (2005): zombie serial killer follow-up to earlier zombie horror film.

Dirty Harry (1971): tough cop with little regard for civil rights of criminals.

Double Bang (2001): honest cop takes law into his own hands when his partner is killed—straight to video.

Double Tap (1998): FBI agent pursuing antidrug cartel vigilante.

DROP Squad (1994): satire about vigilante organisation seeking to bring recalcitrant African Americans back to their heritage—Deprogramming and Restoration of Pride (DROP).

Elektra (2005): an assassin-for-hire who changes to protector of those she has been hired to kill.

Eye for an Eye (1981): ex-cop turns vigilante—see appendix 2.

An Eye for an Eye (1995): a mother avenges her raped and murdered daughter after the killer is released on a technicality—see appendix 2.

Falling Down (1993): sacked executive snaps and takes revenge on anyone who gets in his way.

Force Five (1975): anticrime squad formed by ex-cons in a TVM.

Full Clip (2006): man returns to his home in a small town to claim the inheritance his father has left him. Once there, however, he finds that the local police have corrupted the town and are ruling with an iron fist. With the help of some old friends, he sets out to reclaim the town.

Gang Boys (1997): fight back by local victims after a young man is brutally beaten—straight to video.

Girls Against Boys (2012): college student and her friend take revenge on a man who raped her before the student kills her friend.

Gone (2010): man returns to his home town to avenge the death of his brother.

The Green Hornet (2011): a couple of young men become crime-fighters who pose as criminals in order to infiltrate real criminal gangs in an action comedy.

The Gunman (2003): police officer tasked with tracking down vigilante whose next victim is the person who killed his own wife—straight to video—but starring one of the brothers from *Boondock Saints* (supra).

Hard Candy (2006): photographer tied, threatened, and accused of paedophilia by young Lolita figure he met "online" and finally persuaded to commit suicide to atone for photographing an earlier sex attack and murder.

Harry Brown (2009): ex-marine avenges death of his friend—see appendix 2.

Hobo with a Shotgun (2011): dystopian corrupt town into which a hobo attempts to deal some justice with a gun against the gangsters in control—based on a fake trailer for a Quentin Tarantino film with lots of guns and gore.

Jimmy Hollywood (1994): comedy about would-be actor who accidentally becomes a community vigilante by transforming himself into "Jericho," leader of a mock-vigilante group that videotapes criminals and then turns them over to the police.

Juncture (2007): a woman working for an abused children's charity is diagnosed with a terminal brain cancer with no more than three months decides to spend her final days hunting pedophiles who somehow evaded justice.

Karma Police (2008): young man joins a secret organization who believe in rewarding the good and punishing the bad.

Keeper of the City (1992): son of Mafiosi turns vigilante against the Mob pursued by police and with interest from the media.

Kick-Ass (2010): would-be "superhero" encounters the father of a girl vigilante super-hero—cult following.

Kick-Ass 2 (2013): the follow–up finds "Kick Ass" up against another superhero "Motherfucker."

Land of Plenty (2004): Wim Wenders film involving a paranoid Vietnam veteran who drives around filming and spying on Arabs and people with Arab features.

Latin Dragon (2003): returning war hero seeks to reclaim his neighbourhood from gangs—straight to video.

Mystic River (2003): the theme of the perils of vigilante justice is played out—see appendix 2.

Neighboring Sounds (2012): a middle-class neighborhood in a Brazilian city is beset by petty crime and the neighbors engage an independent private security firm which in turn brings more anxiety.

Noise (2007): a lawyer driven mad by noise takes a baseball bat to cars with car alarms and becomes "The Rectifier" and then engages with the legal system to secure a change in the rules.

Nun of That (2009): murdered nun returns to earth and joins a secret sect of nuns, the Order of the Black Habit, who engage in a battle with the Mob.

One Man Jury (1978): police officer weary of the system's ineffectiveness becomes a vigilante to deal with a serial killer.

Original Gangstas (1996): reclaiming of the old neighbourhood from the gang who have killed a variety of innocent people by returning ex-residents.

Out for Blood (1993): lawyer whose family is murdered by drug dealers becomes a vigilante dubbed "Karateman."

Outlaw (2007): ex-soldier forms a vigilante group with some help from a disillusioned police officer—see appendix 2.

The Outlaw Josey Wales (1976): hunting down by mercenaries of ex-Confederate soldier and the motley crew who follow him as he seeks peace and solitude.

Outrage (1998): young punks terrorize a good citizen who, disappointed with the police response, takes the law into his own hands.

Paparazzi (2004): action star turns vigilante and seeks out those whose pursuit of his family has led to their death in a car crash.

Prey of the Jaguar (1996): vigilante who wears an animal costume and who puts people to sleep with a dart.

The Punisher (1990): revenge for family killed by the mob.

The Punisher (2004): FBI agent, Frank Castle, turns vigilante, known as The Punisher, after a family is killed by a mobster whose son is killed in an FBI sting—from Marvel comics.

Punisher: War Zone (2009): further adventures of vigilante Frank Castle from *The Punisher* (2004).

The Purge (2013): futuristic film set in a world where there is an annual purge day when all crime is permitted and the events in anLos Angeles family home when a gang come in pursuit of a man rescued by the family.

The Purge: Anarchy (2014): a sequel to *The Purge* (2013) with a range of storylines of those at risk during the day of mayhem.

Quiet Cool (1986): revenge for murder of family of girlfriend.

Ransom (1996): ransom sought from millionaire magnate who goes on the offensive.

Raw Deal (1986): FBI agent infiltrates the mob.

Red Riding Hood (2003): young girl takes revenge on the killers of her father—Italian film based on the fairy tale.

Righteous Kill (2008): two long-serving policemen reluctantly have to hunt down a vigilante serial killer.

Rogue Force (1999): vigilante group of ex-police officers being investigated—straight to video.

Seeking Justice (2012): a man accepts an offer to deal with those who have raped his wife and is caught up in a web of vigilantes—see appendix 2.

Self-Defense (1983): city police force strike results in citizens banding together as vigilantes.

Shadows and Fog (1992): comedy with Woody Allen as a clerk woken to join a vigilante band looking for a killer.

Skins (2002): destruction on a native American reservation involving a police officer and his brother in various acts of vandalism/vigilantism in a contemplation on the state of the Native American condition.

SnakeEater (1989): loner cop tracks down killers of his parents.

SnakeEater 2: The Drug Buster (1989): ex-cop fights crime on the streets.

SnakeEater 3: His Law (1992): revenge of woman's beating by a gang of bikers.

The Sniper (1978): Italian film with a law-abiding citizen witnessing a violent crime.

Soldier of the Night (1984): Israeli film with toy store worker who is a vigilante killer by night.

Special (2006): man taking an experimental antidepressant drug believing himself to have supernatural powers become a crime-fighting vigilante.

Steele Justice (1987): revenge on Vietnamese killers of a veteran's friend.

The Stranger Wore a Gun (1953): Randolph Scott Western.

Street Corner Justice (1996): ex-cop comes to the aid of local merchants being terrorized by local drug-dealers.

Street Hunter (1990): ex-cop confronts drug dealers.

Super (2010): comedy-drama superhero film in which a short-order cook becomes a vigilante donning a superhero costume.

Sworn to Justice (1997): After attackers kill her sister and nephew, a female psychologist becomes a defence witness by day and avenger by night.

Target Eagle (1984): mercenary hired to infiltrate drug gang.

Taxi Driver (1976): ex-military taxi driver goes on a rampage against those responsible for child prostitution.

This is Not a Love Song (2002): vigilante group pursue petty criminals after they accidentally kill a young woman.

To Protect and Serve (1992): crooked cops get killed and suspicion falls on a rookie.

Trespasses (1986): crooks commit rape and murder and the families seek revenge.

Watchmen (2009): superhero film set in 1985 where the popularity of masked avengers suffers in a wave of antivigilantism.

When Justice Fails (1998): a detective investigating the murders of two sex offenders gets involved with a beautiful district attorney who becomes a main suspect.

When the Bullet Hits the Bone (1996): doctor seeks to get even with a drug cartel.

The Windsplitter (1971): return of actor from Hollywood to his Texas home town results in vigilante action against him and new-fangled ways.

Zebra Force (1976): army veterans embark on a battle against organized crime.

APPENDIX 2: PRÉCIS OF MAJOR VIGILANTE FILMS

An Eye for an Eye (1981): a police officer is forced to resign from the San Francisco Police Department's Narcotics Division when he goes berserk after his partner is murdered. He decides to fight alone and track down those responsible.

A Walk among the Tombstones (2014): an ex-cop is hired by a Russian gangster to avenge the death of his wife.

Dead Man's Shoes (2004): on his return from the Army a young man seeks revenge on the gang who tormented his vulnerable brother one by one. He ends up, unusually for this kind of film, killing himself at the end of the film, his mission accomplished.

Death Sentence (2006): A young man is killed by a gang member as an initiation rite in front of his executive father in a petrol station. The gang member responsible escapes conviction and the father seeks revenge on the whole gang. Seriously wounded he watches the scenes from his home movies as the police arrive to tell him his injured son has survived.

Death Wish (1974): revenge of murder and rape of wife and daughter by liberal architect, Paul Kersey, ending the lives of those who were responsible after they walk free from court. The police ask him to leave town after his actions in dealing with a variety of punks and lowlife make the unknown vigilante a local hero.

Death Wish 2 (1982): Kersey seeks revenge for trauma to daughter and the rape of his maid.

Death Wish 3 (1985): further revenge on those dear to Kersey.
Death Wish 4: The Crackdown (1987): Kersey attacks crack dealers.
Death Wish 5: The Face of Death (1994): revenge for treatment of business of Kersey's fiancée.
Eye for an Eye (1995): Karen McCann hears her daughter being raped and murdered over the phone and eventually seeks revenge on the killer after he is freed on a technicality and goes on to rape and murder another woman with impunity.
Gran Torino (2009): a misanthropic, xenophobic, retired factory worker learns to appreciate his Asian neighbors and takes action against the local thugs who have sought to recruit the young son into their gang. When the daughter is raped he confronts the gang. In a final showdown he is gunned down and the gang taken into police custody.
Harry Brown (2009): a frail pensioner misses the death of his wife in hospital due to the actions of a local gang of youths and then his friend dies in a confrontation with the youths. He takes revenge against those responsible after initially rediscovering his skills learned as a Marine serving in Northern Ireland.
John Doe: Vigilante (2014): a man becomes a local hero after carrying out vigilante actions and inspiring copycat activity.
Law Abiding Citizen (2009): a happily married man and his family are attacked by two thugs in their home and the wife and daughter are raped and killed. The gang members blame each other and the ambitious prosecutor accepts a plea bargain for a conviction of one of them. The hero some time later seeks revenge against first the gang members and then against everyone who was responsible from the prosecutor to the mayor of the city.
Mystic River (2003): an attempt to visit justice on the killer of the daughter of one of the protagonists, an ex-con. Things are, however, complicated and his childhood friend, a policeman, and one friend is killed suspected of murdering a young girl. Although guilty of another revenge killing this is a mistake. Here vigilante justice is shown as an enterprise fraught with mistakes and uncertainty.
Outlaw (2007): embittered ex-paratrooper, aghast at what has happened to his neighbourhood and the inadequacy of the judicial system enrols a gang of those who have also been let down by the system including a lawyer, a white-collar worker, a student, a hotel security guard, and a football hooligan. Using a police insider to provide information on various unsalubrious individuals the gang deal with them. In a final shootout with the armed and corrupt police, all the gang are killed except the white-collar worker who makes his escape.
Red (2008): a gang kill a man's dog and he comes after them with deadly consequences.

Seeking Justice (2012): An English teacher's wife is raped and doubting the law's ability to deal with the trial, he accepts the offer of help from a vigilante organization. He is then required to kill someone as his part of the bargain and things escalate.

The Brave One (2007): Erica Bain, her boyfriend and dog are attacked in Central Park by a gang and the boyfriend and dog die. She survives and the gang escape justice. She shoots a robber in a corner shop with the gun she has obtained and then a gang of youths on the subway. A police detective tracks her down when she is on her final act of revenge and allows her to escape.

The Equalizer (2014): a blue-collar worker in a warehouse takes a variety of actions to avenge the wrongs done to his fellow workers with which the law has no truck. He turns out to have been involved in special ops and worked for the government and is able to outwit the source of the trouble and dispose of them without the authorities being any the wiser.

The Fourth Angel (2001): Journalist seeks revenge on the terrorists whose actions led to the death of his family in crossfire in a hijacking. The hijackers are released and, having failed to get any cooperation from the authorities the protagonist seeks out the gang and disposes of them.

The Limey (1999): British career criminal flies to California to investigate and take revenge on the sleazy record producer who he has reason to believe was responsible for the death of his daughter. He is able to use his professional skills to gain access to the house of the perpetrator and is in a position to exact his revenge when the truth about the death is revealed.

Vendetta (2013): a soldier with special ability to extract information from the enemy returns from Afghanistan returns too late to save his parents who have been burnt alive by a gang in retaliation for killing the brother of the gang leader in self-defence during a mugging. The soldier takes revenge on each member of the gang and walks free at the end due to the value of his special skills to the state.

NOTES

1. I would like to thank Mike Bruce, Steve Greenfield, Angus Nurse, Guy Osborn, Jenifer Ross, and Alison Young for their comments on earlier drafts of this chapter.

2. The titles in Spain and France for the Denzel Washington film *The Equalizer* (2014) discussed below are *El Justiciero* and *Le Justicier* respectively.

3. Goetz shot four young men on the subway in December 1984 and was convicted of carrying an unlicensed firearm for which he served nine months (Fletcher 1988; Lesly 1988; Rubin 1988)

4. Zimmerman was the neighborhood watch coordinator who shot Trayvon Martin in 2012. A jury accepted his claim that under the Florida 2005 "Stand Your Ground" law, he was acting in self-defense. This permits the use of deadly force when someone reasonably feels he or she is at risk of great bodily harm in a confrontation—www.bbc.co.uk/news/world-us-canada-23304198 and www.cbsnews.com/feature/george-zimmerman-trial-trayvon-martin-case/.

5. It is the name taken by the British long-term prisoner, Michael Peterson when he was a bare knuckle fighter in one of his rare periods of liberty since entering the penal system in 1972 where he remains in 2014.

6. *Blackthorn* (Ibon Cormenzana and Andrés Santana; Mateo Gil 2011), however, finds Butch (Sam Shepard) having somehow evaded the hail of bullets and still in Bolivia and surviving pursuit by the Bolivian army once again.

7. There have been few TV equivalents since *William Tell* and *The Four Just Men* in the 1960s although one might mention Timothy Spall in *Gunrush* (2009) and the *Dexter* series (2006–2013).

8. A sequel game, *Vigilante 2: Rise of John Doe* became available in 2014—itunes.apple.com/gb/app/vigilante-2-rise-of-john-doe/id832866234?mt=8.

9. Although the earlier, *Last House on the Left* (Wes Craven, 1972), seems to be on the same lines involving rape and revenge, albeit by the victim's parents and is so identified by Read (2000) at 41. In addition the film *Lipstick* (1976) involves revenge by Chris McCormick (Margaux Hemingway) for both her own and her sister's rape.

10. Although the aims of vigilante groups are not necessarily always progressive—the anti-Naxalite group Salwa Judum being a case in point (Asian Centre for Human Rights 2006).

11. As classified by *VideoHound's Golden Movie Retriever 2008 and 2015*, with some additions from the author.

REFERENCES

Adorno, Theodor and Max Horkheimer. 1979. *Dialectic of Enlightenment*. London: Verso (1944 first published in German as *Dialektik der Aufklärung*).

Aeschylus. 1984. *Oresteia: Agamemnon: The Libation Bearers; The Eumenides*. Harmondsworth, UK: Penguin.

Anderson, Vincent. 2013. *Bald Knobbers: Chronicles of Vigilante Justice*. Stroud, UK: The History Press.

ArtsReformation.com. 1930. The Motion Picture Production Code of 1930 (Hays Code). Accessed May 2, 2015 at: www.artsreformation.com/a001/hays-code.html.

Asian Centre for Human Rights. 2006. *The Adivasis of Chhattisgarh: Victims of the Naxalite Movement and Salwa Judum Campaign*. New Delhi: Asian Centre for Human Rights.

Asimow, Michael (ed.). 2009. *The Lawyer in Your Living Room: TV Lawyers.* Washington, DC: American Bar Association.

Asimow, Michael, Kathryn Brown, and David Papke (eds.). 2014. *Law and Popular Culture: International Perspectives.* Cambridge: Cambridge Scholars Publishing.

Bergman, Paul and Michael Asimow. 1996. *Reel Justice—The Courtroom Goes to the Movies.* Kansas City: Andrews and McMeel.

———. 2004. *Reel Justice—The Courtroom Goes to the Movies,* Second Edition. Kansas City: Andrews and McMeel.

Berthod, Anne. 2012. *Sampat Pal, Warrior in a Pink Sari: The Inside Story of the Gulabi Gang as Told to Anne Berthod.* New Delhi: Zubaan.

Black David.1999. *Law in Film: Resonance and Representation.* Urbana, IL: University of Illinois Press.

Blackburn, Robin. 2008. "The Subprime Crisis." *New Left Review,* 50 (March-April): 63–106. Accessed December 1, 2014 at: newleftreview.org/II/50/robin-blackburn-the-subprime-crisis.

Booth, Robert. 2014. "Paedophile Hunters: The Vigilantes Taking the Law Into Their Own Hands." *The Guardian,* November 1. Accessed May 16, 2015 at: www.theguardian.com/uk-news/2014/nov/11/paedophile-hunters-vigilantes-peter-mitchell-derby.

Bronson, Charles and Robin Ackroyd. 2000. *Bronson.* London: John Blake Publishing.

Calderon, Veronica. 2014. "Meet the Armed Vigilantes Fighting for Michoacan." *El Pais.* January 26. Accessed May 1, 2015 at: elpais.com/elpais/2014/01/26/inenglish/1390742073_084337.html.

Clover, Carol. 1992. *Men, Women and Chain Saws: Gender in the Modern Horror Film.* Princeton: Princeton University Press.

Dailly, James and Ryan Davidson. 2011. *The Law of Superheroes.* New York: Gotham.

Denvir, John (ed.). 1996. *Legal Reelism: Movies as Legal Texts.* Urbana, IL: University of Illinois Press.

Dillon, Mark. 2013. *Montana Vigilantes 1863–1870 Gold, Guns and Gallows.* Logan, UT: Utah State University Press.

Fletcher, George. 1988. *A Crime of Self-Defense: Bernhard Goetz and the Law on Trial.* Chicago: University of Chicago Press.

Gohring, Nancy. 2007. "Digital Vigilantes: Hacking for a Good Cause." *PC World Magazine,* December 25. Accessed December 9, 2014 at: www.pcworld.com/article/140731/article.html.

Greenfield Steve, Guy Osborn, and Peter Robson. 2001. *Film and the Law: The Cinema of Justice.* London: Cavendish.

Grude, Torstein (producer) and Jain, Nishtha (director). 2012. *Gulabi Gang.* [Motion Picture]. India: Piraya Film. Co-production: Raintree Films and Final Cut for Real.

———. 2010. *Film and the Law: The Cinema of Justice,* second edition. Oxford: Hart.

Guthrie, Woodrow. 1935. *Vigilante Man.* (A song by Woody Guthrie). Accessed December 9, 2014 at: woodyguthrie.org/Lyrics/.

———. 1940. *The Ballad of Pretty Boy Floyd.* (A song by Woody Guthrie). Accessed December 9, 2014 at: woodyguthrie.org/Lyrics/Pretty_Boy_Floyd.htm.

Hartman, Mary and Elmo Ingenthron. 1988. *Bald Knobbers: Vigilantes on the Ozarks Frontier*. New Orleans: Pelican Publishing.

Havery, Gavin. 2015. "Jail for Man Who Tried to Meet 14-year-old Girl but was Snared by Vigilante Group Dark Justice." *The Northern Echo*, March 27. Accessed May 18, 2015 at: www.thenorthernecho.co.uk/news/11885040.Jail_for_man_who_tried_to_meet_14_year_old_girl_but_was_snared_by_vigilante_group_Dark_Justice/.

Hephaestus Books. 2011. *Rape and Revenge Films*. Hephaestus Books (no publishing details on the book number ISBN-13: 9781242972744).

Heller-Nicholas, Alexandra. 2011. *Rape-Revenge Films: A Critical Study*. Jefferson, NC: McFarland and Co.

Henry, Claire. 2014. *Revisionist Rape-Revenge: Redefining a Film Genre*. New York: Palgrave Macmillan.

Hobsbawm, Eric. 1960. *Social Bandits and Primitive Rebels*. New York: Free Press.

———. 1969. *Bandits*. London: Weidenfeld and Nicolson.

IMDB. 2014. "John Doe: Vigilante." *Internet Movie Database*. Accessed May 2, 2015 at: http://www.imdb.com/title/tt1418754/.

Jarvis, Robert and Paul Joseph. 1998. *Prime Time Law: Fictional Television as Legal Narrative*. Durham NC: Carolina Academic Press.

Kamir, Orit. 2002. "Honor and Dignity Cultures: the Case of Hvod Ha-adam (Dignity) in Israeli Society and Law." In *The Concept of Human Dignity in Human Rights Law*, edited by David Kretzmer and Eckart Klein, 231–62. Amsterdam: Kluwer Press.

———. 2006. *Framed: Women in Law and Film*. Durham NC: Duke University Press.

Kenny, Kevin. 1998. *Making Sense of the Molly Maguires*. New York: Oxford University Press.

Lesly, Mark. 1988. *Subway Gunman: A Juror's Account*. Langham, NY: British American Publishing.

Lucia, Cynthia. 2005. *Framing Female Lawyers: Women on Trial in Film*. Austin: University of Texas Press.

Machura, Stefan and Peter Robson (eds.). 2001. *Law and Film*. Oxford: Blackwell.

Marlowe, Christopher. 2002. *Tamburlaine*. Newton Abbott: David and Charles.

May, Lary. 2015. "Redeeming the Lost War: Backlash Films and the Rise of the Punitive State." In *Punishment in Popular Culture*, edited by Charles Ogletree Jnr. and Austin Sarat, 23–54. New York: New York University Press.

Meyer Phil. 1993. "Visual Literacy and the Legal Culture: Reading Film as Text in the Law School Setting." *Legal Studies Forum* 17(1): 73–93.

———. 2001. "Why a Jury Trial is More Like a Movie Than a Novel." In *Law and Film*, edited by Machura Stefan and Peter Robson, 133–46. Oxford: Blackwell.

Ministry of Justice Report. 2013. *Public Perceptions of Crime*. Auckland: New Zealand. Accessed May 1, 2015 at: www.justice.govt.nz/publications/global-publications/p/public-perceptions-of-crime-survey-report.

Minuteman.com. 2014. The Minute Men. minutemanproject.com. Accessed December 9, 2014.

Nevins, Francis. 1996. "Through the Great Depression on Horseback: Legal Themes in Westerns of the 1930s." In *Legal Reelism*, edited by John Denvir, 44–69. Urbana, IL: University of Illinois Press.

Office for National Statistics. 2013. *Focus On: Violent Crime and Sexual Offences, 2011/12*. London: UK Office of National Statistics. Accessed December 9, 2014 at: www.ons.gov.uk/ons/dcp171778_298904.pdf.

Quinn, Arthur. 1997. *The Rivals: William Gwin, David Broderick, and the Birth of California*. Lincoln: University of Nebraska Press.

Radio Times. 2015. *Radio Times Guide to Films 2015*. London: Immediate Media Company.

Rapping, Elayne. 2003. *Law and Justice As Seen in TV*. New York: New York University Press.

Read, Jacinda. 2000. *The New Avengers: Feminism, Femininity and the Rape-Revenge Cycle*. Manchester: Manchester University Press.

Robertson, James. 1989. *The Hidden Cinema: British Film Censorship in Action 1913–1975*. London: Routledge.

Robson, Peter. 1996. "Images of Law in the Fiction of John Grisham." In *Tall Stories? Reading Law and Literature*, edited by John Morison and Christine Bell, 201–22. Aldershot: Dartmouth Publishing.

———. 2001. "Adapting the Modern Law Novel: Filming John Grisham." In *Law and Film*, edited by Machura Stefan and Peter Robson, 147–63. Oxford: Blackwell.

———. 2014. "The Law Through the Eye of the Courtroom Comedy: The Light Legal Procedural in Context." In *Law and Popular Culture: International Perspectives*, edited by Michael Asimov, Kathryn Brown and David Papke, 233–52. Cambridge: Cambridge University Press.

Robson, Peter and Jessica Silbey (eds.). 2012. *Law and Justice on the Small Screen*. Oxford, UK: Hart.

Rubin, Lillian. 1988. *Quiet Rage: Bernie Goetz in a Time of Madness*. Oakland: University of California Press.

Sen, Soumik (director). 2014. *Gulaab Gang* [Motion Picture]. India: Benaras Mediaworks.

Seneca, Lucius Annaeus. 1993. *Thyestes*. London: Nick Hern Books.

Shakespeare, William. 2004. *The Complete Works of Shakespeare*. New York: Barnes and Noble.

Smith, Dominic. 2010. *Public Confidence in the Criminal Justice System: Findings from the British Crime Survey 2002/03 to 2007/08*. Research Series 16/10. London: Ministry of Justice. Accessed May 1, 2015 at: www.justice.gov.uk/downloads/publications/research-and-analysis/moj-research/confidence-cjs-british-crime-survey.pdf.

Sophocles. 2008. *Elektra and Other Plays*. Harmondsworth, UK: Penguin.

Sperling, Cass Warner and Cork Millner. 1998. *Hollywood Be Thy Name*. Roseville, CA: Prima Publishing.

Tunick, Mark. 2012. "Reality TV and the Entrapment of Predators." In *Law and Justice on the Small Screen*, edited by Peter Robson and Jessica Silbey, 289–308. Oxford, UK: Hart.

VideoHound. 2008. *VideoHound's Golden Movie Retriever 2009*. New York: Gale Cengage Learning.

———. 2015. *VideoHound's Golden Movie Retriever 2015*. New York: Gale Cengage Learning.

Vigilante: Speak for the Dead. 2015. *Vigilante: Speak for the Dead HD—iPad Gameplay Video*. Accessed May 1, 2015 at: www.youtube.com/watch?v=VbIJw3P3mX0.
Villez, Barbara. 2005. *Séries Télé: visions de la justice*. Paris: Presses Universitaires de France.
———. 2010. *Television and the Legal System*. London: Routledge.
Wright, Will. 1975. *Sixguns and Society: A Structural Study of the Western*. Berkeley: University of California Press.
Young, Alison. 2010. *The Scene of Violence*. New York: Routledge.

III

LAW AND CRIME IN AMERICAN FILM AND TELEVISION

7

Alfred Hitchcock

Visions of Guilt and Innocence

Mathieu Deflem

In this chapter, I analyze the cinema of Alfred Hitchcock from a sociological perspective that thematically focuses on the themes of guilt and innocence. The analysis relies on some of Hitchcock's more popular movies, but also discussed are some of his lesser-known films and some of his earlier works. While this study is decidedly sociological in orientation, the discussion also builds on insights from the so-called *auteur* theory, popularized by François Truffaut's (1984) interviews with Hitchcock, and centrally revolves around the notion of pure cinema, with which Hitchcock expressed his artistic ideal of movie making.

Working from a sociological perspective, I offer an interpretive analysis of the visions of guilt and innocence in Hitchcock's films that refrains from any psychologistic dream analyses or otherwise reductive introspection. Instead, I rely on the work of Emile Durkheim, one of the central founders of sociology, and the anthropology of Victor Turner to develop an appropriate perspective of film making (and viewing) as a ritual event. I argue that Hitchcock's movies are most centrally to be conceived as liminal experiences whereby both the characters involved in the plot and their viewers go through a series of events and adventures that leave them in an altered state, from what was before, through the pains and pleasures of change itself, to an outcome that is never certain but essentially still ambiguous. Hitchcock thereby portrays attributes of guilt and innocence that involve a demarcation between private guilt and public guilt, a transference of guilt from one to another, and a universality of various degrees and kinds of guilt among many, possibly even all who are involved in a movie (and its viewing). I will substantiate my arguments by means of illustration, relying on analyses of various events and characters from a range of Hitchcock films.

CINEMA AS RITUAL

The sociological analysis of cultural events revolving around ritual and symbolism, especially within the realm of religion, is built upon the seminal work of Emile Durkheim (see Alexander 1988). The work of Durkheim is centrally concerned with the question of social order and integration, especially under conditions of increasing cultural complexity and individualism. No society more than a modern one, which Durkheim described as organic, emphasizes the individual as the core unit of normative prescriptions on rights and responsibilities (Durkheim 1914). How then, Durkheim and any other sociologist since have asked, is social integration achieved? To Durkheim, the answer lies in the fact that there has to be a higher normative force that individuals accept as valid to enable adherence to binding obligations and specifications of rights and duties. Society is this moral force.

In his work on religion and ritual, Durkheim (1912) studied the mechanisms by which societal norms are lived, how they are produced and reproduced. Religion, Durkheim argues, is not only a system of belief, it is also action, particularly ritual action. A central idea in Durkheim's work is that during ritual ceremonies the participating group or community is most consciously and most actively aware of itself as an order higher than the participating individuals. A community is therefore no more truly conscious of itself, displaying itself as a community, than when it celebrates itself. Among the functional implications of this idea is that through ritual practice a community's cohesiveness, exemplified by the physical assembly of people and the focus on a particular symbol during ritual practice, is secured, lived, and maintained. The community is renewed, and the individual, as individual and at once as member of the community, is strengthened by participation in ritual activity. Particularly because of the impact of powerful symbols, a society is celebrated through rituals.

From Durkheim's work, sociologists have learned that rituals, both small or momentous and temporary or more enduring, serve to re-enact the central values and norms guiding a community or society at large. A wedding, by example, is not merely a ritual consecrating the marriage between two romantically or otherwise intimately linked partners, but it is also, because of its public display and legitimation, a central event on behalf of all of society, specifying and celebrating fundamental social norms related to gender, sexuality, and life. Sociologically, a wedding is not about the love between two people, but about the adoration of society for itself.

Durkheim's sociology forcefully argues for the societal constitution and re-integrative functions of ritual. Yet, Durkheim also tends to emphasize the social origins and consequences of ritual at the expense of an analysis of the practice of ritual enactment itself. It is this question of what happens during ritual practice that forms the center part of the work of anthropologist Victor W. Turner, who critically built on Durkheim's oeuvre (see Deflem 1991). Turner developed a unique anthropological perspective of ritual that extended beyond Durkheim's emphasis on the re-integrative functions of ritual (Turner 1967; 1969; 1974).

Turner defines ritual as "prescribed formal behavior for occasions not given over to technological routine, having reference to beliefs in mystical beings and powers" (Turner 1967, 19). A symbol is the smallest unit of ritual which still retains the specific properties of ritual behavior. Importantly, Turner identifies a three-phased process of ritual. Building on the fact that a ritual brings about a transition from one state to another, Turner observes that between these states the ritual subjects are often secluded, spending time in an interstructural situation, which Turner characterizes as liminality. During this liminal phase, the ritual subjects have a no longer/not yet status: the subjects are "neither here nor there; they are betwixt and between the positions assigned and arrayed by law, custom, convention, and ceremonial" (Turner 1969, 95).

Turner argues that the very essence of ritual performances is not, as Durkheim would have it, a celebration of the social order or social structure, but a successful attempt, albeit a temporary one, to escape from the demands and functions of the structures of society in order to create antistructure by means of so-called "communitas" or a new sense of belonging. Communitas is defined in opposition to structure. Whereas social structure refers to the normatively proscribed arrangement of social positions, communitas refers to liminality, marginality, inferiority, and equality. The characteristics of the social structure are no longer applicable during the period of liminality that is displayed in ritual and other forms of communitas. Yet, eventually, the fate of communitas is a "decline and fall into structure and law" (Turner 1969, 132), upon which a new form of communitas may arise. A view of cinema, in particular the films of Alfred Hitchcock, as liminality can enable a sociologically illuminating vision surrounding the legal and moral themes of guilt and innocence.

THE CASE OF ALFRED HITCHCOCK

A reading of Hitchcock's movies as rituals of liminality has at least two dimensions, involving the cultural place of his films in their social environment as well as the specific form that Hitchcock gave to his individual films and the response they were meant to invoke on the part of the viewer. I begin with a very brief overview of the life and work of Alfred Hitchcock for the reader who may not be sufficiently familiar with this legendary director.

Life and Work

Hitchcock's work counts among the most popular and revered in the history of Western cinema. Hitchcock was also a very famous person during his life, a true celebrity (Kapsis 1992). These days Hitchcock is still a cultural icon, although his work is not as well-known anymore. Hitchcock directed movies for a period of more than fifty years, over a time period when the medium evolved tremendously. He was born on August 13, 1899, in a part of Essex that is now part of London (Chandler 2005, 29–42; Taylor 1978, 25–36). He attended a Catholic (high) school and studied engineering. A fan of the theater, Hitchcock first began working in the cinema world in 1920 as a title card designer for silent pictures. Gradually, he would take on different, more creative roles in the movie-making industry, eventually becoming assistant director and subsequently director.

Hitchcock's first directing effort was in 1922 with a movie called *Number 13*, but the production was canceled because of financial problems (Chandler 2005, 41). In 1925, Hitchcock was assigned to direct *The Pleasure Garden*, which was released the following year (see figure 7.1), when he also directed *The Mountain Eagle*, a movie that is now lost and which Hitchcock himself considered to be "very bad" (Truffaut 1984, 39). While both of these movies were not successful, a year later, Hitchcock released his first commercial success, *The Lodger*, the movie that the director and his admirers often refer to as the first true "Hitchcock movie" (Chandler 2005, 60; Truffaut 1984, 43). Several more silent movies with various themes followed in the years to come. In 1929, Hitchcock released *Blackmail*, the first British "talkie" (Truffaut 1984, 64).

In the early 1930s, Hitchcock directed several more movies with different themes that met with varying levels of success. Then, between 1934 and 1938, Hitchcock made several very successful movies, now often referred to collectively as the "thriller series" (Chandler 2005, 92). Among them are *The Man Who Knew Too Much* in 1934, *The 39 Steps* in 1935 (arguably his best movie of this era), *Sabotage* in 1936, and *The Lady Vanishes* in 1938 (Chandler 2005, 91–119). By the late 1930s, Hitchcock had come

Figure 7.1 The elements of Hitchcock's visual style, which he would eventually come to express under the heading of "pure cinema," are already present in his first movie *The Pleasure Garden*, as shown in this scene indicating fear and guilt by the manner in which the eyes of a woman are looking out from behind a fence. Image in the public domain.

to enjoy an international reputation that was such that he, as the then acknowledged best British director (Gottlieb 2003, 14), could move to Hollywood, the center of the movie industry.

In 1939, Hitchcock and his wife and daughter moved to the United States, where he signed a contract with David O. Selznick, one of the most successful movie producers at the time (Truffaut 1984, 121, 127). Hitchcock and Selznick would go to on to make several pictures together, but, to escape Selznick's control, Hitchcock also worked with other producers (Taylor 1978, 161). Hitchcock's first American movie (largely set in England) was *Rebecca* in 1940, a huge hit, which won the Academy Award for best movie, an honor that went to producer Selznick (Truffaut 1984, 133). Hitchcock never won an Oscar for any of his movies.

During World War II, Hitchcock made several successful films, such as *Suspicion* in 1941, *Shadow of a Doubt* in 1943, and *Spellbound* in 1945 (Truffaut 1984, 145–73). He also directed two small French-language movies that were oriented at occupied Europe, to help in the war effort, and he edited a documentary about the Holocaust that was not seen until the 1980s and has just very recently been restored (The Telegraph 2015). In 1946, Hitchcock directed *Notorious* starring Cary Grant and Ingrid Bergman, followed by his last movie for Selznick, *The Paradine Case* in 1947 (Truffaut 1984, 173). Hitchcock then started his own production company, Transatlantic Pictures, for which he directed *Rope* in 1948, his first color movie, which was an experimental film based on long single-take camera shots (Truffaut 1984, 179–84). Like *Rope*, his next movies, *Under Capricorn* in 1949 and *Stage Fright* in 1950, were not very successful (Truffaut 1984, 185–89).

Returning to the studio system, Hitchcock would, during the 1950s and early 1960s, be at his absolute peak, both artistically and commercially, directing some of the best and commercially most successful movies of his career. Among the films Hitchcock directed in this period special mention can be made of *Strangers on a Train* in 1951, *Dial M for Murder* in 1954, *Rear Window* in 1954, *To Catch a Thief* in 1955 (the year in which Hitchcock became a U.S. citizen), *Vertigo* in 1958, *North by Northwest* in 1959, *Psycho* in 1960, and *The Birds* in 1963 (Chandler 2005, 191–266). Hitchcock had by this time acquired fame, wealth, and complete control over his art. However, because the thriller genre had long been looked down upon in the so-called serious artistic circles of the modern cinema, it was not until the late 1960s that Hitchcock also acquired prestige as an artistically accomplished filmmaker, especially because of the efforts by François Truffaut (whose 1984 book on the director was originally published in 1967) and other directors of the "French new wave."

The movies Hitchcock directed in the 1960s after the release of *Marnie* in 1964 were not as successful, largely because he had lost some of his independence as well as some of his best collaborators, such as film music composer Bernard Herrmann, with whom Hitchcock had a creative falling out, and long-time associates, cinematographer Robert Burks and editor George Tomasini, both of whom had died (Taylor 1978, 273, 277–78). A planned movie in the second half of the 1960s, involving rather explicit depictions of sex and violence, was vetoed by Universal Studios, and Hitchcock had to turn to projects, including scripts and actors, that were more or less forced upon him (Chandler 2005, 287–95).

Hitchcock's last two movies were again more independent manifestations of his cinematic talent (Taylor 1978, 283–305). In 1972, Hitchcock returned to his native England to direct *Frenzy*, a successful movie, that can be regarded his final masterpiece. In 1976, Hitchcock released *Family Plot*, a comedy thriller that was to be his last film. Hitchcock began working on another movie, *The Short Night*, but, because of his failing health, he had to abort the project and he formally retired in the spring of 1979

(Chandler 2005, 326). Hitchcock died on April 29, 1980. He received a Catholic funeral service, and his body was cremated (Chandler 2005, 329).

Hitchcock's Liminal Subjects

At its best, the art of the cinema provides antistructure. Movie viewing is a created environment of excitement and entertainment in which the audience hopes to find what cannot be found elsewhere. Film making and film viewing must be intertwined, and Alfred Hitchcock counts among the directors who are most aware of this central ambition to engage the viewer into the movie. Indeed, the connection with the audience is central in a Hitchcock movie, who argued that a film has to be designed "as Shakespeare did his plays—for an audience" (Truffaut 1984, 283). The director cannot make a movie just for his or her own pleasure, according to Hitchcock, because of the enormous financial cost that is involved as well as because of artistic considerations (Gottlieb 1995, 186–89). The cost of cinematic expression is, according to Hitchcock, the most delicate aspect in finding a balance between the artistic and the commercial. Hitchcock's best movies should therefore also be among his most commercially successful ones. The Hitchcock audience should ideally be (and to a large extent is) a global audience to the extent that viewers respond identically all over the world to the exact same stimuli on the movie screen (Gottlieb 2003, 130). The more specific manner in which Hitchcock seeks to involve the audience in his films is emotional (Gottlieb 2003, 131, 181; Truffaut 1984, 283). The approach is resolutely non-intellectual, not oriented at making people think, but making them feel a certain way, for the duration of the movie and possibly thereafter as well. Hitchcock likened this approach to the experience of being on a roller coaster or visiting a haunted house, indicating the centrality of what he argued to be the audience's quest for "the satisfaction of temporary pain" (Gottlieb 2003, 69). As such an escape into the pleasures associated with danger and suspense, a Hitchcock movie constitutes a ritual performance of liminality, a temporary but nonetheless real experience of communitas.

Hitchcock's films are also manifestations of liminality in a more specific sense. A Hitchcock film typically displays a basic three-fold structure that follows the processual scheme of ritual performances outlined by Turner from social structure (before a ritual) to antistructure (during a ritual) to a return to social structure (upon the completion of a ritual).

First, there is in Hitchcock's films typically an event that triggers the action. The filmic device Hitchcock most preferred was the so-called MacGuffin, a rather banal (ideally even a completely banal) and hardly noteworthy object or event that is introduced to move the rest of the story forward but that is otherwise not relevant to the experience of the film (Gottlieb 1995, 124; Truffaut 1984, 137–38). The typical example of a MacGuffin mentioned by Hitchcock is the government secret the spies are after. The wine bottle with uranium in *Notorious* (Hitchcock 1946), the love letter in *Dial M For Murder* (Hitchcock 1954), and the stolen diamond in *Family Plot* (Hitchcock 1976) are examples. In the movie *North by Northwest* (Hitchcock 1959), Hitchcock felt he had come up with the best MacGuffin yet (Truffaut 1984, 139). In that story, a man played by Carry Grant is mistakenly believed to be a U.S. agent and subsequently chased across the country by a group of spies. Why the spies justify their pursuit is deadly important to them but wholly irrelevant to the emotional experience the viewers undergo while the hero is being chased. At some point, rather late in the movie, an American agent explains only in passing that the spies are chasing the hero because they are looking for "government secrets, I suppose" (Hitchcock 1959).

In a next phase, Hitchcock's subjects are typically held captive in some situation of extreme danger, involving illness, panic, confusion, and other intense states, both mental and physical, of despair and destitution. The heroes are now stripped of their worldly status and are caught in an adventure that is not of their own choosing, but which is forced upon them by circumstance. In *North by Northwest* (Hitchcock 1959), the hero on the run is continually tortured and victimized by the spies who are chasing him—first when they force him to drink a bottle of liquor and try to get him killed in a staged car accident, subsequently when they involve him in many kinds of tortures throughout the movie, and eventually when they try to kill him on top of Mount Rushmore.

In a final phase, the Hitchcockian heroes return to the world of social structure. Yet, they are never the same as they were before their adventure. They return to the world differently, not necessarily better, not necessarily worse, but always changed. For example, in *North by Northwest* (Hitchcock 1959), the hero is in the end united with the woman he fell in love with throughout his ordeal. In the last scene of the movie, as they are sitting in a train that enters a tunnel, he refers to her as his wife, "Mrs. Thornhill." From the story, we know that she is his third wife. While it is therefore the third time our hero will give up on his bachelor lifestyle, it will be the first time, so the story implies, that he will be happy in matrimony.

The *Auteur* Theory and Pure Cinema

There are two technical aspects of Hitchcock's film to be mentioned that are useful to explain for my analysis. First, thanks to Truffaut and other directors and movie critics associated with the French film magazine *Les Cahiers du Cinema*, the so-called *auteur* theory of film making has been much discussed in connection with Hitchcock's work. What this perspective boils down to is that certain, artistically accomplished films, including those directed by Hitchcock, are to be conceived as manifestations of the creative talent and vision of the director. The director is the author of the film as much as the writer is of a book (Kapsis 1992, 13–14)

While the *auteur* perspective need not lead to analyze Hitchcock's movies on the basis of the assumed traits of his inner psychology (Wood 2002), it is also important to realize that a film is not a natural phenomenon but a purposely constructed reality. In Hitchcock's case, the control and command of the director in assembling the various pieces that make up the movie are the most important principles of the various techniques he applies. The cinematic vision of Hitchcock is achieved not only through the actual directing of scenes, but also through his choice of the script, his choice of actors, his choice of set decorations, and other demands placed by the director on those who work for him on making a movie (Gottlieb 2003, 177–78). Hitchcock's increasing stature and fame over the course of his career gradually enabled him to fulfill this ambition more perfectly.

Hitchcock referred to his ideal form of film making as pure cinema (Truffaut 1984). The concept of pure cinema conveys the notion that film cannot be reduced to any other art form than itself. A film is not a novel, not a painting, not music, though it contains narrative, visual, musical, and other elements. When he was making a particular movie, Hitchcock, therefore, usually only very loosely relied on the ideas presented in a short story or book. Hitchcock's movie *The Birds* (Hitchcock 1963), by example, relies on a short story of which Hitchcock retained nothing except the birds (Taylor 1978, 266). As a result, also, Hitchcock did not make movies of any of the great books of world literature. The very notion of a movie version of a book is antithetical to the Hitchcock style.

Ideally, also, Hitchcock seeks to accomplish pure cinema in a purely pictorial form, emphasizing the images, along with the corresponding sounds, and how they are framed and assembled to be presented to the audience (Truffaut 1984, 31). The director does not say anything, but instead must show something. The Hitchcockian cinematic emphasis is entirely on the visual aspects of a movie. Pure cinema places the emphasis on the assembly of pieces of film both to communicate an idea and to invoke an emotion (Gottlieb 1995, 288). Therefore, also, the director should have complete control over the actors, of which Hitchcock was famously fond of saying that they are to be treated like cattle (Truffaut 1984, 140). Actors are but one element in a Hitchcock movie, neither more nor less important than the lighting, the set design, and other formal aspects of the movie. Actors should therefore be directed, that is, they should be told what to do as a function of the movie, especially the placement of the camera. Hitchcock's reliance on a carefully prepared script, often accompanied with a detailed storyboard, are the technical expressions of the ideal of pure cinema (Gottlieb 1995, 288–92; 2003, 35–37, 68–69). The underlying notion is that a movie to Hitchcock is most essentially a presentation of assembled slices of film projected on a white large rectangular screen in a movie theater. The advent of the talking picture, therefore, had an ambivalent effect to Hitchcock, although he did use sound (and music) creatively in his movies as well, but always in connection with the presentation of visual images (Kapsis 1992, 143).

While Hitchcock preferred to work meticulously on the form of his movie, his films nonetheless also rely on content, on a plot and various themes that work as the narrative devices of pure cinema. The best form to engage the audience, as Hitchcock discovered early on in his career, was by means of suspense (Gottlieb 2003, 61–64). Unlike a sudden moment of intense shock, suspense is accomplished by giving the audience full knowledge about what is going on, so that the viewers will become emotionally involved. In the case of shock, by contrast, something unexpected happens, gripping the audience for a few seconds. But in suspense, the members of the audience know everything. They are, as Hitchcock said, allowed "to play God" (Gottlieb 1995, 113), precisely when and because the characters in the story are unaware of what is going on. However, the audience also has to be relieved and, in sociological terms, be allowed to leave their liminal experience behind and return to social structure. The themes of Hitchcock's movies therefore relate to very basic emotions, involving fear, death, sex, and indeed guilt (see figure 7.2).

THE ORDER OF GUILT AND INNOCENCE

Guilt and innocence are constitutive principles of a society's legal and moral order. A central notion of a modern system of law holds that no one can be held accountable for a breach of law unless the offender, who has been held to have factually committed the crime, also had the intention to commit the illegal act. More specifically, the mere intention to commit a crime cannot be held as a ground for prosecution, but a *means rea* (criminal mind) must be present for there to be an offense for which a court of law can formally pronounce guilt (Hall 2005).

A central clue to the understanding of liminality in Hitchcock's films revolves around the dual nature of guilt. There is, on the one hand, the guilt formally declared by society. This is what can be called public guilt. It is the public, official, and legal branding of a person to be accountable for an illegal act. Typically in Hitchcock's films, public guilt is applied to a person who is factually innocent, someone of whom the viewer knows that he or she did not do what they are accused of having done. Most typically, also, the act for which public guilt is declared is a matter of a

Figure 7.2. Hitchcock's emphasis on sexual desire and fear and, in particular, on the ambiguity that can exist between them is typically expressed in purely visual terms, such as in this scene from *The Pleasure Garden*. Image in the public domain.

society's formal normative order as manifested in a system of laws. The display of public guilt in Hitchcock's movies immediately involves the audience on an emotional level as the viewer sympathizes with the hero who is wrongly accused.

Intimately relating to but distinctly contrasting public guilt, another form of guilt is portrayed in Hitchcock's films as a condition relating more closely to the sentiments and thoughts people have about their own conduct. It is the private guilt subjects experience when, as members of a normative order which is not necessarily synonymous with that of society at large, they recognize themselves for what they have done wrong, typically in a more generally moral rather than a strict legal sense. They can, therefore, often no longer hide themselves from their immediate others as they truly are. Most typically, private guilt in Hitchcock is rigidly separated from public guilt. Private guilt refers not to a formal and objective order of law but to codes of conduct in the realm of private and subjective morality and ethics. It is a matter of individual consciousness. Strikingly, private guilt applies in Hitchcock's universe to almost everybody, even and especially those who are victims of circumstances.

In the remainder of this chapter, I substantiate my arguments on the liminal nature of Hitchcock films and the modalities of guilt and innocence by means of illustration, relying on analyses of events and characters in several of the master's fifty-three movies.

HITCHCOCK'S LIMINALITY AND GUILT

What is readily striking from the viewpoint of ritual introduced in this chapter is that the process of liminality and the notions of public and private guilt are very closely related in the Hitchcock universe. Public guilt is the guilt of a person so labeled by some authoritative agents or institutions of the social order, representing a formal system of laws. Most often in Hitchcock's films, public guilt implies factual innocence, manifested by the image of the hero who is wrongly accused. By contrast, private guilt occurs when the characters in a story recognize themselves as guilty. In Hitchcock's movies, private guilt is experienced by those who committed the illegal act of which the hero is falsely accused, but also by the hero, albeit it for other reasons. Importantly, both forms of guilt in the world of Hitchcock entail a process that evolves through several successive stages. In the following pages, I present examples of the various phases most typical in this process of liminality through public condemnation.

Involvement and Affliction

For the drama of a movie to unfold successfully from the viewpoint of Hitchcock's pure cinema, a person who is legally innocent of a crime (through not innocent in all, moral respects) will typically get involved in an adventure that is someone else's. Often times, mistaken identity leads to involvement through a rather silly but very consequential misunderstanding.

I have already used several examples from *North by Northwest* (Hitchcock 1959), the masterful comedy / romance in which the character played by Cary Grant is chased across northern America, for no reason apparent to him, but straight into the arms of the beautiful cool blonde played by Eva Marie Saint. Many observers find this movie to be quintessential Hitchcock both in contents and form. The involvement in *North by Northwest* occurs through a seemingly very innocuous and silly coincidence. The Cary Grant character is in a hotel bar having a drink with colleagues. At some point he stands up to make a phone call just at the precise moment when a certain Mr. Kaplan is being paged as part of a clever trick by a group of spies who are looking for a covert American agent. As the spies now mistake him for the agent, a process is set in motion that entails a long and arduous series of strange events, which will greatly and emotionally involve the viewer in the hero's trials and tribulations.

Similarly, in *The Man Who Knew Too Much* (Hitchcock 1956), Hitchcock's remake of his own 1934 movie, a man played by Jimmy Stewart is on vacation with his wife and son in Morocco. Out of nowhere, he is suddenly approached by a dying man, who tells him of a plot to kill a statesman in London. Now the man knows too much, even though he does not even know so himself. Once the hero is involved upon the kidnapping of his son, a series of unexpected events, full of danger and suffering, are forced upon him and his family.

The labeling of guilt in Hitchcock continues from an initial involvement through a process that, through several stages, includes various public instruments and symbols of condemnation. Examples of this unfolding of the ritual process in Hitchcock's movies are far too numerous to mention, for the obvious reason that no movie would be of any cinematic merit were it not to involve this essential processual aspect of drama. While in the social order at large, liminality is a relatively temporary process that is reserved only for special occasions such as rites of passage, in the world of the cinema (as in art in general), the emphasis shifts entirely from structure to the process and experience of anti-structure. In Hitchcock's own words, drama is "life with the dull bits cut out" (Truffaut 1984, 103).

Two cinematic types of Hitchockian affliction can be specially mentioned: the wrong man and the chase. As already indicated on several occasions, the archetypical affliction in Hitchcock's movie pertains to is a hero wrongly accused. In his movie *The Wrong Man* (Hitchcock 1957), Hitchcock brought this theme to the center of attention, additionally strengthening the impact of the story by the fact that it was based on real-life events. In the movie, an innocent man played by Henry Fonda is mistakenly identified as a thief and from then on subjected to all the humiliating degradations of criminal justice, from arrest through booking and arraignment to detention. As the man is questioned by the police for a crime he did not commit, one of the officers observes: "An innocent man has nothing to fear, remember that" (Hitchcock 1957). Although the man is eventually cleared, his wife suffers a mental breakdown.

The chase in Hitchcock's universes involves a process whereby the initial involvement leads the publicly condemned guilty person to go on the run (Gottlieb 1995, 125–32). The Hitchcockian chase is not simply an exciting adventure, although it is that too. It involves a transference of guilt from one person (who did commit a crime) to another (who did not) (Truffaut 1984, 203). The chase is seen by representatives of the social order, typically the police as well as the ignorant public, as a confession of guilt. Yet, because of circumstances, for the protagonist the chase is the only possible means to search for the true culprit and rid himself of the guilt society has inflicted upon him. The chase involves a cleansing. Additionally, the tormented hero will have to find the real wrongdoer, because the police in Hitchcock's world are often incompetent and outright stupid, and usually only implicate the falsely accused even more.

In Hitchcock's prototypical chase movie *The 39 Steps* (Balcon and Hitchcock 1935), a Canadian man visiting London accidentally meets a woman who, unbeknownst to him, is running away from secret agents. He agrees to hide her in his flat, but during the night she is murdered. Fearing (quite rightly as it soon turns out) that he will be accused of the woman's murder, the man goes on the run and finds himself in various situations of danger. Though he will be able to clear (and cleanse himself) in the end, the price he has to pay is an involvement in immoralities and even illegalities that result from the accusations to which he is subjected. At some point, he has to bribe a man he despises but whose help he desperately needs so he does not get caught and is able to close in on the real culprit.

At the end of the chase, the Hitchcockian hero is cleared of all formal charges and legal accusations. But this cleansing always comes at a price, after a long and intense period of suffering and loss. In *The Lodger* (Balcon and Hitchcock 1927), a man is mistakenly held to be Jack the Ripper (see figure 7.3). Just when the real murderer is discovered by the police, an angry crowd chases him and forces him off a bridge, barely staying alive because his handcuffed hands snag, catching him hanging over a fence. Only in the final moment, after he has been beaten repeatedly by the mad mob can he be rescued, not by the police but by his love interest. Hitchcock portrays the return to the social order as serious and weighty, such as in *The Wrong Man* (Hitchcock 1957) where the hero's wife in the end has gone insane, but at other times the director shows the cost of the return to the social order in more humorous terms. The hero in *To Catch a Thief* (Hitchcock 1955), by example, in the end has the beautiful Grace Kelly running into his arms, only to be told that her mother will be coming along as well.

Symbols and Techniques

Relying on the basic technique of suspense, Hitchcock most always reveals to the audience, typically at the very beginning of the movie, who the real villain is. The cinematic technique thereby is primarily visual so that the audience can literally see the guilt of the offender's crime, typically through some small, intimate, or otherwise seemingly innocent symbol. For example, in *Frenzy* (Hitchcock 1972), the audience knows who the real murderer is very early on in the story when a man is seen

Figure 7.3. The hero in the 1927 silent movie *The Lodger*, portrayed by Ivor Novello, looks guilty in a city gripped by fear for a serial killer who targets blonde women. Image in the public domain.

brutally raping a woman. Yet, the man's guilt is seen most sharply in his eyes, which is to say, through the manner in which Hitchcock's camera captures those eyes and projects their filming onto the screen. In the early thriller *Murder!* (Maxwell and Hitchcock 1930), the only explicit whodunit directed by Hitchcock, the killer's guilt is betrayed not despite but precisely because and when his head and eyes turn away from sight. In *Psycho* (Hitchcock 1960), the murderer is surrounded by stuffed birds, especially owls, who, as Hitchcock himself argued, are watchers of the night through whom "he can see his own guilt reflected in their knowing eyes" (Truffaut 1984, 282). In *Suspicion* (Edington and Hitchcock 1941), a man whose own wife thinks he is out to kill her is symbolically visualized as guilty by means of an illuminated glass of milk thought to be poisoned. The movie *Shadow of a Doubt* (Skirball and Hitchcock 1943) leaves little doubt as to who the guilty person is as the opening scene of the film shows a man lying in bed, fully clothed, during the daytime, smoking a cigar, with several dollar bills carelessly placed next to him.

As parents often tell their children to look into their eyes when they suspect a lie, the Hitchcockian symbols of private guilt are especially powerful and critically contribute to lead to the unmasking of the real culprit. In *Young and Innocent* (1937), we know of the killer only the one tiny detail that he has a nervous twitch in his eyes. Toward the end of the movie, we see the wrongly accused hero's love interest looking for the murderer in a hotel. While she is desperately looking around, Hitchcock's camera takes us a through a long tracking shot closer and closer to the eyes of the drummer in the hotel band. At the final moment, when the close-up can go no tighter, we see his eyes starting to twitch.

Hitchcock did not make any movies containing shock or horror except *Psycho* (Hitchcock 1960), which Hitchcock himself described as a "shocker" (Kapsis 1992, 63). It is not altogether unfortunate that Hitchcock is sometimes today known only for this movie, especially among a younger generation today, for even though *Psycho* is an a-typical movie in many respects, the film does vividly demonstrate the ideal of pure cinema and some of the cinematic techniques Hitchcock used to portray guilt. In typical Hitchcock fashion, the movie is only very loosely based on a novel derived from the real-life story of a serial killer. Hitchcock radically shifts the focus in his movie from the killer, a mentally disturbed young man, to the victim, an attractive female. The woman is romantically and sexually involved with a man to whom she is not married and at some point steals money. The first half of the movie is essential in its very lengthy, drawn-out and rather distracting build-up toward the woman's sudden and violent killing while she is taking a shower.

The shower scene in *Psycho* is rightly discussed as a stellar example of pure cinema as there is simply no way to convey in words the experience of viewing the scene in the film and its impact for the remainder of the story. Less discussed, but critical to unravel Hitchcock's visions of guilt and innocence, are the many scenes in *Psycho* where the characters of the offender, on the one hand, and the victims as well as her loved-ones, on the other hand, can be viewed standing or sitting opposite from one another. The characters are either filmed from left and right angles, respectively, or, more often and more poignantly still, they are each positioned on one side of the screen. This Hitchcockian technique can be referred to as doubling, that is, the splitting or multiplying into two, such as two characters representing good and evil, respectively, or two sharply contrasting sides of one character (Sterritt 2002, 106). While this narrative device is hardly specific to Hitchcock, what is much more particular about Hitchcock is the visual manner in which doubling is achieved. Indeed, a straightforward but very effective device of pure cinema, doubling accomplishes by purely pictorial means that which at once separates and connects, specifically guilt versus innocence and private guilt versus public guilt.

Hitchcock's most striking use of doubling is when the technique is used to convey the separation of guilt on one side of the screen and innocence on the other. The splitting of the subjects over the screen shows that guilt is what innocence is not, that they are in opposition to one another. Thus, importantly, they are also connected as there is no guilt without innocence. In *Psycho*, the splitting of the characters over the screen is very rigid and omnipresent throughout the movie to distinguish clearly and repeatedly the offender from the victim, further augmented by the sharp black and white photography and Bernard Herrmann's accompanying music score. This splitting is additionally used to visualize the dual personality of the offender and the ambiguities of the victim, most distinctly by the use of mirrors that pop up time and time again throughout the movie to visualize the dual nature of a character. Hitchcock often uses the doubling technique at various levels at once. This creates not only an added dimension of splitting or separation but also conveys an ambiguity of guilt and innocence or a transference of guilt. On these rare but poignant occasions, there is, rather than a mere separation of guilt from innocence, a vagueness and ambiguity of who is guilty and who is innocent.

Doubling to demarcate guilt from innocence is, in both narrative and visual form, most clearly seen in the Hitchcock movie *Shadow of a Doubt* (1943). The story involves a man who romantically befriends widowed women, only to kill them and rob them of their wealth. To hide from the police, he visits the family of his sister, whose daughter, Charlie, is named after him. The entire unfolding drama concerns the relation between the uncle and his niece, the killer and the young woman who must and will reveal his true identity. Uncle and niece not only have the same name, they also share a very close, at times, telepathic bond. The dilemma for the two is whether to love or to hate, to belong or to leave, to hold or to push away, and their portrayals throughout the movie accordingly constantly position them left and right of the screen, moving closer to and removing themselves from each other, holding hands and letting go.

The role of symbolic doubling is particularly well-realized in a scene from Hitchcock's movie *Strangers on a Train* (Hitchcock 1951) because here the technique is displayed in entirely pictorial means. In the story of the movie, a man has killed another man's cheating wife, hoping for him to kill his annoying father in return. After he has committed the murder, the man visits the unsuspecting beneficiary of his crime and informs him of what he has done. Their meeting takes place with the murderer standing behind the bars of a fence, as if he is in a jail cell, shown to the left of the screen, and the unsuspecting hero standing beside the fence to the right-hand side of the screen. As the hero becomes aware he has gotten involved in the crime because he did not take the plan of the mad murderer seriously but now stands to benefit from it anyway, a police car comes to the house, whereupon the hero moves to the side and is shown standing next to the murderer behind the fence. Now, both are guilty.

HITCHCOCK'S UNIVERSE OF GUILT

In Hitchcock's world, nobody is ever truly innocent. This theme in Hitchcock is strikingly congruent with a basic tenet of the church in which he was raised. For the separation between public and private guilt not only corresponds, as mentioned before, to a distinction between formal law and individual morality, it is at times also expressed by Hitchcock in terms of a secular versus a higher, indeed sacred order of normativity. Most distinctly, the notion of original sin is on display in Hitchcock in the idea of universal guilt.

Even the most dashingly handsome and courageous heroes and the most tragic of victims are in Hitchcock's cinema also portrayed as guilty in some other discernable sense. The examples that can be mentioned are numerous and stretch the entire length of Hitchcock's career. For example, in *The Paradine Case* (Selznick and Hitchcock 1947), a man defends a woman accused of killing her husband. The woman is guilty and the lawyer loses the case. Yet graver is his moral loss, because he fell in love with his client despite his being a married man. In *Strangers on a Train* (Hitchcock 1951), the hero may not actually have killed his wife, but he did at some point scream that he wanted to strangle her. In *Torn Curtain* (Hitchcock 1966), the hero lies to his girlfriend to hide his identity as a double agent. He later kills a man. In *Family Plot* (Hitchcock 1976), a woman and her boyfriend manage to uncover a couple of kidnappers. The woman herself, however, is a fake medium and takes advantage, emotionally and financially, of an aging widow desperately looking for a family member.

In Hitchcock's world, private guilt in a moral, if not always legal sense is generalized to apply to everybody. It is Original Sin. This private guilt can often also be observed to refer to a moral code that is of a distinctly sexual nature. The examples are again numerous. In *Rich and Strange* (Maxwell and Hitchcock 1931), a married couple suddenly gains a fortune and decides to travel the world. Before they find happiness together at the movie's end, they cheat on each other. In *The Lady Vanishes* (Black and Hitchcock 1938), the heroine manages to help uncover a spy ring and along the way falls in love with a man even though she was engaged to someone else. In *Strangers on a Train* (Hitchcock 1951), the hero benefits from the killing of his wife by being free to marry a woman he was already having a romantic liaison with. In *Marnie* (Hitchcock 1964), a man marries a woman he knows to be a thief. He later forces himself upon her during their honeymoon, when it turns out she is frigid.

In Hitchcock's universe, a sexually charged sense of private guilt can apply to heroes as well as to villains and their victims. In *Dial M for Murder* (Hitchcock 1954), a man tries to kill his wife through a hired hit man. The wife manages to survive the failed murder plot, but she was cheating on her husband. The woman who is killed in *Psycho* (Hitchcock 1960) not only stole money, she was also sexually involved with a divorced man. In *The Birds* (Hitchcock 1963), an attractive, affluent woman falls in love with a down-to-earth, handsome man. Despite the objections from the man's jealous mother, the two are in the end brought together, even receiving the approval of the man's mother. The affluent woman is spoiled and arrogant. The man was unable to maintain a relationship with another woman, a school teacher, because he lacked the courage and strength to resist the interference of his mother. Still in love with the man, the school teacher remained single and eventually is killed during a bird attack, allowing the man to pursue the affluent woman. In *Topaz* (Hitchcock 1969), a French secret service agent uncovers a communist espionage ring. The agent cheats on his wife with an informant, while his wife is cheating on him with a close friend, who is later discovered to be the head of the spy ring.

BETWEEN STRUCTURE AND ANTI-STRUCTURE

Hitchcock made fifty-three movies and despite the fact that he uses certain re-occurring plot devices and techniques of visualization, the stylistic range of his movies is broad. Sometimes the emphasis is on romance, comedy, and adventure, while at other times the themes are more seriously concerned with fear, death, and despair. Almost never did Hitchcock use the thriller genre to focus on a crime. To Hitchcock, the thriller was about form, not substance. From the viewpoint of the framework adopted in this chapter, two very different kinds of Hitchcock movies deserve special consideration as they represent the two polar opposites of structure and antistructure.

Representing the normative demands of the social structure are most clearly those Hitchcock movies that are closely related to reality. This approach is atypical of Hitchcock as his style lends itself best to realistic portrayals of fantasy stories. Only the very special and tragic circumstance of World War II forced and allowed Hitchcock to break with this approach. Indeed, Hitchcock made several movies during World War II that explicitly dealt with the theme of war and that served to function as contributions to the war effort. In 1944 Hitchcock made two short propaganda movies (in French) for the British Ministry of Information. Moreover, Hitchcock made three regular features during the war that can be additionally conceived as part of the director's "little contribution to the war effort" (Truffaut 1984, 159): *Foreign Correspondent* (Wanger and Hitchcock 1940) about the coming of the war in Europe; *Saboteur* (Lloyd and Hitchcock 1942) about Nazi infiltrators in the United States; and *Lifeboat* (Macgowan and Hitchcock 1944) about the triumph of American democratic culture over Nazism. Because of their focus on a disturbing reality that nobody could avoid, Hitchcock's wartime movies break with his usual quest for liminality. These films do not present any ambiguity in moral or legal respects and instead clearly and resolutely demarcate guilt from innocence. There are villains who are to be defeated and there are heroes who will defeat them. The moral order of Hitchcock's wartime movies have boundaries that are precise, unquestionable, and unshakeable.

Contrasting his wartime work, Hitchcock's other movies entail a search for liminality in varying ways and to various degrees. In the vast majority of Hitchcock's movies, guilt and innocence shift and change. In at least two films, *Blackmail* of 1929 and *Sabotage* of 1936, Hitchcock even went as far as to portray and justify a radical and near complete reversal of some of the most central principles of the social order, to present an antistructure in which even murder is justified. In *Blackmail* (Maxwell and Hitchcock 1929), a young woman is displeased with her boyfriend's lack of attention for her and his preoccupation with his job at Scotland Yard. One night, she secretly meets with another man and goes to his apartment to look at his paintings. When the man forces himself upon her, the woman defends herself and kills her assailant with a bread knife (see figure 7.4). When the body is discovered, the woman's boyfriend is assigned to the case and quickly discovers that his girlfriend is the killer. However, after a man with a criminal record who witnessed the killing blackmails the

Figure 7.4. The heroine of the 1929 movie *Blackmail*, played by Anny Ondra, kills a man when he is trying to rape her. Image in the public domain.

woman, it is the blackmailer who is thought to be the killer. He accidentally dies, and the young woman goes free.

The film *Sabotage* (Balcon and Hitchcock 1936), which in the United States was released under the title *The Woman Alone*, portrays a woman who discovers that her husband is involved in a gang of foreign saboteurs.

The woman has a younger brother whom she adores. When the woman's husband is assigned to let a bomb explode in the heart of London, he conceals the bomb in a package he gives to the young boy. As the boy is delayed taking the package to its destination, the bomb explodes and the boy is killed. Hitchcock later regretted this scene as a "grave error" (Gottlieb 2003, 70), because the boy's death followed a lengthy suspense scene that at the end offered no sense of relief for the audience. However, the boy's death does serve to justify the extraordinary event that will occur later in the story. After the boy's older sister finds out her own husband was responsible, she holds a knife while preparing dinner and looks at her husband. When the man stands up in amazement from the look in his wife's eyes and approaches her, she stabs him to death. A police detective finds out about the woman's involvement, but he has fallen in love with her and, with the police assuming her husband died in a subsequent explosion, the woman goes free.

HITCHCOCK'S SEARCH FOR LIMINALITY

Hitchcock's movies, like other noteworthy expressions of art, offer reversals of the structured and rigid principles of the social order to create a distinct if temporary sense of communitas. Additionally, within the stories of Hitchcock's cinema, the dramatic characters are submitted to a process of liminality, a drama that takes them through a process of moving from one state to another. Cinematically, Hitchcock is very effective at displaying liminality because his movies cannot be exhausted by reference to the story that is told. Instead, the prime element of his cinema is the experience of the inter-structural journey through which Hitchcock makes his characters undergo for the benefit of the viewer. As guilt and innocence are constitutive principles of a society's normative order, liminality infuses the order of guilt and innocence with ambiguity and fluidity. The liminal subjects are on the run because they are publicly condemned. Heroes who are victims in some respect are guilty of wrongdoings at another level of normativity. Only in Hitchcock's wartime movies is there a lack of ambiguity over guilt and innocence, because war is an exceptional state of turmoil that precludes liminality.

The singularly most ridiculous thing that has been written about Hitchcock is that his films are the result of some deeper psychological state, a mental disorder almost, oriented at inflicting pain, particularly upon females. Not surprisingly, this viewpoint is typically couched in highly sexually charged terms (Wood 2002). In truth, Hitchcock's supposed torture of his subjects represents a ritual of affliction that is a necessary component of the quest for a new existence. Hitchcock identified with the victims in his movies, especially when they were women, who he also reckoned to make up the major part of the audience (Gottlieb 1995, 73). Shame, loss, and moral guilt are needed as part of a ritual process in order to accomplish a new life. To heighten the sense of loss and disorder, Hitchcock typically introduces the liminal subjects in a setting of complete order, a surrounding filled with familiar symbols. To accomplish a new existence, the final phase of the ritual performance must end in some tragedy, which in other respects represents liberation.

Realistically connecting to fundamental principles of the normative order of society, Hitchcock's films contain elements of a social and cultural identity that do not necessarily belong to the director, but to the society from which the viewing audience is drawn. Thus Hitchcock's films reproduce elements of a social order from which the audience can successfully part during the experiential process of cinema. In search of another reality, Hitchcock and his audience sought to escape from the normative bounds imposed by society as the essential purpose and desire of his movies. The success of the cinematic accomplishment of spontaneous communitas in which the artist successfully involves the audience is the measure of Hitchcock's genius.

REFERENCES

Alexander, Jeffrey C. (ed.). 1988. *Durkheimian Sociology: Cultural Studies*. London: Cambridge University Press.

Balcon, Michael (producer) and Alfred Hitchcock (director). 1927. *The Lodger* [Motion Picture]. United Kingdom: Gainsborough.

———. 1929. *Blackmail* [Motion Picture]. United Kingdom: British International.

———. 1935. *The 39 Steps* [Motion Picture]. United Kingdom: Gaumont-British.

Black, Edward (producer) and Alfred Hitchcock (director). 1938. *The Lady Vanishes* [Motion Picture]. United Kingdom: Gaumont-British.

Chandler, Charlotte. 2005. *It's Only a Movie: Alfred Hitchcock, A Personal Biography*. New York: Simon & Schuster.

Deflem, Mathieu. 1991. "Ritual, Anti-Structure, and Religion: A Discussion of Victor Turner's Processual Symbolic Analysis." *Journal for the Scientific Study of Religion* 30(1): 1–25.

Durkheim, Emile. (1912) 1965. *The Elementary Forms of the Religious Life*. New York: The Free Press.

———. (1914) 1973. "The Dualism of Human Nature and Its Social Conditions." In *Emile Durkheim on Morality and Society*, edited by Robert N. Bellah, 149–63. Chicago: University of Chicago Press.

Edington, Harry E. (producer) and Alfred Hitchcock (director). 1941. *Suspicion* [Motion Picture]. United States: RKO.

Gottlieb, Sidney (ed.). 1995. *Hitchcock on Hitchcock: Selected Writings and Interviews*. Berkeley, CA: University of California Press.

——— (ed.). 2003. *Alfred Hitchcock: Interviews*. Jackson, MS: University Press of Mississippi.
Hall, Jerome. 2005. *General Principles of Criminal Law*. Second edition. Clark, NJ: The Lawbook Exchange.
Hitchcock, Alfred (producer/director). 1946. *Notorious* [Motion Picture]. United States: RKO.
——— (producer/director). 1951. *Strangers on a Train* [Motion Picture]. United States: Warner Brothers-First National.
——— (producer/director). 1954. *Dial M For Murder* [Motion Picture]. United States: Warner Brothers-First National.
——— (producer/director). 1955. *To Catch a Thief* [Motion Picture]. United States: Paramount.
——— (producer/director). 1956. *The Man Who Knew Too Much* [Motion Picture]. United States: Paramount.
——— (producer/director). 1956. *The Wrong Man* [Motion Picture]. United States: Warner Brothers-First National.
——— (producer/director). 1959. *North by Northwest* [Motion Picture]. United States: MGM.
——— (producer/director). 1960. *Psycho* [Motion Picture]. United States: Paramount.
——— (producer/director). 1963. *The Birds* [Motion Picture]. United States: Universal.
——— (producer/director). 1964. *Marnie* [Motion Picture]. United States: Universal.
——— (producer/director). 1966. *Torn Curtain* [Motion Picture]. United States: Universal.
——— (producer/director). 1969. *Topaz* [Motion Picture]. United States: Universal.
——— (producer/director). 1972. *Frenzy* [Motion Picture]. United States: Universal.
——— (producer/director). 1976. *Family Plot* [Motion Picture]. United States: Universal.
Kapsis, Robert E. 1992. *Hitchcock: The Making of a Reputation*. Chicago: The University of Chicago Press.
Lloyd, Frank (producer) and Alfred Hitchcock (director). 1942. *Saboteur* [Motion Picture]. United States: Universal.
Macgowan, Kenneth (producer) and Alfred Hitchcock (director). 1944. *Lifeboat* [Motion Picture]. United States: 20th Century-Fox.
Maxwell, John (producer) and Alfred Hitchcock (director). 1930. *Murder!* [Motion Picture]. United Kingdom: British International.
———. 1931. *Rich and Strange* [Motion Picture]. United Kingdom: British International.
Selznick, David O. (producer) and Alfred Hitchcock (director). 1947. *The Paradine Case* [Motion Picture]. United States: Selznick International-Vanguard Films.
Skirball, Jack H. (producer) and Alfred Hitchcock (director). 1943. *Shadow of a Doubt* [Motion Picture]. United States: Universal.
Sterritt, David. 2002. "The Diabolic Imagination: Hitchcock, Bakhtin, and the Carnevalization of Cinema." In *Framing Hitchcock*, edited by Sidney Gottlieb and Christopher Brookhouse, 93–112. Detroit: Wayne State University Press.

Taylor, John Russell. 1978. *Hitch: The Life and Times of Alfred Hitchcock*. New York: Da Capo Press.

The Telegraph. 2015. "Alfred Hitchcock Holocaust Film to go on General Release 70 Years After Suppression." *The Telegraph*, Accessed January 26, 2015, www.telegraph.co.uk/news/uknews/11368569/Alfred-Hitchcock-holocaust-film-to-go-on-general-release-70-years-after-suppression.html

Truffaut, François. 1984. *Hitchcock*. Revised edition. New York: Simon & Schuster.

Turner, Victor W. 1967. *The Forest of Symbols*. Ithaca, NY: Cornell University Press.

———. 1969. *The Ritual Process: Structure and Anti-Structure*. Ithaca, NY: Cornell University Press.

———. 1974. *Dramas, Fields, and Metaphors: Symbolic Action in Human Society*. Ithaca, NY: Cornell University Press.

Wanger, Walter (producer) and Alfred Hitchcock (director). 1940. *Foreign Correspondent* [Motion Picture]. United States: Wanger Productions.

Wood, Robin. 2002. *Hitchcock's Films Revisited*. Revised edition. New York: Columbia University Press.

8

Heroes for Hard Times

The Wire's *"Good Police"*

John Denvir

In an earlier paper, I praised the Emmy-Award-winning television series *The Wire* for its searing critique of the American justice system (Denvir 2014). I in no way retreat from my praise for the series' insights into the systemic dysfunctions of our bureaucratic and political systems as they affect enforcement of the criminal law, but I feel now that I did not show proper attention to another aspect of *The Wire*—its ability to inspire efforts at reform. Here we must pay less attention to what the series' heroes' failed to accomplish and more to what they did accomplish for themselves and the larger community.

As the critical insights of *The Wire* make clear, we live in hard times in urban America. That's why we need heroes for hard times. Otherwise we become inured to the idea that injustice is the norm and any attempts to change it are fated to fail. I think *The Wire* provides such heroes.

Sometimes our heroes can come from real life, like Gandhi or Martin Luther King Jr. But today we mostly find heroes in popular narratives shown to us on television and in the movies. Unfortunately, these "heroes" are designed more to entertain than to inspire. While it is comforting to see them prevail, the facile narratives in which they operate misinform us about both the true problems we face and what would be effective remedies for them. Instead we spend long hours watching unrealistic heroes win improbable victories by incredible means.

We would be better served by stories about believable protagonists whose efforts are heroic even if they do not always prevail, or at least do not prevail as much as they had hoped. Even their defeats can have value. At a minimum their failures remind us that injustice is not easily uprooted, itself an improvement on a psychology of denial about how our society actually operates. But these stories also show us that intelligent efforts at reform offer rewards that a resigned passivity to the status quo can never deliver.

The creators of the series, David Simon and Ed Burns, have provided us just such stories in *The Wire*, which refuses to give its audience a contrived happy ending. It insists that the causes of crime are deeply embedded in our social structure and cultural values. The heroes seldom triumph in the sense of winning a clear-cut victory, but still show us that "losing" can be a form of winning for those courageous enough to make the attempt.

BALTIMORE: THE BIG PICTURE

The Wire's five seasons take place in post-9/11 Baltimore, a former industrial giant slowly turning to rust. The unemployment and crime rates continue to rise while the tax base shrinks. It's a hard place to earn a living if you are under-educated or African American. The plot mostly consists of stories of Baltimore's various professional "tribes"—the drug dealers, the police, and the politicians—struggles to expand their areas of influence. The terrain upon which this competition is often fought is West Baltimore, a slum whose poor, African American residents have few resources to use to advance their own interests. These are the people who are the true victims of the drug trade being conducted on their doorsteps.

This sad state of affairs is most affectingly chronicled in season 4, which focuses on the failures of the Baltimore public school system. The Baltimore schools have more than their share of problems. They lack adequate funding and are squeezed by local and state educational bureaucracies that seem indifferent to their fate. In addition, the drug trade in West Baltimore also has a deadening effect on the academic potential of the students.

In season 4, we meet four junior high school classmates, each of whom is negatively impacted by drug trade. Duquan ("Dukie") Weems (Jermaine Crawford) (IMDB.com 2014) is very poor, even by the low economic standards of West Baltimore. He has no clean clothes and no place to clean up before coming to school, where he is teased by his schoolmates about his body odor. A concerned teacher not only buys Dukie new clothes, but also arranges for him to shower at school before class. Later the teacher asks a classmate why Dukie never wears his new duds; the reply is that that both Dukie's parents are addicts and they had sold the new clothes for drugs.

Namond Brice (Julito McCullum) (IMDB.com 2014) has a different connection with the drug trade. His father Roland "Wee-Bay" Brice (Hassan Johnson) (IMDB.com 2014), is in prison for life for murders he committed as a drug cartel "soldier." Namond's mother fully expects that her son will follow the family "trade" as soon as he leaves school. The problem is that Namond is not cut out for the life of a drug dealer. He's more a clown than a junior gangster.

Michael Lee (Tristan Wilds) (IMDB.com 2014), the brightest of the group, also comes from a family devastated by drugs. His father, when not in jail, regularly beats up his mother. Michael attracts the attention of a drug gang that is always happy to find fresh new talent. By the end of the year, he has left school to take an entry-level job with a drug gang. Our last view shows him brandishing a pistol.

The fourth member of the group is Randy Wagstaff (Maestro Harrell) (IMDB.com 2014). Randy is the runt of the group, but popular and entrepreneurial; he sells snacks to his fellow students. Randy's fatal mistake is to witness a drug gang murder. When questioned about the slaying by authorities, Randy is branded a "snitch" by his peers and effectively ostracized at the school. He ends the season an angry teenager living in a dysfunctional group home.

The mini-narratives of these four boys show how the futures of the students of West Baltimore are impacted by the drug war. They are crippled academically because their home lives have not prepared them to perform successfully in school, and they lack the self-esteem and discipline necessary to do well in school. Beyond the handicaps created by the past, there is also despair about the future. The students are fully aware that the only decent-paying jobs for West Baltimore teens are novice slots in the drug gangs, employers who don't care much about good grades in school.

THE BARKSDALE PROSECUTION

Good police work alone can never solve the problems of the West Baltimore schools or their students, but it could play an important part in providing a space for normal social interactions like schooling to take place. So the attempt by a group of Baltimore police officers to send the leaders of the major local drug gang to jail for long terms would have a positive impact on the lives of kids like Dukie, Namond, Michael, and Randy.

At this point in the series, the laws have mostly lain dormant because the police department's leaders have not ranked aggressive prosecution of the drug lords a high departmental priority. Controlling the drug scene would require a large commitment of department resources, and the return on this investment to the department would be minimal because drug crime in West Baltimore is not one of the issues that the local politicians who fund the department regard as important. They see the sale of drugs as a victimless crime and drug-related killings as isolated instances of black on black violence of little interest to the press, and therefore invisible to voters.

Season 1 tells the story of how a group of officers (the "good police") attempt to reverse this policy of bureaucratic inattention. The two leaders of this group are Lieutenant Cedric Daniels (Lance Reddick) (IMDB.com 2014) and Detective Jimmy McNulty (Dominic West). They are an odd pair. Daniels is a "company man," an African American who appears to be quickly climbing the bureaucratic ladder to a high position within the department. McNulty is mercurial by temperament, sometimes charming and often infuriating. One of his consistent traits is an innate suspicion of authority figures, such as people like Daniels. Nevertheless, Daniels and McNulty share a commitment to good police work.

The plot is triggered by McNulty's proclivity to be in the wrong place at the wrong time. Out of curiosity, McNulty drops in on the murder trial of a young drug gangster named D'Angelo Barksdale (Lawrence Gilliard Jr.). He listens as an eyewitness to the murder recants her statement identifying Barksdale as the killer. This is no surprise to McNulty who knows that D'Angelo is the nephew of the drug gang boss Avon Barksdale (Wood Harris) (IMDB.com 2014). He also sees that Stringer Bell (Idris Elba) (IMDB.com 2014), the other leader of the Barksdale drug gang, is in the courtroom—a presence that reminds the witness that the Barksdale gang has a well-established policy of killing witnesses who testify against them.

After dismissing the case because there is no longer evidence to convict, Judge Daniel Phelan (Peter Gerety) (IMDB.com 2014) calls McNulty into his chambers to help him better understand the strange events he has just witnessed in his courtroom. McNulty tells Phelan that the witness recanted because if she had not done so, she would have been murdered. To McNulty, it's just another day in West Baltimore, but Phelan is shocked and outraged that such a travesty of justice could take place in his courtroom.

He calls Deputy Police Commissioner Ervin Burrell (Frankie Faison) to demand that the department take action to remedy this intolerable situation. This places Burrell in a difficult position. He knows little about the drug trade in West Baltimore and has no interest in learning more. It is not an area that warrants many departmental resources, but Burrell also recognizes that a Superior Court judge is an important political actor, someone the department does not care to offend.

Burrell devises a clever plan to mollify Phelan without undue interference with the department's traditional priorities. The department will create a special task force to go after drug crime. This will appease Phelan. The task force will be headed by Cedric Daniels (Lance Reddick) (IMDB.com 2014), a loyal lieutenant with ambitions to ascend the bureaucratic ladder. Daniels can be trusted to keep the investigation low key. The rest of the officers appointed to the task force, except one, will be mostly rookies or the dregs of the police force.

The one exception is Jimmy McNulty, who must be disciplined for committing the bureaucratic sin of discussing internal police matters with an outsider. As punishment, McNulty will be transferred from his prestigious position on the homicide squad to the dead-end Daniels unit. Burrell figures that after a month or two of investigations leading to the prosecution of some low level dealers, he will be able to disband the task force without offending Phelan.

But it turns out that Burrell has made some miscalculations. Daniels decides to push back against the leadership that has given him a mission designed to fail. McNulty decides that his "demotion" will actually allow him to do some good police work in combatting the drug violence in West Baltimore. And some of the police assigned to the task force prove to be excellent officers when operating within a supportive organizational structure.

Up until this time, the department's standard practice has been to ignore the drug trade in West Baltimore except for making occasional "buy and bust" arrests and prosecutions to show the press that the department is on the job. These prosecutions lead to short prison terms for low-level "soldiers" who the Barksdale gang quickly replaces on the streets. The convictions have no impact on the drug gang's leaders, Avon Barksdale and Stringer Bell. They continue to reap a million dollars or two a month from the drug sales and pay no taxes.

The Daniels unit, at McNulty's urging (and without Burrell's knowledge) adopts a new strategy for enforcing drug laws. They want to connect Avon Barksdale and Stringer Bell to the drug-related murders that are routinely committed in West Baltimore or to the purchases of large quantities of drugs, offenses that will take them off the streets for good.

McNulty, and later Daniels, realize that they are going to have to do a different type of police work than departmental routine calls for. They are going to have to engage in intelligence work to understand how the Barksdale gang operates. At the beginning they don't even know what Avon Barksdale looks like. So they start to build a database of information on the gang, its personnel, and its operating procedures. Here they find there is a role for imagination and creativity sadly lacking in the bureaucratic "buy and bust" tactics.

One of the detectives assigned to the unit, Shakima ("Kima") Greggs (Sonja Sohn) (IMDB.com 2014), has recruited a confidential informant ("snitch"). He is a drug addict named Reginald ("Bubbles") Cousins (Andre Royo) (IMDB.com 2014), who is considered harmless by the Barksdale gang and therefore has easy access to the areas where they hang out. Bubbles, pretending to be selling hats to finance his drug habit, is able to identify the key players by playfully placing hats on their heads, allowing Greggs and her partners to create a photo gallery of the gang's members.

The unit also recognizes that the gang members communicate by beepers rather than cell phones; upon receiving a beeper message, the gang member goes to a pay phone to call the beeper number. McNulty figures out that if they could clone a gang member's beeper, they too would know who the gang member was calling. Judge Phelan gives them authority to clone a beeper found on a gang member.

But this victory is soon threatened by the realization that gang is using a code to disguise the called number. So they are still in the dark as to whom the phone calls are being made. But this problem soon yields a solution. To everyone's (including his own) surprise, rookie Roland Prezybylewski ("Prez") (Jim True-Frost) (IMDB.com 2014) is able to break the code. Now by using the beeper information and rooftop surveillance the unit is able to follow the gang's activities. The information gleaned from the beepers has another function; it provides the "probable cause" that permits Judge Phelan to authorize a wiretap on selected pay phones used by the gang. The unit can now monitor the gang's internal communications, which will eventually yield evidence of Barksdale and Bell's involvement in serious crime.

McNulty is also able to forge a relationship with a gunman named Omar Little (Michael Kenneth Williams) (IMDB.com 2014), who earns a good living, not by selling drugs, but by robbing those who do sell them. The gang has gruesomely killed Omar's young lover Brendan Walsh (Brendan Walsh) (IMDB.com 2014; Alvarez 2009, 529) as payback for stealing the gang's drug revenues. Omar is willing to provide the Daniels unit inside information on some of the gang's murders. Even more encouraging news emerges. McNulty tracks down an unhappy gang soldier named Wallace (Michael B. Jordan) (IMDB.com 2014), who can actually place Stringer Bell at the scene of Omar's lover's murder. And suddenly it appears that Avon Barksdale himself might be tied to a murder. An investigation of an old murder discloses that the victim was a former girlfriend of Avon Barksdale who had threatened to talk to the police about his activities.

But while most of the task force is investigating the gang's drug dealing and murders, Lester Freamon (Clarke Peters) (IMDB.com 2014), supposedly one of the "dregs" assigned to the unit, pursues another line of attack. He traces the profits that the gang reaps every month to see where they go. It turns out that closely held corporations headed by Barksdale confederates and represented by Barksdales' attorney, Maurice Levy, have been buying up a large number of abandoned properties in West Baltimore that are located within a proposed "redevelopment zone" primed to receive government grants (Alvarez 2009, 530). Barksdale confederates also turn out to be generous contributors to the campaigns of several important local politicians who will have a say on how the redevelopment funds will be allocated. Freamon sees here the potential for prosecuting Barksdale and Bell for a variety of "white collar" crimes ranging from money-laundering to bribery of public officials.

But while there is a good deal of potential in these investigations, none of them are ripe for prosecution. The Daniels unit needs time to allow the wiretap to slowly amass the evidence they need to win a major trial before a jury. This, of course, is not the script that the department leadership had planned for the unit.

Then an incident that at first seems to be a success blows up in the unit's face. Using information gleaned from the wiretap, the unit stops a limousine departing from a Barksdale drug location; the driver has twenty thousand dollars in small bills. The limousine turns out to be licensed to a State Senator named Clayton ("Clay") Davis (IMDB.com 2014). It appears to Daniels, McNulty, and Freamon that the Barksdale gang is using the revenues from its drug trade to bribe politicians.

At first, the members of the unit are elated by their discovery, but they soon discover that their joy was premature. They have inadvertently crossed into very dangerous territory. They are now investigating how politicians acquire their funds. Politicians do not want any investigations into their financial activities and they let Burrell know of their displeasure. Since the politicians determine the department's budget and the career prospects of its leaders, Burrell takes quick action. He directs Daniels to return the seized funds and also tells Daniels to close down the "wire" that produces information that the department would rather not know about.

Luckily this threat to the larger investigation is thwarted by Judge Phelan, who threatens to hold Burrell in contempt if the wire he has authorized is terminated before its allotted time has expired. But Burrell gets a second chance when the Daniels unit seems to catch a break in the apprehension of the titular owner of a Barksdale "men's club" for an attempted drug buy. Orlando (actor name not given), the front man, felt that he was not being treated fairly by Avon and decided to sell some dope on his own. He is quickly ensnared in a state police sting operation and finds himself looking at some serious jail time.

When he mentions his connection to Barksdale, the state narcs bring in the Daniels unit. Burrell insists that the unit use Orlando in a "buy and bust" operation. He will pretend to buy a large quantity of drugs from a Barksdale lieutenant who will be arrested when he delivers the drugs. But the plan backfires; Orlando is killed and Kima Greggs, who was working undercover, is seriously wounded. The members of the unit, especially McNulty, are inconsolable in their knowledge that they put their colleague and friend in harm's way.

Burrell has a different reaction. Embarrassed by the news reports that drug dealers have shot a police officer, he demands a dramatic departmental response. He orders a mass "bust" of all known drug venues in Baltimore. He decides to include the Barksdale's gang's primary drug depot. Daniels tries to persuade him to exclude this one property because arrests there will clearly signify to the Barksdale gang that the police are using a wire to listen to their conversations. Once they are aware of this fact, information gleaned from the wire will dry up, and the major prosecution Daniels is hoping for will never take place.

But Burrell refuses to relent. McNulty even attempts to get Judge Phelan to intervene, but the judge refuses. It seems that the politicians have gotten word of Phelan's role in the wiretap and have threatened to remove him from the Democratic ticket in the upcoming judicial elections.

The mass dragnet takes place and, as predicted, the wire goes silent. But there is s an unexpected benefit to the Daniels unit from the mass bust. The Barksdale gang suddenly has no dope to satisfy its customers' needs. This emergency causes them to be less careful in their drug purchases. Coincidentally, Freamon successfully installs a hidden camera in the gang's offices. It immediately picks up a conversation in which Avon directs his nephew D'Angelo to make a large "buy" in New Jersey to restock the gang's supplies. D'Angelo's car is then followed and he is arrested after the purchase with a sizeable amount of drugs, making both he and his uncle vulnerable to prosecution.

The good news is that the "good police" finally have admissible evidence implicating Avon Barksdale in a crime that calls for jail time. The bad news is that it will not be long term, and Stringer Bell will be free to run the gang's operation until Avon is released. More immediately, it also gives Burrell an opening to close down the whole Barksdale investigation in the wake of a great publicity event for the department. The Baltimore police will have sent a major drug dealer to prison, an unprecedented event in Baltimore. In Daniels and McNulty's minds, this is too small a prize won at too high a price.

But Burrell prevails and a complicated plea bargain is worked out with Barksdale's attorney. The major points are that Avon Barksdale will go to jail for a seven-year term, but is eligible for parole in about four years. His nephew D'Angelo accepts a twenty-year term, and the gang's primary assassin "Wee-Bay" accepts of plea of life without the possibility of parole in return for a state promise that he not be executed.

Series creator Simon and writer Burns in the final scenes of the first season portray the Barksdale prosecution as a huge failure. The gang keeps all its money and Stringer Bell is free to run the gang's businesses in Avon's absence. Moreover, all the investigations into political corruption are aborted. But Burrell is more than satisfied. He has used information gleaned from the troublesome "wire" to put a major drug lord in jail. This will show the department is serious in combatting drug crime. And, of course, he didn't want the investigations into campaign finance to go forward anyhow.

This resolution also has repercussions within the department. Burrell uses the "victory" as political proof that the special drug unit has done its job and can be closed down. Daniels returns to his old job in narcotics. McNulty is assigned to a police boat patrolling Baltimore's harbor where Burrell expects he will spend the rest of his career inhaling diesel fumes. And Stringer Bell moves into his new offices to resume business as usual. It appears that bureaucratic narrowness had frustrated the attempts by the Daniels unit to do good police work.

LOSING AS WINNING

But maybe there is a different way of looking at what has transpired. In determining whether a reform effort has been successful or not it is necessary to judge from more than one perspective. For example, Simon and Burns seem to see the Barksdale prosecution as a case history in the failure of the American justice system. There is every reason to agree with them if we demand that our reforms be both quick and total. The series shows a group of intelligent and hard-working police officers attempt to shut down the leaders of a major drug gang that is destroying the lives, sometimes literally, of the residents of West Baltimore. They are unsuccessful, not because they didn't try to do their job, but because they did. The police leadership frustrates their efforts, not because putting Barksdale and Bell in jail would not have served the public interest, but because the investigation was making the local politicians nervous. Politics trumped good police work.

So the Barksdale prosecution did not accomplish all the goals that the "good police" had hoped for. But that doesn't make it a failure. "Successes" come in more than one size. If the Barksdale prosecution did not succeed in ridding West Baltimore of the drug trade, it did improve the situation. The major drug dealer in West Baltimore was sentenced to a seven-year prison term, and the gang's most dangerous gunman, Wee Bay, went to jail for life.

These are substantial accomplishments in their own right, but they take on added significance if seen through the wider lens of history. We find out in season 2 that Avon's imprisonment triggers events that eventually bring the break-up of the Barksdale gang. Tensions grow between Barksdale in jail and Stringer Bell running the operation outside that eventually turn them against one another. By the end of series, each has engineered the murder of the other, and the gang has ceased to be a player in the West Baltimore drug scene.

So too Wee Bay's time in jail seems to have a beneficial effect on how he sees his career in the drug trade. In season 1, Wee Bay is quite cavalier in accepting the fact that he will spend the rest of his life in prison, but he seems to have had a change of heart when he re-enters the narrative in season 4. His wife visits him in jail to tell him that a retired police officer has offered to adopt his son Namond Brice (Julito McCullum) (IMDB.com 2014) and raise him as his own child. She is angry at the very thought of her child leaving the life (of crime) she has planned for him, but Wee Bay tells her to "let the boy go." He knows the heavy price that the "game" can charge, a knowledge the "good police" forced upon him. One imagines that Wee Bay's experience may also register with other young men contemplating the drug game as a career option.

Another perspective we can take is how the "good police's" reform attempts affected their own lives. Sometimes a reform effort fails to achieve its immediate goals, but still serves as an inspiration for future victories. The Equal Rights Amendment is a good example. In the 1970s feminists were never able to get the required number of states to ratify the amendment to make it law. But the energy that fight generated inspired others who witnessed it to dramatically change the national discussion about women's rights in the decades that followed (Rosen 2001, 267–71; Francis 2015).

To judge whether the exploits of the Daniels unit were a success for its individual members, we have to take account of the career opportunities from which they had to choose. One of *The Wire*'s most valuable contributions to our understanding of contemporary America is its portrayal of dynamics of the police bureaucracy in Baltimore. Here we do not have the usual pop culture picture of a coterie of heroes who pass the time exchanging one-liners between successes. Instead *The Wire* shows us how the administrative structure of a workplace determines the career opportunities open to its employees. Like most Americans today the members of the Daniels unit work in a large bureaucracy, and the structure and politics of that bureaucracy set the parameters of their career options.

In Simon and Burns's portrait of the Baltimore Police Department, most employees fit into one of two categories—"careerist" or "lifer" (Hoath, Schneider, and Starr 1998). The daily routine within either category creates few opportunities for police officers who want to do excellent police work. Careerists gauge all their actions by how they will impact their progression up the bureaucratic career ladder. Deputy Commissioner Burrell is an excellent example of the successful careerist. He started as a novice in the police academy and ends up as chief of police. The careerist has talents, but not the talents that would entice a Daniels or a McNulty to become a police officer. Successful careerists like Burrell are no more than clever internal politicians, weighing carefully the effect that any proposed action might have on their careers.

The culmination of the Barksdale prosecution is a good example of how the careerist mind functions. Here was a chance for Burrell to win some good publicity for the department, but at the same time he terminated investigations dangerous to powerful politicians and disciplined "disloyal" employees like McNulty. We might call that a careerist trifecta.

At the lower levels of the bureaucratic ladder, the careerist makes sure to measure his or her own success by the metrics espoused by the leaders of the department. If the leadership wants to "close" as many cases as possible, that's what the careerist does. Unfortunately this leads to a down-sizing of the department's mission. For instance, the ideal of protecting the citizenry is translated into a policy of successfully closing a large percentage of the case files opened. Unfortunately, this mindset creates a tendency to not open cases not easily solved and to settle cases prematurely in order to improve statistics. Major Edward Rawls (John Doman) (IMDB.com 2014) is a good example of the careerist in action in this regard. He does not want his underlings like McNulty taking time for police work other than working and closing open cases. And his strategy works from a careerist perspective. At the end of the series Rawls succeeds Burrell as chief.

Lifers are the "soldiers" of the Baltimore Police Department. The lifer is not interested in advancement to the highest level of the bureaucracy because the lifer's true ambition is retirement with pension. That does not mean that some lifers are not conscientious workers. "Bunk" Moreland is a good example of a righteous lifer; he just wants to stay within the operating orders handed down. He knows that the policies are short-sighted, but does not see it as his role to deviate from them. Other lifers, some of the older officers assigned to the Daniels unit, are prime examples, and want to do the least amount of work that the bureaucracy will accept. This leads to a cynicism that undermines the morale of everyone in the organization. McNulty sums up the lifer credo well when he reminds

Moreland early on in season 1, "Never give a f—k when it's not your turn to give a f—k."

At the beginning of the series Daniels is a model careerist and McNulty a disgruntled lifer. But neither is comfortable with his situation. The formation of the drug task force gives each a chance to experiment with a third career option—the "professional." The professional may work for a bureaucracy, but he or she maintains independent standards for judging how he or she should act. And while department policies are serious constraints on his or her actions, they do not determine how he or she goes about "policing." In a well-functioning bureaucracy, a compromise will be silently reached between "chain of command" authority and the individual officer's need for autonomy to do his or her job well. This flexibility serves the best interests of the department, the officer, and the public.

None of the Daniels unit see themselves as pursuing a new professional identity; they just want to do good police work. But I think they provide good examples of how "professionals" would conduct themselves. My earlier description of their tactics show that they demonstrate a good deal of both creativity and tenacity in their conduct of the Barksdale prosecution.

Now I would like to focus on the personal benefits their new approach brought them. One is the joy of doing an important job the way they think it should be done. They are no longer wage slaves unreflectively performing actions prescribed by superiors who may have less information about and interest in the case at hand. Instead of resignedly complaining about how bad things are, they take action to make them better. They are personally engaged in their work, and they also have the satisfaction of belonging to a community dedicated to a common goal to which each member contributes. Working together on important projects creates bonds of personal trust and loyalty that lifers and careerists never experience.

And in facing new problems without clear solutions, many of the "good police" start to discover skills they did not know they had. Lester Freamon did not know he had the organizational skills to run a sophisticated investigation because the department leadership had had him buried away in a dead-end job. Prez's discovery that his facility for solving puzzles enables him to break the Barksdale beeper code is just the start. He proves an able partner in Lester Freamon's investigation of the Barksdale gang's assets. When he eventually discovers he is not cut out to be a police officer, we rediscover him in season 4 using his math and game skills as a talented and respected junior high math teacher.

And the "good police" are not the only people who benefit from their work. Kima Greggs establishes a friendship with her snitch Bubbles that supports him in his eventually successful break from the drug life. Lester Freamon helps his snitch Shardene Innes (Wendy Grantham) (IMDB.

com 2014) escape her life as bar girl soliciting men to buy drinks. And, whatever their immediate success or failure, the "good police" shake up the bureaucracy, providing new role models for other officers who feel frustrated by the "careerist' and "lifer" options. Season 2 shows one of the unit's "soldiers" bragging to new recruits about his role in the Barksdale prosecution.

Of course, there are risks involved. One should not expect the leaders of a bureaucracy to reward employees who challenge their authority. Daniels is passed over for a promotion he coveted. McNulty is demoted to a less prestigious assignment. Later in the series Daniels voluntarily resigns from the department on a matter of principle and McNulty is fired for misconduct that he agrees warrants termination. But other less vocal "good police" like Lester Freamon and Kima Greggs remain in good standing.

I suggest that the ultimate test of whether the gamble they made in pushing the bureaucratic envelope was worth the effort is whether anyone regrets his or her decision. By that measure, it seems clearly a success.

HEROES FOR OUR TIME

We live in hard times when social problems are difficult and many, and easy solutions few. That's why we need more than super-heroes who only make sense at the level of fantasy. We also need heroes we can identify with and hope to emulate. Most times popular narratives fail us on that score. There's no way to copy Batman.

I think the "good police" of *The Wire* are heroes for our time. They work (like we do) within bureaucratic structures that inhibit creativity. I am not saying that we don't need careerists and lifers; an agency staffed only with McNultys would be a disaster. But I do think we need professionals who push back against bureaucratic dysfunction, professionals with the creativity and grit to make the organization strive to do the job the way it should be done. They don't always fully succeed, but we are better off for their attempts, and so are they. Heroes are always welcome, but it is in hard times that we really need them.

REFERENCES

Alvarez, Rafael. 2009. *The Wire: Truth Be Told.* New York: Grove Press.

Denvir, John. 2014. "Seeing the Big Picture: Why Law Fails in *The Wire*." In *Law and Popular Culture: International Perspectives*, edited by Michael Asimow, Kathryn Brown, and David Ray Papke, 121–40. Newcastle Upon Tyne, UK: Cambridge Scholars Publishing.

Francis, Roberta. 2015. "The History Behind the Equal Rights Amendment." Mount Laurel, NJ: Alice Paul Institute. Accessed April 30, 2015, www.equalrightsamendment.org/history.htm

Hoath, David, Frank W. Schneider, and Meyer W. Starr. 1998. "Police Job Satisfaction as a Function of Career Orientation and Position Tenure." *Journal of Criminal Justice* 26(4): 337–47.

IMDB.com. 2014. "The Wire Full Cast and Crew (2002-2008)." *IMDb.com* (Internet Movie Database.com). Accessed December 4, 2014, www.imdb.com/title/tt0306414/fullcredits?ref_=tt_ql_1.

Rosen, Ruth. 2001. *The World Split Open: How the Modern Women's Movement Changed America.* New York: The Penguin Group.

Simon, David (producer). 2002–2006. *The Wire.* [television program]. New York: HBO.

9

Documenting Crime

Genre, Verity, and Filmmaker as Avenger

Matthew Sorrento

Scholarship on the documentary is a lot like anthropological work. Writers in the field study existing phenomena (nonfiction cinema) to theorize how it captures the truth. Narrative fictional film seems more inclined for commentary, since scholars can grasp the concept of story and a given storyteller's approach with relative ease. With the documentary, which aims to portray "reality," critics must posit the best means for doing so (a heavy philosophical prospect) and then, assess how films manage the task. Different filmmaking movements did as much by revising their approach: the "direct cinema" trend of the 1960s resisted the narrative conventions of the traditional style, credited to Scottish documentarian, innovator, and theorist John Grierson (Ward 2005, 9). Errol Morris's *The Thin Blue Line* (1988) was a call for such revisionist theorizing. In a film depicting a true miscarriage of justice (one man sentenced for a crime that another, also featured in the film, actually committed), Morris interviews several parties related to the case to include various accounts of it, with varying amounts of credibility. His approach is to present a text of shifting versions of the truth, what Linda Williams has described as postmodern and worthy of the moniker "the new documentary" (1993, 11).

Williams's analysis is compelling, and serves to documentary scholarship a dish of its dreams, though it doesn't address the film's revealing association to the crime genre. Alternate versions of the truth, though novel in nonfiction film, were nothing new in narrative filmmaking: consider the most famous example, Akira Kurosawa's *Rashomon* (1950), in which four characters provide contradictory accounts of the death of a samurai and the rape of his wife. The inclination to read *The Thin Blue Line* as a statement on the shifting nature of truth is strong enough to overlook Morris's presence in the film beyond his filming and directing the admittedly stylized interviews and dramatizations. As a true crime narrative, Morris questions the participants and witnesses not to reveal sensationalism (though his film is thrilling), but to investigate the crime itself, after the fact, in the only role he is able to do so, since the law has already passed judgment. With a camera, Morris operates as a meta-investigator/"avenger," taking one of the three principal roles in crime films, the other two being the "criminal" and the "victim" (Leitch 2002, 16). Thus, the key to Morris's approach has more to do with the tradition of crime cinema in America (and how documentary fits into the tradition) than any discussions of "truth" on film. In lieu of a neat resolution to the mystery, as in an Arthur Conan Doyle mystery, Morris reveals the tortuous steps of a *film noir*-style investigation centered on an unofficial investigator/private eye, while serving his revelations as steps in the narrative. It's no surprise that Morris worked as a private investigator in the 1980s, when trying to supplement his income as a struggling documentary filmmaker (Criterion Collection 2015). Through his job as a private investigator, he encountered Dr. James Grigson, a.k.a. "Dr. Death," profiled in *The Thin Blue Line* as the psychiatrist who testified that Randall Dale Adams, whom Morris eventually proved to be wrongfully accused, could "work all day, and creep all night," hence helping to convict him. The encounter led Morris to doubt the judgment of the Adams case, and hence the investigation became a duty for documentarian/investigator Morris.

In the documentary's greater goal to deliver absolute truth to the viewer,[1] the crime documentary has developed, thanks largely to Morris's film, as a collective attempt for filmmakers to assume the role of avenger when no actual one could solve, or failed to solve, a problematic case. Here we see the crime genre bring the wrongfully accused, the victim(s) in front of the camera, and a filmmaker shaping a narrative of truth. Since this role failed to appear in the original "backstory" investigation (in its place, usually an inadequate or corrupt police investigation), it is completed by the one creating the text of truth, whether it be the truth of the crime, or the actual state of the surviving victims or the criminals. The best of the crime documentary is undoubtedly Morris's film, as it managed to help free the wrongfully accused Adams by proving the guilt of David Harris, a teenager whom Adams encountered in Dallas. The tradition following the film includes films not always as successful, though they challenge the public narrative's verdict to present a nonfiction storyteller's telling of the truth.

This chapter discusses how crime documentaries since *The Thin Blue Line* (a solidified genre tradition, though ignored in scholarship) modify the crime film conventions, with filmmakers serving as meta-avengers, like Morris, to use the medium of the feature film documentary to investigate a case. With the filmmaker working as avenger to complete the crime film narrative, the style is informed especially by detective-centered fictional narratives. At its onset, this style was inspired by the well-made mysteries by Arthur Conan Doyle and Agatha Christie, which present our need for logical reasoning to interpret evidence related to problematic crimes for a clear resolution. And yet, by the 1940s, the style revealed the anxiety of such a search, in the fiction and film associated with the *noir* tradition (the films centered on an urban "unofficial investigator" working in place of police deemed ineffective in the contemporary American city and failing to solve the enigmatic problems). The filmmaker/avenger in the recent crime documentary genre descends from the strained presence of the *noir* unofficial avenger: the former's task is an inherently frustrated one, in that it aims to undo the law's treatment of justice, and yet must be done to bring truth to the medium of cinema.

I will discuss how narrative crime film styles, always concerned with verity, evolved into documentary-inspired *noir* films that portray true crime, at a time when crime documentary, per se, was prohibited by the Production Code and laws about filming in court.[2] As setting is important to crime films, this chapter details the traditional crime film's relation to place (in the city) and how this place aims for verity. I will then address how narrative filmmakers modify their style into near-actual accounts of true crime to question the public accounts of cases, with special attention to Richard Brooks's adaptation of Truman Capote's *In Cold Blood* (book 1966, film 1967). These narratives working within the American studios were essential in developing Morris's approach, which in turn lead to a rich, if scattered, crime documentary movement. With a close look at standout works in the contemporary genre, I will detail the role of the avenger/filmmaker in a given case, and how their vision of "truth in crime" addresses the accused's situation, either as a bid for retrying the accused (the *Paradise Lost* series 1996–2011) or offering an account of the convicted's humanity, often for those living on death row (documentaries on Aileen Wuornos by Nick Broomfield and Werner Herzog's *Into the Abyss*, 2011), in a society obsessed with victim culture.

VERITY AND PLACE IN THE CRIME GENRE

Discussing the crime documentary as a genre is problematic, in several ways. For one, "crime documentary" suggests the practice of recording the phenomena of crime in various media, though principally in prose. Criminologists study the "documents" of crime for the content they reveal in lieu of the method of portrayal—that is, what can be learned about crime from its portrayal in media. "Crime documentary," to them, refers to the evidence of crime more than the method of delivery of the evidence. Before the publication of Truman Capote's *In Cold Blood*, references to the term "true crime" are scant in criticism, in favor of the term "crime documentary," which leaves the medium unclear (nonfiction prose, television reportage, short subject documentary film, etc.). The means and the goals of documenting the crime are similarly vague. In film scholarship, the rare discussion of crime actuality is especially scarce, and when mentioned, leads to more confusion. For example, Raymond Borde and Étienne Chaumeton (1955, 18) mention "crime documentary" by referring to the works of "Hathaway, Kazan, Dassin"—ostensibly, referring to docudramas based on true crime.[3] I use the term "verity" in the following discussion of early fictional crime films not to argue that these films show "truth" (hardly the case), but to underscore their *aims for realism*, so as not to confuse the term with "*verite*" (relating to the documentary style).

In his pioneering, comprehensive study of crime films, Thomas Leitch (2002) does not consider the crime documentary, nor does Kirsten Moana Thompson (2007). Like other scholars who see documentaries as a very different beast, Leitch and Thompson focus on the rich fictional tradition that works by varying the uses and roles of the criminal, victim, and avenger. The avenger often takes the central role in the narrative, as in the police thriller, or *policier*; the criminal is central in many works of *film noir*, such as Billy Wilder's *Double Indemnity* (1944); while the victim is central in films like Fritz Lang's *Fury* (1936) and Jonathan Kaplan's *The Accused* (1988). American narrative films featuring an injustice rarely show passive victims (Leitch 2002, 80), as figures like Spencer Tracy's Joe Wilson, in Lang's film, and Jody Foster's role in Kaplan's fight back through the justice system, in court, or as rogue avengers taking law and justice into their own hands. This very American inclination to avenge, unlike many other national cinemas that settle with passive victims, satisfies the viewer's desire for injustice righted. The "avenging" role of documentarian is a natural inclination, and I discuss below how American fictional works, in the history of sound film, grew closer to true crime, as they focused on actual accounts of cases to remedy assumptions drawn from murky "public" narratives.

Early Gangland, in Sound

The tradition of films adapting true crime begins with the "torn from the headlines" tradition at the early 1930s Warner Bros. studio. Crime film buffs delight in seeking out earlier gangsters from the silent film tradition: the first most likely appears in D. W. Griffiths's *Musketeers of Pig Alley* (1912), a short film concerning the victims of New York gangsters, though underworld hoods are better realized in Raoul Walsh's *Regeneration* (1915), now distinct from the mustachioed villains chasing damsels in earlier one- / two-reelers based on stage melodramas. Before it reached for prestige status later in the 1930s, Warner Bros. developed a streamlined style of film influenced by the pressures of the Great Depression (Schatz 2010, 136–37). These gritty works, designed to need only one star (such as James Cagney and Edward G. Robinson, whereas romantic tales would require at least two), preferred consistent "male" action without a drop of sentimentality (138). While a social problem film like *I Am a Fugitive from a Chain Gang* (LeRoy 1932) was inclined toward the prestige product later embraced by the studio, as a narrative driven by crime and its consequences fit in well with the studio style.

Warner Bros. and other studios taking on the gangster tale were capitalizing on the sensationalism of the gangland news stories. Often delivered as headlines followed by blurbs or brief articles, these stories of 1920s gangland activity whetted the appetite of readers. Not until the advent of sound as a mainstream filmmaking practice (begun in 1927, but widespread by the 1930s) could the gangster's tommy gun rattle and tough talk come alive on the screen. Viewers wanted the gun shots, wisecracks, and molls in full, and yet these films work as a study of character in action. The portrayal of ambition-cum-demise surely served the Hay's Code's need for law and justice, with the rouge hood who reaches the top (after downing his boss) finally falling by the end (after the bond between him and a right-hand man is broken). While Mervyn LeRoy's *Little Caesar* (1930) and Howard Hawks's *Scarface* (1932) reflect Al Capone (the former, in Robinson's baby face looks; the latter, in the title character's facial flaw), we see a new national narrative, boundless ambition and serving a moralistic desire for punishment, aiming to reframe true crimes.

The notable advance in the gangster picture is the hood taking the central role. The police or opponents would get him in the end (as was required by censorship), though this wouldn't happen until the narrative clearly delineated his passions and flaws. The full view of criminality provided something fresh and revealing to viewers, a first taste of crime upfront onscreen long before true crime was possible and noteworthy in that the central criminal was more often than not based on a real figure.

For many, the gangster film was an expose on the American city—exaggerated and myopic as such, the narratives presented the nearby cities as a concentration of seamy folks, the boldest of which would become the central criminal figure. With the central criminal as a Catholic immigrant, racism certainly had something to do with it. Recent disdain for immigrant workers in urban factories fueled the temperance movement, which would lead to the Volstead Act and, naturally, the criminal underworld centered on bootlegging. The city would remain central to the crime film in all its styles, through all the developments, with exceptions like the non-urban entries such as Robert Montgomery's *Ride the Pink Horse* (1947) and the Coen brothers' *Fargo* (1996) working as deliberate variations to the norm. The permanent presence of the city in crime films results from its place in the *noir* style, beginning in the era of World War II. While the gangster pic presents the criminal as a central role, the *noir* style submerges the film's perspective in a criminal psychology.

Film Noir and Neo-Realism

Film noir, in its most effective form, displays criminal psychology (Hirsch 1981, 172), and hence, criminal centered films, in which the central character has that role, are the most powerful for the viewer. Made during the reign of the Production Code Administration (PCA), these films had to incorporate elements of law and order, and yet, a tenet of the style was the ineffectiveness of the police. Enter the unofficial avenger (most often a private investigator, though other figures fit the role—see Edward G. Robinson's Barton Keyes, an insurance claims manager, in *Double Indemnity*), whose job is nearly insurmountable. The unofficial investigator often learns of the truth after missing the mark. Keyes personally vouches for the character of Walter Neff (Fred MacMurry), and thus his trust, hardly enough in this bleak worldview, prevents him from discovering the culprit and reaching the truth. In contrast to the well-made Conan Doyle mystery, his feelings cloud his judgment. With the PCA demanding law and order, the criminal would fall by other means. Any attempts to film true crime are filtered through fiction in this era. As the following section shows, true crime began to emerge more directly in the *noir* style.

The influence of neo-realism on the *noir* style has been well documented (Schrader 1972, 10). A style rooted in Hollywood expressionism that became a trend in the 1930 horror works of Universal Studios—which was then refined by Orson Welles's films for RKO Studios, *Citizen Kane* (1941) and *The Magnificent Ambersons* (1942)—*noir* captured the gritty verity of the American city in crisis or decline, details of which are prevalent in the gangster films of the early 1930s and continued in the G-Men films, featuring a gangster in disguise. Though committed to realism, *noir* also employed a shadowy mood of chiaroscuro lighting that depicts not the (actual) nightmarish energy of Murnau's *Nosferatu: A Symphony of Horror* (1922) or *Faust* (1926), but a dark view of relatable images in urban settings. The American crime style shares something with Murnau (who immigrated to the United States in 1926, eventually influencing various homegrown directors) and especially his 1922 film, which captured the dreadful in everyday nature. Though nightmarish in its own way, *noir* remained a style committed to bleak tones of actuality.

As the style developed in the late 1940s and into the 1950s, the influence of post-war films from Europe, especially those by Italian filmmakers, showed American filmmakers that the stylization of Hollywood studio sets in exterior shots (those in Howard Hawks's *The Big Sleep* [1946] are prominent examples) could be set aside for location work. If *Double Indemnity* briefly placed the actual Los Angeles in mind, when Neff pulls up to Phyllis Dietrichson's (Barbara Stanwyck) house, then Robert Aldrich's *Kiss Me Deadly* (1955) committed to documenting the city in full, its commercial center and outlying housing tracts in an eerie gloaming and at night, as did a budget film like *Roadblock* (Daniels 1951), with its famous chase in the Los Angeles River. Thus, by the mid-1950s location shooting, with the help of lightweight cameras and that would help avoid costly set construction, becomes the trend. Stanley Kubrick's low-budget, self-produced feature, *Killer's Kiss* (1955), used New York in a similar fashion. As cameraman in addition to writer-director, he filmed exteriors to reveal the vertical confinement of Manhattan's streets. *Film noir* became the everyman's tough-guy genre made away from the Hollywood studios and in the great cities of the east, west, and anywhere in between, now our collective homegrown nightmare. Reaching for verity, *noir* began to find it in "place."

Docu-noir

Noir's new verity, related to place, in the late 1940s/1950s suggested that the most unlikely crime stories are tied to reality (think of the bizarre atomic age plot in *Kiss Me Deadly*, depicted alongside Los Angeles neighborhoods familiar at the time). The style also drew film storytellers away from the nightmares of the dream factory and toward true crime. In a sense, it was a return to the "torn from the headlines" spirit of the 1930s gangster films of Warner Bros., even if those films remain a glamorized vision of "roaring '20s" bootlegging. Docu-noir was an attempt to bring "true crime" to the screen, at a time when the story form was restricted to the page and true crime, at best, could be adapted as narrative film, with courtrooms forbidden from filming.

Docu-noir films feature the police and their work to solve crimes; with stories told from law enforcement's perspective, we see a style that, more than likely, led to the creation of the modern police procedural film, or *policier*, and its television counterpart. This treatment shows a marked departure from the earlier *noir* styles, which preferred crime stories centered on criminals (largely inspired by the gangster films of the 1930s) or those centered on unofficial investigators/avengers—mostly, the private detective, whose presence reflected a distrust of the police. With docu-noir favoring the official avenger, mostly detectives employed by the police departments, it's as if the criminal figure had previously received too much focus in the Eisenhower era of rebuilding post-war America, as the administration urged citizens to return to traditional family values. For law and justice to tackle the dark crimes of *noir*, the perspective on the police's quest would need verity. Earlier backlashes against the surge of the gangster in the 1930s included *Beast in the City* (1932), in which Captain Jim Fitzpatrick (Walter Huston) uses violent means to take on gangsters, and the various G-Men films that followed. And yet these films worked in the same studio-bound style, the vision of the dream factory. Docu-noir that arrived in the 1950s used actual locations to assert itself as official accounts of police work. With the official avenger as the most prominent figure, the classic *noir* style began its fall.

Anthony Mann is credited for helping to launch the semi-documentary style of *noir*. His 1947 film *T-Men* (produced by Eagle-Lion Films, a British company that acquired Producers Releasing Corporation and continued its style of budget films) begins with an introduction by Elmer L. Irey, former U.S. Treasury Department director, who lead agents investigating fraud against the Internal Revenue Service. The film moves to a fictional case inspired by a number of prominent Treasury Department investigations of the time. To reach the criminal psychology necessary to *noir*, agents disguise themselves as hoods to infiltrate a gang, which leads to the film's famous scene of one agent being killed by the gangsters while the other watches, horrified but not breaking his cover. Allegiance to the police meant that justice would be served, while Mann details the crimes occurring on location in Detroit and Los Angeles, capturing urban verity but not a clarified location and milieu.

He Walked by Night (1948, also from Eagle-Lion), a film of lesser value and effect, is nonetheless more famous for inspiring Jack Webb, who had a minor role in the film, to create the documentary-style police thriller series *Dragnet* (radio, 1949–1957; television, 1951–1959, 1967–1970). *He Walked by Night*, with direction by Mann—originally uncredited, having taken over the project from Alfred L. Werker—is adapted from the hunt for World War II veteran and former police employee William Erwin Walker, who went on a crime spree that included burglary and the fatal shooting of a police officer. Walker's case—undoubtedly an extreme one, in that he proved that an everyman can prove criminal and deadly—is the kind that would necessitate official avengers taking the spotlight, as would later tales of extreme killers: *The Boston Strangler* (Fleischer 1968) and *Dirty Harry* (Siegel 1971), the film largely responsible for creating the rogue cop genre. *He Walked by Night* uses verity and detail to present societal order falling away, until capable law enforcement rights the wrongs.

As *noir* goes quasi-documentary, we see the crime films adapting to address questions of how best to depict the truth. If crime was, and will remain, a subject that studios loved to exploit, the aim to present fact and verity grew. While police thrillers of the 1950s continued the style, the rise of courtroom dramas based on real cases began, in films like *A Place in the Sun* (Stevens 1951), *Anatomy of a Murder* (Preminger 1959), and *Compulsion* (Fleischer 1959; a subject of further discussion below). Though not sparing the thrills of crime stories, filmmakers are now concerned with portraying justice. Featuring films detailing the judicial process, the trend is long before documentary crime films could argue for a just reassessment of the accused, though here we see the initial steps.

FINDING THE ACTUAL PLACE: BASED ON TRUE CRIME

The trend of docu-noir surged when docudrama was, oddly, treated as nonfiction cinema, that is, the equivalent of documentary. A problem specific to documentary studies, especially for scholars who aim to clarify the medium's style and commitment to truth, the docudrama treated as actuality spans from early films (questions of Robert Flaherty's reenacted scenes he filmed with Nanook, the fictional name of Allakariallak which also titled his 1922 film) up through Michael Moore's handling of content fashioned into what some describe as propaganda. An especially problematic example of the docudrama (admittedly a loose term as it is) treated as actuality came at the 1951 Academy Awards. A nomination for Best Documentary went to Gordon Douglas's *I Was a Communist for the FBI*, a narrative film loosely (and suspiciously) based on the records of communist party infiltrator Matt Cvetic that were published in the *Saturday Evening Post* in 1950. While glamorizing Cvetic's presence (played by Frank Lovejoy), the film depicts communists undercover in America exploiting racial conflict while admitting their own racism; they even deploy a bizarre schoolteacher who, while disseminating her ideology to children, even offers sexual services to potential enlistees! While *I Was a Communist for the FBI* leads to other issues in film study (politics in American propaganda, the influence of the Academy in politics and film culture, propaganda as camp, and such), the example points to a desire to address deviance in a "nonfiction" format, and how "modified" true story narratives were treated as such. With the high-profile *I Was a Communist for the FBI* more of an exception, "true crime" of the era was limited to narrative features, mostly low-budget entries made for the second half of a double bill. While Mann's films discussed earlier fall into this category, others more directly based on fact (though still made as narrative features) appeared and would lead to the most notable narrative film to inspire the artist-as-avenger crime documentary, Richard Brooks's *In Cold Blood* (discussed in detail later).

Phil Karlson's *The Phenix City Story* (1955), a procedural noir, is based on the assassination of Albert Patterson in 1954, who when elected as Alabama attorney general, promised to clean up the crime in the mob-controlled, eponymous city. The murder of a politician by gangsters touched the nerve of a public, in fear of similar assassinations at the hands of communists (see Douglas's earlier film), who would soon obsess about such possibilities after the 1963 assassination of John F. Kennedy in Dallas. Like *T-Men*, this film begins with an introduction featuring journalist Clete Roberts interviewing actual witnesses (still available on some prints of the film), a stunt to claim the following dramatization as actual crime documentary. Another stunt in the narrative appears in the role of Zeke Ward (James Edwards), a fictional character who helps John Patterson, son of the murdered attorney general elect, escape thugs; Ward's young daughter is later murdered and thrown on Patterson's lawn. That Zeke decides to help, in spite of the racism from those around him and extreme violence (both delivered in a casual manner), is a narrative device to minimize the anti-Civil Rights ideas of John Patterson, here creatively reimagined as compassionate (Alabama Archives and History). While a critic native to the state, Jonathan Rosenbaum, asserts the portrayal of mid-century Alabama to be realistic, the other exaggerations and misconceptions, in service of melodrama, underscore the problems of true crime adapted into fictional narrative, and present the miles to go, still, before actual true crime could arrive to screen.

The Phenix City Story was filmed at real locations of the titular Alabama city, thus in kind with the docu-noir style, while other films looked to the aftermath of crime, in the "theater" where justice aims to serve: the courtroom. Two 1959 films, Richard Fleischer's *Compulsion* and Otto Preminger's *Anatomy of a Murder*, depicted criminal acts—a murder modeled on the 1924 Leopold/Loeb murder case and a 1952 murder, respectively—as events to be analyzed in court. Courtroom films were prominent by the early sound era, when the oratory of lawyers could be adequately related onscreen. The courtroom drama uses official testimony (or adapts it) as filmic text, the approach of both 1959 films noted above. The main focus of both films is the courtroom's ability to deliver justice, while the actual crimes remain in backstory and content for interpretation (though *Compulsion* depicts the criminals' actions and motivations before the event). *Compulsion* uses Orson Welles's role, inspired by Clarence Darrow, to depict a complex argument against capital punishment, with the two accused obviously guilty and possibly facing execution. (The actual closing argument lasted twelve hours; Werner Herzog would take up his own kind of argument against the death penalty in his 2011 documentary, *Into the Abyss*, discussed below.)

Compulsion and *Anatomy* appeared during a last hurrah for monochrome cinema, which show a refinement in grayscale presentation; it was a final golden age for the medium as it was phased out, like the stellar silent era in the late 1920s. In the case of the two films in question, monochrome was used for its otherworldliness, its eerie quality to depict crime with its ties to the *noir* style, while newsreel associations helped to sell it as actuality. Writer-director Richard Brooks would insist on using monochrome in 1967 when adapting Truman Capote's bestselling nonfiction novel, *In Cold Blood*, to the screen. A pioneering work in the true crime genre, the book is a compelling true account with strains of editorializing by the author. Certain statements therein urge the reader to buy into Capote's stance against capital punishment, like Fleischer's 1959 film (itself inspired by Meyer Levin's 1956 fictional account), while Capote altered facts for dramatic effect.

The 1959 films use the courtroom to deliver the suspense and psychology of the parties involved, especially the accused and the defense counselor, with the prosecuting attorney more removed and more threatening (especially in George C. Scott's Oscar-nominated role in *Anatomy*). Preminger's film aims to depict crime via courtroom analysis, as suggested by its title. In this case, the avenger figure aiming to free his charge—either from conviction (*Anatomy*) or from execution—remains onscreen, as a character. *In Cold Blood* the film presents the true avenger as storyteller, the figure delivering the narrative. In adapting Capote's already famous medium, the film presents a reporter—Capote's surrogate (Paul Stewart)—as the one recording the perspective of the detained and investigating their motivation for a robbery-cum-murder in the heartland, far from the seamy city that popular culture asserted was the realm of crime. That Stewart's role is hard-boiled (a far cry from the Capote) underscores the strong influence of *noir* remaining after the movement and the homophobia of bringing Capote's eerie-alluring presence onscreen.

Brooks's insistence on actuality is striking for the time. Flatly refusing to shoot the film in color to maintain its presence as a stark collective memory, Brooks also rejected studio pressure to cast stars as the two leads—according to him, Paul Newman and Steve McQueen (Brooks). Knowing that a Hollywood treatment would detract from the film's effect, he stuck with his choice to cast Robert Blake and Scott Wilson as the two criminals. The style helps to sell the account as one sympathetic to Perry Smith, who was himself a victim to abuse (from his father) and rape (during military service). Capote's suggestion, clarified by Voss, that Smith feels rejection from his alleged lover/partner in crime, Dick

Figure 9.1. Robert Blake as Perry Smith in Richard Brooks's *In Cold Blood* (1967). Image in the public domain, optimized by Susan Gilbert.

Hickcock (Wilson), when he wants to rape Nancy Clutter (Brenda C. Currin) before her murder, recalls the parental rejections Smith experienced when younger. Brooks's film, working in flashback (beginning with the arrest of Smith and Hickcock), focuses on the criminals' apprehension as a launching point for their analysis. The means for insight influenced the true crime documentary to come, especially its aim for the storyteller to act as avenger for the accused (wrongfully, in some cases), especially in the film that launched the style, Errol Morris's *The Thin Blue Line*.

TAKING UP FROM HOLLYWOOD: THE DOCUMENTARY AVENGER

At the closing of *The Thin Blue Line*, Morris includes a monologue from David Harris. He discusses his childhood trauma of his older brother drowning in a swimming pool, and how it left his father cold to him after the death. Williams (1993, 20) notes that this paternal rejection, like the one experienced by Smith before his murders, likely resounded for Harris when Adams refused to offer him a place to stay. With the homoerotic readings aside (though worth note as another connection to *In Cold Blood*), the relationship between Harris and Adams contains a motivation behind the former's killing of the patrolman, as delivered by storyteller/avenger Morris. In the spirit of Capote and Brooks's filmed account of that case, Morris's aim is to avenge the wrongful conviction of Adams. Working as a private detective to supplement his income making documentaries, Morris encountered Dr. Grigson, which led him to the case of Adams. The fact that Morris managed to get a confession (on audio) from Harris, thus helping to exonerate Adams, makes the film one of the most noteworthy in the miscarriage of justice tradition. Another important concern is that, also in the tradition of Capote, Morris takes the role of storyteller-as-avenger to interact with the true crime narrative, making him an extra-textual crime narrative figure. Like Capote, Morris takes the role missing from the crime narrative framework, to complete the foundation on which the genre tradition had stood. Morris's example led to new collective goal in documentary crime, in which the storyteller (documentarian) creates the tale to avenge for the parties depicted, both the wrongfully accused and the guilty-but-misunderstood. As the traditional crime genre's onscreen avenger seeks an answer to a mystery and hence, the truth, the documentary avenger assembles a nonfiction narrative to seek, and hopefully unveil, the same.

A striking difference between the documentary avenger style and the detective films that inspired it—aside from the obvious one concerning nonfiction versus fiction—is narrative space. While criminal-centered *noir* films like *Double Indemnity* incorporate a narrative-long flashback, and thus show an obsession with the past and "lost time" (Schrader 1972, 11), unofficial-avenger films in the *noir* style tend to work in the present, the private eye set to an immediate task, though an issue related to the past is often revealed (see the past criminal acts in Roman Polanksi's *Chinatown*, 1974). Documentary avenger films, also set upon the immediate task of engaging with the wrongfully accused or the misunderstood criminal through interviews or profiles, depict the accused and case details long after the crime, during what's termed the "deliberation" in law film studies (i.e., the court case), or the "disposition," the incarceration (Greenfield, Osborn, and Robson 2010, 47). In other words, while the documentary avenger's focus is a past crime, he must create a "narrative of the present" by interviewing/profiling criminals and victims. By analyzing history and the psychology of available figures, the documentary avenger unifies the criminal-centered and the unofficial investigator styles of *noir*, making the nonfiction descendant a grand example of the genre, in scope.

Documenting "Deliberation"

Since Morris encountered the case of Adams (via Grigson) long after his conviction, he lacked the ability to film during the trial, though documentarians following him did. (*The Thin Blue Line* would fall into the category discussed below this one.) The filmmaking team of Joe Berlinger and Bruce Sinofsky, best known for the *Paradise Lost* series (discussed below) were trained in the "direct cinema" style as employees of Albert and David Maysles. Berlinger and Sinofsky came across the story of the death of William Ward, sixty-four, by the hands of his brother, fifty-nine-year-old Delbert, which they would feature in *Brother's Keeper* (1992). As two farmers of minimal education occupying a shack in Munnsville, New York (a farming community near Syracuse) without central heat or plumbing, the Wards' insular lifestyle was like those of farmers in the nineteenth century. Raised to farm the land they owned, the brothers continued the simple life of their family that went back generations. The case became an example of crime with an historical context occurring in the present, though read in the context of mainstream society.

Delbert said that he killed his brother to end his chronic pain, which sympathetic citizens nearby described as a "mercy killing." Hardly a new idea, "mercy killing" is a concept not familiar to Delbert, who with a low IQ made the decision out of desperation and duty to his brother (Kolbert). The slaughtering of a pig onscreen (in which Delbert assists, but cannot do himself) reveals the Wards' experience with death common to the nineteenth-century lifestyle, in animal slaughtering and funerals held in the home; with death an "overwhelming fact of everyday life" (Bryant 2003, 569); it was an immediate choice for Delbert to stop his brother's pain. Investigators discover semen on the deceased's leg, as William shared a bed with Delbert, and argue that the death was some kind of post-sex crime of passion. The Wards chose not to adhere to the conservative idea of traditional family by remaining a family unit of siblings. Their home, which investigators and news media described as squalid (really an example of rural poverty), also caused alarm. Their lifestyle was read out of context of a simple farming system, in addition to the obvious fact that bachelors occupied the place.

Berlinger and Sinofsky aim to present the fact (clear to some, but not all) that the Ward brothers, who were inseparable and working in an antiquated agricultural system (they have tractors but not advanced comforts of home, like plumbing and central heat) used the best method to solve William's chronic pain. While current medical practice would prescribe pain medication to address the problem, the film argues that such a decision was beyond the brothers' reach. Like many crime documentaries, the filmmakers provide a visual/aural evidence to the record that is dominated by sensational print journalism and contrived soundbites and images in television and radio reporting. The film's overall goal, to show the present legal system's failure to interpret historical culture, is shown with the detail of a *verite* approach, and a relaxed tone of letting the full defense—Delbert's articulate peers and neighbors who understand him—have its say. The courtroom footage adds suspense, leaving viewers wondering whether contemporary politics will judge Delbert, or if a sympathetic reading of his case will prevail. When Delbert is acquitted, the film presents an example of humanity prevailing in a system eager to convict, since the New York State Police were found to have coerced a signed confession from Delbert—who is illiterate—which he later retracted.

The filmmaking team later encountered the case of the teens who would become known as "The West Memphis Three" during the deliberation stage of their case, a grisly murder of three boys in West Memphis, Arkansas. With a goal similar to that in *Brother's Keeper*, Berlinger and Sinofsky wanted to follow the lead of Errol Morris and "blow the doors off the case" which, from current reportage, they sensed was misguided (Rothbart 2012).[4] *Paradise Lost* (1996) begins as a story about three likely guilty teenagers, Damien Echols, Jason Baldwin, and Jessie Misskelley—a case of youth devouring youth—as viewers wonder whether the filmmakers exploit the sensationalism of the murders, though the filmmakers use the sensationalistic drive as a foil to unveil the flawed investigation and trial. While Morris begins *The Thin Blue Line* with similar goals—using suspense to describe the case and welcome the viewer into a bizarre historical narrative—the film soon presents Adams as victim, while Harris, the other interviewee incarcerated for another crime, grows more suspicious of the case in question. *Paradise Lost*, in contrast, begins in the perspective of a judgmental onlooker, with Berlinger and Sinofsky using clips from media coverage, in which Echols, the accused, appears nonchalant, though probably enjoying some of the attention as a bored teenager from poverty.

Paradise Lost soon reveals another suspect—John Mark Byers, the stepfather of murdered Christopher Byers—and reclaims a thread of suspense. West Memphis Chief Inspector Gary Gitchell delivered what surely is one of the most misguided statements that any representative of the law ever gave to the press. An interviewer asked sharply: "On a scale of one to ten, how solid do you think your case is (against Damien Echols, Jason Baldwin, and Jessie Misskelley)?" Gitchell's hyperbolic answer, "eleven," would prove absurd once other facts were unveiled. That the response accidentally invokes Rob Reiner's faux documentary, *This Is Spinal Tap* (1984), featuring a parodic heavy metal band with amps that go to eleven, shows how law enforcement can become more foolish than an innocent/goofy interest like heavy metal. Since the accused were fans of the music, the prosecution demonized and exploited the interest. Once the accused are brought to trial, which the filmmakers had access to film, prosecutors based their case against the three on fear of teen rebellion and heavy metal culture, vaguely equating the latter with Satanism (itself a vague and unrealized threat against the religious Right). To demean Damien's mental state before the murders, a prosecutor addressed his interest in Shakespeare's famous "Tomorrow" soliloquy from *Macbeth*[5] as suspicious—from a passage that many high school teens are assigned to memorize!—and the trial again returns to absurd "amp it up to eleven!" territory. Viewers think the same of a false "expert" on cults called by the prosecution, an expert allowed by the judge though this alleged expert was certified through a brief correspondence course.

Testimony reveals that evidence related to a bleeding man, who showed up at a local restaurant, was lost by investigators. With this evidence, and others presented by the filmmaking team, the three boys appear victims of an unfair trial, one not respecting their innocence until proven guilty. Audiotape from the interrogation of Jesse Miskelly, which was recorded only *in part*, records him confessing, though his defense asserts the statement came after hours of interrogating a teen with a limited IQ. The false confession, also prominent in the case of Adams, conducted over a the prolonged time (especially harmful considering the mental capacity of the subject), bears resemblance to early methods of confession via torture to reveal truth, devised in Roman law and continued in the medieval church (Enders 2002, 3). The prosecution also withheld mention of Jesse's "confession" until the end of the trial, in an attempt to shock and surprise the jury into convicting him. Once the location of the bodies is revealed to be a dumpsite, and not the site of the crime, with no blood or tissue found, the case against the "three" seems barely stable, and yet enough to get a conviction. The film reveals issues of injustice still in place after *The Thin Blue Line*: a need for videotaped interrogations, the criminal case judge and the appeals judge to be separate parties, the elimination of elected judges in service of public opinion and, naturally, a continuation of the argument against the death penalty (furthering Capote's legacy).

With help from the first film (*Paradise Lost*), the case gained extensive exposure: the 1996 Sundance Film Festival, airtime on HBO, and a strong following on home video. As a filmmaker-as-avenger piece, it didn't achieve the immediate success of Morris, with the 1996 film becoming an act of advocacy that would grow with the second and third installments. Like *Brother's Keeper*, the first entry in the series would underscore the influence of place, prominent in crime films overall and especially in *The Thin Blue Line*: Adams's line, that "if there's a hell on earth, it's Dallas County," could easily apply to West Memphis. Along with helping to promote the Innocence Project (www.innocenceproject.org/), which "is dedicated to exonerating wrongfully convicted individuals through DNA testing and reforming the criminal justice system to prevent future injustice," *Paradise Lost* set a strong precedent for crime documentaries that would follow: in the *verite* style, with no authorial voice, the viewer must judge the case documented onscreen by the truth of the film's narrative more than the instant success it achieves.

Jean-Xavier de Lestrade's *The Staircase* (2004), an eight-part miniseries, offers an in-depth account of a murder trial. With significant attention to the prosecution, de Lestrade details the defense attorney's process to assure that the court considers reasonable doubt (the perspective and goal in Berlinger and Sinofsky's films, though they were more removed from the defense attorneys). The film develops the theme as the narrative gradually reveals the details of the case, as the defense attorneys learn of them, to create sizable suspense. The film becomes a political statement almost unwittingly, in that the defense takes a liberal stance for a closeted gay man (novelist Michael Peterson, accused of murdering his wife), a lifestyle that his sympathetic children claim they knew, against the family values approach of the prosecution. While sympathetic to powerful defense attorney David Rudolf, the series reveals him to be basking in the spotlight, hence questioning where duty ends and personal promotion begins for criminal attorneys. He and his team do such a fine job of defending Peterson that the verdict, after days of deliberation, finding him guilty, is a shattering denouement, a fine portrayal of the ambiguity of justice in the American legal system. As his daughters burst into tears, we realize that on one hand, they believe in their father's innocence (the aim of the defense team and, seemingly, the objective filmmaking) and mourn the decision. On the other hand, now missing both parents they fear the truth of how they lost their mother and if the prosecuting team in fact had their best interests at heart.

Life of the Convicted: The "Disposition" Films

Documentaries featuring the convicted take us from the ritualistic venue of the court—orderly and just to some, fearful to others, thus a kind of "purgatory" to the American psyche—into American prisons, obviously serving the role of "hell." Often used to represent an oppressive system (with Frank Darabont's *The Shawshank Redemption* [1994] a prominent example, and, it is worth noting that a film featuring an asylum, like *One Flew Over the Cuckoo's Nest* [1975], works in a similar fashion), prisons onscreen call for sympathy in a framework where the walls are less literal than metaphorical, and viewers yearn for innocence. While in *The Thin Blue Line*'s rare case the innocence of the condemned was proven, other filmmakers enter this "forbidden" realm without a chance of proving innocence, but with the hope of portraying humanity. That "disposition" documentary films feature death row cases heightens associations to hell as the convicted look toward the end of their lives.

The subject of *Aileen Wuornos: The Selling of a Serial Killer* (Broomfield 1992) drew sensationalism as a female serial killer. In a recent trend of films that use tabloid narratives for deeper investigation—including Danny Boyle's *127 Hours* (2010), Stuart Gordon's *Stuck* (2007), and Sean Penn's *Into the Wild* (2007)—Broomfield's documentary, and its 2003 follow-up, *Aileen: Life and Death of a Serial Killer*, work as proto-examples. Broomfield aims to bring to screen the woman (executed in 2002) beneath the excessive sensationalism, fueled by news accounts serving both those thirsty for her blood and the Oprah Winfrey-type viewer obsessing over victimization (Lucia 2008, 14–15). As a serial killer convicted in Florida, a firmly death-penalty state, the film's setting accentuates the hellish associations, in light of her apparent guilt.

The focus of Broomfield's first film, prominent in the title, features Wuornos as a spectacle that became an item for sale by the media. Her lawyer sells the rights to an exclusive interview (the first film was later used by a new defense team to present her first lawyer as incompetent), while local police involved in the case cut deals with producers to make a Hollywood film. Amidst the media craze, director Broomfield (2004) argues that he really believed Wuornos killed in self-defense (though murders were probably planned), after years of bad encounters as a roadside prostitute. Broomfield seems intent on profiling the "true" Aileen, though footage from his follow-up film portrays lawyers at Wuornos's final appeal trial accusing him of manipulating footage in the earlier film.

Such accusations also came to Andrew Jarecki for his 2003 Oscar-nominated documentary, *Capturing the Friedmans*, which pleads for the innocence of Jesse Friedman, convicted along with his father, Arnold Friedman, of child molestation, though they are possible victims of a witch hunt. Portraying a case that seemed decided by negative publicity, the film failed to include Geraldo Rivera's interview with the incarcerated Jesse, who details how his father forced him to sexually abuse children.

The crime documentaries of Berlinger and Sinofsky, and the Wuornos films by Broomfield, play like workmen's entries next to *Into the Abyss*, a meditative feature by film poet Werner Herzog. His goal from the onset, to celebrate life of those seeing their death approaching, seems far from the intent to avenge the wrongly accused by telling their stories fairly and objectively. Herzog, noting that he doesn't necessarily like his subjects—he even says this to one, during a prison interview—reveals their psyche facing death, in the spirit of Capote and Morris, to challenge America's obsession with the death penalty, and with crime itself.

Needing to follow the tradition of the crime documentary, Herzog profiles the story of the case, allowing the grisly details to unfold, even if he has other goals. When approaching the two principal interviewees of the

Figure 9.2. Werner Herzog, the filmmaker/avenger behind *Into the Abyss* (2011). Photo provided by IFC, copyright permission granted courtesy of Sundance Selects.

film, convicted murderers Michael Perry and Jason Burkett, Herzog was clear about his intentions:

> I told the perpetrators that I was not in the business of guilt or innocence and this film was not a platform for them to prove their innocence. . . . I think in this particular case, with this very senseless crime, so senseless it's staggering, what fascinated me was that it points to a decay in family values and the cohesion of society, all these things that looked so big and beyond this case. It was not a question of proving their guilt or innocence. (Olson 2011)

He visits the scene of the triple murder—Conroe, Texas—and interviews his guide, Lieutenant Damon Hall of the Montgomery County Sheriff's Department, who explains the evidence and how it helped them conceive of the crime (murders for a Camaro, which involved the theft of a second car, as well). Empty eggshells and uncooked cookie dough in the deceased's home underscore traces of death, and the impending execution. Herzog tests viewer resilience and moral objectivity by detailing an especially loathsome and foolish murder. Perry and Burkett went to a house of a friend to steal his Camaro—but then, when realizing that their friend was out, decided to kill his mother and take the car. Perry and Burkett couldn't get into the neighborhood gate to get the Camaro,

Figure 9.3. Lieutenant Damon Hall recounts the discovery of murder victims in *Into the Abyss* (2011). Photo provided by IFC, copyright permission granted courtesy of Sundance Selects.

after they had gotten rid of the remains of fifty-year-old Sandra Stotler, whom Jason had shot. They decided to kill her son, Adam Stolter, and his friend Jeremy Richardson after luring them to woods to get the clicker for the gate. The two bragged about the robbery and murders to friends, and Perry even impersonated Adam, his murder victim, by showing the deceased's identification when arrested for a traffic misdemeanor in the Camaro; as a result he was let out on bond.

Herzog profiles the crime via the accounts of the lieutenant, family members, and others to survey their feelings about having been involved. The lieutenant, required to collect the remains and work with the prosecution, is a professional but is quietly bewildered by the events; we sense the same about his feelings for the justice system's choice of how to sentence the criminals, more of which comes from other professionals involved (a preacher, and an executioner who had to leave the job). Herzog's trademark shot, in this case, of the sheriff—looking at the camera while Herzog's records whatever external/internal character appears—shows a man called into action by deviance, though feeling out of place in spite of his duty.

Hardly a theist, Herzog—assisted by cinematographer Peter Zeitlinger—view the landscape for any signs of life or distress. That it is a quiet, wooded area, partially developed by sprawl since the 2001 murders, implies Herzog's atheism and insistence that morality is a humanist endeavor, too often misguided by passions and a lack of judgment.

Herzog provides as little of the crime narrative as possible, and largely ignores the trial, a mainstay in the crime documentary. Instead he focuses on immediately available content: mainly, interviews. Though Welles's role in *Compulsion* delivers an anticapital punishment closing argument in court, Herzog's take is to assess those affected by it, the victims as much as the condemned. Of the two convicted men, one was sentenced to die (Michael Perry), while the other, Burkett, escaped the death penalty with a life sentence. Burkett's sentencing resulted from testimony from his father, a criminal throughout his adult life who admits that his son, lacking a solid home and sick as a child, never had a chance for anything better. Herzog interviews the father, also in prison, for an account of his testimony, which asserts his son's victimization in youth. Considering the lack of courtroom content in the film, the father's account—like the others in custody, given from behind plexiglass—is raw truth-telling by Herzog and some of the most compelling footage in the film (along with other accounts of crime from family and citizens of Conroe). Portraying Herzog's commitment to deliver "ecstatic truth," in a clear, immediate method, the footage offers the finest example of nonfiction storytelling from the filmmaker. We see a similar life-and-death testimony from Dieter Dengler, as he reenacts his capture and torture in Laos in Herzog's *Little Dieter Needs to Fly* (1997, adapted as a narrative film by Herzog as *Rescue Dawn* 2006), and in the destructive footage of self-assuaging, mentally ill Timothy Treadwell cohabiting with bears (*Grizzly Man* 2005). But a father's successful attempt to save the life of his son, who will at best die in prison, revealed in *Into the Abyss* shows immediacy not present in the long-freed Dengler and in the memory of the deceased Treadwell, though both films deliver compelling accounts in their own right. Morris's successful pressing for the truth from Harris, which in fact freed Adams, makes Herzog's account all the more tragically full of life.

There is another trace of Morris's famous case in *Into the Abyss*, when Perry swears he didn't kill anyone, thus suggesting Burkett is to blame. The urge to save oneself is delivered with as much compassion as blame, in Herzog's account, when the viewer recalls the clear evidence against Perry that the sheriff had described earlier in the documentary narrative. Herzog draws this kind of "truthful" account by rejecting the planned question approach to interviewing in lieu of exploring their psychology at the moment, in spontaneity and feeling through the discussion (Rose 2012). Herzog engages in religious discussion with Perry, mainly, to reveal his feeling, and perhaps his desperation, in a belief in an afterlife, while the matters are of little concern to the artist. As Perry describes feeling lethargic, as if he is already dying by realizing what is ahead, we realize that Herzog is filming him at the very end: his final conversations with Perry took place just eight days before his execution (Olson 2011).

Herzog's film is a triumphant rendering of the crime documentary, not in that it exonerates the wrongly condemned, but that it reveals life, in full, as it is exposed to crime. The project could have been conducted in prisons all over the United States, which are filling up and leaving us to wonder if and how the corrections systems can be repaired. Herzog's approach was not a rare situation, like Macky Alston's in *The Killer Within* (2006), which profiles a murder(er), in retrospect, by featuring an aged university professor who shot dead a dorm mate back in college, and was treated psychologically and released in his twenties. By portraying him revealing the news to his friends and the college community, the film shows how the event must be interpreted in the present. Alston's film was an opportunity rarer than *Happy Valley* (2014), which investigates the aftermath of the molestation scandal at the Pennsylvania State University (a.k.a., Penn State). Herzog's film triumphs as a record that could have come from anywhere, and he wisely continued the project with four fifty-minutes documentaries, in a series called *On Death Row*, made for the usually sensationalistic television channel Investigation Discovery. His style in the greater project asserts to the filmmaking communities worldwide that verity is an essential in filmed crime narratives, especially when the filmmaker is the narrative's only true avenger.

NOTES

1. In a video interview on the Criterion Collection's video release, Morris notes that he had always abhorred the postmodern idea that truth is shifting, and that his main interest is in finding "absolute" truth. See also Ward (2005, 8).

2. While filming in U.S. courts had been prohibited since 1946, in 1990 judges were allowed to authorize "broadcasting, televising, recording, or taking photographs" in the courtroom and in adjacent areas (United States Courts).

3. The confusion in popular film culture between the categories of documentary and docudrama has not helped. In 1951, a nomination for the Academy Award for Best Documentary went to Gordon Douglas's *I Was a Communist for the FBI*, a narrative film loosely (and suspiciously) based on the records of communist party infiltrator Matt Cvetic that were published in the *Saturday Evening Post* in 1950.

4. The second (2000) and third (2011) entries in the series focus on the "disposition" of the "Three" as the filmmaking team abandons the *verite* style when focusing on the growing movement to free them. The second and third entries show the growing campaign to free "Three," and the third presents their release via controversial "Alford Pleas" once new DNA evidence proved their innocence.

5. Echols misidentifies the quote as coming from *A Midsummer Night's Dream*.

REFERENCES

Alabama Department of Archives and History. No Date. "Alabama Governors: John Malcolm Patterson." Accessed February 18, 2015, www.archives.state.al.us/govs_list/g_patter.html.

Berlinger, Joe and Bruce Sinofsky (producers and directors). 1992. *Brother's Keeper* [Motion Picture]. United States: New Video Group.

——— (producers and directors). 1996. *Paradise Lost.* [Motion Picture]. United States: Home Box Office.

——— (producers and directors). 2000. *Paradise Lost 2: Revelations.* [Motion Picture]. United States: Home Box Office.

——— (producers and directors). 2011. *Paradise Lost 3: Purgatory.* [Motion Picture]. United States: Home Box Office.

Bischoff, Samuel (producer) and Phil Karlson (director). 1955. *The Phenix City Story.* [Motion Picture]. United States: Warner Home Video.

Borde, Raymond and Étienne Chaumeton. 1955. "Towards a Definition of *Film Noir*." In *Film Noir Reader*, edited by Alain Silver and James Ursini, 19–25. New York: Limelight.

Brooks, Richard (producer and director). 1967. *In Cold Blood* [Motion Picture]. United States: Columbia Pictures.

———. "Richard Brooks: Hollywood Juillet." Accessed March 22, 2015, www.youtube.com/watch?v=7HTngdwb1jw.

Broomfield, Nick (producer and director). 1992. *Aileen Wuornos: The Selling of a Serial Killer* [Motion Picture]. United States: Strand Releasing.

——— (producer and director). 2003. *Aileen: Life and Death of a Serial Killer* [Motion Picture]. United States: Columbia TriStar Home Entertainment.

———. 2004. "Interview of Nick Broomfield by Paula Zahn." CNN Transcript, February 28. Accessed February 15, 2015, www.webcitation.org/5bGcGsAcy.

Bryant, Clifton D. (ed.). 2003. *Handbook of Death and Dying*. Thousand Oaks, CA: Sage Publications.

Capote, Truman. 1966. *In Cold Blood*. New York: Random House.

Criterion Collection. 2015. "Interview with Errol Morris." Supplement to DVD Release, 2015.

Enders, Jody. 2002. *The Medieval Theater of Cruelty: Rhetoric, Memory, Violence*. New York: Cornell University Press.

Greenfield, Steve, Guy Osborn, and Peter Robson. 2010. *Film and the Law*. Second Edition. Oxford: Hart.

Herzog, Werner (producer and director). 2011. *Into the Abyss* [Motion Picture]. United States: IFC Films.

Hirsch, Foster. 1986. *Film Noir: The Dark Side of the Screen*. New York: Da Capo Press.

Kolbert, Elizabeth. 1990. "A Dairy Town Doubts Brother Killed Brother." *New York Times,* July 19. Accessed February 13, 2015, www.nytimes.com/1990/07/19/nyregion/a-dairy-town-doubts-brother-killed-brother.html.

Leitch, Thomas. 2002. *Crime Films*. Cambridge: Cambridge University Press.

Lipson, Mark (producer) and Errol Morris (director). 1988. *The Thin Blue Line* [Motion Picture]. United States: Criterion Collection.

Lucia, Cynthia. 2008. "Sexual Politics and Awakenings in *Towelhead*." *Cineaste* 33(4): 14–19.

Olson, Mark. 2011. "Toronto: Werner Herzog Looks *Into the Abyss* of Death and Crime." *24 Frames*, September 10. Accessed February 28, 2015, latimesblogs.latimes.com/movies/2011/09/toronto-2011-werner-herzog-looks-into-the-abyss-of-death-and-crime.html#sthash.4qShDPAM.dpuf.

Preminger, Otto (producer and director). 1959. *Anatomy of a Murder* [Motion Picture]. United States: the Criterion Collection.

Rose, Steve. 2012. "Werner Herzog on Death, Danger and the End of the World." *The Guardian*, April 13. Accessed February 2, 2015, www.theguardian.com/film/2012/apr/14/werner-herzog-into-the-abyss.

Rosenbaum, Jonathan. 2002. "Reality and History as the Apotheosis of Southern Sleaze: Phil Karlson's *The Phenix City Story*." *The Oxford-American* 42. Accessed March 25, 2015, www.jonathanrosenbaum.net/2002/01/reality-and-history-as-the-apotheosis-of-southern-sleaze-phil-karlson%E2%80%99s-the-phenix-city-story-tk/.

Rothbart, Davy. 2012. "Q&A: *Paradise Lost* directors Joe Berlinger and Bruce Sinofsky." *Grantland*, January 18. Accessed February 15, 2015, grantland.com/features/child-murders-robin-hood-hills-directors-joe-berlinger-bruce-sinofsky/.

Schatz, Thomas. 2010. *Genius of the System: Hollywood Filmmaking in the Studio Era*. Detroit: University of Minnesota Press.

Schrader, Paul. 1972. "Notes on *Film Noir*." *Film Comment* 8(1): 8–13.

Thompson, Kirsten Moana. 2007. *Crime Films: Investigating the Scene*. London: Wallflower.

United States Courts. "History of Cameras in Courts." Accessed May 11, 2015, www.uscourts.gov/aboutfederal-courts/cameras-courts/history-cameras-courts.

Voss, Ralph F. 2011. *Truman Capote and the Legacy of In Cold Blood*. Tuscaloosa: University of Alabama Press.

Ward, Paul. 2005. *Documentary: the Margins of Reality*. New York: Wallflower.

Williams, Linda. 1993. "Mirrors without Memories: Truth, History, and the New Documentary." *Film Quarterly* 46 (3): 9–21. Collected as "Mirrors without Memories: Truth, History, and *The Thin Blue Line*." In *Documenting the Documentary*, edited by Barry Keith Grant, 379–96. Detroit: Wayne State University Press. 1998.

Zanuck, Richard D. (producer) and Richard Fleischer (director). 1959. *Compulsion* [Motion Picture]. United States: 20th Century Fox Home Entertainment.

10

Screening the Law

Ideology and Law in American Popular Culture[1]

Naomi Mezey and Mark C. Niles

Imagine for a moment you are watching television: a detective you know and trust from previous episodes brings a young black man into the interrogation room to tell him that his friend has already confessed, implicating him; the detective lets him know they have good prints. You can usually tell by casting and costume, and sometimes by musical score, whether they have the right guy, and if they don't, you know he won't go to jail. If they do have the right guy, he probably will go to jail. If he doesn't, it will be because of some identifiable and fixable failing in the legal process. You know when the show begins how it will end, you have the formula memorized without even thinking about it; the fun is in how you get there, or perhaps in the comforting familiarity itself. Now imagine watching a similar scene in a movie theater. Depending on the kind of film and the director, there may be considerably less confidence about the defendant's guilt or innocence, and if those are established, there are usually still more narrative possibilities. The guilty might go free and the innocent might still be implicated. In its portrayals of criminal law and civil law alike, film offers the possibility of less sanguine images of law's failures.

This chapter attempts to think critically about the pop cultural life of law, to investigate the legal and ideological messages that cultural images of law bear, and to explore how, why, and to what extent television and film differ in their portrayals of law. While many legal scholars have addressed the legal content of popular culture in recent years, few have explored the field expansively or interrogated the significant differences in the images of law and legal institutions produced in the different popular media. In this chapter we take seriously the differences in legal content between film and television and attempt a broader and more theoretically informed account of the differences and similarities between these two important media.

American popular culture is saturated with legal themes. The "courtroom drama" has been a staple of American commercial cinema for more than sixty years (Bergman and Asimow 1996). "Private eye" and "cop" shows, and the "lawyer" shows they spawned, have always been reliable dramatic devices well-suited to network television. These shows have proliferated in recent years to the effective exclusion of other dramatic television genre. As Lawrence Friedman has quipped, "television would shrivel up and die without cops, detectives, crimes, judges, prisons, guns, and trials" (1989, 1588). Furthermore, law and legal issues play a central though sometimes subtler role in the plot development of an impressive percentage of the films and other televisions shows produced by mainstream Hollywood studios and producers every year.[2]

One focus of this chapter is the nature of law's popular appeal and the possible cultural and ideological meanings that attach to these pervasive images of law. Millions more people watch trials or oral arguments in *Ally McBeal, Law & Order, A Few Good Men, Liar Liar, The Practice,* or even short lived shows like *First Monday* or *The Court,* than will ever visit a real court, attend an oral argument in the Supreme Court, or even have the faintest idea of what actually goes on there. This is not to suggest that all or even most of the viewers of these shows will assume that the depictions of law they see in popular culture are completely or even essentially accurate. While many may make just this assumption, many others will see these images for what they are—fictional stories produced by people much more interested in telling a compelling tale than in providing a documentary of our legal system.[3]

We are decidedly uninterested in whether popular culture gets law "right." As Stanley Fish has rightly argued, images of law in television and film are as much about television and film as they are about law (2000, 769–70). What we do care about are the uses to which law is put in popular culture. For whatever the level of sophistication the audience brings to these shows, they are nonetheless the dominant images of the law and its institutions that many Americans, within certain demographic categories,[4] will experience. And they are not without their effects on collective expectations, societal myths, and the national psyche (Stern 2002). So, assuming that we as lawyers and legal scholars ultimately care what the abundant cultural images of our legal system suggest about law and culture, then we need to look closely at the kinds of ideological messages communicated by these pervasive cultural texts.

THE COMPLEXITY OF POP CULTURE INTERPRETATIONS OF LAW

Since the emergence of the first mass-produced entertainment media, scholars have struggled with similar questions in an effort to make sense of the power of the popular media and to explore their influence on individual consumers and communities. The dominant critical analysis of popular culture, developed by the Frankfurt School in the early twentieth century, has suggested that the primary role of popular culture in our society is to communicate, promote, and perpetuate the "dominant ideology," that worldview which provides a conceptual framework and foundation for a particular social order, and which tends to serve the interests of those with power. This theory follows a Marxist model and views popular culture as a means of convincing the masses that their interests are aligned with the broader capitalist political and economic agenda. According to this theory, the ideology communicated by popular culture encompasses "distinct biases, interests, and embedded values, reproducing the point of view of their producers and often the values of the dominant social groups," and consequently serves to "reproduce social domination, . . . legitimate rule by the prevailing groups over subordinate ones, and help replicate the existing inequalities and hierarchies of power and control" (Gigi Durham and Keller 2001, 6).

Applying this traditional conception to an analysis of the depiction of law in American popular culture produces interesting, though somewhat contradictory results. While instructive, this traditional analysis is insufficient, on its own, to explain why law is depicted the way that it is across the full spectrum of contemporary popular culture. While television images of law frequently do serve to reinforce the dominant ideology in a relatively crude way—providing consistently idealized and mythic images of law and government which support the status quo—many images of law in popular film, in contrast, depict law in a way that calls into serious doubt the ability of law to be neutral and just. This more complex and critical view of law, while still essentially "ideological" in its reliance on a legitimate and authoritative legal order and a common and coherent moral order, calls for a more nuanced analysis than that offered by the earliest popular culture critics.

In an effort to bring a more sophisticated analysis to bear on popular culture depictions of law, we invoke the cultural critiques of the Birmingham School in order to assess the subtle ideological content more often found in film. Our focus here is not only on how popular culture functions as a mechanism for communicating and reproducing ideologies, but on the range of ideological meanings in images of law and legal justice on both the small and large screens of popular culture. Yet for all the interpretive variety, there is a virtual absence of seriously controversial or oppositional images of law, particularly on television. We partially link this insight to media consolidation and suggest the ways in which both the theory and practice of popular culture bear on the issue of media regulation and why they matter to democracy.

In one sense our conclusion, stated in its most basic terms, is that for reasons relating to their idiosyncratic profit and aesthetic structures, the dominance of the particular images of law depicted on television are what we refer to as "crudely" ideology-reinforcing, in that they portray the law as a (if not *the*) primary vehicle for achieving justice.[5] In contrast, the ideological content of portrayals of law and justice in popular film is more nuanced, in that film is more likely to portray the law as fallible, as either ineffective at reaching justice, or worse, standing in the way of it. But this more complex view still understands the law as fundamentally legitimate and authoritative, situated within a coherent moral universe. In another sense, however, we don't fully subscribe to such a neat alignment of theory and medium. Indeed, the Birmingham School's insistence on the multiple meanings available in cultural texts forces us to modify a pat conclusion about television's uniform content. At the same time, the very differences between television and film readings and the force with which the dominant readings of television shows in fact dominate suggest the limits of our theoretical tools.

CULTURAL THEORY[6]

It is useful to distinguish at the outset between "popular culture" and "mass culture" (Carroll 1998, 186). We use mass culture to mean the commodities sold by the culture industries, whether they are a pair of jeans, a romance novel or a television show. Following John Fiske (1989, 25), we use popular culture to refer to what people actually do with mass culture, particularly what they do to adapt and reinterpret mass cultural products according to their needs and desires. Popular culture is neither the production of mass culture nor the passive consumption of mass cultural products. It is "the creative, discriminating use of the resources that capitalism provides" (Fiske 1989, 28). Where mass culture represents the dominant cultural production, popular culture is cultural consumption that struggles with and against the meanings of mass culture. It should be evident that mass and popular culture are interdependent; popular culture makes use of the mass cultural resources and mass culture often coopts and markets pop cultural practices.

Both mass culture and popular culture can likewise be distinguished from folk or artisan culture, in which production and consumption are not disaggregated (the ritual Sun Dance, for example, is performed, attended, and given meaning by the same Lakota Sioux community) and which tend to be divorced from the modes of production and consumption common to high technology and high capitalism. Popular culture can also be distinguished to some extent from "high" culture—theater, opera, and the like—which tends to be produced and consumed by the social elite.[7] But the distinctions between high culture and folk culture have broken down considerably as both high and folk cultures circulate through, interact with, and are dependent on popular and mass culture.

While this description ought to help identify mass culture and popular culture and distinguish them from other cultural phenomena in our society, it doesn't tell us anything about how these categories should be deployed, what kinds of questions they enable, or what sorts of answers they might provide. When we use the term popular culture in this chapter, we do not mean it only in the refined sense used by Fiske, but as a shorthand for mass-mediated popular culture, television, and film that is mostly mass produced but open to popular meanings and sometimes exploited for popular purposes.

The first serious critiques of the new popular culture that arose at the turn of the twentieth century in response to the dynamics of industrialization and urbanization identified the primary role played by popular culture images as the communication, promotion, and perpetuation of a dominant societal "ideology" which served the same purpose as other societal, economic, or political structures—to further the interests of the powerful. Ideology came to represent the way "systems of social domination seize control of the consciousness of citizens in such a way that they find domination acceptable" (Carroll 1998, 361).

This Marxist concept of ideology had a deep and lasting impact on the theoretical criticism of popular culture, but the true emergence of modern popular cultural criticism post-dated and expanded on Marx. It grew out of the so-called "Frankfurt School," a group of theorists connected with the Frankfurt Institute of Social Research in the 1920s and 1930s, most of whom later fled Nazi Germany and immigrated to the United States. Writers like Max Horkheimer, Theodor Adorno, Herbert Marcuse, and Walter Benjamin focused their analysis on what they referred to as the "culture industry" and the ascendance of the mass production and mass consumption of culture. "Popular culture," according to the Frankfurt School, was the name given to mass culture by the culture industry in order to make it sound organic and democratic rather than a marketing strategy for products whose main purpose was to proliferate an idealized image of the capitalist economic structure and reconcile those who were subordinated by it to their own subordination (Jay 1973, 216).[8]

The Frankfurt School's almost universal distaste for mass culture was based on its view that the political power of art—mass art in particular—had found a new and alarming role, that of affirmation rather than critique.[9] As the line blurred between work and leisure, and further between worker, consumer, and individual, the ideological role of the culture industry in the reproduction of modern society could not be underestimated (Gigi Durham and Keller 2001, 9). While this fundamental insight about the ideological role of culture remains a central component of modern critical cultural analysis, modern media scholars have questioned the Frankfurt School understanding of the culture industries, directing their skepticism at the ability of those industries to effectively impose ideological indoctrination and at the inability of cultural consumers to exercise any independent judgment.

The Birmingham Centre for Contemporary Cultural Studies initiated and advanced a critical approach to culture that insisted on more negotiation and complexity in the relationship between mass culture texts and the audiences that consume and reproduce them. This approach, developed at the University of Birmingham in Britain during the 1960s, 1970s, and into the 1980s, was second only to the Frankfurt School in its innovation and influence. Stuart Hall, who was director of the Centre for a decade, identified at least three ways in which their work parted company with the Frankfurt School model. The first was a rethinking of ideology that was more aware of discourse, power, consent, and subjectivity (Hall 1992, 121). Second, the Birmingham School "challenged the notions of media texts as 'transparent' bearers of meaning" (Hall 1992, 117), emphasizing the necessity of analysis and interpretation and taking account of contestation over meaning. Third, they "broke with the passive and undifferentiated conceptions of the 'audience' as it has largely appeared in traditional research" (Hall 1992, 118). The Birmingham School allowed for agency among cultural consumers in making and revising the meanings of the cultural products that engaged them. But the agency that the Birmingham School brought to the study of culture was not unqualified; its work acknowledged that cultural meanings were constructed both from above and below—what Hall calls encoding and decoding—and hence subject to negotiation and contestation (Hall 1992, 128).

The Birmingham School adopted a notion of ideology that went beyond the Marxist formulation of false consciousness or misrepresentation of material reality for the purpose of legitimating unequal social relations. Following Louis Althusser and post-structuralism, they tended to use ideology to mean the whole conceptual system or set of stories and images through which people make sense of themselves, their lives and the material conditions of their existence (Althusser 1977, 123). British cultural studies and Althusser were additionally indebted to the thinking of Antonio Gramsci, who added complexity to the discussion of the social and political reproduction of ideology with his theory of "hegemony." By hegemony Gramsci meant the ways in which the institutions of civil society (education, religion, and culture) exercise power by inducing consent rather than through outright coercion (Hoare and Smith 1971, 242–46). This idea is particularly important for illuminating the ways in which mass-mediated popular culture gets its ideological power: it doesn't force people to believe one thing or another, it merely makes certain ways of thinking and acting and being seem utterly normal and natural (Hoare and Smith 1971, 242). Popular culture informs our common sense, and for Gramsci, common sense is a form of ideology; it is "the conception of the world which is uncritically absorbed by the various social and cultural environments in which the moral individuality of the average man is developed" (Hoare and Smith 1971, 419).

For our purposes, we are interested in the ideological roles of two mass cultural media, television and film, as well as the extent to which the legal products of these media are accessible to alternative readings by viewers, readings which suggest more complex ideological meanings or even resistant themes of law's illegitimacy or moral indeterminacy. While the Birmingham School emphasized the importance of actual interpretations by cultural consumers, studies of television and film viewers' understandings of legal images are virtually nonexistent, thus we take this insight merely as an imperative to allow for multiple readings of any cultural text.

WHAT'S SHOWING?

We now turn to the central question of our analysis—given the classical theoretical critique of popular culture and the industries that produce it, what images of law and justice would we expect to see in American popular culture? If the Frankfurt School theorists are correct, mass-mediated popular culture is not popular in the sense that it bears much imprint of popular beliefs and opinions. Rather, the culture industries manufacture mass entertainment that uniformly and effectively communicates a legal ideology that is consistent with the economic and political interests of an elite industry of which they are apart. It is uniform in the sense that cultural producers flood the market with images and messages that support a dominant legal ideology to the exclusion of competing images and messages. It is effective in the sense that consumers understand the images and messages in the way they are intended, and as the Frankfurt School theorists believed, mass culture was so effective precisely because it created a mass public of consumers who adopted wholesale the ideological position of the culture industries and who were thereby reconciled to their own subordination. The spectators and audiences of popular culture were just one more cultural commodity.

Applying this conception of mass culture to television and film images of the law, one would expect a somewhat crude model of ideological communication and content. Under a crude model, these images of law would provide clear, strong, unambiguous, and ultimately comforting images of law and legal institutions. These images would suggest that law usually gets at the truth and most often promotes justice. We say "usually" and "most often" because even within a crude model of legal ideology, popular culture images of the law can be said to perpetuate a crude ideology of law without every aspect of that portrayal conforming to the model. Ideological structures, like the cultures that produce and are reproduced by them, are not monolithic.

Under the crude model, one might expect images of law that are both deeply formulaic and cathartic. They might, and often do, resemble circumscribed and overly dramatic "highlight" clips, with ready-made, predictable heroes and villains, and consistently just resolutions to conflict. According to this model images of law would promote the advertising "environment" of mass media by dampening political doubt and dissent, replacing it instead with status anxiety. The legal images we have in mind here are the stock legal characters and plot lines of popular culture: faithful, honest, working-class cops; clever, talented, and fundamentally humane lawyers, who ultimately put away the guilty and free the innocent; wronged and powerless individuals who against all odds triumph over faceless, corporate wrongdoers; fair and impartial judges (whose fairness and impartiality is reinforced by the occasional exposure of judicial bias or corruption which is promptly punished, purifying the ranks of judges and rendering the aberrant behavior all the more aberrant); and dedicated, dutiful, and sometimes brilliant political leaders, who notwithstanding understandable differences of opinion, all try to do the greatest good for the greatest number of citizens. At its most basic, the images of law and legal institutions that a crude version of legal ideology supports would reassure cultural consumers that existing legal institutions and actors can be counted on to produce something that feels like justice.

The Birmingham School critique, however, suggests that the power of the culture industries is less uniform and effective, mediated as it is by popular reinterpretation and resistance. If they are right, one would expect a good deal more variation in the ideological commitments of producers and in the kinds of images of law that are produced. In addition,

British cultural studies allowed room for popular understandings of cultural images and messages that were less aligned with the dominant legal ideology. Thus, in contrast to the Frankfurt School, a Birmingham theorist would expect to see a more varied range of legal images and meanings, generated by both pop cultural producers and consumers. One would expect many of those legal images to be consistent with a dominant legal ideology and some to be ideologically challenging and subversive. By rethinking power as fundamentally discursive and insisting on a role for cultural consumers in the meaning-making process, the Birmingham School necessarily allowed for more variation and inconsistency in the ability of popular culture to reproduce dominant ideological ideas. Ideological reproduction is varied here because cultural producers are only partly responsible for the meanings generated by cultural products.

As Birmingham scholars make clear, however, not all critical or ambivalent portrayals of law and legal institutions are inconsistent with a dominant ideology of law. Indeed, there is a venerable tradition of law bashing that we think is nonetheless consistent with a dominant ideology of law. One reason for this is because ideology itself is not monolithic. For example, one tension that runs through American legal ideology is between respect for law as a social organizer and distrust of law as antagonistic to deep individualism and libertarianism. So some kinds of criticism of law or legal institutions are merely supportive of one version of the dominant ideology (individualism) over another (important constraints imposed on individuals by the law). That said, not all popular critiques of law are ideologically reinforcing. To take the agency and critical capacity of viewers seriously, in the way suggested by the Birmingham School's cultural theory, means allowing for and identifying the ways in which critiques of law tend to support or erode a dominant legal ideology.

A complex version of legal ideology suggests that some critical engagements with law and popular culture are still ideology reinforcing. These critiques might take a number of different forms. For one, pop cultural portrayals might present images that seem more plausible and realistic than the caricatures outlined above but nonetheless dampen critical, political engagement. Or critical presentations of law might be used to show how in tolerating individual dissent and critique the authority of legal institutions is made stronger. Finally, portrayals of law's failures might be ideology reinforcing if they maintain a sense of moral order that is not eroded by the occasional failing of legal order. Sometimes we can live with law not tracking morality, as long as we agree about what the right outcome should be, and who the good guys and the bad guys are. Portrayals of law's total failure to achieve justice often reflect just this sort of complex version of legal ideology in that they depend implicitly on a shared and self-evident vision of justice. It is the rarest of popular culture texts that posits an ambivalent sense of the requirements of justice, while any number provides images of law as incapable of producing a readily apparent justice. Indeed, in a sense, one version of a dominant reading of law is precisely its ineffectuality, its technicality, its fussiness, and its complexity in the face of a clear moral order. And one thing that makes this dichotomy possible is the presumed common sense about justice that forms the foundation of mass-mediated popular culture.

Jessica Silbey, in her analysis of the ideological posture of trial films, finds what we are calling a complex version of legal ideology.

> The trial film deliberately choreographs the viewer-subject's participation in and critique of law to produce and sustain the ideology of liberal legalism: an understanding that law's recursive structure sustains its authority and power, but also an insistence on the possibility of (as the liberal legal subject claims to embody an example of) individual resistance and agency despite law's engulfing presence. (Silbey 2001, 98)

As Silbey suggests, one reason that individual critique and resistance to law can be ideologically reinforcing is because they support liberalism, one of the first principles of American legal ideology. Silbey's conclusion is that the trial film genre's visual and narrative patterns fit within the ideology of liberal legalism in one of two forms that map onto what we are calling crude and complex legal ideologies: either because law achieves justice, or because even when law fails justice, these films perpetuate "law's reputation as an ever-present social organizer—not because the law is always right, but because it is always the law, the last sanctioned force, the foundation upon which everyone has dared to stand" (Silbey 2001, 112).

Under the complex model, one would expect to see very different images of law and legal institutions than what one would see under a crude model of legal ideology. Here, pop cultural images of law would be more likely to convey "popular" attitudes toward the law, attitudes which reflect the complexity, ambivalence, and disdain that people feel about the law. To the extent that the consumers of popular culture find their interactions with the law and legal institutions to be frightening, intimidating, incomprehensible, or alienating, and to the extent that consumers believe or even suspect that legal institutions may not be consistently producing just resolutions to societal disputes, one would expect to see a far more nuanced and ambiguous, and sometimes deeply negative, depiction of law and its relationship to justice in our popular culture.

However, even under the complex model, many popular cultural portrayals of law will still be consistent with a dominant legal ideology. What one would not expect to see because they are fundamentally inconsistent with legal ideology are images that portray the legal system as fragile, arbitrary, illegitimate, or lacking in authority. Representations of law that question the naturalness or existence of a shared moral order, or that allow for the possibility of an anarchic rejection of law as we know it, would not be ideologically reproducing at all; they would be oppositional and counterhegemonic.

We find some texts and some media more open to ambiguous or oppositional readings. For example, we find that the vast majority of network television is most easily and naturally understood as crudely ideological; that is, viewers probably tend to read the visual and verbal narratives much as the producers intend: there are good guys, bad guys, and law usually works pretty well. There are, to be sure, occasional exceptions in television, shows that allow for more negotiated or even oppositional readings and where the ideological production is more complex. In contrast, we find more film texts to be less ideologically determinative than much of the content on network television. There are simply a greater percentage of films that allow for readings that find the moral framework more ambiguous, and the legal system more unreliable, more random, more corrupt. Films that allow for these sorts of readings tend to be those which reinforce a more complex version of legal ideology or which subvert the dominant forms of legal ideology altogether.

Law on Television

To an overwhelming extent the images of law and legal institutions that have been depicted on television have followed the model that the Frankfurt School scholars would have predicted. A brief but comprehensive survey of the legally themed programs aired on network television during its relatively short history demonstrates the dominance of crude ideology-reinforcing images of the law and legal institutions in the medium.[10] With a few arguable exceptions, the images of law and legal structures depicted on television serve to reinforce the most reassuring conceptions of the relationship between law and justice, and even offer comforting mythologies as alternatives to the more complex and disturbing legal images presented elsewhere, in popular film, in other entertainment media, or in the real world.

With the notable exception of *Dragnet,* which aired in some form until 1970 (and returned to network television in 2002), the first television shows in the 1950s to feature law enforcement officials[11] or private detectives[12] were never particularly successful or long-running, but all provided the same basic storylines: just, intelligent, even heroic law enforcement officials quickly solving crime and fostering justice. The first network show to feature attorneys as central characters was the short-lived *Justice,* which aired on NBC from 1954 to 1956 and centered on

National Legal Aid Society lawyers' representation of indigent clients. But the first truly significant popular culture depiction of an attorney on television came in 1957 when CBS first aired *Perry Mason*. The show, based on the characters in Erle Stanley Gardner's novels (McNeil 1996, 651), focused on the practice of the eponymous criminal defense attorney, and was the most successful legal drama, and one of the most popular shows of any kind, in network television history.

Perry Mason had such a strong cultural influence that millions of people born after its last episode aired are still familiar both with the character, and with his signature talent for dramatic and successful cross-examination. Mason was not depicted merely as a remarkably successful lawyer during the course of the series. He was *perfect*. Each episode of the series culminated in the exoneration of Mason's always innocent client and the conclusive exposure of the guilty party, sometimes as a result of a dramatic courtroom confession or merely through the undeniable power of Mason's deductive reasoning (Brooks and Marsh 1999, 798). Mason's perfect record demonstrated his heroic character. But the true hero was the legal system itself. In the end, Mason's clients might have benefited from his exceptional legal acumen, but they were acquitted because they were always innocent.

Perry Mason aired on CBS for ten seasons and fit the crude model of an ideology reinforcing image of lawyers and the legal system neatly. The innocent were never convicted, and the guilty were always exposed in the end, and these just results were produced by officers of the court working within the boundaries of the system. The unflagging consistency of this kind of system-procured justice fostered both a kind of hero worship of the attorney, and an abiding faith that the justice system could be expected (even relied upon) to produce a just result. However, alternative readings of even such a legal standard-bearer are possible. One is that with a foolish prosecutor and a misguided homicide detective, those clients who did not have the good fortune of having Mason as their lawyer were at the mercy of other unreliable law-enforcement figures. Another possibility is that suggested by Norman Rosenberg: with a classic show that endures in syndication one is likely to see younger viewers reading the show "with very different sensibilities and through equally different ideological frameworks from older fans of the show" (Rosenberg 1998, 116). Rosenberg suggests, for example, that younger viewers read *Perry Mason* as legal camp (1998, 116).

In the 1960s, the most significant legally themed show was *The Fugitive*, the ongoing saga of a man falsely accused (and doggedly pursued by law enforcement officials) for the murder of his wife (*The Fugitive* 1963–1967).[13] Although only airing for four seasons, it was a remarkably popular series and had an uncommonly powerful impact on the popular culture as demonstrated by the response to its August 29, 1967, final episode which garnered more viewers than any other television show up to that time and would not be matched by a network television show for another thirteen years (Brooks and Marsh 1999, 441). Albeit in a slightly more subtle way than the predictable *Perry Mason, The Fugitive* provided a similarly effective ideological image of the law, law enforcement, and their relationship with justice. While it took four years, the ultimate resolution of the dramatic conflict in *The Fugitive* served to reinforce the faith and confidence in the nation's legal system, and in its ability to produce just results. In the final episode, the falsely accused main character, Richard Kimble, finally corners the true killer, and, Phillip Gerard, the law enforcement official who has been pursuing Kimble during the series, finally realizes the truth, interjecting himself in a climactic confrontation between Kimble and the real killer, shooting and killing the latter. So, while justice was tantalizingly delayed, it was nonetheless ultimately achieved and, perhaps most importantly, by the symbol of the legal system himself. Kimble's vigilantism was subdued and law's power regained.[14]

The 1970s and early 1980s saw a string of lightly regarded and even less successful legal dramas, but in 1986, during a period when network programming was dominated by situation comedies, nighttime soap operas, and a stunning array of private investigator series, a seismic shift occurred when Stephen Bochco, fresh off the remarkable critical and commercial success of *Hill Street Blues* (NBC 1981–1987) created the first show in almost two decades centered on a group of lawyers in a legal practice. Unlike the legal dramas of a generation before, which had primarily told the stories of lawyers fighting for the rights of the indigent and alienated, Bochco's new show, *L.A. Law* (NBC 1986–1994), was set in a high profile private firm in Los Angeles that catered to the rich and powerful. And with the possible exceptions of its predecessor *Perry Mason*, and its successor *Ally McBeal*, *L.A. Law* had a deeper and broader impact on popular culture than any other legally themed show in the history of network television.

L.A. Law, which aired on NBC's powerful Thursday night schedule from 1986 to 1994, provided a significantly different image of both lawyers and the legal system than had *Perry Mason* or *The Fugitive*, but it nonetheless provided an effective vehicle for communication of a crude, ideology-reinforcing image of lawyers and their role in the legal system. The show fit its historical moment—the economic boom times of the mid 1980s—and provided the kind of model figures one would expect in that context. The lawyers in the show's central law firm, McKenzie, Brackman, were not admirable because of their legal talents, as Perry Mason had been, or even because of their moral or personal attributes. Their stature came from other features that were highly regarded: wealth, influence, and physical beauty. To its credit, the series represented law practice in a new way, by making the legal issues both central and engaging (Gillers 1989). However, the primary subject of the show's ideology reinforcement was the legitimization and glorification of the lifestyles and social status of young legal professionals. Both messages were very successfully communicated given that many have credited the high profile success of the show, and its particular depiction of the private law firm practice, with an upsurge in applications to law school during its run (Austin 2002, 57; Glass 1990, 407).

In 1999, NBC premiered *The West Wing* (NBC 1999–2006), a critically and commercially successful dramatic series about a current day, fictional, Democratic White House, which provided viewers with inspirational images of government and government officials. The show focused on a brilliant, noble, and at times heroic president, surrounded by a devoted staff who, while politically motivated, worked to serve the president because of their belief that he was the best thing for the country. Even for those viewers who did not share the notably moderate-to-left lean of the depicted administration, the show reinforced the message that our leaders place the interest of the nation above their personal or political agendas. The show also provided a storyline of the embattled president facing impeachment, and provided the audience with a kind of mythic retelling of the Clinton scandal as well as a fictionalized catharsis in which the show's president acknowledged his mistakes and accepted the consequences.

The ubiquitous *Law & Order* franchise, with its exceptionally long run from 1990 to 2010, provided a similarly mythologized picture of our criminal justice system (NBC 1990–2010). While the main characters of the series were far from the pillar of virtue that Perry Mason was, the show nonetheless projected a reliable and predictable message that law and legal institutions are essentially effective at attaining justice and that legal professionals are dedicated to achieving just ends. The flawed human characters, gritty street scenes, multiracial cast, and the dark shots (for some reason the prosecutors' offices had an inadequate supply of lamps) gave the visual impression of a realism that was mostly belied by the plots.

Though lauded for its "moral ambiguity" (Keetley 1998, 33), *Law & Order* used fallible characters and morally interesting storylines to give an impression of more moral complexity than it actually delivered. The speed and efficiency with which the crimes were investigated was dazzling, and the formula of the presentation was transparent. While politics or prejudice often influenced the specific decisions of the prosecutors, that influence was almost always eventually acknowledged, if only to provide the attorneys with the opportunity to triumph over their own personal flaws, doing justice despite themselves and reinforcing a faith in the system that ensures justice even when the individuals involved are imperfect and human. The prosecutions in the *Law & Order* series did not result in the conviction of the guilty quite as reliably as the innocent were acquitted in *Perry Mason*, but prosecutions of anyone of ambiguous guilt were all but nonexistent, acquittals were rare, and when they did happen, they could be explained. In this way the show placated viewers by differentiating between specific, explainable problems that occasionally influence the outcome of a case and a more general and serious suggestion that our legal system is fundamentally arbitrary or corrupt. The first type of the problem is the bread-and-butter of the modern gritty crime drama. The second sort is almost nonexistent on network television.

While very different in approach, the two modern network shows that most often approached legal themes through comedy also offered more varied images of law and lawyers and sometimes they even suggested scathing critique. The wildly popular and critically controversial *Ally McBeal* (FOX 1997–2002) was one of the very few comedies on television with lawyers as main characters. *The Simpsons* (FOX 1989–present), while not a show whose central theme is law, regularly offers some of the most hilarious and devastating depictions of lawyers and the legal system on television.

Ally McBeal, another David E. Kelley show, premiered in 1997 and ran for five seasons on FOX. Much like the upstart network itself, *Ally McBeal* was a different kind of law show: quirky, amusing, and fundamentally bland. While the show did not seem primarily concerned with legal or social critique, the comedic form and its own self-consciousness allowed for a greater range of interpretive possibilities than most television shows about law. The characters were socioeconomically the same characters that populated *L.A. Law*; they were attractive, wealthy professionals who got to spend their time worrying about face bras, show frogs, and apparitions of soul singers. But one of the things that made *Ally McBeal* different not only from *L.A. Law* but from most other shows was the fact that the principle characters were unreformed neurotics whose sense of longing and incompleteness were central to their professional lives and whose neuroses were exposed through parody. Moreover, in its parodies of legal cases and courtroom performances one could also read in *Ally McBeal* a larger critique of law: that it was as flawed, as human, and as subject to social prejudice and psychic chaos as the lawyers that practiced it. It is plausible to interpret *Ally McBeal* to suggest that law is not about justice, but about the performance of inner and outer controversies, the articulation of psychological and social trauma.

Visually the viewer inhabits both the realities and the fantasies of the characters. The camera often shows what the characters only imagine, fear, or desire. Whether hallucinations of Barry White or a dancing baby, many of these visual images of inner anxiety became late-1990s cultural icons. In addition, the lawsuits were exaggerated and absurd, and it rarely mattered whether the lawyers won or lost their cases, because they were about the performance of certain ideas. In so many of the cases portrayed on the show, the law is either the site of farce—as when Ally goes to court with her fingers stuck in a bowling ball ("You Never Can Tell" 1998), or Richard Fish conducts a vaudevillian cross-examination ("Angels and Blimps" 1999)—or law is shown to be a rather inconsequential sideshow in the larger dramas of our lives. The cases rarely matter as much as Ally's doomed romances and the ongoing office hijinks. The most consistent critique the show ever mounts is that the law simply doesn't matter that much. Perhaps the best example of this is when Ally and Ling agree to represent a young boy dying of leukemia who wants to sue God ("Angels and Blimps" 1999). In a sense suing God is the ultimate confession of law's impotence (and arrogance). Though ostensibly very mild in its critique of law, through humor and preoccupation with the human psyche the show made room for alternative and more critical readings.

Whereas *Ally McBeal* was a show ostensibly about law in which law played a relatively minor role, *The Simpsons* is a show ostensibly not at all about law in which law sometimes plays a central role. For twenty-five seasons and counting *The Simpsons* has been depicting lawyers and the legal system in a profoundly satiric and critical light. It is one of the few examples in either television or film of a show that is at once popular and potentially subversive. The show's secondary characters are the various townspeople of the fictional Springfield, and the recurring characters involved with law and governance are uniformly among the most incompetent and corrupt (Groening 1997, 44, 160). Lionel Hutz is Springfield's ambulance-chasing lawyer who displays diplomas from Harvard, Yale, MIT, Oxford, the Sorbonne, and the Louvre in his strip mall office. Hutz carries an apple core in his empty briefcase and solicits business by handing out sponge cards and smoking monkey statuettes. The Mayor of Springfield is the corrupt and promiscuous Diamond Joe Quimby. Styled on any number of Kennedy men, Mayor Quimby is known for wife swapping, pot smoking, and declaring meaningless holidays. Quimby's nemesis is Clancy Wiggum, the bumbling and incompetent Chief of Police who rivals Homer for the character with the lowest IQ and highest interest in donuts. Chief Wiggum often talks into his wallet and confuses DOAs with DUIs.

Perhaps more than any other show on television, *The Simpsons* is about popular culture itself and is full of allusions to movies and other television shows. In fact, in striking contrast to the main thesis of this chapter, *The Simpsons* has on a number of occasions taken classic and idealistic legal movies and turned them into brutally satiric television. In his comment on the role of law in *The Simpsons*, Kevin Ho has called the series a grand legal satire in that "truth and justice are never attained through the efforts of traditional legal actors. Rather, truth and justice are attained only through the efforts of children, or by abusing, sidestepping, or simply ignoring the legal system" (Ho 2003, 276). For this reason, *The Simpsons* may be the one show on television in which the portrayal of law does not always reproduce, in either crude or complex fashion, a dominant legal ideology. It is quite capable of being read as openly subversive in that it consistently finds legal and governmental institutions fundamentally corrupt. It can do this on television because it is animated, satirical, and always closes with a happy ending. It thinly masks its brutal social commentary with humor and entertainment. *The Simpsons* can get away with subversion because it is equally capable of alternate readings in which it is understood only as a looney cartoon aimed at cynical children. As Homer says (while revealing the top of his butt), "Oh Marge, cartoons don't have any deep meaning. They're just stupid drawings that give you a cheap laugh" ("Mr. Lisa Goes to Washington" 1991).

While we believe there is tremendous critical potential in humor, it is less clear that that potential is fully realized in television comedies about the law. What is clear is that ideological messages are usually more unstable in comedy, allowing for complex and even subversive ideological readings by viewers. Although series like *Ally McBeal* and *The Simpsons* prevent the assertion of a truly monolithic picture of crude ideological reproduction on network television, they are the exceptions rather than the rule. The Birmingham School was right to insist on the possibility of multiple meanings, as they give us a richer account of television images and narratives. Yet for all the possible alternative readings of legally themed television shows, taken as a whole their rather consistent messages suggest a limit to the theory of decoding. The vast majority of past and current images of law on television support the conclusion that television serves as a consistently effective instrument for the communication of the kind of crude ideological vision of law and its relationship to justice that the Frankfurt School envisioned.

Law at the Movies

Perhaps the best evidence that the film industry was also thoroughly involved with the ideological portrayal of law and legal institutions was the Hays Code and its impact on the substantive depiction of law in American popular film for more than four decades. While network television may have perfected the crude form of ideology reinforcement, the film industry originated it in the Hays Code, which is an instructive example of just how crude ideology reinforcement and legal mythologizing can be.

The Hays Production Code was adopted by motion picture production companies in 1934 and regulated the film portrayal of a number of topics, including law and crime.[15] The production code grew out of the social reform movements of the 1920s, which objected to portrayals of sex and violence in movies, and which were able to exert substantial political pressure in favor of federal regulation of the film industry (Parker 1996, 82–85). In response to threats by Congress to implement movie censorship statutorily, Hollywood executives agreed to implement the Hays Code. Because one of its primary purposes was to respond to the violent gangster films of the Depression era, the Hays Code included numerous provisions regulating movie portrayals of the legal system and criminal activity. One of the code's three guiding principles instructed producers that: "Law—divine, natural, or human—shall not be ridiculed, nor shall sympathy be created for its violation" (Motion Picture Producers and Distributors of America 1987, 208). The "Reasons Underlying the General Principles" elaborated:

> By human law is understood the law written by civilized nations.
>
> 1. The presentation of crimes against the law is often necessary for the carrying out of the plot. But the presentation must not throw sympathy with the crime as against the law nor with the criminal as against those who punish him.
> 2. The courts of the land should not be presented as unjust. This does not mean that a single court may not be represented as unjust, much less that a single court official must not be presented this way. But the court system of the country must not suffer as a result of this presentation.

Thus, the code prohibited any positive portrayal of lawbreaking, and in some cases, discouraged any portrayal at all, even if negative. Additionally, the code required the positive portrayal of law enforcement and the justice system as a whole.

Within the motion picture trade association was the Production Code Administration, the office responsible for administering the Hays Code. It exercised substantial power over the content of films produced by association member studios. Studios were required to submit treatments and scripts for every movie they produced for a decision on their compliance with the production code, direct any appeals to the trade association board, and pay a $25,000 fine for releasing films in violation of the code; additionally, member theaters were prohibited from showing films without approval by the Production Code Administration (Leff and Simmons 1990, 52). Between 1934 and 1968, when the production code was replaced by the MPAA ratings system still in use today, the administration reviewed over five thousand motion pictures (Motion Picture Producers and Distributors of America 1987, xi).

The Hays Code was, in essence, ideological control by the culture industries in its crudest sense. And the control was remarkably effective, at least for a while. The Production Code Administration deployed these provisions of the code to censor such well-known crime-related and "*noir*" movies as *The Maltese Falcon* (Wallis 1941), *The Postman Always Rings Twice* (Wilson 1946), *Double Indemnity* (DeSylva 1944), and *Angels with Dirty Faces* (Bischoff 1938) (Motion Picture Producers and Distributors of America 1987, 38–49). Letters from the Hays office instructed the producers of *The Maltese Falcon*, for example, that "[Sam] Spade's speech about the district attorney should be rewritten to get away from characterizing most district attorneys as men who will do anything to further their careers" (39). In another instance, the Production Code Administration objected to the original script for *Double Indemnity* because "[a]t the end of the story, the crime is confessed . . . to the auditors of the insurance company, who proceed thereupon to withhold this information from the proper legal authorities and successfully effect a gross miscarriage of justice by arranging for the escape of the two murderers" (45–46).

The Hays Code was an example of a very public and concerted effort on the part of the motion picture industry to promote a particular ideological vision of the law and legal institutions, one that censored realistic portrayals of criminal activity, prohibited critical depictions of law enforcement officials and attorneys, and mandated that law be portrayed as a means to justice. The sheer volume of these images helped to naturalize the ideological messages that were so heavily encoded in many of these cultural texts. Yet for all its influence, the Hays Code was not monolithically enforced. In one sense it under-enforced its own rules, by paying less attention to low-profile films and by its own intimate engagement with high-profile films. This may be most evident in the case of film noir, the stylized Hollywood thrillers of the 1940s that dealt consistently with the law (Rosenberg 2001, 1450). As Norman Rosenberg points out in his assessment of the Production Code Administration's ongoing negotiations over *The Big Sleep* (Hawks 1946), the Code became "something of an enabling mechanism for classical Hollywood movie making" (1456). Because the Production Code Administration could not begin to thoroughly sanitize a movie about blackmailers, pornographers, slutty society girls, homosexuals, drug addicts, and murderers, it instead transferred some of its objectionable material to the unredeemable characters and reduced other material to innuendo. Indeed, the visual innuendos only enhanced the multiplicity of readings these regulated films afforded. Rosenberg asserts that the motion picture industry worked with the Production Code Administration "to devise an extensive array of cinematic codes and conventions through which Hollywood movies could represent code-regulated issues such as law and sexuality" (1456). The classic example is the fade-to-dark after a couple embraces to signal that sex follows (1456).

Perhaps most amazing is how consistently current law-related television shows and movies still conform to the edicts of the now defunct Hays Code. In this sense the Hays Code could be said to have over-enforced in the ongoing censoring power of its cultural imprint (Post 1998). The fact is that despite the relative freedom in film making in the post-Code era (the Code and its enforcement mechanisms were effectively dismantled in the mid-1960s), much of the content of contemporary popular American film continues to fit the crude model of ideology reinforcement that we associate with Hollywood film during the Hays Code and with the vast majority of network television. Movies like *Class Action* (Shelby 1991), *The Untouchables* (Linson 1987), *A Few Good Men* (Reiner 1992), *Philadelphia* (Saxon 1993), *The Client* (Milchan 1994), *Runaway Jury* (Milchan 2003), and *Minority Report* (Molen 2002), among others, while likely to portray some negative images of lawyers or the legal system, continue to tell pat stories of good guys defeating bad guys, the triumph of the law and the attainment of justice.

Like television, crude ideological reproduction in law-related movies is not the only story one can tell. Unlike television, however, there are abundant examples of films which are open to a greater variety of ideological readings and some which are fundamentally critical of the legal system, the government or the prevailing moral order. We discuss a number of these in detail in the next section. One example will help illustrate both the greater political and ideological license that has historically been available in film, as well as the power of the Hays Code to determine cultural messages. The cinematic history of *Chicago* (Richards 2002), winner of the 2003 Academy Award for Best Picture, is long and varied. The story, which centers on the murder trials of two women charged with killing their lovers, was originally written as a play by Maurine Watkins, an African American reporter, who had covered the trials in 1924 (Sweeney 2003, 27). Her fictionalized play was produced on Broadway (Watkins 1926), and was soon made into a film called *Chicago* (DeMille 1927), released before the Hays Code in 1927 (Seiler 2003, 3D). In the play and the original movie two clearly guilty murderers succeed in manipulating the legal system in order to avoid punishment.

However, when the film was remade in 1942, during the Code years, the title changed and so did the story. In *Roxy Hart* the lead character does not commit the murder, is falsely charged and succeeds in fighting the charges and winning her freedom (Nunnally 1942). The changes in this version were the result of the "censorship [that] had overpowered Hollywood. The then-powerful Catholic Legion of Decency had blackballed the play, and drastic sanitizing was necessary to get it to the screen" (Seiler 2003, 3D).

The story returned again in 1969, this time back on Broadway as a musical whose plot line closely resembled that of the original play (*Chicago, A Musical Vaudeville* 1975). While the 1969 run was not successful, a 1990 revival was an overwhelming success, "especially after the O. J. Simpson trial made the play's once-shocking concept—that a trial could be entertainment and the guilty could go free—conventional wisdom" (Seiler 2003, 3D). Finally, the recent Academy Award-winning motion picture, adapted from the latest Broadway version, returns to the original premise that law and the legal process are a spectacle prone to manipulation by the clever and amoral, and ends with the triumphant acquittal of the two guilty and remorseless murderers.

The production tale of *Chicago* says quite a bit about the effects of history and political eras on the ideological content of popular culture; namely, that while the potential always exists for a range of messages about the law and legal institutions, in certain times and places powerful corporate and social forces can and do enforce the portrayal of rather crude ideological images of law in mass-mediated popular culture. But this should not be taken to suggest that the reigning ideas and relative restrictions of any historical moment are ever completely represented in popular culture. As *film noir* demonstrates, for all the power of the Hays Code, films critical of law were still released during the period of the Code. There has always been enough artistry in film-making and enough interpretive power located in cultural consumers that monolithic ideological control is impossible. At the same time, however, there has always been enough muscle in the culture industries that radical or subversive ideological messages are still rare. The widespread refusal of distributors and theaters to show *Fahrenheit 9/11* is a case in point (Moore 2004).[16] The film argues that the sitting president stole the election that put him in the White House and then started a war and sacrificed American lives to keep himself there. Not many industry executives wanted to touch this film, and before the rise of the independent film movement it would probably never have been seen, let alone made.

It is striking that before and after (and occasionally during) the Hays Code era, popular American film has provided a much greater array of complex and ambivalent images of law and its relationship to justice than one would expect to see under the Frankfurt School model. Unlike most depictions of law on television, law in film is frequently open to readings that are consistent with the complex model of ideology reinforcement and, every so often, to readings that are simply subversive.

The Man Who Shot Liberty Valance (Ford 1962) was released by Paramount in 1962, in the waning days of the Hays Code. Written by James Warner Bellah and Willis Goldbeck (based on a magazine article written by famed Western author Dorothy M. Johnson) and directed by legendary Hollywood maverick John Ford, the film addresses the relationships of law and legal institutions to the promotion of justice and to the broader development of civilizing social institutions.[17] It looks with ambivalence on the central role of law in civilizing and subduing the mythic American frontier. Lightly regarded by contemporary film critics as, among other things, an unsophisticated "parody of Mr. Ford's best work," the film's stature has grown considerably over the past two decades (McBride 2001, 624–25). A recent biographer of Ford observes that "[w]ith its profoundly skeptical reexamination of American history and mythology, a prophetic quality in anticipating the public's loss of faith in government, and an acknowledgement of the growing brutality in American life and in the Western genre, *The Man Who Shot Liberty Valance* now clearly stands out as the most important American film of the 1960's" (McBride 2001, 623).

The film, which Ford shot in black and white long after almost all Hollywood films were produced in color, is told as a flashback through the eyes of an old man, a senator named Ransom Stoddard who recounts to a local journalist the gripping story of why he has returned to the small frontier town of Shinbone for the funeral of the long-forgotten Tom Doniphon. Ford's choice of the black and white cinematography serves many of his goals, not the least of which is providing the kind of surreal and uncertain mood that characterizes distant memory. In this case, the memory is both private and public: the film is the story of these two men, Stoddard and Doniphon, as well as a nostalgic account of a changing nation and the personal and collective costs of that national change. The bare, lifeless sets and the strange, sometimes poor lighting emphasize the story Stoddard tells, as well as his unreliability as a narrator—at least if we are to judge by the visual quality of his remembrance (Anderson 1981, 180–81).[18]

Jimmy Stewart plays the narrator Stoddard, both the older man at the beginning and end of the movie, as well as the young attorney "fresh out of law school, bag full of law books," who as the story begins, is traveling west in a stage coach, expressly inspired by Horace Greeley's challenge to go west to seek fame, fortune, and adventure. But before Stoddard makes it to Shinbone, his stagecoach is held up by a band of outlaws. Stoddard's naiveté and innocence are evident as he confronts the bandits, asking "what kind of men are you?!" The lead outlaw is none other than the famed and feared Liberty Valance (played passionately by Lee Marvin), a local bandit who terrorizes the area, and who responds to Stoddard's question by smacking him across the face with the hilt of a silver-tipped bullwhip. "This kind, Dude. Now what kind of man are you, Dude?" Liberty Valance's question goes to the heart of the narrative, and Stoddard's response, as he picks himself up out of the dust and bravely faces Valance again, provides the starting point for his character's remarkable development, and for the development of the concept of law and legal establishment in the film: "I am an attorney at law, duly licensed by the territory. And you may have us in your guns now, but I will see you in jail for this!"

Valance seems amused at first by the seemingly empty threat of criminal prosecution from such a pitiful and powerless creature (who is infinitely more likely to be dead in a few seconds then to live long enough to see Valance brought to justice), but when he comes across Stoddard's law books he explodes with fury. There is something about the threat of law, however remote, to Valance himself but also to the entire social order, that entirely unhinges Valance. What had been an orderly business transaction becomes frantic and brutal. Valance tears the pages from one book, and then singles Stoddard out for a savage beating that only ends when his lackeys forcibly pull Valance away. But before the attack begins, Valance takes off his bandana, demonstrating his utter lack of concern at being identified, and says, "Lawyer, huh? I'll teach you law. *Western* law!"

This early scene might well lead a first-time viewer to reasonably assume that she is about to witness some version of a stock story in which the neophyte lawyer, against all odds, triumphs over the vicious outlaw in an allegory of the arrival of justice and civilization to the Wild West. But the film, from a director who made many films with those themes and that structure, takes a drastically different turn. Ford offers instead an intriguing version of the stock story but with an oppositional reading built into it; the oppositional reading is not just decoded by the viewer, but clearly encoded by the filmmaker. Indeed, it is an eloquent, elegiac anti-Western by one of the most influential and effective architects of the dominant Western motif of the civilizing influence of legal justice.[19] It is an allegory of sorts, or in the estimation of critic Lindsay Anderson (1981, 181), a parable about two different sorts of civilizations: one ruled by Western law and the other ruled by book law.[20] But the Western law that emerges in *The Man Who Shot Liberty Valance* is not Valance's brutal version, but the moral, resolute, laconic version of Tom Doniphon (played by John Wayne), the only man strong enough to protect the town from Liberty Valance. The stories of these two men, "Tom and Ranse, the man of the past and the man of the future, the man of action and the man of ideas, that form the substance of the parable" (Anderson 1981, 181). And it is as much about the different kinds of law these two men represent. What differentiates this film is not the ending—we know how it ends because history has already decided it—but its elegiac mood: Ford is unusually attentive to the price we have paid for accepting book law.

After being left for dead by Valance and his men, Stoddard is saved by Doniphon, who happens to ride by with his hired man Pompe (Woody Strode). Doniphon takes him into Shinbone and places him in the care of Hallie (Vera Miles), a young waitress at Pete's Restaurant whom Doniphon intends to marry. When Stoddard regains consciousness, he immediately wants to know the outlaw's identity, again expressing his desire to use the law to stop Liberty Valance. Doniphon is amused by Stoddard and hands him a gun saying, "I know those law books mean a lot to you, but not out here. Out here a man settles his own problems." Stoddard is aghast at the idea:

> You know what you are saying to me? You're saying just exactly what Liberty Valance said. What kind of community have I come to? You all seem to know about Liberty Valance. He's a no good, gun-packing, murdering thief. But the only advice you can give to me is to carry a gun. Well I'm a lawyer! Ransom Stoddard, Attorney at Law, and the law is the only . . . , the only. . .

Stoddard is unable to tell us what the law is because he collapses again in mid-sentence. Just as in the first scene, Stoddard's self-identification as a lawyer carries an implicit, though as of yet illusory, assertion of authority and power.

After failing to get help from the town marshall, the buffoonish Link Appleyard (Andy Devine), Stoddard decides that he will have to do something about Valance himself, in the meantime taking a job as a waiter at Pete's Restaurant, under Hallie's tutelage. Early in the film Stoddard is portrayed as powerless, soft, and feminized. His feminization is reinforced by the full-length apron he wears much of the time, not only while he is working at the restaurant, but even, for some reason, on the dusty streets of Shinbone. In another confrontation between Valance and Stoddard at the restaurant, Valance laughs menacingly at Stoddard, saying "Well, lookie at the new *waitress*," and trips Stoddard, sending him and a tray of food sprawling to the floor. Doniphon again intervenes as the only check on Valance's unbridled power within the town. Duncan Peabody, the town's newspaper editor, emphasizes the link between the feminized Stoddard and feminized law by joking that what scared Valance off was the "spectacle of law and order here rising up out of the gravy and mashed potatoes" (Ford 1962). The three men each appear to represent different types of power and authority, each corresponding to different stages of civilization. Valance's power is primitive and uncontrolled. Doniphon's power is also dependent on the gun and private violence, but is executed through a romantic individualistic code of moral maturity and integrity.[21] If Valance is the boy, Doniphon is the man. Stoddard's power, as yet unrealized, is based on books, on codes of written law and on a violence that has been turned over to the state. Stoddard is the woman. The implicit suggestion is that one of the costs of book law is the emasculation of men.

Now a romantic view of a prior quasi-legal order is not necessarily oppositional. There is certainly a strain of nostalgic individualism and machismo to the depreciation of law this posture entails. But Ford doesn't end the story there. He makes both the costs and benefits of "progress" feel real and immediate. As the film progresses, so do Stoddard's character and stature, and so does the town. Stoddard next takes on the role (still a traditionally feminine one) of the new schoolteacher in the community, where he not only teaches old and young to read and to speak grammatically, but also emphasizes civics and democracy. In this environment he is confident and sure. Stoddard's civics lessons are soon put to the test, however: a statehood vote by the residents of the territory is imminent. And although a majority of the residents, including the farmers and townspeople of Shinbone, are supportive of statehood and the civilizing impact it would bring to their lives, the ranchers are adverse to statehood and anything else that would limit the "open range." The ranchers hire Valance to kill several farmers and intimidate the residents of Shinbone into voting against statehood, and Doniphon returns to town to mount a defense. He bursts into school to gather the grown men. Class is quickly dismissed and Hallie, who had become Stoddard's prize pupil and assistant teacher, stands sadly by Stoddard as he erases the phrase "Education is the basis of law and order" from the blackboard. Seeing her disappointment and bitter himself, he says, "You heard what Tom said, when force threatens, talk's no good anymore!"

But force and talk are both far from done. They continue to battle it out in the movie, as do the concepts of liberty and collective governance, competing desires at the heart of legal ideology. At the town meeting to elect delegates to the statehood convention, Doniphon orchestrates Stoddard's nomination. Stoddard first nominates Doniphon, the town's true leader and the only logical candidate, but Tom refuses the nomination saying that he has "other plans, personal plans, Mr. Attorney." The reference is to his plans to marry Hallie, but the explanation is unconvincing. His real motivation is far more complex. The suggestion is that his reluctance is based at least partially on his own ambivalence to the idea of statehood—its impact on the community and his status in it, a status based primarily on his role as a counterbalance to the constant threat posed by Valance. The audience senses that Doniphon understands that he belongs, just as Valance does, to a dying order. States don't need cowboys to deal with people like Valance; they need lawyers. And Doniphon knows as well as Valance that he has just as much to lose from "progress." As Eyman points out, Doniphon "knows that, on some level, when he kills Valance, he is killing himself" (1999, 491).

Once Stoddard is elected as delegate, he and Doniphon are immediately confronted by Valance who again pits force against talk:

> That vote don't mean a thing. Now you stay out of this, Doniphon, he's been hiding behind your gun long enough. You got a choice, *dishwasher*. Either

> you get out of town or tonight you be out on that street alone. You be there. And don't make us come and get you.

Stoddard considers leaving town until he finds his friend Peabody's newspaper office ransacked and Peabody beaten almost to death by Liberty Valance. That night, wearing his apron and carrying the gun Doniphon gave him, Stoddard goes to meet Valance out on the street for a duel which stands to be little more than an execution. Indeed, Valance taunts and toys with Stoddard, shooting the gun out of his right hand—only to have Stoddard retrieve the gun and somehow kill Valance with a left-handed shot.

This mysterious duel is the fulcrum of the film, the point at which the fortunes of Stoddard and Doniphon and the structure of frontier life all change direction. It is the beginning of Doniphon's decline and Stoddard's ascendancy. Stoddard stumbles back to the restaurant where Hallie cleans his wounds and gazes at him with a new sense of respect and affection. After Doniphon walks in on Stoddard and Hallie in an affectionate embrace, he goes to burn down the house he has been building for Hallie, almost killing himself in the process. Stoddard, on the other hand, travels to Capitol City as a delegate to the statehood convention, where he is nominated by Peabody as a delegate to Congress. Peabody offers an intriguingly complex argument for Stoddard's qualifications. Discussing the bold pioneers who settled the West, he notes that:

> The boldest of these were the cattlemen who seized the wide-open range for their own domain, and their law was the law of the hired gun. But now, today, come the railroad and the people, the steady, hardworking citizens. . . . We need statehood to protect the rights of every man and woman however humble. And how do we get it? I'll tell you how. We get it by placing our votes behind one man. And we have that man with us here. He is man who came to us not packing a gun, but carrying instead a bag of . . . *law books*. Yes, he is a lawyer and a teacher . . . but more important, he has come to be known through this territory over the past few weeks as a great champion of law and order.

Stoddard is mortified both by his nomination and its justification. The reason that he is now famous as a champion of law and order and viable as a candidate is because he has become known as the man who shot Liberty Valance. Stoddard is disgusted at the irony: he came to Shinbone to bring law and order, and yet his single dramatic unlawful act is what brought order to Shinbone and made him their legal hero (Post 1998, 382–83). Indeed, the irony is still richer when the opponents of statehood rise to oppose Stoddard's nomination. These proponents of force argue against Stoddard precisely because he used force rather than the mechanisms of law to take down Valance. Major Cassius Starbuckle asks the assembly: "Is it possible that such a representative body of honest, hard-working Americans can endorse a candidate for the Congress of our own beloved country whose only claim to the office is that he killed a man?" Stoddard, who can no longer stand the shame, leaves the assembly room, vowing to return to the East where he belongs.

As Stoddard leaves, he finds Doniphon waiting for him in the hall. Doniphon wants to know why he is leaving: "Valance couldn't make you run away. What is it now, Pilgrim? Your conscience?" Stoddard's response is anguished, "Isn't it enough to kill a man without trying to build a life on it?!!" Doniphon then reveals to Stoddard (and the audience) that he wasn't actually the man who killed Liberty Valance. Through a flashback within the flashback, we see as the ever-present Doniphon shoots Valance from a hidden vantage on the other side of the street. Much as Doniphon orchestrated Stoddard's nomination to the convention, he also seems to have engineered Stoddard's newfound reputation as a man of action. Finally, by telling Stoddard the truth he allows Stoddard to live with the reputation by assuring him that it was falsely earned. Perhaps most surprising is that Stoddard, the man of principle, is willing to take credit for killing Liberty Valance and build a career on it, but only if he didn't really do it. He can build his life on a lie, but not on an act of lawlessness.[22] The change has come, the rules are different now, but Ford refuses to let either the old rules or new feel natural and right.

Stoddard accepts the nomination, marries Hallie, and is elected to Congress. He goes on to become governor, then senator and it is suggested that he may become the vice presidential candidate; over the course of the next few decades he brings Shinbone and the entire state the benefits of civilization that he had so naively dreamed of bringing as a young man, including legal institutions and the justice they protect. During the same period, Doniphon's stature collapses; he becomes long-forgotten in the town he once protected single-handedly and dies a drunken vagrant. Doniphon's death is what has brought them back to Shinbone after so many years and this is where Stoddard concludes the story he is telling the newspaper reporter at the beginning of the film. He and Hallie board the train back to Washington, DC. The train conductor tells them about the special arrangements that have been made for their return trip. Stoddard thanks him, and the conductor replies, "Nothing's too good for the man who shot Liberty Valance." Stoddard has just told the journalist the true story, but the legend lives on.[23]

The final shot of the film shows the train arcing away into the distance, visually defying a more linear narrative of progress. The mood is sad and ambivalent. It is neither nostalgic for the past nor satisfied with the present, leaving the audience with nothing more concrete than the fact of history itself. It was the prophetic Doniphon who called Stoddard "Pilgrim," and he is a pilgrim of sorts. And like the Pilgrims before him, Stoddard brought destruction along with progress. Ford seems to suggest that, seen through the wide lens of history, Stoddard's success in civilizing the frontier is a hollow victory, for he has simply replaced one kind of civilization with another, one legal order with another. The strong message of this heartbreaking story is that loss, costs, and contradiction always lay at the heart of progress.[24] The values of civilization as we know it and book law as we practice it are called into question without recourse to the comforts of nostalgia. One of the costs of the turn to book law is some forms of justice. And unlike most popular depictions of law, even those where law constrains justice, we do not have a comforting sense of who the hero is. In one sense *The Man Who Shot Liberty Valance* is the story of the advent of modern justice, and Lindsay Anderson's assessment describes both the story and its subject: "The hero does not win. The winner is not heroic" (1981, 178). By siding with neither liberty nor collective governance, the film embraces two of the most incompatible strains within legal ideology.

Ford's is an especially dark, poetic perspective that refuses the dominant ideology of law and justice. While relatively rare, his position is far from unique in popular film. The theme of the costs and impotence of law and its inability to achieve consistent justice is evident in a broad range of popular films by American, Canadian, and Australian filmmakers, which achieved commercial and critical success in the United States. Whether an early John Ford film like *The Grapes of Wrath* (Zanuck 1940) or a Frank Capra film of the same era, *Mr. Smith Goes to Washington* (Capra 1939), mainstream directors working in the studio system have portrayed government, governmental institutions, and public officials as venal, corrupt, and hostile to justice. Post-Code era films like Francis Ford Coppola's *The Godfather* trilogy are even more pointed, depicting the limitations of the American justice system, born of prejudice against and disregard for recent immigrants, and the violent lawlessness that such limitations produce (Ruddy 1972; Coppola 1974; Coppola 1990). The *Godfather* movies, much like Fritz Lang's *M*, went so far as to equate the practices of the powerful in the criminal world with their counterparts in "lawful" society. Like Ford, Coppola consciously encoded his films to highlight the moral opaqueness of law by showing the equivalencies between law and lawlessness (Papke 1996); as both directors make vivid, some forms of lawlessness are not anarchic, but simply different systems with different rules and codes of behavior. More recent films like Bruce Beresford's *Breaker Morant* highlight the use of legal structures to circumvent both law and justice in the service of other imperatives (Carroll 1980). In *Breaker*, three Australian soldiers who followed unjust orders are court marshaled. In the interests of larger political objectives, these soldiers are sacrificed to protect the truly guilty parties—the ones who gave the orders. And, in a twist on the same basic theme, in Barry Levinson's *Sleepers*, legal institutions are consciously and carefully perverted to exact righteous revenge (Levinson 1996).

One of the most common and accessible of all popular film formats is the courtroom drama. This genre has been highly successful at conveying accessible legal conflict and resolution to a wide and varied audience. A surprising number of these film narratives, however, provide dark, complex, and occasionally disturbing pictures of the role of the lawyer, and frequently of the law itself. Even when justice is realized, it is often realized in spite of lawyers and the law. No modern American film provides a more challenging and subtle image of the role of lawyers in the promotion of justice and injustice than the 1982 film *The Verdict* (Harris 1982). And no film relies more effectively on a hegemonic, common sense understanding of justice to demonstrate both law's inherent weaknesses and its role as the foundation of justice in our society. Like so many other courtroom dramas, *The Verdict* is not easily read as ideologically oppositional; against all odds justice wins out in the end. It is, however, ideologically complex in the sense that there is an explicit critique of law and lawyers, and that critique depends on a clear and shared moral economy and legal legitimacy—for the most part we know who the good guys and bad guys are, and we know we need law, however flawed.

The film overtly critiques power and the ways in which the most powerful social institutions, like the law, the church and the medical profession—*The Verdict* implicates all of these—have enormous effects on the ordinary people who are dependent on their services. The film suggests that the powerless feel their dependence and constraint even when lawyers, clergy, and doctors act in good faith, but that too often those with power act out of self-interest, greed, and the desire for more power. This line of argument represents the film's most ideologically oppositional strain in that it goes to the heart of power relations and the oppressive effects of power. But to the extent this argument relies on a critique of law's ability to do justice, it is undone by the film's semi-triumphant end.

What makes *The Verdict* even more interesting is that the main character, attorney Frank Galvin, played by Paul Newman, defies moral categorization. He is selfish, desperate, flawed, and willing to act illegally, but he is also portrayed as having deep integrity, compassion, and commitment to justice. Directed by Sidney Lumet, from a screenplay by David Mamet (adapted from the novel by Boston attorney Barry Reed), *The Verdict* is the story of Galvin's attempt to rebuild his life and his career by trying a medical malpractice case. As the film begins, Galvin is at the very bottom, personally and professionally. The opening credits roll over a shot of Galvin playing pinball in a bar at the crack of dawn, a mug of beer his only companion. We then see him slipping a ten dollar bill to an employee at a funeral home so that he can be introduced to bereaved family members in a desperate attempt to drum up business. Next we see Galvin consume a breakfast of powdered donuts and a shot of whiskey, which his hands are not even steady enough to raise to his mouth. At the next funeral home he is exposed and angrily ousted. Galvin pauses for a moment after the rebuke, as if reminded of something that he has long since forgotten—the gap between the lawyer he aspired to be and the one to which he has been reduced.

Not long after Galvin ransacks his own already disheveled office in a drunken stupor, pulling his law school diploma from the wall and bashing it against his desk, his friend Mickey visits. This fellow attorney comes by the office to remind Galvin about the client he threw his way and the court date he has in less than two weeks. Galvin pulls himself together long enough to meet his clients in the exterior room to his destroyed office under the pretension that his secretary is at lunch and his office is full of papers for a big upcoming case. It is but the first of his many deceptive interactions with these clients. The clients, a young working-class couple, tell their story: the wife's sister, Deborah Ann, was severely injured during childbirth, losing the baby and suffering severe brain damage. She is in a permanent vegetative state, and they are suing the doctors and the hospital that they believe are responsible. They need $50,000 for permanent medical care and a bit more money so they can leave town in search of a better job for the husband. Galvin, without having ever seen their file, tells them that they have a great case, and that he doubts that the case will ever come to trial.

The owner of the hospital, the Catholic Archdiocese of Boston, schedules a meeting with Galvin to offer him a settlement. Galvin has by then met with an expert witness willing to testify that the attending physicians were seriously negligent in the case. He tells Galvin that it would be crazy to accept a settlement because the doctors "gave her the wrong anesthetic and she wound up drowning in her own vomit. The doctors murdered her." Galvin is surprised by the willingness of this doctor to testify against the more famous defendants and the powerful church; Galvin asks him why he is doing it, to which the doctor responds: "To do the right thing. Isn't that why you're doing it?" He considers this question and we see on his face a familiar searching look as if he is trying to recall a former self, one who would have taken this case for reasons other than the possibility of a quick settlement.

It seems that some of Galvin's long-dormant idealism is beginning to reawaken. This case against a Catholic hospital just may be Galvin's salvation. Before keeping his appointment at the Archdiocese, Galvin stops by the hospital where Deborah Ann is cared for. He stands by her bedside taking Polaroid shots of her, and as the pictures gradually develop before his eyes, we see a gradual change in Galvin before ours. He sits down, brow furrowed, again as if there is something he is trying to remember. When a nurse tells him that he is not allowed to be in this ward, he looks down and replies, almost shamefully, "I'm her attorney."

At the meeting, the Archdiocese offers a good settlement of $210,000 and the expected disclaimers. But Galvin's response to the offer is unexpected. He notes how neatly the figure can be divided into thirds to accommodate his one-third contingency fee. And Galvin laments that accepting the settlement will prevent the "truth" about what happened to his client from being uncovered. The archbishop asks rhetorically and provocatively, "What is the truth?" But Galvin responds sincerely: "I came here to take your money. I brought snap shots to show you so I could get your money. I can't do it. I can't take it. Because if I take the money I'm lost. I'll just be a rich ambulance chaser."

This is Galvin's first classically heroic moment in the film, and it feels heroic precisely because the movie has made it clear and the audience fully accepts that Galvin's client has been the victim of human wrongdoing. And yet, while the audience can take comfort in the film's general moral coherence, it cannot feel confident in Galvin's heroism. The film is complex exactly in its refusal to let the heroic moment be. At the same time that Galvin manages to rise above his apparent weaknesses, malaise, and venality, to commit himself to fight for justice, he also violates some of the most basic ethical principles that govern the behavior of lawyers. First, he rejects a settlement that would have provided his clients with far more money than they sought as compensation, and worse yet, he does so without even bothering to check with them. And second, he acts in his own interests rather than the interests of his clients. He appears to reject the settlement for reasons that have everything to do with reviving his own lost idealism, his self-respect, and his failing career.

When he tells his colleague Mickey that he has turned down the settlement offer, Mickey thinks he is out of his mind. Galvin says, "They killed her, and they're trying to buy it," to which Mickey responds, "That's the fucking point, Dummy. Let them buy it." But Galvin is undaunted, indeed he is energized, and is beginning to look like a new man, or perhaps like the man he has been trying to remember. In the courthouse, after having withstood the pressure from the presiding judge to settle the case, Galvin runs into the all but forgotten clients who have been told by the other side that he rejected the settlement. The mood changes abruptly. The angry husband confronts Galvin about his lack of communication during the case, noting that he is showing the same lack of regard for them as the hospital and the church.

Alongside the redemption of Galvin, the desperation of this powerless man at the mercy of power is the other central theme of the film. The speech belies any sense that Galvin acted triumphantly or heroically by rejecting the settlement offer, and it also contributes to a larger critique of the classic movie moment when the desire for truth wins out over the desire for money, and the lawyer heroically rejects the settlement in the interests of true justice. *The Verdict* invites the viewer to question the implicit triumph of that moment by suggesting that sometimes money is more valuable than truth, and justice ought to be determined by the needs of the less powerful rather than the needs of power. The same plaintive plea of "who do you think you are" is a refrain throughout the story, addressed to all the holders of power and influence in this narrative: the lawyers and the judge, the doctors and the clergymen. The film ably portrays what the client observes and feels, that people like him, the working class and the poor, are the victims of power rather than its beneficiaries. The law for these people does not offer opportunities for redemption, as it does for Galvin, but slim hope and dependence.

The case begins to unravel for Galvin when he finds out that his star expert witness has abruptly left the country, bound for a resort that one of the defense lawyers had been planning to visit before the trial date was set. The strong implication is that the defendant's legal team, unconstrained by ethics or professionalism, has used its impressive money and muscle to get rid of the witness who was the key to the plaintiff's entire case. Galvin must ask the judge, who he has recently insulted, for a continuance, and the judge refuses, making it clear that his refusal is based on personal pique rather than legal justification.

It is at this point in the story that we hear exactly how Galvin fell from the heights of a once stellar legal career. Early in his career at a high-profile law firm, Galvin discovered that one of the name partners had bribed a juror in an important trial. Galvin was devastated. His friend Mickey recalls how Galvin didn't heed his advice and instead told the firm that he was going to tell the judge what happened. But before he could do it, the firm pinned the jury tampering on Galvin and had him arrested on felony charges. Galvin finally gave up, and sought forgiveness from the firm, which dropped the charges and then fired him on the spot.

Again, Galvin's idealism and unwillingness to act as a "normal" lawyer would act gets him into trouble. In *The Verdict*, the "normal" lawyer is unconstrained by conviction, loyalty, morality, or justice. And yet it is perhaps the singular accomplishment of the film that Galvin's refusal to fall in line as a lawyer by disdaining the rules does not render him heroic. By the time we hear this story we know enough about Galvin to know he is not always noble. Despite the way the film resists heroism, it certainly succumbs to rather clichéd lawyer bashing. The obvious suggestion is that the legal profession is thoroughly corrupt. We are reminded again and again that lawyers do not become wealthy and powerful by helping the weak or serving justice. The defense firm not only hides Galvin's star witness, but even more stunningly they employ a woman to attract, distract, and spy on Galvin so they always know what his strategy is. When the spy becomes remorseful, the partner in charge of the defense attempts to console her by reminder her that winning is the most important thing for lawyers because the resources it generates pays for all the "good" that lawyers can do and the goods they enjoy.

Faced with a missing witness and a judge who won't change the trial date, Galvin is again forced to surrender, as he did in the jury-tampering incident. He calls the Archdiocese's counsel and begs to accept the settlement offer that has now been withdrawn. But settlement is no longer an option. After a near nervous breakdown, Galvin finally pulls himself together and tracks down a replacement expert witness, a two-bit elderly doctor (the fact that he is an African American doctor for a Boston trial only adds to Galvin's woes), and starts his trial. The trial is a dark comedy about the legal professional: the judge, whose personal animosity toward Galvin had only grown during the course of the trial, personally examines Galvin's expert witness with disbelief and hostility; Galvin chastises the judge in open court and again in chambers; then Galvin returns to botch the cross-examination of the treating physician.

Beyond desperate, Galvin breaks a number of laws in an attempt to find the one witness who might provide a chance to win the case—the former admitting nurse at the hospital. After breaking into a mailbox, impersonating a magazine salesman on the phone, and just for good measure lying to a nurse in a Catholic chapel, he finds the former nurse, who has fled to New York. She is reluctant to return and testify to the fact that Deborah Ann had eaten one hour before being admitted, that she had written that down on the form, and that after the accident the doctors forced her to change the admittance form by threatening to prevent her from ever working in a hospital again. But she does return, and in dramatic and unimpeachable testimony, the former nurse not only tells her story, but produces a copy of the original admittance form to dispute the altered version that had been entered into evidence by the defense. Her anguished testimony reasserts the central theme of the story, the utter lack of regard that those in power have for the powerless and the myriad ways that their acts of selfishness wreak havoc in the lives of those less powerful:

> After the operation, when that poor girl, she went into a coma, Dr. Towler called me in. He told me that he had five difficult deliveries in a row and he was tired and he never looked at the admittance form. And he told me to change the form. He told me to change the one to a nine or else, or else

> he said, he said he'd fire me. He said I'd never work again. Who were these men? Who were these men?! I wanted to be a nurse!

The film's dire vision of the relationship between lawyers, the legal system, and the promotion of justice is exemplified not by this dramatic revelation, but by what follows. The defendant's counsel makes a clever and technical legal argument—that the photocopy of the original admittance form should not be allowed as evidence given the existence of the actual original, albeit potentially falsified. Moreover, the attorney argues that since the only evidentiary basis for the nurse's testimony is the photocopy, her entire testimony should be stricken and that the jury should be instructed to totally disregard the centrally relevant information she has provided. The judge accepts both arguments over Galvin's objection, and instructs the jury in the sternest possible terms to disregard everything that the nurse has said.

The substantive evidentiary decision is presented as a reasonable and defensible application of existing law. Galvin's objections seem obligatory and rote, and the judge's demeanor does not betray the bias evident earlier in the trial. Unlike the instances of trial error or misconduct depicted in many other films, such as . . . *And Justice for All*, *To Kill a Mockingbird*, and *Breaker Morant*, where injustice results from the failure to follow the clear precepts of the law, here it is apparently the standard application of the law that produces injustice. Ideologically this is far more damning—legal rules rather than human bias are responsible for unjust results. And yet, as is almost invariably true in popular cultural depictions of legal disputes, there is no doubt where justice lies. In contrast to all the interpretive room available for decoding this movie, the moral demarcations are abundantly clear; we know the doctors are guilty, the lawyers acted in bad faith, and law stands in the way of the plaintiff's relief.

Seemingly defeated, with no admissible evidence to provide the basis for a jury verdict in his clients' favor, Galvin focuses in his closing statement on the reality of what has happened in the courtroom, and on the gap that exists in this case between law and justice. He observes that law by its nature is merely a rough guide for producing justice, and that it should never be mistaken for justice itself. In a stunning and succinct argument, he asks the jury to believe what they have seen, to trust *their own ability* to understand what is just, and to abandon the law in their pursuit of justice:

> You know, so much of the time we're just lost. We say please, God, tell us what is right, tell us what is true. There is no justice. . . . But today, you are the law. You *are* the law. Not some book. Not the lawyers. Not a marble statue, or the trappings of the court. See, those are just symbols of our desire

> to be just. They are, they are in fact, a prayer—a fervent and a frightened prayer.

Not surprisingly the camera stays motionless in the jury box during his speech, putting the audience in the position of the jury, and both juries are meant to be convinced by Galvin's words. They resonate because they appeal to a shared sense of right, a shared sense of powerlessness, and a shared suspicion that the institutions that are meant to protect us really oppress us. But for all its populist resistance, Galvin's speech doesn't ask the jury to break the law or even to ignore it, but to become it and create it. The end is not a rejection of law as much as a triumph of its authority. After reading the verdict in favor of the plaintiffs, the jury foreman asks the judge "are we limited to the size of the award . . . are we permitted to award an amount greater than the amount the plaintiff asked for?"

Although the outcome is different from what legal rules would provide for, the alternative is still legally produced justice, and the conclusion is not only comforting, but authoritative. The law already makes room for common-sense understandings of justice by nonlawyers; that is the heart of the jury system and the acknowledged ability of juries to nullify the legal rules through which they are supposed to judge the case. Thus, although severely and relentlessly critical of the role of the law and the lawyer in the promotion of justice and the oppression of the powerless, *The Verdict* nonetheless relies on a notion of transparent and transcendent justice that is ideologically reinforcing. And through recourse to this sense of justice, the law, even when it is not legitimate, still has the capacity to be authoritative. In this way, *The Verdict* and similar films support the dominant ideological view of law, but in a manner that is far darker and more complex than almost anything available on television.

WHY THIS MATTERS TO DEMOCRACY

Our description of the ideological content of legally themed images in television and film is intended to provide both a broad and nuanced assessment of the styles of ideological communication across two important popular media. More than just descriptive, our analysis implies normative possibilities as well by suggesting the kinds of influence that various ideological portrayals of law might have on our society generally and our democratic institutions specifically. The normative insights are especially important in a world in which our democratic spaces, like the public sphere, are increasingly dependent on popular culture.

In the wake of twenty-first-century technological changes, however, film and television content are increasingly indistinguishable, as both are produced by a wider array of entities, accessible by download onto multiple devices, and screened in similar ways. When one can access the entirety of a television series in the first instance, without traditional advertising, the significant differences in profit models that once existed between the two media also begin to collapse. In the original version of this chapter (Mezey and Niles 2005), we elaborated on the differences in production and profit structure between film and network television to help explain the substantial difference in the ideological content between the two. We concluded that the best explanation for why network television was more consistently crude ideologically was its dependence on corporate advertisers. It is still the case that in ways that are not nearly as true for movie studios, television networks make money by producing and airing programming that is a good vehicle for advertising.[25]

Perhaps even more relevant now are the continuing effects of the deregulation of the late 1980s and 1990s, which has allowed major conglomerates (which also own major film studios) to buy up television networks and local stations throughout the country, resulting in unprecedented concentrations of media ownership (Carman 2002).[26] Media consolidation is one development that gives the Frankfurt School approach startling salience today. On the one hand, the culture industries have never looked more dominant in their ideological production. On the other hand, these industries operate through the same virtual fora of mass communication that provide their viewers with opportunities for public critique and resistance.

Jurgen Habermas, a second-generation Frankfurt School theorist, focused attention on what he called the "bourgeois public sphere," a realm of accessible institutions for public discussion among private individuals, the space in which public opinion is formed (2001, 102). The public sphere emerged with the development of territorial states and their distinctions between public authority and private life, mediating between private society and the state by allowing for robust yet informal political participation in the form of discussion and debate among citizens (Habermas 2001, 104). A public sphere depends on some democratic rights, such as freedoms of association, assembly and speech (Habermas 2001, 102), and democracy depends on a public sphere in which private individuals come together to form a politically engaged public. "Citizens behave as a public body when they confer in unrestricted fashion . . . about matters of general interest. In a large public body, this kind of communication requires specific means for transmitting information and influencing those who receive it" (Habermas 2001, 102).

Today, newspapers, radio, television, and the Internet have replaced coffee houses, assemblies, and pamphlets as the media of the public sphere. As the public sphere has expanded, it has become more diverse and more contested, functioning as a site for the mediation of competing group interests (Habermas 2001, 102). The channels of communication, however, which facilitate the public sphere, have become more privatized and commercial (Habermas 2001, 105). While the impact of media consolidation is disputed, the fact of it is not. It is clear that since the 1980s there has been a significant deregulation of media ownership, facilitated by both the Federal Communications Commission (FCC) and Congress (Baker, C. Edwin 2002, 841).[27] The result of increasing deregulation has meant greater concentration of all media in the hands of a few global conglomerates. Twenty years ago, about fifty media companies owned more than half of all film and film distribution companies, broadcast media, newspapers, radio stations, music, and publishing companies (Bagdikian 2000). Today fewer than ten major media conglomerates own almost all the major network television and cable channels, film production and distribution companies, many of the major theater chains, music labels, radio stations, newspapers, and publishing houses (*Columbia Journalism Review*).[28] Although the Internet potentially opens up additional avenues for democratic exchange, the fact is that most people spend most of their online time on sites whose content is dictated by the same media conglomerates which own the other media venues (Baker, C. Edwin 2002, 895–99).[29]

More recent scholars have focused on the effects of an invasion of the public sphere by modern media conglomerates, specifically asking what the impact might be on popular culture content (Herman and McChesney 1997). While much of that impact remains speculative, this chapter is in part an attempt to show how consistent the ideological messages have been, on television certainly, but also at the movies. Where ideological communication is more varied, the public sphere has a better chance of providing a forum for thought and debate on matters of importance. While images of the law are just one set of many ideological images that appear on television and film, they give a clue to the range of ideas that are out there about our society and its governing institutions. And the evidence is not encouraging. Along with an abundance of crudely ideological messages come an even greater abundance of consumption opportunities. The "marketplace of ideas" so necessary to democracy is increasingly a marketplace that no longer trades in ideas but only sells things. Media consolidation has played an unmistakable role in that transformation.

Despite the public distaste for media consolidation and the partial check provided by the judiciary, the overall legal and regulatory trend is shifting away from protecting the public sphere and toward nurturing the private sphere and the economic interests of media conglomerates. C. Edwin Baker, for example, has gone beyond documenting the effects of media concentration on the public sphere per se and has focused on the ways in which such concentrations effect a robust democracy. Baker notes a historical shift in the way legal institutions in general, and courts in particular, have thought about the media: where once they were seen as entities primarily valued for their ability to facilitate public, democratic communication, they now tend to be viewed as "rights-bearing units in their own right" (Baker, C. Edwin 2002, 842). The effect, according to Baker, is that law is "giving up on democracy" through the privatization of the public sphere (842). The public sphere has become a perfect environment not so much for public debate but for private commerce; democratic values have been replaced with market values (Baker, C. Edwin 2002, 5).

Viewed from the perspective of the public sphere, one can better see how the producers of mass culture and the ever-diminishing number of entities for which they work, have enormous influence on the political, sociological, psychological, and cultural identity of our society. Given this reality, it is critically important to assess what these entities are doing with this power. In this chapter we have canvassed and assessed what kinds of images of law and legal institutions are being depicted by the mass culture industries, and what impact these depictions are having on the society that helps to produce them. Our conclusion is that in both crude and complex ways television and film communicate and reproduce a dominant legal ideology that relies on an ambivalent sense of law and an increasingly unquestioned commitment to a moral order with which law only sometimes aligns itself.

CONCLUSION

The basic conclusion of our analysis is that American popular culture is far too diverse and complex to lend itself credibly to one description of the role that ideology plays in the substantive content of popular texts. We have aimed in this chapter to bring together a more precise assessment of the specific features of the two dominant popular media, film, and television, with a nuanced understanding of the various ways that legal ideology is developed, communicated, and recreated in mass-mediated popular culture. More specifically, we have canvassed the substantive content of television and film for their abundant images of and arguments about the law in order to assess what those images and arguments can tell us about the legal ideology and popular understandings of legal institutions and the role of law in society.

Our analysis indicates that while all mass-mediated popular culture serves a pervasive ideology-reinforcing role in our society, the models of ideological production endemic to television and film are decidedly different. Due we think to their differences in structuring production, profits, and narrative, television more consistently produces quite crude versions of legal ideology while film is more likely to portray more complex images of law and legal institutions. Notwithstanding these differences, a strong ideological message about law's ability to achieve justice in our society is consistently communicated by both media, and neither offers many subversive or counterhegemonic perspectives on law, although film has the greater potential, tantalizingly if rarely realized, to offer truly oppositional messages to at least some viewers.

Viewers of network television see images of law and legal institutions that almost invariably provide a comforting picture of the role that law and legal professionals play in the promotion of justice. Viewers of popular film, on the other hand, encounter a more diverse set of images, some genuinely challenging to the notion that law is a reliable or effective mechanism for achieving justice. But most of us are avid viewers of both media, and the images of law in both rely, as popular texts must to a great extent, on thematic and structural features that are familiar across a wide spectrum of the culture. Thus, even when the audience is allowed to harbor doubts about the integrity of the hero or is deprived a real hero at all, it still shares a common moral foundation that is rarely questioned. When law is screened, a commonly accepted notion of where justice lies is rarely if ever challenged, even in the course of some of the more disturbingly negative depictions of the role of law in our society.

So while film audiences may despair at the sight of the seeming failure of the legal system to bring justice to a paralyzed woman robbed of her life and baby by arrogant and negligent doctors, and cast aside by stingy, disinterested clergy, they are still called upon to have "faith in justice," to rely on an innate understanding of justice (the "justice in our hearts"), and to "act with justice." And not only do viewers know what that means, but in fact that "justice" is done. Frank Galvin's closing argument in *The Verdict* provides an able summary of the prevailing attitude toward law communicated in our popular culture—notwithstanding the relative success or failure of our legal institutions and professionals—there is a mythic, shared and hegemonic sense of justice to which we can turn, and upon which we can all rely. And it is this simple faith in justice that is the primary ideological product of our popular media images of law.

NOTES

1. A longer version of this chapter was published originally in 2005 in the *Columbia Journal of Law and Arts* (Mezey and Niles 2005). The authors retain the copyright and this version has been adapted by them. The authors wish to thank Muneer Ahmad, Pamela Bridgewater, Christine Haight Farley, Mitu Gulati, Lisa

Heinzerling, Vicki Jackson, Jason Loviglio, Penny Pether, Nina Pillard, Mike Seidman, Rebecca Tushnet, and Leti Volpp for their comments on earlier drafts, as well as the extremely helpful suggestions received at the Georgetown Summer Workshop and the Virginia/Georgetown Junior Faculty Exchange. We are especially indebted to our research assistants: Kim Einzig, Emily Friedman, Brian Frye, Jette Gebhart, Melissa Millikin, Andrea Stover, Sarah Westergren, Carol Willette, and Debra Wolf.

2. Of course the thematic primacy of law is not restricted to film and television. Law is also an overwhelmingly common subject of American mass-produced fiction.

3. It must be emphasized that while popular cultural depictions of law are pervasive and influential, they don't necessarily tell us what cultural consumers actually think about what they see and read. As Lawrence Friedman rightly cautions, "What people actually think about law, what they worry about, what they hope for, what they use, what they contend with, are not congruent with what goes into the picture tube, or with what comes out" (Friedman 1989, 1589).

4. While there are many different "realities" in peoples' relationship with and feelings toward the law, race, and class are two significant cleavages. For example, most white popular culture consumers from a middle and upper middle class background are overwhelmingly likely to experience our legal system, particularly the criminal justice system, as television and movie viewers. However, recent studies indicate that an alarming percentage of African American males experience the legal system first hand, usually in form of incarceration or probation. It would be interesting and worthwhile to investigate the meanings that popular images of our legal system hold for people much more intimately subjected to the most disciplinary forms of law, and particularly for African Americans, whose membership in the popular culture audience far outstrips their relative percentage of the population. But that is another article.

5. This statement of course assumes that we know what justice means, and that we can agree about what it consists of in any given circumstance. While we don't intend to render the notion of "justice" unproblematic, we think that within most television programs and films the narrative generally sets up a set of assumptions about what is just. And yet outside a particular narrative world, what we mean by "justice" when we demand it of law and lawyers is profoundly unclear. In his analysis of popular images of lawyers, Robert Post succinctly and elegantly shows how the very mixed emotions Americans feel toward lawyers captures a deep longing for shared justice and community as well as a contradictory longing for autonomy. Yet as Post makes clear, the betrayal we accuse lawyers of is a betrayal by our own "wildly pluralistic culture" in which we do not share a coherent set of values or a coherent notion of justice (Post 1987, 385). Outside cultural texts, the content of "legal justice" is also shifting and contested (West 2002, 333–44).

6. A longer version of this section appears in the originally published article (Mezey and Niles 2005).

7. "High art" is controversial as both a term and a category. It is used most often to mean those art forms ordinarily consumed by the well-educated elite (Gans 1974, 10). Carroll, on the other hand, distinguishes high art and avante guarde art from mass art forms not by the class of its consumers but by its purpose, which

he claims is to resist easy reception and stretch or disrupt common sensibilities (Carroll 1998, 190–91).

8. Writing in the United States in the mid-1940s, Adorno and Horkheimer published perhaps the most famous and furious essay against the American culture industry (1999, 31). They saw what was once the individual, artisanal production of art become a monopolistic industry that mass produced not just identical cultural products, but identical cultural consumers (32–34). "The culture industry as a whole has molded men as a type unfailingly reproduced in every product" (35). In essence, the culture industry had manufactured a totalitarian society in which real life was merely the disappointing extension of the movie version, and real people were commodities modeled on the commodities they consumed (40).

9. It is worth noting that whether mass art was employed to affirm the power structure or critique it, these writers saw it as "mass culture" in the sense we identify it, culture or art whose meanings are essentially controlled by those who produce it with little attention to mediating institutions and no attention to the signifying practices of cultural consumers.

10. Our specific reference to network television is both intentional and important to our analysis. The crude ideological model of popular culture fits the dynamics of network television more readily than either popular film or newer television business models such as pay cable, satellite, and Internet television, which do not rely on advertising revenue to make a profit. As we discuss at length in the original version of this chapter, it is reliance on advertising as the profit engine that partially accounts for some of the differences in ideological reproduction between film and network television.

11. The earliest were *Captain Video* and *Dick Tracy*, and were followed by *The Plainclothesman, Crime Syndicated, The Man Behind the Badge*, and *Dragnet*.

12. These included including *Ellery Queen; Rocky King, Detective; Charlie Wild, Private Detective; Inspector Mark Saber; Martin Kane, Private Eye*. The "private eye" drama remained a popular staple of network television, through the 1950s and 1960s (with shows like *M Squad, The Thin Man, The Naked City, Peter Gun*, and *The Untouchable*).

13. There were some notable cop and crime shows such as *The Man from U.N.C.L.E.* (NBC 1964–1968) or *Get Smart!* (NBC 1965–1969).

14. There is an alternative reading of *The Fugitive* that is more disturbing and more complex. That reading suggests that if it weren't for Kimble's vigilantism, the legal system would have put an innocent man to death. There is a strong suggestion in *The Fugitive* that law cannot get it right alone, but that suggestion lies mostly dormant in the television show. It is much more evident in the film adaptation (Kopelson 1993).

15. The code was named after Will Hays, head of the motion picture trade association, who was instrumental in forming the association's Committee on Public Relations in response to public demands regarding the moral content of movies (see generally, Leff and Simmons 1990, 290).

16. After Disney, the parent company of Miramax, refused to distribute the film, it took some time to find another distributor. Even then, some theaters declined to show it (Higgins 2004). The film was finally distributed by Lion's Gate and became a surprise financial success.

17. These themes have inspired a number of legal scholars to write about the film. See, for example, O'Neill 2004 (discussing the film's portrayal of the role of the law in the development of civilization); Bohnke 2001 (exploring the interrelated concepts of myth, law and legitimacy in the movie); Marini 2001 (characterizing Ranse Stoddard and Tom Doniphon as embodiments of the public and private and the role of both in the rule of law); Lubet 2000 (imaginatively recreating of the trial generated by Liberty Valance's murder); Post 1987 (using the film to investigate the cultural link between law and lawlessness).

18. Anderson argues that Ford's work suffered from his impatience with the demands of spectacle and his almost complete disregard for the set and lighting, but that the visual starkness, the lack of "decorative distraction," also threw the power and richness of the story into relief (1981, 180–81).

19. Various Ford biographers have suggested that "Ford's vision of America had darkened" late in his life, and *The Man Who Shot Liberty Valance* can be seen as a kind of reexamination of themes that he had presented, in what in retrospect seemed a far too uncritical manner (McBride 2001, 631–34).

20. As Post notes, this opposition continues to be a contradiction at the heart of our culture and is expressed in our ambivalence toward lawyers. "The lawyer is the public and unavoidable embodiment of the tension we all experience between the desire for an embracing and common community and the urge toward individual independence and self-assertion." (Post 1987, 389).

21. As one critic notes, however, Doniphon's statute in the town is just as dependent on its relative lawlessness and individualized power as Valance's. Once Valance is killed, the "only world in which [Doniphon] can exist, the world of the gun rather than the book" is destroyed (McBride 2001, 633).

22. In his essay on the film, Cheyney Ryan argues that this perpetuated misidentification of the man who actually shot Liberty Valance is what makes the movie about ideology, "in the sense that Louis Althusser used the term—a structure of misrecognition that necessarily animates the interactions and unfolding of an ordered community" (Ryan 1996, 23).

23. As Scott Eyman notes in his biography of Ford, "In *The Searchers*, as well as *Liberty Valance*, the kind of men needed to master the wilderness are the kind of men that can only function in wilderness; they are men who civilization must expel. If society is to benefit from someone's sacrifice, legend must take precedence over truth. Ford may celebrate America's history and values, but he also articulates the contradictions that can easily lead to a mournful pessimism. Ford is too complex an artist to assert that the modern world is a 180-degree betrayal of the past; rather, he believes that history is organic and the present is the logical extension of the past" (1999, 492).

24. Discussing the central theme of *The Man Who Shot Liberty Valance*, McBride notes that "Ford makes a film with a populist thrust but an ultimate skepticism about the value of 'progress.' In terms of psychohistory, the killing of Valance, a rampant Western id-figure . . . means the purging of the unbridled force of the libido from the frontier town of Shinbone, leaving in its wake Tom's coffin, the feeble old Pompey, and the desiccated Stoddard couple. The wilderness may have become a garden, but it has become poisoned at its heart. Ford strikes this theme from the opening shot of the train bearing the Stoddards back to Shinbone: as the

train leaves the frame, Ford lingers a moment on its black smoke hovering over the otherwise pristine landscape, visually showing that 'progress' is a polluting force" (2001, 632).

25. The pressures of advertiser preferences are not limited to entertainment programming. As media columnist Lisa de Moraes attests, "more than half of [local] news directors interviewed said they'd been pressured by advertisers to kill negative stories—especially ones about their industries—and to run puff pieces about sponsors" (2001, C7).

26. A few corporations own not only most of the mass media venues, such as TV, film, radio, books, magazines, and newspapers, but they also own the delivery systems for those venues (networks, cable, satellite, etc.) (Baker, William F. 2002, A33).

27. Most notably, in 1996 Congress passed the Telecommunications Act, which directed the FCC to revisit and justify its ownership limitations in the interests of a more competitive, deregulated national policy aimed at accelerating private investment in media technologies (Telecommunications Act, 1996, Pub. L. No. 104-104, 104th Cong. [February 8, 1996]).

28. The Columbia Journalism Review Web site is exhaustive and fairly current.

29. See also, *Prometheus Radio Project v. FCC* (noting "a critical distinction between Web sites that are independent sources of local news and Web sites of local newspapers and broadcast stations that merely republish the information already being reported by the newspaper or broadcast station counterpart") (*Prometheus Radio Project v. FCC* 2004, 405–6).

REFERENCES

Adorno, Theodor and Max Horkheimer. 1993. "The Culture Industry: Enlightenment as Mass Deception." In *The Cultural Studies Reader*, edited by Simon During, 31–41. New York: Routledge.

Ally McBeal [Television Show]. 1997–2002. FOX.

Althusser, Louis. 1977. "Ideology and Ideological State Apparatuses (Notes towards an Investigation)." In *Lenin and Philosophy, and Other Essays*, translated by Ben Brewster. London: New Left Books.

Anderson, Lindsay. 1981. *About John Ford*. London: Plexus Publishing Limited.

"Angels and Blimps." 1999. *Ally McBeal*. Fox Video, February 8.

Austin, Arthur. 2002. "The Postmodern Buzz in Law School Rankings." *Vermont Law Review* 27(1): 49–80.

Bagdikian, Ben H. 2000. *The Media Monopoly*, 6th ed. Boston: Beacon Press.

Baker, C. Edwin. 2002. "Media Concentration: Giving Up on Democracy." *Florida Law Review* 54(5): 839–919.

Baker, William F. 2002. "Big Business is Devouring Television." *Newsday*, March 13.

Benjamin, Walter. 1969. *Illuminations*. Translated by Harry Zohn. New York: Harcourt, Brace & World.

Bergman, Paul and Michael Asimow. 1996. *Reel Justice: The Courtroom Goes to the Movies*. Kansas City: Andrews McMeel Publishing, LLC.

Bischoff, Samuel (producer). 1938. *Angels with Dirty Faces* [Motion Picture]. United States: Warner Brothers.
Bohnke, Michael. 2001. "Myth and Law in the Films of John Ford." *Journal of Law and Society* 28(1): 47–63.
Brooks, Tim and Earle Marsh. 1999. *Complete Directory of Prime Time Network and Cable TV Shows, 1946–Present*. New York: Ballantine Books.
Capra, Frank (producer). 1939. *Mr. Smith Goes to Washington* [Motion Picture]. United States: Columbia Pictures.
Carman, John. 2002. "Goliaths for TV Likely to Get Fatter: Ruling Good for Giant Firms." *San Francisco Chronicle*, February 21.
Carroll, Matt (producer). 1980. *Breaker Morant* [Motion Picture]. Australia: South Australian Film Corporation and New World Pictures (distributor).
Carroll, Noel. 1998. *A Philosophy of Mass Art*. New York: Oxford University Press.
Chicago, A Musical Vaudeville. 1975. Maurine Watkins. Directed by Bob Fosse. 46th Street Theater, Broadway, New York, June 3, 1975–August 27, 1977.
Childers, Joseph and Gary Hentzi (eds.). 1995. *The Columbia Dictionary of Modern Literary and Cultural Criticism*. New York: Columbia University Press.
Columbia Journalism Review. Last accessed April 15, 2015 at www.cjr.org/resources/index.php?c=index.
Coppola, Francis F. (producer). 1974. *The Godfather Part II* [Motion Picture]. United States: Paramount Pictures.
———. 1990. *The Godfather Part III* [Motion Picture]. United States: Paramount Pictures and Zoetrope Studios.
De Certeau, Michael. 1984. *The Practice of Everyday Life*. Berkeley: University of California Press.
DeMille, Cecil B. (producer). 1927. *Chicago* [Motion Picture]. United States: DeMille Pictures Corporation.
De Moraes, Lisa. 2001. "There's Not Much News that's Good News." *Washington Post*, November 16.
DeSylva, Buddy and Joseph Sistrom (producers). 1944. *Double Indemnity* [Motion Picture]. United States: Paramount.
Eyman, Scott. 1999. *Print the Legend: The Life and Times of John Ford*. New York: Simon and Schuster.
"Fahrenheit 9/11." *Box Office Mojo*. Last accessed April 15, 2015 at www.boxofficemojo.com/movies/?id=fahrenheit911.htm.
Fish, Stanley. 2000. "Theory Minimalism." *San Diego Law Review* 37: 761–76.
Fiske, John. 1989. *Understanding Popular Culture*. London: Unwin Hyman Ltd.
Ford, John and Willis Goldbeck (producers). 1962. *The Man Who Shot Liberty Valance* [Motion Picture]. United States: Paramount.
Friedman, Lawrence M. 1989. "Law, Lawyers, and Popular Culture." *Yale Law Journal* 98: 1579–1606.
The Fugitive [Television Show]. 1963–1967. ABC.
Gans, Herbert J. 1974. *Popular Culture and High Culture: An Analysis and Evaluation of Taste*. New York: Basic Books, Inc.
Get Smart! [Television Show]. 1965–1969. NBC.
Gigi Durham, Meenakshi and Douglas M. Kellner (eds.). 2001. *Media and Cultural Studies: KeyWorks*. Hoboken, NJ: Blackwell Publishing Ltd.

Gillers, Stephen. 1989. "Taking L.A. Law More Seriously." *Yale Law Journal* 98(8): 1607–23.

Glass, Diane M. 1990. "Portia in Primetime: Women Lawyers, Television, and *L.A. Law*." *Yale Journal of Law and Feminism* 2(2): 371–434.

Groening, Matt. 1997. *The Simpsons: A Complete Guide to Our Favorite Family*, edited by Ray Richmond and Antonia Coffman. New York: HarperPerennial.

Habermas, Jurgen. 2001. "The Public Sphere: An Encyclopedia Article." In *Media and Cultural Studies: KeyWorks*, edited by Meenakshi Gigi Durham and Doublas M. Kellner, 75–79. Hoboken, NJ: Blackwell Publishing Ltd.

Hall, Stuart. 1992. "Encoding/Decoding." In *Culture, Media, Language: Working Papers in Cultural Studies, 1972–79*, edited by Stuart Hall et al., 128–38. New York: Routledge.

———. 1992b. "Introduction to Media Studies at the Centre." In *Culture, Media, Language: Working Papers in Cultural Studies, 1972–79*, edited by Stuart Hall et al., 117–21. New York: Routledge.

Harris, Burtt, David Brown, and Richard Zanuck (producers). 1982. *The Verdict* [Motion Picture]. United States: 20th Century Fox.

Hawks, Howard (producer). 1946. *The Big Sleep* [Motion Picture]. United States: Warner Brothers.

Herman, Edward S. and Robert W. McChesney. 1997. *The Global Media: The New Missionaries of Corporate Capitalism*. New York: Bloomsbury Academic Press.

Higgins, Charlotte. 2004. "*Fahrenheit 9/11* Could Light Fire under Bush." *The Guardian*. May 17.

Hill Street Blues [Television Show]. 1981–1987. NBC.

Ho, Kevin K. 2003. "*The Simpsons* and the Law: Revealing Truth and Justice to the Masses." *UCLA Entertainment Law Review* 10 (2): 275–88.

Hoare, Quintin and Geoffrey Nowell Smith (eds.). 1971. *Antonio Gramsci, Selections from the Prison Notebooks*. Translated by Quintin Hoare and Geoffrey Nowell Smith. Paris: International Publishers Co.

Hobson, Dorothy. 1982. *Crossroads: The Drama of a Soap Opera*. London: Methuen London Ltd.

Jay, Martin. 1973. *The Dialectical Imagination: A History of the Frankfurt School and the Institute of Social Research 1923–1950*. Boston: Little Brown and Company.

Johnson, Nunnally (producer). 1942. *Roxie Hart* [Motion Picture]. United States: 20th Century Fox.

Keetley, Dawn. 1998. "Law & Order." In *Prime Time Law: Fictional Television as Legal Narrative*, edited by Robert M. Jarvis and Paul R. Joseph, 33–54. Durham, NC: Carolina Academic Press.

Kopelson, Arnold (producer). 1993. *The Fugitive* [Motion Picture]. United States: Warner Brothers.

LA Law [Television Show]. 1986–1994. NBC.

Law & Order [Television Show]. 1990–2010. NBC.

Leff, Leonard J. and Jerold L. Simmons. 1990. *The Dame in the Kimono: Hollywood, Censorship, and the Production Code from the 1920s to the 1960s*. New York: Grove Weidenfeld.

Levinson, Barry and Steve Golin (producers). 1996. *Sleepers* [Motion Picture]. United States: Warner Brothers.

Linson, Art (producer). 1987. *The Untouchables* [Motion Picture]. United States: Paramount Studios.
Lubet, Steven. 2000. "*The Man Who Shot Liberty Valance*: Truth or Justice in the Old West." *UCLA Law Review* 48(2): 353–73.
The Man from U.N.C.L.E. [Television Show]. 1964–1968. NBC.
Marini, John. 2001. "Western Justice: John Ford and Sam Peckinpah on the Defense of the Heroic." *Nexus—A Journal of Opinion* 6: 57–66.
McBride, Joseph. 2001. *Searching for John Ford*. New York: St. Martin's Press.
McNeil, Alex. 1996. *Total Television: The Comprehensive Guide to Programming from 1948 to the Present*. 4th ed. Baltimore: Penguin Books.
Mezey, Naomi and Mark C. Niles. 2005. "Screening the Law: Ideology and Law in American Popular Culture." *Columbia Journal of Law and Arts* 28: 91–186.
Milchan, Arnon and Christopher Mankiewicz (producers). 2003. *Runaway Jury* [Motion Picture]. United States: 20th Century Fox.
Milchan, Arnon and Steven Reuther (producers). 1994. *The Client* [Motion Picture]. United States: Warner Brothers.
Modleski, Tania. 1984. *Loving with a Vengeance: Mass-Produced Fantasies for Women*. London: Methuen, Inc.
Molen, Gerald R., Bonnie Curtis, Walter F. Parkes, and Jan de Bont (producers). 2002. *Minority Report* [Motion Picture]. United States: 20th Century Fox and Dreamworks Productions.
Moore, Michael, et al. (producers). 2004. *Fahrenheit 9/11* [Motion Picture]. United States: Miramax Films.
Morely, David. 1980. *The "Nationwide" Audience: Structure and Decoding*. London: BFI.
Motion Picture Producers and Distributors of America, Production Code Administration. 1987. "The Motion Picture Production Code." In *The Censorship Papers: Movie Censorship Letters from the Hays Office, 1934 to 1968*, edited by Gerald Gardner. New York: Dodd Mead and Company.
"Mr. Lisa Goes to Washington." 1991. *The Simpsons*. Fox Video, September 26.
O'Neill, Timothy P. 2004. "Two Concepts of Liberty Valance: John Ford, Isaiah Berlin, and the Tragic Choice of the Frontier." *Creighton Law Review* 37(3): 471–92.
Papke, David Ray. 1996. "Myth and Meaning: Francis Ford Coppola and Popular Response to the Godfather Trilogy." In *Legal Reelism: Movies as Legal Texts*, edited by John Denvir, 1–22. Champaign: University of Illinois Press.
Parker, Alison M. 1996. "Mothering the Movies: Women Reformers and Popular Culture." In *Movie Censorship and American Culture*, edited by Francis G. Couvares, 73–96. Washington DC: Smithsonian Institution Press.
Post, Robert C. (ed.). 1987. "On the Popular Image of the Lawyer: Reflections in a Dark Glass." *California Law Review* 75: 379–90.
———. 1998. *Censorship and Silencing: Practices of Cultural Regulation*. Los Angeles: The Getty Research Institute.
Prometheus Radio Project v. FCC, 2004, 373 F.3rd 372. WestLaw Next.
Radway, Janice. 1987. *Reading the Romance: Women, Patriarchy and Popular Literature*. North Carolina: UNC Press.

Reiner, Robert, David Brown, and Andrew Scheinman (producers). 1992. *A Few Good Men* [Motion Picture]. United States: Columbia Pictures.
Richards, Martin (producer). 2002. *Chicago* [Motion Picture]. United States: Miramax Films.
Rosenberg, Norman. 1998. "Perry Mason." In *Prime Time Law: Fictional Television as Legal Narrative*, edited by Robert M. Jarvis and Paul R. Joseph, 115–28. Durham, NC: Carolina Academic Press.
——. 2001. "Looking for Law in all the Old Traces: The Movies of Classical Hollywood, the Law, and the Case(s) of *Film Noir*." *UCLA Law Review* 48(6): 1443–71.
Ruddy, Albert S. (producer). 1972. *The Godfather* [Motion Picture]. United States: Paramount Pictures.
Ryan, Cheyney. 1996. "Print the Legend: Violence and Recognition in *The Man Who Shot Liberty Valance*." In *Legal Reelism*, edited by John Denvir, 23–43. Chicago: University of Illinois Press.
Saxon, Edward and Jonathan Demme (producers). 1993. *Philadelphia* [Motion Picture]. United States: Tristar Pictures.
Seiler, Andy. 2003. "Pssstttt! 'Chicago' Has a Secret Past." *USA Today*, March 24.
Shelby, Carolyn, Christopher Ames, Kim Kurumada, and Robert W. Cort (producers). 1991. *Class Action* [Motion Picture]. United States: 20th Century Fox.
Silbey, Jessica. 2001. "Patterns of Courtroom Justice." *Journal of Law and Society* 28(1): 97–116.
The Simpsons [Television Show]. 1989–present. Fox.
Stern, Gary. 2002. "Courtroom Life Imitates Art." *The National Law Journal*, July 22.
Sweeney, Annie. 2003. "The Truth Behind *Chicago*: Glitz was Fleeting for the Women of 'Murderess Row.'" *Chicago Sun-Times*, March 23.
Telecommunications Act, 1996, Pub. L. No. 104-104, 104th Cong. (February 8).
Turner, Graeme. 1996. *British Cultural Studies: An Introduction*. New York: Routledge.
Wallis, Hal B. (producer). 1941. *The Maltese Falcon* [Motion Picture]. United States: Warner Brothers.
Watkins, Maurine. 1926. *Chicago* [Play].
West, Robin. 2002. "Re-Imagining Justice." *Yale Journal of Law and Feminism* 14: 333–44.
The West Wing [Television Show]. 1999–2006. NBC.
Wilson, Carey (producer). 1946. *The Postman Always Rings Twice* [Motion Picture]. United States: MGM.
"You Never Can Tell." 1998. *Ally McBeal*. Fox Video, November 23.
Zanuck, Darryl F. and Nunnally Johnson (producers). 1940. *The Grapes of Wrath* [Motion Picture]. United States: 20th Century Fox.

IV

FILM, CRIME, AND THE SOCIAL WORLD

11

Race and Serial Killing in the Media

*The Case of Wayne Williams**

Caroline Joan "Kay" S. Picart

In an iconic scene from the 1995 movie *Copycat*, criminal psychologist Helen Hudson (played by Sigourney Weaver) is giving a lecture on serial killing. She first requests all males in the room to stand up, explaining that serial killing is principally a male trait. Then, she asks all African American and Asian males to sit down. Those who remain, the white men, become the iconic image of serial killers. The popular misconception or media fallacy that arises from this cinematic depiction is that all serial killings are done by white males.

This chapter is not about profiling serial killers racially. It is about analyzing media myths in relation to serial killing, against the backdrop of the interaction between popular culture and the criminal justice system.[1] Ultimately, the chapter's moral compass relies upon returning the focus to the victims, who are often forgotten in the media circus that follows highly publicized violent crimes. In specific, this chapter is about analyzing monstrous media myths and remembering the principal lesson from this case: that racially stereotyping serial killers can have dangerous consequences, especially for a group vulnerable to victimization.

Most black serial killers are relatively unknown. Unlike Ted Bundy and Jeffrey Dahmer, Coral Watts, Milton Johnson, Calvin Jackson, and Alton Coleman are not household names (Jenkins 1998, 17). One of the well-known myths, as illustrated in the *Copycat* scene discussed earlier, is that nearly all serial killers are white males; yet, the reality is that one in every five serial killers is black, and nearly 16 percent of all serial killers are female (Hickey 2010, 5). The main exception to the relative media obscurity of black serial killers is Wayne Williams, a then-twenty-three-year-old African American music promoter.

Williams, popularly dubbed by the mainstream media as "America's first black serial killer," was arrested as the killer of over twenty black children, though he was formally charged and convicted of murdering just two of his victims (Hickey 2010, 2). The case increased the visibility of serial killers in the media and drew attention to the fact that there are nonwhite male serial killers and that even children could be targets (as the stereotype was again that adult women were the group most in peril) (Hickey 2010, 1–2). Technologically, fiber evidence was a key feature of the prosecution's case against Williams; but profiling was a new investigative technique, which also featured prominently in both the arrest and eventual media coverage of Williams's arrest (Hickey 2010, 2).

The questions this chapter seeks to explore are the following:

1. Generally, why are black serial homicide cases not given as much media coverage as white serial killer cases?
2. In particular, why was the case of Wayne Williams different from the general media pattern of ignoring black serial killers?
3. What does the case of the Atlanta Youth Murders tell us about how whites and blacks perceive the media coverage of the trial of Wayne Williams and the criminal justice system?
4. Is there a relation between media narratives concerning race and serial killers, and media coverage of racial hoaxes?

METHOD

This chapter finds its center of gravity in the focus on media constructions of blackness and whiteness in relation to serial killing, as found in the case of Wayne Williams. The analysis relies principally upon the approaches of two well-established legal theorists and law professors. First, law professor and criminologist Katheryn Russell-Brown focuses on "how the racialized images of black skin have become embedded within the American fabric" (2008/2009, 3). Russell-Brown's work focuses both on racialized contemporary popular cultural constructions as spawned by media depictions and on the operation of the criminal justice system (2008/2009, 3–4). She covers both the historical genealogy and the influence of race in the formation of the criminal justice system, from the slave codes to Jim Crow legislation (2008/2009, 35–52). Given the limitations of a chapter, I will not be able to have the depth Russell-Brown has in her book, but I am indebted to her for the clarity of the analytical methods she uses, which are both empirical and qualitative.

The second law professor I rely on is Kimberlé Crenshaw. Acknowledging the complexity and mobility of racial construction in relation to power, Crenshaw proposes an "intersectional" approach: one that takes into account how race, gender, and class, for example, are not isolated indicia of personhood and privilege, but operate as concrete foundations of power, which interact much like variables (Crenshaw 1995, 350). Crenshaw's focus is less on whiteness and identity politics than on one of its counterparts, the experiences of violence lived by poor African American women, who are institutionalized through an accretion of norms (1995, 358). Although I look more at constructions of masculinity rather than femininity in this chapter, one thing to draw from Crenshaw is a recognition of the reductive quality of identity politics and its failure to grapple with lived power differentials, institutionalized through legal practices and social norms. Crenshaw argues that the problem with identity politics is that, at a basic level, it "frequently conflates or ignores intragroup differences," which in turn "contributes to tension *among* groups" (1995, 357).

However, this chapter also grows out of a prior project, which is crucial to my analysis, and in specific, my focus on the use of monstrous metaphors, and how these monstrous metaphors function rhetorically in media narratives (Picart and Greek 2007, 5, 11, 13).[2] Drawing from Stanford Lyman's "Gothic sociology," (1990, 29–108)[3] Cecil Greek, a professor of criminology and criminal justice, and I, a social and political philosopher, used a Gothic criminological approach to analyze how Gothic metaphors and imagery rhetorically work to describe crime, as depicted by the media (Picart and Greek 2007, 11–12). Yet the objective was less to show that media myths are simply "fiction" (Picart and Greek 2007, 12).[4] Rather, our focus was on the complex interaction between the "fact" of public policy and the "fiction" of media depictions that constitutes lived reality, such that one realm cannot be absolutely demarcated from the other (Picart and Greek 2007, 13–14).[5] This is not to say that there is no such thing as "fact," or that "fact" and "fiction" are the same thing; rather, it is to point out that fact and fiction do not form a simple binary, especially in media depictions.

To some extent, it is precisely the dynamic that contributes to the complex unfolding of the story of the Atlanta Youth Murders, in so far as the "Monster" of the narrative, as told by the prosecution and the media, was a fair-skinned black man who identified so much with whites that he hated his own race and remorselessly killed off those whom he deemed unworthy of life. This narrative exploded into widely varying reactions from predominantly white and black communities.

THE ABSENCES OF BLACK MALE SERIAL KILLERS IN THE MEDIA

Examples of Black Male Serial Killers

While they are not the majority of serial murderers, there are black male serial killers. Eric N. Hickey (2010, 192), a criminologist, conducted a recent study, in which he identified that black males comprise about 23 percent of the serial murderer population, while white males occupy 72 percent of the population (2010, 5). To name a few recent examples of black male serial killers, Henry Louis Wallace raped and strangled at least nine African American women from 1993 until his capture in 1996 (though he confessed, to his psychiatrist, to raping between thirty-five and one hundred) (Hickey 2010, 196–97). Maury Travis was apprehended in 2002 and subsequently hanged himself in his jail cell. Travis had built a secret torture chamber in his basement, where the police found bondage equipment, videotapes recording his rape and torture sessions, and clippings covering police investigations of his murdered victims (most of whom were prostitutes and crack addicts) (Shinkle 1992). Derrick Todd Lee, arrested in 2003, was convicted of killing seven women by strangulation (Holmes and Holmes 2010, 45). More recently, Anthony Sowell, a convicted sex offender, was charged with killing eleven black women in Detroit in 2010 (Lindsay 2010).

What is puzzling is why the mainstream media, in general, does not pay as close attention to these stories, as they do to white male serial killers. One could argue that these men have not killed as many as Ted Bundy (twenty-plus victims) (Holmes and Holmes 2010, 156–57) or John Wayne Gacy (thirty-three victims) (Holmes and Holmes 2010, 68). But there are other white male serial killers, with a comparable victim body count who have been more thoroughly covered, such as David Berkowitz (six victims) (Holmes and Holmes 2010, 96) and Ed Kemper (nine victims) (Holmes and Holmes 2010, 2). One could also conjecture that it is because these lesser known serial killers were neither as violent nor as savage in their attacks. Yet Coral Watts, the Detroit "Sunday Morning Slasher," a sexually motivated serial killer whose exploits made him "comparable to Ted Bundy" remains relatively unknown (Jenkins 1998, 17, 25).[6]

The "Marketability" of Stories About Black Serial Killers

Philip Jenkins, a criminologist who has done extensive work on serial killers, poses two compelling reasons why there is less coverage of black serial killers. First, Jenkins shrewdly points to publishers' attitudes regarding how "newsworthy" or "saleable" the story will be (Holmes and

Holmes 2010, 26–27). Precisely because the popular perception is that psychopathic serial killers are white, there is a prevailing assumption that books on black serial killers will be relegated to the "Black Studies" sections of bookstores and never have mass appeal (Holmes and Holmes 2010, 27). To illustrate his point, Jenkins compared the very similar cases of Gary Heidnik and Harrison "Marty" Graham (Holmes and Holmes 2010, 27). Both men imprisoned and murdered several victims in their houses in poor urban areas, and the hideous details of both crimes (involving sex slavery) were initially heavily reported upon by the media (Holmes and Holmes 2010, 27). Heidnik achieved notoriety: he is the subject of a book-length study (Englade 1988). In 1991, he was interviewed on *60 Minutes*; his profile was partially used to create the *Silence of the Lambs*'s Buffalo Bill, who trapped women in his basement (Jenkins 1998, 27). In contrast, save for some coverage in Philadelphia, Graham sunk into obscurity (Jenkins 1998, 27). The only difference between the two men: Heidnik is white; Graham is black (Jenkins 1998, 27).

The Race and Class of the Victims

Second, Jenkins points to a well-known phenomenon among criminologists, social scientists, and lawyers, among others. If the victims the serial killer chooses are poor and black, their deaths are less likely to be seen, by law enforcement, as part of a serial killer pattern (Jenkins 1998, 28). For example, Albert Fish, a white man who predatorily molested and killed black children in Washington, DC, and New York from 1910 to 1935 remained at large for a quarter of a century because of his victim choice (Jenkins 1998, 28). In his final confession, he stated that the police simply did not care about poor, "colored" children and were not as vigilant when they died or disappeared (Jenkins 1998, 28). Significantly, Fish got caught only when he murdered the child of his white, middle-class neighbors (Jenkins 1998, 28). The *Fish* case illustrates the important interactions between race and class (i.e., that race could not be isolated from class, in terms of Fish's choice of victims) and shows the analytic power of Crenshaw's intersectional approach.

Along a parallel track, the Baldus study shows that black defendants who kill white victims have a 22 percent chance of getting the death penalty, as opposed to 1 percent for black defendants killing black victims (*McClesky v Kemp* 1987)[7], showing that black deaths caused by black violence are punished less rigorously. Similarly, James W. Clarke arrives at a similar indictment of the criminal justice system, which, in his view, replaced the slaveholders' authority (1998, 210).[8] He states that the "warped criminal justice system" has three destructive and enduring consequences: (1) it granted an "immunity for crimes committed against black victims" (1998, 210); (2) it condoned black-on-black violence as a way of settling disputes (1998, 210); and (3) it "contributed directly to disruption, disunity and rising rates of violent crime within the black community and, not incidentally, black families" (1998, 210). Jenkins concurs and goes even further, in terms of serial killing and blackness:

> Discriminatory police attitudes go some way toward explaining the low priority attached to African-American murder victims, and this benefits any offender who chooses to pursue minority victims. As homicide is primarily an intra-racial crime, this would mean that African-American serial killers would be far more likely to escape detection. Racial attitudes here are profoundly linked to social stereotypes. (1998, 28)

Thus, Jenkins conjectures, if a killer of "moderate intelligence" were to plant money, drugs, or even gang insignia at the scene of the crime, the crime would likely be viewed as simply urban homicide, rather than serial killing (1998, 29). Particularly if the means of killing were subtle (such as suffocation), the murderer would probably go undetected for years (1998, 29).

Monstrous Metaphors and Serial Killer Stereotypes

Convincing as Jenkins's theses are, the Atlanta Youth Murders are in direct contradiction to the patterns Jenkins outlines. In spite of Wayne Williams's blackness, the story of the Atlanta Youth Murders produced documentaries, television interviews, a fictional film, and numerous books. In 2010, Soledad O'Brien conducted an updated interview with the incarcerated Williams (CNN Documentary).[9] The victims, whose decomposing bodies were dumped in poor neighborhoods, the woods, or the Chattahoochee River were predominantly poor, black children, and the accused was a black man. Using the patterns Jenkins drew, this case should also have eventually been forgotten. But there is something about this case that continues to touch a very raw nerve in the American psyche.

There is a third reason Jenkins touches on briefly and tentatively to suggest why black serial killers are discussed less in media coverage. Speaking of why there have been no black *Psycho* films, for example, Jenkins remarked that filmmakers are "anxious to avoid being accused of depicting crude or controversial racial stereotypes" (1998, 24); nevertheless, it is curious that in many other areas, the media's depictions of black skin with criminality are ubiquitous. While I think this thesis may be simplistic, there is a heuristic value to tracking or mapping the rhetorical framing of how the "Atlanta Monster" was detected and convicted, and from whose point of view these narratives were constructed. Thus, I analyze metaphors of monstrosity that abound, in relation to the narrative of the Atlanta Youth Murders. That is, since the stories concerning Williams either depict him as a psychopath or another victim diverge so strikingly, it is important to track how such wildly different interpretations of the "monstrous" emerge. Finally, applying Russell-Brown's and Crenshaw's methods, the chapter will track how race, class, gender, and sexuality are connected in the vastly different white and black narratives that emerge concerning Williams, in retrospect. The value of this exercise is less about taking sides, than simply documenting both points of views and grounding them rhetorically, in order to reveal what lies underneath the monstrous metaphors. To do so, I analyze the logic behind the narratives concerning race, monstrous metaphors, and the criminal justice system.

The Case of the Atlanta Youth Murders: General Facts

For twenty-two months, from the summer of 1979 to the spring of 1981, Atlanta residents lived in increasing fear and outrage as thirty victims, mostly poor black children (twenty-eight males and two females), were killed. The ages of the victims ranged from seven to twenty-eight, and most were youths of a similar build; they were all black. Some of the victims were shot or strangled; others were stabbed, bludgeoned, or suffocated (Hickey 2010, 192).

Though Atlanta authorities were initially reluctant to believe these deaths were linked, partly because of the activism of the mothers of the missing or dead children, they eventually conceded that perhaps these deaths were part of a pattern, and a special task force was formed (Hickey 2010, 192). Because all the victims were black, some speculated that this was part of a white supremacist plot to systematically kill all black children (Hickey 2010, 192). Others conjectured that the culprits were Satan worshipers, blood cultists, or even copycat murderers (Hickey 2010, 192). The Ku Klux Klan (KKK) was placed under surveillance, but there were no clear links that could be established between the KKK and the increasing deaths.[10] Bernard Headley paints a clear picture of the atmosphere of fear that suffused the city.

> Some believed, for instance, that the murders were the handiwork of white supremacist groups like the Ku Klux Klan. Others held that an agency of the federal government was carrying out the killings. Or that one government agency, like the FBI, had been in conspiracy with another—say, the Central Intelligence Agency (CIA) or the Atlanta-based Centers for Disease Control (CDC)—to commit mass murder. Or worst of all, the FBI and CIA were in diabolical cahoots with the Klan to murder black male children, whose bodies the CIA needed for penile experimentation. (1998, 2)[11]

As the tension mounted, Atlanta became a city under siege. In a startling newscast, the mayor offered a $150,000 reward, stacked invitingly high, for tips leading to the trial (Headley 1998, 98). Boxing legend Muhammad Ali donated $400,000 (Headley 1998, 98). Sammy Davis Jr. and Frank Sinatra raised more money through a benefit concert (Headley 1998, 98). Then-President Ronald Reagan appointed then-Vice President George Bush Sr. to coordinate efforts (Headley 1998, 106). As the turmoil increased, Atlanta's convention income decreased (Headley 1998, 123).

It was at this point, when nude bodies began showing up at the Chattahoochee River (as if in response to news reports that police were gathering trace fiber evidence from the bodies of the victims) that the police conducted a three-week stakeout of bridges over the river (Headley 1998, 130). On May 22 1981, shortly before 3 a.m., Robert Campbell, an Atlanta police recruit, was approximately eight feet from the water under the James Jackson Parkway Bridge when he heard a "loud splash." In Campbell's testimony, as narrated by Jack Mallard (the prosecutor), Campbell, the former lifeguard, accustomed to hearing the sound of human bodies hitting the water, said that the "splash" he heard sounded different from the sound of beavers diving in. He used a flashlight to follow the ripples in the river when he looked up at the bridge and saw car lights come on "right there above where the splash originated" (Mallard 2009, 96). Campbell called Freddie Jacobs, another Atlanta police recruit, who was also on stakeout in the bushes above the rail. Jacobs testified that he saw a station wagon close to the rail, as it came across the bridge from a parked position very slowly. After crossing the bridge, the vehicle turned around and came across the bridge; patrolman Carl Holden and FBI agent Gregg Gilliland stopped the station wagon at I-285 (Mallard 2009, 97). When Wayne Williams, the driver, stepped out of the car, Williams inquired into what "this [was] all about" (Headley 1998, 132) When Gilliland responded that he couldn't tell Williams at this time, Williams remarked, "I know this must be about those boys" (Headley 1998, 132).

According to FBI records, Williams then "voluntarily consented" to a routine search of his station wagon (Headley 1998, 132). According to patrolman Holden, when he was interviewed by Soledad O'Brien during a 2010 CNN interview (CNN Documentary 2010), a flashlight, a pair of dirty gloves, and a nylon cord were on the front passenger seat. In the same documentary, Williams vehemently denied that there had been a nylon cord, and said that if there had been, it would have shown up later. According to Headley, there were also a knapsack of men's clothing, a large open bag of women's clothing, and a white bedspread with a black and green design; in addition, the car was a "mess" because it looked like it had been used to "transfer animals" (Headley 1998, 132). Williams admitted that his parents' fourteen-year-old German Shepherd had been in the car a number of times.

Despite the disagreements, the accounts concur that Wayne Williams was detained for about an hour and a half, as he was questioned about why he was on the bridge at that hour (Headley 1998, 132). Wayne's story, at that time, was that because he was a musical talent scout, he had an early appointment with a woman called Cheryl Johnson; he claimed he was simply trying to check out the neighborhood to find her address, purportedly at the Spanish Trace Apartments in Smyrna (Headley 1998, 147). Unfortunately, no such woman ever turned up, despite the intense media coverage of Williams's activities before he was officially charged (Headley 1998, 132).

Though there was not enough evidence to hold or charge Williams at that time, word leaked to the press (Headley 1998, 149). The *New York Post* went straight for the racial button with the headline: "Atlanta Monster Seized; Police Nab Black Suspect" (Headley 1998, 149). A three-week media circus ensued, which Williams partially helped generate by handing reporters a five-page resume of himself during a "news conference" he held at his parent's home (Headley 1998, 150–51); Williams also liked leading the police who were tailing him on eighty-mph wild goose chases down one-way streets (Headley 1998, 163).

On June 21 1981, Wayne Williams was arrested for the murder of Nathaniel Cater (Headley 1998, 165) (see figure 11.1). Eventually, Williams was indicted for the murders of Jimmy Payne and Nathaniel Cater (Headley 1998, 169). The forensic fiber evidence pointed to a link between Williams and ten of the homicides (Headley 1998, 183–85). Judge Clarence Cooper ruled the evidence admissible (Headley 1998, 178–79). A jury of eight blacks and four whites found Williams guilty of the two murders, and the judge sentenced Williams to two consecutive life sentences (Headley 1998, 197). On March 1, 1982, two days after Williams's guilty verdict, law enforcement officials declared, via a "preponderance of incriminating forensic evidence," that Wayne Williams was responsible for murdering Alfred Evans (thirteen); Yusef Bell (nine); Eric Middlebrooks (fourteen); Christopher Richardson (twelve); Aaron Wyche (ten); Anthony Carter (nine); Earl Terrell (ten); Clifford Jones (twelve); Charles Stephens (ten); Aaron Jackson (nine); Lubie Geter (fourteen); Terry Pue (fifteen); Patrick Baltazar (twelve); Curtis Walker (thirteen); Joseph "Jo-Jo" Bell (fifteen); Timothy Hill (thirteen); Eddie Duncan (twenty-one); Larry Rogers (twenty); Michael McIntosh (twenty-three); John Porter (twenty-eight); William Barrett (seventeen), Jimmy Payne (twenty-one), and Nathaniel Cater (twenty-seven) (Headley 1998, 197).

Figure 11.1. Wayne Williams under arrest. Image in the public domain, optimized by Susan Gilbert.

ANALYZING METAPHORS OF MONSTROSITY

Monstrous Metaphors in the Prosecution's Profile

Profiling as a New Investigative Tool

The prosecution's fiber evidence, then a relatively new forensic technique, was and continues to be much touted as circumstantially airtight by those who believe Wayne Williams to be the Atlanta Youth Murderer. Conversely, detractors impugned and continued to reject the evidence, especially the fibers derived from bodies in the river, as open to too much contamination to be credible. Yet what lies underneath the disagreement regarding the credibility of the fiber evidence is something more fundamental and can be found in the monstrous metaphors that lurk in what appear as purely rational discourses.

At the height of the crisis, the "big city super-cops," and a new breed of crime fighters, profilers, were called in to assist the Atlanta police (A&E 2000). The Atlanta Youth Murder investigation was the "first major test" for profiling (A&E 2000). The profile they produced was that the killer not only had to be intelligent, but also black, because he could move around comfortably in these neighborhoods and get these children into dangerous circumstances without detecting attention (A&E 2000). He was a con man (someone charismatic, who inspired trust in his victims), and who probably had an obsession with the police and police work and was media-savvy (as the killer seemed to be responding to leaks about the fiber evidence the police were collecting by throwing the nude bodies of the victims into the river, to wash away any fiber evidence) (A&E 2000).

After Williams was apprehended at the bridge, the police began collecting information on the self-proclaimed music promoter and freelance photographer. They found a large degree of convergence between the profile of the unknown killer and Williams. Table 11.1 reveals a tabulated summary of the convergences between the profile and Williams's biography.

A Black Man Who Hated Blackness

Yet the profile, to be persuasive enough to make the circumstantial evidence compelling and to convince a predominantly black jury of Williams's guilt, needed one thing: a motive. To be credible, such a motive would have to be powerful enough to rhetorically conjure the most hideous of monsters. The profilers predicted a black man filled with an intense loathing for poor members of his own race; a man who was "racist with his own kind" and out to "terminate them" (A&E 2000). And indeed, despite Williams's vehement denials, there appear to be several sources

Table 11.1.

Profile	**Wayne Williams**
Intelligent but with unfulfilled dreams	Virtual child prodigy (ran an amateur radio station); dropped out of Georgia State University
Tried to impersonate the police	Arrested for impersonating police when he was 18
Prone to exaggerations	Resume filled with exaggerations
Prone to deception	Failed polygraph tests
News-savvy; kept close watch on police	Had police scanners in his car, which he used to take photos of fires during the overnight beat for a local news organization
Could lure poor street-wise kids	Posted ads for auditions to aspiring young musicians or dancers, aged 11-21, all over the Atlanta housing project, without any financial benefit to himself

that independently corroborate Williams's contempt for poor, black kids, whom he saw as "dragging down his race" (A&E 2000). For example, Bernard Headley, a professor of criminology and criminal justice, extensively documented some of the corroborating evidence.

> Wayne often expressed negative feelings toward blacks; he frequently did so to the white emergency workers around whom he freelanced. He seemed "resentful of being black," recalled one white police officer. White ambulance driver Bobby Toland said "it was common knowledge that Wayne was not crazy about the black race." Another emergency worker said Wayne often would portray black people as a "sorry lot—the way they lived, the way they acted, leeching off the government." . . .
>
> Once when the entire nation seemed genuinely affected by the mysterious youth slayings and disappearances, an associate of Wayne's recalled him "putting down the idea" of people raising money for victims' families. Wade Marcus would remember mentioning to Wayne in January or February 1981 that he was considering sending money to assist in the investigation of the Atlanta murders. Wayne, Marcus recalled, told him not to waste his money because the kids were "just prostitutes hanging around all night long." (1998, 141–42)

"Drop Shots"

Additionally, the profilers predicted that given the psychopathic and narcissistic qualities of the killer, Williams would most likely crack after extensive cross-examination (A&E 2000). After two days of intense cross-examination, Williams exploded, calling the police "goons" and the prosecutor a "fool" (A&E 2000). That sudden change in character, from composed to combative, seemed to be a decisive factor in the jury's belief that Williams was guilty; it was as if underneath a civil and "normal" exterior, a creature of anger and unnatural appetites had lurked, and been unmasked, to the shock and horror of the principally black jury.

Furthermore, Jack Mallard, the prosecutor, picked up on a derogatory term Williams had used in relation to Ken Kimbro and his friend, young black males who lived in the projects (like the other street kids Williams had referred to in his "June 4 News Conference") (2009, 293–94). Mallard asked if the term referred to people who live in the projects; Williams denied that and transferred the epithet to Mallard, calling him a "drop shot" (2009, 293). Mallard did not know the meaning of the term until a few years later, when Assistant Prosecutor Chuck Clay of Cobb County came across the genealogy of the term (2009, 293). Quoting *The Story of Georgia and The Georgia People*, Williams cited the definition:

> A large plantation was a little kingdom. The overseer was in charge, a black driver was under him, there were hoe-hands, plowmen, quartermasters, cooks, gardeners, blacksmiths, carpenters, shoe-makers, a midwife, nurses,

> dairy maids, spinners, weavers, seamstresses, chicken-and-turkey raisers, and even a gang of little negroes, called the "drop-shot gang," who carried water and food to the hands in the field. (Mallard 2009, 294)[12]

Despite the fact that the true meaning of the term did not emerge until later, there was a striking resonance between the prosecution's profile of Williams as the killer and the derogatory meaning of the term. "Drop shots" were the "little negroes" at the bottom of rung on the plantation, who were only worthy of carrying water to those even lower than themselves in the hierarchy: the field hands (Mallard 2009, 294).

Men Who Eat Their Own

Thus, the prosecution painted the monstrous image of a man who hated the color of his own skin so much that he killed others who reminded him of his own self-loathing (A&E 2000). District Attorney Lewis Slaton did the closing arguments: he portrayed Williams as "doing away with inferiors as Attila the Hun, Adolf Hitler, Idi Amin from Uganda" (Mallard 2009, 294). For the most part, it is this monstrous picture that is accepted by most whites, and has entered criminology textbooks and the mainstream culture.

METAPHORS OF MONSTROSITY IN CRITIQUES OF THE TRIAL

The Legal Lie of the One Drop Rule

James Baldwin, a well-known African American author and civil rights activist, responded to the prosecution's profile of both Williams and his victims, with eloquent fury:

> The imagination is poorly equipped to deal with this action because self-hatred is so common, and takes so many forms. . . . [G]iven the bottom-line realities of life in these so ambiguously United States, the missing, menaced, murdered children were menaced by color and locality: they were—visibly Black, which, in this Republic, is a kind of doom, and actually poor—which condition elicits from the land of opportunity and the work ethic a judgment as merciless as it is defensive. (1985, 6)

Baldwin recounted that "half-breeds" or "mulattoes," using the "elegant" terms of the "Civilized," were "legal creations"—fair-skinned blacks who were pale enough to "hope to be treated as white" (1985, 6). Thus, what was principally monstrous, for Baldwin, was the lie strictly demarcating black blood from white blood: "Underlying the tremendous unwillingness to believe that a Black person could be murdering Black children was the specifically Southern knowledge and experience of how much Black blood is in White veins—and how much White blood is in black veins" (1985, 8).

In addition, to Baldwin, the black survival strategy of "passing" became appropriated as a (white) profiling tool to trap a murderer "dark enough to pass unnoticed in Black neighborhoods" (1985, 8). That is, instead of a fair-skinned black person passing as white in an environment dominated by privileged whites, the picture the profile painted, which the mainstream media adopted, was of a monstrous fair-skinned black man passing as a normal black man in poor black neighborhoods. To Baldwin, that was a monstrous appropriation of a black survival strategy.

The Criminal Justice System as Juggernaut

The next monstrous metaphor that lurks in Baldwin's book is that of a system that like a juggernaut, levels inconsistencies in order to maintain its self-perpetuating hierarchy. In conjunction with this metaphor of the system-as-monstrous, the view that Williams was simply a scapegoat for authorities under intense pressure is a common one (A&E 2000), as was the peculiarly Southern knowledge that "Atlanta policemen had to join the Ku Klux Klan if they ever hoped to become accepted members of the force" (Headley 1998, 17).

Indeed, there seems to be evidence that Lubie Geter, one of the victims, was killed by a Klansman, Sanders (A&E 2000). In addition, a witness claimed that he saw another victim, Clifford Jones, being sexually tortured and strangled by a white man, Jamie Brooks, who was later seen in a hooded robe, carrying something "heavy wrapped in plastic," and who reportedly walked to a further dumpster to drop off the heavy load (Mori 2010). Unfortunately, the witness, Freddie Cosby, was not deemed credible because he was mentally retarded (Mori 2010).

Williams as Another Victim

The results from years of fruitless appeals have led,[13] until possibly recently, many to view Williams as simply another victim, alongside the murdered Atlanta youths, especially Clifford Jones, whose death, like Emmett Till, raised the hue and cry. "Jones, like Emmett Till, in 1955 . . . was an out-of-state visitor from . . . the North. Had he been a 'Mississippi boy, his bones might yet be irrecoverable at the bottom of the river" (Baldwin 1985, 40). Baldwin's reference to Emmett Till is another civil rights–related battle cry. This allusion becomes even more potent because it juxtaposes images of the mutilated body of a young boy, whose image is burnt into public memory, alongside the numerous, violated bodies of the Atlanta Youth Murder victims. If the violence inflicted on Emmett Till's body could stoke such national indignation, Baldwin's juxtaposition seemed to imply, how much more righteous anger could the virtual Holocaust of discarded bodies of Atlanta Youth Murder victims awaken?

The Monstrous Within

Yet Baldwin's ultimate metaphor of monstrosity is less something "out there" such as a racist criminal justice system. For Baldwin, the most ghastly of monstrosities is not some external order or superhumanly evil person. That ultimate metaphor of monstrosity resides within, complicit with an unjust and racist order.

> The author of a crime is what he is—he knows it, can make no more demands, nor is anything more demanded of him. But he who collaborates is doomed, bound forever in that unimaginable and yet very common condition which we weakly suggest as *Hell*. In that condition, and every American should know it, one can never again summon breath to cry *let my people go*! (Baldwin 1985, 125)

The Uniqueness of the Media Coverage of the Atlanta Youth Murders

To this day, Williams's conviction as the Atlanta youth serial murderer remains controversial and continues to generate a steady stream of updated documentaries. Part of the rhetorical uniqueness of the case is tied up with the sheer proliferation of Gothic tropes used in conjunction with its coverage. For example, the prosecution used another monstrous metaphor I did not discuss: that of being a homosexual pedophile. Similarly, the monstrous specter of a KKK plan to start a race war has refused to be dispelled, and remains a persistent feature of the media coverage of this story. Additionally, experts of various sorts either praise or criticize the trilobal fiber evidence and the criminal profile, resulting in either a laudable judgement of justice or of hideous injustice, keeping the case in the national spotlight.

Hypothesizing on why this case received as much media coverage as it did (see figure 11.2), perhaps Wayne Williams's case became nationally noteworthy because before the profile had been created, there was rampant suspicion that the killer was white; the media thus initially treated it as such. Additionally, probably because the activism of the victims' mothers created such a powerful grassroots movement, the resultant public visibility (combined with the effect on the city's tourist-oriented economy) forced local and federal authorities to respond to their cries for justice. Finally, perhaps the case was as heavily covered because the At-

Figure 11.2. Wayne Williams (center right) being led to trial. Image in public domain, optimized by Susan Gilbert.

lanta youth serial murders took place in the aspiring "jewel of the south," showcasing the drama of an upwardly mobile black administration pitted against its poor black constituents, in a city where racial tensions were high and the political balance of power could tip.

What is clear is that the Atlanta Youth Murders touched a raw nerve, in relation to race relations, perceptions of the criminal justice system, and rhetorical constructions of monstrosity. And what has been lost in the media parade of monstrous metaphors are the quiet voices of the victims, seven of whose cases remain officially unsolved. In analyzing the monstrous metaphors at work in the sensationalization of the Atlanta Youth Murders, the moral fulcrum of this chapter has been to help prevent attacks on victims with the same profile that made them easy marks: being poor and black.

LOOKING BEYOND THE ATLANTA YOUTH MURDERS: MEDIA DEPICTIONS OF FACT AND FICTION IN RELATION TO RACE AND SERIAL KILLING

Recent criminological data has begun to document black serial killers. For example, professor of criminal justice, Anthony Walsh, compiled data on approximately ninety African American serial killers and the time periods and states in which they committed their crimes (2005, 271, 278). Walsh concludes,

> Based on these figures, there were approximately five times more African American serial killers operating in the 1980s than there were from 1945 to 1979. Likewise, the 13-year period between 1990 and the first half of 2004 revealed 32 African American serial killers—an average of about 2.3 per year. (Walsh 2005, 271, 278)

Walsh's figures correspond with Hicks's findings that black serial killers make up about 21.8 percent of his study of black and white serial killers. An earlier study by criminologists Michael Newton and Judy Ann Newton in 1991 came up with a 16 percent estimate of the number of blacks in the serial murderer category (Newton and Newton 1991, 40).

While it is clear that white males remain the majority in the serial murderer category, recent studies have begun to document the existence of black male serial killers. The value of studies, such as these, is to demystify racist cultural myths, one of which is the view that serial killers are "white and brilliant, thus alluding that Blacks aren't smart enough to carry out organized murder" (Chehade 2001/2003, 2). Such a myth has a long history, starting with Samuel Morton's *Crania Americana* (Morton

1839). In brief, Morton claimed that there was a direct correlation between intelligence and the size of the skull/brain (Morton 1839). He also claimed a correlation between intelligence and race, with whites at the top of the pyramid and blacks at the bottom (Morton 1839). The derogatory racist implication is that only white males are "brilliant" enough to plan and commit serial murders. However, legal scholars and historians, such as Russell-Brown (2006, 23–24) and Schiebinger (2004, 135), have also demystified this cultural fallacy concerning intelligence dressed in a pseudoscientific veneer.

The history of the negative stereotyping of African Americans and the resultant harmful social, legal, and political consequences of these cultural myths are well documented. Serial killing, a particularly violent form of homicide, is one area where stereotypes imply a different type of stereotyping. Though criminologist Walsh attributes this relative media reluctance to cover stories of black serial killers to a liberal fear of being labeled "racist," (which he compares to the situation of untenured assistant professors afraid to publish anything explosive that could get them fired) (Walsh 2004, 42), I believe the situation is more complex than that.

For example, there is a striking affinity between the narrative patterns yielded by the Atlanta Youth Murders and racial hoaxes, as analyzed by Russell-Brown.

Russell-Brown described a racial hoax as occurring when:

(a) someone fabricates a crime and blames it on another person because of his race, or
(b) an actual crime has been committed and the perpetrator falsely blames someone because of his race. (2008/2009, 100)

Among other findings, Russell-Brown found that white-on-black hoaxes (where whites blame blacks for real or imagined crimes) are perpetrated based on the myth of the "criminalblackman"—an aberrant individual capable of random acts of violence with "menacing, demonlike details" (2008/2009, 107). In contrast, black-on-white racial hoaxes, such as the cases of the Duke lacrosse team and Tawana Brawley (though Brawley has never recanted), usually appeal to a different type of narrative: one bound up with a conspiracy bound up with white privilege or white supremacy (Russell-Brown 2008/2009, 111–12).

Similarly, in the Atlanta Youth Murders, for example, the prosecution's racial profile of Wayne Williams, as a self-hating light-skinned black man who preyed on the poor black kids whom he regarded as society's scum, corresponds with the racial narrative characteristic of white-on-black hoaxes. In other words, it is the narrative of the criminalblackman, writ large. It is this story of the Monstrous Black Man that a mostly white community and the mainstream media propagated, miming the rhetorical patterns of a white-on-black hoax. In contrast, a predominantly black community then believed that the murders of the poor black children were tied up in a KKK conspiracy to kill one black child every month in order to spark a race war. This rhetorical pattern corresponds with the general narrative form of black-on-white hoaxes.

In other words, the mainstream media coverage of the Atlanta Youth Murders constructed the story, not as a typical/normal "black-on-black" assault, but as something more akin to a "white-on-black" assault, writ "monstrously" large. As journalist and author John Perazzo writes regarding popular media representations, "*white*-on-black transgressions are testaments to racism, while *black*-on-black offenses are meaningless" (1999, 49). This differed radically from the black community's reaction to the media coverage.

Furthermore, in keeping with a Gothic criminological approach, the spheres of "fact" and "fiction" in relation to race and the criminal justice system, as reported in the media, are complexly intertwined. Empirically, there is a rough correlation between the proportion of whites to blacks in Newton and Newton's (1991, 40), Walsh's (2004, 278), and Hickey's (2010, 5) studies of serial murderers (between 16 and 23 percent black and 72 percent white) and Russell-Brown's findings on the proportions of the reported cases of white-on-black hoaxes (20 percent) and black-on-white hoaxes (67 percent) (2008/2009, 105). That is, the racial breakdown of the serial killer population, based on the factual accounts gathered by criminologists, roughly corresponds with Russell-Brown's racial breakdown of hoaxes (thus "fictional" accounts). What this simply shows, in my view, is the media's choices regarding what "deserves" coverage, reinforcing racial stereotypes, as well as reflecting their influence.

Though these statistical racial correspondences may be coincidental, what is clear is that cultural myths (often simplistically labeled "false") and "factual reality" (often simplistically characterized as "truth") are not related in a simple oppositional binary. Often, it is the media that shapes how perceptions of "truth" and "lie" interrelate, and popular perceptions, in turn, influence public policy, which flow back to affect trends in media representations and cultural stereotypes (Picart 2007, 11). As Raymond Surette, professor of criminal justice and legal studies, noted,

> We live in a multimedia web that has resulted in the common practice of media content looping. . . . Real events migrate to entertainment media and the public sees fictional events as real. The . . . prevalence of *Frankensteinian* as an adjective . . . and the trope of being a bloodsucking vampire as a political description are all examples of content looping in the multimedia web and the associated ascension of the popular version of Gothic criminology. (Surette 2007, 222)

The racial dimension of such narratives is particularly crucial to document because as journalist Jared Taylor states,

> In our multiracial society, race lurks just below the surface of much that is not explicitly racial. Newspaper stories about other things—housing patterns, local elections, crime, antipoverty programs, law-school admissions, mortgage lending, employment rates—are also, sometimes only by implication, about race. When race is not in the foreground of American life, it does not usually take much searching to find it in the background. (1992/1993, 10)

And given that one of the cultural myths is that black-on-black violence does not matter, and its correspondent factual reality is that poor black youths are the most vulnerable to violent crime, it is important to address the popular cultural racial (mis)perceptions about serial murderers. The popular stereotype of the serial killer being a white male is, as criminologist Jenkins argues, as "inaccurate and as pernicious as any of the more familiar racial slurs" (Jenkins 1998, 30). Perhaps ultimately destroying this simplistic stereotype may help prevent the often invisible perpetration of violence against these types of victims. As Walsh soberly conjectures, "one wonders how many additional victims have been lost because law enforcement succumbed to the stereotype and concentrated their efforts on White males" (2004, 287). Ultimately, the greatest danger of silencing stories concerning nonwhite serial killers is, as Jenkins points out, the possibility that "[u]nderestimating minority involvement in serial homicide can thus lead to neglecting the protection of minority individuals and communities who stand in greatest peril of victimization" (Jenkins 1998, 30).

Of course, these types of stories must be treated with caution, as they could be sensationalized to further the already harmful stereotype of the "criminalblackman" so prevalent in other media narratives. But that is a risk well worth taking, given what the price of silence demands, of those victims chosen because they are most likely to go unnoticed and forgotten, by both the media and the criminal justice system.

SUMMARY OF FINDINGS AND CONCLUSION

In summary, this chapter has explored the following theses, in relation to the questions it posed in the introduction.

First, generally, black serial homicide cases are not given as much media coverage as white serial killer cases because of three principal reasons: (1) publishers do not think stories about black serial murderers will prove as commercially successful as stories about white male serial killers, so they usually choose not to cover it; for example, even though Gary Heidnik and Marty Graham committed comparable crimes (sexual enslavement and murder in their urban homes) in Philadelphia at roughly the same time, Heidnik achieved media immortality, while Graham is now virtually unknown; (2) if the victims are poor and black and the suspect is also black, the police are less likely to view the case as a serial murder; (3) the media, like untenured professors, are afraid of publishing and perishing, because the conjunction of monstrous metaphors with blackness leave them open to the charge of racism.

Second, in particular, the case of Wayne Williams was different from the general media pattern of ignoring black serial killers partly because of the prevalence and severity of monstrous metaphors in the coverage and reactions to the story, as evidenced in the rhetoric used by the predominantly white prosecution and the predominantly black civil rights community in relation to a mysterious, fairer-skinned black man. Yet there were other factors as well that contributed to the "newsworthiness" of the story: the initial suspicion that the killings were associated with a KKK-inspired plot to spark a race war; the political activism of the victims' mothers who ignited a grassroots movement; the detrimental effect of the stories on Atlanta's economy; the spectacle of a progressive city with a black mayor and a black police chief pitted against poor black constituents, in a city where racial tensions were rampant and the balance of power was tenuous.

Third, for the most part, whites tended to identify with the prosecution's narrative concerning Wayne Williams, while blacks tended to be skeptical. Both sides engaged in a battle of warring monstrous metaphors. For the prosecution/predominantly white community, Wayne Williams was the same kind of creature as Attila the Hun, Adolf Hitler, and Idi Amin. For the predominantly black civil rights community, the monsters were the racist criminal justice and legal systems that produced the lies of one drop rule; the "half-breeds" who could hope to be treated as white; and the mentality of complicity with these institutional structures and cultural myths.

Fourth, factual media narratives concerning race and serial killers and media coverage of racial hoaxes seem to intersect in two ways: (1) In this particular case, the mainstream coverage of the prosecution's arguments resembled the narrative pattern of white-on-black hoaxes, focusing on the monstrosity of the criminalblackman; in contrast, the coverage of those opposed to the prosecution rhetorically mimed the narrative pattern of black-on-white hoaxes, emphasizing the monstrosity of white supremacy and/or white privilege. (2) More generally, the proportion of blacks to whites in the male serial killer population as reported by criminologists (20:72) roughly corresponds with the proportion of black-on-white hoaxes compared with white-on-black hoaxes (20:67), as analyzed by

Russell-Brown. Thus, the realm of "fact" as reported by criminologists, in some ways, statistically mirrors the "fiction" of hoaxes, and vice versa; this is not to conflate fact with fiction, but to show the complexity of their relationship, especially when refracted through the prism of media depictions, which often reinforce and attest to the strength of racial stereotypes.

Ultimately, this chapter on the media depictions of race and serial killing constitutes one attempt to grapple with the effects of racism and white privilege. Thus, to achieve a more effective engagement with racism and white privilege and their influence on media accounts of what is "real," what is necessary is a structural and political critique that is sensitive to the power of metaphors and the rhetorical construction of reality. To borrow from Robert Jensen, a professor of journalism:

> The fundamental frame for pursuing analyses of issues around race, ethnicity, gender, sexuality and class should not be cultural but political, not individual but structural. Instead of talking about diversity in race, class, gender, and sexual orientation, we should critique white supremacy, economic inequality in capitalism, patriarchy and heterosexism. We should talk about systems and structures of power, about ideologies of domination and subordination--and the injuries done to those in subordinate groups, and the benefits and privileges that accrue to those in dominant groups. (Jensen 2005, 78)

Crucial to such an analysis would be a study of how the rhetorics of monstrosity interact with the institutional and political factors that create the matrix of power in which we all partake and participate.

NOTES

*Acknowledgments. The views expressed in this chapter are purely of the author's and do not represent the views of the firm for which she works. This chapter was originally published as Caroline Joan "Kay" S. Picart, "Race and Serial Killing in the Media," *Speaking of Monsters: A Teratological Anthology*, Caroline Joan "Kay" S. Picart and John Edgar Browning, eds. (New York: Palgrave Macmillan, 2012), 173–91. The author thanks Palgrave Macmillan for granting a license to republish the chapter. This chapter was derived from an essay that was originally awarded a Book Award for a seminar on Race, Law, and Justice at the University of Florida Levin College of Law. The author is indebted to Katheryn Russell-Brown for her insightful comments on earlier drafts, and to Lani Guinier and Raymond Fleming for their earlier acute mentorship on Critical Race Theory. The author thanks Margaret Petty for her kind assistance with re-formatting this chapter for this anthology, Harry Keyishian for his support and collegiality, co-editors Cecil Greek and Michael Hviid Jacobsen for their professionalism and cordiality, and the editorial staff of Fairleigh Dickinson University Press (Rowman & Littlefield) for their patient guidance during the editorial process. She dedicates this chapter to the Picart, Terrell, and Rivera families, and especially her loving husband, Jerry Rivera.

1. Criminologists Ronald M. Holmes and Stephen T. Holmes (2010, 7, 9) recount a dinner conversation with Tom Harris, the author of *Red Dragon* (1981) and *Silence of the Lambs* (1989). Harris's books were the source of the cinematic myth of Hannibal Lecter as "dark knight" and hyper-intelligent savage iconized by Anthony Hopkins's performances in *Silence of the Lambs* (1991) and *Hannibal* (2001). When Ronald's wife and Stephen's mother remarked that they did not read Harris's books because they "scare the hell out of [them]," Harris, smiling over the rim of his wine glass, responded, "They scare the hell out of me, too!"

2. (Picart and Greek 2007, 11). In *Monsters In and Among Us*, Cecil Greek, a criminologist, and the author collaborated on examining the plethora of books and films connecting violence, fear, visualizations of the "monstrous," and Gothic modes of narration in popular culture, academia, and even public policy. Using an interdisciplinary approach, and a variety of essays from invited specialists in film criticism, media studies, and rhetoric, as well as communication, criminology, and sociology, Picart and Greek analyzed contemporary visualizations of the Gothic and the monstrous in film and media. Contributors included media and film specialists Edward Ingebretsen, Jason Grant McKahan, and Pat Gill; rhetoricians Davis Houck and Thomas Benson; and sociologist-criminologist Raymond Surette. The "media monsters" Picart and Greek chose to focus on were the pedophilic homosexual priest (Ingebretsen's chapter); the hypermasculinized rogue cop (Houck and Greek's chapters); the masculinized mother (Benson's chapter); the drug addict (McKahan's chapter); the white-collar criminal (Gill's contribution); the serial killer (Picart and Greek's chapter); and the terrorist (Picart and Greek's chapter) (Picart and Greek 2007, 5, 13).

3. See generally, (Lyman 1978).

4. Ultimately, Picart and Greek also found that the class, gender, and sexuality of the serial killer resulted in different Gothic metaphors: Hannibal Lecter was associated with the glamorous vampire. In contrast, in the case of Wuornos, reputedly "America's first female serial killer," instead of the powerful and glamorous vampire, Picart and Greek found the pitiful and ugly outcast of the Frankensteinian monster. Wuornos was depicted as white trash eternally in search of companionship and love; tragically, she did everything for the lover who eventually betrayed and abandoned her (Picart and Greek 2009, 93, 94, 102).

5. In the case of the celebrity of the *Hannibal* films, for example, Surette (2007, 220–21) argued that the media-induced frenzy over the menace of serial killers funneled more funding for the special FBI Behavioral Science Unit featured in *Silence of the Lambs* and fostered crucial criminal justice policy changes, boosting the image of profilers as modern-day heroes.

6. Of course, one could also point out that some cases, regardless of the race of serial killer, remain of purely regional interest, such as the case of Danny Rolling, the "Gainesville Ripper," whose name does not even appear in Hickey's (2010, 5) book. Rolling is briefly mentioned in Holmes and Holmes (2010, 46).

7. See also Eric Monkkonen (1995, 101, 110–11).

8. See also Stephan Thernstrom and Abigail Thernstrom (1997/1999, 54).

9. See also "CNN Viewers: Williams 'guilty' in Atlanta Child Murders," *CNN Justice*, June 11, 2010, articles.cnn.com/2010-06-11/justice/atlanta.murders.poll.ireport_1_atlanta-child-murders-two-life-sentences-killings/2?_s=PM:CRIME.

10. The hypothesis of a federal cover-up of evidence implicating the KKK because of fear of a race war within the United States is the animating idea of the fictional film, *Echo of Murder* (Carner 2001).

11. The Tuskegee study on syphilis, where black men were used like guinea pigs to study the onset and progression of the disease, while denying them the cure (penicillin), was exposed in July 1972 (Headley 1998, 219, n3).

12. Mallard (2009, 294) citing George Gillman Smith (1901/1968, 350).

13. Additionally, on September 26, 1990, Williams's new defense team filed a 184-page Amended Petition for writ of habeas corpus. One of the major issues raised was that Williams's counsel was denied access to a secret independent investigation of the Ku Klux Klan in relation to the Atlanta Child Murders. On July 10, 1998, Superior Court Judge Hal Craig denied the defense petition, effectively ruling that the KKK probe had not yielded any evidence relevant to the outcome of the Williams's trial, and that its exclusion from Williams's trial did not constitute harmful error (Headley 1998, 345, 349).

REFERENCES

A&E Studios. 2000. *American Justice—The Atlanta Child Murders.* [Television Broadcast.] New York.

Baldwin, James. 1985. *The Evidence of Things Not Seen.* New York: Henry Holt and Co., LLC.

Carner, Charles (director). 2001. *Echo of Murder.* [DVD]. New York: Showtime Entertainment.

Chehade, Carol. 2001/2003. *Big Little White Lies: Our Attempt to White-Out America.* Kearney, NE: Nehmarche Publishing, Inc.

Clarke, James W. 1998. *The Lineaments of Wrath: Race, Violent Crime and American Culture.* New Brunswick, NJ: Transaction Publishers.

"CNN Documentary: The Atlanta Child Murders." *CNN*, June 1, 2010.

"CNN Viewers: Williams 'Guilty' in Atlanta Child Murders." *CNN Justice*, Accessed June 11, 2010, articles.cnn.com/2010-06-11/justice/atlanta.murders.poll.ireport_1_atlanta-child-murders-two-life-sentences-killings/2?_s=PM:CRIME.

Crenshaw, Kimberlé. 1995. "Mapping the Margins: Intersectionality, Identity Politics, and Violence Against Women of Color." In *Critical Race Theory: The Key Writings That Formed the Movement*, edited by Kimberlé Crenshaw, Neil Gotanda, Gary Peller, and Kendall Thomas, 357–83. New York: The New Press.

Englade, Ken. 1988. *Cellar of Horror.* New York: St. Martin's Press.

Headley, Bernard. 1998. *The Atlanta Youth Murders and the Politics of Race.* Carbondale, IL: Southern Illinois University Press.

Hickey, Eric W. 2010. *Serial Murderers and Their Victims*, 5th ed. Thousand Oaks, CA: Sage Publications, Inc.

Holmes, Ronald M. and Stephen T. Holmes (eds.). 2010. *Serial Murder*, 3rd ed. Thousand Oaks, CA: Sage Publications, Inc.
Jenkins, Philip. 1998. "African-Americans and Serial Homicide." In *Contemporary Perspectives on Serial Murder*, edited by Ronald M. Holmes and Stephen T. Holmes, 17–32. Thousand Oaks, CA: Sage Publications, Inc.
Jensen, Robert. 2005. *The Heart of Whiteness: Confronting Race, Racism, and White Privilege*. San Francisco, CA: City Lights Books.
Lindsay, Paul. 2010. "Anthony Sowell, Alleged 'Cleveland Strangler': Is Race a Factor in Serial Killer Probe?" *Crimesider*. Accessed April 14, www.cbsnews.com/8301-504083_162-20002361-504083.html.
Lyman, Stanford M. 1978. *The Seven Deadly Sins: Society and Evil*. New York: St. Martin's Press.
———. 1990. "Rereading Robert E. Park: Toward a Gothic Perspective on Capitalism and Imperialism." In *Explorations: The Age of Enlightenment*, edited by M. W. duQuesnay, 29–108. Lafayette, LA: University of Southwestern Louisiana Foundation.
Mallard, Jack. 2009. *The Atlanta Child Murders: The Night Stalker*. Charleston, SC: BookSurge Publishing.
McCleskey v. Kemp, 481 U.S. 282, 275 (1987).
Monkkonen, Eric. 1995. "Racial Factors in New York City Homicides, 1800–1874." In *Ethnicity, Race and Crime: Perspectives Across Time and Place*, edited by D. F. Hawkins, 99–120. Albany, NY: State University Press of New York.
Mori, Mark (producer and director). 2010. *Wayne Williams and the Atlanta Child Murders*, for Court TV [Television Broadcast]. Single Spark Pictures, Inc.
Morton, Samuel George. 1839. *Crania Americana; or, A Comparative View of the Skulls of Various Aboriginal Nations of North and South America: To Which Is Prefixed an Essay on the Varieties of the Human Species*. Philadelphia: J. Dobson.
Newton, Michael and Judy Ann Newton. 1991. *Racial and Religious Violence in America: A Chronology*. New York: Garland.
Perazzo, John. 1999. *The Myths That Divide Us: How Lies Have Poisoned American Race Relations*, second ed. Briarcliff Manor, NY: World Studies Books.
Picart, Caroline Joan "Kay" S. and Cecil Greek. 2007. *Monsters In and Among Us*. Madison, NJ: Fairleigh Dickinson University Press.
———. 2009. "When Women Kill: Undead Imagery in the Cinematic Portrait of Aileen Wuornos." In *Draculas, Vampires & Other Undead Forms: Essays on Gender, Race and Culture*, edited by John Edgar Browning and Caroline Joan "Kay" S. Picart, 93–112. Lanham, MD: Scarecrow Press.
Russell-Brown, Katheryn. 2006. *Protecting Our Own: Race, Crime and African Americans*. Lanham, MD: Rowman & Littlefield Publishing.
———. 2008/2009. *The Color of Crime*, 2nd ed. New York: New York University Press.
Schiebinger, Londa. 2004. *Nature's Body: Gender in the Making of Modern Science*, 2nd ed. Piscataway, NJ: Rutgers University Press.
Shinkle, Peter. 1992. "Serial Killer Caught by His Own Internet Footprint," *St. Louis Post-Dispatch*. Accessed June 17. www.rense.com/general26/serial.htm.
Smith, George Gillman. 1901/1968. *The Story of Georgia and the Georgia People, 1732 to 1860*. Baltimore: Genealogical Publishing Co.

Surette, Raymond. 2007. "Gothic Criminology and Criminal Justice Policy." In *Monsters In and Among Us*, edited by Caroline Joan "Kay" S. Picart and Cecil Greek, 199–226. Madison, NJ: Fairleigh Dickinson University Press.

Taylor, Jared. 1992/1993. *Paved with Good Intentions: The Failure of Race Relations in Contemporary America.* New York: Carroll and Graf Publishers, Inc.

Thernstrom, Stephan and Abigail Thernstrom. 1997/1999. *America in Black and White: One Nation, Indivisible.* New York: Touchstone.

Walsh, Anthony. 2004. *Race and Crime: A Biosocial Analysis.* Hauppauge, NJ: Nova Science Publishers, Inc.

———. 2005. "African Americans and Serial Killing in the Media: The Myth and the Reality." *Homicide Studies* 9(4): 271–291.

12

Globalization and the Rise of the Behemoth

A Study in Gothic Criminology

Cecil Greek

Why does it appear to be so difficult for the social sciences, and in particular criminology, to discuss evil? Is it possible that film might offer an avenue to expand our understandings of evil, particularly when global societal actions result in massive human harm? This chapter will expand upon earlier efforts to describe a Gothic Criminology (Picart and Greek 2007) to discuss monstrous human activity. Embedded within certain Hollywood films' themes related to how modern militarized societies attempt to maintain order, often by using overwhelming force and domination, there appears to be an effort to offer a unique sociological interpretation of understanding postmodern international relations. I will call this phenomenon Behemoth, and offer a historical, theological, and sociological perspective on the potential usefulness of this concept for understanding contemporary global evil. Four films will be focused upon in this chapter: *The Constant Gardener* (2005), *Battle in Seattle* (2007), *Lord of War* (2005), and *Syriana* (2005); all films were made at the height of president George W. Bush's campaigns against terrorism at home and abroad, 2002 to 2008. Each film deals with a different aspect of chaos (international medical policies, global economic policy, terrorism and the Middle East, and illicit weapons sales and their impact on ongoing civil strife), and how the West perpetuates chaos, while claiming to be trying to ameliorate it, to justify its Behemoth strategies. The explanation for why these four particular films are seen as critical to understanding globalization and evil will become evident.

CRIMINOLOGY'S RELUCTANCE TO PERCEIVE THE PERSISTENCE OF EVIL

The traditional academic discipline of criminology has two major research foci: (1) the causes of criminal behavior (biogenetic, psychological, and sociological) and (2) officially sanctioned state responses to crime (law, police, courts, and corrections). The now dominant methodology for researching these aspects of modern social life is based upon quantitative data analysis. However, it becomes obvious to those who study criminology that the discipline is discussing implicitly the ongoing existence of evil in the world, but without ever directly addressing this issue. For a number of reasons criminology almost never refers to evil or other value-loaded phrases, and limits itself to the discussion of the legally constructed categories of crime. Criminology, like its parental discipline sociology, sought to become value neutral early in the twentieth century in order to prove its scientific worth (Greek 1992). Second, etiological models developed by criminologists, be they biological, psychological, or sociological, served as "salvation devices" removing blame from the actual perpetrators of harm on others (Matza 1990). For example, in the psychological world, sin became sickness (Menninger 1973), resulting in the medicalization of deviance (Conrad and Schneider 1992). Paradoxically, at the same time, the criminal justice system ignored most criminological discussions of causality and continued to function primarily on a free will model, believing punishment was both justifiable and functional. Nevertheless, the legal system must separate willful and intentionally harmful actions from those that are excusable or justifiable, such as those committed during moments of insanity. Thus, the law must grapple with deciphering evil intent from the accidental, unavoidable, and such, on a daily basis. On the other hand, it appears that criminologists largely retreated from legal discussions of the utility of punishment, hoping that by not adding to the deterrence debate their alternative positivistic position advocating prevention, prediction, and control might ultimately be given a hearing by policy makers. While rarely called upon to add insight into policy debates, the criminological focus on prevention, treatment, and rehabilitation of offenders had a difficult time fighting off conservative attacks that "nothing works" (Martinson 1974). Meanwhile, politically constructed wars on drugs, gangs, crime, and terrorism, based upon free will views of human behavior as corrupted, became dominant in the public sphere, with the result that the United States now has one of the largest per capita prison populations in the world (Currie 1998).

While the social science research community largely has abandoned discussion of evil for the reasons detailed above, one only has to look at the events of the last century to see that the advance of technological society has increased dramatically the human potential for intentional harm on a mass scale. A century of total war and mass genocide only now is being recognized adequately by the criminological community as a significant research concern (Maier-Katkin, Mears, Bernard 2009; Hagan and Rymond-Richmond 2009).

If academic social science to date has responded inadequately to the ongoing problem of social evil, then perhaps we might turn elsewhere to locate other perspectives that could possibly reopen the discussion. Literature and film, while not scientific in a positivistic sense, nevertheless offer explanations for the human condition that often resonates with mass audiences as truthful (Leavy 2009). As Rafter (2006) has demonstrated, sometimes Hollywood films borrow existing criminological models of deviant behavior, while on other occasions offering alternative explanations for evil. In particular, a number of Hollywood film traditions seem to begin from the premise that evil is a permanent part of social existence, and that the world trend toward greater civilization and social complexity has not eliminated our most base instincts, but rather increased their damage potential. These anti-Enlightenment cinematic traditions have been described variously by film scholars as expressionistic, *film noir*, absurdist, postmodern, and Gothic. While these cinematic motifs have been readily identified in the terror and horror genres, they have also made their way into contemporary films, which might be placed in the docudrama category, in that they take facts and events from everyday life and weave these components into tales that audiences find realistic rather than fantastic. From the point of view of the films' producers and directors, it is essential that audiences emotionally identify with the stories being told as true. This chapter examines a small subset of these films, focused around the general topic of globalization and evil, building upon earlier work in Gothic Criminology (Picart and Greek 2007), by adding a new concept (Behemoth) to those discussions.

The first section includes a brief comparison of the ongoing discussions and debates regarding globalization to Hollywood's overall perspective on the negative consequences of modernization, followed by a description of the models and concepts that are employed here to analyze these films. Of particular relevance is Franz Neumann's (1963) concept of the Behemoth, a theory he developed to explain Nazi evil as organized chaos. The original tale of the Behemoth, which has origins in Jewish literature, can also be interpreted as a chaos theory. The specific topics that appear in the four films discussed here include global economic exploitation, human rights abuses, the mass marketing of weapons, terrorism, as well as efforts to control these chaotic elements of modern life, sometimes through draconian political and military intervention.

The importance of this project lies in its recognition that traditional criminological models used to explain transnational mass-inflicted harm, such as white-collar crime, state crime, and critical criminology, appear inadequate to comprehend evil on such a global scale. As an alternative, the use of film as a visual social medium for describing the behemoth nature of postmodern wrongdoing in ways that resonate with public social consciousness is worthy of exploration. Despite efforts to banish evil from criminological discussion, these films may be linking to a more primordial understanding of chaotically induced evil and efforts to control chaos through both legal and extralegal means such as massive force.

HOLLYWOOD FUTUROLOGY AND THE IMPLIED CRITICISM OF THE PRESENT

When analyzed as a whole, Hollywood presents an overwhelmingly pessimistic image of the earth's current state and near future possibilities. Film viewers certainly would recognize this outlook in the science fiction genre, as blockbuster films such as The Matrix trilogy and Terminator series predict that in the not so distant future civilization as we know it will all but disappear, leaving only a remnant of humanity struggling for survival. The human race had sown the seeds of its own demise through overdependence on dehumanizing industrialization, depersonalizing technology, environmental negligence, and uncontrolled global struggling over weapons of mass destruction. Machines, robots, and computers (which seem to have no on-off switches) ultimately dominate a post-apocalypse planet. At their most benign the planet's new techno–machine rulers create dream worlds in which human beings are offered a digitally constructed existence, but are denied true freedom or individuality. At worst, the machines attempt to rid the planet of any human remnants as if they were some sort of cancer. Dystopia has firmly replaced utopia as the predominant future predicted state of humanity (on dystopia theory see: Lyman 2001; Jacobsen and Tester 2012; Britto and Greek 2016). Even Disney's weak attempt to combat this trend, *Tomorrowland* (2015), informs us that the predominant response to warnings of global apocalypse likely will be complacency, until it is too late.

But, what of films that do not consider themselves science fiction in that they focus realistically on recent past and contemporary events of global significance? In these films humanity is impacted by historical forces frequently academically described under the umbrella term *globalization*. Within contemporary films, globalization's major facets are depicted as leading to terrible social consequences that appear to be beyond human amelioration. Thus, Hollywood's depictions of globalization offer additional insight (and emotional resonance due to their visual and auditory styles) from those embedded in academic literature or even politically motivated writings. In contrast, overall, social theorists and policy makers have been more positive in their interpretations of global modernization and the planet's future than filmmakers. In addition, neither pro- nor anti-globalization constituencies appear to have made their cases convincingly to the public, and continue to debate combatively, leading in some cases to highly publicized street encounters outside global summit meetings. Globalization films have stepped into this debate, offering a more holistic view of the relationship between modern economic and technological forces and their impact worldwide. In the process, these films have presaged a new criminological theoretical perspective for describing and analyzing evil.

While Hollywood has featured a number of globalization's components, this chapter will focus selectively on particular thematic topics. These will include the end of the Cold War and resulting migration and trade problems, including illegal arms, global economic, and financial markets, and global terrorism and the world's response to it. A focus on how filmmakers embed human rights issues within their descriptions will be included, as these films are often meant to serve as wake-up calls for citizens and politicians. The films elected for discussion here include *The Constant Gardener* (2005), *Battle in Seattle* (2007), *Lord of War* (2005), and *Syriana* (2005). While each has a different set of themes, what unites them is their overall employment of a Behemoth perspective on the current world condition.

As an overall interpretive theoretical model this chapter will offer a new strand of a recently developed perspective, Gothic Criminology, to amplify the postmodern implications of Hollywood's treatment of globalization (Picart and Greek 2007a). While previously used to explain individualistic forms of *monstrous* evil such as vampiric serial murderers (Picart and Greek 2003; Picart 2014), suicidal mass-murdering terrorists (Picart and Greek 2007b), and Golem-like corrupted law enforcement agents (Greek 2007), a more encompassing model is developed here to describe "massive evil."

Given that globalization is depicted in the films to be discussed here as harbinger of chaos rather than order, the Behemoth may prove to be an apt theoretical metaphor to describe this phenomenon. The concept, derived from Jewish folklore and eschatology, representing "controlled chaos," was first employed by Thomas Hobbes (1990) to describe the lawlessness associated with English Civil War, and more recently by refugee scholar Franz Neumann (1963) in his then-contemporary analysis of the Nazi regime. Paradoxically, Neumann documented that the Nazi fixation with order was based upon an artificially created chaos, both within Germany and the countries it conquered. Neumann's approach to understanding totalitarianism was largely forgotten for half a century, but has recently been revived in revisionist histories of Nazi Germany (Kershaw 1999; 2000; Longerich 2015). Just as Hitler and the Nazis took advantage of maintaining an ongoing state of chaos, globalization films argue that chaos within the modern world allows for continuing mass exploitation and human rights abuses. For example, critics have questioned how the United States as the leader of the Western world has responded to the threat engendered by terrorist generated chaos? To global drug cartels menacing our communities? To mass migrations of unwanted immigrants illegally living among us? In its efforts to remain the dominant nation state on the globe, has America adopted a Behemoth approach to such problems, and then attempted to gain the world's support for its corresponding draconian policy responses?

Within the Hollywood films to be discussed here is embedded a working theory of how global chaos has been socially constructed in the modern world, and then responded to as if a real condition. This does not mean that the filmic depiction of the modern world as chaotic is not based on facts, but these facts are selectively assembled and interpreted in cinematically compelling ways to tell menacing stories of evil that moviegoers will accept as truthful. In order for these movies to be taken seriously by audiences, rather than as entertaining variations on James Bond and other spy and action films, the globalization films must document a verisimilitude to real world events and behaviors. To accomplish this, these films combine techniques borrowed from multiple sources: the documentary film to indicate reality; hyper-linked film editing styles to signal simultaneous localized events that will later prove to be interconnected; and classic Gothic horror film locations, cinematography, lighting, and sound techniques to signify the ongoing persistence of evil.

While Hollywood globalization films attempt to expose the transnational problems we now face, the films are dramatic constructions that can be analyzed by using a combination of film and sociological/criminological techniques. In this regard, the approach to be used here seems quite useful in deciphering the Gothic components of the Behemoth subgenre (Picart and Greek, 2007a). These films present a consistently bleak interpretation of global events. The importance of this project may lie in its recognition that traditional criminological models used to explain transnational crime such as white-collar crime theory, state crime theory, and critical criminology appear inadequate to comprehend evil on a global scale. As an alternative, the use of film as a visual social medium for describing the Behemoth nature of postmodern wrongdoing in ways that resonate with public social consciousness is worthy of exploration. Despite efforts to banish evil from criminological discussion, these films may be linking to a more primordial understanding of this phenomenon as part of the human condition.

DEFINITIONS AND CONCEPTS

Before commencing with analysis of the selected films, it is essential to define key concepts that will be employed here and give a brief overview of the theoretical approach to be used. Globalization, Gothic Criminology, and Behemoth will be discussed in turn.

The Pros and Cons of Globalization

Globalization, once an academic term, has now entered everyday usage. As will be seen here, globalization has now come to refer to a broad spectrum of social changes engendered by modernity; these changes can be interpreted in positive or negative ways. Within the academic community, globalization has been defined both in a literal sense and as a sociological phenomenon. Both pro- and anti-globalization writings appear in the academic literature and are debated publicly (compare Sachs 2005 to Podobnik and Reifer 2005).

In its literal sense, globalization refers to the ongoing process of transforming local and regional phenomenon into global ones through a combination of economic, technological, political, and sociocultural forces. Some argue that economic globalization has been the major driving force, and that national economies have been integrated into an international one through global trade, world banking systems, foreign investments and related technological support (Bhagwati 2004). Others give additional credit to the spread of mass media including films, television, and music, and the rapid expansion of the Internet in speeding global cultural transmission (Crane and Kawashima 2002).

Sociologically, globalization both depends upon and fosters the unification of all peoples into a single society that functions together. Cultural globalization has been understood as a process of homogenization, but often interpreted by opponents as the impending global hegemony of Western/American culture and the demise of traditional cultures and diversity. For instance, Thomas Friedman (2007) has referred to the latest phase of social globalization brought on by mass communications technologies as a "flattening" of the world.

Pro-globalization writers focus on the potential benefits, both current and future, of directed economic and cultural change while anti-globalization opponents highlight the negative consequences for significant portions of the human population. Free trade is seen by proponents as leading to economic opportunity and prosperity, a greater sharing of world resources, and increased civil liberties for individuals. Everyone benefits from greater employment, lower prices, and higher standards of living (Sachs 2005). The spread of liberty and capitalism are seen to go hand-in-hand—a viewpoint turned into a policy by neo-conservatives during the Bush administration.

Anti-globalization arguments come from a broad spectrum opposing this utopian version of recent world history as overly optimistic and misusing facts and statistics for the benefit of financial and business leaders (Podobnik and Reifer 2005). As well as being an umbrella term for general opposition to modernization, anti-globalization is demonstrated by single movement issues that oppose components of modern social change. Some critics look at the dangers to the planet questioning the bio-sustainability of unfettered economic growth. Others focus on the perceived negative consequences to indigenous cultures. Among the list of economic negatives frequently described are: outsourcing of jobs from one society to another, the weakening of labor unions worldwide, and the exploitation of foreign impoverished laborers and children (Chossudovsky 2003). Overall, poorer countries suffer greater disadvantages from globalization than more advanced ones. Finally, global poverty is stated as increasing rather than decreasing, despite the claims otherwise of the World Bank and IMF (Chossudovsky 2003).

Nevertheless, both pro and con sides still would need to explain the past three decades' historical events and how these events either support or invalidate their theories. These events are more problematic for the pro-globalization side, which ends up treating history as obstacles blocking the inevitable arrival of global peace and economic prosperity. As first noted by historian Frederick Teggart (1916), historical events often run counter to teleological predictions about the outcomes of social forces. Pro-globalization supporters must explain how history does not falsify their belief system.

Since the 1980s we have witnessed the end of Cold War and its resulting releases of peoples and "products," the spread of terrorism from a local phenomenon to a global menace, and use of existing rapid transportation and communication systems to transfer illicit goods like drugs, weapons, and illegal immigrants. Global electronic banking routinely permits money laundering its ill-gotten profits. Once financial systems have been globalized, failures in one segment have dire international consequences, such as the domino effect created by massive bankruptcies in the American home mortgage market and the resulting devaluation of derivatives in 2007 and 2008 (MacLean and Nocera 2011).

Globalization theorists offer two competing interpretations of these events. Pro-globalization advocates discuss these events as if they were unpredicted anomalies, and continue to predict brighter days ahead once these phenomena are dealt with. The upward path of globalization was bound to encounter some bumps in the road. If the global community is willing to unite to eliminate terrorism, transnational drug distribution networks, and flows of illegal money, and such, everyone will be better off as the promises of globalization are allowed to come to fruition in a world inching toward utopia (Jacoby 2005). But, such an interpretation tends to minimize history and the human potential to do evil, which may be a root cause of some of these problems. The international financial collapse of 2007 was as much due to greed as it was poor financial market modeling (Morley 2007).

Anti-globalization theorists interpret these same events as directly related to processes already set in motion. For example, Noam Chomsky (2004) recognized that while Bush's 2003 invasion of Iraq drew worldwide criticism because it seemed to present a new philosophy of preemptive war combined with an appearance of global empire building, it was, according to Chomsky only further evidence of the long-established operating philosophy of American foreign policy. While other anti-globalization commentators may have failed to predict the exact path that history would take, they did recognize that while past negative trends might be regionally isolated, increased global interaction allowed these events to have much greater impacts (Naim 2010).

Gothic Criminology and Globalization

As we will see, the anti-globalization perspective appears to be the underlying predominant assumption of Hollywood globalization films. Bringing the world closer together has multiplied the possibilities for evil doing. The dominant cinematic interpretation of these events takes on a particular Gothic characterization, focusing on the perceived unleashing of "chaos" in the world and the responding efforts to restore control and order.

What is a Gothic Criminological approach? As previously detailed (Picart and Greek 2007c), Gothic Criminology is a hybrid theoretical model that combines elements of Gothic literature and film studies with criminological theories that focus on certain monstrously banal aspects of modern society. As Arendt (1963) documented, the simultaneous existence of monstrous evil and banal human participation in such behaviors is not oxymoronic. For example, Golem-like police officers directed to protect the public and maintain order may in the process violate law and commit crimes (Greek 2007). As a heuristic model Gothic theory represents a cultural criminological approach (Ferrell and Hayward 2008) aimed at comprehending film's role in explaining the dark side of postmodern society to itself (Denzin 1991). As such, film, in its efforts to encapsulate reality represents a form of mass-distributed sociodicy, replacing theodicy's former role in documenting the continuing evil presence on our planet (Lyman 1995). While the global movie moguls may recognize that films seemingly glamorizing evil (and pyrotechnics) often do quite well at the box office, the writers and directors producing globalization-themed movies are involved in a more complex storytelling process. However, unlike the ongoing debate between pro- and anti-globalization writers, Hollywood's predominant interpretation of modernization is quite pessimistic, functioning as a harbinger of the coming dystopic era depicted in Hollywood's futurist science fiction films.

In general the films discussed here do not rely upon established criminological theories, such as genetic predispositions, Freudian psychology or social environmental factors to explain current events. Instead they draw upon a Gothic sense of evil. Nicole Rafter (2000, 11) identified such a trend within "critical crime films." These, she stated "are rooted in the traditions of *film noirs*, the brooding mysteries and gangster films of the 1940s and 1950s that take corruption for granted, assuming that brutality and criminality are part of the human condition." Visually literate film watchers recognize an encounter with a Gothic movie. Over time, Hollywood developed a set of stock techniques, originally borrowed from German expressionist film, for lighting, camera locations, depth of field and angles, set design, music and sound, special effects, and editing (Philips 2001; Rabiger 2003), most famously associated with the Hollywood horror/terror genre pictures and *film noir* (Borde and Chaumeton 2002; Hirsch 2001). While many of these techniques are used in Hollywood's most recent globalization films, they are transferred to new background locations, replacing haunted houses and dark forests with deserts (the Middle East), torture-inflicting interrogation facilities, abandoned gun warehouses of the former Soviet bloc, African slums, or American urban streets where military equipment-enhanced police battle unarmed protestors, as examples of what is depicted in the referenced films.

In addition to the film tradition, one can presage aspects of a Gothic approach to globalization in certain criminological researchers. For example, Robert Park, early twentieth-century sociology chair at the University of Chicago, developed a global perspective on economic exploitation, later identified as "vampiric capitalism," in his journalistic critiques of Western appropriation of African peoples and resources (Lyman 1990; 1992). The life blood of capitalism is profits. Without profits, capitalism ceases to function. In its quest for profits Park pointed out that early capitalism used imperialism to attain the cheap natural resources and access to labor power needed to fuel it. To compound matters, in American law, corporations came to be treated like persons, yet live on beyond the deaths of their founders. Thus, like a vampire a corporation cannot be killed as it is an immortal entity, as it lives beyond its initial founders. It should not be surprising to find that at the turn of the twenty-first century, corporations, to maintain high profits, have harnessed the forces unleashed by post–Cold War globalization to once again locate cheap labor and displace workers in more developed societies, while moving their global corporate headquarters to countries that offered the lowest overall tax rates (Sullivan 2013). Hollywood's globalization films frequently focus on these trends.

Why employ a Gothic Criminological approach to docudrama type films on globalization? The interplay of "fact" and "fiction," as discussed by Picart (2014, 173), can be seen as heightened in these films which purport to be based upon real world events:

> A Gothic criminological approach analyzes how Gothic metaphors and imagery rhetorically work to describe crime, as depicted by the media. Yet the objective was less to illustrate that media myths are reducible to "fiction." Rather, our focus was on the complex interactions between the "fact" of public policy, and the "fiction" of media depictions that constitutes lived reality, such that one realm cannot be absolutely demarcated from the other. This is not to say that there is no such thing as "fact," or that "fact" and "fiction" are indistinguishable; rather, it is to point out that "fact" and "fiction" do not form a simple binary, especially in media depictions.

Chaos Theory and the Behemoth: A Short Historical Introduction

The predominant perspective on the contemporary world as depicted in films such as *The Constant Gardener*, *Battle in Seattle*, *Lord of War*, and *Syriana* is one of chaos. Emile Durkheim might have referred to this phenomenon as an aspect of anomie, but in these films the issue is not that individuals do not understand the predominant social mores, or that mores are even in flux; instead there is something deeply amiss at the very core of modernity itself resulting in a dis-ease or "liquidity" felt by all (Bauman 2006). When viewing any of the above films one feels an uneasy queasiness that seems to build dramatically as the films progress, driven by the filmmakers' toolkit of suggestive lighting, disorienting background music and sounds, as well as the interplay of foreground and background visual and textual elements keeping the viewer off centered. What is the source of this feeling that the world is not right and that chaos might overtake us at any time?

Franz Neumann (1963) first offered the social sciences the concept of the Behemoth to explain a particular historical manifestation of chaos, the Nazi state. Neumann (vii) noted the origin of the Behemoth in Jewish eschatology—of Babylonian origin—as the monster, sometimes depicted as a giant beast or ox, ruling the land (the desert). Described in Job 40 and Psalm 50 as the first of God's creation, and elsewhere in Jewish literature as "so big he sits on a thousand mountains," with an insatiable thirst able to "drink up all the waters of Paradise" (Dennis 2007, 31), Behemoth was partnered with the Leviathan, the sea monster, featured also in the book of Job (Mathewson 2008). Both are monsters associated with chaos, making this concept an essential part of the ancient Jewish understanding of reality (Whitney 2006). According to Levenson (1988, 17), even though God's creation had established the world in an orderly manner, the potential for the rise of chaos as part of the continuing existence of evil was a given part of the earthly condition. "The confinement of chaos rather than its elimination is the essence of creation, and the survival of orderly reality hangs only upon God's vigilance," ensuring that the cosmos remains orderly. Thus, the world is not inherently safe, instead it is inherently unsafe and precarious.

According to the apocalyptic writings, Behemoth and Leviathan would reappear shortly before the end of the world. Leviathan emerges from the sea while Behemoth comes from the desert (Whitney 2006, 53) (the Middle East being often cited as the epicenter of global chaos). The monsters will establish a rule of terror—but the monsters ultimately will battle each other and both be destroyed, according to one account ushering in the reign of a new messiah (Torrey 1947). The day of the righteous and just will have come and the beasts will be eaten as part of a celebratory feast (Torrey 1947; Wallace 1948). Thus, within Judaism the ending will be happy. Nevertheless, in between God's creation and the end point of history, God's chosen people are left to struggle on their own in a world often chaotic, resulting in the great diasporatic tragedies of Jewish history such as European ghettoization, the Russian pogroms and finally, the Holocaust (Levenson 1988, 50). In this theology, God is "a semiotiose deity, one who can still be aroused, who can still respond to the anguished cry of a cultic community to affect together a new victory." The Behemoth figure remained a component of late second millennium Jewish theology, even making its appearance in the wall paintings of synagogues, often in its oxen format (Hubka 2002; Gwozdziec Synagogue 2014).

A contemporary theological interpretation of Jewish chaos theory appears in the largely unseen (even though nominated for best picture 2009) Coen Brothers' (2009) feature *A Serious Man*. Based loosely on the book of Job, and the brothers' own experiences of growing up in the modest size Midwest town where Jews were a distinct minority, physics lecturer Larry Gopnik (Michael Stuhlbarg) experiences a series of life shaking events. His wife leaves him for a nebbish, both of his children become ungovernable, and his job and potential tenure at the university is threatened by a student claiming he accepted a bribe. As his life increasingly falls apart Gopnick seeks audiences with higher and higher ranking rabbis, but is only given a series of platitudes rather than any real answers or explanations. Just when it seems he might be getting his life back in order, the film dramatically terminates with the town about to be torn apart by a tornado, demonstrating that Behemoth-like chaos will rule in the end.

The specific linking of the Behemoth to political and social conditions begins with Thomas Hobbes (1990). His lesser-known work, *The Behemoth*, served as a companion book to his much more famous *The Leviathan*, though the former was never published during his lifetime as King Charles II would not permit it (Malcolm 1994, 771). *Behemoth* tells a story of the chaotic conditions, including sedition, rebellion, and the breakdown of authority, associated with the English Civil War under Cromwell. Hobbes's wish was for the orderly return of the monarch, as featured in *Leviathan*, who would put an end to chaos.

Neumann (1963, vii) borrowed from this earlier work, citing that Hobbes's *The Behemoth* "depicts a non-state, a chaos situation of lawlessness, disorder and anarchy." In his prolonged description of the Nazi state, Neumann argues that the Third Reich expressed neither a consistent ideology nor possessed a coherent structure. Thus, Hitler's regime was a chaotic, lawless, and amorphous monster that depended upon ongoing conflict between four power groups (the Nazi party, the German state bureaucracy, the Armed Forces, and big business). Together these four groups created the Behemoth that was Nazi Germany. The BBC documentary, *The Nazis: A Warning from History* (1997), also clearly demonstrates the use of chaos as a controlling technique employed by the Third Reich. Citizens were encouraged to spy upon each other and turn their neighbors into the SS; conquered territories were ruled by a combination of competing factions made up of traditional military, SS units, and local paramilitary style law enforcement; and Hitler often assigned multiple individuals the same tasks rather than employing Weberian bureaucratic principles, hoping that the competition in attempting to carry out his orders would result in the best suited rising to the top (Longerich 2015).

CONTEMPORARY GLOBALIZED BEHEMOTHS

In the chaotic worlds of the present, constructed for film audiences as realities rather than science fictions, there is little hope for improvement of contemporary conditions. In order to restore control, and in some cases perpetuate and capitalize on political and economic chaos, a Behemoth-like response structure emerges, one that requires going beyond the rule of law and traditionally accepted political activities, moving on to the condoning of violence, murder, and in some cases, the threat and use of massive force. In each of the films, "conspiracies of power" are the norm. In *Lord of War* (2005), the end of the Cold War has resulted in the inability of the five permanent members of the United Nations Security Council, who are also the five major sellers of weapons, to control the illicit distribution of arms. Massive amounts of weapons, previously under Soviet control, have flooded onto the market and been sold to third world regimes involved in civil wars or political strife. While the global community uses Interpol agents to try to control the gunrunning, ultimately as long as the receivers are politically aligned with current U.S. interests, the weapons shipments are allowed to continue. In *Syriana* (2005), oil companies, government officials, and the CIA all conspire to make sure that the flow of oil from the Middle East to the West continues unabated. Moderate or reform Arab leaders must be eliminated, to ensure that Western control of oil is maintained. In *The Constant Gardener* (2005), the conspiracy involves a global drug company, a drug testing company, British political officials, and the British Secret Service. Together they are willing to kill investigators who might reveal their plot to unwittingly test hazardous new drugs on impoverished African populations. In *Battle in Seattle* (2007), in order to ensure continued world economic policy domination, the global superpowers must employ the local police and political officials to ensure that counter messages conveyed by protesters are successfully silenced. Voices of dissent must not be allowed to unite. The continuance of the Behemoth-like structures ultimately depends upon such conspiracies going largely unrecognized by the public and the use of propaganda to demonstrate that the battle against chaos must continue unabated.

In each film, the conspiracy must be uncovered and revealed, and it is the role of the chief protagonist(s) to do so before themselves being killed or silenced. At heart, all are variations on the classic detective *noir* film, and employ classic *noir* techniques of lighting, camera placement, sound, and editing to ensure that the audience remains disoriented while hoping for an investigative success. In *Syriana*, CIA agent Bob Barnes (George Clooney) goes rogue and races to inform the progressive Arab leader of his impending assassination. In *The Constant Gardener*, British diplomat Justin Quayle (Ralph Fiennes) discovers that his activist wife is murdered to hide a drug testing conspiracy and attempts to reveal the murder, thus putting his own life in jeopardy. In *Battle in Seattle*, a TV news local reporter (Connie Nielson) switches her allegiance from her bosses who wish to depict the protesters as thugs to the side of the protesters themselves, seeing their victimization by police as unjustified. Finally, the *Lord of War* antihero Yuri Orlov (Nicolas Cage) exposes the sanctioned weapons supplying activities of first world powers. Nevertheless, despite the eye opening revelations, each film ends with the dystopian conclusion that chaos will continue as it is in the best interest of the Behemoth powers to allow such a condition, rather than strive for a more utopian world or a classic Hollywood happy ending. The detectives' discoveries land on deaf ears and warnings ultimately go unheeded. Law is of little or no use, and in fact can be a hindrance as the rule of law prevents arrests and prosecutions as seen in *Lord of War*. How these themes are specifically treated in each of the four films is discussed next.

LORD OF WAR

Lord of War (2005) makes an interesting starting point for these discussions, as it clearly demonstrates an unintended outcome of the overall success of globalization, in particular the ending of the Cold War and the dissolution of the Soviet Union. It could be argued that the termination of the need for ever increasing military buildup of guns, bombs, and military vehicles resulted in an obscenely, absurdly gargantuan stockpile of now largely useless killing equipment; but, rather than destroy these weapons, opportunists looked for ways to sell off these items at bargain basement prices. The film begins with an indictment of the illicit arms trade, but also tends to glorify the antihero who is able to thwart the global superpowers.

The film begins by showing the ground littered with spent shell cases, looking almost like an army of cockroaches. Gunrunner and narrator Yuri Orlov (Nicolas Cage) stands in the middle of a war-torn scene, announcing there is one gun for every twelve persons on the planet, sarcastically asking how we can arm the other eleven. The intro scene, shot entirely from the point of view of a bullet, follows a single round being manufactured in a Russian factory in what is now Ukraine, its departure inspection, and eventual arrival in a war-torn section of Africa. When the bullet is finally fired it goes directly into the head of a preteen child soldier, killing him instantly. The carnage caused by the tens of thousands of guns and millions of bullets is brought home dramatically in this one single death.

In a key moment in the film, entrepreneurial arms dealer Yuri celebrates Mikhail Gorbachev's 1991 announcement of the breakup of the Soviet Union, as if it is Christmas, recognizing that the ensuing chaos over establishing independent governments and re-organizing military units will be a boon to his business. Finally, the gunrunning behemoth of the five permanent voting members of the UN Security Council (the United States, China, the Soviet Union, the United Kingdom, and France) can be competed with by private entrepreneurs.

As Yuri is a Ukrainian immigrant, he goes immediately to the newly free Ukraine to make major arms deals to purchase leftover Cold War guns, tanks, and so forth, which are being housed there, and sell them globally to whoever wants to use them to engage in civil wars (mostly in Africa, but also Afghanistan and Columbia), insurgencies, ethnic cleansing, and genocide. The Ukraine military was no longer being paid, and a new government had not fully taken over yet. Yuri uses this period of chaos to do his own buying and selling, using his high-ranking military uncle to get unlimited access to weapons. As Yuri himself states, forty-five years of the Cold War had led to the biggest buildup of military hardware in history. He recognizes that "this state of chaos won't last forever," and the superpowers will react to restore order. Over the next ten years, $32 billion worth of arms were stolen and resold from Ukraine alone.

The rule of law is shown to be entirely ineffective. Efforts to control the burgeoning private arms trade by Interpol (an agency that typically only provides logistics and tactical support rather than actual law enforcement), and its ineffective representative agent Jack Valentine (Ethan Hawke), prove futile in stopping the arms trade. During their various encounters throughout the film Yuri continues to easily thwart Interpol, because without overwhelming evidence, the agent must respect the rule of law and allow the arms dealer to continue his ventures. Yuri is a master at manipulating the required documentation for arms sales, and uses a number of deceptive tactics as well. Even when Yuri is arrested at the film's conclusion, he informs Valentine that he will soon be released, because his personal efforts are in line with the overall political positions of the U.S. government regarding these third world civil wars. When caught, Yuri is unapologetic, and justifies his own actions, stating: "I do rub shoulders with some of the most vile, sadistic men calling themselves leaders today. Some of those men are the enemies of your enemies. The biggest arm dealer in the world is your boss, the president of the United States who ships more merchandise in a day than I do in a year." Thus, as in *Syriana*, United States foreign policy ensures that chaos rather than stability is the norm in many places on the globe. Yuri is just another cog in the Behemoth that controls the world by perpetuating instability. Released from arrest, Yuri immediately goes back to selling more guns. The film allegedly is based on the real life arms smuggler Viktor Bout, who unlike Yuri Orlov, was arrested in Thailand in 2008, extradited to the United States in 2010 and convicted in a federal courthouse in Manhattan in 2011 (BBC News 2012).

SYRIANA

Syriana clearly represents the American effort to maintain control over world oil through sustaining the image of the Middle East as a place of ongoing chaos. This is indicated in the very first scene of the film that shows the sun rising over a misty desert location, finally focusing in on a bus stop scene in which poorly dressed guest workers from Pakistan fight over who will get on the bus going to work in the oil fields of an Arab country. Giant oilfields have risen out of the desert as have accompanying modern cities with giant skyscrapers. As we learn in the film, the status quo is maintained by a combination of American display of force, secret CIA operations, bribery-laced deals between American oil company executives and ruling political elites, all the while ensuring that only the right political leaders are permitted to rule. The American government also "forces" these regimes to buy American arms and military equipment (one of the central themes of *Lord of War*), rather than spend their money on improving the lives of their own citizens. Against such a Behemoth, the true emergence of increased democratization and liberalization in the region has been permanently thwarted.

In a second opening scene, supposedly taking place simultaneously, CIA agent Bob Barnes (George Clooney) appears. He has set up a fraudulent sale of a missile in order to bring out into the open and kill alleged terrorists. While he lets one of the missiles slip away he is able to set off a bomb in the car of one of the purchasers. The powerful image of that first explosion of the bomb dealers' car represents the abstract force of the U.S. government, destroying everything around in favor of their own interests. Hence, as the car explodes, Bob continues walking as if nothing happens, fearless and with an arrogant air.

A series of seemingly unrelated stories are told in *Syriana*, keeping the viewer in chaotic suspense, only coming together in the climactic final scene. An American financial derivatives expert, Brian Woodman (Matt Damon), enters into a relationship with the son and heir apparent, Prince Nasir Al-Subaai (Alexander Seddig), of an aging emir of an Arab country. At first Woodman criticizes Nasir for his country's poor use of the massive wealth made from oil export, but later recognizes that Nasir is highly educated; and has plans for creating a parliament, giving women the right to vote, setting up an independent judiciary, and improving the lives of all his citizens by maximizing oil profits through cutting out the middlemen. The prince intends to dramatically extend the rule of law, making his country into a Western-style democracy. At that point Woodman fully signs up to be Nasir's advisor, not knowing that such a decision might prove fatal.

The middlemen to which Nasir refers are actually two American oil companies, one of which, Killen, has bribed government officials to get an oil contract, and then allowed itself to be bought out by a larger oil company, Connex, resulting in the creation of a huge conglomerate with employees in 160 countries, a Gross National Product the size of Pakistan or Denmark, or the equivalent twenty-third largest economy in the world. Executives from the two companies promise that their merger will result in reduced costs and ultimately major consumer benefits.

Word that some of the oil contracts involve bribery makes its way to Congress, resulting in a major investigation. When one of the oil executives involved in the bribery scandal is finally located and encountered, he is bewildered that the matter is being treated seriously. As he states, "Corruption is why we win. We have laws against corruption precisely so we can get away with it. Corruption is our protection." The Justice Department attorney sent to investigate the merger ultimately uncovers corruption and bribery at both companies. In a climactic scene with a high ranking government official, the lawyer is required to give up one person at each company to satisfy the Justice Department in what is referred to as the "illusion of due diligence." With one person from each company going off to jail, the merger is allowed to take place without further legal or government interference. Thus, corruption is vindicated and corporations are allowed to profit, as long as they turn in a scapegoat.

Meanwhile, CIA agent Barnes is sent to Beirut to assassinate Nasir, as the agency insists he is a known terrorist. Nasir was labeled a terrorist because he did an oil deal with China. Barnes's efforts prove unsuccessful, and a Lebanese double agent sells out CIA operative Barnes to the Arabs, who brutally torture him and broadcast widely that the CIA is practicing assassination. To cover up, the CIA develops a counter story that Barnes is a rogue agent, and proceeds to destroy his career. Once he uncovers the truth, Barnes decides to warn Nasir of yet another assassination attempt on his life, but ends up being killed in the targeted missile attack on Nasir, who has decided to unseat with military support, his brother, now the new emir after his father's death. Nasir was informed by his dying father that his obviously inferior brother will be named emir, because that's what the Americans wanted. As Nasir had signed oil contracts with the Chinese, the United States determined it could not possibly support his becoming the country's leader. Also, in contrast to Nasir, his brother would allow the Americans to continue to have military bases in their country while it was believed that Nasir would not. The brother was perceived as much more willing to be a friend of the United States, thus the CIA perceived it was in the best interests of the United States to assassinate Nasir.

The film's overall theme is that chaos in the Middle East is good for oil companies. The political background of the film is often being discussed in the background on television, radio, and in presentations at various government meetings, while the main characters in the film take up actions which may be in direct opposition to their political statements. For example, a number of oil company executives appear at a meeting before

Congress representing the Committee for the Liberalization of Iran. Yet, they know that continued instability in the region will result in greater American military presence and thus more easily facilitating forced compliance with American initiatives.

The real instability in the region is shown to be the oil companies themselves, whether they be American or of some other nationality. For example, the new Chinese owners fire all of the guest workers from Pakistan who are working at the refineries in Iran. The Pakistani workers had been forced to live in tiny cabins, and after their firing some become willing adherents to radical Islamic thought. Ultimately, several take part in a terrorist suicide attack as the first tanker filled with oil from the new American-leased oil fields leaves port. Thus, in the end, the film invalidates its own criticism of the Behemoth policies of the United States and its Western allies. With no end to terrorism in sight, what else are we left to do, but prop up regimes that promise to keep the oil flowing while killing off any that would threaten Western domination? There appears to be no way out of this circle. Stability is falsely promised while chaos is maintained.

THE CONSTANT GARDENER

The Constant Gardener is another film set in the present featuring a Behemoth-type conspiracy being carried out in a place characterized as being in chaos. Instead of American interests and oil companies attempting to influence worldwide oil markets, British drug companies are using impoverished African civilians as guinea pigs in testing newly developed, but as yet unproven, drugs.

The film opens with Justin Quayle (Ralph Fiennes), a lower-level British diplomat assigned to an African country, finding out that his wife Tessa (Rachel Weisz) has died, and in fact been killed, while on a medical missionary journey alone with her black driver. The film flashes back to his first meeting with his wife, as he is giving a diplomatic speech in London on the positive aspects of diplomacy and the rule of law: "Diplomacy as we've demonstrated is the very map and marker of civilization, pointing nations to the safest way through country fraught with peril."

Tessa verbally attacks Justin after his speech, questioning why the United Kingdom (UK) would follow the United States' lead and become part of a war with Iraq over oil. Very soon, they are in bed together, and will ultimately marry. We later discover that her concern is not over "blood for oil" as in *Syriana*, but over the illegitimate testing of unproven drugs on impoverished populations.

Discovering that he is to be posted to Africa, Tessa begs to go along even though they hardly know each other. They quickly marry, and Justin only gradually learns the many secrets that Tessa harbors. Justin seems much more committed to his plants (a constant gardener) than to other human beings, but Tessa has a true compassion for humanity. In the film's first shot in Africa we see a place that is overpopulated, dilapidated, and extremely impoverished. Tessa, now pregnant, attends an outdoor play put on to spread the message against AIDS. Children seem to love her, and offer her a homemade gift, one that can be hung above the baby's crib. Poverty, contaminated water, and lack of medicine to deal with AIDS are repeated themes. We quickly come to see that Justin represents law and order and gradual reform while Tessa represents the revolutionary, out to expose the evils of first-world capitalist societies on the third world.

Tessa and Justin go to a party where British representatives of drug companies meet with Kenyan public health officials. Tessa immediately starts criticizing both the drug company representatives and the public health minister (Bernard Otieno Oduor), for failing to get AIDS medication that has already been paid for actually to the people who need it. She insinuates that the minister is selling the medication himself for personal gain. This reflects poorly on both Justin's ability to manage his wife, and his competence as a state diplomatic official.

While on a medical mission in the community, now one week from giving birth, Tessa become suspicious when she sees villagers being tested for both AIDS and tuberculosis for free. She suspects that the drug companies are up to something. In the very next scene. Tessa is in a hospital bed, suckling an infant. We find out that her own fetus has died, and she is suckling the child of the woman in the bed next to her, a fifteen-year-old girl who is dying. She tells Sandy (Danny Houston), the British diplomatic official who seems much taken by her, that she is going to reveal to him that the girl is being murdered, and that he must do something to stop this type of action. He reluctantly promises to do so. Instead Sandy informs Justin that his wife is quite mad and needs to be moved to a better hospital. The young mother in the bed next door does indeed die, and we find out she has been given something by the doctor that may have killed her.

Justin thinks he overhears Tessa telling her friend that hers is a marriage of convenience that will only produce dead offspring. Meanwhile, Justin continues to tend to his plants. Later we find out that Tessa was actually referring not to her own relationship, but to the marriage between the drug producing company and the drug testing company, which together were manufacturing and testing a drug, that has killed a number of infants.

Tessa talks to online activists who convince her that the drug companies test their drugs illegitimately on impoverished populations. She, as the initial discoverer of the deadly conspiracy, aspires to prove that this is true. Tessa gives Sandy a report on what the drug companies are doing, which Sandy promises to send on to government officials in London. However, when Tessa questions Sandy about what response he has gotten, he admits that he has been told to watch her and monitor everything she is doing. He begs her to stop her investigations.

By mid-film, the flashbacks are over and we are into the legal investigation of Tessa's death. The news media informs Justin that her body and that of her companion were locked inside a car and had been mutilated. The film gradually reveals why Tessa was murdered as Justin is forced to give up his docile persona and become a man of action to solve the mystery.

The police confiscate all of Tessa's computers and papers. Justin finds a few remaining items hidden in a box in the closet. There he finds that she has been investigating Dypraxin, a drug created by the fictional company KDH Pharmaceuticals. It is being tested on poor Kenyans by another fictional company, ThreeBees, in exchange for free medical treatment. It is intended to treat tuberculosis, and was created in anticipation of a future TB epidemic.

As Justin continues to investigate his wife's death on his own, he discovers the conspiracy involving the drug companies, local police, British diplomatic officials, leading British politicians, and the British equivalent of the CIA. Ultimately Justin himself becomes the target, and his diplomatic passport is taken away, forcing him to go undercover to find out the truth. The drug company is ultimately preparing for a major tuberculosis epidemic that could kill off one third of the human population. If their new drug is successful, it will be worth billions.

Justin goes to Germany to meet with one of Tessa's Internet associates. This associate informs him that the Kenyan government has been bribed to allow the drug testing. The company intends to hide the results of the secret drug tests, even if side effects are discovered, so that they can get the drug to market more quickly. As diplomatic official Sandy tells Justin, he should simply forget what he has found out, ultimately justifying the conspiracy by employing a denial of victim neutralization technique: "We're not killing people who wouldn't be dead otherwise."

In the final segment, Justin goes to the Sudan (Darfur) to find Dr. Lorbeer (Peter Postlethwaite), the creator of the drug to tell him about the conspiracy, only to find out that the doctor is involved in it as well. The film offers no positive resolution, as what Justin discovers is never revealed to the public. Thus, the medical and political chaos of the underdeveloped world allows the Behemoth policies of the drug companies and their political allies to triumph. Rather than facing the legal issues related to new drug testing and patient consent that are firmly in place in most Western democracies, the drug companies seek out chaotic global locations to get around these rules, killing patients in the process without any repercussions.

BATTLE IN SEATTLE

The next film to be discussed, *Battle in Seattle*, directly confronts globalization and its Behemoth representative, the World Trade Organization (WTO), head on. The film's prologue begins with a historical discussion of the creation of the General Agreement on Trades and Tariffs (GATT) and the WTO after World War II to create stability and a sense of global community, but almost immediately the overview turns negative. The World Trade Organization is described not only as a single global economic community made up of 150 nations controlling 90 percent of all world trade, but as "a system of global governance that none of us voted for and none of us control." According to director Stuart Townsend's view, the organization allows human rights and the environment to be subordinated to the needs of global corporations. One of the few opportunities ordinary citizens had to comment on WTO policies, was by showing up as protesters at the economic summit meetings regularly held by the organization. This 2007 docudrama film claims to be based upon facts of what happened at the Seattle Summit in 1999, pitting the Behemoth structure of the organization, backed by leading American political officials and intelligence agents and muscled by the coopted, military outfitted local police against a group of unarmed protesters, themselves struggling to put up an organized resistance.

In the film's opening scene protesters dressed like terrorists risk life and limb on a giant crane in order to unfurl a banner proclaiming their opposition to the WTO meetings and their support for democracy. In the film's final framing scene, we see that the banner is still in place and has not been taken down by the police or political officials despite the horrific battle that ensues during the film.

The first thing the assembled protesters do is meet to discuss how they have a fantastic group of lawyers to support what they're doing, and get them out of any trouble in case they happen to be arrested. The protesters stress that their efforts will be nonviolent and any actions they take will be done on the basis of consensus. They intend to follow the rule of law.

Certainly the protesters are not the bringers of chaos. In fact, throughout the film, they are depicted as orderly and methodical. Their six months of preparations include detailed maps of where they will set up their blockades around the convention site.

Meanwhile, the police go over the who's who of protesters (mostly citing their environmental protest efforts which have branded them as eco-terrorists), treating them as if they are major criminals. In comparison to the protesters' extensive planning, the Seattle Police Department discusses controlling only a small area where they will set up barricades to keep the protesters back. Individual police officers worry about chemical or biological attacks by the protesters, assuming them to be like terrorists, but in the end it is the police that use teargas against the protesters.

As the action part of the movie begins, the protesters methodically block all entrances to the conference setting by interlocking their arms together in a show of unity; the only way the police can dissuade them is by "breaking their arms." It appears that the police are not ready for any activities that take place outside their own barricade. To combat the organization of the protesters the police will need to resort to creating chaos.

Although the night before the protests began the mayor (Ray Liotta) had promised the protesters that he would not gas them or act violently against them, as soon as he is told that all the intersections have been barricaded, he is informed by federal political officials that he may have no other options but to respond aggressively.

Although the protesters have blocked access to the conference, the approved protest parade (actual archive footage) they carry out makes them appear harmless (Moore 2008). College students dressed in colorful outfits with balloons, butterfly wings, and such—all reminiscent of the hippie and yippee movements of the 1960s—predominate. For the first day the protesters are able to shut down the initial ceremonies and pride themselves on carrying out the first successful Internet protest in history, as apparently they had flash mobbed the event.

Unfortunately, a fringe group of the protesters who consider themselves anarchists break from the organized peaceful main group and start to destroy shop windows downtown. Protest leaders attempt to stop the window smashers, but aren't able to do so. The media immediately appears on the scene, and heads straight for the mayhem, sending out media reports that chaos has broken out in the city. The media records the protest leader's political message about corporate executives raping the world, but simply erases the recording rather than putting it on the news. The corporate news media is not going to look kindly on the protesters.

The police can be held back no longer. The riot squad comes attired in garb looking like a cross between the Teenage Mutant Ninja Turtles and Robocop. They march on the street beating their long sticks in unison, anxious to take on the protesters. When faced with the ultimatum of dispersing or being gassed, the protesters hold their ground and continue to play and dance. The protesters are first gassed and then beaten and arrested.

To demonstrate the collateral damage to ordinary citizens of the forced enforcement of such economic policies, Ella (Charlize Theron), pregnant wife of one of the riot police officers, Dale (Woody Harrelson), gets caught up in the crowd by mistake, and is hit in the stomach by a police officer with a baton, ultimately terminating her pregnancy. When the police officer visits his wife at the hospital he looms over her in his black Robocop uniform, his bald head showing clearly his protruding veins in a scene reminiscent of the original German version of Nosferatu the vampire, who has brought pestilence to the nation. His wife pushes him away in revulsion when he tries to console her over the loss of their child.

As the film progresses, it becomes evident over and over again that law enforcement, in the guise of restoring law and order, only brings chaos, violence, and death. Meanwhile, (in a scene that could easily have appeared in *The Constant Gardener*) at the conference itself a speaker a from Doctors Without Borders (Rade Serbedzija) pleads for the WTO to fund public health initiatives, including AIDS-related drugs for Africa and other third-world areas, but conference participants simply walk out on his talk and ignore him. In another scene, conference organizers, in order to stop an African coalition at the conference from forming a subgroup against the overall goals of the meeting, remove their interpreters, thus forcing the group back into a Babel-like status. The organization thus creates chaos and then uses it to its own advantage.

By day two the police are ordered to arrest anyone who will not disburse. Officers go through the crowd spraying them at point-blank range with tear gas, as though they were exterminating bugs. Despite the chaos brought by the police, the protesters remain as calm as they can, helping each other to wash the teargas from their eyes, and in no way taking on the police. In one particularly pointed scene police officer Dale chases the protest leader (Martin Henderson), and even when he enters a church, traditionally a sanctuary from state authority, the police officer chases him out and beats him senseless outside the church.

The rule of law is ultimately jettisoned. All of the protest group's lawyers are arrested as part of the protest, leaving the group without anyone to get them out of jail. Once arrested, the protesters are not allowed access to counsel, to make phone calls, or given medical attention. When they are finally freed from jail, and an alliance is formed with the self-expelled third-world conference members, the film celebrates its only victory for the downtrodden. The other major victory by the protesters is that they are able to convince a reporter (Connie Nielson) to shift her allegiance from her corporate backers to empathetically covering the point of view of the protesters. However, in the process she loses her job.

During the film's credits, the writer Stuart Townsend, presents what happened after Seattle, focusing mostly on the WTO's failed promises to better respect third-world trade partners and to provide medicines to poorer countries. The struggle of the people continues against the Behemoth world disorder.

CONCLUSION

In the films discussed here we see the origin of a perspective that continues to be used by Hollywood to discuss U.S. foreign policy and globalization themes. As with other strands of Gothic Criminology, combining elements of historical, theological thought (Jewish apocryphal literature), social science (Neumann's analysis of the use of chaos as a justifying control technique), along with recognition of certain film styles and techniques, assists in developing a heuristic model useful in explaining the predominant ethos of this set of films. As the Behemoth only has use for law only when the imposition of that law is in the best interest of the monster, it can be quickly jettisoned for the use of force or violence whenever necessary. These films point out our inability to cope with "liquid global fears," described by Bauman (2006) as the "the highly selective globalization of trade and capital, surveillance and information, coercion and weapons, crime, and terrorism, all now disdaining territorial sovereignty and respecting no state boundary." As Hollywood has now turned to making a series of partly fictionalized, partly factual films about the U.S. invasions of Iraq and Afghanistan (e.g., *The Hurt Locker* [2008], *Jar Head* [2005], *Generation Kill* [2008], *Green Zone* [2010], *Brothers* [2009], *American Sniper* [2014]), other variations of the Behemoth perspective will in all likelihood continue to emerge.

REFERENCES

Abberley, Jeff (producer) and Fernando Mierelles (director). 2005. *The Constant Gardener* [Motion Picture]. USA: Focus Features.

Aloe, Mary (producer) and Stuart Townsend (director). 2007. *Battle in Seattle* [Motion Picture]. USA: Metropolitan Films.

Arendt, Hannah. 1963. *Eichmann in Jerusalem: A Report on the Banality of Evil.* New York: Viking Press.

Bauman, Zygmunt. 2006. *Liquid Fear.* Boston: Polity Press.

BBC News. 2012. "Viktor Bout: Profile." BBC News Online. April 5. Accessed June 1, 2015 at: www.bbc.com/news/world-europe-11036569.

Bhagwati, Jagdish. 2004. *In Defense of Globalization*. Oxford: Oxford University Press.

Bird, Brad (producer and director). 2015. *Tomorrowland* [Motion Picture]. USA: Walt Disney Pictures.

Borde, Raymond and Etienne Chaumeton. 2002. *A Panorama of American Film Noir (1941–1953).* New York: City Light Books.
Britto, Farah and Cecil Greek. 2016. "A Depiction of Evil, Order and Chaos: The Symbiotic Relationship of Law and the Supernatural in Film and Television." In this volume.
Cage, Nicholas (producer) and Andrew Niccol (director). 2005. *Lord of War* [Motion Picture]. USA: Lions Gate Films.
Clooney, George (producer) and Stephen Gaghan (director). 2005. *Syriana* [Motion Picture]. USA: Warner Brothers.
Chomsky, Noam. 2004. *Hegemony or Survival: America's Quest for Global Dominance.* New York: Holt Paperbacks.
Chossudovsky, Michel. 2003. *The Globalization of Poverty and the New World Order.* Shanty Bay, Ontario: Global Outlook.
Coen, Ethan and Joel Coen (producers and directors). 2009. *A Serious Man* [Motion Picture]. USA: Focus Features.
Conrad, Peter and Joseph Schneider. 1992. *Deviance and Medicalization: from Badness to Sickness.* Philadelphia, PA: Temple University Press.
Crane, Diana and Nobuko Kawashima. 2002. *Global Culture: Media, Arts, Policy, and Globalization.* New York: Routledge.
Currie, Elliot. 1998. *Crime and Punishment in America.* New York: Holt Paperbacks.
Curtis, Adam (producer and director). 2004. *The Power of Nightmares: the Rise of the Politics of Fear* [Television Documentary]. London: British Broadcasting Company (BBC).
Dennis, G. W. 2007. *The Encyclopedia of Jewish Myth, Magic and Mysticism.* Woodbury, MN: Llewellyn Worldwide.
Denzin, Norman. 1991. *Images of Postmodern Society: Social Theory and Contemporary Cinema.* Newberry Park, CA: Sage Publications.
Ferrell, Jeff and Keith Hayward. 2008. *Cultural Criminology: An Invitation.* Newberry Park, CA: Sage Publications.
Friedman, Thomas. 2007. *The World Is Flat 3.0: A Brief History of the 21st Century.* New York: Picador.
Greek, Cecil. 1992. *The Religious Roots of American Sociology.* New York: Garland Publishing, Inc.
———. 2007. "The Big City Rogue Cop as Monster." In *Monsters In and Among Us: Toward a Gothic Criminology*, edited by Caroline Joan "Kay" S. Picart and Cecil Greek, 164–98. Plainsboro, NJ: Associated University Presses.
Gwozdziec Synagogue Painting Blog. Accessed February 14, 2015 at: gwozdziec.tumblr.com/page/5.
Hagan, John and W. Rymond-Richmond. 2009. *Darfur and the Crime of Genocide.* New York: Cambridge University Press.
Hirsch, Foster. 2001. *The Dark Side of the Screen: Film Noir.* New York: DaCapo Press.
Hobbes, Thomas. 1990. *Behemoth or the Long Parliament.* Chicago: University of Chicago Press.
Hubka, Thomas. 2002. "Medieval Themes in the Wall Paintings of 17th and 18th Century Polish Wooden Synagogues." In *Imagining the Self, Imagining the Other,* edited by Eva Fromjmovic, 200–19. Boston: Brill.

Jacobsen, Michael Hviid and Keith Tester (eds.). 2012. *Utopia: Social Theory and the Future*. Surrey: Ashgate Publishing Ltd.
Jacoby, Russell. 2005. *Picture Imperfect: Utopian Thought for an Anti-Utopian Age*. New York: Columbia University Press.
Kershaw, Ian. 1999. *Hitler, 1889–36: Hubris*. New York: W. W. Norton.
———. 2000. *Hitler, 1936–45: Nemesis*. New York: W. W. Norton.
Leavy, Patricia. 2009. *Method Meets Art: Arts-Based Research Practice*. New York: The Guilford Press.
Levenson, John D. 1988. *Creation and the Persistence of Evil: The Jewish Drama of Divine Omnipotence*. New Haven, CT: Princeton University Press.
Longerich, Peter. 2015. *Goebbels: A Biography*. New York: Random House.
Lyman, Stanford. 1990. "Rereading Robert E. Park: Toward a Gothic Perspective on Capitalism and Imperialism." *Explorations: The Age of Enlightenment* (Volume IV), edited by M. W. duQuesnay, 29–108. Lafayette, LA: University of Southwestern Louisiana Foundation.
———. 1992. *Militarism, Imperialism, and Racial Accommodation: An Analysis and Interpretation of the Early Writings of Robert E. Park*. Fayetteville, AR: University of Arkansas Press.
———. 1995. "Social Theory and Social Movements: Sociology as Sociodicy." In *Social Movements: Critiques, Concepts, Case-Studies*, edited by Stanford Lyman, 397–435. New York: New York University Press.
———. 2001. *Roads to Dystopia: Sociological Essays on the Postmodern Condition*. Fayetteville: University of Arkansas Press.
MacLean, Bethany and Joe Nocera. 2011. *All the Devils Are Here: The Hidden History of the Financial Crisis*. New York: Portfolio.
Maier-Katkin, Dan, Daniel Mears and Thomas Bernard. 2009. "Towards a Criminology of Crimes against Humanity." *Theoretical Criminology* 13(2): 277–55.
Malcolm, Noel (ed.). 1994. *Thomas Hobbes: The Correspondence*. Vol. 2 1660–1679. Oxford: Clarendon Press.
Martinson, Robert. 1974. "What Works?— Questions and Answers about Prison Reform." *The Public Interest* 35(Spring): 22–54.
Mathewson, Dan. 2008. "Between Testimony and Interpretation: The Book of Job in Post-Holocaust, Jewish Theological Reflection." *Studies in the Literary Imagination* 41(2): 17–39.
Matza, David. 1990. *Delinquency and Drift*. St. Louis: Transaction Publishers.
Menniger, Karl. 1973. *Whatever Became of Sin?* Portland: Hawthorn Books.
Moore, Roger. 2008. "Review of *Battle in Seattle*." *Orlando Sentinel*. October 15. Accessed June 1, 2015 at: www.orlandosentinel.com/entertainment/movies/orl-movie-review-battle-in-seattle-story.html.
Morley, Robert. 2007. "The Con That Turned the World against America." *theTRUMPET.com*. Accessed June 10, 2009 from www.thetrumpet.com/index.php?q=4288.2525.0.0.
Naim, Moses. 2010. *Illicit: How Smugglers, Traffickers and Copycats are Hijacking the Global Economy*. New York: Random House.
Neumann, Franz. 1963. *Behemoth: The Structure and Practice of National Socialism, 1933–1944*. New York: Octagon Books, Inc.
Philips, William. 2001. *Film: An Introduction*. New York: St. Martin's Press.

Picart, Caroline Joan (Kay) S. 2014. "Media Myths Regarding Serial Killers: A Gothic Criminology." In *The Poetics of Crime: Understanding and Researching Crime and Deviance through Creative Sources*, edited by Michael Hviid Jacobsen, 173–92. Burlington, VT: Ashgate.

Picart, Caroline Joan (Kay) S. and Cecil Greek. 2003. "The Compulsions of Serial Killers as Vampires: Toward a Gothic Criminology." *Journal of Criminal Justice and Popular Culture* 10(1): 39–68.

———. (eds.). 2007a. *Monsters In and Among Us: Toward a Gothic Criminology*. Plainsboro, NJ: Associated University Presses.

———. 2007b. "The Terrorist as a Gothic Criminological Case Study." In *Monsters In and Among Us: Toward a Gothic Criminology*, edited by Caroline Joan "Kay" S. Picart and Cecil Greek, 256–88. Plainsboro, NJ: Associated University Presses.

———. 2007c. "Introduction to Gothic Criminology." In *Monsters In and Among Us: Toward a Gothic Criminology*, edited by Caroline Joan "Kay" S. Picart and Cecil Greek, 11–42. Plainsboro, NJ: Associated University Presses.

Podobnik, Bruce and Thomas Reifer (eds.). 2005 *Transforming Globalization: Challenges and Opportunities in the Post 9/11 Era*. Boston: Brill Academic Press.

Rabiger, Michael. 2003. *Directing: Film Techniques and Aesthetics*, 3rd edition. New York: Focal Press.

Rafter, Nicole. 2000. *Shots in the Mirror: Crime Films and Society*. New York: Oxford Press.

———. 2006. *Shots in the Mirror: Crime Films and Society*, 2nd edition. New York: Oxford University Press.

Rees, Laurence (producer and director). 1997. *The Nazis: A Warning from History*. [DVD]. London: BBC.

Sachs, Jeffrey. 2005. *The End of Poverty*. New York: The Penguin Press.

Sullivan, Martin. 2013. "If Ireland Is Not a Tax Haven, What Is It?" *Forbes Magazine*. Nov. 6. Accessed on June 1, 2015 at www.forbes.com/sites/taxanalysts/2013/11/06/if-ireland-is-not-a-tax-haven-what-is-it/.

Teggart, Frederick. 1916. *Prolegomena to History: The Relation of History to Literature, Philosophy, and Science*. Berkeley, CA: University of California Press.

Torrey, Charles C. 1947. "The Messiah Son of Ephraim." *Journal of Biblical Literature* 66(3): 253–77.

Wallace, Howard. 1948. "Leviathan and the Beast in Revelation." *The Biblical Archaeologist* 11(3): 61–68.

Whitney, K. William. 2006. *Leviathan and Behemoth in Second Temple and Early Rabbinic Judaism*. Winona Lake, IN: Eisenbrauns.

13

A Depiction of Evil, Order, and Chaos

The Symbiotic Relationship of Law and the Supernatural in Film and Television

Farah Britto and Cecil Greek

Diametrically opposed issues such as good versus evil or order versus chaos pervade the worlds created by horror genre tales, whether in film or serialized television offerings. But there appear to be differences in the ways film and television take on these issues. Similarly, Stanley (2014) posited that dystopian worlds are constructed differently in television dramas versus films:

> Television shows posit a hideous future with a silver lining; good or bad, are more or less equals. Movies like *Divergent*, *Snowpiercer* and *Elysium* foresee societal divisions that last into Armageddon and beyond that define a new, inevitably Orwellian world that emerges from the ruin of civilization. (Stanley 2014, C1)

The divide described here between media platform and the visual construction of dystopian societies may also appear in other facets of the social world as depicted in television versus film fiction. The popularity of the horror genre in film and its growing presence on television networks provides a new area of research, particularly in the context of popular representations of law and the legal system. Law, as a feature of the human social world, is seen as incongruous to the supernatural realm from which evil often emanates. The approach to religious content, framed through the supernatural context in television and film, will be examined here first through an anthropological lens, and then through a criminological one. This approach, described below, allows a deep examination of visual media, employing new theoretical perspectives that are rarely applied to media studies.

The anthropology of religion has been a major subfield in anthropology since its colonialist beginnings. Following the phenomenologically rooted perspective of Lambek, "religious worlds are real, vivid, and significant to those who construct and inhabit them" (2008, 4–5). Further, when analyzing films and TV shows that portray religious activity and dogma, the position employed here supports that these expressions of religion are "symbolic construction[s] of the world" rather than functionalist constructions responding to societal needs (Lambek 2008, 8). Given the visual and storytelling nature of both film and television, it is appropriate to approach the study of religion in this way (i.e., as symbolic constructs), since film and television allow writers, directors, and producers to construct worlds and fill those worlds with meaning. However, while film and television formats are themselves human constructions of the world as we understand it, these products can also be interpreted as responses to the human condition embedded in the mysteries of the universe, and beyond the sense described by Lambek (2008). The themes and discourse present in fictionalized media can be responding to or critiquing the social construction of religion, namely traditional religious practice and belief. In other words, these films can critique, describe, and assert beliefs about specific elements that are considered religious, including the supernatural, by defining their relationship to elements of the human world, such as law, expressed as part of the criminological order of human societies.

Religion as a social system component is only one way it is depicted in horror fiction. All themes that might be considered as having a religious subtext, including the supernatural, which at its roots requires a belief in the possibility of an afterlife or otherworldly realm of existence, are also considered. Thus, when referring to religion or religious elements, these include not only references to religious institutions and religious practice, but also to all manner of supernatural appearances such as the Judeo-Christian God, ghosts, demons, possessions, and miraculous occurrences. A related aspect of these depictions are the religious dichotomies expressed as sacred versus profane or good versus evil, sometimes pitted as God versus the Devil (Durkheim 1915; Douglas 1966; Russell 1987; 1990). As such, although some themes may relate directly to codified, recognized religions, such as Christianity or Judaism, themes in the referenced media depictions relating to evil or the supernatural are nonetheless considered to be religious subtexts. For the sake of clarity, these themes/subjects/ideas are denoted here as "religious/supernatural."

Moving from the anthropological to the criminological, what roles do popular representations of law and justice play in the recurring depictions of the supernatural realm featured in visual horror fiction, and is there a difference between feature films and television serials in this regard? Mirroring the dichotomy of good versus evil, the dichotomy of order versus chaos is a major component of the horror genre, and becomes a primary framework from which law enters into the discussion. A predominant perspective is that law produces, as one of its major positive effects, order. Thus, the enforcement of the law is the backbone of a system in which chaos is kept at bay. According to the Classical School of criminology, the law instills a sense of fear in individuals who might be contemplating harming others—whether by stealing, injuring, or murdering—through a set of laws and punishments commensurate to those crimes (Vold, Bernard, and Snipes 1998). Without law and law enforcement, chaos and fear might ensue, as there is no system for moral regulation to protect humans from one another. The dichotomies of order versus chaos and good versus evil are tightly bound, therefore also closely linking law and religion/the supernatural. While good versus evil is a question of moral behavior and norms, order or chaos may result from the ability for humans to choose between good over evil behaviors. Typically, law and law enforcement act as purveyors of what society considers "the good," punishing evil deeds and evil people, condoning good actions and protecting good people. Of course, in the real world, there may be exceptions, such as law enforcement agents who go beyond the law to produce a semblance of order (Greek 2007) or themselves induce chaos to justify overly violent control responses (Greek 2016).

In combining religious/supernatural and criminological/legal themes within the horror genre, patterns begin to emerge that can be discussed through the application of several theoretical perspectives, including Gothic Criminology, monster theory, and dystopia theory. All three of these theories prove useful in analyzing the films and television episodes discussed here. Within these theoretical frameworks, the following research questions can be addressed: (1) Is there a difference in the way religion/the supernatural is portrayed between the television and film formats? (2) If so, what distinguishes the messages present in film versus television programing? (3) What are the identifiable patterns and themes of horror films that utilize the religious/supernatural as a subject? And (4) Does law play a role in these discussions, or does the depicted supernatural realm exist outside an ordered universe governable by law?

THE DATA AND ITS ANALYSIS

The data for this research include six films and eight episodes of two television series. All data are from the horror genre, and were released between 2011 and 2014. The films include: *The Awakening* (2011), directed by Nick Murphy; *Sinister* (2012), directed by Scott Derrickson; *The Possession* (2012), directed by Ole Bornedal; *The Conjuring* (2013), directed by James Wan; *Oculus* (2013), directed by Mike Flanagan; and *Deliver Us from Evil* (2014), directed by Scott Derrickson. The two television series included are *The Walking Dead* (season 2, October 16, 2011–March 18, 2012) and *American Horror Story: Asylum* (season 2, October 17, 2012–January 23, 2013). While both series were viewed in their entirety for content and context, four episodes in each series were screened critically for further analysis. For *The Walking Dead*, episodes 2, 4, 7, and 8 served as primary data, and for *American Horror Story*, episodes 1, 2, 6, and 10 served as primary data. All specific episodes were randomly selected, but the two series themselves were selected because they fit the horror-themed visual fiction category, started broadcast in the same approximate time frame, and featured ongoing plot lines rather than separate episodes that concluded weekly. These elements are an important point of discussion, as they distinguish themselves from other television series and were therefore chosen purposefully for analysis. Unlike television series that are only a few years older, the sample selected are among a new trend of television programing structures that are more cinematic in nature: they are not contained episodes with clear closure, a departure from the work brought forth by Mezey and Niles in their chapter *Screening the Law: Ideology and Law in American Popular Culture*, in which television series comprise a predictable, containable structure where viewers do not necessarily need to tune in weekly to follow the plot of the show. In addition, the programs fit squarely within the realm of the horror genre, another unique trend that is not often seen on traditional network television due to the nature of the genre's adult content (which is why the series analyzed here are found on cable networks). Finally, the look of these series, and the technology used to create these programs, aim for a cinematic look (with the use of artistic shots, DSLR cameras, and slower frame rates that mirror film visually).

To be more specific, the selected films and television episodes were not chosen based on any overtly religious themes (although the titles of some like *The Possession* and *The Conjuring* certainly suggest that religious elements may be present in them). Nevertheless, it is clear that there are subgenres (serial killers, slasher/gore, etc.) within the horror category that would have allowed for a broader sample of monster-themed visual fiction. For this project, films and television episodes were chosen based on stories situated within the realm of the paranormal (a very prominent subcategory) as opposed to serial killer films, for example. Within this limitation, the six "most popular" horror films between 2011 and 2014 were selected, based on Web sites that rate film popularity (Rotten Tomatoes, Internet Movie Database [IMDb], and Google). Due to the sheer popularity of *American Horror Story* and *The Walking Dead*, which are two series that first premiered at about the same time (2011 and 2010 respectively) and both prominently bear the horror genre distinction on IMDb, these television series were chosen for review (Hibberd 2013; Venable 2015). The horror genre distinction is an important aspect of these shows, as other television series (such as *Supernatural*, *Dominion*, etc.) may include monsters and even religious themes, but they can be more typically characterized, in our view, adopting and modifying Picart's (2004) description, as "hybrid genres," combining drama, action, and fantasy with horror motifs, though Picart is talking about hybrid films with a Frankensteinian motif, not television series. While this research does not claim that the chosen series under study are indicative of a "purely" horror genre, these series, taken at face value, are self-proclaiming horror stories, with zombies, a classic symbol of the horror genre, as the central characters of *The Walking Dead*, and *American Horror Story* making explicit claims in the series title for what the programing aims to be. As mentioned above, the modern storytelling format that has become popularized on cable networks, where each episode of the series does not bear the traditional television format in which each episode comes to a conclusive end, is another important point of distinction that bears repeating. In these series (and other series on cable channels like FX and AMC, such as *Breaking Bad*, *Sons of Anarchy*, and *Justified*, all of which have a large viewing audience and critical acclaim), the episodes feature ongoing storylines that mimic the deep characterization and plot development seen in filmmaking. Given the expansion of delayed viewing made possible through DVRs, DVDs, and Web-based on-demand services, television producers recognized the need for more sophisticated fare and plots geared to long-term "fan" viewers (Tyron 2008, 310). This format is more similar to film, so that differences in the story and messages cannot simply be attributed to structural differences that have traditionally existed between film and television programing. It could be argued that this modern television structure, in which stories are developed over months and even years, allows for even more in-depth storytelling than films. By using television series that mimic film in several ways, an analysis of television versus film precludes major structural differences that would normally stand to explain differences in each medium's message and story.

The selection of only new productions, specifically those premiered between 2011 and 2014, was made in order to understand the application of religious/supernatural and criminological/legal themes in the horror genre in their most recent iteration. Earlier research has historically documented the horror genre (Brophy 1986; Dixon 2010; Freeland 1996). While this study discusses the most recent examples in popular horror film and television, these results could be employed for future comparative research.

Discourse and narrative analyses were used to analyze the data. All sample films and episodes were screened and critically evaluated multiple times. A Foucauldian discourse analysis was applied inductively, in which prominent themes and discourses were drawn from screening the films and episodes. According to Moore, such discourse analysis:

> identifies how discourses construct ideas about ourselves and the world in which we live, but also how they instruct us to "participate in social life" and "furnish us with subject positions." In other words, from a Foucauldian perspective, discourses inform things like social roles and interaction by sketching out a social order and our place within it. Put differently, discourses help keep us in our place. For those who follow the Foucauldian approach to discourse analysis, this method is a critical tool for revealing both the constraining and socially constructed nature of discourse. It is customarily a tool in a broader project aimed at social critique. (2014, 198–99)

While Foucault focused on how religion, politics, and social mores together formed predominant discourses in real societies, we are interested in how film and television can both posit alternative fictional realities by employing their own discourses.

Narrative analysis was utilized to construct each film's or episode's structure and overall message. Based upon Moore (2014, 181–82), a holistic-form and holistic-content approach to narrative analysis that focused on the film or episode as a whole product or message, as opposed to the categorical approach that focused on individual characteristics and themes, was utilized. The combination of Foucauldian discourse analysis and holistic-form and holistic-content narrative analysis provides a comparison of the overall stories and visual content among the sampled films and programs, while also focusing in on the messages present in each film that might lead to overall trends in the horror genre dealing with religious/supernatural themes and their intersection with law. As Blumer (1954, 7) in Moore (2014, 198) suggests, when employing such qualitative methodologies, the chosen theoretical frameworks (in this case Gothic Criminology, monster theory, and dystopia theory) can be drawn upon as "sensitizing concepts" to construct categories for analysis.

GOTHIC ELEMENTS IN HORROR FILM AND TELEVISION

Gothic Criminology, as a theory, has proven useful in its application to the religiously inspired terror genre (Picart and Greek 2007b). More broadly, Gothic Criminology includes two critical elements for these discussions: the portrayal of the perpetrators as monsters and the criminal justice system/legal response to monstrous evil, whether that evil is generated by ordinary humans or supernatural entities. We will turn to these themes shortly.

First we address the issue of how the viewer knows that they have left the everyday, mundane world and entered into a Gothic realm. Gothic visual representations have become a staple, if not a cliché element of the horror genre (Picart and Greek 2007a, 16). According to its literary tradition, the Gothic has been represented by a number of place-specific tropes (and their accompanying sounds, smells, and mood setting elements), where evil may either be lurking or more easily accommodated:

> The graveyard and the convent, the moats and the drawbridges, dungeons, towers, mysterious trap doors and corridors, rusty hinges, flickering candles, burial vaults, birthmarks, tolling bells, hidden manuscripts, twilight, ancestral curses. . . . Gothic scenes are heavily populated with images of decay, decadence, disease and death: crumbling architectural remains, rotting old houses, ancient relics, and even decrepit, senile people are always quintessential. (Picart and Greek 2007a, 16–18)

Thus, the depictions of the Gothic in film follow their literary counterparts as words have been transformed into moving images:

> Through the use of both visual and sound techniques, film became an effective vehicle for re-envisaging Gothic stories. Over time, a set of stock techniques for lighting, camera locations, depth of field and angles, set design, music and sound, special effects, and editing were developed. (Picart and Greek 2007a, 20–21)

Building upon the visual and sonic mood-inducing techniques, Gothic Criminology allows an avenue for expressing and discussing what evil is socially, as "it potentially provides both a vocabulary and a set of theories that analyze how 'evil' becomes what it is representationally" (Picart and Greek 2007a, 14). Gothic Criminology can thus be used to discuss how evil is represented in religious/supernatural ways in horror film, as seen in the following types of examples: "body-snatching, claustrophobia, the devil, imprisonment, exorcism, the grotesque, the Inquisition, masochism and sadism, necromancy, possession, the pursued protagonist, pursuit of heroines, revenge, reason, somnambulism, superstition, transformation/metamorphosis, and witches and witchcraft" (Picart and Greek 2007a, 24). A number of these themes appear in our sample, showing expressions and representations of evil inhabiting the contemporary world. A number of these examples, particularly those that come from the Hollywood films, locate evil as of supernatural origin, and sometimes directly impacting on the natural world. Thus, these representations of deviance are portrayed not in terms of sicknesses inside individuals as the social sciences might (Conrad and Schneider 1992), but in terms of religious/supernatural expressions that may exonerate an individual from blame ("the Devil made me do it" or "the Devil did it").

Filmic examples that reveal Gothic visualization and mood abound within the samples used here. Films like *Deliver Us from Evil* immediately bring the viewer to a dark place, and the majority of the film takes place at night, following a police officer who routinely works the night shift, which is also when, at least in popular imagination, the strangest and most horrific acts of evil take place (Katz 1980). Rain and cloudiness are also indications of Gothic visualization. In films like *The Possession*, *Sinister*, and *The Awakening*, the sun is almost never directly evident, and instead the atmosphere appears grey and muted. These films utilize the use of blue tones to set the scene, which is in fact a natural lighting technique that also gives off an ominous, high contrast effect. Further, in *The Awakening*, the blue tones that are associated with natural light are brought inside, and used to light the space rather than red/orange light that is most associated with artificial light, indoor light, and an altogether lighter mood in filmmaking.

The two television serials both feature Gothic visual elements as well as camera and lighting techniques. Season 2 of *American Horror Story* takes place at an insane asylum overseen by the Catholic Church, so that the scenery is both asylum and convent at once, visually portraying what can be distinguished as overlapping Gothic locations. In *The Walking Dead*, both characters (the zombies) and the setting provide visuals of death and decay, again showing Gothic tropes while also portraying a dystopian future in which the last remaining humans must fight to survive.

All the films reviewed here follow standard Gothic visualization, in which much of the film is set in darkness, lit by either stark artificial light, or completely in blue tones. While blue tones suggest natural lighting, the instances in which blue tone is used gives an air of artificiality, as there is also high contrast, making the visualization dim and unearthly. Images from *The Awakening* and *Deliver Us from Evil* show the same use of blue tones and high contrast, revealing the eeriness of the scenes that align with Gothic depictions. Further, the use of shadows is very important in setting the scene and mood of the films, and shadows are also depicted in many images from *Deliver Us from Evil*. In cases such as *Deliver Us from Evil*, *Oculus*, and *The Possession*, the shadows manifest as a character in its own right, representing evil and supernatural forces as a tangible and engulfing force that overtakes the main characters of these films, upon which the shadows allow a space for possessions to occur and supernatural occurrences to take place (Kracauer 2004).

The use of artificial light and darkness further the high contrast and can be considered as demonstrative of a battle between good and evil.

In *Oculus*, the characters fight to keep the lights on, which are constantly being put out by a supernatural entity present in an old mirror. As the film progresses, the lighting gets dimmer and dimmer; in essence as the characters slowly lose their hold on reality. It is reminiscent of a *Heart of Darkness* scenario, and as the sun goes down and the artificial lights begin to wane, the characters lose hold of what is real and what is not.

Similarly, lighting is used in *Deliver Us from Evil* to show how the family of the central character, Detective Ralph Sarchie (Eric Bana), falls into darkness. In the beginning, the family (mother and daughter) is shown in warm lighting and is depicted as happy and wholesome. As the film progresses, the family falls into darkness. One scene close to the climax of the film shows the young daughter in the light, which abruptly goes out as the "monster" comes out. In the subsequent scene, the mother and daughter are both in darkness.

The lighting and mood induced by these filmic techniques are enhanced by other elements used in several of the films analyzed here. Many films preface as their first introduction to audiences a full screen graphic that presents a truth element to the story about to be told, then juxtapose this with a film technique that seems to undercut such a statement. For example, *The Possession* opens with a wide aerial shot that eerily meanders over a residential neighborhood. This immediately sets the scene that an otherworldly element is looking down on the human race, showing the way that camera angles are used in horror films to create a mood and introduce Gothic and supernatural elements. These opening scenes linked with truth proclamations immediately present the supernatural as real, beckoning the audience to believe that the story about to unfold before them could have happened, that religious/supernatural occurrences should be both feared and recognized as genuine. While this story development is likely a tool by filmmakers to make their horror films even more scary, whereby making their audiences believe the story they are watching as believable in order to induce fear, these films also send a clear message about religious/supernatural beliefs and the place of evil in the world that audiences might also take to be true. To give one example from the film *Deliver Us from Evil*, viewers are informed that evil does not reside in persons, even if that person is possessed; rather, evil resides in the supernatural entities that haunt the characters in the films. One piece of dialogue from the film is very telling about the place of evil in horror films. The priest informs the cop that: "I've experienced two types of evil in this life. Secondary evil, the evil that men do. . . . And primary evil, which is something else entirely." The cop replies: "Okay? I've seen some horrible things but nothing that can't be explained by human nature." The priest responds: "Then you haven't seen true evil."

Of course, a discussion of Gothic visualization cannot be divorced from auditory devices widely utilized in both the films and television series to induce fear and promote the eerie and dark worlds visually depicted in the horror genre narratives. Arguably, the sound in these horror films and television shows is what induces fear for viewers, as the sound effects are often a cue that something evil or supernatural is about to happen. The suspense of understanding that something frightening, albeit it is unclear exactly what, is about to happen to the characters in the story can cause anxiety and fear for the viewers, even before they see any visual manifestations of the evil or supernatural appearances. In all of the films and television episodes reviewed here, audio devices are used in this way. In *The Walking Dead*, for example, dangerous situations are often preceded by no sound at all, until a rising bass can be detected and culminates into a loud, low sound when a zombie unexpectedly appears. Oftentimes, it is the culmination of this leitmotif, reminiscent of a rising heart rate, which induces fear for viewers. In other examples, such as *The Possession* and *Sinister*, where the prime religious/supernatural elements are evil manifestations, such as a demon (*The Possession*) or an ancient deity (*Sinister*), the sound effects denote the presence of evil, even when it cannot be seen visually. In this case, the sound effects are auditory cues for viewers, so that when they are watching a film like *The Possession*, they understand that the little girl on screen is not just a little girl, the presence of evil is within her in the form of a demon. Thus, sound effects help make the evil representations feel real for viewers.

Depicting religious/supernatural elements does not always require special effects that create a visual monster on screen. Like sound, *invisible* forces act as evil representations. In *The Possession*, some scenes require the viewers to believe that evil forces are not physical manifestations: in the opening scene, a woman is attacked by an invisible entity, thrown to the ground and into the air by nothing apparently visible. The following scene introduces a basketball coach telling his players to use an "invisi-ball" to practice. The players proceed to play with this "invisible" ball, which is actually nothing at all. Symbolically, this scene is important, begging the question of what is real and what is imagined, dealing directly with the opening scene of the film. Later in the film, when a teacher is attacked by this invisible evil force, a shot showing a flag blowing in the wind is depicted. Wind, which is a real, but invisible force, is juxtaposed by this invisible evil. This symbolic illustration forces viewers to consider that invisible evil is also real, since, like the wind, just because an entity cannot be seen does not mean that it does not exist. Just as auditory cues are nonvisual ways of depicting Gothic tropes and contributing to Gothic visualization, special effects that create an invisible evil are also Gothic representations of monsters and a way to make viewers question the notion of real versus imaginary forces.

How is it possible for modern humans living in a secularized, consumer-driven society to take seriously the existence of an evil supernatural realm as depicted in these films and shows? Historian W. Scott Poole (2014b) argues that modernity has not ruled out the mysterious, instead arguing that contemporary "religion and Gothic are in alliance"; in other words, religious and Gothic imagery have a kind of symbiotic relationship within our current social and media spheres. Going back to the 1950s, Vampira and other popularizations of Gothic preternaturalism emerged at the same time in history as Billy Graham's crusades. Graham, an Evangelical preaching of the imminent return of Jesus, subsequently preached against the film *The Exorcist*, while the Catholic Church simultaneously endorsed it as showing verifiable aspects of demon possession (Poole 2014b). The intersection of religion and films with religious/supernatural themes represents the less than antagonistic relationship between these two cultural elements. Echoing this sentiment, Picart and Greek (2007a, 19) state, "Gothicism and Christianity have always had a strong and intimate relationship characterized by an ambivalent blend of kinship and rivalry."

GOTHIC WORLDS AS DYSTOPIAS

Another framework that offers significant insight into the Gothic realm as depicted in these films and television shows has been broadly labeled as dystopia theory (Jacobsen and Tester 2012; Lyman 2001). The world of religious deviance, fear, and the inability of the law to protect us from evil, which are the foci of horror films and television, exist within a society characterized as dystopian. Film viewers would easily recognize that a whole generation of Hollywood films set in the near future prophesize a coming dystopia, but what of these horror films set in the present? Blockbuster films such as The Matrix trilogy and Terminator series predict that in the not so distant future civilization as we know it will all but disappear, leaving only a remnant of humanity struggling for survival. The human race has sown the seeds of its own demise through its own sins: overdependence on dehumanizing industrialization, depersonalizing technology, environmental negligence, and uncontrolled global struggle over weapons of mass destruction. Machines, robots, and computers ultimately dominate a post-apocalypse planet. At their most benign, the planet's new rulers create artificial dream worlds in which human beings are offered an alienated existence, but are denied true freedom or individuality. At worst, the machines attempt to rid the planet of any human remnants. Dystopia has firmly replaced any possibility of utopia as the predominant future state of humanity (Greek 2016).

Dystopia as an aspect of contemporary society is rooted in a postmodern understanding of human societal existence as one of fighting off the creeping suspicion that the world is really an absurd place (Lyman and Scott 1970). Capitalist constructed, consumer-oriented realities offer a thin veneer that only partially shields citizens from recognizing the precariousness of the world we have socially constructed. Within the films and programs discussed here, as in the world in which we live itself, the dystopian elements of existence are continuously pointed out, often by the media. All dimensions of media, from news to Hollywood film and television, thrive on the dystopic elements of life, including natural disasters, high-profile crimes, and globalized images of mass violence, health epidemics, as well as class and religious conflict (Jacobsen and Tester 2012). Only by practicing a form of ongoing civil inattention, characterized by Georg Simmel (1971) as the blasé attitude of urbanites, can citizens ignore the dystopic elements of modern existence.

In the horror genre, dystopia is especially present, not only in the background noise of media news broadcasts of ever present catastrophes and such, but in particular in the realms in which death, darkness, and evil permeate the Gothic spaces of the stories. Dystopic imagery seems particularly suited to the development of religious/supernatural themes, as the dystopia both creates a space for the existence of evil and provides a discourse for religiosity and the supernatural. A dystopian world allows monsters to enter it; but these worlds may not also be beyond salvation, as some of the films allow the hope of religion to conquer evil. In *Deliver Us from Evil*, the world is a dark place seen through the eyes of a cop working the night shift. It is in this grotesque world that Detective Sarchie (Eric Bana) is able to find religiosity as his only hope and light. Similarly, in *The Conjuring*, evil is only vanquished by the good memories of the past, despite the dystopic world that the characters now inhabit. It is only through this dystopia that the characters in *The Conjuring* might find religiosity. Dystopia is necessary to set the scene of a horror film or television series. It is difficult to imagine bad things happening when the world is harmoniously at peace. Even when a family seems happy (such as in *Sinister*) it soon becomes clear that the father (Ethan Hawke) is an alcoholic, emotionally removed from his family (on dystopia within the family, see Lyman 1997, 210–33). It is through these dystopic scenarios that evil enters and monsters dwell. A dystopic world is also the culmination of a society that has become lawless, as it depicts a place that the law cannot infiltrate or protect. When agents of the law attempt to restore order in such realms, what chance do they have for success, particularly when battling unleashed supernatural forces?

MONSTERS AND THE LAW

Having identified what typifies these cinematic stories as Gothic, we return to the two most important elements for our analysis: the portrayal of the perpetrators as monsters and the criminal justice system/legal response to the presence of monstrous evil. Although none of the films/episodes reviewed here could be categorized as a "crime dramas," elements of law, the justice system, and criminological themes are present in the majority of them and are an important point of analysis. What role could the law possibly play when faced with the possibility of monstrous, supernaturally induced evil? This theme will be highlighted in the upcoming discussion section.

The monstrous must be included in the analysis toolkit, as monsters (both real and psychological) are important, arguably the main, characters of all the stories in this sample. While "the monstrous" is a major component part of Gothic Criminology, monster theory as further developed by Cohen (1996) assists in better understanding the monstrous as an element of horror genre religious/supernatural themes.

In his Preface to *Monster Theory*, Cohen (1996, xi) explains that "'human' and 'monster' are co-incipient, mutually constitutive, monstrously hybrid" entities. This description presents the idea that the monster is not separate from the human, but that people can and do become monsters. The transformation of human into monster, or the struggle of human versus monster to inform how the monster is portrayed in the religious/supernatural guise been the focus of both narrative and discourse analyses. Cohen (1996) provides seven theses for his monster theory, some of which include the possibility of supernatural realms impinging on the natural world, at least in the mind of the monstrous offender: (1) "The Monster's Body is a Cultural Body," in which "The monster's body quite literally incorporates fear, desire, anxiety, and fantasy" (Cohen 1996, 4). (2) "The Monster Always Escapes," so that "We see the damage the monster wreaks, the material remains . . . but the monster itself turns immaterial and vanishes, to reappear someplace else" (Cohen 1996, 4). (3) "The Monster is the Harbinger of Category Crisis," as it cannot be easily categorized as one known thing (Cohen 1996, 4). (4) "The Monster Dwells at the Gates of Difference," as "it is an incorporation of the Outside, The Beyond" (Cohen 1996, 7). In terms of religiosity, this *other* may refer to angels and demons, the afterlife, or realms where humans do not understand or cannot go. (5) "The Monster Polices the Borders of the Possible," in which "curiosity is more often punished than rewarded" (Cohen 1996, 12). (6) "Fear of the Monster Is Really a Kind of Desire," so that "the monster is continually linked to forbidden practices in order to normalize and enforce. The Monster also attracts" (Cohen 1996, 16). Finally, (7)

"The Monster Stands at the Threshold . . . of Becoming," meaning that while monsters can be "hidden away at the edges of the world and in the forbidden recesses of our mind . . . they always return" (Cohen 1996, 20). It is this framework that serves as a starting point for the analysis of the monstrous.

Monsters are omnipresent in all the films and television episodes. There are several examples of the seven monstrous forms presented by Cohen (1996). Importantly, and alluded to above, monsters are depicted differently in television than they are in film. In television, it is clear that the monsters are humans. In *American Horror Story*, both the religiously righteous and the educated (the doctor and the psychiatrist) are monsters. The monsignor is a murderer; the asylum doctor was once an SS officer and now conducts gruesome experiments on patients; and the psychiatrist is a serial killer. Several in-episode quotes support this narrative: "All monsters are human." "I've dealt with bigger monsters than you" (*American Horror Story*, episode 1). In *American Horror Story*, the monsters are linked to an innate, animal desire: sex, lust, greed, which aligns with Cohen's (1996) thesis 6, "Fear of the Monster Is Really a Kind of Desire." In *The Walking Dead*, the monsters were literally once people who are now zombies. Some of the human characters, such as Shane, are also monsters, or are forced to become monstrous and murder other human survivors to save themselves. In Kyle William Bishop's (2010, 24) analysis of the zombie narrative in the horror film *Dawn of the Dead* (1978), he suggests that after the survivors learn to live in their zombie-infested environment, they "cease to be much of a direct threat," and in fact the "real fear comes from the other human survivors, those who can still think, plot, and act." This observation is true for *The Walking Dead*, blurring the lines between who the monsters really are: the zombies or the human survivors. This distinction reflects on the human capacity for violence and monstrosity.

In film, the monsters are all based in the religious/supernatural realm, which aligns with Cohen's (1996) thesis 4, "The Monster Dwells at the Gates of Difference." The monster is always a *real* monster, the Devil, a demon, or a pagan deity. In most of the films, the monster escapes capture (thesis 2). In *Oculus*, the main characters trying to destroy the evil either die or go to prison. The monster in the mirror survives to torment future people. In *The Possession*, the Rabbi is in a fatal car accident at the end of the film, and the box with the evil spirit is free to find another victim. In all examples, the monster embodies fear, anxiety, and fantasy (Cohen's thesis 1), and is personified through the horror genre in which the very nature of the visual medium, with its music and darkness, creates monstrous fear within the viewer as well.

In the films chosen for this study, a pattern arose in the way that evil is framed. In each case, evil is addressed as a real "monster," not as something that *people* do. In all the films, demons, possessions, pagan deities, or objects are the sole sources of evil, with the human characters fighting against the evil using their limited natural defenses. The skeptical or non-religious character type (described in detail below), by not recognizing the supernatural powers, essentially welcomes an evil presence to enter their life. The skeptic thus pays the ultimate price for not believing. This theme can be seen repeatedly. In *Sinister*, writer Ellison Oswalt (Ethan Hawke) states, "I never believed in this stuff" and subsequently becomes the victim of supernatural forces. In *Deliver Us from Evil*, Detective Sarchie (Eric Bana) becomes the object of a haunting, but must be transformed into a believer (through confessing his sins), before given the ability to vanquish the evil entity. The supernatural does not have to directly possess a human being in order to insert itself into the natural world, such as *Oculus*. Nevertheless, failure to recognize such evil in any form that it takes may doom those who encounter it.

EVIL, LAW, AND THE SUPERNATURAL: COMPARING FILM AND TELEVISION HORROR

Applying the three theories described above, there is substantial overlap in the way that monsters are depicted, the scenes are set, and the stories are told. While supernatural religiosity is a major element to the analysis of these horror films, this cannot be unwed from the presence of criminality and law. Depictions of law and treatment of criminological themes are intimately tied to the religious/supernatural analysis of the horror films and television programs, and can be analyzed using the combined application of Gothic Criminology, monster theory, and dystopia theory. There are several striking points of analysis worth discussing here, including such depictions of religion/the supernatural and the law, and the character types present in many of the films, which in some cases differ considerably from the television episodes, as well as the overarching similarities in visual representation, sound, and story elements that have been described above.

Film Characterization and the Element of Truth

There are three primary character types present in all the sample films. The first character type is often the main character, and is normally depicted as a skeptic loner. This individual is always set apart from the rest of the characters around which the major action in the film revolves. The character is necessarily solitary, and may become more isolated from friends, family, and society as the story develops. In *Sinister*, this character is the father, played by Ethan Hawke, who is writing a crime novel about a murdered family. In *Deliver Us from Evil,* it is again a father, a police officer attempting to solve a major investigation. In *The Awakening,* it is a woman, Florence Cathcart (Rebecca Hall), who works to reveal that there is no such thing as ghosts. In *The Possession,* it is arguably two individuals; first a father, Clyde (Jeffrey Dean Morgan), removed from his family through a divorce, and then later his daughter, Hannah (Madison Davenport), who becomes possessed by an evil spirit. In all such cases, these individuals have something in common: they are all skeptical about anything religious/supernatural. The female lead in *The Awakening* does not believe in the supernatural and actively works to show that ghosts do not exist. In *Deliver Us from Evil,* there is a scene where the father/main character, Det. Ralph Sarchie, does not attend church with his wife and daughter. In this scene, the mother tells her daughter, both of whom are preparing to leave for church, "Daddy doesn't go to church," which depicts him as a nonbeliever. Several other scenes depict his secular outlook. However, Sarchie does have an ability he calls his "radar," which is described as a kind of intuition about when bad things are going to happen. What is initially presented as a sixth sense is later described in religious terms, and is discussed below.

The second character type is the knowledgeable religious individual who already is educated about the "real" supernatural events that the main characters are witnessing but dismissing as scientifically explainable. This individual, who may be dismissed as a crackpot or religious fanatic at first, ultimately becomes the main character's counselor and trusted advisor. In *Deliver Us from Evil,* this individual is a Catholic priest (Edgar Ramirez) who performs an exorcism with officer Sarchie. In *The Conjuring,* the family seeks the aid of the Warrens, a husband and wife duo (Patrick Wilson and Vera Farminga) who help to expel evil spirits, one being a demonologist and the other being a psychic able to see supernatural entities. In *The Possession,* the Hasidic Rabbi Shah (Armin Chaim Kornfeld) is sought out to help perform an exorcism.

The third film character type is the evil entity itself. It is always a supernatural being or force, but never beneficent, and the evil it unleashes is mostly tied to demonic (nonhuman spirits) or the Devil. In some examples, the supernatural entity is tied to a thing (evil spirits embedded in a mirror in *Oculus*) and in other examples the supernatural entity is a pagan deity (as in *Sinister,* although the evil presence has also embedded itself inside super 8 film). In only one instance is the supernatural entity not the source of evil (*The Awakening*); as this film focuses on the evil actions of people, even though ghosts are present. In all other examples, the evil resides in entities from the religious/supernatural realm and not in the monstrous actions of persons. This becomes important in the discussion of monsters below.

In each of the sampled films, an important element that frames their supernatural explanations is an assertion that the story that unfolds is based in "truth." Part of the creation of fear and believability for monsters and religious/supernatural themes is the necessity to make the viewers believe what they are seeing is in the realm of possibility and may actually have already transpired. In nearly every film, there is a full screen graphic proclaiming its truthiness:

> "Based on Actual Accounts"—*Deliver Us from Evil*
>
> "The Following is Based on a True Story. This is what happened to one family over the course of 29 days"—*The Possession*
>
> "OBSERVATION: Between 1914 and 1919 war and influenza have claimed more than a million lives in Britain Alone. CONCLUSION: This is a time for ghosts"—*The Awakening*

Of course, other visual devices, such as the use of super 8 film as documentary evidence (*Sinister*) and the insertion of case studies and real, historical figures (*The Conjuring*) also add to this sense of realism.

The verisimilitude of natural reality, which always frames the beginning of these films before they shift into Gothic realms, adds to the intended discourse that religion/supernatural entities are indeed real. Even when films have descended into the realm of Gothic evil, we are offered reminders that the monstrous supernatural is part of our everyday lives. In *Deliver Us from Evil*, a monologue from the Catholic priest uses "logic" to show that evil is real. The priest, early in the film, states sarcastically, "You outgrew God," revealing a discourse that proclaims the truth of religion and spirituality. The closing frame of the films that typically takes the viewer back from the Gothic world to the naturalistic one represents another truth claim about what the viewer has experienced. For example, the final scene of *The Conjuring* shows a graphic stating, "The fairy tales are true. The Devil exists. God exists." In all films, a discourse that supports the supernatural as a genuine aspect of everyday life is found. Thus, being a nonbeliever or skeptic in the film's world becomes itself a form of aberration, and will put the individuals at great risk.

Finally, the filmic treatment of law and law enforcement serves to validate the presence of ongoing supernatural evil. However, in order to instill a sense of realism for the supernatural, law enforcement and the criminal justice system must be depicted as ineffective. Humans, even police officers, cannot fight the forces of supernatural evil. The justice system cannot capture, judge, or punish that which is preternatural, and thus cannot reform, deter, or incapacitate a demon or spirit. The supernatural exists beyond the realm of natural law's jurisdiction. In many of the films, the possessed human being cannot be held accountable for their evil actions, since it was the demon within, and not their own free will decision-making, that caused deviant behavior. The legal similarity here is to temporary insanity, which since the M'Naghten Rule—which focuses on whether a criminal defendant knew the nature of the crime or understood right from wrong at the time it was committed—has been used to remove blame from the accused (Findlaw 2015). Similarly, one could also question whether persons under the influence of supernatural entities could actually form criminal intent, *mens rea*. While the latter is not a defense in court and quite different from the M'Naghten Rule, which argues that a person cannot be held "cognitively" responsible for his or her acts under certain conditions, without *mens rea* the criminal intent nexus between the accused and the criminal action is broken. Finally, in these films, in punishing or executing a possessed individual the criminal justice system would only be destroying the temporary receptacle of evil, rather than removing such evil from the world itself. In many of the sample films, therefore, law enforcement can offer little assistance to victims, and is subsequently portrayed as inadequate, foolish, and naïve in the face of supernatural evil. Only police officers, such as Ralph Sarchie in *Deliver Us from Evil,* willing to ask for the assistance of religious experts who comprehend supernatural evil have a chance at restoring law and order.

The film *Deliver Us from Evil* offers a good example of the inadequacy of law enforcement to combat the supernatural, and yet these two forces are thrust together repeatedly in the film. In the film's climax, for example, the final act to rid a demon from a man through exorcism is performed at the police station, in a holding cell where the detective was previously attempting to obtain information from the accused man. The methods of the law dealing with detainment and questioning is subverted in favor of an exorcism, as this is a supernatural matter that goes above and beyond the power of the law. In the film's conclusion, through the exorcism, which is described in meticulous stages by the priest as if describing a scientific method, the law enforcement officer is transformed into a true believer. The transformation of the law enforcement officer into a Christian believer is indicative of his realization that human law enforcement cannot combat supernatural evil, and so must accept religious methods and beliefs to rid the world of this evil. As a culmination of the foreshadowing in the film leading up to this point, the law enforcement officer, who drove night after night looking for evil *people,* now realizes that the true evil he must combat actually resides in the supernatural realm. He subsequently transforms himself from a law enforcement officer to a religious disciple.

In the film *Oculus*, a similar tension exists between the law and the supernatural world. Here, traditional science is also shown as inadequate against the forces of the supernatural. The female lead character, Kaylie Russell (Karen Gillan) is convinced that a mirror is responsible for the death of her parents, as well as many deaths throughout history since the mirror was first constructed. In the start of the film, it is apparent that Kaylie's brother, Tim Russell (Brenton Thwaites), was accused of the juvenile murder of his father and sentenced to stay at a mental institution for years until he becomes an adult. His doctors convince him that he did indeed murder his father, despite his own memories of the supernatural experiences he had in his home before the murder occurred. Upon his release, Kaylie is determined to set the record straight, exonerate her brother, and show that the mirror and its supernatural powers are to blame. Kaylie uses video cameras and other devices to scientifically document the supernatural qualities of the mirror. These tools subsequently malfunction and yet by recording only observable behavior actually only show that Kaylie and Tim may truly be insane. In the film's conclusion, Kaylie is inadvertently murdered by Tim, who was experiencing visions induced by the mirror and did not see that Kaylie was in the way of his attempts to destroy the mirror with a large boat anchor. In this plotline, the issues of the supernatural, law, and science intersect, but the supernatural succeeds in overcoming both law and science. The law cannot indict a mirror for murder as it certainly cannot have criminal intent; instead, criminal responsibility must be placed upon a person. At the film's end, the brother is again arrested and accused of murdering his sister. Due to his past conviction and recent release from the mental facility, Tim will likely be convicted for his sister Kaylie's murder. The forensically recorded evidence that Kaylie was sure would prove that the mirror is the true evil entity only results in convicting Tim of the crime. This film reveals several important points fundamental to law but counter to supernatural causality: (1) the law cannot and does not accept material objects as evil or able to commit murder; (2) the law must place blame on a person for such crimes, unless an accident or other breaks in the causal chain are evident; and (3) the supernatural is powerful enough to influence tools that humans believe to be incorruptible, such as video and audio recordings and other electronic devices. This film thus subverts our ideas of proof, which is so vital to law, conviction, and punishment. If the supernatural can induce humans to see and experience things beyond the realm of evidentiary visual capture with cameras, then traditional law enforcement truly is useless in fighting such powerful forces.

In a similar vein, the film *The Awakening* also uses scientific recording devices to capture evidence. The main character, Florence Cathcart (Rebecca Hall) works to debunk supernatural claims and instances of ghosts.

She uses photography and other tools that are commonly accepted as scientific modes of gathering "real" evidence. She is clearly the skeptic character type, and believes in science over religion, stating early in the film, "without science, people believe in everything, including spirits." This foreshadowing leads to unexplainable occurrences that she cannot prove with her scientific tools, forcing her to accept the supernatural as real. Thus, science, like law, is useless in this reality. The film culminates with an unsolved murder, solidifying the inexactitude of law and its inability to protect and reveal the truth. In this film, it is the supernatural and religion that expose the truth behind the murder in a way that the law is unable to do.

Even when the law itself is not being dismantled, law enforcement officers are often repudiated. In *The Conjuring*, a nonbelieving law enforcement officer, Brad (John Brotherton) is employed to help with the Warrens' investigation of a demonic haunting at the home of the Perron family. Early in the film, the law enforcement officer claims that gusts of wind are to blame for doors slamming. By the end of the film, after he and the film's audience have witnessed possession, apparitions, and an exorcism; neither he nor the audience can deny the reality of the supernatural entity or the sole power of religious methods to combat such evil entities. At the end of the film, one of the characters helping the Warrens, Drew (Shannon Kook), asks the police officer, who was grazed in the neck by a shotgun fired by an unexplainable force, "Did a draft do that to your face?" The police officer responds, "I'd take a guy with a gun any day," thus solidifying the inability for law enforcement to enter and combat the world of the supernatural.

The Case of Horror Television

The television series analyzed here reveal quite different interpretations than the films, particularly when offering explanations of the true sources of monstrous evil. Ultimately, such horrific evil is not the result of supernatural entities acting within the world, but resides instead inside human beings themselves, thus showing that humans commit atrocious acts because they choose to do so. Bishop (2010, 119) explains that in zombie narratives like *The Walking Dead*, fear is directed inward, "that deep down, we may be little more than animals, concerned only with appetite," and that in a world of zombies, it is not so much a struggle against monsters, but a "struggle to retain [a] sense of humanity." Even in instances when the monsters are zombies, these creatures are not supernatural beings, but were once people (often recognizable as former friends or family members) now simply mindless corpses that have risen from the dead (Bishop 2010).

Given the nature of the long form television series, there are less neat stereotypic character types than compared to those found in film. The much longer length of time writers have to develop serial television characters allows them to construct and provide in-depth backgrounds for a wide variety of personality types, sometimes conflicted combinations of good and evil. In the episodes analyzed here, a major difference from horror film narrative appears, in particular, with the presence of religiously motivated characters who themselves represent evil rather than opponents of it. In *American Horror Story*, the religious characters (the nuns and the monsignor) have strayed from the faith while keeping up appearances, and are often more deviant than the nonreligious characters. In episode 6, the monsignor murders a woman to cover up his wrongdoing, as he was attempting to acquire a higher position and more power within the Catholic Church hierarchy. One of the nuns, Sister Jude, wears suggestive red lingerie under her habit, and scenes in which she fantasizes about having sex with the monsignor are featured. The other nun, Sister Mary Eunice, is possessed by the Devil and seduces the monsignor to have sex with her, even though both are supposed to be living under vows of celibacy. In the series, the Catholic Church, and arguably religion in general, is seen as backward and farcical. Further, an exorcism that takes place in episode 2 of *American Horror Story* ends badly, killing the boy being exorcised. This could be a discourse against religious dogma as well, as it could be interpreted as the boy not receiving proper medical care and dying due to religious superstition. It is important to note in comparison that none of the possessed characters in the films previously discussed here died after being exorcised; they were all restored to normalcy.

Despite the differences in the way that religious persons in film versus television are depicted, law enforcement is portrayed in the same way in both instances, as largely ineffective. A serial killer depicted on *American Horror Story* is able to frame an innocent man, who is sentenced to death, allowing the serial killer to move on to his next victim, who is held captive in his basement. The ability of the serial killer to continue unabated is propelled by law enforcement oversight and the failure of the justice system in arresting and prosecuting an innocent man. The season 2 back-story on *American Horror Story* reveals that the innocently accused character Kit Walker (Evan Peters) was actually abducted by aliens, as was his wife, Alma (Britne Oldford), but was subsequently accused of murdering her because she never returned. Since this supernatural event could not be explained or proven in ways comprehensible to the structure of the justice system, this character is doomed to prosecution. In this example, the law, whose structure, rooted in the real world, aims to ascertain the truth in assigning criminal motivation before passing judgment, cannot function in cases of extraterrestrial causes and events.

Turning to *The Walking Dead*, we see the same negative views of the religious and of the legal and law enforcement communities. The spiritual character, Hershel (Scott Wilson), is presented as a steadfast believer, seen in some scenes as reading the Bible and quoting scripture or mentioning God in other scenes. His view about the "walkers," as the zombies are called, is presented as backward and wrong. He believes that the "walkers" are sick people who need a cure, rather than the undead who can only be dismembered to defeat them. His religious ineptitude is further signified in episode 7, when he doesn't allow Rick (Andrew Lincoln) and his cohort to stay with him on his farm, showing no mercy to fulfill his Christian duty to "love one another." Here, he is cast as a sheltered, selfish, uneducated individual. This distinction between his unchristian personal behavior and his piety is placed in sharp relief, as he is seen in shots reading his Bible and proclaiming to be a devout believer. In the dystopian world in which ordinary persons have become mindless creatures, Christians are equally zombielike in not recognizing their own hypocrisy and stupidity. Thus, religious believers are themselves part of the problem in such a chaotic world, rather than offering any hope of a utopian post-apocalyptic earth or in an afterlife. The very world of *The Walking Dead* can thus be considered a direct affront to the end time promises of premillennial Christianity, as believers might understand this apocalyptic world as the "End of Days" described in the Book of Revelations (Blomberg and Chung 2009). In this hopeless rendering, Christians and non-Christians alike are forsaken, to either become zombies or survive in this dystopic world, rather than being saved by the return of Jesus and safely brought into his kingdom.

Again, as in *American Horror Story*, the law is depicted in *The Walking Dead* as useless and unable to maintain social control or restore order. The law is alluded to repeatedly by the main character, Rick Grimes (Andrew Lincoln), a police officer before the zombie epidemic ensued. Rick continues to wear his police uniform in the post-apocalyptic world, despite the obvious fact that the zombies do not recognize the uniform as a symbol of law and order. As the season progresses, Rick, who does not seem to own a change of clothes, allows his uniform to become covered in blood and dirt, representing the disintegration of law and its ability to maintain stability in society. In several episodes, Rick not only shoots and kills zombies, who were once people, but he also murders people who have survived the zombie apocalypse without succumbing to the "virus" in order to preserve his family. These scenes are symbolic of the breaking down of the law and its inversion, as the police officer who once protected and served now murders for self-preservation. The zombie dystopia disintegrates toward a Hobbesian war of all against all. Bishop (2010, 141) suggests that the zombie subgenre, which often aligns with an apocalyptic narrative, necessitates the breaking down of law and social structures, stating that the zombie narrative "depict[s] the chaotic decay of two of the most powerful institutions in America: the media and law enforcement" (here using he uses the *Dawn of the Dead* film as an example, but is equally valid for *The Walking Dead*). Bishop reiterates that once thrown into this apocalyptic scenario, the surviving characters "take both the law and their protection into their own hands" (Bishop 2010, 24).

While the depiction of law is similar in both film and television horror formats, the two offer different perspectives about evil and religion. What might account for the latter? If television is truly a more widely accessible medium than film, might it be as Poole (2014b, 17) describes "helping to reinforce dominant ideals" since its emergence as a mass form of entertainment? Perhaps, like the 1950s, when television was used "to argue that, despite religious differences, unity could be found" (Poole 2014b, 17), the lack of faith in religious explanations and solutions is now used by television producers and writers as a uniting principle among the masses. Poole (2014b, 17), ever pessimistic, states, "religious faith [is] always in danger of accelerating into a roaring blaze of . . . apocalyptic flames," a possible explanation for the post-apocalyptic world in which zombies are the norm. Perhaps, in the wake of the wane on religiosity, television discourse mirrors larger sentiments about religion. Recent news articles echo the loss of religiosity among the American public, as one states, "One in five American adults now have no religious affiliation" (Kaleem 2012). And another reports, "the number of atheists, while still small, has nearly doubled from 900,000 to 1.6 million" (Harris 2009). Although it cannot be shown empirically, the combatant-like discourse present in popular television programing shown here could be a mirror for current religious sentiment.

Despite the difference in religious message present in film and television, the similarity of the way law is depicted in both forms of media reveals an inability for law and state-sanctioned justice to exist in the horror genre's Gothic dystopian universe. This is due in part to the strict parameters under which law exists, which cannot possibly accept the supernatural as the root cause of evil and which must single out persons, and not forces (be they sociological or supernatural), as responsible for committing crimes. In a post-apocalyptic world like that depicted in *The Walking Dead,* law cannot exist if the population does not recognize the symbols of law, or respect the persons that attempt to employ them. The horror genre thus sends a disturbing message to its audience: law and order are not sustainable, as they are not grounded in the realities of a universe subject to the intervention of Gothic forces. Only as long as people believe in this construction of society and the consensus of the power of symbols can a semblance of order be maintained. Bishop (2010) states that narratives that involve monsters, such as zombies, reflect contemporary Gothic themes, playing on the fears that audiences have of the breaking down of law and military structures. He suggests that the absence of viable governmental and law enforcement institutions in these apocalyptic filmic examples exacerbates "repressed cultural anxieties," pointing to national security emergencies such as the 9/11 terrorist attacks and even earlier with the Vietnam War as instances that coincide with a renewal of zombie narratives in popular television and film media. Thus, when disasters happen in the real world, widespread fear and anxiety is played out visually in film and television through the horror genre and Gothic visualization. Bishop contends that "such monsters would not prove much of a threat if actualized in the modern-day world; most probably the police or military could quickly exterminate these aberrations" (Bishop 2010, 22). But, there is an interesting inversion of reality present in the content of these films and television shows: in a Gothic universe the supernatural is real; thus making the law one of the structures of the natural world that is ineffectual, if not an outright illusion. This nihilistic revelation of human existence is the ultimate outcome of the dystopic reality in which the characters dwell.

CONCLUSION

Paradoxically, the overall effect of these depictions may be to support rather than undermine the legal status quo. Given that evil is omnipresent, whether in a supernatural or preternatural form or plainly rooted in human nature, what other response can there be but to use the existing powers imbued within our world's authority structures to try to keep dystopic forces at bay? Giving in to the irrational forces of the universe would only result in the disastrous dystopic dissolution of society, a message that is clearly portrayed and explored by filmmakers and television producers in the samples analyzed here. In any case, this discussion of the horror genre in film and television raises questions of how such media depictions are a reflection of culture and a depiction of religious and law enforcement sentiments in the American psyche, exemplified by Bishop's (2010) discussion above regarding the waves of past zombie media narratives in popular culture aligning with major national security disasters, such as the Vietnam War and the 9/11 terrorist attacks. This point raises questions for further inquiry about real-world fear and anxiety being expressed, and possibly relieved, through visual representations and depictions in the horror genre (Grant 1996; Wood 2003). And how, combined with alarmist media accounts, these fears become fodder for politicians who might manipulate them (Curtis 2004; Greek 2015).

REFERENCES

Bishop, Kyle William. 2010. *American Zombie Gothic: The Rise and Fall (and Rise) of the Walking Dead in Popular Culture.* Jefferson, NC: McFarland & Company, Inc.

Blomberg, Craig and Sung Wook Chung (eds.). 2009. *A Case for Historic Premillennialism: An Alternative to 'Left Behind' Eschatology*. Baker Academic.

Blum, Jason (producer) and Scott Derrickson (director). 2012. *Sinister* [Motion picture]. Montreal: Alliance Films.

Blum, Jason (producer) and Mike Flanagan (director). 2013. *Oculus* [Motion picture]. Hollywood: Blumhouse Productions.

Blumer, Herbert. 1954. "What is Wrong with Social Theory?" *American Sociological Review* 18: 3–10.

Bowie, Fiona. 2008. "Anthropology of Religion." *Religion Compass* 2(5): 862–74.

Brophy, Philip. 1986. "Horrality—The Textuality of Contemporary Horror Films." *Screen* 27(1): 2–13.

Bruckheimer, Jerry (producer) and Scott Derrickson (director). 2014. *Deliver Us from Evil* [Motion picture]. Hollywood: Screen Gems.

Cohen, Jeffrey Jerome (ed.). 1996. *Monster Theory: Reading Culture*. Minneapolis: University of Minnesota Press.

Conrad, Peter, and Joseph W. Schneider. 1992. *Deviance and Medicalization: From Badness to Sickness*. Philadelphia: Temple University Press.

Curtis, Adam (producer and director). 2004. *The Power of Nightmares: The Rise of the Politics of Fear* [Television Documentary]. London: British Broadcasting Company (BBC).

Dixon, Wheeler Winston. 2010. *A History of Horror*. New Brunswick, NJ: Rutgers University Press.

Douglas, Mary. 1966. *Purity and Danger*. New York: Routledge.

Durkheim, Emile. 1915. *The Elementary Forms of the Religious Life*. London: George Allen and Unwin, Ltd.

Findlaw. 2015. "The M'Naghten Rule." *Findlaw.* Accessed June 18, 2015 at criminal.findlaw.com/criminal-procedure/the-m-naghten-rule.html.

Freeland, Cynthia A. 1996. "Feminist Frameworks for Horror Films." In *Post-Theory: Reconstructing Film Studies*, edited by David Bordwell, 195–218. Madison: University of Wisconsin Press.

Grant, Keith Barry. 1996. *The Dread of Difference: Gender and the Horror Film*. Austin, TX: University of Texas Press.

Greek, Cecil. 2007. "The Big City Rogue Cop as Monster." In *Monsters In and Among Us: Toward a Gothic Criminology*, edited by Caroline Joan "Kay" S. Picart and Cecil Greek, 164–98. Plainsboro, NJ: Associated University Presses.

———. 2016. "Globalization and the Rise of the Behemoth: A Study in Gothic Criminology." In This Volume.

Harris, Dan. 2009. "America Is Becoming Less Christian, Less Religious." *ABC News*, March 9. Accessed January 3, 2015 at abcnews.go.com/US/story?id=7041036.

Hibberd, James. 2013. "*The Walking Dead*: How to Comprehend Its Massive Ratings." *Entertainment Weekly*. November 11. Accessed June 18, 2015 at www.ew.com/article/2013/11/11/the-walking-dead-ratings.

Hurd, G. A. (producer). 2011–2012. *The Walking Dead* [Television series]. New York: AMC

Jacobsen, Michael Hviid, and Keith Tester (eds.). 2012. *Utopia: Social Theory and the Future*. Surrey: Ashgate Publishing Ltd.

Kaleem, Jaweed. 2012. "'No Religion' Is Increasingly Popular Choice For Americans." *Huffington Post*, October 9. Accessed March 30, 2015 at www.huffingtonpost.com/2012/10/09/no-religion-pew-report_n_1949598.html

Katz, Jack. 1980. *Seductions of Crime*. New York: Basic Books.

Kracauer, Siegfried. 2004. *From Caligari to Hitler: A Psychological History of the German Film*. Princeton, NJ: Princeton University Press.

Lambek, Michael. 2008. *A Reader in the Anthropology of Religion*. 2nd edition. Oxford: Blackwell Publishing Ltd.

Lyman, Stanford. 1997. "Anhedonia: Gender and the Decline of Emotions in American Film, 1930–1988." *Postmodernism and a Sociology of the Absurd*, 210–33. Fayetteville, AR: University of Arkansas Press.

———. 2001. *Roads to Dystopia: Sociological Essays on the Postmodern Condition*. Fayetteville, AR: University of Arkansas Press.

Lyman, Stanford, and Marvin Scott. 1970. *A Sociology of the Absurd*. New York: Appleton-Century-Crofts.

Monahan, Susanne C. 2013. "Seeing Religion Sociologically Through Film." In *Cinematic Sociology: Social Life in Film*, 2nd edition, edited by Jean-Anne Sutherland and Kathryn Feltey, 305–19. Thousand Oaks, CA: Sage Publications, Inc.

Moore, Sarah. 2014. *Crime and the Media*. New York: Palgrave Macmillan.

Picart, Caroline Joan "Kay" S. 2004. "The Third Shadow and Hybrid Genres: Horror, Humor, Gender, and Race in *Alien Resurrection*." *Communication and Critical/Cultural Studies* 1(4): 335–54.

Picart, Caroline Joan "Kay" S. and Cecil Greek (eds.). 2007a. *Monsters In and Among Us: Toward a Gothic Criminology*. Plainsboro, NJ: Associated University Presses.

———. 2007b. "Profiling the Terrorist as a Mass Murderer." In *Monsters In and Among Us: Toward a Gothic Criminology*, edited by Caroline Joan "Kay" S. Picart and Cecil Greek, chapter 9. Plainsboro, NJ: Associated University Presses.

Poole, W. Scott. 2014a. *Vampira: Dark Goddess of Horror*. Berkeley, CA: Soft Skull Press.

———. 2014b. "From Vampira to Slenderman: The Return of the Gothic." USF Humanities Institute Lecture, October 30.

Raimi, Sam (producer), and Ole Bornedal (director). 2012. *The Possession* [Motion picture]. Hollywood: Ghost House Pictures.

Rigby, Kate. 2012. "Utopianism, Dystopianism and Ecological Thought." In *Utopia: Social Theory and the Future*, edited by Michael Hviid Jacobsen and Keith Tester, 141–60. Surrey: Ashgate Publishing Ltd.

Russell, James Burton. 1987. *Devil: Perceptions of Evil from Antiquity to Primitive Christianity*. Ithaca, NY: Cornell University Press.

———. 1990. *Mephistopheles: The Devil in the Modern World*. Ithaca, NY: Cornell University Press.

Safran, P. K. (producer) and James Wan (director). 2013. *The Conjuring* [Motion picture]. Hollywood: New Line Cinema.

Simmel, Georg. 1971. "The Metropolis and Mental Life." In *Simmel: On Individuality and Social Forms*, edited by Donald Levine, 324–39. Chicago: University of Chicago Press.

Stanley, Alessandra. 2014. "In a Hell, But in It Together: The Social Split Between TV and Movie Dystopias." *New York Times*, October 13. Accessed April 27, 2015 at www.nytimes.com/2014/10/13/arts/the-social-split-between-tv-and-movie-dystopias.html?_r=0.

Thompson, David (producer) and Nick Murphy (director). 2011. *The Awakening* [Motion picture]. London: StudioCanal.

Tyron, Charles. 2008. "TV Time Lords: Fan Cultures, Narrative Complexity, and the Future of Science Fiction Television." In *The Essential Television Science Fiction Reader*, edited by J. P. Telotte, 301–20. Frankfurt, KY: University of Kentucky Press.

Venable, Nick. 2015. "*American Horror Story: Freak Show* Is Even More Popular Than We Thought." *CinemaBlend*. Accessed June 18, 2015 at www.cinemablend.com/television/American-Horror-Story-Freak-Show-Even-More-Popular-Than-We-Thought-67828.html.

Vold, George, Thomas Bernard and Jeffrey Snipes. 1998. *Theoretical Criminology*. Oxford: Oxford University Press.

Wood, Robin. 2003. *Hollywood from Vietnam to Reagan and Beyond*. New York: Columbia University Press.

Woodall, A. M. (producer). 2012–2013. *American Horror Story: Asylum*. [Television series]. USA: FX.

V

PEDAGOGY, EPISTEMOLOGY, AND ETHICS IN FILMS OF LAW AND CRIME

14

Contours of a Cinematic Criminology

Distillation, Dramatization, Distortion, and Anecdotal Data

Michael Hviid Jacobsen and Anders Petersen

American sociologist Robert A. Nisbet once wrote a wonderful and insightful book titled *Sociology as an Art Form*, which—at the time of its publication—was both applauded and criticized because it went directly against the ingrained notion that sociology was, first and foremost, a science with only limited or no resemblance with the world of art whatsoever. In his book, Nisbet debunked this notion and instead documented, delineated, and discussed the sociological indebtedness to some of the great novelists of the preceding centuries for inspiring the ability to paint "sociological portraits" and portray "sociological landscapes." Without denying the scientific status of sociology, Nisbet thus concluded:

> Sociology is, without question, one of the sciences, but it is also one of the arts—nourished, as I argue in this book, by precisely the same kinds of creative imagination which are to be found in such areas as music, painting, poetry, the novel, and drama. . . . The problems, insights, ideas, and forms which come to the artist and to the scientist seem to come as often from the unconscious as the conscious mind, from wide, eclectic, and unorganized reading, observing, or experiencing, from musing, browsing, and dreaming, from buried experiences, as from anything immediately and consciously in view. They come . . . as often from the "left-handed" processes of feeling and intuition as from "right-handed" processes of logic, empirical directness, and reason. (Nisbet 1976, 9–19)

As is obvious from this—at the time daring—statement, Nisbet proposed a close historical, intellectual, and practical affinity between the world of art and the world of social science in their mutual endeavor to describe and understand the social world—an affinity confirmed also by Wolf Lepenies (1988). In his acclaimed and oft-cited masterpiece *The Sociological Imagination*, another American sociologist C. Wright Mills urged his colleagues to become "intellectual craftsmen" instead of performing the role of mere "technicians." Mills stated that in order to "be a good craftsman: avoid any rigid set of procedures," "avoid the fetishism of method and technique," and "seek to develop and use the sociological imagination" (Mills 1959, 225). This "sociological imagination" should aspire to develop and nurture a new kind of intellectual curiosity and consciousness—inherited from the great classics and founders of sociology—that, if deployed, would allow for a better grip on what was going on in society and in the lives of individuals. What Nisbet, Lepenies, and Mills, as well as quite a few others, stated to be the pressing need within sociology, obviously also pertains to the needs within the discipline of criminology (see, e.g., Frauley 2015). Although the birth of the discipline of criminology can be dated as far back as the eighteenth century (DiChristina 2012), further than the establishment of sociology, criminology is nevertheless often regarded and described as the offspring, the younger sibling (sometimes even the methodologically crippled sibling) or the understudy of sociology. The intimate relationship between the two disciplines of sociology and criminology has been described and analyzed in great detail throughout the years; thus, we argue that what pertains to sociology when it comes to drawing on and learning from creative, imaginative, or poetic sources of inspiration is also of relevance to the discipline of criminology.

Throughout large proportions of its history, and at least until relatively recently, criminology as a discipline has relied upon and predominantly been identified with a positivistic philosophy of science and its often accompanying quantitative methodologies (see, e.g., Presdee 2000; Young 2011). Although such a view may seem rather narrow and even misleading—no least contemplating the valuable qualitative and especially ethnographic work conducted under the auspices of criminology—it nevertheless captures a common understanding and critique, primarily voiced by the ranks of critical and cultural criminology, that the discipline privileges a positivistic methodology and scientific worldview. Thus, in a text much inspired, and not only in its title, by Mills's aforementioned argument for the "sociological imagination," British sociologist Jock Young in *The Criminological Imagination* warned against "voodoo criminology," "the bogus of positivism," and its concomitant "closing down" of this imagination in contemporary criminology (Young 2011). Additionally, others have recently argued for and urged a revitalization and expansion of the criminological imagination moving it beyond its frequent association with quantification, measurement, objectivity, causality, and state-sponsored research allowing for a more creative and open-minded methodological mentality to flourish and ferment the field (see, e.g., Barton, Corteen, Scott, and Whyte 2007; Ferrell 2009; Jacobsen 2014a). Nevertheless, criminology *is* not an exact science—it simply cannot be as its very subject matter, crime, is not only controversial, but it is also a matter of social definition, negotiation, and indeed power relations and discursive struggles incessantly leaving the world open to interpretation. Such a controversial phenomenon as crime—perhaps especially in liquid-modern times like ours that are constantly disembedding everything without re-embedding them again—calls for a reconsideration and reorientation of the criminological imagination (see Jacobsen and Walklate 2016).

Obviously, the criminological imagination can be set in motion or sparked by many different sources and experiences. Scientific evidence is, however, merely one of them. Fiction is and has throughout modern history remained another important source of imagination. Fiction comes in many different guises, ranging from classical literature via the modern novel, to films and cartoons, to contemporary Internet imagery. One of the main imaginative sources available to criminologists concerned with investigating crime is indeed the media of film in a culture increasingly characterized by the "spectacle" of visual and figural signification contrary to the predominantly discursive signification of the past (Debord 1970; Lash 1990). Popular cultural images thus abound everywhere and provide us with a multitude of visions and stories of fact as well as of fiction.

Although nowadays there is an almost unfathomable proliferation of images, in such a "viewer society" or "synoptic culture" as ours, we all seem to watch, and be moved by, as well as controlled by, the same images (Mathiesen 1997). Today, more so than ever before, film features in the public imagination—perhaps, arguably, even more than books as books increasingly also seem to be adapted to the silver screen. "Going to the movies" has long since superseded going to the theater as "the favorite American pastime" (Sutherland and Feltey 2012, 1). And if there is nothing going on at the theater or the cinema, fortunately oversized satellite TV-packages or video-machines at home are certain to provide all the entertainment needed. Moreover, with the recent rise and rapid spreading of popular streaming services such as HBO, Netflix, or Viaplay available to viewers 24/7 (as of 2015 Netflix has more than 65 million global subscribers), we come to live in an increasingly visually oriented and mediated culture culminating in what American sociologist Norman K. Denzin aptly labelled a "cinematic society" (Denzin 1995; see also Denzin 1991).

Such a cinematic society requires a cinematic imagination because a large proportion of the film material produced and consumed nowadays is concerned with depicting crime-related topics ranging across inmate prison life, crime solving puzzles, courageous or corrupted police forces to violent gang culture, murder mysteries, and the depraved minds of murderers. Crime films thus equally cover the nature, origins, processes, and consequences of crime, as it were, in the round. Consequently, we live in what has been termed a "criminological society" (Jacobsen 2014b) in which everybody seems to be craving their daily dose of crime entertainment and also to some extent view themselves as accomplished amateur detectives. The so-called "cinematic gaze" (Denzin 1995)—just as the aforementioned criminological imagination—is therefore not the privileged property of the professional criminologist but is used by all of us whenever we contemplate what is going on in the world around us. Since the supply and demand of crime film is, as mentioned, rapidly increasing, the criminologist ought to take this gaze and this imagination into consideration and use it for research purposes whenever he or she seeks to investigate and understand crime-related matters. This is the main argument of the subsequent parts of this chapter.

The backbone of this chapter is constituted by three metaphors proposed by two American sociologists, Penney C. Hills and L. Rust Hills, in the edited volume *How We Live*—a book devoted to showing how fiction is particularly suitable for shedding light on social and cultural changes and pinpointing how fiction can inspire thinking about a variety of sociological themes (Hills and Hills 1968). In the postscript to their book they tentatively proposed three complementary ways in which social scientists might benefit from, be inspired by and learn from works of fiction—*distillation*, *dramatization*, and *distortion*. In this chapter we elaborate on, expand, and adopt these three metaphors to show how criminologists could inspire, buttress, and refine their analyses as well as their teaching through the use of fiction and, in this chapter, specifically use insights from film. This is what we in the title of the chapter refer to as "cinematic criminology." Before we by way of these three metaphors specifically venture into discussing how criminology might be inspired by filmic images and stories, let us briefly look at the rise of interest in film in criminology.

THE RISE OF THE CINEMATIC IMAGINATION

There are multiple ways of obtaining knowledge about and gaining understanding of the social world. This is also true when it comes to the worlds of crime. In social science research, surveying, interviewing, or participant observations seem to be the privileged methods in providing access to knowledge and understanding. Crime is indeed a tangible and factual phenomenon—something that is measured in official statistics, something that costs society a certain amount of money each year, something that is subject to political interventions and juridical sanctions, and something that has real-life consequences for individuals and societies—and thus is something that can be captured by conventional social science methods (such as surveys, interviews, or participant observation). However, crime is also an elusive phenomenon because it, at least most of the time to most of us, takes place far away from public scrutiny and direct observation. Fortunately, crime is something most of us mostly see, hear, or read about in the media rather than something of which we have first-hand experience. To a certain extent this may even also be the case for some criminologists who may primarily know about crime from statistics, documents, or other secondary data sources. This elusiveness and sequestered character of crime makes it relevant and at times even necessary to access knowledge and information from alternative sources. Here fiction—as a kind of "vicarious experience" supplementing, substantiating, corroborating, completing, or animating other types of "certified" or empirically generated knowledge—can prove particularly useful. Despite the thousands of books and feature films now devoted to depicting crime as a fictional topic, the reception of doing "filmic ethnography" or using the "cinematic imagination" in criminology has been a rather slow and delayed process. In contrast, despite a protracted labor process and a by no means uncontroversial birth, within the sibling discipline of sociology, there has for decades been a lively and by now longstanding tradition for cherishing and appreciating how film may inspire and ignite the sociological imagination.

The notion that social scientists, sociologists as well as criminologists, can learn something valuable from watching and studying film is in fact far from new. One of the first to point specifically to the intimate interconnections between social science and film was American novelist Philip Roth, whose review in *New Republic* showed how a host of films provided prejudicial and biased commentaries on acute social problems such as drugs and race (Roth 1957). From time to time, films would be cited in sociological research without any systematics or an overall agenda. The rise of the subgenre, the "sociology of film," was a natural offspring of the "sociology of literature." Later, the "sociology through literature" movement particularly surfaced throughout the 1970s on the American continent, insisting on showing the important interconnections between sociology and literature and variously pointing to the potentials of literary knowledge, literary technique, and literary analysis for sociologists (see, e.g., Berger 1977; Brown 1977; Coser 1972; Ofshe 1970; Rockwell 1974; Wilson 1979).

As American sociologist Lewis A. Coser convincingly argued in his introduction to "sociology through literature": "Sociologists have but rarely utilized works of literature in their investigations. And yet it would appear obvious that the trained sensibilities of a novelist or a poet may provide a richer source of social insight than, say, the impressions of untrained informants on which so much sociological research currently rests" (Coser 1972, 2). Presumably due to the rise and proliferation of satellite television throughout the late 1970s, the arrival and availability of the video-machine to ordinary people and the increasing supply of films in the cinema, this initial sociological interest in literature as an alternative source of knowledge later expanded also to include the realm of film during the 1980s (see, e.g. Demerath III 1981; Miller 1990; Prendergast 1986; Smith 1973). Some sociologists started seeing film as "social facts" through which to document social change, stratification, power structures, the causes behind socio- and psychopathologies, and so forth. Some even engaged in critically dissecting film as an integral part of the modern ideological state-apparatus or as a cog in the gigantic wheel of capitalist market culture, whereas others just allowed themselves to be inspired by film in their own research and teaching. For some, watching and investigating film thus became an important vehicle for starting to think sociologically about a variety of social topics, as vivid illustrations of social theory or as inspiration for theorizing. As Danish sociologists Bülent Diken and Carsten Bagge Laustsen stated in their *Sociology Through the Projector* regarding the way they approached films as so-called "emblems" aimed at enhancing a sociological imagination: "We treat the themes, the people and the objects inhabiting the films as emblems whose interactions produce meanings relevant to social theory. Such fragments taken from the films and placed in the field of social theory can stimulate sociological imagination" (Diken and Laustsen 2008, 12–13). Thus, the very notion of "cinematic sociology" (Sutherland and Feltey 2012) is today much less controversial, sensational and indeed—at least to some practitioners of the discipline—less frightening than when it was first introduced.

The situation seems to have been somewhat different in the field of criminology. Besides a few early and scattered film reviews and attempts at showing how film could possibly be used for scientific purposes (see, e.g., Nathe 1978; 1981; Swart 1985), the notion that film should become part of the teaching curriculum or be used as "data material" in research apparently took longer to mature for criminologists than for sociologists. Film references were therefore far from commonly found in criminological work and the "turn to films" begun by sociologists during the late 1970s and early 1980s was—perhaps due to the aforementioned quantitative predilection in the discipline—delayed within the field of criminology for a decade or two. With a few exceptions, it was not until the 1990s that more and more titles devoted to film analysis slowly started to appear in academic journals and book catalogues from publishing houses (see, e.g., Denvir 1996; Sparks 1992).

Today, things have changed rather drastically—perhaps not only due to the increased availability of film in our culture but also due to the important impact on the criminological discipline made by critical and cultural criminology. Now, courses on criminology and film are offered at several colleges, and universities and articles and books dealing with film are not regarded with the same indifferent shoulder shrug or suspicion as earlier. Within criminology and legal studies, researchers in recent years have undertaken serious and groundbreaking explorations of the cinematic imagination in relation to a multitude of different topics and with the use of a variety of different methods (for illustrative examples of this new interest in film, see, e.g., Bergman and Asimow 2006; Chase 2002; Clarens 1997; Frauley 2009; Greenfield, Osborn, and Robson 2010; Jacobsen and Petersen 2014: Jenkins 1992; Kauffman 2010; Leitch 2002; Rafter 2006; Tzanelli, O'Brien, and Yar 2005; Welch, Fleming, and Dowler 2011; Yar 2010). However, particularly a few recent and important publications really testify to the new status and increased acceptance of cinematic criminology. For example, American sociologist Mathieu Deflem's edited volume *Popular Culture, Crime and Social Control* (2010) shows how a multitude of popular cultural phenomena, manifestations, and artefacts such as film, music, paintings, television, sculptures, photographs, and Internet material can be meaningfully used to tease out information about crime topics. Additionally, in *Criminology, Deviance and the Silver Screen* (2011), Canadian sociologist Jon Frauley provides an in-depth argument for using fictional realities (including film) for conceptual development, theorizing, and pedagogical purposes in criminology and deviance studies, and American criminologists Nicole H. Rafter and Michelle Brown's book, *Criminology Goes to the Movies* (2011), displays a compelling use of central concepts and analytical tools of criminology are used to uncover previously unnoticed or neglected meanings in film in what is described as an increasingly mass-mediated culture. Although these volumes are perhaps not part of the criminological mainstream, and although some of them are indeed composed by trained sociologists, criminologists apparently and finally seem to have begun to appreciate that film provides a bountiful treasure trove for whoever wants to study, acquire knowledge about, and understand worlds of crime past and present.

Obviously, there are many potential uses of fiction, literary as well as filmic, in criminology. Here we will delimit our outlining and analysis to four uses—three of which are directly inspired by the work of Hills and

Hills (1968) who briefly proposed three metaphors to illustrate the fertile interplay between fiction and factual sociological or cultural analysis—what they termed *distillation, dramatization,* and *distortion*. To this trinity we below add *anecdotal data* as a fourth way of using film imaginatively to describe, understand and analyze crime-related topics. Each of these strategies will be exemplified and discussed with reference to a relevant film material.

DISTILLATION: FILM AS REALITY-CONCENTRATOR

Just as whiskey is distilled in order to provide the tasty depths to the mixture of quite ordinary ingredients, social reality, too, can be distilled by way of fictional imagination. Hills and Hills describe the method or strategy of *distillation* as follows:

> Distillation . . . is as good a name as any for the way in which the writer transforms the reality of what he knows into the reality of the story. Fiction gives the author the license to abstract from the raw material of what he knows, feels and believes (including his direct experience with people and things as well as his reading, his dreams and phantasies—the whole encyclopedia of his mind) an essence that takes on the shape of reality in the story. (Hills and Hills 1968, 892)

But distillation is not the domain of only the fiction writer. Distilling the essence of social reality into something more tangible and comprehensible is also what many film directors seek to achieve. Distillation is by no means an endeavor upon which only contemporary film directors have embarked. It has more or less always been the case that some films have tried to densify social reality for the audience, or at least aspects of it. British social realism is perhaps one of the most well-known genres where this is the case. Better than most other genres, social realism has shown the British self-portraits of and to themselves (and to the rest of the world), pushing the boundaries in the effort to put the experiences of real Britons on the screen. In the postwar period, films such as *Blue Scar* (directed by Jill Craigie), *It Always Rains on Sunday* (directed by Robert Hammer), and *Together* (directed by Lorenza Mazetti and Denis Horne)—just to mention a few—portrayed the seamy sides of life in Britain for especially working-class people in the years after World War I. Now, social realism is not constrained only to focusing on the everyday hardship of so-called ordinary people. Portraits of a less bleak nature have also been painted and nowadays humor is a great part of British social realism. For instance, filmmakers such as Ken Loach, Shane Meadows, and Mike

Leigh are all well-known for their roles in directing social realist films and television series and for their usage of humor and irony.

When it comes to social realism and films of interest to criminology, the case of Denmark is actually quite interesting. For many years (from 1968 until the beginning of the 1980s), the survival of Danish cinemas was almost entirely dependent upon a series of crime-comedies about *Olsen Banden* ("The Olsen Gang"), directed by Erik Balling (1968–1998). Shortly speaking, the series is about three petty-thieves—all of whom are portrayed in an almost comic-book manner—who dream about stealing millions of Danish Crowns (the national currency) that would allow them to kick back and spend the rest of their lives living comfortably in sunny Spain. The gang is organized around Egon Olsen—the crime genius and leader of the gang—who always has brilliant plans for how to steal the money, diamonds, and such and thus realize their dreams. The plans are always very creative, involving the usage of various odd artifacts that aid the gang in getting what they want. The metropolitan milieu within which the gang operates is always very cozy—one almost gets a sense of joining Danny Kaye in singing "Wonderful, wonderful, Copenhagen" from the 1952 musical *Hans Christian Andersen*. But alas—it always ends badly. Hence, every film (fourteen all in all) ends with Egon being captured by the police and sent off to prison. For many years, these films were a huge part of the Danish imaginary when it comes to crime in films. One of the main reasons for their success—besides being funny—was due to their harmless nature. Even though they revolved around crime, nobody was really hurt in the films. Nobody really got injured—physically or mentally. Nobody died. Furthermore, all the persons in the films were caricatures instead of "real persons," which ensured that the audience could laugh at them instead of properly relating to them.

Whereas the *Olsen Banden* films distilled crime in a comedic fashion, other directors later turned to a more sinister angle when distilling the world of crime. In 1996, Danish filmmaker Nicolas Winding Refn launched his film *Pusher*, which in many ways can be seen as a milestone in Danish film history. First of all, the film is publicly conceived as the first Danish gangster film (Blicher 2011), which uses violence in unprecedented ways in Danish cinema. Second, the film portrays two drug-dealers from the outskirts of Copenhagen who actually look and act like drug-dealers—something that we might call an "archetypical representation" (Greenfield 1983). Thus, the audience gets a sense of connection with Frank (Kim Bodnia) and Tommy (Mads Mikkelsen), the main characters. Third, Frank and Tommy are portrayed as stereotyped heterosexual omega males, acting male (Bingham 1994) in a rather different way than the Danish audience were used to seeing in the cinema. The very out-spoken—and in many ways unsympathetic—raw masculinity of Frank and Tommy stirred up real emotions and feelings: disgust, fascination, indignation, and so forth. But the social reality portrayed in the film also has its limitations. In *Pusher*, the audience is neither invited into the deeper layers of the main characters' psychology, nor are the social milieus in which the film takes place familiarized. That is, although the spectators get a glimpse of what reality could look like—and get a sense of connection with the main characters—they also become aware of the fact that this reality is limited to very few. Not a lot of people in Denmark are actually involved in dealing drugs, hardcore violence, and a daily struggle for survival.

Pusher certainly paved the way for other Danish filmmakers who aspired to engage themselves in this social realistic crime genre that distilled the worlds of crime in a sinister manner. Hence, in the last couple of decades, several Danish films have revolved around similar issues as *Pusher*—some with more successful outcomes than others. One very successful film of interest to this chapter in general—and to the strategy of distillation in particular—is *Nordvest* (Northwest), a 2013 film directed by Michael Noer. *Nordvest*—named after a rather notorious area in the northwest of Copenhagen—takes its point of departure in the life of eighteen-year old burglar Casper who lives in Nordvest with his mother and two younger siblings. Casper spends most of his time breaking into houses in the posh areas in the north-coast of Copenhagen. Casper sells the loot to third-generation immigrant Jamal, who runs a smaller gang in the neighborhood. However, in the opinion of Casper, Jamal is constantly cheating him—simply not offering him enough money for the stolen goods. Therefore, Casper sees it as a window of opportunity when bike-gang related pimp Bjørn offers him a better pay for the goods. But not only that—Casper also gets a chance to rise in the world of crime and subsequently, he quickly gets more and more ingrained in the hardcore criminal milieu of drugs, prostitution, trafficking and so forth. Jamal does not take Casper's new business agreement lightly, beating up Casper's little brother to show Casper that he means business; Jamal wants Casper to work for him exclusively. But Casper has reached a point of no return—he is simply not in a position to leave Bjørn's organization (he knows too much) and thus, he is gradually caught in a conflict that threatens to destroy not only him but also his immediate family.

The social reality distilled in *Nordvest* is more intimate than in *Pusher* and in many ways more relevant to more people. First of all, we get a clear sense of what class relationships in contemporary Danish society can entail. It is absolutely no coincidence that Casper burglarizes the rich, of whose life he can only dream. Additionally, he can rationalize his stealing by saying things like "they won't miss their stuff anyway" and "they got it coming for being so rich." Ultimately, what is really interesting is that the rich (or even middle-class) are not portrayed in the film as "normal." One often gets that impression in welfare-state Denmark that everybody is pretty much middle-class or even financially stable. *Nordvest* is painting a different picture of people who struggle to make ends meet and sometime engages in criminal activities to do so. Second, *Nordvest* is also a film about the hardships involved in raising a family as a single mother. One really gets the impression that Casper's mother is trying her best. But dealing with three kids alone, working late hours, and living in a tough neighborhood is a dangerous cocktail. Casper's mother wants to participate actively in the daily activities of her oldest son, but she does not have the ability to do so. Hence, Casper is "allowed" to pursue his criminal career. Maybe one could argue that the family is short of the resources that Pierre Bourdieu so famously called social capital, which he considered to be one of the pivotal aspects of successful social integration (Bourdieu 1986). Or, perhaps the analysis should be more acutely focused. Casper does not lack social capital—he has friends, networks, acquaintances, and so on—but he lacks the right kind. His social capital, seen from this perspective, has a negative impact on him rather than a positive one. There is no single answer to why this is the case. The film does not give its audience any unequivocal explanation as to why Casper and his family are in this position; rather, the perspective is multilayered.

We would argue that this is one of the reasons why *Nordvest* had such a positive reception in Denmark. Watching a struggling family, who is not portrayed as cynical, narrow-minded, or indifferent, but simply caught in difficult social situations and life-circumstances, is something to which a lot of people can relate and with which they can sympathize. To judge Casper and his family is therefore not made easy—something which attests to the relevance of the film when discussing even wider social aspects in contemporary Denmark. The film can be seen as raising issues of social exclusion during a historical epoch in which the criteria for social inclusion are narrowly defined by the ability to perform according to normal standards of education, the labor market and so forth. Those who fall short of normalcy are, more or less, on their own and can very easily find themselves in the same position as Casper and his family. By using films such as *Nordvest*—that distill complex social reality into a social realist drama—criminologists, in their research, can certainly raise attention to such issues in a very lively and interesting manner to the benefit of both students and researchers.

DRAMATIZATION: FILM AS PLOT AND CHARACTER CREATOR

It has once boldly been proposed that "reality is a drama, life is theater, and the social world is inherently dramatic" (Lyman and Scott 1975, 3).

Although we do not necessarily subscribe to such a dramaturgical view, there is no doubt that social life, to lesser or larger degrees, can appear rather dramatic, understood in the way that everyday life as well as structural levels of society every now and then are engaged in performances, negotiations, struggles, and the downright use of force, which are ultimately dramatic in character. At other times, however, everyday life, as well as structural levels of society, is characterized by anything but drama—repetition, staleness, dullness, and utterly undramatic occurrences. However, the interesting point in this particular connection is how we may learn about the dramas of social reality from the dramas of movies. The second possible use of fiction for criminologists is thus that of *dramatization*. Hills and Hills define this method or approach in the following way:

> Dramatization is the method by which the imagination is directly engaged . . . [in] making something happen in a story, of bringing alive the elements of character, plot, and setting, not only making them seem important, interesting and believable, but also putting them in motion, making them dynamic. (1968, 892–93)

Developing or inventing plots, storylines, characters, props, and such can in that perspective be seen as tools used to making something dynamic and hence lively. The endeavor of dramatization is therefore crucial and thus in constant need of reflections on "how to dramatize." Of course, several sources of inspiration can be used in completing this task. In relation to this chapter, however, we believe Robert J. Kelley has written something noteworthy when suggesting similarities between criminology and artistic endeavors:

> Like the criminologist, the novelist tends to break down a phenomenon, or a personality, into its interrelated parts for analysis. To seek larger meanings, to widen the scope to include other events, to offer hypotheses or speculations is to provide interpretation. Though the style of presentation differs, the logic of analysis and the intuitive understanding of interpretation fill the works of the artist and the scientist. Scientists create hypotheses, test them and draw conclusions; writers create plots and develop characters. In both styles of work, inspiration and imagination are the driving forces. (Kelly 1991, 56)

The same goes for the film director. His work is similar to that of the novelist—and arguably, the criminologist: to create believable stories and depict life-like personalities that have some similarities to real life persons. If he overly dramatizes, he risks the danger of caricature, ridicule, or even indifference.

In a jointly written piece (see Jacobsen and Petersen 2014) we have analyzed aspects of identity formation in the French prison drama *A Prophet*, which was released in 2009. In the article we first and foremost concentrate on the concept of prisonization and what that entails when analyzing the film through a prism of identity theory. In relation to this article, *A Prophet* is also interesting. When creating the main character of the film, Malik (Tahar Rahim), director Jaques Audiard was certainly aware of crucial aspects of dramatization. Malik, a young small-time crook of Arab decent is sentenced to six years in prison in Brécourt (a maximum security prison). Here, he is very quickly caught up in the prison hierarchy in which age-old Corsican mobster César Luciani (Niels Arnfred) is at the pinnacle. At the beginning, Malik is naturally scared of the Corsican gang—and in particular of their leader—and therefore very reluctant to engage in any sort of confrontation or arrangement with them. Moreover, due to his Arabic descent, Malik is almost obliged to take side with the other Arabs in the prison in the everyday battle between Arabs and whites. But the story is much more complex than that. It does not want to portray a uniform rivalry between two opposing sides. Rather, it wants—via Malik—to engage in the multifaceted nature of contemporary prison life. It does so in the following way.

One day, Reyeb (Hichem Yacoubi), an Arab who is temporarily in the same prison and who is to testify against the Corsican gang with which César Luciani is associated, notices Malik in the showers. Reyeb tries to make friends with Malik—offers him a joint—but also makes an advance with sexual intent. Malik accepts the joint but rejects the sexual offer, something that is observed by the Corsican contingent. After this incident, the Corsicans send for Malik; they have an offer he cannot refuse. They suggest that Malik try to gain Reyeb's trust, albeit only for the purpose of killing Reyeb. It takes a while before Malik understands the direness of his predicament, the fact that he is caught in a kill-or-be-killed situation. In a very extreme way, what is being portrayed in the film is a full-fledged rite of initiation. One can actually see this as a bizarre "male initiation ceremony" (Young 1962), whose function is to transform Malik from a youngster to a "real man." While the roving camera shows the unwatchable—a violent struggle that culminates in Malik cutting the victim's carotid artery with a razor blade—the spectators become aware of the drastic transition that Malik's life is undergoing. With the attack on Reyeb, Malik's apprenticeship really begins. So, while having saved his own life by taking a life, Malik is also entering a life of submission: he is now at the mercy of the Corsicans.

For us, at least two different and dramatized sorts of analysis can be deduced from this. First of all, it is made painfully obvious that prison life—more often than not—makes you become a hardcore criminal rather than turning you into a "good" citizen. To director Audiard (2009), there is simply no need to overdramatize this. It is almost a social fact. Time and time again it has been shown that prisons are hotbeds for criminal careers, conclusions that criminological research is sure to back (Burnett and Maruna 2004; Needels 1996). Second—and even more interesting in connection with the theme of this section—the transformation in Malik's life situation is not static. Rather, Audaird is concerned with the dynamic nature of Malik's journey toward becoming somebody he—more or less—chooses to be. As the film progresses, it becomes more and more evident that Malik does not intend to be an apprentice for all of his prison life. He does not want to be repressed by the Corsicans—to be a pure instrument in their hands. To escape this situation he uses different tools. He learns the Corsican language so that while he serves his masters at the dining table, he can understand their jargon and their private conversations. They, on the other hand, cannot understand what he is saying when he speaks in Arabic to other Arabs or to them. He learns the tricks and the trades of prison life—he becomes street-wise. Slowly but surely, Malik expands his prison activities and engages with others outside the Corsican gang. By dominating the language of his masters and maneuvering in other waters than those controlled by the Corsicans, Malik not only becomes aware of his situation, but he also paves the way to overturning the power relationship and thus (re)claims his own identity. César Luciani is not unaware of this development. One of Audiards's great accomplishments is that he allows the dynamism of Malik's development to have an impact on the old mobster. Luciani is also forced to adapt to the changed circumstances, which he does by gradually giving more personal and complex orders to Malik, thereby addressing Malik more as an equal partner. Moreover, Malik is invited into the inner circles of the mobster organization, thereby gaining a position of irreplaceability. The playing fields gradually level out. Of course, this is not a lasting situation. Equality between Malik and Luciani is unthinkable in a prison environment. Consequently, one of the two needs to be victorious. Eventually, Malik is the conqueror. He does not replace Luciani as the new boss *per se*, but he ensures that the old mobster is made an outcast, with Luciani getting a serious beating by some of his former confidants. Hence, the film is also a story about how power relationships in prisons can be altered—how old regimes can be replaced by new ones in an unconventional setting.

To us, there is no doubt about the fact that criminologists could very easily be inspired by *A Prophet* in their analyses of the aspects—and even others—we have taken into consideration here. Thus, the dramatization technique employed in the film can certainly aid and give life to criminological descriptions—making them even more dynamic and thus paradoxically perhaps also more believable.

DISTORTION: FILM AS DELIBERATE DECEIVER

The third strategy mentioned by Hills and Hills is that of *distortion*. Distortion is defined as a by-product of distillation and dramatization—as something that takes place whenever these two methods are exaggerated:

> The analogy is to the difference between the flat, white-light "accuracy" of a photograph and the painting of a fine artist, who gives dimension by emphasizing depths and shadows, who subtly distorts or even exaggerates features so as to point up that which, according to his vision and technique, he sees as significant, as the real nature of his object. (Hills and Hills 1968, 893)

Caricature, disproportion and so on are not uncommon features in films about criminals or criminality. Since the birth of this filmic genre, distortion has been a very important instrument in the toolkit of filmmakers. Of course, there are various problematic aspects that might follow in the wake of using the technique of distortion. Let us point at two—by no means exhausting the issue under consideration—problems. Filmic distortion—or the production of fictitious images as such—may lead to misconceptions of criminals that can jeopardize social and legal justice, as Steven Kohm and Pauline Greenhill have argued for in their article *Pedophile Crime Films as Popular Culture: A Problem of Justice?* (see Kohm and Greenhill 2011). This means that cinematic distortion may create an environment of hostility toward certain criminals; nevertheless, distortion can also have the opposite effect and present hardcore criminals as human beings rather than as monsters. A rather different problem is scrutinized by American sociologist Nicholas J. Demerath III. In his review of the uses of film in sociology, Demerath III quoted Daniel Bell's observation on the distorting technique involved in modern cinema:

> The influence of the cinematic technique . . . creates a distortion of common sense perception in the total range of human experience. The effect . . . is to dramatize each moment, to increase our tension to a fever pitch, and yet to leave us without a resolution, reconciliation or transforming moment. (Demerath III 1981, 74)

Distortion can thus lead us astray and perhaps even blur our focus to a point of blindness. But it can also sharpen our attention toward specific issues upon which a filmmaker wants to shed additional light. Seen in this perspective, distortion can help to raise moral, ethical, aesthetic, and critical issues that otherwise have a hard time getting the necessary attention of the public. Let us give an example.

In 2002, Brazilian filmmaker Fernando Meirelles released the internationally acclaimed movie *City of God*. The film is based on author Paoulo

Lins's book from 1997, *Cidade des Deus*. Generally speaking, the book—and hence the film—is about the hardship of life in the infamous *favela* (slum, shantytown) *City of God* in Rio de Janeiro. For people growing up in this *favela*—as well as in many others—education, jobs, and a safe existence are hopeless dreams. Instead, the road to recognition, respect, and money is paved with guns, violence, murder, and drug dealing. At the age of eight or nine, the kids in the *favela* begin their criminal careers as lookouts, while their older friends commit various crimes. In this brutal environment, kids find work in organized crime. A "normal" career is that of working your way through the ranks: from lookout to teenage thug to finally becoming a genuine ice-cold and deadly street-warrior. Normaly, this consists of reproducing a vicious circle of organized crime that seems extremely hard to break. At the beginning of the book Paoulo Lins makes a very poetic description of the *favela*. He writes:

> *City of God* lent its voice to ghosts in the abandoned mansions, thinned out the flora and fauna, remapped little Portugal and renamed the marsh: Up Top, Out Front, Down Below, The Other side of the River and the Blocks. Even now, the sky turns blue and fills the world with stars, forests make the earth green, clouds whiten landscapes and mankind innovates, reddening the river. Here, now, a slum, a neo-slum of concrete, brimming with dealer-doorways, sinister-silences and cries of despair along its lanes and in the indecision of its crossroads. (Lins 2007, 6)

The picture painted is extremely grim. But then again, the reality in Brazilian *favelas* is grim. The tagline in *City of God* is: "If you run, the beast catches you; if you stay, the beast eats you," a proverb analogous to the English: "Damned if you do, damned if you don't." So, why should Meirelles use any form of distortion when making a film out of the book? The conditions portrayed in the book are hard enough as it is. So why not just make a one-to-one transformation of the book into a film? To be fair, Meirelles is very true to the intentions of the book. But he also stresses something very clearly—one could say distorts it—namely the ways in which Brazilian society *per se* turns the blind eye to the outrageous social situation in the *favela*. More specifically, Meirelles directs attention to the ways in which the police plays a big part in supporting the possible reproduction of the social illnesses in the *favela*. As vividly shown in the film—something the director quite obviously is anxious to highlight for his audience—the main goal of the police is not to put an end to the crimes committed in the City of God. It is not to make things better for the inhabitants. Rather, the police take advantage of the situation and use the *favela* as a source of income. Hence, the only time the police enters the *favela* is when they collect their bribes. Otherwise they do not care about what is happening in the *favela*, as long as the criminal activities are being contained within the geographical limits of the *favela*, that is. The political economy of the situation is thus understandable for both parties and status quo is easily maintained. This is a status quo that seems much more beneficial to the police than to the ordinary people living in the *favela*. Of course, there is a direct line from corruption within the police force to political corruption as such. Additionally, the audience is left with no doubt that this connection actually exists.

What Meirelles does, when focusing on these issues, is not only point out how nauseatingly rotten the Brazilian police force and political establishment apparently are. Rather, he also addresses wider issues of social inequality that are inherent in the problems of the *favela*. In that sense, Meirelles uses the film as a societal critique, thereby highlighting one of the most obvious social problems in Brazilian society that for some odd reason was not a huge part of the public consciousness prior to the book or the film. In the introduction to an entire anthology concerned with *City of God*—the book as well as the film—Brazilian social scientist Else R. P. Viera pays tribute to the ways in which Meirelles's film has strengthened and amplified the public awareness of *favela* problems. She writes:

> "Is the camera mightier than the word and the sword?" is the question that has hovered over our journey. The voices in this book, disparate as they may be, in unison seem to imply the need for the recovery of the social and political ethos. Cidade de Deus, before Paulo Lins's book, was an open letter that no one cared to read. The camera and the sound technology of Meirelles's *City of God* further hit our eyes and ears with the magnitude of the problem of dire poverty encountering drug traffic, in our days unimaginably aggravated as it has fallen into the hands of global narco-guerrillas. (Viera 2005, xxv)

The power of the film to raise public awareness is, in this perspective, pivotal. It is somewhat tragic/comical that the film also raised awareness in other areas, for example, in the tourist industry. As Bianca Freire-Medeiros (2011, 21) has shown, *City of God* gave a regular boost to this industry, raising the numbers of foreign visitors to the *favela* considerably. There seems to be no doubt about the fact that Meirelles—somewhat due to using the technique of distortion—has managed to open doors (to the public as well as to various political milieus) that were otherwise closed. By doing so, this film made a significant contribution to public debates about important social problems. Indeed it was to a large extent agenda-setting for reality. Moreover, the film highlighted particular aspects about organized crime in the *favelas* of Brazil that could be intriguing for criminologists to investigate even further.

ANECDOTAL DATA: FILM AS IMAGINATIVE AND INDIRECT EVIDENCE

Besides the three aforementioned uses of fiction as sources of inspiration (as well as sources of potential distortion) for criminologists—*distillation, dramatization*, and *distortion*—we propose a fourth strategy for using fiction in general and film in particular that might be added. We call this *anecdotal data* (sometimes referred also to as "anecdotal evidence" in research methodology books). Whereas the three previously listed strategies describe processes that in some way are "internal" techniques through which films function, film as "anecdotal data" can be used as an "external" strategy from which the criminological researcher can directly draw. Such anecdotal data can illustrate his or her own analysis with experiences or events that are difficult to come by through empirical studies either due to the sequestered nature of these experiences or because, in complex reality, they seldom seem to occur in such a clear-cut and "pure" manner as in filmic depictions. Anecdotal data comes in many different guises and with differing levels of substantiation, depth, and scope such as: personal life stories, rumors, gossip, recollections, testimonials, newspaper clippings, drawings, film, graffiti, posters, music, and such. In short, the world is full to the brim with tiny bits and pieces that may provide important insights or prove to be documentation of human activity—factual or fictional. Anecdotal data are generally not held in high regard in sociological or criminological circles, because it is seen as unscientific and subjective—it is also controversial because it is often found in an unsystematic process of association and is difficult to validate (see, e.g., Moore and Stilgoe 2009). For example, as stated in the introduction to a criminological theory primer, "criminology is based not on authority or anecdotes but on empirical research" (Tibbetts 2015, 10). However, anecdotal data every now and then still ends up—either in a systematic or more often an impressionistic manner—in scholarly work, and generally for a good reason. Everyday life is to a large degree made up of this kind of material. As British criminologist Mike Presdee once so memorably described the approach of cultural sociology and its use of everyday "data":

> Cultural criminology uses the "evidence" of everyday existence, wherever it is found and in whatever form it can be found; the debris of everyday life is its "data." It uses cultural artefacts whenever and wherever they present themselves, examining the cultural "trail" they leave behind. Life histories, images, music and dance, all have a story to tell in the unravelling of crime. (Presdee 2000, 15)

Although Presdee did not specifically mention film as part of these useful cultural artifacts, films are indeed some of the most widespread and globally consumed cultural items containing important information about our culture, society, lifestyles, and subjective experiences. Borrowing for the vast pool of popular cultural inputs should be seen as possessing research potential rather than as a problem for criminology (Young 2008). Moreover, few would claim that the generally recognizable "anecdotes" from everyday life used by Canadian sociologist Erving Goffman—despite his own admission that they were neither "proof" nor "evidence"—were entirely irrelevant or utterly useless for theorizing (see, e.g. Goffman 1974, 15). Notwithstanding this, very few researchers openly admit that their studies or analyses draw on such anecdotal data. One notable exception with specific reference to criminology is British criminologist Dennis Chapman's classic *Sociology and the Stereotype of the Criminal* in which he initially testified how "this study will present tentative arguments based on fragmentary and anecdotal data not crucial in themselves but pervasive enough, it is hoped, to compel consideration of the argument" (Chapman 1968/2001, 7). Despite such an admission, anecdotal data is seldom consulted or used directly as a source of evidence in journal articles or research reports because such information is seen as lacking the rigor, quantity, and scope characteristic of what is generally regarded as "real" data.

As C. Wright Mills once reminded his readers regarding an integral quality of being an "intellectual craftsman," much can be gained from encouraging and pursuing "an attitude of playfulness towards the phrases and words with which various issues are defined," which will often "loosen up the imagination" (Mills 1959, 212). So why would we then deliberately diminish the research potential of that which is not conventionally counted as "data"? What could possibly be gained from narrowing "data" down only to what has been "officially" harvested during ethnographic fieldwork? Why limit the research parameters to what—at times quite sporadically—has been collected as interview material, what has been predefined as "documents" or to the—at times quite shallow—information gathered in a survey? Using anecdotal data as imaginative evidence serves a purpose precisely because the dividing line between factual data and other types of knowledge is dotted rather than double drawn. As British sociologist Joan Rockwell once suggested in her book *Fact in Fiction*, "social fact may be revealed by fiction, even fiction of the most wildly improbable kind" (Rockwell 1974, 117). The quality of anecdotal data thus consists in the fact that film can often tell us more with one well-put example, such as from a film sequence compared with ten in-depth interviews or a comprehensive survey material. Anecdotal data allows us as "outsiders" to "get inside" people or situations that are difficult to sample, to access or to follow over extended periods of time.

Let us take a few film examples to illustrate this contention. How can we use anecdotal data such as film in order to understand release from prison and problems relating to rehabilitation? Obviously, we could ask ex-convicts about what they see as the main obstacles to successful social reintegration and the primary dangers for recidivism. However, there are also other options. Most movie aficionados are familiar with the unforgettable halfway house scene from *The Shawshank Redemption* (directed by Frank Darabont, 1994). Here we see the character Brooks Hatlen (James Whitmore), an old man released from jail who after years of imprisonment had become a thoroughly "institutionalized man" completely unable to make it on the outside, deciding to commit suicide. Standing on a ramshackle chair on feeble old legs, he carves "Brooks was here" into the ceiling beam before hanging himself. The scene is indeed a thought-provoking and dramatic testimony of the difficulties of rehabilitation and reintegration of ex-criminals.

As another example of using anecdotal data, how can we try to understand what goes on in the hermetically closed world of everyday life in multi-ethnic and gang-dominated prisons when somebody is breaking the rules? In the Danish prison film *R* (directed by Tobias Lindholm, 2010) the collective punishment and bestial murder of the main character, Rune (Pilou Asbæk) (hence the film title *R*), is an illustrative example of how snitches and cheats are treated in a closed and violent prison environment, about which it would be difficult to obtain first-hand research information due to fear of retaliation from other inmates. The same goes for knowledge about juvenile correction facilities. For example, watching Canadian film *Dog Pound* (directed by Kim Chaprion, 2010) provides an intriguing insight into the hidden world of making and breaking power hierarchies, friendships, violence, harassment, and revolt among youth offenders. Or how can we access knowledge about the possible causes and consequences of street prostitution? Of course, we can turn to reports on the experiences and human costs of long-term prostitution or we can interview practicing or previous prostitutes or even experts in the field. However, in order to get into and capture the interwoven and complex connections between disturbed sexuality, childhood traumas, petty crime, prostitution, alcohol problems, emotional troubles, stigmatization, and a string of murders (in self-defense) we might have to turn to film. Here watching the reality-based film *Monster* (directed by Patty Jenkins, 2003) could allow the researcher to witness and understand some of the disheartening social and personal experiences driving women into, out of, and back to prostitution. The same saturated insights would undeniably be difficult to obtain from survey material or participant observation alone.

Based on these few selected examples above, there are obviously many useful applications of anecdotal data such as, for example, films in criminological research. Thus, we summarize six such potential and general uses will be summarized:

1. Anecdotal data may function, for the individual researcher as well as for an entire research community, as imaginative "kick-starters" for thinking about a neglected or overlooked topic. This is the generative potential of anecdotal data.
2. Anecdotal data may problematize and confront doxic or supposedly self-evident knowledge within a field of study by putting things into perspective and offering creative or counter-factual openings for innovative thinking.
3. Anecdotal data may highlight hidden dimensions or fill out knowledge holes in existing research literature.
4. Anecdotal data may serve purely ornamental purposes of academic texts or provide illustrative or poetic sources of alternative data material to supplement, substantiate, corroborate, complete, or animate other more conventional types of data.
5. Anecdotal data may make reading research much more interesting, pleasurable, thought-provoking, recognizable, or accessible (perhaps particularly to non-academic audiences) than the often tedious, pretentious, or technical presentation of findings normally found in scientific journals or research volumes.
6. Anecdotal data may provide ingenious illustrations of how the world potentially could be and could have been different from what it currently is. This is the utopian potential of anecdotal data.

All of the above—by no means exhaustive—points pertain to and summarize what has been stated so far in this chapter regarding the potential use of film in criminological research. Although we have generally applauded the distilling, dramatizing, distorting, and anecdotal qualities of film as sources of inspiration and as "data," we also urge caution and careful consideration. Without detracting from the value of anecdotal data, the criminologist, when for example using film sources as "data," naturally needs to be wary not to confuse the fictional world with the empirically verifiable or validated world. These worlds are not necessarily the same—even though they at times overlap quite considerably. So although anecdotal data may be persuasive and telling for criminologists, such data can also lead criminologists to follow false leads, or lead to their findings being questioned or even downright refuted by existing research. Good anecdotal data is data that allows us to move beyond the confines of what we already know or think we know with the uncompromising reservation that this source of "data" necessarily needs to be supported, corroborated, or substantiated by other types of data in order to acquire scientific status.

TEACHING CRIMINOLOGY THROUGH FILM

As should have become clear by now, the main purpose of this article is to show how social scientists—especially criminologists—might benefit from, be inspired by and learn from the strategies of *distillation*, *dramatization*, *distortion*, and *anecdotal data*. Furthermore, we have elaborated on these techniques to show how criminologists could inspire, buttress, and refine their analyses through the insights from film. Now, we will move on to showing how criminologists can benefit from using films in their teaching.

More than four decades ago American sociologist Lewis A. Coser insightfully observed how reading fiction for students—as well as for everybody else—may provide "an opportunity to clothe the dry bones of social theory with the living and plastic tissue which grows from literary imagination" (Coser 1972, 5). However, reading fiction is not the only way forward to securing more interesting and perhaps even more enlightening teaching. In an article entitled "Creativity in the Classroom—The Poetics of Pedagogy and Therapeutic Shock in Teaching Sociology" we outlined a series of suggestions that would (could) make university teaching more interesting to the students as well as to the teachers (Petersen, Jacobsen, and Antoft 2014). The starting point of the article was something that a lot of university teachers (probably) can relate to, namely the somewhat formal, dry, and dusty affair of teaching. Or, perhaps one could even say the rigidity of teaching. Often, lecturers, speaking in a large auditorium, provide compressed information to a number of students sitting in rows of chairs, in the expectation that the knowledge thus imparted will guide them as well as possible to pass their future examinations. In many cases, teaching is not a dialogue, but rather a monologue. The teaching environment can, sometimes, be blamed for this. Perhaps the location and the actual form of teaching do not permit more active involvement from the students. Sometimes curriculum pressures can lead to everything being targeted and focused on providing relatively specific keywords or concepts that are easy to remember. This is hardly something that ignites the imagination of the students—nor of the teachers, for that matter. And we know this. Or, we should know it. Several years ago, the critical German social scientist Oskar Negt spoke of the phenomenon of "exemplary learning" (Negt 1981), by which he meant that through experimentation with the form of learning—including group and project work—it should be possible for students (and in his perspective, particularly working-class students) to come to understand themselves as subjects in a wider social context, and thereby be made aware of their own (revolutionary) potential. Seen in this perspective, teachers have an obligation to make the students learn about society—in this case about criminology—through unusual, unconventional, and at times provocative, challenging, and boundary-shifting pedagogical means, such as film.

We hope that we have more than hinted at this throughout this chapter. Films are able to "do something" to the audience as well as to social scientists. Moreover, they can make some things happen: ignite social, political and cultural debates and instigate societal critique. Films are thus able to be influential on a larger—structural—scale. Films mentioned in this chapter have done so. A lot of other films have done the same. Just think of how John Badham's controversial 1981 film *Whose Life Is It Anyway?* which proved to be seminal in relation to discussions about euthanasia, or how entirely fiction-based films like *Lord of the Rings* (2001–2003) or *The Da Vinci Code* (2006) in recent years have helped to stimulate popular and politicoreligious discussions of right and wrong, good and evil, among a worldwide audience. The important thing is that the films do not need to be of a specific kind. It is our view that, in principle, all films can be used as an analytical basis or as inspiration for criminological thinking—they do not need to be particularly intellectual or avant-garde. Of course, we are not the only ones of this opinion. Within the discipline of sociology the journal, *Teaching Sociology*, has been instrumental in showing and arguing for the importance of using film in teaching a variety of topics. For example, C. Emery Burton (1988) argues that films not only have the advantage of stimulating alternative takes on social issues, but also can overcome the apathy and boredom of some students. Furthermore, Lauraine LeBlanc (1997) stipulates how teaching ethnographic methods can benefit from using films. As she writes:

> Using feature film as a common basis of experience is one way instructors can prepare students for field research. . . . The use of feature films to teach ethnography is really quite distinct from the content of the film, so almost any feature film could be used to teach observational skills. (LeBlanc 1997, 66)

In criminology, the *Journal of Criminal Justice Education* has performed an analogous role to what *Teaching Sociology* has done in the discipline of sociology when it comes to proposing strategies and methods for using film as sources of inspiration. A multitude of examples from this journal can be shown (for example Cook and Bacot 1993; Pino, Brunson, and Stewart 2009; Rockell 2009); nevertheless, other journals have taken the issue into consideration (see Atherton 2013; Rogers 1986). However, we believe one of the best arguments for using films in teaching criminology is provided by Diana Bretherick. She observed:

> It is often [people's] own cultural experience of crime and criminals that excites their interest. They read about crime in the press and fictional and non-fictional literature. They see it on television, on the news, in drama, documentaries and reconstructions. It is a favorite subject for film makers. The Internet is full of apposite websites. Culturally we are saturated by crime to the extent that it almost excludes any other subject. This is what brings most students to study criminology and yet, ironically, the academic discipline has, until recently, tended to neglect crime as popular culture, preferring to adhere to the tried and tested formula of sociological theory, psychological insights and criminal justice considerations. (Bretherick 2006, 6)

Indeed, this is bizarre. Why not use this source of information, this source of data, even more so than seems to be the case? Why not meet the students of criminology on their own turf? Of course, we cannot claim that this is not being done already. We do not have any empirical data suggesting that criminologists around the world are not following these suggestions. All we have is a strong hunch.

If using films in teaching still sounds a bit awkward to some teachers, we would like to pin-point some rather concrete pedagogical benefits that this endeavor can attain. As American sociologist Cheryl Laz once suggested, fiction—although she particularly referred to the genre of "science fiction"—has a variety of important functions when used in sociology teaching sessions:

1. *Making strange*—a process through which it defamiliarizes the already and apparently well-known and commonsensical world and sheds light on that which is taken for granted.
2. *Making believe*—a process through which hypothetical-speculative or creative thought-experiments are conjured up about how social life and social institutions could otherwise look like and maybe one day will end up looking like.
3. *Making real*—a process through which the use of abstract sociological concepts or "anonymous" theories is brought into play with concrete descriptions of actual individuals and their actions, motives, wishes, dreams, etc. from the world of fiction. (Laz 1996)

As mentioned earlier, what pertains to the discipline of sociology when it comes to the use of film in teaching is also of relevance to the field of criminology due to their close disciplinary affinity. We hope to have shown that films—in criminological analysis as well as teaching—can be very beneficent to both students as well as teachers.

CONCLUSION

As we, in this chapter, have aspired to argue, illustrate and discuss, criminology—in its research endeavors as well as in teaching contexts—could quite possibly benefit from acknowledging the value of crime-related topics found in fiction in general and particularly in film. Although such an argument is perhaps less controversial today as it may have been a decade or two ago—especially as more and more volumes continue to be published documenting the utility of fiction in social science research—it is nevertheless still relatively rare that film is specifically used as "evidence" or what might be termed "vicarious experience" in criminological research. This "methodological limitation" (Mills 1959) means that important sources of knowledge are routinely overlooked or downright rejected in favor of more certified types of information such as what can be obtained through conventional methods of interviews, surveys, or fieldwork.

In the chapter we have, by adopting some insightful strategies once suggested by Hills and Hills (1968) in their book on how fiction can shed light on and enhance our understanding of different dimensions social life, attempted to show the multiple potential uses of fiction and particularly film as an indispensable part of the methodological toolbox of the practicing criminologist. Hills and Hills proposed *distillation, dramatization,* and *distortion* as three ways or processes through which fiction can assist us in understanding what goes on in society as well as in the lives of individuals and groups. To this trinity we have added a fourth strategy termed *anecdotal data* suggesting that although film—their characters, storylines, plots, settings, and such—are indeed fictional accounts that are not to be confused with the raw data one collects, such as data gathered during fieldwork, interviewing or surveys, the potentials for a creative inclusion of cinematic insights into criminological research is indeed present. Moreover, we have argued that spicing up criminology teaching through the use of films might not only benefit the students' understanding of crime but it could also help focus their attention during occasional dull introductions to criminological theory.

Some might object that such a permissive perspective is unnecessarily confusing science with art or and that it can only be regarded as an adventure in some sort of artsy or quirky criminology. However, if used wisely, creatively as well as with analytical ingenuity and rigor, then film may serve as an important source of knowledge whenever studying areas that are either under-theorized or under-researched. Additionally, when filmic images, characters, and plots might provoke new understandings or generate overlooked insights to supplement, substantiate, clarify, complete, corroborate, or animate existing knowledge. This could be the case in a variety of different areas of criminology, for example when studying criminal identity, gang crime, white collar crime, prostitution, street violence, or aspects of the juridical or penal systems. In short, filmic material can, in various parts of the research process, constitute a useful source of knowledge.

Here we have specifically argued for the use of film as such as source of inspiration for criminological research. At times like these in which the crime genre looms large in the public mind and in which everybody can now easily access excessive amounts of crime films and television series via suppliers such as Netflix, HBO, or Viaplay, we might just as well take advantage of these relatively new available sources of popular cultural information and interpretation and—though obviously subjecting them to sober assessment and critical inquiry—use them for analytical purposes.

However, social life holds much more in promise for the observant and imaginative criminological researcher than merely film. British sociologist Wilhelm Baldamus once suggested that sociologists, not to mention criminologists, ought to trace and embrace alternative sources of knowledge in our pursuit of making discoveries or covering new territory in the social sciences. In order to do so, we would need to recognize that narrow understandings or notions of "research," "method," "data," and "validity" need to be sidestepped. In Baldamus's own words: "We would have to presume that side by side with the *official* methodology that one finds in the textbooks on systematic theory, formal logic, statistical methods, survey design or interviewing procedure, there exists a reservoir of *unofficial*, non-formalized techniques of inquiry" (Baldamus 1972, 281). According to Baldamus we should recognize and perhaps even plunge ourselves into this reservoir of "unofficial" knowledge; furthermore, he believes that such alternative sources could importantly contribute to so-called "informal theorizing" which, to him, formed "a large and indispensable element of all empirical research" (Baldamus 1972, 295). Thus, as we have proposed, there are ample reasons for even the empirically oriented criminologist to consult film as input which might aid and abet attempts at theorizing. Moreover, and more generally, as Dutch philosopher Jan Jakob A. Mooij once proposed in his defense for so-called "fictional realities," "they produce a marvelous complement to the acknowledged realities and the received truths of the scientific world-view" (Mooij 1993, 5). Imagination, according to Mooij, is an integral part of such fictional realities that "is based on a free, creative use of the relevant data" (Mooij 1993, 6). Imagination can thus serve many purposes for the criminologist, particularly pointing him or her to that which, in Murray S. David's (1971) wise words, is "interesting" rather than necessarily "true." However, we need to stress that fiction, and in this case the cinematic imagination, is not a substitute for scientifically grounded criminological knowledge;

rather, it is a supplement that, whenever it seems appropriate, fruitful, or necessary, and can assist us in comprehending crime-related matters more closely or more creatively.

This chapter has aspired to argue that criminologists ought to look beyond the cramped confines of conventional methodology and data sources and deploy a more playful attitude toward what they are studying and how they are teaching. This is not to suggest that criminology cannot proceed without paying attention to unofficial methodologies but it is a way of proposing that nothing can be lost from trying to expand one's methodological and analytical horizon. Whether we have succeeded in our endeavor will ultimately have to be decided by the reader.

REFERENCES

Atherton, Matthew C. 2013. "Teaching Criminology Through Film: Utilizing Popular Criminology in the Classroom." *Journal of Excellence in College Teaching* 24(2): 1–24.

Audiard, Jacques (director) and Martine Cassinelli and Antonin Dedet (producers). 2009. *A Prophet* [Motion Picture]. France: AGC Distribution.

Baldamus, Wilhelm. 1972. "The Role of Discoveries in Social Science." In *The Rules of the Game: Cross-Disciplinary Essays on Models in Scholarly Thought*, edited by Teodor Shannin, 276–302. London: Tavistock.

Balling, Erik (director). 1968–1998. *Olsen-banden* [Motion Picture Series Consisting of Fourteen Films]. Denmark: Nordisk Film.

Barton, Alana, Karen Corteen, David Scott, and David Whyte (eds.). 2007. *Expanding the Criminological Imagination—Critical Readings in Criminology*. Cullompton: Willan.

Berger, Morroe. 1977. *Real and Imagined Worlds: The Novel and Social Science*. London: Harvard University Press.

Bergman, Paul, and Michael Asimow. 2006. *Reel Justice: The Courtroom Goes to the Movies*. Kansas City: Andrews McMeel Publishing.

Bingham, Dennis. 1994. *Acting Male: Masculinities in the Films of James Stewart, Jack Nicholson, and Clint Eastwood*. New Brunswick, NJ: Rutgers University Press.

Blicher, Mattias. 2011. "Rebellen der drog fra andedammen." Retrieved June 23, 2015 from www.ekkofilm.dk/artikler/rebellen-der-drog-fra-andedammen/.

Bourdieu, Pierre. 1986. "The Forms of Capital." In *Handbook of Theory for the Sociology of Education,* edited by John E. Richardson, 241–58. London: Greenwood Press.

Bretherick, Diana. 2006. *Crime from Below: An Examination of the Role of Popular Cultural Representations of Crime in Criminology*. Unpublished PhD thesis, University of Portsmouth.

Brown, Richard H. 1977. *A Poetic for Sociology: Towards a Logic of Discovery for the Human Sciences*. Cambridge: Cambridge University Press.

Burnett, Ros, and Shadd Maruna. 2004. "So 'Prison Works,' Does It? The Criminal Careers of 130 Men Released from Prison under Home Secretary, Michael Howard." *The Howard Journal* 43(4): 390–404.

Burton, C. Emory. 1988. "Sociology and the Feature Film." *Teaching Sociology* 16(3): 263–71.

Chapman, Dennis. 1968/2001. *Sociology and the Stereotype of the Criminal*. London: Routledge.

Chase, Anthony. 2002. *Movies on Trial: The Legal System on the Silver Screen*. New York: New Press.

Clarens, Carlos. 1997. *Crime Movies*. New York: Da Capo Press.

Cook, Kathy L., and Hunter Bacot. 1993. "Movies in the Classroom: Popular Images of Criminal Justice, Criminology and the Law." *Journal of Criminal Justice Education* 4(1): 199–209.

Coser, Lewis A. (ed.). 1972. *Sociology Through Literature*, 2nd edition. Englewood Cliffs, NJ: Prentice-Hall.

Davis, Murray S. 1971. "That's Interesting!—Towards a Phenomenology of Sociology and a Sociology of Phenomenology." *Philosophy of the Social Sciences* 1(4): 309–45.

Debord, Guy. 1970. *The Society of the Spectacle*. New York: Black & Red.

Deflem, Mathieu. 2007. "Alfred Hitchcock and Sociological Theory: Parsons Goes to the Movies." *Sociation Today* 5(1), online version.

———. 2010. *Popular Culture, Crime and Social Control*. Bingley: Emerald.

Demerath III, Nicholas J. 1981. "Through a Double-Crossed Eye: Sociology and the Movies." *Teaching Sociology* 9(1): 69–82.

Denvir, John. 1996. *Legal Reelism: Movies as Legal Texts*. Champaign, IL: University of Illinois Press.

Denzin, Norman K. 1991. *Images of Postmodern Society: Social Theory and Contemporary Cinema*. London: Sage Publications.

———. 1995. *The Cinematic Society: The Voyeur's Gaze*. London: Sage Publications.

DiChristina, Bruce (ed.). 2012. *The Birth of Criminology: Readings from the Eighteenth and Nineteenth Centuries*. New York: Wolters Kluwer Law and Business.

Diken, Bülent, and Carsten Bagge Laustsen. 2008. *Sociology through the Projector*. London: Routledge.

Ferrell, Jeff. 2009. "Kill Method: A Provocation." *Journal of Theoretical and Philosophical Criminology* 1(1): 1–22.

Frauley, Jon. 2009. "The Fictional Reality and Criminology: On Ontology of Theory and Exemplary Pedagogical Practice." *Current Issues in Criminal Justice* 21(3): 438–59.

———. 2011. *Criminology, Deviance and the Silver Screen: The Fictional Reality and the Criminological Imagination*. London: Palgrave/Macmillan.

———. 2015. *C. Wright Mills and the Criminological Imagination: Prospects for Creative Inquiry*. Farnham: Ashgate.

Freire-Medeiros, Bianca. 2011. "I Went to the City of God: Gringos, Guns and the Touristic *Favela*." *Journal of Latin American Cultural Studies* 20(1): 21–34.

Goffman, Erving. 1974. *Frame Analysis—An Essay on the Organization of Experience*. Boston: Northeastern University Press.

Greenfield, Barbara. 1983. "The Archetypal Masculine: Its Manifestation in Myth and Its Significance for Women." *Journal of Analytical Psychology* 28(1): 33–50.
Greenfield, Steve, Guy Osborn, and Peter Robson. 2010. *Film and the Law: The Cinema of Justice*. Oxford: Hart Publishing.
Hills, Penney C., and L. Rust Hills (eds.). 1968. *How We Live—Contemporary Life in Contemporary Fiction*. New York: Macmillan.
Jacobsen, Michael Hviid (ed.). 2014a. *The Poetics of Crime—Understanding and Researching Crime and Deviance Through Creative Sources*. Farnham: Ashgate.
———. 2014b. "Introduction: Towards the Poetics of Crime: Contours of a Cultural, Critical and Creative Criminology." In *The Poetics of Crime—Understanding and Researching Crime and Deviance Through Creative Sources*, edited by Michael Hviid Jacobsen, 1–25. Farnham: Ashgate.
Jacobsen, Michael Hviid, and Anders Petersen. 2014. "The Poetics of Prisonization: Creative Criminology Through the Projector." In *The Poetics of Crime—Understanding and Researching Crime and Deviance Through Creative Sources*, edited by Michael Hviid Jacobsen, 209–36. Farnham: Ashgate.
Jacobsen, Michael Hviid, and Sandra Walklate. 2016. *Liquid Criminology*. Farnham: Ashgate.
Jenkins, Elizabeth M. 1992. "Documentary Film as a Resource in Teaching Criminal Justice: The Case of Female Terrorists." *Journal of Criminal Justice Education* 3(2): 341–50.
Kauffman, Kent. 2010. *Movie Guide for Legal Studies*. Englewood Cliffs, NJ: Prentice-Hall.
Kelly, Robert J. 1991. "Mapping the Domains of Crime: The Contribution of Literary Works to Criminology." *International Journal of Offender Therapy* 35(1): 45–61.
Kohm, Steven A. and Pauline Greenhill. 2011. "Pedophile Crime Films as Popular Culture—A Problem of Justice?" *Theoretical Criminology* 15(2): 195–215.
Lash, Scott. 1990. *Sociology of Postmodernism*. London: Routledge.
Laz, Cheryl. 1996. "Science Fiction and Introductory Sociology: The *Handmaid* in the Classroom." *Teaching Sociology* 24(1): 54–63.
LeBlanc, Lauraine. 1997. "Observing Reel Life: Using Feature Films to Teach Ethnographic Methods." *Teaching Sociology* 26(1): 62–68.
Leitch, Thomas. 2002. *Crime Films*. Cambridge: Cambridge University Press.
Lepenies, Wolf. 1988. *Between Literature and Science: The Rise of Sociology*. Cambridge: Cambridge University Press.
Lins, Paulo. 2007. *City of God*. London: Bloomsbury Publishing.
Lyman, Stanford M. and Marvin B. Scott. 1975. *The Drama of Social Reality*. New York: Oxford University Press.
Mathiesen, Thomas. 1997. "The Viewer Society: Michel Foucault's 'Panopticon' Revisited." *Theoretical Criminology* 1(2): 215–34.
Mereilles, Fernando (director) and Andrea Barata Ribeiro and Mauricio Andrade Ramos (producers). 2002. *City of God* [Motion Picture]. Brazil: 02 Filmes/VideoFilmes.
Miller, Mark Crispin (ed.). 1990. *Seeing Through Movies*. New York: Pantheon Books.
Mills, C. Wright. 1959. *The Sociological Imagination*. New York: Oxford University Press.

Mooij, Jan Jakob A. 1993. *Fictional Realities: The Uses of Literary Imagination*. Amsterdam: John Benjamins Publishing Company.

Moore, Alfred and Jack Stilgoe. 2009. "Experts and Anecdotes—The Role of 'Anecdotal Evidence' in Public Science Controversies." *Science, Technology, Human Values* 34(5): 654–77.

Nathe, Patricia. 1978. "Private Eye and Public Eye: Criminal Justice Movie Review." *Journal of Contemporary Criminal Justice* 1(2): 25–26.

———. 1981. "Private Eye and Public Eye: The Prison Film Genre." *Journal of Contemporary Criminal Justice* 2(1): 34–35.

Needels, Karen E. 1996. "Go Directly to Jail and Do Not Collect? A Long-Term Study of Recidivism, Employment, and Earnings Patterns among Prison Releasees." *Journal of Research in Crime and Delinquency* 33(4): 471–996.

Negt, Oscar. 1981. *Sociologisk fantasi og eksemplarisk indlæring*. Copenhagen: Kurasje.

Nisbet, Robert A. 1976. *Sociology as an Art Form*. London: Heinemann.

Noer, Michael (director) and Rene Ezra and Tomas Radoor (producers). 2013. *Nordvest* [Motion Picture]. Denmark: Nordisk Film.

Ofshe, Richard. 1970. *The Sociology of the Possible*. Englewood Cliffs, NJ: Prentice-Hall.

Petersen, Anders, Michael Hviid Jacobsen, and Rasmus Antoft. 2014. "Creativity in the Classroom—The Poetics of Pedagogy and Therapeutic Shock in Teaching Sociology." In *Imaginative Methodologies in the Social Sciences*, edited by Michael Hviid Jacobsen, Michael S. Drake, Kieran Keohane, and Anders Petersen, 197–216. Farnham: Ashgate.

Pino, Nathan W., Rod K. Brunson, and Eric A. Stewart. 2009. "Using Movies to Illustrate Ethical Dilemmas in Undergraduate Criminal Justice Classes." *Journal of Criminal Justice Education* 20(2): 194–202.

Prendergast, Christopher. 1986. "Cinema Sociology: Cultivating the Sociological Imagination through Popular Films." *Teaching Sociology* 14(4): 243–48.

Presdee, Mike. 2000. *Cultural Criminology and the Carnival of Crime*. London: Routledge.

Rafter, Nicole H. 2006. *Shots in the Mirror: Crime Films and Society*, 2nd Edition. New York: Oxford University Press.

Rafter, Nicole H., and Michelle Brown. 2011. *Criminology Goes to the Movies: Crime Theory and Popular Culture*. New York: New York University Press.

Refn, Nicolas Winding (director) and Henrik Danstrup (producer). 1996. *Pusher* [Motion Picture]. Denmark: Balboa Entertainment.

Rockell, Barbara A. 2009. "Challenging What They All Know: Integrating the Real/Reel World into Criminal Justice Pedagogy." *Journal of Criminal Justice Education* 20(1): 75–92.

Rockwell, Joan. 1974. *Fact in Fiction: The Use of Literature in the Systematic Study of Society*. London: Routledge and Kegan Paul.

Rogers, Joseph W. 1986. "Teaching Criminology." *Teaching Sociology* 14(4): 257–62.

Roth, Philip. 1957. "Film as Sociology." *New Republic*, October 21: 21–22.

Shipley, Wes and Gray Cavender. 2001. "Murder and Mayhem at the Movies." *Journal of Criminal Justice and Popular Culture* 9(1): 1–14.

Smith, Don D. 1973. "Teaching Introductory Sociology Through Film." *Teaching Sociology* 1(1): 48–61.

Sparks, Richard. 1992. *Television and the Drama of Crime: Moral Tales and the Place of Crime in Public Life*. Buckingham: Open University Press.

Sutherland, Jean-Anne and Kathryn M. Feltey (eds.). 2012. *Cinematic Sociology: Social Life in Film*. London: Sage Publications.

Swart, Stanley L. 1985. "Neutralization Theory in Popular Film: A Criminological Perspective on *Save the Tiger*." *Studies in Popular Culture* 8(1): 79–85.

Tibbetts, Stephen G. 2015. *Criminological Theory: The Essentials*. Newbury Park, CA: Sage Publications.

Tzanelli, Rodanthi, Martin O'Brien and Majid Yar. 2005. "'Con Me if You Can': Exploring Crime in the American Cinematic Imagination." *Theoretical Criminology* 9(1): 97–117.

Viera, Else R. P. 2005. "Introduction: Is the Camera Mightier than the Word?" In *In City of God in Many Voices: Brazilian Social Cinema as Action*, edited by Else R. P. Viera, v–xxviii. Nottingham: CCCP.

Welch, Andrew, Thomas Fleming and Kenneth Dowler. 2011. "Constructing Crime and Justice on Film: Meaning and Message in Cinema." *Contemporary Justice Review* 14(4): 457–76.

Wilson, Robert N. 1979. *The Writer as Social Seer*. Chapel Hill, NC: University of North Carolina Press.

Yar, Majid. 2010. "Cultural Criminology Goes to the Movies." In *Framing Crime: Cultural Criminology and the Image*, edited by Keith Hayward and Mike Presdee, 68–82. London: Routledge.

Young, Alison. 2008. "Culture, Critical Criminology and the Imagination of Crime." In *The Critical Criminology Companion*, edited by Thalia Anthony and Chris Cunneen, 18–29. Annandale: Hawkins Press.

Young, Frank W. 1962. "The Function of Male Initiation Ceremonies: A Cross-cultural Test of an Alternative Hypothesis." *American Journal of Sociology* 67(4): 379–96.

Young, Jock. 2011. *The Criminological Imagination*. Cambridge: Polity Press.

15

Fact, Fantasy, Fallacy

Division between Fanciful Musings and Factual Mutterings

Jon Frauley

In teaching and writing in the areas of epistemology and methodology as well as the criminological imagination and creative analytics through film and novels, one thing that has struck me as strange about criminology is how fiction films and (less so) novels are widely accepted as teaching tools while only documentary films, diaries, and letters are taken as legitimate sources of information for research. Several scholars have challenged the view that fiction film and literature do not make for legitimate sources of information for social inquiry, so although cogent arguments have been made for the use of (filmic and literary) fiction as both sources of information and as tools for reflection, criminology has been very slow on the uptake (see Berger 1977; Boyd 2009; Brown 2004; Cohen 2013; Coser 1972; Ferrell 1995a; 1999; Frauley 2010; 2011b; Mills 1959; Potter 1998; Rafter 2006; Rafter and Brown 2001; Rockwell 1977; Ruggiero 2003; Sagarin 1980; Visano 1997; Young 2010). One likely explanation for why this work hasn't made significant inroads within criminology is that it challenges a very entrenched and naturalized proposition that most criminologists tacitly accept as true: the fact–fiction dichotomy.

What fuels this fact–fiction dichotomy (or science–art, fact–theory, or even research–theory dichotomy) is a belief in a "correspondence view" of truth that holds authentic sources of data to be those that correspond directly to some real, lived experience. Since works of art are held to be fabricated and may employ metaphor as a technique of analysis, they are not considered to correspond to an extra-discursive world in the same way as those thought to be "factual."[1] Therefore fiction and art are considered irrelevant as data sources for social scientific enquiry. This not only assumes that some cultural artifacts reflect or mirror reality in a way that others do not, but it sets up a rigid division between art and science, which makes little sense if we view creativity and its expression as central to scientific enquiry, as the latter requires speculation and abstract conceptualizing (see Mills 1959; Williams 1984).

Diaries, letters, photographs, and documentary films have no more or less value than do novels, works of art, or fiction films. This is because "factual" works do not simply reflect reality more truthfully or authentically than fiction. Each reflects *upon* reality and so in this way they do not mirror or *correspond* directly to reality but are made to *refer* to reality in a particular way (Carrabine 2012; Pearce 1978; Woodiwiss 1990; 2001). This chapter aims to demonstrate that because all cultural artifacts, whether diaries or novels, documentary or fiction films have the same ontological status, it makes little sense to categorize them as "factual" and "fictive." They are outcomes of the creative energies and the experiences of the author as well as objective material and discursive relations that situate the author. Those works conventionally perceived as fictive can be rich with criminological insights that can be unlocked, if you will, through the use of the analytical languages available to criminologists, especially by those willing to engage their criminological imagination (Barton, Scott, Corteen, and Whyte 2007; Frauley 2010; 2011b; Frauley 2015; Jacobsen 2014). Those works imagined as factual may be bereft of any insight altogether.

I am approaching "reality" from the point of view of a stratified ontology. In using the term "reality" I do not have in mind the naïve realist view of reality that informs positivism, that there is a brute reality that we can access through scientific methods. I have in mind a stratified ontology like the kind advanced by Critical Realists, which I have elsewhere discussed (2004; 2008; 2011a; Frauley and Pearce 2007; Rigakos and Frauley 2011). The notion that reality is stratified or multifaceted and that what we do experience is an outcome of perhaps partially obscured processes and that this experience does not exhaust what actually does or could exist—frames the position advanced here.[2] I also draw on previous work where I (2010; 2011b) have advanced the notion of "fictional realities," which implicitly rejects the fact–fiction distinction as unhelpful for social science inquiry. In what follows I will discuss the fact–fiction dichotomy and the fallacy of the correspondence view that supports this dichotomy (and its empiricist underpinning) and then enlist a brief discussion of texts and films that may be familiar to the reader to help me illustrate the faulty premise on which much sociology and criminology rests.

FACTS AND FICTIONS

In social science we teach students that diaries and letters are legitimate sources of primary information for research because they are records of past experiences and events. Implicit in this view is the assumption that these sources are truthful or factual representations of reality. However, there is sometimes no way to determine if a diary or a photograph is a factual record of life experience or faithful rendition of events. For instance, the Depression-era desert photograph, "Cattle Skull, Badlands," caused a heated debate about "truthfulness" in documentary photography: does the image reflect reality or is it merely an artistic reflection upon reality? Although the image is of something "real," claims that the skull had been moved and manipulated informed a right-wing backlash against the photo as nothing more than "a prop and [Republicans] labelled the picture New Deal propaganda" manipulated to help "pass contentious legislation through Congress" (Carrabine 2012, 472). *My Secret Life* (1888), by an anonymous author, serves as an example of similar concerns surrounding written texts. This text is said to be a memoire of one man's sexual exploits in Victorian England, but some argue that it is a work of erotic fiction and thus demote its status from something truthful or factual to that of fabrication. Whether or not this text is fact or fiction or the skull photograph is authentic or contrived will likely never be definitively resolved, nor does it really matter. Both are outcomes of some historically and politically situated social practices and therefore they will bear traces of gendered, classed, and racialized structures of power and domination at work in the positioning of their author within his or her social hierarchy. Thus they are likely to have some historical and social value as a cultural artifact of twentieth-century America or of nineteenth-century England.

Let us take the work of Charles Dickens as another example of the problem with this fact–fiction (but also art–science) dichotomy. Dickens's works have long been held to not only *reflect the reality* of his times but to also be a *reflection upon those realities*. Indeed, it has been argued that Dickens was a kind of proto-social scientist (Brussel 1938; Hanson 2012; Squires 1938; see the journal *Dickens Studies* for papers on how Dickens routinely blurred the boundaries between "fact" and "fiction"). Moreover, he possessed the quality of mind that, according to radical sociologist C. Wright Mills (1959), all social scientists ought to possess. That is, Dickens had a keen "sociological imagination" and was a kind of "intellectual craftsman" who offered historically and socially tempered insights into the human condition.

According to Garry Potter (1998, 185):

> Writers, good writers, as well as possessing a creative facility with language, have insights into the human condition, insights into the dynamics of social grouping, [etc.] . . . the sort of knowledges achieved through other, through actually sometimes very similar, means, by psychologists, sociologists, historians, philosophers . . . when crafting a work of fiction they do not attempt these insights in a formalised analytical form. Rather they utilise their insight in their creation of fictional universes. (see also, Sagarin 1980)

Potter captures the argument put forward by Mills (1959). Although Mills didn't think artists and novelists could offer the kind of penetrating social analysis that sociologists could and ought to offer, he did nevertheless recognize in much of their work the quality of mind he believed necessary for insightful social science (see Frauley 2015). Within the fictional reality crafted by Dickens we find serious treatment of social problems of industrialization such as mass poverty, crime, imprisonment, and homelessness, and, with this, insights about life in Victorian England.

The argument that divisions between fact and fiction and between science and art have no analytical purchase for social science does not mean that we should, for instance, take novelists as offering historical accounts of their times. We would not take, for example, Herman Melville's *Moby Dick* as a first hand factual historical account of whaling practices in the nineteenth century, but it does offer insights on crime and society that are there but embedded in the text to be extracted, if you will, through analysis using the conceptual tools available to social scientists. These insights, as Sagarin (1980, 82) has remarked "do not merely dramatize reality but inform us as well and deepen our knowledge of the world and of humanity." Pearce argues similarly in his analysis of filmic portrayals of organized crime:

> The greatness of novelists, a parallel art form to film, often lies not only in their concrete evocation of life but also in the maturity of their understanding of it, the ways in which individuals relate to their own and other milieu and how these are affected by social structural constraints. (1978, 262)

As Ruggiero (2003, 136) has demonstrated, *Moby Dick* does contain insights on what were considered to be "acceptable and unacceptable economic practices." Thus, although *Moby Dick* is a work of fiction, not everything contained within the text or to which the text refers is fictional (see Potter 1998). *Moby Dick* is analyzed by Ruggiero as a text containing cogent sociological insights "about the achievements and destructiveness of economic undertakings, the development of productive forces and power, and ultimately the distinction between legitimate enterprise and the crimes of the economy" (2003, 136). Thus there is knowledge of reality to be extracted from works of fiction not least because the historical conditions under which the work and author are produced find their way into the text (Potter 1998). That is, social scientists can identify traces of the material and discursive realities that impacted authors and thus even the most fanciful musings will contain within them traces of dominant social and political sentiments, institutional organization, language conventions, and also authors' own views on particular social issues (see also Potter 1998). Of course, Ruggiero reads the novel through a criminological lens and that shapes the interpretation, but the issue here is that there is present in that "fictional reality" (see Frauley 2010; 2011b) traces of conditions external to that narrative that can be unlocked, so to speak, with the help of the social scientist's conceptual tools.

APPREHENDING REALITY AND THE REALITY OF BOUNDARIES

One reason for the exclusion of works of fiction from the world of legitimate social science source material lies with how the connection between these materials and the world beyond them has come to be perceived. According to Sagarin, even though many of the portraits painted of criminals by criminologists "are in the form of endless tables and statistical correlations, sometimes important even when boring, but seldom punctuated by anything deserving to be called insightful, this has not always been the case" (1980, 78–79). During the eighteenth and nineteenth centuries the interest in social science, especially criminology, began to grow and this lead to the eventual development of parallel inquiries into the sorts of things that have preoccupied criminologists. One line of inquiry developed as the empiricist scientific tradition with another rooted in the arts and literature (Berger 1977, 11; Cohen 2013, 3; Sagarin 1980, 75). This is an account of a split between different styles of inquiry that have come to be recognized as "science" and "art."

How we conceptualize the connection between lived experiences and diaries and novels, or reality and documentary film, is really just a particular way of organizing ideas in order to make the world orderable in some way that is intelligible within a much larger epistemological framework, one that is perhaps unknown to the reader or viewer. According to Pearce:

> Reality is not self[-]evident—there is no such thing as a naïve, pre-conceptual apprehension of the world. We experience and know the world through socially derived categories which are themselves constantly open to revision as our conditions of existence and our knowledge are transformed through

> history. This applies both to our taken-for-granted knowledge and its counterpart—science upon which intellectual work has been expended. (1978, 246–47, references omitted)

If we do not view films or read novels according to the categories, concepts, and analytical frameworks of our respective disciplines to unlock the insights of authors or filmmakers or to reveal the traces of reality that subtend the work, this doesn't mean that we utilize none at all or that we do not uncover or extract meaning from the texts, films, or images. It simply means we utilize common sense, everyday thinking, or "everyday theorizing" as Craib (1984) called it, rather than a more disciplined variety of thought.

Film theorists such as Eitzen (1995) have argued, similarly. Our experiences of what constitutes a documentary, for instance, are not somehow unconnected to the discursive resources we have at our disposal:

> Every representation of reality is no more than a fiction in the sense that it is an artificial construct, a highly contrived and selective view of the world, produced for some purpose. . . . Even our "brute" perceptions of the world are inescapably tainted by our beliefs, assumptions, goals and desires. So, even if there is a concrete, material reality upon which our existence depends (something very few actually doubt) we can only apprehend it through mental representations that at best resemble reality and that are in large part socially created. . . . [T]here is no such thing as a text that is intrinsically and necessarily a documentary. It is a particular kind of reading frame that makes a text a documentary. (Eitzen 1995, 82, 98)

As Eitzen has argued, there cannot be any firm line that divides fictive from fact-ive films. For example, a fiction film does attest factually to the body of work of an actor, so in that regard we can understand fiction films as documenting an actor's career or acting style. It is the reception of the film—how it is processed through our conceptual framing—that will determine its status. Similarly, Sobchack (1999) has argued that the term "documentary" makes reference to a viewing *experience*, one that is different from that of viewing fiction films, one that is characterized by a "documentary consciousness" so that one perceives what is depicted in the film to actually exist elsewhere unlike with works of fiction.

Given the perception of some films as "documentaries" and others as "fiction," Eitzen's definition of documentary film is "any motion picture that is susceptible to the question 'Might it be lying?'" (1995, 81). Watching a documentary on the tobacco industry, for example, leaves us with a sense that we have gained an "insider's perspective" on that industry and have learned something. Watching an entertaining fiction film such as *Thank You for Smoking* (Reitman 2005), despite the fact it is quite similar to the documentary, *The Tobacco Conspiracy (Tabac, la conspiration)* (Collot 2006), leaves us with fond musings of its mischievous rapscallion of a protagonist and feel-good Hollywood ending. The former film does not evoke the issue of truth or question of trust. This is because the "documentary consciousness" is not present when we view *Thank You for Smoking*.

Documentaries are intended by their directors and producers to invoke questions of truth and trust unlike fiction films. Mockumentaries, although fiction, are also made to invoke this consciousness and raise the question, "Might it be lying?" One such "fake" documentary is William Karel's 2002 French film, *Dark Side of the Moon (Opération lune)*, about how the CIA, with the help of Stanly Kubrick and the set of *2001: A Space Odyssey*, faked images of the Apollo 11 moon landing. This film will compel viewers to wonder whether or not it is "lying" because it employs the cues conventionally associated with documentary film (including interviews with high profile experts, U.S. officials, and Kubrick's widow). This mockumentary (which is a documentary, according to Eitzen's definition) is a spoof of all manner of conspiracy theories and hammers home the untenability of adhering to any rigid division between "fact" and "fiction." Similar themes are explored by Peter Hyams in his 1978 thriller, *Capricorn One*. This film bears none of the cues associated with documentaries so its plot, that NASA and the U.S. Air Force faked images of a Mars landing, is received as entertainment. The premise of the film, however, invites viewers to ponder the reality of the 1969 moon landing and corresponding conspiracy theories surrounding it. Although clearly fiction, the film raises issues similar to those contemplated in *Dark Side of the Moon* and trades on pop culture musings about the nature of government conspiracies. Other films, such as Rob Reiner's (1984), *This is Spinal Tap*, are blatant satires that play on the documentary format. The viewing frame set out by Reiner is clearly different than that of Karel but both are "fake" documentaries. Still other films (and books for that matter) blur boundaries further and are sometimes inventive of new genres. Take for instance Truman Capote's (1965), *In Cold Blood*, the first "nonfiction novel" (Berger 1977, 251) or Harold Becker's (1979) true-crime fiction film, *The Onion Field*. Perhaps the best and greatest example, though, of the analytical impotence of the fact-fiction dichotomy for social science is illustrated by the 1938 radio dramatization of H. G. Welles's book, *The War of the Worlds*. Broadcast on CBS, Orson Welles and his Mercury Players were so believable that many listeners were terrified that Martians and their death rays were actually invading the United States (Potter 2002; Ndalianis 2012, 170).

This idea that reception is never unmediated does not simply refer to how we read novels or view films (or listen to radio). Academic works, too, can be approached in the same way. This is demonstrated by the "Sokal hoax." In 1996, the prestigious cultural studies journal *Social Text* published an article written by physicist Alan Sokal. After its publication Sokal admitted it was a work of fiction, strategically invented to appeal to cultural studies aficionados, especially postmodernists. His objective was to prove that humanities journals were not rigorous and that the postmodern critique of science was bereft of any practically adequate understanding of what constituted "science." The point is that when the article was submitted and reviewed it was received as a "factual" paper as it had all the necessary cues to trigger the use of a particular reading frame. After the reveal, however, that original reading frame was no longer adequate as the paper was clearly a parody of postmodernist arguments. The paper is still available and without knowing otherwise, it would be read today as an authentic scholarly paper rather than an imposter.

In keeping to the view that creative and poetic works have the same ontological status as scientific texts, whether Sokal's paper was indeed fake makes no difference to its ontological state. It was the product of a scientist's intellectual and creative labor within an historical and institutional context and in that regard isn't any different from the chapter I am writing now. As Eitzen has suggested, fiction films can be taken as a documenting of an actor's style or career or as to how filmmakers have treated particular subjects or issues. Thus whether a documentary film or text is "fake" or not, it is a reflection upon reality and reflects to some degree the reality under which it was produced.

Problematizing the usefulness of a fact–fiction dichotomy for social science is a call to transgress the use of this entrenched convention. Coincidently, Sokal's parody is called "Transgressing the Boundaries." Much like *Dark Side of the Moon*, Sokal's paper was written to invoke the question, "Might it be lying?" and in so doing, and in a strange irony, he ended up producing a piece of art that helped transgress the boundaries between science and poetics, between fact and fiction. "The aesthetic experience of reading literary works of art," Cohen argues, "activates the imagination to visualize other worlds existing in the past, present, or future blurring binary oppositions between reality/fiction, objective/subjective, or logic/affect. These dichotomies . . . are transgressed in artistic production" (2013, 2). Transgressing conventional conceptual boundaries is what I have been discussing here and what I am advocating for criminology.

CONCEPTUALIZING AND PERMEATING BOUNDARIES

Some texts and films are so heavy with symbolism and deal with such intimate human experiences that it may be very difficult not to view the narrative as a commentary on real life despite the lack of cues that would have us pose, "Might it be lying?" Take, for example, Lynne Stopkewich's (1996) *Kissed*. The story resonates with us not because of any dramatization of events that we might have experienced personally but because we have all experienced on some level the abstract conceptions and feelings symbolized in the film. *Kissed* uses metaphor to reflect on and puzzle over powerful themes and issues that transcend the narrative, such as love, loss, control, life, death, morality, and spirituality, among other things. Because I have an interest in governance and regulation, I view the film as an allegory about the pluralistic nature of governance in contemporary Western societies.

Frequently interpreted as a film about necrophilia, *Kissed* presents necrophilia as metaphor for transgression, specifically for the transgression of the boundary that is thought to divide life from death. It requires us to contemplate life and love as deeply spiritual and mystical. The film explores states of being human and presents life and death as sensual experiences existing on a continuum, intermingled and defying the conventional boundaries that are thought to separate them. Manifestly, the film positions necrophilia as a form of sexual transgression, "sex that crosses or threatens to cross boundaries and . . . that flout social, moral and cultural convention" and which "have the potential to challenge or confirm the moral, legal, social, economic, political, ethnic, racial and other limits in any particular cultural context" (Donnan and Magowan 2012, 1, 4; see also O'Neil and Seal 2012). Yet it also illustrates how transgression is conceptualized and responded to within three dominant models of social control: a medical-scientific model; a spiritual-moral-religious model; and a political-legal model. These three ways of framing transgression are the prominent ones at work within Western societies today for understanding and judging human conduct. Each of these corresponds to distinct modes of norm production—medicalization, moralization, and criminalization—which authorize specific ritualistic and institutionalized practices of domination and boundary maintenance and therefore make possible three types of transgression. Each of these modalities has transgressed the boundaries of its initial institutional existence (including the precepts they presuppose) and has become ubiquitous and overlapping in the regulation and governance of Western social life.

A circumspect criminological reading of the film reveals tensions between these differing regulatory processes and precepts that play a role in shaping understandings of transgression and death. Transgression is imagined differently depending on which framing we adopt. Legal transgression is premised upon a voluntary and rational calculation to violate the law; the transgression of psychiatric norms is imagined to evidence mental illness and thus one is sick and not criminal, compelled to transgress;

the violation of widely accepted moral imperatives is considered a transgression of natural order (one is more "evil" than ill). Thus, the political-legal, science-medical, and moral-spiritual each are different systems of thought and expert practice that inform different forms of domination, stigmatization, and potential experiences of transgression. *Kissed* offers a view of how these different models of transgression operate, interact, and sometimes conflict.

The protagonist, Sandra Larson, represents a *moral-spiritual* framing. She views death as a transformation process not simply as the end of life, as death is a different state of being, rather than simply a lack of being. Sandra attempts to understand this different state of being experientially, through her senses, by viewing, touching, smelling, and tasting death incarnate. Sandra views death as a transformation of energies and as sacred, seeing in it something deeply spiritual. Death requires a ritual that includes her "loving" the corpses, which she stipulates "comforts" them and helps them "cross over." The ritual of "shroud, chant, bury" that she engages in aids in this transgression of the boundary between life and death. Sandra is consumed by and seems compelled by the cadaver's energy, by its final release of life, which is shrouded in mystery.

The second, more conventional framing of transgression and of domination is represented by Mr. Wallis, Sandra's employer, her college teachers, as well as her boyfriend, Matt, a former medical student. These characters represent a clinical *scientific* approach to death. Matt attempts to gain understanding and produce an explanation of Sandra's attraction to death. He is obsessed with her fascination and attempts to understand in a systematic and somewhat detached manner by recording his observations. He attempts to role-play (or engage in simulation) to gain insight into Sandra's behavior. At one point in the film Matt suggests that Sandra "grafts personalities onto the bodies," that perhaps her "delusions" about the dead are in part about control and that she perhaps is a schizophrenic. Thus, because of Matt's conceptual framing he views her as sick, as suffering from a compulsion, as having an "addiction." This aligns with the views of death held by Sandra's professors and employer who view death in clinical terms as a lack of life and the dead as "patients" and "dead flesh." This view, contra Sandra's, is detached, cold, and sees no meaning in death that would be significant for understanding life. Thus the science-medicine model of understanding love, death, and life casts the spiritual as fanciful, fictive, and deviant. The ritual central to the medicine-science model, unlike that of the spiritual-moral-religious, isn't to help in the crossing over of the dead or the transmission of their "energy" as it is for Sandra but rather it is to prepare dead flesh for display (in the mortuary or medical school). The controversial travelling *Body Worlds* and *Animal Inside Out* exhibitions come to mind.[3] The embalming ritual is a clinical procedure to produce a representation of death (or of bodies in death that are life-like and in a way attempting to mask their "altered reality").

At the end of the film *legal* discourse enters the frame with the police examination of Matt's death. A different kind of ritual is performed here—a forensic ritual wherein the body and crime scene are analyzed for clues as to cause of death and determination of whether his death is a suicide, accident, or homicide. The set of categories used to frame death are different from the others. Statements are taken, photographs produced, notes made and compared, evidence detected and evaluated. The concern is limited to preserving the setting and context of death, not with the exploration of the meaning of death itself. The ritual to determine suicide, accident, or homicide requires a cause of death, which is premised upon a correspondence theory of truth. Direct correspondence also underpins the medical-scientific: one either has a pulse and brain activity and is alive or lacks these and is dead. The spiritual-moral-religious does not hold life and death to be binary oppositions but as intertwined, making it illogical to distinguish living from dying.

What we come to understand is that Sandra Larson is only truly alive when she is consumed by death, that transgression of the life–death boundary does not yield an end to life but is productive of new forms of existence (see Katz 1988), and that neither of the three dominant framings of transgression are alone adequate for understanding this. We are thus lead to transgress the conventional boundaries that frame everyday thinking about life, death, and transgression.

How we make sense of or experience a film, text, or image—as if it is somehow telling us something about actual events, people, or things or as not making reference to anything but itself—requires a conceptual framing and this framing manages to some degree the expectations and impressions of readers and viewers. Whether fiction or documentary, each is the outcome of some set of situated practices and guiding framing. They are productions that reflect reality (but do not mirror it) and reflect upon reality. The fact–fiction dichotomy has very little if any analytical purchase because it says little about how viewers might experience a film, text, or image or render these intelligible, and says even less about their value for how they *reflect upon reality*. The dichotomy simply distracts us from any hard thinking around the value of cultural artifacts for social science. Again, this is not to suggest that there is no reality or that we cannot distinguish fantasy from reality. It is to suggest that classifying cultural artifacts as fact-ive or fictive is problematic for social science because both have the same ontological status: they are both products of a conceptual framing and the creativity and productive energies of their authors, as cultural criminologists argue (Ferrell 1999; 1995a; 1995b; Ferrell, Hayward, and Young 2008). Moreover, they both contain traces of the reality under which they were produced and they reflect upon reality in some way or other (see Potter 1998; Pearce 1978).

REALISM AND ONTOLOGY

John Tagg's (1988) work on photography further illustrates the complexity of apprehending reality and the inadequacy of a correspondence view of truth. In his text, *The Burden of Representation: Essays on Photographies and Histories*, he describes the history of photography, including how photographs came to be accepted as evidence within criminal courts. The apparatus of the camera is discussed for how it shapes the images that come to be viewed as truthful and authentic representations of reality. All photographs, he argues, are in part the result of "specific and, in every sense, significant distortions which render its relation to any prior reality deeply problematic and raise the question of the *determining level of the material apparatus and of the social practices* within which photography takes place" (Tagg 1988, 2, emphasis added). The claim is not that photographs are distortions of reality, but rather that they are outcomes of the distortions produced by the apparatus of the camera and of a social practice of photography. Therefore to say that pictures correspond directly to the material reality the photographer attempts to capture is highly problematic. The camera and its manipulation are intermediaries and this mediation is not benign, as professional photographers and marketers are well aware. The point here is that photographs are more closely related to the apparatus and practice that produces them than to the material reality to which we might suppose the image unproblematically corresponds.

One further example of the breakdown of the correspondence view that I hope will further clarify what I am getting at is found in historian Ernst Gombrich's (1977), *Art and Illusion: A Study in the Psychology of Pictorial Representation*. Here he argued that representations do not correspond to the thing that one might be trying to capture—the extra-discursive material reality—but rather to one's largely unconscious or unthought "schemata," because this is an intermediary that lies between us and our empirical object. In contrasting two different images of the same landscape, one produced by a Chinese artist and one by an Englishman, Gombrich offers an example of how "schemata" operate.[4] Gombrich attributes the differences to the culturally relative schemata that each artist sees the world through. Sayer suggests as much when he states that these differences are indebted to the "'conceptually-saturated' character of observation" (1992, 53). That is, observations are always "theory-laden":

> What a layperson and a biologist claim to be able to see under a microscope will differ considerably, not just in the sense that they see the same shapes but interpret them differently . . . but because they have learned to see or "discriminate" different patterns in the first place. (Sayer 1992, 53)

Thus, observers do not experience the same thing despite looking at the same thing. One way to experience works of fiction is to perceive them as illegitimate data sources for social scientific enquiry. The notion that there are inherent differences that would require us to exclude poetic texts from the realm of social science rests on a simplistic and inadequate epistemological framing and rather shallow model of ontology.

What I've outlined above—the fallacy of direct correspondence—is well-known and in keeping with what Woodiwiss (1990; 2001) has called a "non-representationalist" (i.e., non-empiricist) approach to social theory and sociology. This position takes seriously the Saussurian understanding of signifiers (and variations such as that of Roland Barthes) as signifying not empirical things but concepts. The implication of this is that our criminological languages are used to make reference to extra-discursive things and in doing so we produce a representation of those things and this representation becomes the object of criminological scrutiny. This is discussed in the next section. What is worth pointing out here is that although this view—that language is not neutral and that it shapes and constrains not only what is understood but how we visualize and experience the world—is so well-known that it is hardly worth repeating here but nevertheless it seems to have escaped the purview of a great many criminologists. Criminologists will readily admit that the world is not "black and white" and that there are many gray areas, but they have long struggled to admit that the theory–fact, fiction–fact, and art–science dualities are really just products of a particular way of conceptualizing and of the nature of our language. This struggle suggests that many either choose to ignore what is well-known or that this isn't well known within criminology.

Although sociology, anthropology, and other social sciences underwent a "linguistic turn" in the 1980s and 1990s, this seems to have had relatively little impact on criminology (Arrigo, Milovanovic, and Schehr 2005). The significance of this extends beyond the more sophisticated understanding of the nature and role of linguistic categories in constructing representations of reality that is overlooked. This oversight is significant because it suggests that the naïve empiricist ontology that underpins the less adequate correspondence or representational view of language has not been broken with to any great degree.

> According to the traditional, representational theory best exemplified in Wittgenstein's *Tractatus*, language consists of humanly created symbols

> which name and so may be understood, more or less complicatedly, to stand for the things that humans wish to talk about. By contrast, according to the significatory theory first enunciated by Saussure, words (including theoretical terms) do not represent extra-linguistic things. Rather, they are arbitrary combinations of systematically differentiated aural and/or graphic images (signifiers) with similarly differentiated mental ones (signifieds), which owe their existence as elements of language, not to human beings but to such additional non-human but equally active and substantive systems of difference and opposition as syntaxes and lexicons, which in turn are better conceptualised as the properties of social formations than as the products of individual or collective subjects. (Woodiwiss 1990, 3)

What Woodiwiss reminds us of here is not simply that language is never neutral and that it constrains our representations of empirical reality, but that because social structures such as language are not reducible to human beings, but always *position* human subjectivity and action, we must move away not only from a correspondence view of language but from the empiricist ontology on which this view is based. What is needed is a more sophisticated conception of ontology as stratified that can account for differences between "analytic" (i.e., conceptual) entities and "extra-social" (i.e., concrete material) entities to which the former make partial reference (Woodiwiss 1990, 7–8).

As Sayer (1992) and Woodiwiss (1990) (and countless others) have argued, reality is stratified, meaning there is much more to reality than what we might be able to perceive. Our perception is limited both conceptually (by our viewing frame) and physiologically (by the structure of our sense organs).

> Our senses of sight, hearing, touch, taste and smell are so taken for granted in everyday life that it is tempting to assume that they connect us to the world in a simple, straightforward manner: hence the common-sense faith in the neutrality of observation. . . . Research on perception has shown it to be complex. . . . What we therefore claim to be able to perceive is the outcome of a complex set of factors; not just the nature of the object, but the condition of the physical mechanisms which are sensitive to certain types of energy (e.g., the condition of our eyes) and the types of concepts we have for making sense of the "sense data." (Sayer 1992, 51)

Thus as Sayer and Woodiwiss hold, our visual fields are already "conceptually saturated" making it impossible to perceive anything in an unmediated fashion. This complicates the criminological common sense that some cultural artifacts directly correspond to reality in ways others do not.

The division between fact and fiction is really only a convention and these terms do not make reference to anything other than some conceptual distinctions, but powerfully embedded distinctions that to many social scientists are not conceptual at all but actually obtaining in an extra-discursive reality.

In this light, how can we reasonably argue that diaries or documentaries are legitimate data sources but that novels and fiction films do not meet the threshold of "scientificity" (Foucault 1976/1980; 1977/1980)? What, as Foucault asks, are we really doing when we make these kinds of distinctions?

> It is surely the following kinds of questions that would need to be posed: What types of knowledge do you want to *disqualify* in the very instant of your demand: "Is it a science"? Which speaking, discoursing subjects—which subjects of experience and knowledge—do you then want to "*diminish*" when you say: "I who conduct this discourse am conducting a scientific discourse, and I am a scientist"? (Foucault 1976/1980, 84–85)

Sayer's position that, "Precisely because we are accustomed to thinking in terms of a particular set of concepts, we rarely recognize their influence" (1992, 53), dovetails with Foucault's idea about the disqualifying of some forms of understanding versus others as a way of naturalizing a particular epistemological framing. In this context, the use of the fact–fiction division is about upholding the legitimacy of one set of concepts to the detriment or denigration of others. For Foucault we must address this promotion of one framing over another as a "politics of knowledge" because every truth-claim has a political stake (1976/1980; 1977/1980). This is why, for example, he viewed the sciences as dominant and powerful systems of truth production that operated through rituals of exclusion. It should be said that I am not advocating some postmodern argument for anything goes or a radical relativism that denotes that there are multiple truths or perhaps no truth at all. The point here is that what we understand by "fiction" or "fact" does not capture the reality of the states so designated. That is, what we *know* and what we *perceive* are different from the things we are attempting to know and to perceive. "Data" cannot and should not be taken to mean "given things" (Sayer 1992, 52) for the reasons already outlined. Thus the theory–fact, fiction–fact, or art–science distinctions are at their very core conceptual. These terms are positivistic "sponge words" as Mills (1959) might have argued. They give the appearance of being analytical but have very little if any social scientific import. They reflect an outdated and inadequate epistemological and ontological framing.

Let us consider Sayer further:

> The invocation of "facts" in popular discourse plays upon a hidden ambiguity, between "facts" as states or properties of the world itself, and "facts" as

> "factual statements" putatively made about those states. A factual statement like "the Earth is spherical" is not the same thing as the thing to which it refers. One is a "thought object," the other is a "real object," something which exists regardless of whether we happen to know it. We can of course only think about the real object in terms of a thought object . . . we cannot get outside language or knowledge to see how it compares with the object. The illusion of the appeal to facts in popular discourse involves collapsing statements into their referents, thought objects into real objects. It thereby appears to appeal to the facts themselves, the way the world is, in an unmediated fashion, but it is actually an appeal to a particular way of talking about the world in some conceptual system. (Sayer 1992, 47; see also Woodiwiss 1990; 2001)

Collapsing statements into their referents is a form of empiricism and thinking a photograph, film, or text corresponds directly to what it depicts is a form of empiricism. Empiricism as a theory of knowledge has difficulty with the idea that theoretical statements have the same ontological status as the empirical or observational statements that are made about the state of material, concrete things. That is, both are "analytical" statements and both *refer* to something concrete, but they do not *correspond* directly to the extra-discursive concrete thing (Sayer 1992, 54; Woodiwiss 1990, 7–8). Although observational statements or "statements of fact" (e.g., crime rates are falling) are often thought of as simply facts and divorced from theory as a result (because they are thought to be concrete rather than abstract), both belong to the realm of thought objects and therefore the theory–fact division is untenable. This same argument holds for the fact–fiction dichotomy.

What is happening with the collapse of the space between concepts and concrete things, according to Sayer and Woodiwiss is that, for instance in the case of empiricism, social scientists forget that things such as "validity" and "fact" are concepts and thus this forgetfulness leads to treating "validity" and "fact" as things beyond reproach. This is also often done with the category "crime." There are quite a few different things to which "crime" is made to refer in the criminological literature, but the majority of people likely perceive "crime" according to a legal framing, holding it to be the willful violation of the criminal law. In the same way, the fact–fiction division is conceptual but is often taken by social scientists to describe a material reality and thus one type of cultural artifact is demoted to the status of invalid source for social research. What we really have is a distinction between abstract concepts and concrete concepts. Again, this is not to say that *Moby Dick* is "real" or that anything goes. There will inevitably be more or less accurate statements about things or some rendition of events will encompass more and explain more than others. The point Woodiwiss and Sayer and others are making is that as social scientists or lay persons we must perceive the world and make statements and judgments about the world by using some sort of schemata or conceptual system and that even the selection of this schemata or conceptual system is done from within an already existing schemata or conceptual system. Statements made about the world are theoretical statements that utilize abstract or concrete concepts, making it problematic to insist that some accounts are "factual" and others "fictional." This however does not mean we cannot rank or identify in order of importance factors in the production, reproduction, or transformation of whatever we are trying to understand or explain.

CONCLUSION

Carrrabine has recently written on the growing visual criminology movement, remarking that criminology must now, given the "relentless flow of images" that have come to characterize contemporary Western societies, "develop a more sophisticated understanding of the visual and confront the ways in which contemporary societies are saturated with images of crime" (Carrabine 2012, 46; see also Hayward and Presdee 2010). If criminology does not yet possess a sophisticated way to understand the visual then it likely hasn't developed a sophisticated way to understand the relationship between our knowledge of reality and reality itself and along with this the fact–fiction, fact–theory, or science–art dichotomies. Thus, it suffers from an underdeveloped conception of social ontology, not just from a lack of sophistication regarding images. As ontology is central to methodology (but often taken for granted), if criminology is to come to terms with existing and more sophisticated approaches to texts, images, and films ontology must become an important criminological pursuit.

A way to understand differences between an empiricist "correspondence view" of truth—which underpins the fact–fiction dichotomy—and what Woodiwiss and Sayer discuss as the process of "reference" is to think again of the photograph as discussed by Tagg. Photographs, and certain types of films, are widely accepted to be coherent and authentic representations that correspond directly to reality; a record of facts if you will. Thus they are thought to be a *reflection of reality*. There is held to be a one-to-one correspondence that gives them a factual, somewhat scientific status in law and which gives diaries and letters a certain status in social science. This status makes the photograph or documentary film a *technology of regulation*. For example, photographs sometimes operate as *instruments* of criminal law, used to secure a conviction. Diaries and letters and other primary source material are used the same way in social science, to secure a point of view, explanation, or generalization.

At the same time, however, the same photograph, text, or film can be taken to be an artistic piece whose primary status is not that of reflection of reality, but rather *reflection upon reality*. As a *reflection upon reality* the image operates more like a statement made by the author or artist about some aspect of lived experience. It is held to be a creative expression that makes *reference* to some external condition. As an *object of to be regulated*, the object's ownership and use is legally regulated through contract law, intellectual property law, and copyright law, for instance as in cases of copyrighted materials of professional photographers and artists. Sources for inquiry are similarly regulated by the conventions of social science. So even though a photograph, letter, diary, or documentary might be thought to mirror reality it is important not to collapse statements into their referents and to recall that these are also commentaries on reality in that they are works that make *reference* to reality in some way, and this raises the problem of dividing filmic and textual materials using the fact–fiction scheme.

In thinking about the things that criminologists and sociologists think about, we must dispense with the fantasy that there is a hard or firm distinction between fact-ive and fictive cultural artifacts. I have offered a comparative examination of fictive and fact-ive works to illustrate the problem with holding to any firm ontological division between works of fantasy and those that are held to be the result of or which capture "real" experiences or events. This is because both of what we term "fiction" and what is often referred to as "fact" are emergent outcomes of situated social practices, use of available discursive resources and the physiological structure of sense organs and thus have the same ontological status. The terms themselves are both concepts and do not correspond directly to actually existing empirical states, but rather make reference to a particular epistemological framing.

This chapter has adopted a reflexive realist approach to the study of literature and film, arguing that novels and fiction films contain within them traces of empirical reality and reflect upon that reality. As fictional realities are empirical entities, and contain within them traces of the actual material and discursive conditions under which they were created, they are amenable to criminological analysis and are just as valuable as "factual" works. This casts the familiar fact–fiction division as an obstacle to criminological knowledge production and as a challenge to be overcome.

NOTES

1. I employ the adjectives "factual" and "fiction" as well as "fact-ive" and "fictive." A "fictive" or "fiction" text is one that is, as one would expect, a work of

fantasy. A "fictional" text is a text that exists within the fiction or fictive narrative; that is, within what I (2010; 2011b) have elsewhere termed "fictional realities" (see also Woodward 2011). Thus we must distinguish between the status of cultural artifacts (e.g., films and texts) themselves and distinguish between the status of things within these fictive worlds. Thus immediately we are confronted with the issues of stratification and ontology when discussing "fact" and "fiction." This will be discussed throughout.

2. Critical realism offers a tripartite model of reality. There are three intersecting domains or orders:

> *the empirical* (the limited set of events and phenomena that human beings can experience), *the actual* (all the phenomena and events that have been produced), and *the real* (which includes not only the actual but also the stratified systems of generative structures and mechanisms that have the capacity, which may or may not be exercised, to produce these and possibly other events and phenomena). (Frauley and Pearce 2007, 6, emphasis added)

All phenomena that are emergent have been actualized, but not all actualized potential will be apprehended empirically. I have written about how this ontology can be applied to think about criminological enquiry (Frauley 2011a; Rigakos and Frauley 2011), methodology in the social sciences (Frauley 2008; Frauley and Pearce 2007), epistemological problems in social science (Frauley 2004; 2005) as well as Foucault's conception of power (Frauley 2007). It is important to note that in practical terms these three domains or orders cannot be neatly separated but they can be treated analytically as distinct, so we are better off conceptualizing these as interacting and overlapping rather than as a hierarchy of determinations (see Bohm's [1978; 1980; Bohm and Hiley 1993] idea of "implicate" and "explicate" orders of reality).

3. See www.bodyworlds.com/en.html; www.animalinsideout.com/en.html.

4. The two images, "Cows in Derwentwater" and "Derwentwater," can be viewed and compared at landscapes.indigenousknowledge.org/exhibit-2.

REFERENCES

Anonymous. 1888. *My Secret Life*, vol. 1–11. Accessed 11 February 2015 from www.globalgrey.co.uk/my-secret-life-complete-volumes-1-11/.

Arrigo, Bruce, Dragan Milovanovic, and Robert Schehr. 2005. *The French Connection in Criminology: Rediscovering Crime, Law, and Social Change*. Albany, NY: SUNY Press.

Barton, Alana, David Scott, Karen Corteen, and Dave Whyte (eds.). 2007. *Expanding the Criminological Imagination: Critical Readings in Criminology*. Portland, OR: Willan Publishing.

Becker, Harold (director). 1979. *The Onion Field* [motion picture]. United States: Black Marble.

Berger, Morroe. 1977. *Real and Imagined Worlds: The Novel and Social Science*. Cambridge, MA: Harvard University Press.

Bohm, David. 1978. "The Implicate Order." *Process Studies* 8(2): 73–102.
———. 1980. *Wholeness and the Implicate Order*. London: Routledge.
Bohm, David and Basil Hiley. 1993. *The Undivided Universe: An Ontological Interpretation of Quantum Theory*. New York: Routledge.
Boyd, Susan. 2009. *Hooked: Drug War Films in Britain, Canada, and the United States*. Toronto: University of Toronto Press.
Brown, Michelle. 2004. "Crime Fiction and Criminology." *Criminal Justice Review* 29(1): 206–20.
Brussel, James. 1938. "Charles Dickens: Child Psychologist and Sociologist." *Psychiatric Quarterly* 12(1): 163–74.
Capote, Truman. 1965. *In Cold Blood*. New York: Random House.
Carrabine, Eamonn. 2012. "Just Images: Aesthetics, Ethics and Visual Criminology." *British Journal of Criminology* 52: 463–89.
Cohen, Marilyn (ed.). 2013. *Novel Approaches to Anthropology: Contributions to Literary Anthropology*. Lanham, MD: Lexington Books.
Collot, Nadia (director). 2006. *The Tobacco Conspiracy* [Tabac, la conspiration, motion picture]. France & Canada: Kuiv Productions/National Film Board of Canada/ France 2.
Coser, Lewis (ed.). 1972. *Sociology Through Literature*, 2nd edition. Englewood Cliffs, NJ: Prentice-Hall.
Craib, Ian. 1984. *Modern Social Theory*. New York: Harvester Wheatsheaf.
Donnan, Hastings, and Fiona Magowan. 2012. "Sexual Transgression, Social Order, and the Self." In *Transgressive Sex: Subversion and Control in Erotic Encounters*, edited by H. Donnan and F. Magowan, 1–24. New York: Berghahn Books.
Eitzen, D. 1995. "When is a Documentary?: Documentary as a Mode of Reception." *Cinema Journal* 35(1): 81–102.
Ferrell, Jeff. 1995a. "Culture, Crime, and Cultural Criminology." *Journal of Criminal Justice and Popular Culture* 3(2): 25–42.
———. 1995b. "Style Matters: Criminal Identity and Social Control." In *Cultural Criminology*, edited by J. Ferrell and C. Sanders, 169–89. Boston: Northeastern University Press.
———. 1999. "Cultural Criminology." *Annual Review of Sociology* 25: 398–418.
Ferrell, Jeff, Keith Hayward, and Jock Young. 2008. *Cultural Criminology: An Invitation*. Thousand Oaks, CA: Sage.
Foucault, Michel. 1976/1980. "Two Lectures." In *Power/Knowledge*, edited by Colin Gordon, 78–108. New York: Pantheon.
———. 1977/1980. "Truth and Power." In *Power/Knowledge*, edited by Colin Gordon, 109–33. New York: Pantheon.
Frauley, Jon. 2004. "Race, Justice, and the Production of Knowledge: A Critical Realist Consideration." *Canadian Journal of Law & Society* 19: 177–97.
———. 2005. "Representing Theory and Theorising in Criminal Justice Studies: Practising Theory Considered." *Critical Criminology* 13(3): 245–65.
———. 2007. "Toward an Archaeological-Realist Foucauldian Analytics of Government." *British Journal of Criminology* 47(4): 617–33
———. 2008. "Heterodox Criminology: Rethinking Methodology and Criminological Knowledge Production." In *Criminology: Challenges for the 21st Century*, edited by W. Ventura, 1–25. New York: Nova Science Publishers.

———. 2010. "The Fictional Reality and Criminology: An Ontology of Theory and Exemplary Pedagogical Practice." *Current Issues Criminal Justice* 21(3): 437–59.

———. 2011a. "Critical Realist Criminology." In *Criminology: Critical Canadian Perspectives*, edited by Kirsten Kramar, 145–58. Toronto: Pearson.

———. 2011b. *Criminology, Deviance and the Silver Screen: The Fictional Reality and the Criminological Imagination*. New York: Palgrave Macmillan.

———. (ed.). 2015. *C. Wright Mills and the Criminological Imagination: Prospects for Creative Enquiry*. Farnham, UK: Ashgate Publishing.

Frauley, Jon and Frank Pearce. 2007. "Critical Realism and the Social Sciences: Methodological and Epistemological Preliminaries." In *Critical Realism and the Social Sciences: Heterodox Elaborations*, edited by J. Frauley and F. Pearce, 3–29. Toronto: University of Toronto Press.

Gombrich, Ernst Hans. 1977. *Art and Illusion: A Study in the Psychology of Pictorial Representation*. London: Phaidon Press.

Greenhill, Pauline, and Steven Kohm. 2010. "'Little Red Riding Hood' Crime Films: Criminal Themes and Critical Variations." *Annual Review of Interdisciplinary Justice Research* 1: 77–93.

Hanson, Julienne. 2012. "Presentiment, Contrast and Ambiguity in Fictional Space: The London Novels of Charles Dickens and Peter Ackroyd." *The Journal of Space Syntax* 3(1): 81–124.

Hayward, Keith, and Mike Presdee (eds.). 2010. *Framing Crime: Cultural Criminology and the Image*. New York: Routledge.

Hyams, Peter (director). 1978. *Capricorn One* [motion picture]. USA: Associated General Films.

Jacobsen, Michael Hviid (ed.). 2014. *The Poetics of Crime: Understanding and Researching Crime and Deviance Through Creative Sources*. Farnham, UK: Ashgate Publishing.

Karel, William (director). 2002. *Dark Side of the Moon* [Opération lune, motion picture]. France: Arte France/Centre National de la Cinématographie.

Katz, Jack. 1988. *Seductions of Crime: The Moral and Sensual Attractions in Doing Evil*. New York: Basic Books.

Mills, C. Wright. 1959. *The Sociological Imagination*. New York: Oxford University Press.

Ndalianis, Angela. 2012. *The Horror Sensorium: Media and the Senses*. Jefferson, NC: McFarland and Co.

O'Neil, Maggie and Lizzie Seal. 2012. *Transgressive Imaginations: Crime, Deviance, and Culture*. Palgrave Macmillan.

Pearce, Frank. 1989. *The Radical Durkheim*. London: Unwin Hyman.

———. 1978. "Art and Reality: Gangsters in Film and Society." *The Sociological Review* 26(S1): 245–70.

Potter, Garry. 1998. "Truth in Fiction, Science and Criticism." *Journal of Literary Semantics* 27(3): 173–89.

Potter, Lee Ann. 2002. "The War of the Words: Letters to the FCC regarding Orson Welles' 1938 Broadcast." *Social Education* 66(4): 198–204.

Rafter, Nicole. 2006. *Shots in the Mirror: Crime Films and Society*, 2nd edition. New York: Oxford.

Rafter, Nicole, and Michelle Brown. 2011. *Criminology Goes to the Movies: Crime Theory and Popular Culture*. New York: New York University Press.

Reiner, Rob (director). 1984. *This is Spinal Tap* [motion picture]. USA: Metro-Goldwyn-Mayer.

Reitman, Jason (director). 2005. *Thank You For Smoking* [motion picture]. USA: Room 9 Entertainment.

Rigakos, George, and Jon Frauley. 2011. "The Promise of Critical Realism: Toward a Post-Empiricist Criminology." In *Critical Criminology in Canada: New Voices, New Directions*, edited by A. Doyle and D. Moore, 243–68. Vancouver: University of British Columbia Press.

Rockwell, Joan. 1977. "A Theory of Literature and Society." *Sociological Review* 25(S1): 32–42.

Ruggiero, Vincenzo. 2002. "Moby Dick and the Crimes of the Economy." *British Journal of Criminology* 42(1): 96–108.

———. 2003. *Crime in Literature: Sociology of Deviance and Fiction*. New York: Verso.

Sagarin, Edward. 1980. "In Search of Criminology Through Fiction." *Deviant Behavior* 2: 73–91.

Sayer, Andrew. 1992. *Method in Social Science: A Realist Approach*, 2nd edition. New York: Routledge.

Sobchack, Vivian. 1999. "Toward a Phenomenology of Nonfictional Film Experience." In *Collecting Visible Evidence*, edited by J. Gaines and M. Renow, 241–54. Minneapolis: University of Minnesota Press.

Sokal, Alan. 1996. "Transgressing the Boundaries: Toward a Transformative Hermeneutics of Quantum Gravity. *Social Text* 14(1/2): 217–52.

Squires, Paul Chatham. 1938. "Charles Dickens as Criminologist." *Journal of Criminal Law and Criminology* 29(2): 170–201.

Stopkewich, Lynne (director). 1996. *Kissed* [motion picture]. Canada: Boneyard Film Company/British Columbia Film.

Tagg, John. 1988. *The Burden of Representation: Essays on Photographies and Histories*. Minneapolis: University of Minnesota Press.

Visano, Livy. 1997. "Dracula as a Contemporary Ethnography: A Critique of Mediated Moralities and Mysterious Mythologies. In *Bram Stoker's Dracula: Sucking Through the Century, 1897–1997*, edited by P. Simpson-Housley and Carol Margaret Davison, 331–50. Toronto: Dundurn Press.

Williams, Frank. 1984. "The Demise of the Criminological Imagination." *Justice Quarterly* 1(1): 91–106.

Woodiwiss, Anthony. 1990. *Social Theory After Postmodernism*. London: Pluto Press.

———. 2001. *The Visual in Social Theory*. New York: Athlone Press.

Woodward, Richard. 2011. "Truth in Fiction." *Philosophy Compass* 6(3): 158–67.

Young, Alison. 2010. *The Scene of Violence: Cinema, Crime, Affect*. New York: Routledge.

16

Tobias Beecher

Law as a Refuge from Uncertainty?

Steve Greenfield

Analysis of the representation of cinematic and television lawyers has often focused on the portrayal of the individual lawyer's qualities and professional ethics. Two consistently asked questions have been if the portrayals are "realistic" and whether they reflect lawyers in a positive or negative light (Asimow 2000; Greenfield 2001)? Lawyer behavior in court and toward clients as well as competence may be examined to determine if a lawyer is shown as being a "good" or a "bad" lawyer. Much of this work has been driven by a paradigm that correlates a trend toward "bad" portrayals with an increasing public unpopularity of lawyers measured through surveys. However, little academic work has though been undertaken to demonstrate a causal link between the screen characteristics and subsequent perception. It is a problematic relationship; one study that sought to address the issue specifically among law students was not able to draw firm conclusions (Asimow et al. 2005). This approach is, perhaps, something of a dead end and arose from a different period when screen lawyers appeared to have moved from heroic to flawed (Asimow 1996). It is of course possible to argue that both positions are open to challenge; see for example the revisionist work on Atticus Finch (Freedman 1994). Finch (Gregory Peck) is often cited as the ultimate heroic screen lawyer, a single parent and an upholder of the rule of law a lawyer in a racist community prepared to represent a black defendant. Freedman (1994, 482) takes the view that this is a simplistic rose-spectacled view and that we ought to have a more critical reading of the character:

> In short, Atticus Finch is both more and less than the mythical figure that has been made of him. He is human-sometimes right and sometimes wrong. This in line with the view that characters are often more complex than a good/bad perspective permits. Shifting from both the realist and causal perspectives does though allow film and law to progress from a simple "law as legal practice" based approach; " . . . to embrace subjects such as psychology, literature, sociology or even film studies." (Greenfield, Osborn, and Robson 2010, 48).

Different ideas and concepts can be applied to the portrayal of law and lawyers to build a more dynamic and expansive approach beyond a simple classification.

LAWYERS FACING PERSONAL UNCERTAINTY

This chapter contributes a small step on this move to interdisciplinary work by adopting ideas from social psychology encompassing self and social identity in a period of uncertainty. Oz and indeed Tobias Beecher (Lee Tergesen) could be analyzed from a number of different perspectives rooted in concepts drawn from sociology or criminology *inter alia* white collar criminals, prison gangs, prison violence, inmate relations, and such. The rationale for using an uncertainty-identity theory is to consider the significance of law itself to the characteristics of the portrayal. There are other cinematic examples of the importance of law in terms of personal crisis. For example, Frank Galvin (Paul Newman) in *The Verdict* uses one last case to resurrect not just his career as a lawyer but his own personal life. His reengagement with law is the means of salvation on both a personal and professional level. Lincoln (*Young Mr. Lincoln*) is also shown finding solace in the law after the devastating death of his first love, Ann Rutledge. Thus law becomes much more than professional practice to the characters but something more integral to their lives and personality. The essence of the adopted approach is to consider the influence of both law and the professional status of being a lawyer to the construction of the identity that is portrayed.

There is an existing body of work developing that explores the general film/psychology relationship and covers a wide variety of standpoints. Young's (2012) book *Psychology at the Movies* provides a detailed introduction to a whole range of issues including a chapter on "The Psychology of Filmmakers." He notes: "Movies are not just about people, they are made by people—brilliant, egocentric, passionate, and maybe a little crazy" (2012, 64). However, in terms of law films and psychology the field is somewhat limited. There is the excellent *Batman and Psychology: A Dark and Stormy Night* (Langley 2012) that includes the portrayal of Two-Face, the former District Attorney of Gotham City. Harvey Dent (Aaron Eckhart) is an interesting character that moves from law enforcement to law breaking. In *The Dark Knight Rises* it transpires that Dent has given his name to a piece of legislation, the Dent Act, that has led to the suppression of crime gangs. More recently my own essay on the film *Pierrepoint* considered the portrayal of the infamous British executioner, Albert Pierrepoint (Timothy Spall), by applying theories of moral disengagement (Greenfield 2013). This is an emerging area within film and the law that has potential to be developed in different ways and provide new perspectives on law films and legal personnel.

This chapter focuses on one very specific lawyer, Tobias Beecher, who represents an extreme screen depiction as one of the principal figures in the brutal and violent television prison series *Oz*. Beecher's character is very prominent and one of only ten who last the entire show from start to finish. This is a lawyer who from the outset clearly can't fit into an obvious good/bad classification. He is a Harvard educated lawyer originally working in private practice who has been convicted, imprisoned and subsequently debarred. The additional context to the normal lawyer portrayal is the changed environment and status; prison and prisoner. This ties in to some of the original problems of genre and whether a film with a legal character but not necessarily acting professionally as a lawyer, qualifies as a law film. Similarly, at the other end of the spectrum, whether a film without professional lawyers but centered around "law" in some shape or form was within the definition. Beecher is a central character and many of the storylines revolve around both him, his wider family, and his relationships with other prisoners, notably Vern Schillinger (J. K. Simmons), the leader of the Aryan Brotherhood, and his love affair with Chris Keller (Christopher Meloni). According to Santo (2008, 38): "the character of Beecher . . . has been described as the viewer's point of identification inside the prison." Wlodarz similarly notes: "the viewer is positioned to share Beecher's horror as he is thrust into this hotbed of racial conflict and violence, presented here as alien territory for middle-class white men" (2005, 68). The program unusually has a narrator, Augustus Hill (Harrold Perrineau), but many of the visual experiences are seen through Beecher's eyes.

Beecher has been convicted of vehicular manslaughter, killing a nine-year-old girl, and sentenced to fifteen years with the prospect of parole in four years. He was given the option prior to his trial of serving his sentence in a minimum-security prison but rejected the deal seeking an acquittal. As a result he is given a more severe sentence and sent to the maximum security prison, Oz. Beecher enters Oz with an existing alcohol problem and his induction into the prison starts with violence as one from the group awaiting admission, Miguel Alvarez (Kirk Acevedo), is stabbed in the chest. Before the audience knows anything about him Beecher is singled out through his distinctive dress, business suit, and glasses, in stark contrast to the casual wear of his fellow inmates. He is the first prisoner introduced to the viewer:

> Prisoner number 972 Tobias Beecher convicted on July 5th driving whilst intoxicated and vehicular manslaughter sentenced to fifteen years up for parole in four. (Season 1, episode 1)

The group is introduced to the rules of Emerald City which are distinct from the rest of the penitentiary, Head Guard Diane Whittlesey (Edie Falco) explains:[1]

> Your cell is your home, keep it clean, spotless. You are to exercise regularly, attend classes in drug and alcohol counseling. You are to work in one of the prison factories, you are to follow the routine, we tell you when to eat, to sleep, when to piss there is no yelling, no fighting no *fucking* (my emphasis). (Season 1, episode 1) (figure 16.1)

At this point the director cuts to the perplexed figure of Beecher who clearly cannot comprehend his situation and has no notion of what awaits him. A white-collar criminal thrust into a violent gang culture can in itself be dramatic. What is of additional interest here is Beecher as an ex-lawyer and how his relationship to the law and ideas of justice alters in a society that is governed by a different set of regulatory norms while he is undergoing a period of personal crisis. The chapter first outlines the nature of the program and notes some of the academic analysis that has been produced. Second, it briefly sets out the parameters of uncertainty-identity theory and then considers Beecher in the context of his uncertainty and view of the law.

OZ

> The HBO TV series provided a controversial, hyper-violent depiction of life inside a maximum security prison, complete with a weekly carnage of inmate fatalities, male rape, and other prison violence. (Wilson and O'Sullivan 2004, 148)

Figure 16.1. Beecher on arrival is introduced to the violence of Oz. Image found on http://www.hum.aau.dk/~shb/closet_wlodarz.pdf, and optimized by Susan Gilbert.

The HBO drama was first shown in the United States in July 1997 and ran for six seasons totaling fifty-six episodes with the final episode shown in February 2003. According to Chris Albrecht, president of HBO Original Programming; "we were looking for a show about retribution and rehabilitation that could not be done on network television but we didn't want 'Homicide' set inside a prison" (Elias 1997). Homicide refers to the Fontana drama *Homicide: Life on the Street* that was based on David Simon's book (Simon 1991). *Oz* never attracted the same level of popularity as other HBO series such as *The Sopranos* or *The Wire,* but did receive some critical acclaim. John Patterson (2008) noted the difference between British and U.S. prison drama:

> "In American movies, prison is serious business: it's all rape, shivs, inter-gang wars, racial segregation, punishment blocks, chain gangs, razor wire and machine-gun towers. Among British movies set in prisons, the only comparable entries—in terms of pessimism and brutality, at least—are Alan Clarke's *Scum* and John Mackenzie's *A Sense of Freedom*. Everything else is Porridge.

For Schauer (2004, 36), *Oz* was worthy of analysis "because of its cult status as prison-fiction in North America and because it articulates a number of interesting symbolic challenges to the prison film genre." The setting is the Oswald State Correctional Facility, originally named the Oswald State Penitentiary, a maximum security level-4 prison. Inside Oz the focus is on the activities within one self-contained unit, Emerald City, where the minutiae of daily prison life is depicted. Emerald City is an experimental unit, Cell Block 5, governed with almost total autonomy by Tim McManus (Terry Kinney), who personally selects the prisoners he wants as part of his liberal rehabilitation program. One of the elements of interest in the construction of the program is the lack of any defined time periods. There are few outside events and accordingly time becomes a fluid concept. Episodes do not seem to reflect a day or any measurable point in time. For example a prisoner might be sentenced to a month in solitary confinement (the hole) as a punishment and this passes without any other reference points and the prisoner may return with little or nothing apparently having happened. Interestingly this may also be found in the real world, Sykes argues that prisons and particularly those housing the most serious offenders "have a remarkable tendency to over-ride the variations of time and place" (1956–1957, 131).

Oz has been the subject of some academic analysis that has touched on a number of different aspects. For example, Peter Dickinson used its portrayal of the sexual dimension of male imprisonment to review Harvey Hart's film version of John Herbert's work, *Fortune and Men's Eyes*.[2] Yousman (2009) considered *Oz* in terms of the representation of incarceration as hyperviolent and the links to criminal justice policy, whilst Jarvis (2005) also discusses the imagery. Wlodarz (2005) explores the program within a context of male erotica and the prison genre more generally, but also considers the audience dimension. David Marc (2008) notes that the freedom in production permitted exploration of contentious issues:

> Tom Fontana's *Oz* (1997–2003) adapts an old film chestnut for TV, the prison story, and revitalizes it with a psycho-realist dynamism not felt in the genre since *I am a Fugitive from a Chain Gang* (1932). Taking advantage of HBO's relaxed language restrictions, *Oz*, penetrates the setting's inherent homoeroticism, a topic previously reserved for porno novels. (2008, 102)

Rapping's (2003) analysis explores the political and ideological dimension to the show. She draws upon the work of McNeeley (1996) and argues that during the period when the ideology of prisons was connected to correction and rehabilitation there was little need or desire to see this process dramatized. It is perhaps though difficult to measure changes in audience demand for prison dramas and there have been some notable examples.[3] Rapping argues that a changing political context to criminal justice requires portrayals that go beyond the investigation and deliberation phases:

> It demands that we see, with our own eyes, that those who break the laws that represent community values are not merely sent away, but punished. Incapacitation and retribution have replaced deterrence and, certainly rehabilitation as the penal theories of choice. . . . And so we get *Oz*, as big if not bigger, than life in its graphic of the "just deserts" that retributive penal theory requires. (2003, 88)

Wilson and O'Sullivan (2004, 148) also contend that "*Oz* featured no heroes and no villains." This may be true in a traditional rather one-dimensional sense of the definition of a hero or villain that requires a consistency of behavior representing one or the other traits. However, it sidesteps the concept that characteristics and actions need not be fixed and may alter and change according to context and circumstances. There is also the question of whether this classification is determined by the viewer or some other "audience." For example Beecher's initial violent attack on Schillinger is applauded by a large group of prisoners who are clearly happy to see his racist persecutor humiliated and might well see Beecher as "heroic," certainly brave. Even on the more simplistic analysis Sister Peter Marie (Rita Moreno) exhibits courageous qualities in, for example, her refusal to submit to the threats of dismissal to prevent her protesting against the reintroduction of capital punishment. She actually joins the demonstrators outside the prison in spite of Warden Glynn's (Ernie Hudson) ultimatum and loses her job, though is later reinstated. It is hard to see Sister Marie as anything less than heroic. Throughout there are individual acts of both good and evil, Jefferson Keane's (Leon) personal sacrifice being a good example of the former and Keller's embittered betrayal of Beecher the latter. One of the qualities of the program is the complexity of many of the characters; clearly all the prisoners have some element of "evil."[4] Many of the officers are shown to have different sides to their characters and there are examples of officers conspiring with prisoners, with whom they have some association or sympathy. For example, in season 2, Schillinger approaches Diane Whittlesey, the guards' supervisor, and offers to pay her to kill Beecher. Schillinger is desperate having had his offer rejected by all of the prisoners he had asked. There is a high level of unremitting violence throughout the program and numerous serious assaults and murders of both inmates and guards. Killings are also carried out beyond the walls of the prison because of unfolding events inside. In one case O'Reily (Dean Winters) persuades his brother Cyril (Scott William Winters) to murder Dr. Nathan's husband because of his infatuation with her and in another Kenny Wangler (J. D. Williams) has his wife (Lauren Valez) and her lover murdered. Law and justice or rather the absence of "official" law and justice is a continuous theme as an alternative regulatory regime, often governed by the prisoners, operates.

Despite being a prison drama there are a surprising number of lawyers and legal figures rather than just correctional officers. *Oz*'s lawyers feature in a number of guises. First as the representative of prisoners; for example, there is a brief appearance by Schillinger's lawyer when the prisoner is charged with conspiracy to murder a fellow inmate (Beecher). Shirley Bellinger (Kathryn Erbe) (the only woman prisoner who is incarcerated on death row) has a lawyer, Lawrence Bailey, working on her appeal, as does Augustus Hill, Clifford Sprague, and Jaz Hoyt, Ms. Lang. Katherine McClain (Sandra Purpuro) who acts for a prisoners rights organization at times represents both Beecher (parole) and Keller (appeal). Arnie Zelman (Larry Pine) has a significant role representing Kareem Said (Eamonn Walker) and Cyril O'Reily as well as litigating a civil suit after the riot. There is also, in addition to Beecher, Kareem Said who acts as the unofficial adviser to a number of prisoners such as Augustus Hill and indeed, surprisingly at one point, the racist Schillinger. The phenomenon of jailhouse lawyers extorting payment for services identified by Spector (1968) isn't obvious though those helping prisoners with legal cases may have their own motives. It is in this connection of the prosecution of prisoners and appeals, that a number of state lawyers appear and even Judge Grace Lema (Elaine Stritch), who was not only the judge at Beecher's original trial, but is also the judicial figure who overturns Hill's appeal. After a serious riot that leads to the deaths of both inmates and staff, a committee is appointed by Governor Devlin to investigate. This is led by a further legal figure, Professor Alvah Case (Charles S. Dutton), dean of a law school. There is thus a mixture of professional lawyers, lay figures, an academic, and a judge in addition to quasi-judicial figures such as the parole board members. This is not to suggest that *Oz* is a legal drama akin to shows such as *Shark, JAG, L.A. Law, Suits, Damages,* or numerous others as it shows only the end phase of the criminal justice system, though a place where legal personnel do still operate.

UNCERTAINTY: IDENTITY THEORY

Theories within social psychology seek to explain the process of the development of individual identity and also the relationship of individuals to groups. Tajfel (1982) developed the influential idea of "in" and "out" groups that encompasses relations between and within groups and the role of the individual. This division offers the opportunity for individuals to differentiate between groups, identifying with the "in group." Individuals can align themselves with the in group and thus enhance or validate their social identity. This in turn may elevate self-esteem (Hogg 2000). Group membership provides an important dimension for the creation of social identity and there may be a host of relevant groups, some more important and influential than others. Membership or strength of affiliation to groups may change over time or within different circumstances. Undoubtedly social identity and consequent behaviors can alter and change particularly when there is an extreme alteration to the environment and context within which that individual operates. Hogg outlines the importance of certainty in life: "certainty renders existence meaningful and gives one confidence in how to behave, and what to expect from one's physical and social environment" (2000, 227). Certainty is not a universally sought after concept across all areas of life only where it is has subjective importance. Clearly where certainty matters consequent reduction of uncertainty within that sphere will also be important unless the cost of reducing the uncertainty outweighs the need.

The idea of "uncertainty" influencing social identity has been developed to explain a number of different situations where individual behavior alters. Hogg notes that: "Subjective uncertainty is produced by contextual factors that challenge people's certainty about their cognitions, perceptions feelings and behaviours, and ultimately, certainty about and confidence in their sense of self" (2000, 227). So as social context alters this extends to worries and concerns an individual feels about their own position and identity. A key feature is the extent to which the uncertainty impacts upon feelings around "self":

> We are particularly motivated to reduce uncertainty if we feel uncertain about things that reflect on or are relevant to self or if we are uncertain about self per se; about our identity, who we are, how we relate to others and how we are socially located. (Hogg 2012, 65)

One obvious cause of uncertainty is a change in employment, with both a new physical and social environment, and employers will often take steps to reduce this insecurity and promote socialization though induction programs (Hogg 2000). Individual characteristics can play a role in how the changes to the social context, such as the environment, are viewed and acted upon. Some personality types may adjust more easily to change and in any event feel more secure about their own identity and so are less affected by changing circumstances.

Hogg explains the central principle of the attraction to groups in a period of uncertainty:

> The core tenet of uncertainty-identity theory is that feelings of uncertainty, particularly about or relating to who one is and how one should behave,

> motivate uncertainty-reduction, and that the process of self-categorization as a group member reduces self conceptual uncertainty because it provides a consensually validated group prototype that describes and prescribes who one is and how one should behave. (Hogg 2012, 65)

Where uncertainty exists it is suggested that individuals will then be motivated to change their behavior to reduce the problem. Thus uncertainty becomes a driving factor in behavioral transformation notably in relation to group identity, which becomes more important to reduce the unease. Personal uncertainty may be related to other concepts such as confidence, control, meaningfulness, and insecurity (van den Bos 2009). Uncertainty may be permanent or short term and is context dependent (Hogg 2012). The insecurity produced by the situation may lead to critical reflection of self, as van den Bos observes; "encountering feelings of personal uncertainty may trigger serious questions about meaning and one's place in the world" (2009, 200). Van den Bos proposes that one means of managing uncertainty is to reinforce cultural perspectives and values:

> the uncertainty management model argues that under conditions of heightened personal uncertainty people's cultures and the values they convey become especially important to them. Thus, they will value it particularly if persons or events adhere to the norms that are important in their culture or subculture, and they will hate it when people or events violate these norms. (2009, 203)

Uncertainty and consequent group affiliation has been applied to explain the contemporary problem of the radicalization of individuals (Doosje, Loseman, and van den Bos 2013; Hogg, Kruglanski, and van den Bos 2013). It is proposed that when an individual is suffering uncertainty radical or extreme groups appear to offer some solution:

> They provide uncertain people with a clear Black-and-White-ideology, including norms and values (what is good and what is bad) and strict codes of behavior. In this manner, these norms, values and behavioural rules can reduce their uncertainty. (Doosje, Loseman, and van den Bos 2013, 590)

Similarly, the radical organization is perceived in Tajfel's terms as "in group" and the authorities the "out group" and a strict ideology and dogma are clear and definite. With respect to social identity and youth gang membership Goldman, Giles, and Hogg (2014) note what alternative groups need to offer to replace the attraction of gangs:

> a sense of significance and positive reputation, and a sense of status, power, and security; create a sense of belonging; and provide protection or offer

> something that mitigates perceptions of threat. Such groups might coalesce around conservation, politics, religion, music, community and social action, and sports and exercise activities. (2014, 14)

Again this relates to group dynamics and qualities rather than individual engagement with activities. The literature however also points toward the attraction of groups that have fixed and certain ideas during personal uncertainty, hence the link to extremism. These beliefs in the cases of radicalism are based on ideological orthodoxy with an inward looking rigid world view (Hogg and Adelman 2013).

To summarize, uncertainty-identity theory posits that individuals, in the face of uncertainty, are drawn toward groups in order to validate their own social identity and reduce insecurity. The uncertainty may be as a result of a changing physical or social environment. Rigidity and order as well as ideological certainty may be an attractive dimension. Groups that display these characteristics may fulfill a need for certain individuals. The next section considers how Beecher is portrayed in his relationships with the prison authorities, strong individuals within gangs, and, more importantly, the law in his quest to reconstruct his social identity.

BEECHER'S RELATIONSHIP WITH THE GANG CULTURE

Beecher's whole world has been shaken and he finds himself in a new and hostile physical environment. He has lost his family and his career, having being disbarred on conviction. He also has to deal with guilt; Beecher has recurring flashbacks over the death of Kathy Rockwell and believes he deserves to be punished. The highly emotional and failed reconciliation with the victim's mother brought home to him the enormity of the consequences of his actions. The root cause of his predicament is the alcohol addiction that is also part of his personality. Beecher's loss increases throughout the program as further tragedies envelop him. After his initial incomprehension at both the organization and administration of Oz, the unrestrained behavior of the inmates and his brutalization at the hands of Vern Schillinger spirals Beecher downward into darkness and despair (figure 16.2).

The structure of Oz, both physically in terms of the pods the prisoners share, and the lack of overall control by McManus and the guards mean that Beecher is unable to feel any security in his surroundings. A lack of security and support has been identified as a cause of adjustment problems for some prisoners (Wright 1991). This increases his uncertainty. His mental distress becomes obvious and he plunges into emotional discord toward a state of anomie, partially drug fueled. This is seen most obvi-

Figure 16.2. Beecher is degraded by Schillinger before he starts to fight back. Image from http://www.hbo.com/oz/episodes/1/06-to-your-health/index.html, and optimized by Susan Gilbert.

ously when he almost throws himself from the upper level after attacking Vern Schillinger. Beecher has no control over his physical environment and more importantly no means of seeking any restraint over the behavior of the other inmates who threaten him. He has lost the discipline and stability that his previous life provided. The legal processes and rule of law that was central to his position as a lawyer has disappeared, to be replaced with a system that he cannot understand or relate to. He survives, though is scarred both physically and mentally, but is still plagued by the unstable situation.

A crucial part of this instability is the dominating role of the different gangs or groups to whom he has no allegiance. Intergroup relations and affiliation to groups is clearly important inside Emerald City; indeed it is a means of survival given the ongoing conflicts. Gangs are a fundamental part of Oz's make up and provide an alternative system of governance. Inmate need for additional governance structures has been identified as a reason for the growth of prison gangs (Skarbek 2012). There are a number of powerful alliances specifically represented: the Aryan Brotherhood, the Bikers, the Latinos, the Muslims, the Gangstas, and the Italians. More minor groups include the Gays and the Christians. In season 2, episode 2, McManus formally establishes a Council of Representatives that explicitly recognizes the importance of the different interest groups. Despite the apparent tight knit nature of the groups and closed nature of membership they are still wrought with internal wrangling and disputes. Both the Latinos and the Italians replace their leaders because of the incumbent's apparent weakness.[5] Schauer (2004, 38) criticizes the stereotypical construction of the different groups and individuals:

> The skinny Irish live by their wits and their gift of the gab; the "built" African Americans by their physical size, aggression and gang-banger know-how—a bit like the white-supremacists; for the Italians it is a question of Mafia connections on the outside and honor; the Muslims and Hispanics are physically able, but it is through their religion and solidarity that they are able to maintain social status, whereas for the middle-class punk-turned-psycho, space becomes a question of unpredictability and "snapping"—into hyper aggressive identity—from repeated assault and insult.[6]

The problem for Beecher is that he doesn't have any natural internal affiliations given his "sheltered" life on the outside. The uncertainty literature proposes that in times of crisis over personal identity, "people cleave to authority and majority norms and derogate minority and disadvantaged groups that represent alternative values and orientations" (McGregor, Zanna, Holmes, and Spencer 2001, 485). The problem inside Oz is that it is the prisoners themselves who to a large degree "represent" one of the two streams of authority and set the behavioral norms. In theory the governor and McManus set the rules, but the number of murders and violent acts indicate that despite the formal structures there is a parallel system of power and authority. There is no formal authority for Beecher to turn toward for refuge. He doesn't find the degree of control he anticipates and McManus is not always sympathetic to him; for example, when he returns from the hole after attacking Schillinger for the second time he requests a move for his own safety:

> *Beecher:* You've got to transfer me to another cellblock.
>
> *McManus:* All the other cellblocks are full.
>
> *Beecher:* Well transfer me to another prison.
>
> *McManus:* Do I look like a travel agent to you? (Season 1, episode 7)

Denied access to the various gangs, he cannot reduce his uncertainty through group identification. Neither can he embrace traditional authority within the prison nor the actual authority that is the gangs, who are, in any event, inconsistent in their behavior and alliances. Beecher is very much a loner and whilst there are some other examples, such as Ryan O'Reily, he is not anywhere near as well-equipped to survive. Ryan O'Reily also ends up with his brother Cyril, an established gang member and adroit at the political maneuverings between the competing groups in Oz, alongside him. Beecher cannot join the gangs based around ethnic origins and doesn't have the requisite connections for the others. In short he is an individual in a group-centered world and the key question is how his personality inside Oz can be (re)constructed to keep him more secure.

One method of negotiating his relationship with the gangs is through extreme physical violence, a respected trait inside Oz. Beecher is initially portrayed (albeit for a short period) as very meek and mild but is quickly involved in numerous violent incidents. In season 1, episode 7 he brutally attacks Vern Schillinger in the gym, knocking him unconscious before defecating on his face. In a reflective moment Beecher says to McManus "I shat all over a man. That's not normal." Van den Bos notes that in response to uncertainty reactions are more likely to be "visceral and intuitive (instead of more reasoned and rationalistic)" (2009, 198). This is certainly true with respects to Beecher's violence that is unrestrained and manic and certainly not calm and measured. His guttural primeval scream at the end of the gym scene indicates the animalism of the act; this is far more than clinical display of force for self-protection. His violence appears as an attempt to regain some control over his life by establishing himself within the prison population.

BEECHER'S AMBIGUOUS RELATIONSHIP WITH THE LAW

> I love the law, even though it didn't work in my favor and I ended up in here. I thank god every night for the laws we have as it keeps people like Adebisi, Hernandez Schillinger away from my children. (Tobias Beecher, season 4, episode 2)

Beecher's relationship with the law and legal processes provide a means of reconstructing his identity and finding more security. Within this demoralizing situation his legal knowledge and negotiating skills ought to provide him with some limited advantages. Beecher starts to reengage with law but this is not the civil law he practiced on the outside. Despite his "unjust" circumstances he is still drawn to the process of law as a means of achieving justice. While in the midst of the blackness caused by the physical abuse, which he suffers at the hands of Schilllinger, Beecher becomes enlivened by the law. He relishes the prospects of overturning the death sentence imposed on Jefferson Keane, the former leader of the Homeboys, for the killing of another prisoner. Beecher learns from O'Reily and Schillinger that the guards, on behalf of another inmate, set up Keane to fight Martinez and another Latino prisoner, with the expectation that Keane would be killed. However, Keane won the fight and is convicted of murder and sentenced to death, as the conservative state Governor Devlin has just restored capital punishment after thirty-four years. Beecher discusses the case with Bob Rebadow (George Morfogen) who advises him that taking the story to McManus would be dangerous and he would be killed. Beecher places his faith in law.

> *Beecher:* What I should do is represent Keane and appeal his conviction.
>
> *Bob Rebadow:* What, you?
>
> *Beecher:* I'm a lawyer.
>
> *Bob Rebadow:* The State disbarred you.
>
> *Beecher:* The State can't take away what I do, who I am—I can help. He killed Martinez in self-defense. He shouldn't die.

Beecher sees this case as part of his own rehabilitation and clearly still sees himself as a lawyer not just in terms of "what I do," but more importantly as "who I am." Beecher deliberately gets himself placed into protective custody so he can talk to Keane who is awaiting execution. Keane has since converted to Islam and become a measured and thoughtful figure, he is not interested in any appeal and wants to sacrifice himself to end the feud and stop further killing. He also believes he will now go to heaven.

> *Keane:* I am at peace right now. Beecher, please don't take that from me.
>
> *Beecher:* Look I am not responsible for your soul but as a lawyer I am responsible for justice. I don't need your cooperation to file an appeal on your behalf.
>
> *Keane:* Beecher please don't.
>
> *Beecher:* It's something I have to do.

Beecher places the law, justice, and consequently his own salvation above Keane's wishes. The crucial point is that Beecher feels he has a duty, as a lawyer, to see that justice is done. This demonstrates just how important the law is to his identity, even though he is formally no longer a lawyer, and this wider duty transcends the loss of his personal professional position. When Beecher reemerges into the general population Schillinger, the leader of the Aryans, finds out what he is doing. This provokes a furious outburst that culminates in forcing Beecher to eat the pages of the law book he is consulting. Schillinger is outraged by the nature of Beecher's "client" as Keane is the ex-leader of the Homeboys, the gang most politically diametrically opposed to the Ayrans. Interestingly before Beecher throws himself into Keane's appeal, in which Keane has no interest, Beecher doesn't even want to look at O'Reily's papers, telling him as a litigator he has no knowledge of the criminal law. Beecher seems genuinely motivated by the injustice that he has personally found out about and not O'Reily's case, though he pretends to Schillinger that this is what he is working on when he finds him in the library. A disillusioned and depressed Beecher is found by O'Reily who is clearly impressed by his efforts.

> *O'Reily:* You starting to grow some balls Beecher?
>
> *Beecher:* I had some balls—a long long time ago. I thought I could get the balls back again by saving Jefferson Keane but the lawyer in me got stretched out on the rack and hung by the neck until dead. You got any dope?

It is this failure of the law and his failure as a lawyer that sends him into drug use and later the drug-fueled attack on Schillinger. Beecher accepts, largely through guilt, the punishment he has received but has a clear contempt for Judge Grace Lema, his trial judge, who he meets again inside Oz.

> *Judge Lema:* I've been a judge for sixteen years. I've made over twenty-five-hundred decisions. Most of them were good. But only one has haunted me, yours. You see I've always prided myself on being fair and in my court justice was truly blind. But in your case, that little girl, the parents crying, you being a member of the Bar, your prior arrest for DUI, the senseless of it all it caught up with me. I was quick tempered spiteful to the point. I can't tell if I gave you a fair trial. Well seeing you like this I think maybe the punishment exceeded the crime.
>
> *Beecher:* You're what? Sorry? Your Honor you used all your power to crush me. The truth is I did kill Kathy Rockwell and as much as I tried to manipulate the legal system according to the law each crime is worth a maximum number of years. You gave me a maximum of fifteen years in this fuckhole. You say you are haunted by this?

Judge Lema is left looking bewildered muttering "I'm sorry" even though Beecher has left the room. She is clearly surprised by Beecher's forcefulness and also his disinterest in the injustice of both her attitude at his trial or his sentence. He acknowledges, with seemingly some regret, his attempt to manipulate the law to obtain an acquittal for which he feels terrible regret and continuing guilt. It is as if Beecher still believes in the law but not for him, his injustice is deserved. Beecher becomes further involved in the class lawsuit against the state over responsibility for the riot. He believes that Karim has ulterior motives and wants the case to fail so he can point to the inherent bias of the system itself. Beecher strongly defends the legal system even though he is a victim of it.

Inside Oz, Beecher enjoys a very different relationship to the law than outside. He has to contemplate a society where legal rules have little significance when compared to the rules of survival. Beecher finds himself forced to reevaluate his perspective on legality and morality, arguably he just acts instinctively with little thought, again contrary to his legal training. His original desire to conform and obey the rules is quickly eroded as he finds himself drawn deeper into the culture of violence and murder. He still however hopes that the legal processes will provide a route for both his freedom via parole and the ability to be with his lover, Keller, through a successful appeal. Thus Beecher treads an uneasy line acknowledging the importance of the law but simultaneously realizing that to survive he must reject the rule of law as he knew it. At each point that the law seems to provide an escape or some salvation he is thwarted and elects to choose lawlessness while still retaining faith in the law. Beecher's external battle with the system is mirrored with his internal conflicts and descent into depravity. As the law abandons him Beecher abandons the law, and unharnessed seeks release through self-destructive behavior. However he still finds some solace in the order of law, the precedents and the procedure; it is as if through the prospect of saving Keane that Beecher thinks he will find personal redemption. Beecher is drawn back toward the law as both an ideology and a process despite the empirical evidence in front of him that justice is unlikely to result. After all, he was imprisoned and Keane was wrongly convicted and executed. Beecher seems to retain an underlying commitment to the idea of law despite the personal anguish and loss its application had caused him. In his period of uncertainty it is the idea and order of law that attracts him despite its obvious failings. Throughout he still sees and refers to himself as a lawyer and clearly wants to retain his professional identity. Law is not seen in isolation, but makes up perhaps a third component of his new identity, alongside violence and physical homosexual love. The faith in justice and law is maintained despite its inconsistency with his now violent tendencies.

CONCLUSION

What the analysis of Beecher and uncertainty-identity theory does draw out is the significance of law and being a lawyer even in the most extreme circumstances. Both provide a degree of certainty in an insecure environment. Wlodarz (2005, 59) describes *Oz* as "unrelenting in its attention to prison violence and *conflicts of identity*" (my emphasis). Furthermore, he identifies season 2 of *Oz* as constructing a series of binaries: "between minorities, straights and realism at one pole, and whites, gays and artifice at the other" (2005, 87). Beecher is full of contrasts; gay/straight, violent/timid; but most interesting is his binary relationship to law and Beecher clearly defies the simple good/bad classification of lawyer. He is undoubtedly a complex character portrayed as a far more multidimensional than the overwhelming majority of screen lawyers. The long period of time permits his character to emerge and change. Both his physical appearance and sexuality alter as well as the surprising revelation that he has a capacity for extreme violence, when required, and not purely as a defensive measure. He seems happy to exact brutal revenge when necessary, illustrated by his vicious murder of the head correctional officer, Karl Metzger. Beecher was originally unaware of his own ability to inflict pain and seek vengeance and it reveals a different side to not only the viewers but also to himself. Yet he still remains thoughtful, gentle and caring, even loving. He is clearly surprised as to what he has found he is capable of, and has slipped easily into the violent culture embracing the new set of norms that govern his daily life.

He defies direct comparison with other screen lawyers; there is the indirect violence of Sam Bowden in *Cape Fear* though perhaps the better connection to Bowden is the idea of loss that Max Cady emphasizes. Again the loss suffered by Beecher is far more extreme as it goes beyond the long term of imprisonment. Aside from the physical abuse and pain inflicted on Beecher within Oz his wife commits suicide, his father and son are both murdered, and his brother stabbed. For Beecher, unlike Bowden, there is no redemption but just more pain and loss; parole is finally granted but then taken away because of his love for Keller.[7] Perhaps the nearest example is Ned Racine in *Body Heat*, who commits murder and is incarcerated, though this is the end of his story rather than the beginning (McMillian 2009). The alcoholic Frank Galvin is a small rather insignificant comparison though he also finds redemption through law (Greenfield, Osborn, and Robson 2010).

There is a legitimate argument as to whether the audience view Beecher as a lawyer or just another inmate, an ex-lawyer. However, he is still clearly attached to the law and the profession of lawyering. Law is a means of restoring his own self-esteem and draws him back toward his old values. He is certainly flawed and his resort to physical violence takes him into a darker place than when he was admitted into Oz, following his original manslaughter conviction. Beecher explains his character "change" to TV producer Lisa Logan:

> *Logan:* You once tied a fellow inmate down and defecated on his face.
>
> *Beecher:* Yeah.
>
> *Logan:* Is that what it takes to survive?
>
> *Beecher:* I'm not the man I was. Or maybe now, I'm the man I always was and never knew. (Season 4, episode 9)

Tobias Beecher transcends the good lawyer versus bad lawyer dichotomy and provides a perspective about the limitations of law, even for those raised under its wing, in a society where a very different set of moral values come to the fore. The most obvious link of *Oz* is to prison drama but the character of Beecher does also offer challenges to thinking about law film genre and the role of lawyers within it.

NOTES

1. Whittlesey is an interesting character and has an eventful time. She features in twenty-three episodes, has a relationship with McManus, kills a prisoner (Scott Ross) during the riot, but is one of the few characters to both survive and leave on a happy note.

2. Dickinson noted: "Given the acclaim that Tom Fontana's television series *Oz* has recently garnered for its frank depiction of life on the inside, including sexual life on the inside, it seems only appropriate, thirty years after its initial release, to reconsider Hart's film in light of its own, equally complex, interrogation of the prison system's queer subculture" (Dickinson 2002, 19).

3. See for example: *Prisoner Cell Block H* (1979–986), *Bad Girls* (1999–2006), *Porridge* and *Hogan's Heroes* (though these latter two are comedies), Colditz (1972–1974), *Tenko* (1981–1985), *Within These Walls* (1974–1978), *The Prisoner* (1967–1968), and of course the more contemporary *Prison Break* (2005–2009).

4. Tom Fontana discussed characterization in the context of the events of September 11th: "On *Oz* we have several Muslim characters whom we've tried to draw as fully dimensional human beings, sometimes flawed, sometimes righteous. When Timothy McVeigh bombed Oklahoma City, I had the impulse to start writing the Aryan prisoners differently. Will I react the same way now regarding the Muslims? I hope not, but honestly, I don't know." *New York Times*, September 23, 2001.

5. In the case of the Latinos Miguel Alvarez, who also has his father and grandfather in prison, is replaced by El Cid because of Alvarez's perceived vulnerable leadership. With the Italians Peter Schiabtta has replaced his father, Nino, who has been killed by O'Reily and Adebesi. However Peter is unable to control events and has been told by an Italian guard, loyal to the family, that he will be replaced unless he kills Simon Adebesi. Schiabatta fails in this attempt and ends up being raped by Adebesi and consequently his leadership is finished and is then replaced by a more senior figure, his godfather Antonio Nappa.

6. She extends this criticism: "*Oz* does make comments about race and, I would argue, generates stereotyped masculinities. To illustrate how and why this is problematic, one need only look at the character development and pigeonholing of Adebesi, the hugely muscular Nigerian whose accent connotes foreignness" (39).

7. Keller persuades him to collect some pharmaceuticals for his "dying" ex-wife and then informs on him getting him arrested and returned to Oz. When he returns Beecher says to the judgmental McManus and Sister Pete "I got fucked in the ass again."

REFERENCES

Asimow, Michael. 1996. "When Lawyers Were Heroes." *University of San Francisco Law Review* 30(4): 1131–1138.

———. 2000. "Bad Lawyers in the Movies." *Nova Law Review* 24: 533–591.

Asimow, Michael, Steve Greenfield, Guillermo Jorge, Stefan Machura, Guy Osborn, Peter Robson, Cassandra Sharp, and Robert Sockloskie. 2005. "Perceptions of Lawyers—A Transnational Study of Student Views on the Image of Law and Lawyers." *International Journal of the Legal Profession* 15: 407–36.

Dickinson, Peter. 2002. "Critically Queenie: The Lessons of *Fortune and Men's Eyes.*" *Canadian Journal of Film Studies* 11(2): 19–43.

Doosje, Bertjan, Annemarie Loseman, and Kees van den Bos. 2013. "Determinants of Radicalization of Islamic Youth in the Netherlands: Personal Uncertainty, Perceived Injustice, and Perceived Group Threat." *Journal of Social Issues* 69(3): 586–604.

Elias, Justine. 1997. "From the People of *Homicide,* Life Off the Street." *New York Times,* July 6.

Fontana, Tom (producer). 1997–2003. *Oz* [television program]. New York: HBO.

Freedman, Monroe H. 1994. "Atticus Finch-Right and Wrong." *Alabama Law Review* 45: 473–482.

Goldman, Liran, Howard Giles, and Michael A. Hogg. 2014. "Going to Extremes: Social Identity and Communication Processes Associated with Gang Membership." *Group Processes & Intergroup Relations* 1: 1–20.

Greenfield, Steve. 2001. "Hero or Villain? Cinematic Lawyers and the Delivery of Justice." *Journal of Law and Society* 28(1): 25–39.

———. 2013. "State Executioner Pierrrepoint: A Cinematic Portrayal of Moral Disengagement." In *The International Library of Essays on Capital Punishment,* Volume III, edited by Peter Hodgkinson, 391–410. Ashgate: Aldershot.

Greenfield, Steve and Guy Osborn. 1999. "Film, Law and the Delivery of Justice: The Case of Judge Dredd and the Disappearing Courtroom." *Journal of Criminal Justice and Popular Culture* 6(2): 35–45.

Greenfield, Steve, Guy Osborn, and Peter Robson. 2001. *Film and the Law.* London: Cavendish Publishing.

———. 2010. *Film and the Law.* London: Hart Publishing.

Hogg, Michael, A. 2000. "Subjective Uncertainty Reduction through Self-Categorization: A Motivational Theory of Social Identity Processes." *European Review of Social Psychology* 11: 223–55.

———. 2012. "Uncertainty-Identity Theory." In *Handbook of Theories of Social Psychology,* Volume Two, edited by Paul A. M Van Lange, Arie Kruglanski and E. Tory Higgins, 62–80. London: Sage.

Hogg, Michael A., Arie Kruglanski, and Kees van den Bos. 2013. "Uncertainty and the Roots of Extremism." *Journal of Social Issues* 69(3): 407–418.

Hogg, Michael A. and Janice Edelman. 2013. "Uncertainty–Identity Theory: Extreme Groups, Radical Behavior, and Authoritarian Leadership." *Journal of Social Issues* 69(3): 436–454.

Jarvis, Brian. 2005. "The Violence of Images: Inside the Prison TV Drama *Oz*." In *Captured by the Media: Prison Discourse in Popular Culture*, edited by Paul Mason, 154–71. Devon: Willan.

Langley, Travis. 2012. *Batman and Psychology: A Dark and Stormy Knight*. Hoboken, NJ: Wiley.

Leverette, Marc, Brian L. Ott, and Cara Louise Buckley (eds.). 2008. *It's Not TV: Watching HBO in the Post-Television Era*. New York: Routledge.

Marc, David. 2008. "*Carnivale: TV Drama Without TV Genre.*" In *It's Not TV: Watching HBO in the Post-Television Era*, edited by Marc Leverette, Brian L. Ott & Cara Louise Buckley, 101–7. New York: Routledge.

Mason, Paul (ed.). 2005. *Captured by the Media: Prison Discourse in Popular Culture.* Devon: Willan.

McGregor, Ian, Mark P. Zanna, John G. Holmes & Steven J. Spencer. 2001. "Conviction in the Face of Personal Uncertainty: Going to Extremes and Being Oneself." *Journal of Personality and Social Psychology* 80(3): 472–488.

McMillian, Lance. 2009. "Tortured Souls: Unhappy Lawyers Viewed Through the Medium of Film." *Seton Hall Journal of Sports & Entertainment Law* 19 (1): 31–103.

McNeeley, Connie. 1996. *Public Rights, Public Rules*. New York: Routledge

Patterson, John. 2008. "If Only . . . British Prison Dramas Were as Hard-Hitting as their American Counterparts." *The Guardian,* Saturday 14 June 2008. Accessed June 10, 2015 at: www.theguardian.com/film/filmblog/2008/jun/14/ifonlybritishprisondramaswereashardhittingastheiramericancounterparts.

Rapping, Elayne. 2003. *Law and Justice As Seen on TV*. New York: New York University Press.

Santo, Avi. 2008. "Para-Television and Discourses of Distinction: The Culture of Production at HBO." In *It's Not TV: Watching HBO in the Post-Television Era*, edited by Marc Leverette, Brian L. Ott & Cara Louise Buckley, 19–45. New York: Routledge.

Schauer, Terrie. 2004. "Masculinity Incarcerated: Insurrectionary Speech and Masculinities in Prison Fiction." *Journal for Crime, Conflict and the Media* 1(3): 28.

Simon, David. 1991. *Homicide: A Year on the Killing Streets.* New York: Houghton Miffin.

Skarbek, David. 2012. "Prison Gangs, Norms and Organizations." *Journal of Economic Behaviour & Organization* 82: 96-109.

Smith, Dinitia. 1999. "Prison Series Seeks to Shatter Expectations." *New York Times*, July 12. Accessed June 15, 2015 at: www.nytimes.com/1999/07/12/arts/prison-series-seeks-to-shatter-expectations.html?pagewanted=all.

Spector, Herman, C. 1968. "A Prison Librarian Looks at Writ-Writing." *California Law Review* 56: 342, 365–70.

Sykes, Gresham, M. 1956–1957. "Men, Merchants, and Toughs: A Study of Reactions to Imprisonment." *Social Problems* 4: 130–38.

Tajfel, Henri. 1982. "Social Psychology of Intergroup Relations." *Annual Review Psychology* 33: 1–39.

Van den Bos, Kees. 2009. "Making Sense of Life: The Existential Self Trying to Deal with Personal Uncertainty." *Psychological Inquiry* 20: 197–217.

Wilson, David and Sean O'Sullivan. 2004. *Representations of Prison in Film and Television Drama*. Winchester, UK: Waterside Press.

Wlodarz, Joe. 2005. "Maximum Insecurity: Genre Trouble and Closet Erotics in and out of HBO's *Oz*." *Camera Obscura* 20(1): 58–105.
Wright, Kevin. 1991. "A Study of Individual, Environmental, and Interactive Effects in Explaining Adjustment to Prison." *Justice Quarterly* 8(2): 217–42.
Young, S. D. 2012. *Psychology at the Movies*. Chichester: Wiley-Blackwell.
Yousman, Bill. 2009. "Inside *Oz*: Hyperviolence, Race and Class Nightmares, and the Engrossing Spectacle of Terror." *Communication and Critical/Cultural Studies* 6(3): 265–284.

17

Nationalities, Histories, Rhetorics

Real/Reel Representations of the Holocaust and Holocaust Trials and a Poethics of Film and Law[1]

Caroline Joan "Kay" S. Picart

Following Anthony Chase's call to recognize the value of images of law and lawyers generated by mass culture as "legitimate and important subjects for scholarly critique" (1986, 527)[2] and Richard K. Sherwin's observation that "[l]egal reality can no longer be properly understood, or assessed, apart from what appears on the screen," (2000)[3] this chapter attempts a study of film and law in relation to representations of the Holocaust in a twofold manner. First, this chapter historically tracks the functions of film in relation to the collective narrative of the Holocaust, staged against national and international backdrops (Black 1999, 87–95). Within an American context, *Nazi Concentration Camps* (1945), a documentary film, functioned as a self-evident witness (i.e., one that does not require a living witness who can authenticate a document and be subjected to cross-examination) during the Nuremberg International Military Tribunal (IMT), assuming a stance of apparent distance and neutrality. Later, an American cinematic retelling of the Holocaust, *Judgment at Nuremberg* (1961), moved to docudramatic depiction, incorporating documentary footage from *Nazi Concentration Camps* in a fictional rendition. In comparison, *Film Documents of Atrocities Committed by the German-Fascist Invaders* (*Kinodukumenty o zver-stvack nemetsko-fashistskikh zakhvatchikov*; hereinafter *Film Documents of Atrocities* [1945]), the Russian documentary film also submitted to the Nuremberg IMT as evidence alongside the American documentary, encouraged identification with, rather than distance from, the victims of the Holocaust, and was not prominently featured during the trial. Finally, *The Judgment of the Nations* (*Sud Naradov*) (1946), a Russian feature film about the Nuremberg IMT proceedings, was shot as a witness to the trial, again apparently assuming a stance of neutrality while, in fact, propagating the grand narrative of Soviet heroic resistance against the demonic Nazis (Karmen and Svilova 1947).

Second, this chapter examines the language of film as a specific medium and, in particular, how film implicitly references a repository of prior films and also builds from an existing repository of film representations of the Holocaust embedded in public memory (Bergman and Asimov 2006). This complex process of re-visualizing the past opens up new hermeneutic avenues of reading and rewriting these narratives in relation to the present and the future. Thus, in viewing these representations of collective trauma, it also locates the locus of a poethics squarely within both the production and consumption of such images.

More generally, this chapter is aligned with two basic assumptions Orit Kamir (2005, 27) outlined in her study of law and film in relation to her detailed analysis of Roman Polanski's *Death and the Maiden*, a film that sounds similar themes of dramatic trials, the search for justice, and the project of living with trauma. On a superficial level, both law and film "reflect and refract fundamental values, images, notions of identity, lifestyles, and crises of their societies and cultures" (Kamir 2005, 27, 28) and figure prominently in the historically and sociologically grounded construction of "subject, community, identity, memory, gender roles, justice and truth" (Kamir 2005, 28). Furthermore, rhetorically, both law and film provide "major sociocultural arenas where collective hopes, dreams, beliefs, anxieties, and frustrations are publicly portrayed, evaluated and enacted" (Kamir 2005, 28). Holocaust films, whether documentary or fictional, clearly get at these underlying fundamental values, cultural aspirations, and collective anxieties in their staging or simulation of the events of the Holocaust (Aristedemou 2000).[4]

On a second level, as Kamir pointed out, films that connect with depictions of the law engage in "large-scale 'legal indoctrination,'" which Kamir interprets as the training of audiences "in judgment while examining—and often reinforcing—legal norms, logic, and structures" (2005, 28; see also White 1985a; 1985b; 1999). In Holocaust films in particular, "[j]udgment . . . is not merely portrayed but . . . *actively performed* [italics added] by [these] films, together with their . . . constructed and/or actual viewers; it is often a function of film's constitution of a community of viewers and cinematic engagement in the social constitution of primary values, institutions, and concepts" (Kamir 2005, 28–29). And indeed, much as a litigator or defense lawyer carefully chooses how facts are arranged and highlighted as well as the tone or tenor of the storytelling and pays close attention to the defendant's demeanor and dress (Sherwin 2000, 41),[5] a film director may utilize a broad spectrum of tools to foster audience identification with a particular character or to elicit almost automatic emotional reactions to a particular scene or character. Examples of such tools include "cinematic choices regarding genre, editing, methods of narration, plots, points of view, rhythm and casting" (Kamir 2005, 29). The key issue, though, especially in films as potentially emotion-laden as Holocaust films, as I show, is whether this spectatorial interaction is genuinely engaged and critical even as it conjoins the pleasures of viewing with the horrors of collective memory and the aspirations of a grand, national narrative.

Finally, an added dimension to Holocaust films in particular is the question of realism, whether construed as "true," "accurate," or "realistic."[6] One extreme, of course, is the problem of literal accuracy. As Chase rhetorically states in relation to trial films, for example: "Legal realism as a form of film criticism quickly threatens to careen off into deep theoretical space, leaving deconstruction, virtual reality and the science of complex systems dead in their tracks. Are trial films to be measured against the actual legal rules and procedures in existence (1) at the time when the film is historically set, (2) at the time when the film is released in theaters, or (3) at the time the critic is viewing the film?" (1986, 176).

Nevertheless, there is a pragmatic way out of this quagmire: the verisimilitude of the world of film, much like literature, provided it does not pretend to be a literal historical document, allows for some suspension of the rules of literal accuracy. However, that artistic license is laden with both ethical and educational choices and implications[7]—and both film directors and audiences of film, this chapter argues, should be critically aware of these choices and their ramifications. Film attaches to "reality" in complex ways, especially when it performs the function, as Holocaust films do, of witnessing an event of great social magnitude. To reduce witnessing to minutiae is folly; to careen into hyper-imaginative flights, devoid of any connection to reality, is just as dangerous, given the weight of historical memory on "reality."

Ultimately, this chapter attempts to navigate a way of interacting with Holocaust films and films about Holocaust trials such that there is a limit to both identification and detachment, which are the twin dangers faced by spectators of such films. Such a careful balance can be maintained by a critical openness to a dialectical tension between multiple frames or points of view and a certain amount of irreducibility. In other words, this project finds an analogue in Ariella Azoulay's analysis of the hermeneutic of the photographic moment: "With the assistance of the spectator, the point of view under consideration . . . permits the event of photography to be preserved as one bearing the potential for permanent renewal that undermines any attempt to terminate it or to proclaim that it has reached its end" (2011, 79).

While the approach this chapter describes is consonant with a reader-response theory as applied to film, it differs in some significant ways. For example, Kamir, in her analysis of reader-response in relation to establishing a readership of film, distinguishes between flesh-and-blood viewers and "the ideal[/implied] reader sought and invited by the text through textual construction and manipulation" (2006, vxi). Kamir places greater emphasis on the ideal/implied reader than actual audiences, though she does describe her approach as a feminist reading of law and film, implying an audience sympathetic to that orientation (2006, xvii). Notwithstanding the many merits of Kamir's approach, this chapter returns the emphasis to the development of a critical poetic ethics of (actual) reception, not necessarily bound solely to a feminist orientation, though that is a significant dimension.

In addition, although written for a different type of audience, Carol Clover's (1998) essay "God Bless Juries!" focuses on the trial film in order to point out the double structure of trial narratives on film. Generally summarized, conventional trial narratives, for Clover, have a double structure: they include an official legal trial and a second, unofficial "trial" that is central to the narrative and focused on some crucial dimension of the legal system. For example, in Jonathan Kaplan's *The Accused* (1988), the dramatic tension of one such second "trial" lies in whether a single determined female lawyer can sufficiently unsettle a male-oriented system of law that is structurally biased against rape victims (Clover 1998). Clover's principal focus, therefore, is a certain "necessary blank space"[8] that trial movies structurally create and that the audience must necessary fill in hermeneutically. Phrased more simply, trial movies invite audiences to become jurors and pass judgment.

While acknowledging the value of Clover's approach, the poethics with which this chapter grapples is concerned with not only the reception of films, but also their production. And when the audience is simultaneously invited to judge a history of trauma, violence, and hatred, but given familiar rhetorical tropes that assume the "look of reality" and can potentially over-determine responses, much more is at stake. An audience that is critically aware of the rhetorical devices and conventions of film in conjunction with history is just as essential as a filmmaker who is critically conscientious while being imaginative and artistically vibrant in his or her production of images that both depict and recast history.

AMERICAN DOCUMENTARY FILM AND THE NUREMBERG TRIALS: *NAZI CONCENTRATION CAMPS* (1945) AS SELF-AUTHENTICATING WITNESS

The Nuremberg International Military Tribunal was designed to both educate[9] and create historical record (Taylor 1993, 146–49). Henry Stimson, then secretary of war, and Edward Stettinius, then secretary of state, wrote a memorandum to President Franklin Roosevelt regarding the didactic aims of the tribunal: "The use of the judicial method will . . . make available for all mankind to study in future years an authentic record of Nazi crimes and criminality" (1949). Robert H. Jackson's opening statement heralded the showing of the documentary film, *Nazi Concentration Camps*, shot by the Signal Corps, emphasizing the great evidentiary weight the film bore, as well as its self-evident authenticity:

> We will show you these concentration camps in motion pictures, just as the Allied armies found them when they arrived. . . . Our proof will be disgusting and you will say I have robbed you of your sleep. . . . I am one who received during this war most atrocity tales with suspicion and skepticism. But the proof here will be so overwhelming that I venture to predict not one word I have spoken will be denied. (Douglas 2005, 21–22) (see figure 17.1).

Prior to the Nuremberg IMT, despite the use of crime-scene photography in Anglo-American courts, the use of film, essentially as a witness, not simply as proof, was unprecedented (Barnouw 1993, 173–75; see also Avisar 1988; Zelizer 2000). As Douglas observed, "Although motion pictures have been submitted as trial evidence as early as 1915, prior to Nuremberg one can find no records of any court using graphic film of atrocities as proof of criminal wrongdoing" (2005, 23). James Donovan, assistant trial counsel, announced, "These motion pictures speak for themselves in evidencing life and death in Nazi concentration camps" (Douglas 2005, 23). This procedural and substantive innovation seemed to provide the justification for the view that films used as documentary proof could be treated as transparent, self-evident windows, requiring no explanation or contextualization and devoid of the twin dangers of hyperbole or inaccuracy characteristic of live human witnesses.[10]

In terms of content, *Nazi Concentration Camps* frontloaded its status as presenting undeniable proof by showing stills of various affidavits attesting to the film's authenticity. The problem, of course, is that the means of verification is itself part of the film. Thus, "[t]his gesture of self-authentication supports a novel understanding of the documentary as a privileged witness independently competent to swear to the truth of its images" (Douglas 2005, 29).

Figure 17.1. American soldiers view a pile of corpses found in the newly liberated Buchenwald concentration camp in April 1945. Buchenwald, [Thuringia] Germany, April 14, 1945. United States Holocaust Memorial Museum, courtesy of Warren Brennan. Image optimized by Susan Gilbert.

Procedurally, this elevation of documentary film to self-evident witness was not in line with standard practice. The general rule seemed to be: "Motion pictures are admissible in evidence, within the sound discretion of the court, where such pictures are relevant to the issues, and are an accurate reproduction of persons and objects testified to in oral examination before the jury" (Paradis 1965, 236). Generally, in Anglo-American jurisprudence, an authenticating witness is required in order to admit film as evidence (Paradis 1965, 235–47). In prior instances, film was often barred, not because it was inaccurate, but because it was redundant: it simply replicated live witness testimony and added no new information (Wigmore 1970, 218–19). Thus, under normal circumstances rather than the circumstances of the Nuremberg IMT, the film, without a corroborating witness, would have been barred as hearsay.[11] Furthermore, given the gruesome nature of the images, the film could also have been barred on the grounds of being potentially unfairly prejudicial. Both rules, concerning redundancy and the potentially prejudicial effect of gruesome images, have since been incorporated into an existing federal Rule of Evidence in the United States.[12] And although there were "a few dozen witnesses

[who] were invited to present any oral testimony . . . most of the evidence that was used in the prosecution of twenty-two leading war criminals came from [the] interpretation of German documentary texts," which included film footage (Hasian 2006, 31).

However, the enabling charter of the Nuremberg IMT declared that the trial was not "bound by technical rules of evidence" and that the tribunal had the discretion to "adopt and apply to the greatest possible extent expeditious and non-technical procedure, and shall admit any evidence which it deems to have probative value."[13] Jackson eloquently defended the relaxing of the rules of evidence,[14] reasoning, first, "This Tribunal sits under a Charter which recognized the impossibility of covering a decade of time, a continent of space, a million acts, by ordinary rules of proof, and at the same time finishing this case within the lives of living men" (Douglas 2005, 30). Second, he further argued that judges, unlike juries, are sophisticated enough to sift through and weigh even hearsay evidence for relevance and be less moved by prejudicial material. Thus, for Jackson, as well as the tribunal, allowing the film *Nazi Concentration Camps* in was both time-efficient as well as effective, as it allowed the most reliable and comprehensive visual representation of these atrocities, which, coming from the lips of men, appeared too immense to be credible (see figure 17.2). Indeed, Jackson, in reporting back to President Truman, proudly

Figure 17.2. A broken and twisted mound of emaciated corpses lay strewn in one of three open burial pits during the liberation of Belsen on 15 April 1945. Image in the public domain, optimized by Susan Gilbert.

stated that preparation for the Nuremberg trial involved the collection of over 100 thousand enemy documents, millions of "feet captured [from] moving picture films," and tens of thousands of "still photographs" (Fried 1976, 192).

Hardly surprising, *Nazi Concentration Camps* is not a clear, transparent window, but more like a lens, which magnifies some aspects and obscures others. For example, as Douglas notes, what appear to be the voices of the men who signed the affidavits attesting to the authenticity of the footage are soon replaced by an unnamed and omniscient narrator, who alternates with another such anonymous, apparently all-knowing entity (2005, 31). These two voices then take turns interpreting what the camera is looking at: "The narrator[s] suppl[y] the voice not of a military historian or soldier witnessing the liberation of the camps, but of the camera itself. As such, [they seem] to speak with the same objectivity that the images claim for themselves" (Douglas 2005, 31).

Nazi Concentration Camps then fades into a map of prewar Europe, where what is detailed is not names of nations, but concentration camp sites, focusing on a dozen of these and identifying them in bold block letters and the finely grained black and white images that have since been immortalized. Christian Delage notes the synecdochic nature of the images, which, presented in montage, condense the essentials of what the editors of the film wanted to emphasize visually:

> Leipzig (mass graves), Penig (care provided by Americans to some young women), Ohrdruf (Eisenhower's visit), Hadamar (exhumation and post-mortem examination of bodies poisoned or badly treated; interrogation of the Nazi in charge of the so-called "asylum"), Breendonck (reconstruction of the methods of torture used against Belgian resistants), Nordhausen (a few surviving, albeit very weak, deportees among thousands of dead), Harlan (first meal taken by the deportees in a long time), Arnstadt (exhumation of bodies), Mathausen (account given by an imprisoned American soldier), Buchenwald (compulsory visit of the camp by 1,200 people coming from Weimar; images—including those of the crematoria—linked to that report made by the American Commission in charge of the POWs and of the displaced persons), Dachau (aerial shots of the camp, giving an idea of its size; series of shots explaining the working of a gas chambers) and Bergen-Belsen. (2004, 498)

As an interesting footnote, Douglas points out that *Nazi Concentration Camps* could have been shown in color (2005, 31). However, the army, afraid that the three-track projectors necessary for showing Technicolor film would not be available in both courtrooms and movie houses (a fascinating conjunction of targeted audiences), chose to stick with monochrome footage, a decision that would have immense implications in determining the "look of the real" in cinema.

This concern with making sure that everything looked authentic was a principal animating force. Furthermore, the choices made in editing the documentary coincided with Hollywood film conventions, such as alternating long shots with close-ups or medium shots, deploying narratives focusing on individuals, and emphasizing the happy ending. As Delage notes, "All was conditioned to collect evidence that could then become part of the indictment against war criminals" (2004, 499).

Because the images from the film have been much viewed and overinterpreted, this section will limit its discussion purely to some selected instances in which there appear to be contradictions between the camera's neutral position and the subject matter it presents. This is because this same ambiguity, of hovering between an apparently "neutral" documentary gaze and either a propagandistic or an ethically problematic framing, continues in the later films the chapter tracks, as it oscillates between documentary and docudramatic genres.

For example, first, and absurdly, as Douglas (2005, 32) points out, is a sequence showing three smiling male survivors, dressed in rags. One of them is stripped down to his waist, revealing his skeletal frame; all three attempt to pose for the camera, as if they are in a studio and having their portraits taken. Second, ironically, is the image of a young woman lifting her skirts to reveal puncture wounds on her *derrière* against the backdrop of a similarly violated city (Douglas 2005, 32–33). The woman's tortured body and the damaged landscape disturbingly constitute an inadvertently pornographic display of suffering.[15] These instances reveal fissures in the camera's apparently seamlessly omniscient and detached narrative.

Finally, to fortify the film's claims to authenticity, it records, within its frames, witnesses attesting to what the camera witnesses. These witnesses range from Allied Generals Eisenhower, Bradley, and Patton to German citizens, many of them women, ironically dressed in their Sunday best. These German women, when confronted with undeniable evidence of the atrocities, bury their faces in handkerchiefs in the attempt to stifle waves of nausea and sobs of shock and shame. The women's emotional reactions are staged in stark contrast to the stoicism of the generals, a symbolic metonymy for the Allied Powers' masculinized stoic and detached stance set in contrast to the feminized German acknowledgment of guilt.

Furthermore, to give a name to the immensity of the violence and magnitude of the crimes committed, the Nuremberg IMT also created a new category of crimes: "crimes against humanity."[16] This legal innovation characterized crimes of humanity as: "murder, extermination, enslavement, deportation, and other inhumane acts committed against any civilian population, before or during the war, or persecutions on political, racial or religious grounds in execution of or in connection with any crime within the jurisdiction of the Tribunal, whether or not in violation of domestic law of the country where perpetrated" (Douglas 2005, 44).[17] Nevertheless, it was Hannah Arendt who coined the notion of radical evil, as represented in Nazi totalitarianism, which has evolved into the hyperbolic and simplified trope of Nazis as monsters[18]: "The Nazi crimes . . . explode the limits of the law; and that is precisely what constitutes their *monstrousness* [italics added]. For these crimes, no punishment is severe enough" (Kohler and Saner 1992, 54).

FILM IN/AS AMERICAN DOCUDRAMATIC REINTERPRETATION: *JUDGMENT AT NUREMBERG* (1961)

In Stanley Kramer's *Judgment at Nuremberg*, a seven-minute excerpt of *Nazi Concentration Camps* is shown, embedded into the trial as a film within a film. This time, however, the excerpted documentary fragment is authenticated by the prosecutor-turned-witness, Colonel Lawson (Richard Widmark), who appears to be "very, very loosely based on General Taylor" (Aquino 2005, 130).

But let us reserve the analysis of this montage *mise en abyme* sequence for later. The factual, historical basis for this grand star-studded docudrama is not the famous Nuremberg Trial in which Göring and other well-known Nazi leaders were tried, but one a few years later, in 1947 (Case No. 3, *U.S. v. Josef Altstoelter*), in which sixteen German judges and prosecutors were tried (Aquino 2005, 128–29). The film is set in 1948—closer to the period of the Cold War—and as Judge Dan Haywood (Spencer Tracy) surveys the rubble-strewn pavements of the once grand and mighty Berlin, he remarks, "Well, let's face it: Hitler is gone; Goebbles is gone; Göring is gone—committed suicide before they could hang him. Now we're down to the business of judging the doctors, businessmen and judges. Some people think they shouldn't be judged at all. . . . You had to beat the backwoods of Maine to come up with a hick like me."

The movie opens with a view of the bombed-out city through the eyes of Judge Haywood. For the most part, it is the judge's point of view that is dominant in viewing (and judging) the events that have led to this trial. Still, there are several other key players in this docudrama. One is Ernst Janning (Burt Lancaster), who appears "partially based on Judge Franz Schlegelberger, [who] refuses to stand until he is gently pulled up by the soldiers, indicating he does not recognize the jurisdiction of the court" (Aquino 2005, 129–30). Another is Prosecutor Colonel Lawson, who proclaims in his opening statement that the four defendants are on trial for murder, brutalities, torture, and other atrocities committed during the Third Reich, crimes for which the defendants cannot claim ignorance. A third character of note is Defense Attorney Hans Rolfe (Maximilian

Figure 17.3. Defense Attorney Hans Rolfe (Maximilian Schell) in *Judgment at Nuremberg* (1961). Image in the public domain, optimized by Susan Gilbert.

Schell) (see figure 17.3), who appears to represent all four defendants; this arrangement is not typical in usual practice because each defendant usually has his own counsel to avoid possible conflicts of interest. Rolfe grandly proclaims that the task of the tribunal is to "reconsecrate the temple of justice." Furthermore, the defense attorney argues that both love of country and duty to *follow* the law (not determine the law) trapped all four defendants, thus making them victims rather than active perpetrators.

As an excerpted version of *Nazi Concentration Camps* is shown in this docudramatic depiction of the trial, this time the film is authenticated by the colonel.[19] Although the shock effect of embedding these monstrous images in a high-budget Hollywood film with an all-star cast is clear, the monstrosity of the images is attested to less by the images themselves than by the reactions of the diegetic audience to the footage shown. Instead of allowing the footage to run unedited, Kramer, the director, constantly cross-cuts from it to emphasize various reaction shots: "There is the bug-eyed astonishment of one of the lesser defendants; there is the solemn, riveted glare of Ernst Janning, the former German minister of justice . . . there is the tight scowl of disdain worn by the defense counsel . . . and finally, there is the face . . . [of] Judge Haywood" (Mintz 2001, 87).

The focus on reaction shots, composed principally of close-up head shots, tends to split the focus between the documentary footage and the diegetic responses to the film-within-a-film. However, the use of this technique distances viewers from the footage, replacing the monstrous spectacle of the violence the footage records, with the spectacle of reactions that attest to the monstrosity of the images. And ultimately and pivotally, it is Judge Haywood's gaze that matters most in deciding how this trial will be judged (Mintz 2001, 90).

Of course, there are other eyes that also view and respond to the embedded documentary footage. A crucial supporting figure is Frau Bertholt (Marlene Dietrich), the widow of a general executed in a prior trial and a potential romantic interest for the single and aging judge, who presents a powerful contrast to the judge, visually as well as perspectivally. In this film, Dietrich is often shot with the soft star lighting that made women look like goddesses. With her almond eyes, high cheekbones, and aristocratic breeding, she is the ultimate seductress foil to Judge Haywood's country bumpkin persona. Unlike Dietrich, Tracy is shot in less-flattering light; the judge's integrity and clear-sightedness are emphasized in his openly lined and weathered face, which is often shot in stark high-key lighting. For Frau Bertholt, the documentary footage is simply a "monster show," strutted out by the American prosecutor at the slightest excuse to display them. Frau Bertholt, and eventually Ernst Janning, too, urges Judge Haywood to dismiss the gothic shock value of these images and to believe that they, the German people, were not aware of the extent of the atrocities committed.[20]

The result of using this set of narrative techniques is distancing from the actual documentary footage. Once the documentary's shock value has been exploited, Kramer's use of the film-within-the-film almost dissolves these images. As a result of how he embeds the documentary footage, the audience is not encouraged to inquire further about the victims or their individual stories, but rather to contemplate, through the eyes of Judge Haywood, larger universal questions regarding collective moral responsibility and guilt. As Mintz (2001, 100) perceptively remarks:

> [U]niversalizing is a way to avoid seeing the particular and what is troublingly un-universal about it. . . . [A]lthough we are forced to look at the footage, we are not helped by the film to really see it. The footage is used as a sensational move to shock us into acknowledging the moral enormity of the crimes, but we are not asked to investigate their nature or their genesis or to inquire about the identity of the victims. . . . In the absence of a true argument, our attention does not linger after the initial shock, and our courage is available to be enlisted on behalf of the highest principles.

Nevertheless, there is one nameless minor character whose reaction to the documentary footage deserves mention: that of the only African American G.I. in a courtroom in which everyone is white. The colonel drones on, explaining that the footage with corpses of young children attested to how Nazis would hang children and then, like picture frames, display their young victims' bodies on hooks. For two seconds, the camera lingers on the face of the African American G.I., whose impassivity is momentarily replaced by a flicker of astonishment and recognition, a reference to America's own history of atrocities in its race wars. Repeatedly, the film draws attention to America's own history of violence. For example, the defense attorney takes great pleasure in quoting Judge Oliver Wendell Holmes's justification for the sterilization of the mentally deficient. Later, in attempting to gain Ernst Janning's sympathy and solidarity as a German, Rolfe points out America's own barbarity in the bombing of Hiroshima and Nagasaki.[21]

However, neither the brief allusions to America's own history of atrocities, nor Frau Bertholt's sirenic denial of collective German knowledge of, and collusion with, the Nazi Final Solution, nor Ernst Janning's tragic and impassioned appeal that he, for love of country, felt duty-bound to adapt to the Nazi regime, cloud Judge Haywood's vision. The judge declares all four defendants guilty and sentences all of them, including the tragic Ernst Janning, to life in prison (see figure 17.4.). Interestingly, in expressing this view, Judge Haywood becomes the mouthpiece of Arendt's (2006) later description of the Holocaust as an exercise in the banality of evil, rather than a radical evil that transcends the realms of "human affairs and the potentialities of human power" (Arendt 1998, 241). Even

Figure 17.4. Judge Dan Haywood (Spencer Tracy) in *Judgment at Nuremberg* (1961). Image in the public domain, optimized by Susan Gilbert.

super-ordinately principled Ernst Janning, caught up in the monstrous machine of Nazism, was not without blame.

Interestingly, *Judgment at Nuremberg* was shot at roughly the same time as Adolf Eichmann's trial (Arendt 1998, 92), and there appear to be clear parallelisms drawn by Kramer between the two trials. As Murray Shumach, a writer for the *New York Times*, observed:

> In a somber courtroom set in Hollywood, genocide is as current these days as it is in the Beit Haam, in Jerusalem, where Adolf Eichmann is being tried for responsibility for the deaths of six million Jews. In Hollywood, however, cameras and actors are working in a replica of the courtroom of Nuremberg, where civilized nations set the legal precedent that made a special crime of genocide.[22]

In sum, because of its emphasis on a good man caught in the demonic machinery of Nazism, Kramer's *Judgment at Nuremberg* to some extent displaces Arendt's (1998) initial description of Nazi systematic atrocity as radical evil with Arendt's (2006) re-description of the Holocaust as a result of the banality of evil. Though hints of the more Gothic-tinged explanation for the systematic, totalitarian horrors of the Holocaust persist, these are not the principal concern of the film. Furthermore, Kramer's film moves the narrative focus from witnessing the Holocaust via documentary film (deploying an American lens) to reinterpreting and re-contextualizing the Holocaust against the backdrop of the new challenge of the Cold War.

As this chapter shows, unlike the American films, the lesser-known Russian documentary *Film Documents of Atrocities* (1945) and *The Judgment of the Nations* (1946), the Russian feature film about the Nuremberg trial proceedings, were crafted to position affiliation with, rather than detachment from, the victims of Nazism. The differences between the American films and their Russian counterparts are striking because they rhetorically invite their audiences to assume contrastively different politico-aesthetic vantage points in relation to viewing or witnessing the Holocaust and Holocaust-related trials.

RUSSIAN DOCUMENTARY FILM AND THE NUREMBERG TRIALS: *FILM DOCUMENTS OF ATROCITIES* (1945) AS SILENCED WITNESS

Like its American counterpart *Nazi Concentration Camps*, which was directed by George Stevens and whose grainy black-and-white images have become iconic testaments to the Holocaust, the Russian *Film Documents of Atrocities* is a reedited collection of newsreels and documentaries used for both motivational and propagandistic purposes. It was also submitted as evidence in support of the Nuremberg IMT's indictment of crimes against humanity; however, unlike the American documentary, which came to occupy a prominent and celebrated historical position, the Russian documentary was relegated to the background (Hicks 2012, 258; Weckel 2012, 228), spurred in part by an "unease regarding the film's trustworthiness" (Hicks 2012, 187). It is true that the film had polemical origins and that the Soviet Union was not exactly known as a bastion upholding the rule of law. Nevertheless, it is important to review, through a Russian lens, what it meant to witness the Holocaust and to gather evidence of the monstrousness of its crimes. The point is not so much to emphasize Soviet polemics (as all films have hidden vantage points), but rather to examine the complex historical circumstances that enabled *Nazi Concentration Camps* to rise to the level of being a witness at the Nuremberg IMT while relegating *Documents of Atrocities* to the sidelines.

Unlike *Nazi Concentration Camps*, whose rhetorical perspective hovers in between an omniscient point of view, a third-person point of view, the point of view of the accused, and the point of view of the victors, while appearing to be "neutral," *Film Documents of Atrocities* has a unified perspective, which seeks to move its spectators to identify with the victims of the atrocities and galvanize them to seek justice for them and vengeance against the perpetrators. Thus, "the Soviet films that provided the source material articulated this emotive call to action through a significant degree of reconstruction and conscious manipulation: the dead were chosen, identified carefully, and often posed or rearranged" (Hicks 2012, 191–92). Yet it was not enough to script interactions with the dead and speak for them; even the living were prompted regarding how to react to loss, or even in relation to the camera (Hicks 2012, 192).

Some of the disparities between the American and Russian documentaries may be traced to key differences in their historical genesis. *Nazi Concentration Camps*, which focuses exclusively on the concentration camps that U.S. and British troops liberated in Germany, elides concentration camps and death camps and thus omits any mention of Auschwitz, Majdanek, Treblinka, Sobibór, Chelmno, or Belzec. In contrast, *Film Documents of Atrocities*, after showing the aftermath of a range of Nazi crimes in Russia, the Ukraine, Latvia, Estonia, and Belorussia, climaxes with footage from Majdanek and Auschwitz, featuring the now-iconic details of gas chambers, Zyklon-B canisters, the crematoria, and the piles of personal property left behind by the victims.[23] However, the potential visual power and more comprehensive and varied nature of these images are undercut by the accompanying commentary regarding the casualties of the death camps. Unfortunately, the voiceover details the now-discredited hyperbolic initial Soviet estimates of the dead: 1,380,000 in Majdanek and four million in Auschwitz (as opposed to current figures, which estimate between 80,000 and 250,000 in Majdanek, and 1.1 million in Auschwitz) (Hicks 2012, 190). However, as Delage (2006a, 146) has perceptively pointed out, this chosen rhetorical mode was deployed not necessarily out of compassion, but as a graphic representational strategy in conjunction with the visual exploitation of the suffering of grieving relatives. The result, again, is the conflation of justice with revenge. Part of this can be explained in keeping with the images' genesis as part of a larger national campaign with clear propaganda intent. As Schneer observes:

> [Russian] photographers tried to represent a nearly un[-]representable war. They photographed Soviet triumph, on an individual, collective, and military level and could easily use the tools of socialist realism to do so. At the same time, they pictured the evils of the enemy, both through their actions and deeds and by showing caricatures and posters. Both in print and photojournalism, the Soviet press made Nazi atrocities a primary means of representing the German war against the Soviet Union to Soviet readers. (2012, 98)[24]

Thus, as Schneer (2015) further points out in a recent article, part of the reason why Soviet media was considered unreliable, from a Western point of view, was that it blurred art and photojournalism, always embedding the perspective of the photographer—a living witness, metaphorically implied as present in the frame—within the context of the framing of the narrative, while Western photojournalism requires the effacement of the photographer. Ironically, in stark contrast to *Nazi Concentration Camps*, which attempts to make the video the witness, *Film Documents of Atrocities* uses a legalistic approach, focusing on documents rather than witnesses. Nevertheless, the result accomplishes something the American documentary does not: It grants individual victims their names. *Nazi Concentration Camps* yields no individual portrayals of victims, unlike *Film Documents of Atrocities*, which lingers on individual names and faces and hints at their individual narratives. For example, the Russian documentary shows the alleged thirteen-year-old Vitia Golovgev in Rostov, who, in this mythicized version, was murdered because he refused to give up his dove; surviving images of the dead boy show a miraculously still-living bird on top of the young corpse (see figure 17.5).

Unfortunately, the Soviet imperative to build a narrative of national heroism and resistance to the Nazis became license to modify the facts from which the legend sprang. The boy was actually sixteen, and his real name was Vitia Cherevichkin; he had released the bird, a favorite pigeon, not a dove, before he was shot (Matskin and Sobolev 1941, 2; Migulina 2007). Hicks (2012, 53) argues that the name modification from "Cherevichkin" to "Golovgev," as well as the narrative change from released

Figure 17.5. Vitia Golovgev and his dove in *Film Documents of Atrocities* (1945). Image in the public domain, optimized by Susan Gilbert.

pigeon to the miraculously live dove astride the boy's corpse, were made in order to release the narrative from pragmatic considerations (e.g., a pigeon was an alternative means of communication and rebellion) and mythicize the boy as a national symbol. "Vitia's name change may have been intended to enhance his mythical appeal by shifting from the associations of his real name with the lower sphere of women's footwear (*cherevichki*) to those of the fictional one with the higher realm of the head (*golova*) or possibly the dove of peace (*golub*), for which he was killed, since the same Russian word denotes both pigeons generally and doves specifically" (Hicks 2012, 53)

The focus on the boy also serves a threefold rhetorical emphasis: (1) it demarcates Vitia's identity as a child, a completely innocent victim whose senseless death, in Soviet cinema, justifies "righteous" violence[25] (see figure 17.6); (2) it serves to obscure the issue of the Jewishness of a larger majority of the victims (as Vitia was not Jewish) in favor of a narrative of Soviet triumph; and (3) it produces a monstrous story of Nazi bestiality and brutality. The disappearance of Jewish victimhood and identity into a grand narrative of heroic and resistant Soviet nationhood in turn requires the demonization and inhumanity of not only Nazis, but also, to some, all Germans. For example, in a series of articles, Ilia Ehrenburg, a Jewish Russian, declared that "the Hitlerites" were "not human beings, but

Figure 17.6. Child killed by Germans during the last day during the German occupation of Viazma in *Film Documents of Atrocities* (1945). Image in the public domain, optimized by Susan Gilbert.

murderers, executioners, moral degenerates and cruel fanatics," that the "German fascists" were "not human beings but . . . robots which resemble human beings but do not have a grain of humanism in them," and, in a mirror-imaging inversion of a Nazi anti-Semitic slogan, that all "German invaders" were "vermin."[26] Despite its titling as a "document," the Russian documentary thus eventually arrives at the popular oversimplified narrative derived from Arendt's characterization of Nazism as a totalitarian, dehumanizing system.

RUSSIAN FEATURE FILM AS WITNESS TO THE NUREMBERG TRIAL: *THE JUDGMENT OF THE NATIONS* (1946)

The Judgment of the Nations, a feature film (Barnouw 1993, 175) by Roman Karmen that attempted to transmute what were often dull and tedious legal proceedings into a dramatically engaging narrative, was produced within an atmosphere of increasing suspicion among the fragmenting former Allied forces (Barsam 1992, 266–68). On March 5, 1946, Winston Churchill delivered a speech at Westminster College in Fulton, Missouri, mentioning the "Iron Curtain"; Stalin responded in the Soviet Press on March 16, 1946, effectively confirming Churchill's declaration regarding the Cold War (Hicks 2012, 197). Despite the tense and ambivalent atmosphere, *The Judgment of the Nations* was released in the Soviet Union on November 23, 1946.[27]

Karmen envisaged the film to be a witness *to* the Nuremberg IMT, not a witness *at* the trial. Nevertheless, like Kramer's *Judgment at Nuremberg*, the lens in *The Judgment of the Nations* often focuses, in reaction shots, on the faces of the accused when confronted with evidence of their crimes and the spectacle of the aftermath of those crimes. Much of Karmen's film uses montage, wherein the accused lose their composure, as footage of the consequences of their crimes is shown. Karmen steers a careful path between the popular gothic interpretation of Nazis as virtual beasts slave to bestial and irrational drives and Arendt's later interpretation of Nazis as simply banal cogs in machines. Instead, Karmen's film carefully documents nervous ticks the respondents unconsciously displayed, such as Göring's covering of his face and then wiping his neck during unguarded moments, as if proverbially feeling a hangman's noose (Kolesnikova, Senchakova, and Slepneva 1959, 200), and Hess's gesture of resting his face upon his raised hand in an ambiguous gesture of either apparently claiming to not remember, or attempting to forget, the atrocities he had committed (Hicks 2012, 200). By appropriating the Soviet avant-garde's Kuleshov effect, whereby meaning that is not inherent in individual pieces is generated through their juxtaposition, *The Judgment of the Nations*, coedited by Elizaveta Svilova, sets up the image of Hess's ambiguous gesture of apparent forgetfulness, or attempt to forget, as beginning a contrastive montage of Nazis in their former pomp and glory (Hicks 2012, 200–1).

Nevertheless, in positioning *The Judgment of the Nations* as a witness to the Nuremberg Trial, the film essentially silences all the human witnesses who testified at the trial by cutting out all footage of their testimonies and downplays the centrality and systematic nature of Jewish genocide in the unfolding of the Holocaust. In response, Korol'kov perceptively remarked, "Unfortunately, the witnesses who spoke at the trial are not shown in the film. . . . This is unfortunate, as the subject is a worthwhile one: the testimony of the witnesses, representatives of the widest range of nations, provided exceptionally persuasive confirmation that Fascism brought slavery and death to all the peoples of the world" (1946, 4). Although the muting of powerful visual images, such as the attack on Jewish shops during Germany's Kristallnacht on November 9 and 10, 1938, as simply another indistinguishable "Jewish pogrom," is not surprising, given the elision of Jewish identity in Soviet nationality, the lack of any footage of witness testimony is surprising. Although, as pointed out before, the Nuremberg IMT prosecution essentially treated live eyewitness testimony as duplicative of documentary evidence and thus kept these to a minimum (United States Holocaust Memorial Museum 2015), there were certainly opportunities to include such stirring testimony in Karmen's film. There were, in sum, ninety-four witnesses who testified, thirty-three for the prosecution and sixty-one for the defense (Marrus 1997, v). Among these were, for example, Marie-Claude Vallant Couturier, a former Auschwitz inmate who provided compelling testimony about the death camp (Delage 2006b), and Severina Smaglevskaia, who attested to the large numbers of Jews murdered at Auschwitz (Hicks 2012, 205).

Other than the pragmatic consideration of trying to make the simultaneous translation of witness testimony engaging to a film audience, Karmen may have decided not to use witness testimony because of the overwhelming pressure to make sure the Soviet Party line remained the overarching focus of the film. Within this context, witness testimony, ultimately a private expression of grief, grants its speaker an authority not bequeathed by the state; as such, witness testimony presents the possibility of a counter-narrative that breaks away from a state-sanctioned grand narrative (Felman and Laub 1992, xvi; Wieviorka 2006, 144). That was a risk Karmen could not take, given the pressures under which he had to work.

Less perniciously, Karmen had firsthand knowledge of the documentary footage he made central to his film (Hoffman 1996, 183). He had, himself, taken this footage, with an eye on collecting evidence for a future tribunal. "Karmen was always directly on the front line, facing the enemy. He reached Berlin with the first Soviet tanks" (Hoffman 1996, 183). In his view, the camera's point of view itself spoke for the dead, who pointed accusing fingers at their murderers. Thus, an earlier draft of the planned voiceover accompanying footage of a cameraman standing atop an advancing tank, filming evidence of the Nazis' crimes, had the following prospective commentary:

> Together with the forward units of the Red Army, Soviet newsreel cameramen advanced too. They knew that Hitler's criminals would appear before a court of nations. . . . Filming, we knew that the day would come when these terrifying film documents would be presented as evidence of the inexcusable crimes of Fascism. THIS DAY HAS COME.
>
> . . . .
>
> Pan on the bench of the accused. GŐRING. KEITEL. KALTEN-BRUNNER. FRANK. PAPEN. FRICH.
>
> LOOK! YOUR VICTIMS HAVE COME TO IDENTIFY YOU. (Hicks 2012, 206–7)

Thus, while the Soviet film also treats the camera as a witness, this time to the trial, there remain accompanying issues concerning the politics of the gaze embedded in the film's selected vantage point.

CONCLUSION: ATTEMPTING A POETHICS OF FILM AND LAW[28]

To get a broader sense of the complexity of visualizing representations of the Holocaust in relation to the daunting popularization of Holocaust representations, especially in film, Alan Mintz observes:

> We are desperately in need of a way to understand this daunting complexity [of interpretations]. Yet the model we now have at our disposal is a rigid rhetoric of purity and impurity that compounds the difficulty. . . . We construct an ideal of authenticity and are quick to identify betrayals and exploitations. . . . The result is a contentious politics of blame and self-righteousness rather than a broadening cultural dialectic. (2001, 171)

The crucial question then is: How does one move from a deconstructive turn, which seems simply a revolving door of warring narratives, toward a poethics of producing and viewing Holocaust films that have assimilated the look of the "real" while being unavoidably embedded in the politics and aesthetics of monster-making? By "poethics" I mean, generally, the same kind of project Richard Weisberg alludes to, after the Nietzschean "*Umwertung der Werte*" (Weisberg 1992, xii) (roughly translated, not simply an "overturning" of values but their "re-evaluation" or "trans-valuation"): a project that "endeavors nothing less than to fill the ethical void in which legal thought and practice . . . [in which] literature [and in this paper, film] provid[e] a lively and accessible medium for learning about law in an ethical way" (Weisberg 1992, 4–5).

In so doing, this chapter adopts and adapts some of Weisberg's statements, especially his remarks regarding the indivisibility between "the form of a legal utterance and its substance" (Weisberg 1992, 7). In this chapter, Weisberg's statement is applied to the indivisibility of the rhetorical form (docudramatic techniques of framing) from the message (the historical reality of the Holocaust as over-determined by a focus on Nazis as monsters)—a rhetorical form that has become so invisible and naturalized that its narrative structure has a powerful rhetorical force with concrete effects.

One way to work past this dilemma—to press past the deconstructive mode into a potential "poetic ethic"—is to follow Primo Levi's lead. Levi saw the Holocaust as a gray zone rather than one in stark black-and-white. Thus, Levi's (1989, 37) analyses entail judgments that account for context and degree of complicity, refusing to bow to a Manichaean tendency, which shuns half-tints and complexities." One preliminary way to distinguish across the shades of gray, adapted from both LaCapra and Weisberg, is to balance the aesthetic emphasis with a historical grounding, thus giving the responsibility of accounting for the historical and politically laden rhetorical structures to those empowered to forge them. Within the context of film criticism, the challenge would therefore be for film directors to place the conjunction of history and ethics at the forefront, without sacrificing the use of both aesthetic elements and imagination. Specifically, applied to the films examined, for example, it would mean problematizing, rather than reinforcing, film's status as unproblematic witness or the Nazis' unambiguous status as radically and monstrously "Other," a popular misunderstanding of Arendt's concept of Nazism as a totalitarian system exemplifying "radical evil."[29] Perhaps, like Claude Lanzmann (1985), sometimes it is preferable to choose silences and gaps, rather than overt representations laden with popular cultural connotations that reduce a complex narrative into a simplistic formula.[30] Nevertheless, ultimately, as this chapter has shown, even documentary representations are narratives crafted from carefully selected and arranged shots.[31]

As such, continuing with the process of navigating through the gray zone, this chapter follows LaCapra's call for an "interaction among research, theory, and ethico-political concerns in the critical attempt to come to terms with specific problems" (1998, 210). For LaCapra, a focus on the secondary witnesses' response to encountering representations of the trauma of the Holocaust is significant in this process (1998, 149). Such responses can typically be grouped into two categories: (1) narrative redemption, in which the audience suffers vicariously with the victims to achieve a transcendent affirmation of self or group identity (the Scylla of the Russian films); and (2) excessive or unqualified objectification, an uncompromising demand to get at definitive answers as to what really happened (the Charybdis of the American films). While both responses have some value, it is important not to be swept into the two extremes they represent: one of excessive identification, the other of excessive detachment. Like Weisberg, LaCapra draws inspiration from Nietzsche (1974, 12) and employs the Nietzschean notion of *Schwergewicht* to place limits on both narrative redemption and excessive objectification.[32] Per LaCapra, *Schwergewicht* is an acknowledgment of the "stressful weight in inquiry, and . . . how history in its own way poses problems of writing and signification which cannot be reduced to writing up the results of research" (2000, 105). What LaCapra proposes, and this chapter has adopted as illustrated above, is a limit to both extreme identification and extreme detachment, which is made possible by the adoption of critical openness to a dialectical tension between multiple points of view and the inevitability of some amount of irreducibility.

Thus, while the initial step of this approach entails, as enacted in prior sections, trying to contextualize how these cinematic images were forged, the second step, in attempting to make sense of the landscape in this gray zone, lies in developing a critical readership of (re)viewing such images, navigating between extreme detachment and extreme identification. Uncritical consumption helps perpetuate uncritical narratives of monstrosity (a popular oversimplification of Arendt's concept of radical evil exemplified in Nazi totalitarianism as a system that sought to transform human nature itself) (Bernstein 1997, 135) and of film as providing unmediated access to what is "real." In essence, the process of critically "reading" these images is also simultaneously a way of critically problematizing or "rewriting" them.

NOTES

*Acknowledgments: The views expressed in this chapter are purely of the author's and do not represent the views of the firm for which she works. The author is indebted to John Stinneford and *Dapim*'s editors and two anonymous reviewers for very insightful comments on an earlier draft, and she also thanks the staff of *Dapim* for their helpfulness and professionalism. She owes John Edgar Browning a debt for his invaluable assistance with finding appropriate public domain images, and is grateful to Susan Gilbert for her help with optimizing these public domain images into camera-ready form. She dedicates this chapter to the Picart, Terrell, and Rivera families and especially to her husband, Jerry Rivera.

1. This chapter, in text form, was initially published as: Caroline Joan "Kay" S. Picart (May, 2015), "Nationalities, Histories, Rhetorics: Real / Reel Representations of the Holocaust and Holocaust Trials and a Poethics of Film and Law," *Dapim: Studies on the Holocaust* 29(2): 1–20, copyright © Institute for Holocaust Research, University of Haifa, reprinted by permission of Taylor & Francis Ltd, www.tandfonline.com on behalf of Institute for Holocaust Research, University of Haifa. All images inserted into this chapter are in the public domain. The author thanks Taylor and Francis Press for a license to reprint the initial article in this anthology.

2. For other studies concerning law and film, see Lawrence M. Friedman, "Law, Lawyers, and Popular Culture," *Yale Law Journal* vol. 98, no. 8 (1989): 1579–606; and Jessica Silbey, "Patterns of Courtroom Justice," *Journal of Law and Society* vol. 28, no. 1 (2001): 97–116.

3. Richard K. Sherwin, *When Law Goes Pop: The Vanishing Line Between Law and Popular Culture* (Chicago: University of Chicago Press, 2000), quoted in Anthony Chase, *Movies on Trial: The Legal System on the Silver Screen* (New York: The New Press, 2002), 159. See generally Richard K. Sherwin, (ed.), *Popular Culture and Law*

(Surrey and Burlington: Ashgate, 2006) and Austin Sarat, (ed.), *Imagining Legality: Where Law Meets Popular Culture* (New York: The New Press, 2011).

4. Writing generally about texts of law and history, Maria Aristedemou observes, "Literature, law, and history dissolve into each other while the text creates its own law, and its own history which in turn rewrites the history of the event." Maria Aristedemou, *Law and Literature: Journeys from Her to Eternity* (New York: Oxford University Press, 2000), 180.

5. Richard K. Sherwin, "Legal Storytelling: Culture's Tools for Making Meaning," in *When Law Goes Pop: The Vanishing Line Between Law and Popular Culture* (Chicago: University of Chicago Press, 2000), 41. For an account of the dramatic and visual aspect of trials, see Steve Greenfield, Guy Osborn, and Peter Robson, "Theoretical Underpinnings and Physical Boundaries—Defining the Territory," *Film and the Law* (Oxford and New York: Oxford University Press, 2010), 32–50.

6. For an account that analyzes The Godfather Trilogy as Francis Ford Coppola's attempt to demythologize America as "a pluralistic society living by the rule of law and serving as a model for the rest of the world," see David Ray Papke, "Myth and Meaning: Francis Ford Coppola and Popular Response to the Godfather Trilogy," in John Denvir, (ed.), *Legal Reelism: Movies as Legal Texts* (Champaign: University of Illinois Press, 1996), 1–22.

7. Saul Morson reminds us that in viewing images on screen and television, "alternatives always abound, and, more often than not, what exists need not have existed. . . . Instead of casting a foreshadow from the future, [these cast] a shadow 'from the side,' that is from other possibilities." Saul Morson, *Narrative and Freedom: The Shadows of Time* (New Haven, CT: Yale University Press, 1996), 118.

8. For a restatement and critique of Clover's views, see Chase, "Toward a Legal Theory," 165–68.

9. "The success of the campaign to educate Americans about Nazi atrocities was demonstrated in a Gallup poll taken in early May 1945, one that indicated progress from the poll taken in November 1944. A cross section of the American public was asked, 'What do you think of the reports that the Germans have killed many in concentration camps or let them starve to death—are they true or not true?' Eighty-four percent answered, 'True'; Nine percent believed the statement to be 'true, but exaggerated'; only four percent answered 'doubtful, hard to believe' or 'not true'; three percent couldn't decide." Robert A. Abzug, *Inside the Vicious Heart: Americans and the Liberation of Nazi Concentration Camps* (New York: Oxford University Press, 1985), 135–40.

10. For the view regarding selected films, such as *Nuremberg Concentration Camps*, as "transcending the rules of knowledge," see Anton Kaes, "Holocaust and the End of History: Postmodern Historiography in Cinema," in Saul Friedlander, (ed.), *Probing the Limits of Representation: Nazism and the "Final Solution"* (Cambridge, MA: Harvard University Press, 1992), 206, 208.

11. See Article VIII, "Hearsay," *Federal Rules of Evidence*, Legal Information Institute, accessed at www.law.cornell.edu/rules/fre/article_VIII.

12. Rule 403, "Excluding Relevant Evidence for Prejudice, Confusion, Waste of Time, or Other Reasons," Article IV, *Federal Rules of Evidence*, Legal Information Institute, accessed at www.law.cornell.edu/rules/fre/rule_403.

13. Charter of the International Military Tribunal Section V, Article 19, in Nuremberg Trial Proceedings Volume 1, consulted at avalon.law.yale.edu/imt/imtconst.asp#art19.

14. Hasian remarks regarding the heritage of the legal innovations of the Nuremberg IMT: "The mixing and matching of American and Continental procedural and substantive rules of law has left us with many legacies, and we forget too much when we try to abstract out key principles from the rhetorical contexts that infused them with meaning." Hasian, *Rhetorical Vectors of Memory,* 27.

15. "[T]he cultural capital of trauma victims—their wounds, their scars, their tragedy—is appropriated by the same popular codes through which physical and sexual violence is commodified, sold in the cinema, marketed as pornography, and used by tabloids and novelists to attract readers." Arthur Kleinman and Joan Kleinman, "The Appeal of Experience; The Dismay of Images: Cultural Appropriations of Suffering in Our Times," in Arthur Kleinman, Veena Das, and Margaret Lock, (eds.), *Social Suffering* (Oakland: University of California Press, 1996), 10–11.

16. See Article VII, "Crimes Against Humanity," *Rome Statute of the International Criminal Court,* July 17, 1998, accessed at www.icrc.org/ihl/WebART/585-07?OpenDocument.

17. For disagreement regarding the legal validity of this innovation, see Judith Shklar, *Legalism: Law, Morals and Political Trials* (Cambridge, MA: Harvard University Press, 1964).

18. As Richard Bernstein argues, the common, but mistaken, notion that Hannah Arendt equated the concept of radical evil with the monstrousness of men like Hitler and Stalin is, to some extent, probably traceable to Elisabeth Young-Bruehl's biography of Arendt, in which Young-Bruehl wrote, regarding Arendt's famous shift from "radical evil" to the "banality of evil": "Arendt rejected the concept she had used in *The Origins of Totalitarianism* to point to the incomprehensible nature of the Nazis—'radical evil.' As she did this, she freed herself of a long nightmare; she no longer had to live with the idea that monsters and demons had engineered the murder of millions." Quoted in Richard J. Bernstein, "Did Hannah Arendt Change Her Mind?: From Radical Evil to the Banality of Evil," in Larry May and Jerome Kohn, (eds.), *Hannah Arendt: Twenty Years Later* (Cambridge, MA: MIT Press, 1997), 129. I thank one of the anonymous reviewers for the suggestion of clarifying the distinction between Arendt's notion of Nazi totalitarianism as an illustration of radical evil as opposed to the popular representation of Nazis as monsters and beasts.

19. The Prosecuting Attorney's depiction is generally based on General Telford Taylor, who, played by Richard Widmark, becomes the stereotypic heroic military type. Widmark usually portrayed these kinds of roles in films like *Halls of Montezuma* (1950), *The Frogmen* (1951), and *Hell and High Water* (1954). Aquino, *Truth and Lives,* 133.

20. For a summary of the key scenes involving the interactions between Judge Haywood and Frau Bertholt, see Carolyn Patty Blum, "Film, Culture and Accountability for Human Rights Abuses," in Michael Freeman (ed.), *Law and Popular Culture, Current Legal Issues 2004 Volume 7* (Oxford and New York: Oxford University Press, 2004), 507.

21. For a parallel analyses of possible defenses of the judges embedded in the film, and their eventual rejection, see Paul Bergman and Michael Asimow, *Reel Justice: The Courtroom Goes to the Movies* (Riverside: Andrews McMeel Publishing, 2006), 22–24.

22. Murray Schumach, "Hollywood Trial," *New York Times*, April 30, 1961, Section II, p. 9:1; cited in Mintz, *Popular Culture*, 92. For an insightful analysis of how the daily coverage of the Eichmann trials was handled on television, see Jeffrey Shandler, *While America Watches: Televising the Holocaust* (Oxford and New York: Oxford University Press, 1999), 83–132.

23. Schneer points out that photographs of Majdanek were striking in particular because they pointed out the industrial nature of killing and new means of dealing with the dead, as evidenced by the proliferation of industrial ovens. David Schneer, *Through Soviet Eyes: Photography, War, and the Holocaust* (New Brunswick, NJ: Rutgers University Press, 2012), 159.

24. Also, see generally Harvey Asher, "The Soviet Union, the Holocaust, and Auschwitz," *Kritika: Explorations in Russian and Eurasian History* vol. 4, no. 4 (2003): 886–912.

25. Evgenii Margolit, "Barnet I Eizenshtein v kontekste sovetskogo kino," *Kinovedscheskie zapiski* 17 (1993), 172; for examples of extensive footage showing children murdered by Nazis in Film Documents of Atrocities, see Roberto Muehlenkamp, "The Atrocities committed by German-Fascists in the USSR (2)," *Holocaust Controversies: What Part of the Word Genocide Do you Not Understand?*, May 3, 2011, consulted at holocaustcontroversies.blogspot.com/2011/05/atrocities-committed-by-german-fascists.html.

26. Ilia Erenburg, "O nenavisti," *Krasnaia Zvezda*, May 5, 1942, 4. Reprinted in Erenburg, Voina (Iiun' 1941–aprel' 1942), 178–85, and translated as "Hatred," in Erenburg, *Russia at War*, 127–32, and as "About Hatred," in Ilya Ehrenburg and Konstantin Simonov, *In One Newspaper: A Chronicle of Unforgettable Years*, trans. Anatol Kagan (New York: Sphinx 1985), 145–50; Ilia Erenburg, "Opravdanie nenavisti," May 26, 1942, reprinted in Il'ia Erenburg, Voina (Aprel' 1942–mart 1943) (Moscow, 1943), 3–8. The English translation, published in Moscow in 1942, sometimes replaced the word "German" with "Nazi" or "Hitlerites"; see reprint in James von Geldern and Richard Stites, (eds.), *Mass Culture in Soviet Russia: Tales, Poems, Songs, Movies, Plays, and Folklore, 1917–1953* (Bloomington: Indiana University Press, 1995), 403, 405. On vermin (*gady*), refer to 'Iiun,' June 21, 1942. Reprint in Erenburg, Voina (Aprel' 1942–mart 1943), 286–91. For an extended discussion, see Karel C. Berkhoff, *Motherland in Danger: Soviet Propaganda During World War II* (Cambridge, MA: Harvard University Press, 2012), 182–93.

27. See, for example, a review of the film by Tat'iana Tess, 'Tsennyi fil'm,' *Izvestiia*, November 28, 1946, 2.

28. For a precursor to this exploration of a poethics of reception, see generally, Caroline Joan "Kay" S. Picart and David Frank, *Frames of Evil: The Holocaust of Horror in American Film* (Carbondale: Southern Illinois University Press, 2006). I wish to thank and acknowledge David Frank for our earlier collaboration in developing this concept, as applied to a more historical frame.

29. For a framework that views Arendt's famous shift from "radical evil" to "banal" as cohesive and signaling a "moral turn" characteristic of current trends

in historiography, see George Cotkin, "Illuminating Evil: Hannah Arendt and Moral History," *Modern Intellectual History* vol. 4, no. 3 (2007): 463–90.

30. Claude Lanzmann, *Shoah* (Historia, Les Films Aleph, Ministère de la Culture de la Republique Française, 1985). Lanzmann's documentary deliberately avoids any documentary footage from the war period or docudramatic recreations in favor of probing, close-up interviews with both survivors and non-Jewish bystanders against the backdrop of the ruins of former concentration camps and contemporary European rail lines. However, even Lanzmann's documentary choices are problematic as he not only emotionally manipulates the people whom he chooses to interview, but also shares Spielberg's assumption that his film "represents a kind of ultimate reckoning with the Holocaust." Mintz, *Popular Culture and the Shaping of Holocaust Memory*, 146.

31. For an example of an analysis that shows that problems of representation persist even in a documentary, see William Rothman's reading of *Nanook of the North* (1922): William Rothman, "Filmmaker as Hunter: Robert Flaherty's *Nanook of the North*," in Barry Keith Grant and Jeannette Sloniowski, (eds.), *Documenting the Documentary: Close Readings of Documentary Film and Video* (Detroit: Wayne State University Press, 1998), 25.

32. Friedrich Nietzsche, *The Gay Science*, Walter Kaufmann, (trans.) (New York: Vintage Books, 1974), 12, in Nietzsche, *Schwergewicht*, which Walter Kaufmann translates as "the greatest weight," is the only positive response to the "weightlessness" of nihilism and its utter dissolution of boundaries. The threat of nihilism, envisaged in the nightmare of eternal recurrence, may be overcome only through a joyful and rebellious embrace of this nightmarish vision, which is the ultimate measure of the nobility of one's soul. *Schwergewicht* is therefore Nietzsche's search for a moral imperative in the face of the potential meaninglessness that nihilism portends. See also LaCapra, *History and Memory*, 149.

REFERENCES

Abzug, Robert A. 1985. *Inside the Vicious Heart: Americans and the Liberation of Nazi Concentration Camps.* New York: Oxford University Press.

Aquino, John T. 2005. *Truth and Lives on Film: The Legal Problems of Depicting Real Persons and Events in a Fictional Medium.* Jefferson, NC: McFarland and Company.

Arendt, Hannah. 1998. *The Human Condition.* Chicago: University of Chicago Press.

———. 2006. *Eichmann in Jerusalem: A Report on the Banality of Evil.* New York: Penguin Classics.

Aristedemou, Maria. 2000. *Law and Literature: Journeys from Her to Eternity*. New York: Oxford University Press.

Asher, Harvey. 2003. "The Soviet Union, the Holocaust, and Auschwitz." *Kritika: Explorations in Russian and Eurasian History*, 4(4): 886–912.

Avisar, Ilan. 1988. *Screening the Holocaust: Cinema's Images of the Unimaginable.* Bloomington: Indiana University Press.

Azoulay, Ariella. 2011. "Photography," *Mafte'akh* 2e: 79. Accessed November 3, 2013 at: mafteakh.tau.ac.il/en/wp-content/uploads/2011/01/Photography.pdf.

Barnouw, Eric. 1993. *Documentary: A History of the Non-Fiction Film*, 2nd Revised Edition. Oxford and New York: Oxford University Press.

Barsam, Richard M. 1992. *Nonfiction Film: A Critical History*, Revised and Expanded. Bloomington: Indiana University Press.

Berkhoff, Karel C. 2012. *Motherland in Danger: Soviet Propaganda during World War II*. Cambridge, MA: Harvard University Press.

Bergman, Paul, and Michael Asimow. 2006. *Reel Justice: The Courtroom Goes to the Movies*. Riverside, NJ: Andrews McMeel Publishing.

Bernstein, Richard J. 1997. "Did Hannah Arendt Change Her Mind?: From Radical Evil to the Banality of Evil." In *Hannah Arendt: Twenty Years Later*, edited by Larry May and Jerome Kohn, 127–46. Cambridge, MA: MIT Press.

Black, David A. 1999. "History, Genre, Reflexivity in Law." In *Film: Resonance and Representation*, 87–97. Champaign: University of Illinois Press.

Blum, Carolyn Patty. 2004. "Film, Culture and Accountability for Human Rights Abuses." In *Law and Popular Culture, Current Legal Issues* Volume 7, edited by Michael Freeman, chapter 28. Oxford and New York: Oxford University Press.

Chase, Anthony. 1986. "Toward a Legal Theory of Popular Culture." *Wisconsin Law Review*, 13: 527–69.

———. 2002. *Movies on Trial: The Legal System on the Silver Screen*. New York: The New Press.

Clover, Carol J. 1998. "God Bless Juries!" In *Refiguring American Film Genres: History and Theory*, edited by Nick Browne, 255–77. Oakland: University of California Press.

Cotkin, George. 2007. "Illuminating Evil: Hannah Arendt and Moral History." *Modern Intellectual History*, 4(3): 463–90.

Delage, Christian. 2004. "Image as Evidence and Mediation: The Experience of the Nuremberg Trials." In *Law and Popular Culture, Current Legal Issues*, volume 7, edited by Michael Freeman, chapter 27. Oxford and New York: Oxford University Press.

———. 2006a. *La Vérité par l'image: De Nuremberg as procès Milosevic*. Paris: Denöel.

———. (director). 2006b. *Le Procès de Nuremberg: Les Nazis face à leurs crimes* [DVD]. France: Arte.

Douglas, Lawrence. 2005. *The Memory of Judgment: Making Law and History in the Trials of the Holocaust*. New Haven, CT: Yale University Press.

Erenburg, Ilia. 1942a. "O nenavisti." *Krasnaia Zvezda*, May 5: 4, reprinted in Erenburg, Voina (Iiun' 1941–aprel' 1942), 178–85, and translated as "Hatred," in Erenburg, *Russia at War*, 127–32, and as "About Hatred," in Ilya Ehrenburg and Konstantin Simonov. 1985. *In One Newspaper: A Chronicle of Unforgettable Years*, translated by Anatol Kagan, 145–50. New York: Sphinx

———. 1942b. "Opravdanie nenavisti," May 26, reprinted in Il'ia Erenburg, Voina (Aprel' 1942–mart 1943) (Moscow, 1943), 3–8.

Felman, Shoshana, and Dori Laub. 1992. *Testimony: Crises of Witnessing in Literature, Psychoanalysis, and History*. New York: Routledge.

Fried, John H. E. 1976. "The Great Nuremberg Trial." *American Political Science Review*, 70(1): 192–210.

Friedman, Lawrence M. 1989. "Law, Lawyers, and Popular Culture." *Yale Law Journal*, 98(8): 1579–606.

Greenfield, Steve, Guy Osborn, and Peter Robson. 2010. "Theoretical Underpinnings and Physical Boundaries—Defining the Territory." In *Film and the Law*, 32–50. Oxford and New York: Oxford University Press.

Hasian, Marouf A. Jr. 2006. *Rhetorical Vectors of Memory in National and International Holocaust Trials*. East Lansing, MI: Michigan University Press.

Hicks, Jeremy. 2012. *First Films of the Holocaust: Soviet Cinema and the Genocide of the Jews, 1938–1946*. Pittsburgh: University of Pittsburgh Press.

Hoffman, Hilmar. 1996. *The Triumph of Propaganda: Film and National Socialism 1933–1945*. Oxford: Berghahn Books.

International Criminal Court. 1998. "Crimes Against Humanity, Article VII." *Rome Statute of the International Criminal Court*. Accessed December 14, 2013 at www.icrc.org/ihl/WebART/585-07?OpenDocument.

Kaes, Anton. 1992. "Holocaust and the End of History: Postmodern Historiography in Cinema." In *Probing the Limits of Representation: Nazism and the "Final Solution,"* edited by Saul Friedlander, 206–22. Cambridge, MA: Harvard University Press.

Kamir, Orit. 2005. "Cinematic Judgment and Jurisprudence: A Woman's Memory, Recovery, and Justice in a Post-Traumatic Society (A Study of Polanski's *Death and the Maiden*)." In *Law on the Screen*, edited by Austin Sarat, Lawrence Douglas and Martha Merrill Umphrey, 27–81. Redwood City, CA: Stanford University Press.

———. 2006. *Framed: Women in Law and Film*. Durham, NC: Duke University Press.

Karmen, Roman and Yelizaveta Svilova (directors). 1947. *The Judgment of the Nations* (*Sud Naradov*) [Documentary film]. USA: Artkino Pictures.

Kleinman, Arthur, and Joan Kleinman. 1996. "The Appeal of Experience; The Dismay of Images: Cultural Appropriations of Suffering in Our Times." In *Social Suffering*, edited by Arthur Kleinman, Veena Das, and Margaret Lock, 1–23. Oakland: University of California Press.

Kohler, Lotte and Hans Saner (eds.). 1992. *Hannah Arendt and Karl Jaspers, Correspondence 1926–1969*, translated by Robert Kimber and Rita Kimber. San Diego: Harcourt Brace Jovanovich.

Kolesnikova, N., G. Senchakova and T. Slepneva. 1959. *Roman Karmen*. Moscow: Iskusstvo.

Korol'kov, Iu. 1946. "Vozmezdie i groznoe predosterezhenie." *Literaturnaia gazeta*, November 30: 4.

LaCapra, Dominick. 1998. *History and Memory after Auschwitz*. Ithaca: Cornell University Press.

———. 2000. *Writing History, Writing Trauma*. Baltimore: Johns Hopkins University Press.

Lanzmann, Claude (director). 1985. *Shoah* [DVD]. France: Historia, Les Films Aleph, Ministère de la Culture de la Republique Française.

Legal Information Institute. *U.S. Federal Rules of Evidence*. Accessed December 13, 2012 at www.law.cornell.edu/rules/fre/article_VIII.

Levi, Primo. 1989. *The Drowned and the Saved.* New York: Vintage.
Margolit, Evgenii. 1993. "Barnet I Eizenshtein v kontekste sovetskogo kino." *Kinovedscheskie zapiski* 17: 172.
Marrus, Michael R. 1997. *The Nuremberg War Crimes Trial, 1945–46: A Documentary History.* Boston: Bedford.
Matskin, A., and B. Sobolev. 1941. "K ak khozainichili nemtsy v Rostove." *Pravda,* December: 2.
Migulina, Katerina. 2007. "Golubinyi razvedchik." *Trud,* May 10. Accessed March 19, 2014 at www.trud.ru/article/10-05-2007/115772_golubinyj_razvedchik.html
Mintz, Alan. 2001. *Popular Culture and the Shaping of Holocaust Memory in America.* Seattle: University of Washington Press.
Morson, Saul. 1996. *Narrative and Freedom: The Shadows of Time.* New Haven: Yale University Press.
Muehlenkamp, Roberto. 2011. "The Atrocities Committed by German-Fascists in the USSR (2)." *Holocaust Controversies: What Part of the Word Genocide Do you Not Understand?* May 3. Accessed March 2, 2012 at holocaustcontroversies.blogspot.com/2011/05/atrocities-committed-by-german-fascists.html.
Nietzsche, Friedrich. 1974. *The Gay Science.* Translated by Walter Kaufmann. New York: Vintage Books.
Nuremberg Trial Proceedings. 1945. *Charter of the International Military Tribunal,* Volume 1. Accessed July 7, 2013 at avalon.law.yale.edu/imt/imtconst.asp#art19.
Papke, David Ray. 1996. "Myth and Meaning: Francis Ford Coppola and Popular Response to the Godfather Trilogy." In *Legal Reelism: Movies as Legal Texts,* edited by John Denvir, 1–22. Champaign: University of Illinois Press.
Paradis, Pierre R. 1965. "The Celluloid Witness." *University of Colorado Law Review,* 37(2): 235–68.
Picart, Caroline Joan "Kay" S., and David Frank. 2006. *Frames of Evil: The Holocaust of Horror in American Film.* Carbondale: Southern Illinois University Press.
Rothman, William. 1998. "Filmmaker as Hunter: Robert Flaherty's *Nanook of the North.*" In *Documenting the Documentary: Close Readings of Documentary Film and Video,* edited by Barry Keith Grant and Jeannette Sloniowski, 23–39. Detroit: Wayne State University Press.
Sarat, Austin (ed.). 2011. *Imagining Legality: Where Law Meets Popular Culture.* New York: The New Press.
Schneer, David. 2012. *Through Soviet Eyes: Photography, War, and the Holocaust.* New Brunswick: Rutgers University Press.
———. 2015. "Is Seeing Believing? Photographs, Eyewitness Testimony, and Evidence of the Holocaust." *East European Jewish Affairs,* 45(1): 65–78.
Schumach, Murray. 1961. "Hollywood Trial." *New York Times,* April 30, Section 2: 9:1.
Shandler, Jeffrey. 1999. *While America Watches: Televising the Holocaust.* Oxford and New York: Oxford University Press.
Sherwin, Richard K. 2000. *When Law Goes Pop: The Vanishing Line Between Law and Popular Culture.* Chicago: University of Chicago Press.
———. (ed.) 2006. *Popular Culture and Law.* Surrey and Burlington: Ashgate.

Shklar, Judith. 1964. *Legalism: Law, Morals and Political Trials.* Cambridge, MA: Harvard University Press.

Silbey, Jessica. 2001. "Patterns of Courtroom Justice." *Journal of Law and Society,* 28(1): 97–116.

Stimson, Henry L. 1949. "Memorandum from Secretary of War Henry L. Stimson, Secretary of State; Edward R. Stettinius, Jr.; and Attorney Gen. Francis Biddle for President Franklin Roosevelt (January 22, 1945)." In *Report of Robert H. Jackson, United States Representative to the International Conference on Military Trials: London, 1945.* Washington, DC: Department of State Division of Publications. Accessed March 3, 2012 at avalon.law.yale.edu/imt/jack01.asp.

Taylor, Telford. 1993. *The Anatomy of the Nuremberg Trials: A Personal Memoir.* New York: Little Brown and Company.

Tess, Tat'iana. 1946. "Tsennyi fil'm." *Izvestiia,* November 28: 2.

United States Holocaust Memorial Museum. 1945. *Soviet Film of Atrocities Shown at Nuremberg Trials* [Documentary film]. Washington DC: Steven Spielberg Film and Video Archive. Accessed December 1, 2010 at www.ushmm.org/online/film/display/detail.php?file_num=4998.

———. 2015. "International Military Tribunal at Nuremberg." *Holocaust Encyclopedia.* Accessed on January 20, 2015 at www.ushmm.org/wlc/en/article.php?ModuleId=10007069.

von Geldern, James, and Richard Stites (eds.). 1995. *Mass Culture in Soviet Russia: Tales, Poems, Songs, Movies, Plays, and Folklore, 1917–1953.* Bloomington: Indiana University Press.

Weckel, Ulrike. 2012. "The Power of Images: Real and Fictional Roles of Atrocity Footage at Nuremberg." In *Reassessing the Nuremberg Military Trials: Transitional Justice, Trial Narratives and Historiography,* edited by Kim C. Priemel and Alexa Stiller, 221–48. Oxford: Berghahn Books.

Weisberg, Richard. 1992. *Poethics and Other Strategies of Law and Literature.* New York: Columbia University Press.

White, James Boyd. 1985a. *The Legal Imagination.* Chicago: University of Chicago Press.

———. 1985b. *When Words Lose Their Meaning.* Chicago: University of Chicago Press.

———. 1999. *From Expectation to Experience: Essays on Law and Legal Education.* Ann Arbor: University of Michigan Press.

Wieviorka, Annette. 2006. *The Era of the Witness.* Translated by Jared Stark. Ithaca, NY: Cornell University Press.

Wigmore, John H. 1970. *Wigmore on Evidence,* edited by James H. Chadbourn, 218–19. Boston: Little, Brown and Company.

Zelizer, Barbie. 2000. *Remembering to Forget: Holocaust Memory through the Camera's Eye.* Chicago: University of Chicago Press.

Index

Page numbers that refer to figures appear in italics.

About the Editors and Contributors

EDITORS

Cecil Greek is associate professor of sociology at the University of South Florida, Tampa. His specialty areas include the history of sociology and criminology, mass media depictions of crime and deviance, and qualitative research methodologies. His book, *The Religious Roots of American Sociology*, focused on the founding generation of American sociology and their eventual turn from qualitative to quantitative methods. His second book, an edited anthology, with Caroline Joan "Kay" S. Picart, *Monsters In and Among Us: Towards a Gothic Criminology*, focused on film as a medium in which discussion of the continuing existence of gothic imagery and evil are at the forefront.

Michael Hviid Jacobsen is professor of sociology at the Department of Sociology and Social Work, Aalborg University, Denmark. His main research areas are social theory, qualitative and creative methods, emotions, ethics, death and dying, palliative care, crime, everyday life, and utopianism. Selected recent publications are: *Encountering the Everyday* (edited, 2009), *The Contemporary Goffman* (edited, 2010), *Utopia and Social Theory* (edited, 2012), *Deconstructing Death* (edited, 2013), *What Use Is Sociology?* (edited, 2013), *The Poetics of Crime* (edited, 2014), *Liquid Criminology* (edited, 2016), *Beyond Bauman* (edited, 2016), and *Postmortal Society* (edited, 2016).

Caroline Joan "Kay" S. Picart, M.Phil., Christ's College University of Cambridge, U.K.; PhD, Pennsylvania State University; JD, University of Florida, a scholar-attorney practicing in federal criminal law, publishes on law, criminology, sociology, and film. Prior to practicing law, she was a tenured associate professor of English and humanities, with a courtesy appointment at the Florida State University Law School. She has authored/edited seventeen scholarly books, including recently, *Speaking of Monsters* (edited with John Edgar Browning, 2012), *Copyright in American Dance* (2013), *Law In & As Culture* (forthcoming, 2016), *American Self-Activating Terrorists* (forthcoming, 2017), and numerous articles nationally and internationally. She serves as editor of the Fairleigh Dickinson University Press (FDUP) Series on Law, Culture, and Humanities, and is a member of the FDUP Advisory Board.

CONTRIBUTORS

Susan Boyd is Distinguished Professor in the Faculty of Human and Social Development, University of Victoria, Canada. She is the author of a number of articles and books, including: *Mothers and Illicit Drugs; From Witches to Crack Moms; Hooked: Drug War Films*; co-author of *Raise Shit!: Social Action Saving Lives* and *Killer Weed: Marijuana Grow-ops, Media, and Justice*. She also works with local and national groups that advocate for drug policy reform.

Farah Britto graduated from the University of South Florida *summa cum laude* with bachelor degrees in mass communications and anthropology. She is a professional television producer working primarily for the PBS affiliate in Tampa, Florida. She is working toward her master's degree in applied anthropology at the University of South Florida, specializing in visual anthropology and studying filmmaking in Ghana, West Africa. She is expected to graduate with her master's degree in 2016.

Mathieu Deflem is professor of sociology at the University of South Carolina. His specialty areas include sociology of law, social control, popular culture, and social theory. He is the author of dozens of articles in journals and anthologies, the editor of about ten volumes, and the author of three books, including *Policing World Society* (2002) and *Sociology of Law* (2008). His recent work on popular culture deals with the cinema of Alfred Hitchcock and the fame of global pop star Lady Gaga.

John Denvir is professor emeritus of law and the humanities at the University of San Francisco Law School. Denvir edited *Legal Reelism: Movies* *as Legal Texts* (1996), one of the most cited texts in the field of law and popular culture. He has written two books on constitutional theory: *Democracy's Constitution* (2001) and *Freeing Speech* (2010) and his articles have been published in leading law reviews. Denvir has been a visiting professor of law at the University of California Berkeley (Boalt Hall), the University of Oregon, and the University of Kent at Canterbury. He recently published a book entitled *Guile is Good! Why We Need Lawyers* with a companion blog.

Jon Frauley is associate professor of criminology, University of Ottawa (Canada) and visiting professor (2014–2015) of law, criminology, and criminal justice at Carleton University (Ottawa). Areas of interest include epistemology and methodology; medicalization and medical social control; the powers of private inspectorates; and creative analytics through films and novels. Most recently he has edited and contributed to *C. Wright Mills and the Criminological Imagination* (2015).

Steve Greenfield is currently a reader in law and deputy head of Westminster Law School at the University of Westminster, London. He is one of the foremost British scholars, working in the area of film and the law, having been a key member of the small group that initiated the development of the subject, both in terms of teaching and research. His latest thread of work has further broadened the field through the application of theories from social psychology into analysis of the portrayal of law and lawyers.

Orit Kamir, BA, Hebrew University; MA and PhD, University of Michigan, is the founder and academic head of the Center for Human Dignity in Israel. She publishes, teaches and is socially active in three interdisciplinary areas: (1) dignity, respect, and honor as moral/ethical values; (2) law and film; and (3) gender politics. She has authored six monographs and dozens of articles, in English and in Hebrew, and has taught in universities in Israel, the United States, and Europe. She has participated in drafting legislation in Israel, and is a social activist in gender equality and human rights.

Stefan Machura is senior lecturer at the School of Social Sciences, Bangor University, Wales/United Kingdom. Previously, he was at the Law Faculty of the Ruhr-Universität Bochum/Germany. Since 2014, he is board member of the Research Committee on Sociology of Law, International Sociological Association. He has been teaching classes in crime and the media and law in film since 1995.

Carrie Menkel-Meadow is Chancellor's Professor of Law at the University of California Irvine and A. B. Chettle Professor of Law, Dispute Resolution and Civil Procedure at Georgetown University Law Center. She is the author or editor of over ten books, including *Law and Popular Culture*, 2nd edition (2011), *Dispute Resolution: Beyond the Adversarial Model*, 2nd edition (2013), *What's Fair? Ethics for Negotiators* (2006), a contributor to *Law and Popular Culture*, Michael Freeman, ed. (2005), and over two hundred articles on dispute resolution, feminist legal theory, civil procedure, legal ethics, the legal profession, law and literature and popular culture, international law, and transitional justice.

Naomi Mezey is a law professor at Georgetown University Law Center where she teaches civil procedure, legislation, jurisprudence, gender and sexuality, and seminars on law and popular culture and nationalism and cultural identity. Her interdisciplinary scholarship of law and culture focuses on racial, sexual, and gender identities, film and visuality, and cultural property. She has served on the Organizing Committee of the Association for the Study of Law, Culture and the Humanities and is a co-founder of the Columbia, USC, Georgetown, and UCLA Law and Humanities Junior Scholars Workshop.

Mark C. Niles is professor of Law at American University, Washington College of Law. He teaches and specializes in civil procedure, administrative law, constitutional law, and law and literature. From 2010 to 2013 he served as dean and professor of law at Seattle University School of Law. Prior to his tenure as dean at Seattle University, Professor Niles spent twelve years as a professor at the American University, Washington College of Law, the last six as professor and associate dean for academic affairs. Professor Niles has published numerous articles and essays on subjects including the Ninth Amendment, federal tort liability, the evolution of regulatory administration, the social and legal consequences of pre-crime incarceration, and the depiction of law and justice in American popular culture.

Anders Petersen is associate professor of sociology at Aalborg University, Denmark. His speciality areas include social theory, qualitative research methods, and the sociology of health and illness. He has written (with Michael H. Jacobsen) the article "The Poetics of Prisonization: Creative Criminology Through the Projector," which calls for an expanded usage of films in teaching criminology is called for. His current research is on *Diagnostic Cultures*—on the societal implications of the growing number of people who are diagnosed with mental illness.

Peter Robson, LL.B. (St. Andrews); PhD (Strathclyde University), was coeditor of *Law and Film* with Stefan Machura in 2001; coauthor with Steve Greenfield and Guy Osborn of *Film and the Law* (2010), updating the influential first edition; coeditor with Jessica Silbey of *Law and Justice on the Small Screen* (2012); and author of essays on British TV lawyers, teaching law, and popular culture; law in modern popular fiction; and law and theater.

Matthew Sorrento teaches film and media studies at Rutgers University in Camden, New Jersey and is the author of *The New American Crime Film* (2012). He is interview editor of *Film International,* where he regularly contributes, and directs the Reel East Film Festival.

Majid Yar is an independent scholar who has previously held faculty positions at the Universities of Hull, Keele, Kent, and Lancaster. His recent publications include *Cybercrime and Society,* 2nd edition (2013), *Crime, Deviance and Doping* (2014), *The Cultural Imaginary of the Internet* (2014), and *Crime and the Imaginary of Disaster* (2015).

Lightning Source UK Ltd.
Milton Keynes UK
UKOW02n0623220416

272759UK00009B/207/P

9 781611 477054